4th edition

Strategic Management

Building and Sustaining Competitive Advantage

Robert A. Pitts • **David Lei**
Professor Emeritus, *Southern Methodist University*
Gettysburg College

THOMSON

SOUTH-WESTERN

Australia · Brazil · Canada · Mexico · Singapore · Spain · United Kingdom · United States

To our families.

THOMSON

SOUTH-WESTERN

Strategic Management: Building and Sustaining Competitive Advantage, Fourth Edition
Robert A. Pitts and David Lei

VP/Editorial Director:
Jack W. Calhoun

VP/Editor-in-Chief:
Dave Shaut

Sr. Publisher/Director of Development:
Melissa Acuña

Executive Editor:
John Szilagyi

Developmental Editor:
Denise Simon

Marketing Manager:
Rob Bloom

Sr. Production Project Manager:
Deanna Quinn

Manager of Technology, Editorial:
Vicky True

Technology Project Editor:
Kristen Meere

Web Coordinator:
Karen Schaffer

Manufacturing Coordinator:
Doug Wilke

Art Director:
Tippy McIntosh

Internal and Cover Designer:
Knapke Design

Cover Image:
Epoxy/Getty Images

Production House:
Rozi Harris, Interactive Composition Corporation

Printer:
West Group
Eagan, MN

Library of Congress Control Number:
2005921619

For more information about our products, contact us at:

Thomson Learning Academic Resource Center

1-800-423-0563

Thomson Higher Education
5191 Natorp Boulevard
Mason, OH 45040
USA

Brief Contents

Contents

Preface

Strategic Management: Building and Sustaining Competitive Advantage, fourth edition, is designed as a text for the core class taught as part of the strategic management or business policy component for majors in business. It should also prove useful to managers and professionals who wish to update or refine their knowledge of some vital issues in strategy through self-study.

Strategy is a broad concept that covers a multitude of different issues, concepts, and methods. Many topics are considered in the formulation and implementation of strategy, including industry analysis, competitor analysis, ethics, strengths/weaknesses, value creation, technology, innovation, product development, diversification, balancing the needs of various stakeholders, strategic alliances, organization design, virtual organizations, reward systems, corporate cultures, and corporate governance. Strategy requires a significant amount of work to understand, and even the experts often find themselves searching for new ways to research and think about the topic. For practicing managers and leaders, strategy is at the center of the effort to create value for customers, to respond to competitive challenges, and to build strong organizations. Yet, strategy as a concept is also a ton of fun, and that was the spirit that motivated us to continue writing and revising this text.

As was the case with our earlier three editions, the objective of this book is to encourage the reader to develop an ability to understand and appreciate the major drivers of strategy in organizations. There is no question that business organizations of all sizes must prepare for an increasingly complex future. Companies must deal with a variety of strategic, technological, and organizational forces on a daily basis. All these forces work together to redefine the economic and competitive landscape of not only the United States, but also the entire world. Despite the numerous strategic challenges posed by these developments, they also represent opportunities for companies of all sizes in all industries. Forward-looking firms will seek to create new sources of competitive advantage by participating and shaping how industries evolve in the times ahead. Yet, these same challenges also threaten to erode the long-held competitive advantages of companies that are slow to react or unable to mount an effective response.

To survive and prosper in this new millennium, the need to *build and sustain competitive advantage* will be greater than ever. Every chapter in this book was written with a competitive advantage perspective in mind. We believe that even if a large number of readers were not to pursue a career in management per se, an appreciation of how organizations conceive, formulate, implement, and adjust their strategies would help the reader gain a stronger appreciation for some of the key issues, trade-offs, and decisions that managers must face. Thus, our central focus on competitive advantage provides the rationale driving every aspect of our book—from its application-oriented content, to the organization of concepts, and the integration of illustrative examples.

Topical Coverage

Although the instructional approach of our earlier editions has been retained, several major changes have been made in both coverage and organization. The field of strategic management is becoming a richer topic of study as we speak. Companies are continuing to innovate breakthrough products, services, and technologies to serve customers at ever-faster rates. They are planning and organizing their activities using new methods, techniques, and modes of operation, especially with the pervasiveness of the Internet and the rise of "virtual" ways of doing things. They are also reaching out to customers in new parts of the world they never previously entered. Globalization has become etched in our competitive landscape, including new opportunities and threats from emerging and developing countries that are fast becoming vibrant competitors. As the past few years have witnessed, companies of all sizes in all countries also face a host of issues regarding corporate governance, balancing the competing needs of various stakeholders, and the centrality of ethics in strategy. All of these parallel developments challenge researchers and teachers to become not only more keenly aware of these developments, but also more adept in explaining them in the classroom. As authors, we recognize and welcome this opportunity to bring forth a discussion of both traditional and newly emerging characteristics that define our vibrant competitive environment. We introduce theory wherever it provides the foundation for solid understanding, but to keep the topic of strategy both interesting and relevant, we emphasize an applications-based approach to pedagogy.

Strategic Competencies in Action

Both students and instructors want clarity and an organizing framework to help make complex strategic issues more understandable. The most significant revision to our text accomplishes this. Our text presents and explains the vital strategic competencies that managers and leaders must possess to build and sustain competitive advantage. What are these strategic competencies? We believe there are six:

- Vision
- Value Creation
- Planning and Administration
- Global Awareness
- Managing Stakeholders' Needs
- Leveraging Technology

These six competencies represent a combination of insights, skills, and methods that all businesspeople need to keep their organizations competitive. The immediate benefit to both the reader and the instructor is that we have outlined and defined what these competencies represent, and how they can be used to understand strategic issues from a unifying, holistic perspective. These competencies are demonstrated throughout each chapter as a highlighted "strategic competency in action" box where students can see how firms have dealt with a variety of strategic issues that have confronted them.

Vision Competency. Today's organizations must have a sense of purpose that defines their goals and objectives. All organizations need a vision of where they want to go and how to get there. The seeds of competitive advantage rest in the organization's vision and how the organization translates that vision into reality.

Value Creation Competency. Organizations cannot be all things to all people. Enduring competitive advantage is based on how well a firm can create and deliver value to its customers. Building competitive advantage demands that organizations define what they do best.

Planning and Administration. Organizations may be wellsprings of talent, ideas, enthusiasm, and energy. Yet, you cannot build competitive advantage if people, resources, products, and customers are not in the right place. An effective strategy that builds and sustains competitive advantage must have all its constituent parts working together to move in the same direction to achieve a common goal.

Global Awareness.   There is no doubt that the world is shrinking. Today's business has no geographic boundaries. Shrewd organizations are aware of this. They know they must reach out to new customers in new markets. They also know that new types of competitors can spring up from anywhere around the world.

Managing Stakeholders' Needs.   Today's business environment is much more complex, as managers cannot ignore the needs of their shareholders, employees, communities, and governments to serve their customers. Ethics must become a central part of strategy in every organization. Yet, there are no easy answers when managers must balance the needs of different stakeholders over time.

Leveraging Technology.   Today's largest companies must have the capability to move nimbly and to act like a small competitor to serve even the tiniest customer base. Conversely, today's smallest company must be able to compete and even outmaneuver the economic juggernauts of large corporations. Technological advances have made it possible for firms of all sizes to become more flexible and responsive to compete even faster.

The introduction of these strategic competencies represents the biggest enhancement for our text heretofore. For the sake of space and brevity, every chapter covers a minimum of two strategic competencies in action for the reader. For the instructor, however, there are one to two additional strategic competencies in action that are readily available on the Instructor's Section of the Thomson Learning website. There are nearly forty (40) strategic competencies in action when you include those in the book and what is available on the website. Instructors should feel free to use these additional strategic competencies in action for classroom discussion if they wish. Or, instructors may also use these additional competency examples as the basis for short essay-based examinations or case discussions.

To maintain our competitive advantage focus, we retain the basic chapter sequence of the three previous editions. Every chapter has been thoroughly updated to include some of the most recent, compelling, and revealing examples of strategic competencies in action (up to the time of this printing), as well as developments that are now occurring in all types of firms in all types of industries. At the same time, we also introduce and present some of the latest theoretical concepts and frameworks that are widely discussed and researched in the strategic management/business policy field. This balanced approach allows us to ensure that we can maintain our powerful applications-driven focus with a solid grounding in research.

Competitive Advantage Focus

Part One examines the issue of *building competitive advantage*. Chapters 1 through 5 analyze the particular steps involved in identifying and building upon a firm's strengths and distinctive competencies to create sources of competitive advantage. We examine how firms across different industries formulate strategies that enable them to build on their strengths and distinctive capabilities to compete more effectively. Traditional ways of competing are less likely to be successful in the future as customers demand a higher level of product/service customization faster and at lower cost. Thus, many of the trade-offs associated with conventionally derived, generic competitive strategies may no longer be tenable over time. Instead, firms will need to compete along all three dimensions of value creation: low cost, high quality, and speed to market. Many firms have already recognized this likely development, and in response, have begun formulating alternative strategies based on mass customization, flexibility, and new ways to reach customers. Where possible, we also highlight some of the challenges and opportunities that new technologies, such as the Internet, present to both new and established firms. We also consider the development of other types of technologies that enable all firms to become more responsive to their customers' needs while planting the seeds for future competitiveness.

Part Two focuses on *extending competitive advantage*. Chapters 6 through 8 examine the key roles of corporate strategy, global strategy, and strategic alliances in leveraging the firm's resources to deepen and reinforce its sources of competitive advantage. In particular, we bring forth additional research ideas from many fertile areas of the academic literature, including the resource-based approach to corporate strategy. This approach reveals how firms can use their distinctive capabilities and skills to leverage themselves into new arenas. Diversification and global expansion into new markets are not the only challenges and issues we cover; many companies are also actively restructuring and realigning their businesses to sharpen their competitive focus and to unlock latent sources of strategic and financial value. Thus, we also examine what firms need to consider when undertaking different forms of corporate restructuring (for example, cost reduction programs, corporate spin-offs) to promote this value-creation focus. The chapter on strategic alliances brings forth new material based on research and practice as well. For example, many firms find themselves working with strategic alliance partners where they simultaneously collaborate and compete. Likewise, entire industries (such as automotive, airlines, software, consumer electronics, health care, and telecommunications) appear to be regrouping into larger networks or webs of firms that compete with other similarly organized networks. Allying and partnering with other firms will almost certainly become taken for granted as a normal part of strategic behavior.

Part Three addresses the critical issue of *organizing and sustaining competitive advantage*. Chapter 9 deals with organizational structure, with a special emphasis on how alternative organization designs promote the simultaneous development of distinctive capabilities with the need for fast responsiveness to customers' changing needs. We explain the concept of the virtual organization in great detail, and how firms increasingly are becoming network-based organizations in general. We examine the critical success factors that managers must consider when they organize their firm's value-adding activities on a virtual basis. No less important, Chapter 10 also covers such vital topics as reward systems, performance evaluation criteria, corporate culture, and the notion of the learning organization. Chapter 10 examines how firms can renew their sources of competitive advantage as they grapple with issues related to strategic change.

Part Four introduces the notion of corporate governance. Chapter 11 is an entirely new chapter that deals with the key issues of corporate governance. The numerous scandals of corporate malfeasance and other issues that occurred over the past several years demonstrate that governments, employees, and customers will not tolerate firms that act solely in their own Machiavellian self-interest. Truly enduring organizations are built on solid principles. Although corporate governance itself is an extremely complex topic that covers everything from appropriate accounting methodology to members on the boards of directors, we present the essential concepts that students and practitioners must know about.

Our Distinctive Edge

Within this organizational framework, our coverage of strategic management uses a variety of approaches to examine the topic of competitive advantage. To maintain continuity with the expanding research in the field, we have based our presentation and discussion of key concepts on a thorough review of the theoretical and empirical literature from strategic management. To maintain relevancy and applicability for managerial practitioners, we illustrate our presentation with numerous opening "strategic snapshots" and examples of organizations operating within a variety of different industries. Wherever possible, we use up-to-date, real-world examples to demonstrate how organizations from multiple settings deal with the many complex issues surrounding competitive advantage. Numerous industries (such as financial services, consumer packaged goods, telecommunications, airlines, retailing, electronics, computers, restaurants, automotive, entertainment, software, and multimedia) that are either on the leading edge of change or facing many of these strategic challenges are examined in detail.

Of the eleven chapters in our book, seven are especially distinctive, containing material that we emphasize when compared to other books in the discipline. Examples include the following:

Chapter 4: Building Competitive Advantage Through Distinction
Understanding the trade-offs among various competitive strategies
Developing new competitive strategies based on mass customization
The rise of product design modularity and its impact on fast response
Competing to understand and to create new market segments
Economic characteristics of Internet-based competition
Life-cycle dynamics and its impact on different forms of competitive advantage

Chapter 5: Responding to Shifts in Competitive Advantage
How change affects a firm's distinctive competence
Competence-changing and disruptive technologies
Rise of new Internet-driven and alternative distribution channels
Changes in related or neighboring industries
Strategies and responses designed to accommodate change

Chapter 6: Corporate Strategy: Leveraging Resources
Revisiting the "resource-based view of corporate strategy"
Competence-based focus that forms the pillar of synergy
Key tests for diversification success
Costs of diversification
Corporate restructuring and the rise of spin-offs to unlock value

Chapter 8: Strategic Alliances: Partnering for Advantage
Types of strategic alliances
Competence-based competition and learning
Network vs. network competition
The rise of knowledge webs
The rise of "co-opetition"
Alliance benefits/costs/risks
Japanese keiretsu/Korean chaebols
Using alliances to de-skill competitors

Chapter 9: Designing Organizations for Advantage

Trade-offs accompanying different organization designs

The rise of hybrid network organizations

Key characteristics of virtual organizations

Management practices in virtual organizations

Chapter 10: Organizing and Learning to Sustain Advantage

The impact of reward systems on strategy implementation

Performance evaluation and its impact on strategy

Corporate cultures and strategy implementation

The double-edged characteristic of corporate cultures

How dominant approaches give rise to dominant mind-sets

The concept of a learning organization

Management practices of learning organizations

Organization designs to promote learning

Implementing strategic change

Steps to promote change in static and "dinosaur" organizations

Chapter 11: Corporate Governance: Instilling Long-Term Value

The key roles played by boards of directors

Shareholder activism

Board reforms

The Sarbanes-Oxley Act of 2002

Differing global perspectives on what constitutes effective corporate governance

Learning-Based Features of This Text

To maximize the learning value of this text, we have organized each chapter using a common format that introduces and reinforces key strategic management concepts and terms. Each chapter includes the following organizational features:

Learning Objectives. At the beginning of every chapter, a series of learning objectives helps readers identify key points and ideas. These objectives provide a step-by-step process that guides the reader through the chapter's material.

Opening Strategic Snapshots. Each chapter begins with an opening minicase(s), known as a strategic snapshot. These are designed to introduce the different environmental settings, strategies, and actions that relate to an issue surrounding competitive advantage. We use companies from a variety of different industry settings, including Nokia, Cisco Systems, Eastman Kodak, Kellogg, 3M, Nordstrom, General Electric, IBM, and Morrison-Knudsen. The purpose of these cases is to show how a specific company applies the concepts and principles presented in that chapter, providing a useful bridge between real-world practices and the concepts discussed throughout the book.

Strategic Competencies in Action. Selected strategic competencies in action boxes demonstrate how various organizations act upon the six ingredients of strategy.

Key Terms. Key ideas and terms that are vital to understanding strategic management are boldfaced throughout the book. Of course, a glossary at the end of the text provides a review and handy summary of these terms' definitions.

Chapter Summary. Each chapter ends with a summary that is directly linked to the learning objectives. These summaries are presented in a bullet-point format to reinforce key concepts, tools, and ideas discussed in the chapter.

Discussion Questions and Exercises. At the end of most chapters, students are encouraged to think about what they have learned through the use of discussion questions, exercises, and even the Internet to see how companies are competing in today's fast-changing environment.

Examples. In addition to the opening cases, each chapter includes many up-to-date examples of how different organizations tackle a particular issue related to competitive advantage. These examples are designed to supplement the opening cases and to reinforce the reader's learning. Comprehensive company, author, and subject indexes are provided at the end of the text to facilitate easy accessibility to the examples discussed throughout the chapters, as well as the academic research that provides the intellectual underpinning of this book.

The Package

Instructor's Resource Guide with Test Bank (ISBN 0-324-22622-5) prepared by Craig VanSandt at Augustana College. Much more than an instructor's guide, this all-in-one instructional resource has chapter-by-chapter lecture notes, learning objectives, key terms and concepts, an overview of the chapter material, supplemental resources, and test questions for each chapter.

PowerPoint Presentation: A complete set of PowerPoint slides developed by John P. Orr at McKendree College supports each chapter. The slides include the chapter figures, additional figures, and text slides, and are available for downloading from the book's website at http://pitts.swlearning.com.

Website: This text features a website that offers case updates and other strategy resources. Please see us on the web at http://pitts.swlearning.com.

The Business and Company Resource Center: Put a complete business library at your students' fingertips with The Business & Company Resource Center (BCRC). The BCRC is a premier online business research tool that allows you to seamlessly search thousands of periodicals, journals, references, financial information, industry reports, company histories, and much more.

Acknowledgments

Now we come to the high point of our labor of love. There is no doubt that this is the most important and fun part of writing this book. We want to express our deep and continued appreciation to the many people throughout the entire process who provided assistance in the creation and refinement of this text as our editions have evolved. Over the past decade or more, however, there is clearly one person who stands out. We remain indebted first and especially to our mutual friend, John W. Slocum, Jr., a current colleague of one of us and a former colleague of the other, for his genius in bringing us together to work on this project. John's guidance, help, and inspiration have been vital to not only our previous three editions, but also especially this one. For the first three editions that now span over a decade, John spent hundreds of hours reading some of the earlier drafts of our chapters, making recommendations, and helping us to demystify some of our academic writing tendencies. Because of his own enormous base of publishing experience, we benefited from John's knowledge of how the writing, revision, and publication cycle works in practice. The entirely new approach of this fourth edition in many ways can claim John as its intellectual father. The notion of introducing and using strategic competencies as an organizing framework traces its academic roots to John's own legendary work in the management field. John has always remained a fervent believer and practitioner in ensuring that both the student and the instructor can learn, apply, and use the concepts that we academics write about. Thus, the framework of using strategic competencies in action that are found throughout our eleven chapters represents a pivotal intellectual and spiritual contribution from him. We also learned a variety of very helpful techniques that made our writing experience much more enjoyable and certainly more efficient. John's helpful counsel at critical points and his ready willingness to review many early chapters of all our editions have contributed substantially to this effort. John has also served and remained a valuable role model, a ready source of assistance and advice, and most importantly as a truly valued friend.

The highly professional attitude of the many people at Thomson Business and Economics has greatly enhanced the pleasure of writing this book. Although many people at Thomson have been extremely helpful over the years (and the editions), we certainly want to give our special thanks to John Szilagyi and Denise Simon for their nurturing support, editorial guidance, and quick turnaround on our chapter manuscripts. Academics can always benefit from another keen eye, and we definitely benefited from their suggestions and ideas throughout the entire writing and revision process. John Szilagyi has also provided the organizational guidance and leadership within Thomson to ensure that all aspects of book editing, design, and production work together smoothly like a classical orchestra. Our numerous long-distance conversations with Denise Simon have been fun and full of enthusiasm. Likewise, a warm thank-you is due to Rob Bloom, and Joe Sabatino—all of whom have worked diligently to promote our book to universities and business schools.

Our senior production project manager, Deanna Quinn, has done an absolutely splendid job of managing the rapid flow of copyediting and page proofs during the production phase of this book. In fact, Deanna has worked with us for all editions of our book and should be especially commended for all of her first-rate, ultra-dedicated efforts over the past decade; she remains the utmost paragon of fast turnaround, efficiency, dedication, and innovation. The second author made the strongest personal request that our book would be revised and produced under her auspices. Once a wonderful talent and relationship is discovered, we will do everything possible to preserve and sustain it. Doubtless, she has been a real inspiration for us, and certainly has borne the cumulative effects of many years' listening to the second author's barrage of jokes, requests for schedule clarifications, and his need for continuous production feedback.

We would like to express our sincere appreciation to our numerous colleagues in the fields of strategic management, technology management, and organizational behavior who have encouraged us to pursue and deepen our efforts in working on this project. These include Michael A. Hitt of Texas A & M University; Michael E. McGill, former executive vice president of Associates First Capital (and formerly of Southern Methodist University); Charles R. Greer of Texas Christian University; Richard A. Bettis of the University of North Carolina at Chapel Hill; Joel D. Goldhar of Illinois Institute of Technology; and Mariann (Sam) Jelinek of William and Mary College. A number of our colleagues from business and industry have also contributed their invaluable insights and support to ensure that our examples and ideas were accurate, timely, and on target. More importantly, all of these colleagues have become our friends along the way.

Furthermore, we would like to acknowledge and thank our colleagues who reviewed *Strategic Management* as this new edition was in development.

Michael Claudon, Middlebury College
W. Jack Duncan, University of Alabama at Birmingham
Kenneth Gross, Oklahoma University
Don Issac, Tabor College
Debi Mishra, Binghamton University
John Orr, McKendree College
Daniel Rutledge, Purdue University North Central
Rick Smith, Iowa State
Linda Watson, Warner Southern College
Rex Welling, Drake University

We would also like to acknowledge the people who read and commented on *Strategic Management* in its various earlier incarnations. These colleagues provided valuable suggestions that helped to refine the content and instruction approach: Kenneth E. Aupperle, B. R. Baliga, Amy Beattie, Joyce M. Beggs, Eldon H. Bernstein, Kimberly B. Boal, Thomas M. Box, Garry D. Bruton, Charles M. Byles, James J. Chrisman, Marian Clark, Mary Coulter, Peter S. Davis, Derrick E. Dsouza, Timothy W. Edlund, Alan B. Eisner, Robert R. Edwards, Golpira Eshghi, Ari Ginsberg, Freda Zuzan Hartman, F. Theodore, Helmer, J. Kay Keels, David R. Lee, William M. Lindsay, Franz T. Lohrke, John P. Loveland, Timothy A. Matherly, Paul H. Meredith, Wilbur N. Moulton, William F. Muhs, Newman S. Peery, Jr., Dennis J. Pollard, Jesus A. Ponce-De-Leon, W. Keith Schilit, Dean M. Schroeder, Terrence C. Sebora, Chris Shook, Charles B. Shra der, Marilyn L. Taylor, John Clair Thompson, Larry C. Wall, Robert Wharton, and Jack W. Wimer.

We are grateful to our respective academic institutions—Gettysburg College and Southern Methodist University—for their encouragement and support of this effort. In particular, the second author would like to thank Wanda Hanson, Jeannie Milazzo, and Nancy Williams of Southern Methodist University for their exceptional dedication, cheerful personalities, strong work ethics, and all-around help in putting this manuscript through many stages of rewriting, editing, copying, and retyping. The second author thanks Dean Al Niemi for promoting an intellectual environment conducive to the revision and production of this book.

Finally, and perhaps most important, a special thanks is due to all of the students with whom we have had the pleasure and honor of associating and teaching over many years. It is they who are our fountains of youth, as they have the opportunity to learn from the past and to create a better future! They keep our minds young and enthusiastic for our writing.

Robert A. Pitts
David Lei

Part One

Building Competitive Advantage

The Strategic Management Process

Chapter Outline

What you will learn

- *The importance of strategy and why it matters to organizations*

- *The key roles of vision, value creation, planning and administration, global awareness, leveraging technology, and stakeholders*

- *The four stages of the strategic management process*

- *The concept of a SWOT analysis*

- *The concepts of corporate and business strategies*

- *The central role of ethics in strategy*

- *The different stakeholders of an organization*

Strategic Snapshot

Evolution of the Restaurant Industry[1]

Broadly speaking, there are two main segments of the restaurant industry—full-service restaurants and fast-food restaurants. In 2004, it is expected that Americans will spend about $440 billion eating out. The restaurant industry employs more people in the United States—12 million—than any other industry—with the exception of the federal government. Let us take a look at some developments on the fast-food side of the industry.

Ever since Ray Kroc purchased the rights to use the McDonald brothers' idea of serving fast-cooked, low-cost hamburgers, French fries, and chocolate shakes to customers in 1955, the restaurant industry has never been the same. Since that time, the McDonald's restaurant chain has grown to become a $17 billion business (2003 systemwide sales) and will celebrate its fiftieth anniversary in 2005. Its famous golden arches are a familiar sight across the United States and increasingly much of the world. More broadly speaking, the fast-food restaurant has become a highly complex industry in its own right. Companies such as McDonald's, Burger King, Wendy's, KFC (formerly Kentucky Fried Chicken), Taco Bell, and Domino's Pizza are well-known American and global brand names. All of these restaurant firms typically target customers willing to pay for a low-cost meal with a minimum of service and maximum convenience.

The Fast-Food Restaurant Environment

Despite its continued high growth, competition in the fast-food restaurant industry remains fierce; newer rivals enter the picture to serve both existing tastes and the rise of new segments. For example, restaurant chains such as Bennigan's, Brinker International (better known for its flagship chain, Chili's Bar & Grill), and TGI Friday's are trying to capture customers who want larger and more "deluxe" gourmet hamburgers with table service and a more diversified menu. Their offerings are significantly different (and more expensive) from those provided by McDonald's, Burger King, Wendy's, and Jack in the Box—all of which compete fiercely for the fast-food hamburger segment of the restaurant industry. Local hamburger chains that offer quality burgers in a fast-food setting, such as Steak n Shake, are moving beyond their traditional midwestern locations to expand to the South. Other firms, such as Cracker Barrel, KFC, Pizza Hut, Domino's Pizza, La Madeleine, Papa John's International, Little Caesar's, Sbarro, and Taco Bueno, are attempting to stake out positions in the nonhamburger segment of the industry, where they do not have to compete directly with industry giant McDonald's and other established hamburger-based chains with long-standing market positions.

Behind the rapid rise in the number of fast-food restaurants are some important trends that may change the way the industry competes. Two key macroeconomic factors are redefining this industry. First, most people are becoming more health conscious and selective about what and how they eat. In particular, newer forms of "leaner" cuisine that emphasize balanced nutrition and good taste are dramatically changing the way restaurants are preparing and marketing their offerings. The baby-boom generation that grew up after World War II powered the enormous growth of McDonald's and other hamburger joints. As this generation grows older, it is increasingly turning away from hamburgers and more toward healthier diets. Likewise, many of these same people are choosing ethnic foods also, such as Chinese, Italian, or Tex-Mex. Even McDonald's has begun to offer salads in a recognition of this trend's effect on its core hamburger offering.

The second major trend defining this industry is that the average American family continues to eat about half of its meals outside of home—an ongoing trend that became entrenched during the 1990s. Although this development would seem to suggest that the restaurant industry can continue to grow at a rapid pace, Americans are becoming much more selective about what they want. In general, not only are people becoming more health conscious, but they are seeking value from their meals as well. This has been particularly more evident with the recent economic downturn in 2001–2002.

In response to these broader changes in population demographics and economic spending patterns, the more traditional fast-food chains have persisted in trying to conceive new "value-based meals," or "value pricing," that seek to bundle different food offerings under one lower price. At the same time, restaurants have offered a new selection on their menus, featuring items that are claimed to be "heart-healthy," or "lighter fare" for those who are watching their weight. Many existing and newly entering restaurant chains find these changes in demand and tastes an opportunity because it means that more health- and value-conscious customers are willing to try new types of leaner food, such as rotisserie-cooked chicken as opposed to fried chicken. Thus, the numerous changes in the way people choose their meals are having a significant impact on how these restaurant chains formulate their strategies and compete with new rivals.

Sample Competitors

Let us now look at three different competitors in the fast-food restaurant industry and see how they deal with both their competitors and the larger changes taking place among their customers.

McDonald's. McDonald's is one of the oldest and perhaps the best known of all fast-food restaurant companies. Some of its most popular food offerings range from small hamburgers to such market hits as the Big Mac, the Quarter Pounder, its great-tasting French fries, and rich chocolate shakes. In recent years, it has experimented with a variety of healthier menu items, including its recent line of salads. In many ways, McDonald's is considered the bellwether industry leader because of its enormous reach within the United States and around the world. Many Wall Street analysts view McDonald's as a proxy for the overall restaurant industry, since it is viewed as the "price leader" in defining value for customers. When McDonald's offers a special promotion, all of its fast-food rivals must respond by matching a lower price.

McDonald's competes by offering the same basic types of food offerings in each of its restaurants, all prepared to the same exact specifications of heat, time, weight, size, and presentation. By requiring each restaurant to follow standardized procedures in cooking food and serving customers, McDonald's can ensure a consistent level of quality and service throughout its system. The McDonald's operations manual specifies every step and process inside each of its restaurants. Even the precise amount of time that is needed to toast a hamburger bun is spelled out to guarantee consistency of taste. These procedures and guidelines have also helped McDonald's become a low-cost producer, since each restaurant does not have to "relearn" how to cook its food and serve its customers. In effect, the procedures and basic menus used in each McDonald's restaurant are interchangeable with outlets in other parts of the country. Thus, a customer eating a hamburger at a McDonald's in San Francisco will notice little difference from a hamburger served at a McDonald's in New York or elsewhere.

To compete against such rivals as Burger King, Jack in the Box, and Wendy's, McDonald's focuses on providing fast service with consistent quality and generally low prices. This formula has made McDonald's the largest fast-food provider in the United States. However, McDonald's realized that it could not grow its hamburger business at the same double-digit growth rates of years past. In 2000, McDonald's sought to expand by purchasing Boston Market, Donatos Pizza, and Chipotle Mexican Grill to capture growth in new markets. After three years of disappointing results, McDonald's decided to sell off its interest in these nonhamburger restaurant chains.

Brinker International.

Brinker International is better known for the growing variety of restaurants that it operates, including Chili's Bar & Grill, Romano's Macaroni Grill, Corner Bakery Café, Big Bowl Asian Kitchen, Rockfish Seafood Grill, and On The Border, to name a few. However, Chili's is the largest restaurant chain under Brinker management, making up 70 percent of the company's profit and 65 percent of its nearly 1,500 restaurants. It is probably best known for its deluxe hamburgers, and it certainly competes very differently than McDonald's in trying to win customers. Instead of copying McDonald's formula for low-priced, standardized food with no table service, Chili's has taken the opposite approach. Founded by legendary restaurateur Norman Brinker, Chili's was designed to make eating out a fun and warm experience. Although people pay more to eat at Chili's, customers receive friendly table service with a menu that highlights the many different ways a hamburger can be cooked and served. Its famous gourmet hamburgers are offered with various cheeses, mushrooms, and sauces, generous servings of French fries, and other extras that make for a distinctive, satisfying, but reasonably priced meal.

Despite its high-quality offering, Chili's is certainly not just a hamburger-only restaurant. A customer's selection is not limited solely to hamburgers; large salads, small steaks, grilled chicken dishes, seafood, pasta, and its increasingly popular baby back ribs are also available. These offerings cater to customers who still want the fun of eating at Chili's without the high calories or fat content of hamburgers. Still, if customers should feel the need, generous portions of desserts are also offered to round out the meal. Chili's wants to make its customers feel that eating out can be a fun and relaxing experience. The company emphasizes customer service by training its people to be extremely responsive to customer needs and to get to know their regular customers better.

Yum! Brands.

Yum! Brands was formerly known as Tricon Global Restaurants. Before its name change, Yum! Brands was best known for its three core restaurant chains: Pizza Hut, KFC (formerly Kentucky Fried Chicken), and Taco Bell. Once a part of PepsiCo, Yum! Brands (then known as Tricon) became an independent firm in 1997 when PepsiCo decided to exit from the fiercely competitive restaurant business. Although Yum! Brands is not a familiar name to most customers, its restaurants most certainly are. All three units have decades of experience competing with McDonald's and other restaurant chain giants. Instead of competing directly with McDonald's or Chili's, Yum! Brands' three different businesses—KFC, Taco Bell, and Pizza Hut—target three nonhamburger segments of the restaurant industry.

For example, KFC offers its traditional, distinctive-tasting fried chicken recipes, along with its golden rotisserie-cooked chicken to serve both the conventional fast-food and the growing health-conscious segments. Although KFC is a leader in the chicken segment of the restaurant industry, it faces consistently tough competition from Chick-Fil-A, Church's, Popeye's, and other smaller chicken-based restaurants. To meet these competitive threats, KFC has now begun to offer value-priced meals that feature fried chicken with mashed potatoes or biscuits for a new lower price. In 2003, KFC began to offer roasted boneless chicken. It also periodically introduces new chicken-based products, such as popcorn chicken, spicy wings, and other similar items.

Yum! Brands' Taco Bell unit seeks to carve out a position in the growing Tex-Mex fast-food segment. The higher population growth in the Southwest and the Sunbelt has contributed to making Tex-Mex food more popular throughout the United States. In turn, Taco Bell has benefited by offering different types of tacos, enchiladas, fajitas, and other similar foods through its convenience-oriented outlets. Taco Bell competes with other

Mexican-style food chains, such as Taco Bueno and numerous smaller Mexican restaurant chains found in the Southwest. For much of the 1990s, Taco Bell was one of Yum! Brands' fastest-growing and most profitable businesses, although in recent years its growth has slowed considerably as competition in this market segment intensified.

Pizza Hut has traditionally competed by offering restaurant-style, sit-down pizza meals. Pizza Hut's most distinctive food offering is its specialty pan pizza, which has a special taste and texture. In recent years, Pizza Hut has been a strong performer for both previous owner PepsiCo and current owner Yum! Brands. In fact, Pizza Hut is now experimenting with a variety of different types of pizzas in different parts of the country in order to satisfy more local tastes. Although Pizza Hut retains the largest market share in this segment, it faces fierce competition from new companies such as Domino's Pizza and Little Caesar's. Most recently, Pizza Hut's toughest competitor appears to be Papa John's International, a small company that has grown rapidly over the past decade. All of Pizza Hut's competitors try to offer a different approach to customers. To carve out its own market, Domino's Pizza competes against Pizza Hut by offering only home delivery of pizza, rather than sit-down service. Little Caesar's, on the other hand, competes primarily through innovative advertisements and specially priced pizzas for both pickup and delivery; it does not offer sit-down service, either. Papa John's International offers home delivery, advertises aggressively, and claims to use only the freshest ingredients. To meet these competitive challenges, Pizza Hut refocused its operations more on home delivery service and offers free breadsticks, salads, and even soft drinks in order to win over more customers. Pizza Hut even took Papa John's International to court in 1999 and 2000 in a dispute over food claims and the luring away of existing restaurant franchise owners.

Yum! Brands has continued to grow in the past few years. Under CEO David Novak, Yum! Brands is pushing restaurants to improve food quality and counter service. Employees now are evaluated on how well they treat customers, and they are expected to attend training four times a year. Yum! Brands also expanded beyond its three core restaurants by purchasing Long John Silver's and A&W All-American Food Restaurants.

Multiple Strategic Issues

As an example of some of the different issues facing each type of company, we can look at how the major competitors view and manage their restaurant operations. For both McDonald's and Brinker International, restaurants are their primary business. However, the two companies differ in some important ways. For the most part, McDonald's defines its business through its hamburger-focused offerings to customers, with a particular focus on consistency, good value, and a standardized approach to managing operations. In this sense, McDonald's has a much more targeted approach to growing its business. Brinker International, however, operates a number of different restaurant chains—each designed to reach a different type of customer who wants to satisfy a different type of meal preference or taste. What people want from Chili's may indeed be different from what they want from Romano's Macaroni Grill, Corner Bakery Café, or On The Border. Thus, Brinker International must formulate a strategy for each of its restaurant chains in order to reach out to multiple markets.

When Yum! Brands was part of PepsiCo, restaurants were just one portion of a larger company that also includes Frito-Lay snacks and its traditional soft drinks. Thus, PepsiCo did not actually compete in the restaurant industry; its various units (KFC, Taco Bell, and Pizza Hut) did. Consequently, the strategic issues confronting PepsiCo's senior management differed from those facing McDonald's top management. Senior management at PepsiCo were asking themselves how well did their various restaurant businesses fit with their other snack food and soft drink units. PepsiCo's management faced the additional task of ensuring that the restaurant business worked well with its beverage (cola and non-cola) and snack food (Frito-Lay) units. Throughout much of the 1980s and 1990s, the restaurant business was an important part of PepsiCo's overall strategy. Increasing competitive pressures and slowing of the restaurant industry's overall growth rate, however, made it increasingly difficult for PepsiCo to compete effectively in the industry. The strategic benefits that PepsiCo could once bring to the restaurant industry—marketing prowess, low-cost source of beverages, shared advertising expenditures, and shared management—became difficult to sustain when PepsiCo's beverage business began to lose significant market share to arch rival Coca-Cola, especially in markets outside the United States. By the mid- to late 1990s, severe competition and declining profit margins on both fronts—beverages and restaurants—made it increasingly difficult for PepsiCo to compete effectively in both businesses simultaneously. Deciding that it needed to sharpen its competitive focus and to raise capital for its beverage business, PepsiCo's senior management decided to sell its restaurant operations as a way to exit the restaurant business.

McDonald's appears to be refocusing on its core hamburger business. Although it attempted to transfer much of its restaurant-based expertise to Chipotle, Boston Market, and Donatos Pizza, it faced considerable difficulty in doing so. At the same time, McDonald's neglected its vast hamburger restaurant system for a few years, costing it valuable market share as customers grumbled about the quality of food and service. As it tries to sell off its interests in Chipotle, Boston Market, and Donatos Pizza, McDonald's faces some key strategic issues that are very different from how it previously managed its hamburger-focused business in past years.

Introduction

As the preceding examples illustrate, firms must compete with each other to gain their customers' business. Yet, not all firms will necessarily compete with one another in the same way. Each firm is likely to devise its own strategy to deal with its competitive rivals, to serve its particular base of customers, and to act on the changes that impact the way it operates. Each firm needs to develop a competitive advantage in its strategy that enables it to compete effectively.

Strategy refers to the ideas, plans, and support that firms employ to compete successfully against their rivals. Strategy is designed to help firms achieve competitive advantage. In the broadest sense, **competitive advantage** is what allows a firm to gain an edge over its rivals. Competitive advantage enables a firm to generate successful performance over an extended period. Throughout this book, which focuses on the concepts of strategy and competitive advantage, you will learn how firms from a variety of different industries, settings, and situations develop strategies to achieve competitive advantage. Activities undertaken to achieve this end form the basis of the strategic management process.

Competitive rivalry characterizes economic activity not only in our own country but throughout the free world as well, and it is rapidly replacing government planning across most of the globe. Much organized activity outside the realm of business and commerce is also highly competitive. Nonprofit enterprises such as colleges, churches, and charities, for example, generally face numerous rivals eagerly seeking the same students, parishioners, and contributors. Because rivalry is such a pervasive aspect of so many different kinds of activity, the concepts developed in this text will be useful to managers operating in a wide range of settings. How to construct an effective strategy to deal with competitive rivalry is the primary question addressed in this book.

In our book, we believe that the key to formulating and implementing an effective strategy that builds competitive advantage depends on the firm's attention to a core set of six strategic ingredients:

- vision
- value creation

strategy:
Refers to the ideas, plans, and support that firms employ to compete successfully against their rivals. Strategy is designed to help firms achieve competitive advantage.

competitive advantage:
Allows a firm to gain an edge over rivals when competing. Competitive advantage comes from a firm's ability to perform activities more distinctively or more effectively than rivals.

- planning and administration
- global awareness
- managing stakeholders
- leveraging technology

Each of these ingredients contributes to an organization's strategy in its own special way. However, an organization must ensure that these six ingredients work together to form the basis of an effective, coherent strategy. For each strategic ingredient, a particular set of attributes defines its contribution to the organization's strategy. Thus, each strategic ingredient requires the development of a corresponding strategic competency that represents a particular combination of skills and perspectives that enables a firm to construct a strategy that is centered on competitive advantage. We use the term *strategic competency* because we believe that every organization can steadily enrich its capability to compete. Exhibit 1-1 identifies several important skills and perspectives associated with each strategic competency. In practice, it is difficult to isolate where

---

Six Ingredients of Strategy   *Exhibit 1-1*

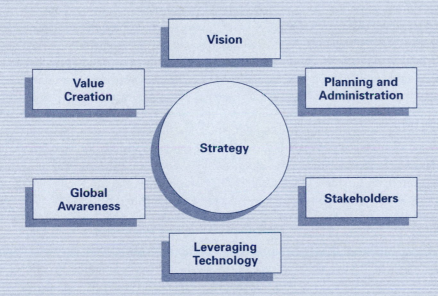

- Each ingredient, in turn, requires the development of a strategic competency.

Vision Competency

- Vision
- Mission
- Goals and Objectives

Value Creation Competency

- Customer Focus
- Competitor Focus

Planning and Administration Competency

- Activity Fit
- Corporate Fit
- Alliance Fit
- People Fit
- Reward System Fit
- Communications Fit

Global Awareness Competency

- Opportunities/Threats Exist Anywhere
- Different Business Practices
- Cultural Awareness

Leveraging Technology Competency

- Faster Innovation
- Big Companies Act Small
- Small Companies Act Big

Stakeholder Competency

- Shareholders
- Customers
- Employees
- Communities
- Senior Managers

one strategic competency begins and another ends. An organization cannot ignore any one of them, nor can it concentrate its efforts on one or two competencies to the exclusion of the others. Laying out these strategic competencies is valuable primarily for helping you to see how the task of strategy formulation and implementation can be complex for any organization. Later in this chapter, we will describe each strategic competency in greater detail.

The Strategy Concept

From a traditional or historical perspective, the term *strategy* reflects strong military roots. Military commanders employ strategy in dealing with their opponents. Throughout human history, numerous military theorists, including Sun Tzu, Alexander the Great, Karl von Clausewitz, Napoleon, Stonewall Jackson, and Douglas MacArthur, have contemplated and written about strategy from many different perspectives.[2] The fundamental premise of strategy is that an adversary can defeat a rival—even a larger, more powerful one—if it can maneuver a battle or engagement onto terrain favorable to its own capabilities and skills.

distinctive competence:
The special skills, capabilities, or resources that enable a firm to stand out from its competitors; what a firm can do especially well to compete or serve its customers.

In this book, we use the term **distinctive competence** to describe those special capabilities, knowledge, skills, technologies, or other resources that enable a firm to distinguish itself from its rivals and create competitive advantage. Ideally, a firm's competence or skill is so distinctive (and even unique) that others will not be able to copy it readily. Capabilities and skills that are valuable in business include such activities as innovative product design, low-cost manufacturing, proprietary technology, superior quality, cultivating organizational practices that facilitate quick response to change, and superior distribution. Thus, a firm may have several skills, areas of activity, or organizational attributes that work in tandem to create competitive advantage. Competitors in the restaurant industry, for example, use a variety of methods for building competitive advantage, including warm and friendly service and special, proprietary recipes (Brinker International's units, including Chili's), consistent quality and low-cost operation (McDonald's), and identification of new marketing segments (Yum! Brands).

terrain:
The environment (or industry) in which competition occurs. In a military sense, terrain is the type of environment or ground on which a battle takes place. From a business sense, terrain refers to markets, segments, and products used to win over customers.

Terrain refers to the environmental setting in which an engagement with an adversary takes place. In the military realm, terrain may be a plain, a forest, a marsh, an urban environment, or the mountains. The characteristics of each of these settings influence which type of troops or deployments can be used most effectively. In the world of business, competitors do not confront each other directly on a battlefield as armies do. Rather, they compete with each other in an industry environment by targeting market segments and attempting to win customers. It is customers who determine, each time they make a purchase, which competitors "win" and which ones "lose." The industry environment thus constitutes the ultimate terrain on which business competition takes place. Accordingly, each firm needs to develop its own set of special capabilities, or distinctive competence, that enables it to win customers in the industry and market environment (terrain) that it chooses.

Because most industries contain numerous customers displaying different needs, firms generally have many different possible terrains from which to choose. Consider the restaurant industry, for example. It contains a number of different groups of customers: those wanting low-cost meals, people desiring gourmet hamburgers, and individuals preferring ethnic or health-conscious menus, as well as those who prefer a special dining experience. Each group thus constitutes a different segment or terrain on which rivals compete. Furthermore, each of these groups can be further divided into smaller subgroups of customers with even more specific needs and characteristics. For example, ethnic food runs the entire range from Chinese to French to Mexican. Each of these individual segments has somewhat different competitive characteristics that define the subterrain.

The Basis of Strategy

The essence of strategy is to match strengths and distinctive competence with terrain in such a way that one's own business enjoys a competitive advantage over rivals competing on the same terrain. In the military realm, the strategic imperative for commanders is to select a battlefield favorable to their force's particular strengths/capabilities and unfavorable to the adversary. A cavalry or highly mobile armored force, for example, should try to fight on flat, open ground where its speed and maneuverability can be put to good use. Units skilled in guerrilla tactics, by contrast, should try to encounter the enemy in dense woods, urban areas, or in the mountains—terrains that favor a hide-and-strike capability. Military strategy thus aims at achieving a favorable match between a military force's internal strengths and the external terrain on which it operates (see Exhibit 1-2).

Military Strategy   *Exhibit 1-2*

Competitive strategy for organizations likewise aims at achieving a favorable match between a firm's distinctive competence and the external environment in which it competes. However, the nature of this match is more complex in the business sphere. Unlike military conflict, competition in business does not always have to result in a win-lose situation. Industry rivals frequently have the opportunity to improve their strengths or skills as competition unfolds. In addition, the value of a firm's distinctive competence that leads to competitive advantage can also decline over time as a result of environmental change. Because of these possibilities, competitive strategy involves not just one but several different imperatives. The most important of these are to discover new opportunities, avert potential threats, overcome current weakness, sustain existing strength, and apply strength to new fields (see Exhibit 1-3).

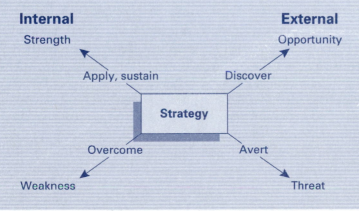

Business Strategy   *Exhibit 1-3*

strategic management process:
The steps by which management converts a firm's values, mission, and goals/objectives into a workable strategy; consists of four stages: analysis, formulation, implementation, and adjustment/evaluation.

Every firm faces the need to deal with these strategic imperatives on a continuous basis. However, some imperatives will be more dominant at a given point in time, depending on the individual firm's particular situation. Before a firm can determine which imperatives are most important, managers must have a strong sense of how the firm can use its distinctive competence to build competitive advantage to succeed in the marketplace.

The Strategic Management Process

A management process designed to satisfy strategic imperatives for building competitive advantage is called a **strategic management process.** It consists of four major steps: analysis, formulation, implementation, and adjustment/evaluation (see Exhibit 1-4).

Exhibit 1-4	Strategy Management Process

Analysis	External environment	Opportunities, Threats
	Internal environment	Strengths, Weaknesses
Formulation	Mission	Customers to be served Capabilities to be developed
	Policies	Goals, guidelines for major activities
Implementation		Organization structure, systems, culture, etc.
Adjustment/ Evaluation		(Cycle to earlier steps)

SWOT analysis:
Shorthand for strengths, weaknesses, opportunities, and threats; a fundamental step in assessing the firm's external environment; required as a first step of strategy formulation and typically carried out at the business level of the firm.

Analysis. The strategic management process begins with careful analysis of a firm's internal strengths and weaknesses and external opportunities and threats. This effort is commonly referred to as **SWOT analysis** (strengths, weaknesses, opportunities, and threats). McDonald's uses SWOT analysis regularly to assess consumer desire for new types of foods. This analysis identified increasing customer desire for new types of food and hamburgers that are "healthier" or have a lower fat content as compared to McDonald's current offerings. McDonald's top management recognizes the rising health consciousness of the American public as a potential opportunity to expand its service to customers. To exploit this opportunity, McDonald's developed, tested, and then marketed a variety of new offerings, including at one point a fat-free hamburger, chicken sandwiches, and different salads that would be instrumental in meeting this need. Had McDonald's not continued its efforts to undertake these modifications, its sales would likely have suffered as a consequence. Consumers' rising health consciousness also represents a potential threat to McDonald's as well as a potential opportunity. Failure to respond to this development could erode McDonald's competitive position in the industry.

McDonald's strengths are its fast, efficient service and its low-cost operations. These strengths give the company a well-known, commanding reputation among many segments of the U.S. population. Moreover, McDonald's spans the entire nation with its golden arches and distinctive restaurant architecture, giving each outlet a special, recognizable presence. McDonald's value-pricing policies instituted several years ago offer a combination of large sandwich, French fries, and large drink for a lower price than if these items were purchased in-dividually. They were designed to overcome a weakness that customers perceived McDonald's food as becoming more expensive over time. These numerous sources of strength, together with aggressive pricing, allow McDonald's to compete effectively with other national hamburger-based chains, such as Burger King and Wendy's, and regional hamburger outlets, such as Carl's Jr. in California and Sonic in the South.

Formulation. Information derived from SWOT analysis is used to construct a strategy that will enable the firm to use its distinctive competence to build competitive advantage. A strategy must be formulated that matches the external opportunities found in the environment with the firm's internal strengths. For each firm, this matchup or coalignment is likely to be different. To gain maximum competitive advantage, individual firms need to identify the activities they per-form best and seek ways to apply these strengths to maximum effect. Effective strategy formu-lation is based on identifying and using the firm's distinctive competence and strengths in ways that other firms cannot duplicate. This is key to building competitive advantage.

McDonald's strategy has long been based on the firm's distinctive competence in serving its customers quality food at reasonable prices. That has enabled McDonald's to become an extremely formidable player in the restaurant industry. The Chili's unit of Brinker International, on the other hand, has formulated a strategy based on providing highly personalized and warm service to each customer. Its approach is designed to make each dining experience memorable with the hope that customers will return frequently. A sit-down meal at Chili's is, however, more costly than a meal at McDonald's. Yet, both firms are prospering in the industry by formulating strategies that use their strengths to pursue somewhat different opportunities in the environment.

Implementation. An organization must commit itself to develop and refine its distinctive competence and strengths. Once an organization has made such a commitment, it must then take steps to implement this choice. Implementation measures or requirements include orga-nizing the firm's tasks, incorporating new technologies to better monitor value-creating activi-ties, hiring individuals to perform designated activities, assigning them responsibility for carry-ing out such activities, training them to perform activities properly, and rewarding them if they carry out responsibilities effectively. At McDonald's corporate headquarters, implementation involves determining such issues as the franchising fees and compensation policies for its restau-rants, hiring policies that individual McDonald's restaurants will use, and an organizational structure that facilitates efficient operations. In the case of individual McDonald's restaurants within the network, implementation focuses on such matters as rolling out new menu items smoothly, hiring able-bodied individuals, training employees to perform specific tasks, motivat-ing employees to perform tasks properly, and treating customers courteously and efficiently.

Adjustment/Evaluation. The industry environment within which a firm operates inevitably changes over time. Also, a firm's performance may fall below desired levels. Either event compels a firm to reexamine its existing approach and make adjustments that are neces-sary to regain high performance. Mechanisms must be put into place to monitor potential environmental changes and alert managers to developments that require a change in strategy and implementation practices.

For example, competition and growth in the restaurant industry may change significantly with the advent of an economic recession that limits people's disposable income. Although fancier restaurants are more likely to suffer from an economic downturn than McDonald's, such a change will also affect McDonald's, though in different ways. More people may initially be inclined to eat at McDonald's because of its value-pricing policies. However, a prolonged recession may lead to a reduction in volume, causing McDonald's to slow down expansion of new restaurants. This development, in turn, will lead to a slower growth of McDonald's earnings in the future.

The issues that managers confront when conducting the strategic management process will differ according to the competitive environments their firms face, the internal strengths and weaknesses they possess, and the number of other businesses their firms operate. Consequently, each firm needs to tailor its strategic management process in ways that best suit its own specific context and situation. In addition, firms that operate in more than one industry face strategic issues beyond those firms that compete in only one industry. These issues can be highly complex, as we will see in later chapters. Thus, firms need to remain constantly attuned to developments and changes in the environment that may warrant further adjustment of their strategies.

Business and Corporate Strategies

To appreciate the comprehensiveness of the analytic approach we will take, consider the organizational chart in Exhibit 1-5. It shows the organizational arrangement used by many firms that operate multiple businesses that span multiple industries. For example, General Electric runs businesses in the power generation, medical equipment, plastics, lighting, water treatment, financial services, home appliances, and transportation industries, to name a few. This type of company is known as a **diversified** or **multibusiness firm.** Diversified or multibusiness firms manage and operate businesses in more than one industry. In contrast, firms such as Domino's Pizza and Papa John's International are known as **single–business** or **undiversified firms.** Undiversified firms limit their activities to products and services in one industry. As indicated in Exhibit 1-5, the major subunits of a diversified, multibusiness firm are entire businesses. Each individual business generally operates in its own specific competitive environment and thus requires a separate business strategy. **Business strategy** attempts to answer the question "How do we build competitive advantage for this particular business?" or "How

multibusiness firm:
A firm that operates more than one line of business. Multibusiness firms often operate across several industries or markets, each with a separate set of customers and competitive requirements (also known as a diversified firm). Firms can possess many business units in their corporate portfolio.

single–business firm:
A firm that operates only one business in one industry or market (also known as an undiversified firm).

undiversified firm:
A firm that operates only one business in one industry or market (also known as a single-business firm).

business strategy:
Plans and actions that firms devise to compete in a given product/market scope or setting; addresses the question "How do we compete within an industry?"

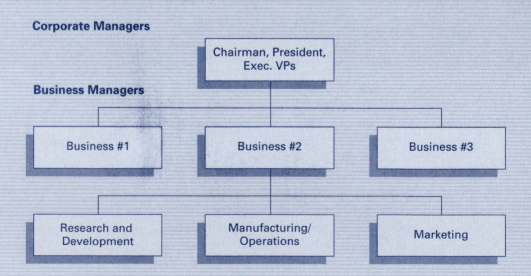

Exhibit 1-5   Multibusiness Enterprise

Corporate Managers

Chairman, President, Exec. VPs

Business Managers

Business #1   Business #2   Business #3

Research and Development   Manufacturing/ Operations   Marketing

should we compete?" For example, the business strategy pursued by KFC, which is part of Yum! Brands, is to provide different types of food based on its famous chicken recipes. By limiting itself to offering primarily chicken-centered recipes, KFC does not compete directly with McDonald's in the larger restaurant industry. Thus, KFC can focus its efforts on competing for an attractive but separate segment that matches its distinctive competence. Some ways that KFC builds competitive advantage include its highly memorable advertising ("finger-lickin' good"), its proprietary recipes (original, extra crispy, skin-free, rotisserie golden chicken), and its ability to share marketing expenses and skills with its sister units Pizza Hut, Taco Bell, Long John Silver's, and A&W All-American Food Restaurants.

Diversified, multibusiness firms also need a higher-level strategy that applies to the organization as a whole. Strategy at this higher level is known as **corporate strategy.** Corporate strategy deals with the question "What set of businesses or industries should the organization operate?" For example, when beverage and packaged foods company PepsiCo owned KFC, Taco Bell, and Pizza Hut for much of the 1980s and 1990s, PepsiCo's allocation of resources and management of the restaurant chains were issues of corporate strategy. When PepsiCo decided to eventually exit the restaurant industry in 1997, that decision also represented an issue of corporate strategy. Thus, corporate strategy was a dominant issue in the minds of PepsiCo's senior management when it considered and acted on such questions as these: Should PepsiCo even have a presence in the restaurant business? If so, what new restaurant (or other) businesses should PepsiCo enter? If not, how should PepsiCo exit the restaurant business to sharpen its focus on its beverage and Frito-Lay snack food businesses? PepsiCo's managers are still asking themselves many of the same corporate strategy questions as related to their current businesses, which include carbonated beverages, snack foods (Frito-Lay), fruit juices (for example, Tropicana), bottled drinks and water (for example, Gatorade), and cereals (Quaker Oats). What resources can PepsiCo's various businesses usefully share to apply and sustain competitive advantage? How can the marketing skills developed at Frito-Lay, for example, be used to help the beverage unit and vice versa?

corporate strategy:
Plans and actions that firms need to formulate and implement when managing a portfolio of businesses; an especially critical issue when firms seek to diversify from their initial activities or operations into new areas. Corporate strategy issues are key to extending the firm's competitive advantage from one business to another.

Strategic Imperatives

Firms facing different strategic situations generally must deal with quite different strategic imperatives. Three common strategic situations and their corresponding strategic imperatives are summarized in Exhibit 1-6.

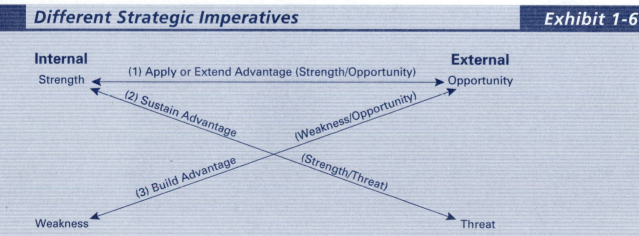

Different Strategic Imperatives **Exhibit 1-6**

Internal **External**

Strength — (1) Apply or Extend Advantage (Strength/Opportunity) → Opportunity

(2) Sustain Advantage

(Weakness/Opportunity)

(3) Build Advantage

(Strength/Threat)

Weakness Threat

Sustain Advantage. In many industries, large established firms possess substantial knowledge, a highly refined distinctive competence, knowledge of their customers' needs, and considerable experience in competing in their respective industries and individual segments. However, changes in the environment can seriously erode these advantages. Consequently, environmental change represents a potential threat to established firms. A major strategic imperative facing such firms is to sustain advantage in the face of environmental threat.

In recent years, McDonald's (as well as its larger rivals, such as Burger King and Wendy's) has had to deal with this kind of strategic imperative. First, the growing health consciousness of American consumers means that McDonald's cannot rely solely on its traditional hamburger-centered menus for sustained growth. Second, the rise of new competitors makes expansion for McDonald's difficult without considering consumers' response. These developments compel McDonald's to devise alternative strategies to sustain high performance and profitability in the fast-food restaurant industry. These include offering salads and lower-priced "value" meals to halt the erosion of its market base.

Build Advantage. Chili's situation is very different for McDonald's. As a much smaller competitor, it lacks McDonald's enormous size, pervasive market presence, and extensive operating experience. The strategic imperative it faces is to build advantage to overcome this initial weakness. To satisfy this imperative, a firm must generally seek market opportunities that do not force it to compete directly with its larger and more powerful rivals. It will generally need to achieve some type of distinction in customers' eyes by offering innovative product features, providing superior service, creating a unique experience, using novel distribution channels, or promoting an unusual image. Such an approach may enable it to satisfy some customers without triggering massive retaliation from well-established rivals. Chili's has adopted this approach by focusing on sit-down customers who want fun, friendly service and good food. Although its restaurant menus initially had a strong hamburger-oriented focus, Chili's now offers alternative meals—such as grilled chicken, salads, and other foods—designed to appeal to different tastes and health-conscious consumers. Chili's has also differentiated itself from McDonald's by offering superior customer service. These modifications enable it to operate without subjecting itself to head-on competition from McDonald's for customers that want a hamburger-based meal. Strong competitive advantage results when firms are able to formulate and implement strategies that make it difficult for rivals to imitate and copy them.

Extend Advantage. Some firms discover that the capabilities they have developed in one business can be used in another. Entry into the new arena enables them to extend advantage beyond their original domain. Yum! Brands found itself in this situation when it concluded that the capabilities developed in its line of pizza, Mexican food, and chicken restaurants could be applied to other fast-food restaurant concepts. These capabilities include extensive knowledge of customer buying habits, market segmentation skills, and market research and advertising prowess. Acting on this belief, Yum! Brands acquired two other fast-food restaurant chains, Long John Silver's and A&W All-American Food Restaurants, in 2002. This strategic move gives Yum! Brands huge exposure to become the world's largest restaurant chain with over 32,000 locations.

McDonald's also believed that its highly refined capabilities for managing a highly disciplined, nationwide system of hamburger restaurants would enable it to enter new restaurant ventures. The 2000 purchases of Chipotle Mexican Grill, Donatos Pizza, and Boston Market Corporation were designed to broaden the company's market reach.

Over time, like many other firms that sought growth by moving into new areas, McDonald's discovered that transferring skills from one restaurant format to another is a very complicated organizational task. Frequently, senior management cannot implement the sharing of skills or capabilities from one line of business to another very effectively or quickly. The economic and organizational costs of managing multiple business units can often outweigh the potential benefits. In recent years, McDonald's suffered from this difficulty. By 2003, growing competition in the hamburger business hurt McDonald's. Earnings dropped and the capabilities and operational processes that work best in the hamburger business did not apply as well to Mexican food and take-home American food. By March 2003, McDonald's was pursuing steps that would allow it to sell its controlling stakes in its nonhamburger restaurant operations.

Text Overview: The Key Challenge of Competitive Advantage. These three challenges provide the primary organizing framework for this text. These strategic imperatives apply to all firms in all industries. See Exhibit 1-7 for a summary of how the different chapters in this book fit into this framework.

Focus on Competitive Advantage		Exhibit 1-7

Strategic Challenge	Key Strategic Management Issues	
Building Competitive Advantage	Ch. 2	Assessing Industry Attractiveness and the Competitive Environment
	Ch. 3	Matching Firm Capabilities with Opportunities
	Ch. 4	Building Competitive Advantage through Distinction
	Ch. 5	Responding to Shifts in Competitive Advantage
Extending Competitive Advantage	Ch. 6	Corporate Strategy: Leveraging Resources
	Ch. 7	Global Strategy: Harnessing New Markets
	Ch. 8	Strategic Alliances: Partnering for Advantage
Organizing for Sustainable Advantage	Ch. 9	Designing Organizations for Advantage
	Ch. 10	Organizing and Learning to Sustain Advantage
Corporate Governance	Ch. 11	Corporate Governance: Instilling Long-Term Value

Chapter 2 begins as the first of four chapters that focus on building advantage. It examines the issue of the business environment. Firms compete in two basic types of environment: the general environment and the more specific industry-competitive environment. We discuss the five forces that determine an industry's structure and how that structure influences the potential for profitability.

In Chapter 3, we present tools to analyze internal strengths and weaknesses. The concept of the value chain is presented, and we discuss some general capabilities that firms use to compete in their industry.

In Chapter 4, we consider how firms develop their competitive strategies. Although each firm must formulate its own set of competitive strategies that best match its situation, most business is developed using one of the three basic strategies: low-cost leadership, differentiation, and focus. The crucial role of the Internet and how the product/market life cycle influences these generic competitive strategies are also presented.

Chapter 5 examines the impact of environmental changes and driving forces on sources of competitive advantage. A competitive advantage developed in one period may often not be as valuable in later time periods. Potential changes in technology, distribution channels, government regulations, and other factors require firms to formulate strategies to deal with change.

Chapter 6 is the first of three chapters that focuses on extending advantage. It introduces the three basic routes firms can take to expand their scope of operations: vertical integration, related diversification, and unrelated diversification. However, not all attempts to extend a firm's competitive advantage to other businesses and activities will be successful. This chapter stresses the point that **diversification** strategies must be based on the extent to which the firm's distinctive competence can be used to enter new lines of businesses. We also examine some steps that firms can take to reinvigorate their core businesses and operations through restructurings and other measures designed to enhance competitive advantage.

diversification:
A strategy that takes the firm into new industries and markets (see related diversification; unrelated diversification).

Chapter 7 presents the crucial topic of global strategy. Firms can expand their operations abroad by using global strategies. The economic basis of global strategies and their benefits and costs are analyzed.

Chapter 8 focuses on strategic alliances. In many industries, firms can no longer afford to assume all the risks of developing new products or entering new markets on their own. In fact, almost every large and medium-sized organization will use alliances in some way during its existence. Strategic alliances enable firms to share the risks and costs of new commercial endeavors, but they also raise important trade-offs that management needs to consider.

Chapter 9 is the first of two chapters that focuses on sustaining competitive advantage through the creation of vibrant and responsive organization designs. In this chapter, we examine the basic dimensions and types of organizational structure. A well-formulated strategy needs a well-designed structure to execute it. In the second part of the chapter, we focus on the emergence of networked and virtual organizations. These new formats are designed to help firms become more responsive to fast-changing technologies and customer needs.

Chapter 10 examines the pivotal roles of reward and performance measurement systems, shared values, and corporate culture in sustaining competitive advantage. These management practices, or organization designs, strongly influence and may even constrain the implementation of a firm's current and future strategy. We also consider the process of managing organizational change. We focus more specifically on how firms can become learning organizations. Learning organizations use change as an opportunity to create new sources of competitive advantage, especially as industry environments become faster moving. Because most companies find organizational change a difficult process to manage, we present some steps senior management can take to make the change process easier.

Chapter 11 addresses the vital issue of corporate governance. We analyze some of the most recent trends that are redefining the practices of boards of directors and consider the impact of the new Sarbanes-Oxley Act on corporate financial reporting and board structure. Corporate governance issues are becoming important issues in other nations as well, as we take a brief look at what trends appear to be surfacing in Europe and Asia.

The Role of Strategic Competencies in Crafting an Effective Strategy

At the beginning of this chapter, we defined a *strategic competency* as a particular combination of skills and perspectives that enable a firm to craft a strategy best suited to its own needs. For each of the six core ingredients of an effective strategy, there is a corresponding strategic competency: vision, value creation, planning and administration, global awareness, managing stakeholders, and leveraging technology.

Although the strategic competency framework is applicable to all types of organizations, the specific makeup and application of each competency is unique to each firm. For example, the way that an automotive firm leverages new types of technology to improve the quality and fuel efficiency of cars and trucks is going to be very different from how a restaurant uses technology to make food better tasting and faster to prepare. Equally important, for all the automotive companies competing in the same industry (for example, General Motors, Toyota, BMW, Hyundai), how each firm leverages technology to create a competitive advantage for itself will depend on factors that are specific to each firm (for example, the way it develops products, the way it works with suppliers, the reputation it has with customers, the way it trains and organizes its work force, the ability to learn new electronics quickly).

Within each chapter, we will examine how organizations from a variety of industries have sought to build competitive advantage or deal with a key strategic/organizational challenge by managing the issues that surround a particular strategic competency. These sections are labeled as "Strategic Competency in Action." A portrait of how a firm cultivates or uses the skills and perspectives associated with a given competency in its own unique way will provide you with a sense of how complex, and yet dynamic, strategy really can be.

Vision Competency: Determining and Setting Strategic Goals

Any organization needs an underlying purpose from which to chart its future. If organizations are to compete effectively and serve their customers well, they need to establish a series of guideposts that focus their efforts over an extended time period. These guideposts will help the firm clarify the purpose of its existence, where it is going, and where it wants to be. Strategies are unlikely to be effective without a sense of direction.

Vision. A **vision** relates to the firm's broadest and most desirable goals. A vision describes the firm's aspirations of what it really wants to be. Visions are important because they are designed to capture the imagination of the firm's people and galvanize their efforts to achieve a higher purpose, cause, or ideal. Some of the most effective visions are those in which the firm seeks to excel or lead in some activity that bonds all of its people together with a common purpose. Visions should have a strong emotional appeal that encourages people to commit their full energies and minds to achieving this ideal. A powerful vision, if fully embraced and executed by the organization, can position the firm for industry-wide leadership. In some cases, a vision may enable the firm to "change the rules" of the industry to one's favor.

vision:
The highest aspirations and ideals of a person or organization; what a firm wants to be. Vision statements often describe the firm or organization in lofty, even romantic or mystical tones (see mission; goals; objectives).

Examples of powerful visions that have changed and redefined entire industries include that of Cable News Network (CNN), now a part of Time Warner. Founded in 1981 by Ted Turner to provide twenty-four-hour news coverage, CNN prospered by aggressively pushing forward its new television format that would ultimately become the fastest news source for corporations and even national governments. Even under recently restructured Time Warner, CNN's vision remains to be the best and most reliable news source on any topic, anywhere, anytime. For example, during the First Gulf War of 1990-1991, world leaders, including Iraq's Saddam Hussein, reportedly tuned in to CNN to receive the most accurate and up-to-date coverage of Operation Desert Storm.

In the restaurant industry example, McDonald's and Brinker International have prospered by pursuing their own visions of what they think the restaurant industry should offer to consumers. The founder of McDonald's Corporation, Ray Kroc, promoted a vision of McDonald's as being the leading provider of moderately priced, quality food to anyone, anywhere. Brinker International, on the other hand, has prospered by pushing forward a different vision of restaurant service; it believes each meal should be a fun and exciting experience.

In the beverage industry, Coca-Cola has a powerful vision that has galvanized the firm's efforts in defining much of the beverage and soft drink industry. Coke wants to make sure that "a Coke is in arm's reach" of any customer, no matter where that customer is around the world. This simple but mighty vision has defined the essence of Coke's purpose and its strategy of entering and serving many markets around the world. No market is too small for Coke to carry out its vision.

In the telecommunications and computer networking industries, Cisco Systems leads in developing state-of-the-art equipment that brings the Internet to everyone—businesses, governments, large organizations, and consumers in the home. A company that is barely twenty years old, Cisco Systems has grown to become one of America's technology leaders and most valuable companies. Under CEO John Chambers, Cisco has a vision that all of the world's activities will eventually be strongly influenced and impacted by the Internet. Over the next few years, Cisco envisions that most business transactions will occur over the Internet, as will a significant portion of job training and education, stock trading and investments for individuals, as well as even health care through telemedicine. Cisco's vision of the Internet can be summarized in its often-quoted commercials: "Are You Ready?" To make its vision happen, Cisco has been extremely aggressive in growing its businesses, especially by acquiring a vast number of promising start-up firms that are developing cutting-edge technologies.

Corporate visions are often lofty and even surrounded by a high level of idealism or romanticism. They provide a consistency of purpose that gives the organization a reason to exist. However, visions do not lay out the actual strategies, steps, or methods by which the firm will pursue its purpose. Missions, on the other hand, are intended to provide the basis for fulfilling a vision.

Mission. A firm's **mission** describes the organization in terms of the business it is in, the customers it serves, and the skills it intends to develop to fulfill its vision. Visions that capture the organization's purpose and ideals become more concrete and "real" in an organization's mission. Missions are more specific than visions in that they establish the broad guidelines of how the firm will achieve or fulfill its vision over a certain time period. Firms will translate their vision into a mission statement that sets the firm's boundaries and provides a sense of direction. Mission statements spell out in a general way some key pillars of building a strategy—the firm's customers, the firm's principal products or services, and the direction that a firm intends to move over a future time period.

For example, the mission at McDonald's can be summarized in four letters originally conceived by founder Ray Kroc and his earliest franchises: QSCV (quality, service, cleanliness, and value). The mission of McDonald's (both at corporate headquarters and in individual restaurants) is to implement each of these four policies to satisfy its customers. High quality of food, fast and courteous service, clean restaurants, and affordable prices are guiding pillars that lay the foundation for all of McDonald's Corporation's strategies and organizational practices. By carrying out this simple mission statement, McDonald's can translate its vision into reality.

Goals and Objectives. Mission statements are designed to make the organization's vision more concrete and real to its people. However, mission statements still do not provide the tangible goals or objectives that must be met to achieve a firm's broader purpose. Thus, **goals** and **objectives** are needed to provide a series of direct, measurable tasks that contribute to the

mission:
Describes the firm or organization in terms of its business. Mission statements answer the questions "What business are we in?" and "What do we intend to do to succeed?" Mission statements are somewhat more concrete than vision statements but still do not specify the goals and objectives necessary to translate the mission into reality (see vision; goals; objectives).

goals:
The specific results to be achieved within a given time period (also known as objectives).

objectives:
The specific results to be achieved within a given time period (also known as goals). Objectives guide the firm or organization in achieving its mission (see vision; mission).

organization's mission. Goals and objectives are the results to be achieved within a specific time period. Unlike the mission statement that describes the firm's purpose more generally, goals and objectives designate the time period in which certain actions and results are to be achieved. Examples of goals and objectives include the following: achieving a 30 percent market share gain in two years, increasing profitability by 15 percent in three years, and developing a new product in six months. Goals and objectives are powerful tools that break down the mission statement into very specific tasks, actions, and results throughout the organization. Each part of the organization is likely to have its own set of goals and objectives to accomplish within a specified time period. When put together, all of these smaller goals and objectives should bring the organization's mission into fruition.

Value Creation Competency: Defining What We Do Best

Central to any organization's existence is how well it creates value in the marketplace. Organizations must deliver compelling economic value to their customers by creating and offering desirable products and services. Equally important, organizations only create value to the extent that their efforts distinguish themselves from similar efforts made by rivals. A firm's strategy is only as valuable to the extent it builds distinction.

Customer Focus. An organization creates competitive advantage only if customers are willing to pay for its products at a price that generates an economic return that is higher than its cost of capital. Indeed, in order to earn the profits necessary to stay in business, firms must identify which customers they can serve best and focus their efforts on developing and commercializing products and services to suit them. This profit-based reality means that it is highly unlikely that a firm can be a provider of all things to all customers. Instead, the firm must develop a **value proposition** that considers what its customers truly want and which products/services the firm will offer at the appropriate price. Developing and implementing this value proposition (right customers + right products/services = economic return) lays the economic foundation for every firm's competitive advantage.

value proposition:
The products and services that meet customer needs at a price that generates a positive economic return.

Competitor Focus. Building competitive advantage requires the organization to do things differently from its rivals. When competitors in any industry all offer the same products to the same group of customers, profitability disappears. Instead, organizations must continue to find ways to prevent rivals from imitating their efforts to become distinctive. Doing so requires an understanding of not only the industry, but also the nature of competition. An effective strategy also anticipates the possibility, even the likelihood, that new types of competitors may enter the industry. New competitors may do things completely different from existing rivals. This is why understanding your competition is such a central idea behind strategy.

Planning and Administration: Getting Everything to Fit

A powerful vision and a compelling value proposition can provide key elements of a firm's strategy. However, a strategy will not deliver high performance and other desired results if all parts of the organization do not work well together to move in a unified direction. The broader competency of planning and administration focuses on the issue of achieving coalignment, or more simply, "fit." Managers must ensure that all parts of the organization fit together to support the strategy. Some of the most important sources of fit are the following:

Activity Fit. Simply put, do we have all the resources in place to perform the activities necessary to create and deliver the organization's value proposition? Is the organization up to task?

Are research and development (R&D) laboratories working on the right projects that will develop winning products and improved production processes? Are factories producing the best possible quality products using the right materials and the right processes? Is the marketing department developing the best message to reach out to our existing and future customers? Are we providing our customers with the level and kind of service that they expect? Should we even be performing some activities that our suppliers might be better doing for us?

Corporate Fit. For companies that operate multiple lines of business, this is a core issue. How do we get our business units to work together? What kinds of activities should our businesses share? How do we transfer resources among business units? Can we lower costs by combining certain activities from different businesses together? Can we enhance our value proposition by performing activities from different businesses together?

Alliance Fit. If we are working together with other companies, do we have the right partners? Are their strategies compatible with ours? Can our partnerships help us to learn and to do new things better?

People Fit. Are our people trained and skilled to perform the tasks they need to accomplish? Are we hiring the right people for our organization? Are we developing our people to do things better?

Reward Systems Fit. Are our people sufficiently and appropriately rewarded for their efforts and output? Are we encouraging our people to perform their best?

Communications Fit. Do we promote clear and honest communication among our people? Do people understand the purposes of our strategy? Are we communicating effectively with our customers? Are we learning from them? Equally important, are we listening and engaging with our broad base of stakeholders, including key people in the communities we serve?

STRATEGIC COMPETENCY *in action*

Planning and Administration: Charles Schwab[3]

In 2000, Charles Schwab Corporation, a leading discount brokerage house, purchased U.S. Trust for $3.2 billion to extend its reach to a new set of customers. U.S. Trust is one of the most exclusive providers of asset management services to the ultra-rich. Facing the prospect that new online brokerages (for example, E*Trade, Ameritrade, TD Waterhouse) were beginning to erode Schwab's competitive position in serving the mass market, Schwab began to pursue a richer customer base. However, the relationship between Schwab's core brokerage operation and U.S. Trust has been tense from the very beginning.

During the 1980s and 1990s, Charles Schwab grew by providing investors discounted pricing to trade stocks and other financial instruments. By offering investors the opportunity to pay as little as $30 per transactions, Schwab grew its account base into the millions. Individual investors preferred Schwab because it offered some of the same services as full-service brokerage houses (for example, Merrill Lynch) without the high commissions. The typical Schwab investor belongs to a "mass-affluent" group that

has about $100,000 to $1 million to invest, and prefers to make his or her own decisions about how to invest.

When Schwab purchased U.S. Trust, it immediately encountered difficulties in working and communicating with financial advisors who provide a very different type of financial service. The average account size at U.S. Trust is about $7 million. However, the management of U.S. Trust differed substantially from Schwab's mass-market approach. Founded by wealthy industrialists in the 1850s, U.S. Trust earned a very loyal following among several generations of well-heeled families who rely on it to provide a full range of services, including asset management, trust and estate services, and even financial planning in the event of family changes (for example, divorces, new births). The relationship between a U.S. Trust advisor and a client is very long term.

Schwab wanted many of its top-tier investors to transfer their assets to U.S. Trust. However, because U.S. Trust charges high annual fees on the amount invested, many of Schwab's customers balked at the idea of paying someone else to manage their money. At the same time, many U.S. Trust advisors disliked the idea of serving a client base that had comparatively small accounts when measured against those of wealthy families.

Concerned with the high costs of U.S. Trust's intimate level of service, Schwab cut the annual bonuses and pay of top advisors and portfolio managers. Mistrust between managers from U.S. Trust and Schwab escalated, as the two sides of the company were unable to cooperate. Strategies that worked for Schwab's mass-affluent customers did not match the needs required for U.S. Trust clients. Many longtime U.S. Trust advisors left the company to join rivals or to start their own wealth-management firms. In the meantime, service at Schwab's core discount brokerage operation began to deteriorate and a growing number of customers began to transfer their accounts to competitors such as Fidelity Investments. To stem the flow of customer defections, Schwab cut its online trading fees by as much as 33 percent in June 2004. At the time of this writing, the fate of U.S. Trust is up in the air, although Schwab denies any interest in selling it.

Global Awareness Competency: Competing in a Smaller World

There is little doubt that every firm is competing in an increasingly globalized marketplace. Consumers around the world are becoming smarter and more selective about what they want to buy. New markets are fast opening up in China and India; these countries are also the birthplace of fierce new rivals in a broad array of industries. With few exceptions, trade barriers among countries and regions continue to decline. This opens up enormous opportunities for U.S. firms to sell in places they previously could not easily reach. At the same time, companies are merging across national borders to form truly multinational enterprises. For example, cross-border mergers, acquisitions, and joint ventures have produced such well-known giants as GlaxoSmithKline, Sanofi-Aventis, and AstraZeneca in the pharmaceutical industry, Daimler-Chrysler and Renault/Nissan in the automotive industry, Airbus Industries in aerospace, and WPP Group in advertising. Although managers need to be aware about global developments in a variety of spheres (for example, politics, diplomacy, regional rivalries), our focus is limited to three different aspects:

Opportunities and Threats Exist Anywhere. Globalization presents a doubleedged sword. On the one hand, the rapid industrialization and emergence of tens of millions of people into the middle class each year present vast opportunities for companies to reach out to new customers. The huge demand for semiconductors, steel, plastics, and industrial machinery in China, for example, offers an unprecedented opportunity for U.S., European, Japanese, and South Korean firms to serve this huge market. Prices are currently rising for many high-technology products and commodities needed in China. At the same time, the enormous growth of the Chinese economy brings with it the blossoming of thousands of local competitors who in turn will likely challenge firms from more developed countries over the next decade. We are already beginning to witness this trend as China begins exporting television sets, textiles, small appliances, clocks, furniture, and even some types of advanced computer networking equipment and integrated circuits.

In a broader sense, globalization means that companies must always remain vigilant for new types of competitors that may spring up from any region of the world. We have already witnessed the rapid rise and success of such diverse companies as Nokia (Finland), IKEA (Sweden), Toyota (Japan), Samsung (South Korea), Wipro and Infosys Technologies (India), and Embraer (Brazil). These companies have begun to compete for global market share at the same time they compete with the biggest rivals anywhere.

Different Business Practices. Companies coming from different regions of the world often bring with them different expectations about how to do business. In many instances, they bring with them exceptional levels of customer service and some of the highest value products (for example, Singapore Airlines in airlines, BMW in automobiles, Samsung in sleek designed phones). The refinement of Toyota's legendary just-in-time inventory system, as well as its distinctive approach to quality improvement, has become a real role model for any industrial company located anywhere. However, globalization also means that firms must be aware of business practices that may not be familiar, and in some instances, may be undesirable (for example, the use of bribes for inside information or preferential market access). Corporate governance practices, in particular, can vary widely across different legal traditions and precedents.

Cultural Awareness. There is no doubt that serving customers in new national or regional markets requires a delicate appreciation of local cultures and sensitivities. Because this topic alone could provide the basis for an entire book in its own right, we offer little direct, concrete guidance here. However, cultural awareness is a very salient issue as it relates to working with suppliers, customers, and alliance partners from different parts of the world. Cultural awareness is a major issue as it relates to cross-border mergers and acquisitions also. An appreciation of how people from various national cultures view complex strategic issues can provide a genuine source of competitive advantage for organizations that seek to broaden their scope of knowledge. Cultivating cultural diversity can help organizations "see" opportunities, challenges, and other issues from multiple "strategic lenses."

Competing in Global Markets: Philips Electronics[4]

Philips Electronics is one of the world's biggest producers of medical equipment, consumer electronics, semiconductors, flat-screen technologies, and home appliances. A European company with a very proud tradition of innovation (it possesses over 100,000 patents), Philips has consistently led the world in developing many important technologies. For example, it helped pioneer medical X-ray technology, the audiocassette, the electric shaver, and today's current compact-disc technology (in conjunction with Sony of Japan). Yet, for all of its creative flair in the labs, Philips has struggled to compete with the likes of Matsushita, Sony, and Samsung in the marketplace.

A big factor behind Philips' outstanding record of innovation is that the company has long encouraged scientific research and big projects that yield potentially big payoffs. While cultivating innovation, Philips has traditionally marketed its products in different parts of the world separately. Although Philips originated in the Netherlands, the company has historically looked to larger markets in the United States, Latin America, Asia, and the rest of Europe for much of its growth. Because the Netherlands by itself provides too small of a home market to expand, Philips was one of the first companies to formulate and implement a worldwide strategy that witnessed the steady growth and profitability of local operations. Many of Philips' innovations over time came from large laboratories located throughout the United States, Europe, Australia, and Canada. Over time, Philips relied heavily on its regional affiliates to manufacture many of its leading-edge products for sale in national and more local markets.

This innovation-driven strategy worked for Philips for many decades. Ultimately, Philips' emphasis on developing products for local markets came under severe economic strain from Japanese competition during the 1980s. Able to rely on a much bigger domestic market to provide critical mass, Japanese rivals such as Matsushita Electric, Sony, JVC, and Toshiba began producing consumer electronics and other high-technology products at lower unit costs. Unlike Philips, Matsushita and other Japanese firms were able to construct much larger factories that were ultraefficient. Over time, they were able to overtake Philips' market position in many markets through the production of quality products at lower costs, even though most production still occurred in Japan. Compared with Sony, Philips also faced considerable difficulties building up a well-recognized brand name with global reach.

Recognizing this competitive challenge, Philips has attempted to restructure its operations to compete more effectively with these rivals over the past two decades. Its current CEO, Gerard Kleisterlee, is overseeing a major reorganization of Philips that seeks to combine disparate operations and organizational practices into a more cohesive system. Kleisterlee wants Philips' traditionally separate business units to communicate and to coordinate their activities to achieve significant cost savings and to deliver leading-edge products to market faster. At the same time, the company has decided to allocate more resources to high-growth opportunities in its core medical, electronics, and flat-screen businesses. Philips is also consolidating its highly dispersed marketing and distribution activities to eliminate duplication and high costs. Managers in each of Philips' regions must now meet and coordinate their strategies and activities more frequently.

In addition, Philips has formed a wide array of technology-sharing relationships with companies throughout the United States and the Far East. With LG Group of South Korea, Philips formed a separate company known as LG Philips LCD, which has become the world's second largest producer of liquid crystal display (LCD) screens that are found in flat-screen televisions, cell phones, and digital cameras. Philips also recently teamed up with a Chinese maker of medical equipment known as Neusoft. Philips-Neusoft Medical Systems, a newly formed company, will produce medical imaging equipment (for example, CT scanners, X-ray machines) for use in China. In the field of advanced integrated circuits, Philips joined with Taiwan Semiconductor Manufacturing Company to codesign and co-produce leading-edge chips that will power next-generation appliances and consumer electronics. It is also working with Samsung Electronics of Korea to produce state-of-the-art digital phones that will allow people to make financial and other secure transactions through an "electronic wallet." Philips also has great ambitions to be an important supplier of new digital technologies for future home entertainment centers. For example, Philips hopes to build the chips, flat-panel displays, sound systems, and other critical components that will transform the way that people enjoy free time in their living rooms. Future home appliances will likely be connected to one another through Internet-like technologies that offer greater ease and convenience of use.

Philips' strategic transition is designed to compete more effectively in an increasingly connected global marketplace. However, the process of changing Philips' organizational practices represents a long-term, ongoing effort that has already helped the company become more profitable and faster moving.

Leveraging Technology Competency: Staying on the Cutting Edge

New technologies and innovations are redefining almost every industry imaginable. Technology by itself has little value; however, technology offers great value and competitive advantage to organizations that can harness it and use it in distinctive ways. Developments in technology occur everywhere everyday. Many people associate the Internet with advanced technology, and businesses are using it to transform their operations and the way they interact with customers, suppliers, and other firms. Yet, technology goes beyond the Internet to include advanced methods to manufacture products with improved quality at lower cost; new ways to treat patients with less pain, risk, and financial costs; new sources of research, information, and knowledge that lay the groundwork for advanced drugs, plastics, environmentally friendly materials, and food products. Remember that technology only produces competitive advantage to the extent that an organization is able to leverage it in a distinctive manner. Some of the most important technology-based impacts on strategy include the following:

Faster Innovation. The arrival of cheaper computing power, the omnipresent reach of the Internet, and the wide availability of talent worldwide makes it possible to create, test, produce, and deliver leading-edge products and services with greater speed and quality than ever before.

Big Companies Act Nimbler. When creatively used, technology can help large companies become more agile to compete more effectively. Technology can help large companies overcome some of the traditional barriers to fast information flows that sometimes occur when operations become large and complex.

Small Companies Act Big. Likewise, when creatively used, technology can help small upstart companies gain the benefits that usually accrue to much larger companies. The Internet, for example, increasingly enables small companies and even individuals to sell directly to much larger companies to search for the best possible pricing for almost every product and service. For example, eBay thrives by offering a global online auction-based transaction system that allows anyone to set up a virtual shop to sell his or her products and services with little overhead costs.

Leveraging Technology: Innovation at Sony[5]

Sony Corporation is one of the world's most consistently successful innovators of consumer electronic products. Throughout its history, Sony has consistently surprised and delighted consumers with superbly designed, user-friendly, high-technology products year after year. Many of its legendary innovations (the pocket-sized transistor radio, Walkman portable radio/cassette player, videocassette recorder [VCR], Trinitron system color television set, camcorder, the compact-disc [CD] player [developed in conjunction with Philips Electronics], and the later MiniDisc) defined state-of-the-art consumer electronics from the 1970s through the 1990s. Its most recent innovations, such as the PlayStation 2 and 3 series of video game systems, PSX DVD (digital video disk) recorder, Cybershot and Mavica digital filmless cameras (using charged coupled devices [CCDs] and flash memories), MP3 players, and advanced flat-screen televisions (using LCD and LCOS technologies) demonstrate Sony's capabilities and commitment to leading innovation. Sony believes that "you don't research demand—you create demand."

In the past, Sony has benefited from technological and market-based changes by learning and leading, rather than following competitors in the innovation race. Sony prefers to deploy its innovation prowess and marketing acumen to create entirely new classes of products and technologies that customers have not even anticipated. Sony often assigns several teams, each pursuing a different technology, to work on the same development problem. For example, five teams worked at various times on the company's CD player and later the MiniDisc project. By encouraging strong competition among teams and product development units, Sony increases the likelihood that a core technology and product idea will emerge as a leader. In addition, working with different technologies helps Sony learn which products are more likely to be easily manufactured and improved over time. By working with different designs and seeing how a customer will likely use a product from different angles, Sony can continuously improve its products over time by incorporating new features and streamlined designs. This innovation approach gives Sony a market edge over its competitors.

Sony's distinctive approach to creating new products and technologies has worked wonders for the company. However, the company's preference to develop its own proprietary

technology also means that Sony faces greater risks if a product idea does not work out. For example, Apple's iPod MP3 player has been initially more popular than Sony's Walkman MP3 player, despite the iPod's higher price. Sony even encountered difficulties in the television business, when other rivals such as Samsung and Sharp beat the company to market in 2003. Nevertheless, Sony regards its strategy of "creating demand" as central to its competitive advantage. Despite these setbacks, Sony's latest gadgets incorporate leading-edge technologies and features from once separate products. New Sony flat-screen televisions, for example, allow watchers to surf channels using a tiny joystick and include a 3-D speaker system to bolster sound. The television development team also worked with Sony's video game division to give the set the feel of a game console. Future versions of the Qualia and Wega brand sets will include image-processing technology that can sharpen picture quality from ordinary standard television to high definition (HD) and even ultrahigh definition.

Sony still believes that it can create future business opportunities by leading customers to entirely new types of products. It competes aggressively with Microsoft's Xbox video game system and is now working on ways to create a "digital living room." In its quest for future dominance over next-generation entertainment hardware standards, Sony is also testing an entirely new class of high-definition DVD systems using what is known as "Blu-Ray" technology. Blu-Ray offers up to sixteen times the storage capacity of conventional DVDs, although Sony must compete against the likes of Toshiba and NEC, which are developing their own version of high-definition DVDs. The ongoing escalating cost of technology development has caused Sony's management to rethink how best to develop leading-edge products in recent years. As Sony attempts to become even faster at innovation, it is seeking new technology and marketing partners, such as Microsoft, to jointly develop new ideas (for example, portable digital music players). Sony is also encouraging its many internal product development teams to work more closely with one another across business units to ensure that good ideas do not get lost.

As next-generation technology products incorporate cutting-edge semiconductors and other display technologies, Sony now works with Toshiba and IBM to develop future microprocessors that will serve as the electronic brains of its PlayStation 3 video game consoles and other appliances. This chip, known as "The Cell," will likely find its first use in new computer technology that will dramatically enhance the creation of special effects and animation for Hollywood—a feature that may change the way that Sony's movie business uses technology to create films. Future television sets that incorporate "The Cell" may even enable watchers to take a television character and insert him or her into a video game. At a minimum, this same chip is expected to better handle the huge volume of video streams and data beamed from satellite and cable systems onto flat-screen televisions.

Stakeholder Competency: What Decision Criteria Are Used?

The strategy concept helps managers deal with competitive realities. However, competition is not the only factor managers must consider. They must also weigh the needs of stakeholders when making strategic decisions. Throughout this book, we will explore some of the dilemmas managers face when attempting to consider the needs of various stakeholders. By way of introduction to this material, let us briefly identify key stakeholders of business organizations and the difficulties senior managers often face when attempting to accommodate stakeholders' needs.

Among the most important stakeholders of any business organization are shareholders, customers, workers, the communities in which firms operate, and top managers themselves.

Shareholders. Shareholders provide the equity capital to finance a firm's operation. Therefore, they have a vital stake and say in its welfare. Although most shareholders are interested in earning a return on their investment, individual shareholders may have differing preferences for the timing of returns (some being interested in immediate benefits, others in long-term returns), varying tolerances for risk taking (some preferring to strictly limit risk, others to assume more risk to reap potentially higher returns), and differing needs for maintaining control of the firm. Feasible strategic alternatives often will have a different impact on these different dimensions. Senior managers must strive to select an approach that reflects the relative importance shareholders attach to each dimension.

How top managers deal with shareholders' concerns is becoming increasingly important to the fate of companies and to the careers of top managers. A growing number of chief executive officers (CEOs) at leading firms have been dismissed in recent years because of their inability to generate sufficient return to their shareholders. For example, companies such as General Motors, Ford Motor Company, Sears, J. C. Penney, 3M, Honeywell International, Procter & Gamble, and The Home Depot have sought new CEOs in the past few years to deal with new challenges that face their respective firms. Shareholders exercise important powers, enabling them to oblige top executives to take the necessary steps to maintain or restore profitability of the firms they manage. Senior management owes a fiduciary responsibility to their shareholders. A **fiduciary responsibility** means that managers must act in the financial interest of shareholders, because shareholders directly or indirectly hire the top management of a company.

At the same time, shareholders take on a degree of financial risk by investing in company stock. For example, a number of well-known companies declared bankruptcy in the wake of serious economic difficulties. Companies such as Montgomery Ward (retailing), Finova (financial services), Tower Automotive (auto parts), US Airways Group (airlines), and Global Crossing (telecommunications) are just a few firms that have experienced very grave competitive issues.

fiduciary responsibility:
The primary responsibility facing top management—to make sure the firm delivers value to its shareholders, the owners of the firm.

Customers. As noted earlier in the discussion of the concept of strategy, competition requires that firms satisfy the needs of customers or go out of business. A firm's responsibility to customers does not simply end there, however. Customers are often unaware of many aspects of the products and services they buy. Product quality, integrity, and safety are essential issues that managers must consider when designing and selling products or services to the buying public. A firm failing to consider such factors risks loss of reputation, potentially onerous legislation, costly liability litigation, and even imprisonment of managers. To avoid such risks, senior managers must keep their broader responsibilities to customers in mind when making strategic decisions.

Employees. Employees typically seek a wide range of benefits that managers must consider when making strategic decisions. These include adequate compensation, benefits, safe working conditions, recognition for accomplishment, and opportunity for advancement. Careful attention to such needs can sometimes produce spectacular results. Leading high-technology firms such as Cisco Systems, Intel, Microsoft, Xerox Corporation, Dell Computer, EMC, and Apple Computer, for example, treat their employees exceptionally well by giving them generous benefits, flexible work hours, and even day care for their children. These progressive companies have achieved considerable success producing state-of-the-art products and technical solutions that are consistently in high demand. By contrast, many U.S. airline companies (for example, Continental Airlines, Delta Air Lines, and American Airlines) have experienced difficult relations with their employees. High labor costs severely eroded the long-term profitability of almost every major U.S. airline. Over time, management's initiatives to cut labor costs resulted in decreased employee morale, shoddier service, and poor management-labor relations. Workers crippled some airlines—specifically Eastern Airlines during the late 1980s—with protracted strikes costing the company millions of dollars.

Employees at many companies serve in the dual role of shareholders as well. For example, the retirement plans used in many companies (known as 401[k] plans because of the tax code) are used to provide a means for employees to save for their futures. However, many of these plans contain a significant amount of company stock, thus directly tying the fate of employees to that of their companies. Over time, however, increased government regulation, triggered in part by the Enron scandal, will likely allow employees to take on less risk as they build their retirement assets.

Communities. Communities rely on firms for tax revenue, employee income to sustain the local economy, and financial and other support for charitable and civic organizations. They are also adversely affected when a firm's facilities pollute the air, burn down, or close down. Thus, communities have a vital stake in the health and integrity of firms operating within their borders. Because communities have legislative authority, they are in a strong position to enforce their wishes. Senior managers must therefore keep community needs in mind when formulating strategies. Cummins Engine, a leading manufacturer of diesel engines for trucks and construction equipment, has paid careful attention to community needs. It traditionally has worked closely with the city of Columbus, Ohio, the site of its corporate headquarters. Cummins is a leading contributor to many civic activities in Columbus; it also is one of the few companies that does not avoid paying a high level of taxes to the city to fund numerous municipal programs. Ben and Jerry's Ice Cream (now a unit of Anglo-Dutch Unilever PLC) works with neighboring communities in its home state of Vermont to promote a clean environment and social programs. Eastman Kodak works closely with government officials in Rochester,

New York, the site of its corporate headquarters, to design community self-improvement programs that enable people to learn skills through education. Corporate and city/state managers often meet together to discuss vital economic and social issues that affect the needs of workers and people in the larger community.

Senior Managers. To lead their organizations and implement strategy effectively, senior executives must be personally ethical, enthusiastic, and committed to the direction of their firms. Managers often have varying preferences for goals such as a firm's size (over $100 million in annual sales), growth rate (at least 20 percent per year), the areas in which a firm competes (high-tech businesses only), and location of facilities (global operations). Top managers need to consider their own personal skills and experiences in developing strategies so that they can feel committed to the course the firm is pursuing. Above their own needs, of course, must come needs of shareholders when evaluating and developing strategies that affect the long-term value of the firm.

Balancing Stakeholders: IBM and Job Creation[6]

STRATEGIC COMPETENCY *in action*

In early 2004, IBM announced that it would begin to increase the amount of software development and other high-technology work performed outside the United States. Lured by markedly lower labor costs in places such as China, Brazil, and India, IBM believed that it needed to hire thousands of engineers and other skilled personnel in these locations to reduce the overall cost of its business operations. As a result, many American employees would face the likely prospect of unemployment. Although scores of large U.S. companies have farmed out work to overseas locations in the past, what was particularly noteworthy about IBM's announcement were the great lengths that senior management took to disguise the full impact on the people most affected by this move. In the past, IBM received great praise for its internal policies that promoted high wages and full employment where possible.

In a series of internal company documents uncovered by the *Wall Street Journal,* IBM employees affected by this "offshoring" of software development work will be compelled to train the very individuals that will ultimately replace them. In other words, a highly skilled IBM manager or engineer, facing the likely prospect of unemployment, will face the additional humiliation of teaching another person how to do his or her job before exiting the company. IBM senior executives, aware of the likely difficulties and sensitive nature of this situation, issued a series of memos to managers to be careful in how they describe the transfer of work to foreign locations. For example, if employees were to ask about whether they would be impacted, IBM managers should use carefully phrased, highly nuanced words to avoid direct discussion of the move. If employees were to request anything in written

form, then all correspondence should be "sanitized" by the human resources department before anything is communicated back to the employee.

The unrest and controversy surrounding IBM's decision demoralized a big portion of its workforce. In addition, for a company that has long enjoyed a tradition of being nonunion, employee interest in forming unions to represent them grew. Membership in Alliance @ IBM, a union that is affiliated with the Communications Workers of America, grew from 5,000 to 6,000 in just a span of six months. Put in a larger context, IBM has over 140,000 employees working in the United States. However, over the past few years, IBM has created only 2,000 jobs annually, while significantly boosting the hiring of overseas nationals at a much faster rate.

From a corporate perspective, IBM has avoided discussing this issue openly with its employees. To keep a lid on bad news, senior executives tried to "paper over" the issue with deliberately vague language. From an employee's perspective, IBM's decision, as well as its handling of the matter, generates considerable mistrust of the company. The requirement to train a replacement for your job adds to the loss of personal dignity. Yet, IBM and many other large U.S. companies feel they have little long-term choice in the matter. Wages in China and India are as much as three-fourths lower than comparable U.S. wages. IBM's competitors, such as Intel, Hewlett-Packard, Dell, and Microsoft, have all commenced or further boosted their employment in lower-wage countries to remain competitive over the past several years. Shareholders and financial markets in general are demanding that companies reduce costs as much as possible to compete globally and to remain profitable.

Responsibility for Strategic Management

Lower-level employees in an enterprise often possess considerable specialized expertise about such issues as technology, customers, and marketing. This gives them an excellent vantage point from which to identify opportunities and threats and to assess a firm's strengths and weaknesses. One might therefore expect senior managers would turn over to them considerable responsibility for conducting the strategic management process. In fact, senior managers do share such responsibility with employees, at least in part. However, top managers generally must play a primary role because of the large financial outlays associated with strategic decisions, the long-term impact of such decisions, and the considerable controversy that such decisions often provoke. Many strategic decisions also bring with them difficult choices on how best to reconcile the needs of various stakeholders.

Who Are Strategic Managers?

business managers:
People in charge of managing and operating a single line of business.

There are two kinds of senior managers most directly responsible for strategy: business managers and corporate managers. **Business managers** are in charge of individual businesses. In a diversified, multibusiness firm (such as IBM), the executives in charge of individual businesses (such as electronic commerce, semiconductors, servers, networking systems, storage systems, and consulting) are business managers. These executives go by a variety of titles, including business manager, general manager, division manager, and strategic business unit manager. The president and chairperson of a single business enterprise (for example, Papa John's International, Domino's Pizza) are also business managers.

corporate managers:
People responsible for overseeing and managing a portfolio of businesses within the firm.

Corporate managers are responsible for portfolios of businesses. Consequently, corporate managers exist only in multi-business firms (for example, General Electric). The president and chairperson of a multibusiness enterprise are corporate managers. Multibusiness firms containing large numbers of businesses often assign executives to positions midway between individual businesses and these senior executives. Each such individual oversees a subset of the firm's total portfolio of businesses. Because each of these individuals has supervisory responsibility for several businesses, these executives are considered corporate managers as well. They go by a variety of titles, including group vice president, executive vice president, and sector executive.

Both business and corporate managers play pivotal roles in the strategic management process. They are the key people who bring all other assets into play when competing with other firms. They also represent the highest levels of authority within the firm or subunit. As a result, they exert enormous influence over the company's capital expenditures to build new plants or to acquire other companies, chart the future direction of the firm's growth, and direct the firm's efforts toward emerging market opportunities. Top managers often serve as the spokespersons for their firms when dealing with the media over such issues as breakthrough technologies, new product rollouts, or potential allegations against the company by shareholders, customers, or communities. Thus, top managers perform multiple tasks at the highest level of an organization and bear the highest responsibility for their firm's strategies and actions.

At the same time, customers, investors, employees, and even the public at large depend on the judgment, experience, and skills of these managers to compete both fairly and within the law. For the vast majority of companies in the United States, senior managers continue to work long hours formulating strategies and action plans that aim to satisfy their customers, reward their investors, develop their employees, and foster a larger sense of public trust. However, business is not immune from scandalous activities that can mar the reputation of entire industries for an extended period.

Characteristics of Strategic Decisions

Large Financial Outlay. Decisions reached through the strategic management process often commit a firm to significant investment of funds. For example, in the high-technology semiconductor (chip) industry, the decision to build a new factory can cost a firm up to $3 billion. In 2001, U.S. semiconductor giant Intel spent over $7.5 billion on capital expenditures alone. Intel sees this huge outlay as a way to learn and apply ever more sophisticated manufacturing techniques to design faster and more powerful chips. In the next few years, a new chip plant will likely cost upwards of $5 billion. Intel continues to invest relentlessly in new manufacturing techniques and scientific breakthroughs to design and produce ever more powerful chips. Other industries face similar situations where high capital expenditures are required to compete in the industry. With its decision to build the Saturn manufacturing plant in Tennessee during the 1990s, General Motors (GM) committed as much as $5 billion over a ten-year period to factory equipment, training, new tools and dyes, robotics, and so forth. Now, GM is trying to use what it learned from the Saturn experience to revolutionize automobile manufacturing in its other divisions; Saturn has already become the "teacher" that shows other GM divisions, such as Chevrolet and Pontiac, how to build small cars effectively. Rolling out a new advertising campaign to promote a new pizza brand at Pizza Hut could cost well over $300 million over several years, with little guarantee that the promotion will be successful. In the pharmaceutical industry, the decision to develop new blockbuster drugs to fight cancer, AIDS, heart disease, diabetes, and other ailments can easily cost upwards of $2 billion. Many leading-edge drugs take over fifteen years to develop before they are considered safe and effective. Pharmaceutical and biotechnology companies must continue to invest in many new technologies to discover new drugs and other compounds that increasingly require more sophisticated methods and techniques. These expenditures also expose the drug maker to great financial risks, and possibly even legal risks. Decisions by Procter & Gamble, Cisco Systems, Citigroup, Microsoft, American Express, Pfizer, Coca-Cola, and PepsiCo to develop new products, launch advertising programs, and acquire other companies often involve very large sums. These are therefore critical strategy issues that fall within the realm of top management.

Long-Term Impact. Decisions reached through the strategic management process are often difficult to reverse. Strategic decisions therefore commit an organization to a particular course of action for an extended period. A decision to build a manufacturing facility, for example, involves choices about location, size, manufacturing technology, training programs, and choice of suppliers. Many factors are difficult to alter once a facility has been built. Investment in physical assets, such as a factory, is just one of many decisions that have a long-term impact. Other hard-to-reverse decisions include acquiring another company, forming a strategic alliance, the creation of industry-wide technical standards for new products, and the amount to spend on research and development to foster innovation.

How a firm allocates resources to strengthen its competitive position thus requires judgment as well as disciplined analysis. Considerable time generally is needed to make changes; during the interim, a firm may not be able to respond to customers' needs or the challenge brought on by new technologies or rivals. Likewise, a decision not to invest in some key activity can also impose its own set of costs. For example, in the late 1990s, IBM's initial inability to expand capacity quickly to produce its highly popular ThinkPad notebook computer gave Japanese competitors easy entry into this extremely profitable segment. Similarly, the difficulty that confronts Eastman Kodak as it struggles to convert to digital photography highlights the inherent risks that senior managers face when allocating resources to new products in fast-changing environments. In many industries, investments in fixed assets are often considered "irreversible." Unsuitable facilities also are often so specialized that they cannot be sold except at a substantial loss. For example, oil companies such as Chevron Texaco, Royal Dutch/Shell Group, and ExxonMobil are saddled with numerous refinery operations that are quickly becoming obsolete because of new technology and numerous environmental regulations that were continuously introduced over the past decade. Cleaning up these refineries will add tremendous costs to these firms, thus raising the cost of gasoline for consumers. Although these firms might like to liquidate some of their facilities, doing so may be difficult; few buyers are likely to be interested in these specialized and increasingly obsolescent assets. Not all strategic decisions are irreversible, but most exert a long-term impact on the organization. Top managers therefore become involved in strategic decisions in an effort to avoid costly mistakes, but there is no guarantee of their success.

Controversial Nature.

Strategic decisions often engender controversy among the firm's managers and employees. Consider a decision by Olympus Optical to customize camera products to meet the needs of individual customers. Sales personnel are likely to favor such a policy, since customization improves their ability to meet customer needs and thereby increases sales volume. It would enable customers to buy different types of cameras with different types of lenses and other features according to their experience level, personal budgets, and color or model preferences. Manufacturing personnel at Olympus would likely resist this move, however, because customization of products significantly complicates the production task, thereby increasing manufacturing costs. Senior managers must oversee and manage controversies of this sort to prevent disagreements from escalating into time-consuming arguments and to ensure that decisions ultimately reached reflect the needs of the overall enterprise.

In recent years, the strategic actions of some companies have invited considerable scrutiny by the government, as well as by investors who question the efficacy of some expenditures. For example, Microsoft faced an inquiry from the Department of Justice in the United States and regulatory bodies in Europe in recent years over its economic behavior and massive expenditures to promote the use of Internet Explorer and Microsoft Media Player as part of its software offerings for personal computers. Competitors such as Sun Microsystems, Time Warner, and other smaller firms charged that Microsoft deliberately spent prodigious sums of money to encourage customers to move away from products offered by rivals, thereby creating a de facto monopoly in key aspects of the software business.

Likewise, many people have questioned the significant marketing expenditures undertaken by U.S. pharmaceutical firms to promote products and brand awareness among consumers. Some people in Congress, as well as public interest groups, wonder why companies such as Pfizer, GlaxoSmithKline, Wyeth, AstraZeneca, Merck, and Schering-Plough advertise their products so aggressively, yet at the same time they have not reduced the price of their drugs. At the same time, pharmaceutical firms are fighting price controls and the specter of increasing government regulation as their profit margins face continued pressures from new competitors, generic drugs, and the escalating costs of research.

In another realm, investors have increasingly become more vocal about what management should do to build competitive advantage. Particularly in the last few years, investors are becoming more active in voicing their opinions about key strategic decisions. For example, investors may signal their approval or dislike of a company's decision to acquire another firm. Consider the case of Hewlett-Packard (HP) in 2001-2002. Investors responded very coolly to HP's announcement that it wanted to merge with Compaq Computer. Believing that the two companies would not make a suitable fit, investors sold off their shares in Hewlett-Packard, thus revealing their distaste for the merger. Even though HP ultimately completed its merger with Compaq, many investors remain skeptical of the combined firm's ability to compete with Dell and IBM. CEO Carly Fiorina, who spearheaded H-P's merger with Compaq, has recently come under greater scrutiny by the company's Board of Directors as H-P continues to face difficulty in competing with Dell Computer and other rivals. By February 2005, the Board asked Fiorina to resign as the company seeks a new direction to revitalize its growth. Many analysts on Wall Street have increasingly called into the question the rationale for the merger and are calling for a major restructuring of H-P's operations.

Difficulties in Reconciling Stakeholders' Needs

The task of accommodating stakeholder needs is complicated by several factors. First, stakeholders have a great variety of needs. Second, the relative strength of such needs is often difficult to determine. The willingness of shareholders to accept risk, or a community's tolerance for pollution, is often exceedingly difficult to judge. Third, individuals within each stakeholder group often have conflicting needs. For example, as noted previously, individual shareholders may have different risk reward preferences: some desiring a risky strategy with high potential returns; others prefer a more conservative approach, even if it offers lower returns. Perhaps most difficult of all are conflicts that arise between stakeholder groups. Shareholders, for example, may favor reducing water pollution control expenditures to increase short-term profitability, whereas the community in which a firm operates disapproves of such a step because of its increased risk of water contamination.

Conflicts such as these are often called ethical dilemmas because they pit the needs of one stakeholder group against those of another. Ethical dilemmas can occur during the strategy selection process and pose some of the most troublesome strategic issues managers confront. To resolve them, managers must carefully weigh the claims of contending parties, a complex task requiring great sensitivity, balance, and judgment. It is not our purpose here to provide definitive guidance in this area. However, it is useful to mention three criteria managers must consider when assessing conflicting stakeholder claims: legal obligations, expectations of society, and personal standards of behavior.

Legal Obligations. At the very minimum, managers must devise strategies that are within the law. Failure to do so can lead to severe consequences such as fines, public censure, and even imprisonment. For example, bond traders at several investment banking and securities firms in the United States, Japan, Singapore, and elsewhere engaged in a wide range of speculative illegal activities to corner various commodity markets during the 1990s. Such illegal actions have exerted a high cost on both the firms and their managers. Even more blatant was the wave of corporate corruption cases that plagued the United States over the past few years.

Consider the recent series of events that surround the collapse of the Enron Corporation, an energy giant that had tremendous ambitions to expand into a variety of businesses. When Enron declared bankruptcy in November 2001, it not only cost investors a tidy sum but also inflicted a calamity on its employees. These people believed that they were working for a firm with a bright future. Moreover, almost all employees had their retirement assets tied to the value of Enron stock, and they were prevented from selling their stock at a crucial time when the company's fortunes were rapidly declining. When Enron ultimately collapsed, all of these employees faced dire financial futures. At the same time, many senior executives were able to sell their stock in the months ahead before the true depth of Enron's financial troubles surfaced in the news. Scandals such as these put American business on the defensive, because the public becomes more skeptical, and even cynical, about the motives (and even the integrity) of senior management.

Names such as Enron, WorldCom, Tyco International, HealthSouth, Adelphia Communications, and others have become notorious, and even synonymous, with corporate greed, fraud, and outright theft. The disastrous impact of corporate corruption on shareholders, employees, and middle managers triggered increased government regulation to prevent future abuse.

Societal Expectations. Managers must also strive to meet the broader expectations of the communities in which they operate, even when such expectations are not explicitly codified into law. Failure to do so can lead to costly litigation. Unfortunately, many companies have taken actions that cost their trust with the public. For example, thousands of patients sued pharmaceutical giant American Home Products (now known as Wyeth) for medical conditions that may well have resulted from the taking of some controversial diet drugs during the 1990s. Now in 2005, patients and shareholders have contemplated and initiated legal action against Merck, a pharmaceutical firm that developed Vioxx to treat arthritic pain. Lawyers for patients claim that Merck allowed Vioxx to remain on the market even when it knew that the drug may well have elevated heart attack risks for some patients. Even more astounding was the constant refusal by tobacco companies to acknowledge a key link between smoking and cancer. Even through much of the 1990s, executives from tobacco companies vociferously defended their companies' viewpoints that smoking was not a major factor related to the high incidence of lung cancer. As a result, the government began to investigate the marketing, product development, and advertising practices of tobacco companies; public pension and retirement funds sold their shares in tobacco companies as a sign of protest; and numerous states began to sue the companies for reimbursement of smoking-related health costs. Over time, the tobacco companies were forced to change their marketing practices and to pay huge sums to different states as part of a larger tobacco settlement that cost the industry tens of billions of dollars. Yet, the tobacco companies face continued legal difficulties as some cancer patients are suing the same companies in court. In the early part of the 1990s, other companies faced a number of different issues related to societal expectations of corporate behavior. The numerous lawsuits that confronted Dow-Corning over the safety of its silicone breast implants emphasize to all firms the importance of prioritizing such issues as safety, health, due diligence, and other social-responsibility matters. In the early 1990s, Dow-Corning spent hundreds of millions of dollars and precious time in court defending its reputation and safety practices and paying fines.

Repeated failure to meet societal expectations often inspires the public to take corrective action in the form of additional legislation. All too frequently, such regulation imposes an even greater burden on firms than socially responsible behavior would have imposed in the first place. These regulations often subject firms to more detailed disclosure requirements, time-consuming paperwork, and stricter product safety and testing practices.

Personal Standards. Senior executives can implement strategy effectively only if they feel comfortable with the actions that the strategy entails. A final ethical criterion for judging strategic decisions is thus managers' own personal standards of behavior. Such standards are generally influenced by the laws and the expectations of the communities in which organizations operate; however, they also reflect many personal factors, such as each manager's upbringing, religious convictions, values, and personal life experiences. These, too, must be brought to bear on strategic decisions.

The task of resolving ethical dilemmas is complicated by changes in ethical criteria that occur over time. Legislation governing child labor, worker safety, and job discrimination, for example, has changed markedly over the years; so have societal expectations about such issues as air and water pollution, treatment of minorities, and sexual harassment. To avoid adopting strategies that will soon be obsolete, managers must anticipate rather than simply react to such changes.

Standards of behavior also vary widely across geographic boundaries. German law, for example, requires firms to provide workers formal representation on the board of directors; U.S. law imposes no such requirement. Test requirements for new pharmaceuticals are very onerous in the United States but are significantly less rigorous in many other countries. As a result, drugs whose efficacy and safety have not been fully established by U.S. standards can be legally sold in many other locations. Payoffs to managers and key government officials are illegal in the United States but are common business practice in other locales. Managers operating abroad must decide which standards to apply in resolving ethical dilemmas: those prevailing in their home country or those of the countries within which they operate. The need to consider such differences will be even more critical over the next decade as industries and firms become more global in scope. Meeting the laws, societal expectations, and cultural traditions of regions around the world will be as important to corporate success as meeting the needs of individual communities at home. Becoming a successful global competitor compels firms to think carefully about their actions and the reputations they project in other lands.

Why Study Strategy?

What benefit can you derive from studying strategic management? If you are currently a senior manager, the benefit is clear: you can immediately apply the knowledge you will gain. Individuals on track to move into senior management positions will likewise benefit. For many readers, though, that eventuality may be a long way off. However, there are two roles that most readers will soon assume for which an understanding of strategic management can be useful: a candidate seeking employment and an employee or manager within an organization.

Candidate Seeking Employment

Someone seeking employment must assess the long-term career opportunities offered by potential employers. Strategic management can assist in this task by enabling a candidate to evaluate a prospective employer's competitive position, the soundness of its strategy, and its future prospects. This knowledge can help a candidate avoid employers that may soon be forced to retrench because of competitive difficulties. It can also provide an edge in the recruitment process; candidates can distinguish themselves from others by showing an interest in and a deep understanding of a company's strategic situation. Demonstrating an awareness of the competitive dynamics of the industry in which a prospective employer operates, the environmental changes affecting its industry, and the challenges these developments pose improves an individual's chances of employment success. Likewise, it is important that prospective employees, as well as current managers and employees, understand some of the key factors that drive the basis for competition in their industry. A heightened awareness of how companies compete, how technologies change, and the decisive role of customers in deciding the fate of companies will help all people become more sensitive as to how they contribute value to their employers. This book will provide a foundation for this kind of awareness.

Employee or Manager

Entry- or lower-level employees and managers are often closer to the action in the specialized areas of a firm's operations than top managers. Consequently, they are in a better position to detect developments with potential implications for strategy. By keeping abreast of such matters, understanding the implications of new developments, and communicating their judgments upward, lower-level employees can provide valuable service to their superiors and senior managers. An understanding of strategic management will help lower-level employees and managers fulfill this function.

Lower-level employees and managers need to understand strategic management for a second important reason. They are critically responsible for implementing company strategy within their own particular spheres of activity. Although superiors will normally provide some guidance on how to do this, their directives cannot anticipate every possible contingency. As a result, lower-level employees and managers must make many decisions on their own. To do so in a way that reinforces rather than undermines what top management is trying to accomplish, lower-level employees need to understand a company's strategy and the requirements it imposes for their particular activities.

A growing awareness and appreciation for strategic thinking can help all employees understand how changes in the industry environment can ultimately affect their company's competitive posture. The need for continuous strategic thinking becomes especially important as every organization in every industry confronts a variety of challenges each day, including new technologies, new forms of competition, changes in regulations, and shifting customer needs. As managers and employees become better versed in understanding the impact of their firms' strategies, they can also play an even stronger role in helping learn, build, and sustain new sources of competitive advantage. Likewise, a growing familiarity and comfort with strategic thinking can help managers and employees advance within their careers. As managers and employees gain increasing levels of responsibility and authority, they will need to be able to think strategically, especially as it relates to allocating scarce resources, people, and time to complete their projects and tasks. Thus, strategic thinking and strategic concepts are by no means the sole domain of senior management; quite the contrary—anyone in any position can benefit from learning and applying key strategic principles to their own roles and lives.

Summary

- Strategy is a powerful concept designed to help firms gain a competitive advantage over rivals. It involves two key choices: the customers a firm will serve and the competences and strengths it will develop to serve customers effectively.
- A firm's choices must reflect its strengths and weaknesses relative to rivals and the opportunities and threats presented by its external environment. Analysis of these four elements is referred to as SWOT analysis.
- All firms must deal with the strategic imperatives facing them according to their own individual situations.
- The management process designed to satisfy strategic imperatives for building competitive advantage is called a strategic management process. It consists of four major steps: analysis, formulation, implementation, and adjustment/evaluation. The issues that managers confront when carrying out these steps will be unique to each firm, depending on the imperatives and situations it faces.
- Because strategic choices frequently involve a large financial outlay, have long-term impact on an organization, and generate considerable controversy among organizational members, top or senior managers generally play a primary role in determining such decisions.
- Executives most directly responsible for strategic decisions are business managers and corporate managers. A business manager is in charge of an entire business; a corporate manager oversees a portfolio of businesses.
- Competitive advantage is one important criterion by which to assess strategic decisions. It is not the only such criterion, however. Strategic decisions must also

satisfy the numerous and often-conflicting needs of various stakeholders: shareholders, customers, employees, communities in which firms operate, and top managers.

- Knowledge of strategic management is useful not only to those who currently occupy or will soon occupy top management positions but also to individuals seeking employment with organizations operating in a competitive environment and to lower-level personnel employed by such organizations.

Endnotes

1. Data and facts for the restaurant industry were adapted from the following sources: "Fat's in the Fire for This Burger King," *BusinessWeek,* November 8, 2004, pp. 69–70; "Can You Really Make Fast Food Healthy?" *Fortune,* August 9, 2004, pp. 134–139; "McDonald's: Fries with That Salad?" *BusinessWeek,* July 5, 2004, pp. 82–84; "As We Chill, Restaurants Cook," *Investor's Business Daily,* April 26, 2004, p. A12; "Midnight Snack: Fast-Food Spots Serve All Night," *Wall Street Journal,* July 15, 2004, pp. B1, B2; "You Want Data with That?" *Forbes,* March 29, 2004, pp. 58-60; "Brinker Has Plenty of Options on the Menu," *Dallas Morning News,* February 22, 2004, pp. 1D–6D; "McDonald's Makeover," *Wall Street Journal,* January 28, 2004, pp. B1, B10; "McDonald's May Exit From Ventures," *Wall Street Journal,* November 10, 2003, p. B4; "McDonald's Aims to Sell Control of Partner Brands," *Wall Street Journal,* March 28, 2003, p. B2; "Hamburger Hell," *BusinessWeek,* March 3, 2003, pp. 104–108; "Happier Meals," *Forbes,* January 20, 2003, pp. 77–78.

2. Many discourses on strategy have evolved over the course of human history. Military history has provided some of the richest sources and "roots" for many concepts underpinning business strategy. Some early examples of discourses on military strategy and history include the following: Sun Tzu's *Art of War,* trans. Samuel Griffith (London: Oxford University Press, 1963); *The Military Maxims of Napoleon,* trans. David G. Chandler (London: Freemantle, 1901; republished, New York: Macmillan, 1987); and Clausewitz's *On War,* from the original German version, *Vom Krieg* (New York: Knopf, 1993). A readable overview of some interesting military strategy concepts with direct relevance to the management of organizations is John Keegan's *The Mask of Command* (New York: Viking Penguin, 1988).

3. Data and facts were adapted from the following sources: "Banker to the Rich, U.S. Trust Stumbles After Sale to Schwab," *Wall Street Journal,* September 17, 2004, p. A1+; "Restore the Core," *BusinessWeek,* August 2, 2004, pp. 72–73; "Is Schwab's Latest Come-On Enough?" *BusinessWeek,* June 7, 2004, p. 44.

4. Data and facts were adapted from the following sources: "World of TV Sets Becomes Flatter—and Bigger," *Wall Street Journal,* January 6, 2005, pp, A13, A14; "Expansion Strategy at Philips Carries Risk," *Wall Street Journal,* January 4, 2005, pp. C1, C2; "Samsung to Use Philips Chips in Transaction-Able Phones," *Wall Street Journal,* August 31, 2004, p. B2; "Philips: Back on the Beam," *BusinessWeek,* May 3, 2004, p. 30+; "LG Philips Raises the Stakes in Production of Flat Screens," *Wall Street Journal,* March 19, 2004, p. B4; "Philips, Neusoft Will Join to Make Medical Gear," *Wall Street Journal,* February 9, 2004, p. B3; "Philips Electronics, Other Companies Plan Web Gadgets," *Wall Street Journal,* August 27, 2003, p. B7; "Can Philips Learn to Walk the Talk?" *Fast Company,* January 1, 2003, p. 44.

An excellent case that examines the competitive and organizational issues facing Philips is "Philips vs. Matsushita: Preparing for a New Round," Harvard Business School Publishing, 9-399-102.

5. Data and facts were adapted from the following sources: "Super Cell," Forbes, February 14, 2005, p. 46; "Microsoft Mulls Sony Partnership to Counter iPod's

Success," *Wall Street Journal,* January 6, 2005, pp. A11, A15; "Stung by iPod," Sony Addresses A Digital Lag," *Wall Street Journal,* December 30, 2004, pp. B1, B2; "Disney to Support Sony DVD Format," *Wall Street Journal,* December 9, 2004, p. B8; "Sony: A Bright Picture?" *BusinessWeek,* November 8, 2004, p. 64; "Alliance Seeks to Get a Stereo to Listen to a PC," *Wall Street Journal,* October 21, 2004, p. B3; "Sony Unveils 70-Inch Television in High-End Battle with Rivals," *Wall Street Journal,* September 10, 2004, p. B3; "Sony TVs Take Sibling Tips," *Wall Street Journal,* August 20, 2004, p. B3; "New Sony TV Chips Give Viewer Control," *Wall Street Journal,* August 12, 2004, p. B1; "Imagine Sony on Steroids," *BusinessWeek,* July 12, 2004, pp. 77–78; "After Long Lag, Sony Puts iPod in Its Cross Hairs," *Wall Street Journal,* July 2, 2004, pp. B1, B2; "Microsoft, Sony Enter Epic Battle," *Wall Street Journal,* May 10, 2004, p. B1+; "Sony Pins Hope on Brainier Gadgets," *Wall Street Journal,* October 8, 2003, p. B5; "Facing a Slump, Sony to Revamp Product Lines," *Wall Street Journal,* September 12, 2003, pp. B1, B4; "New Sony Videogame Camera Sells Well," *Wall Street Journal,* August 29, 2003, p. B6; "Sony's Big Bazooka," *Fortune,* December 30, 2002, pp. 111–114; "Past as Prologue: New CEO to Seek Synergies," *Wall Street Journal,* March 8, 2005, pp. B1, B9; "Sony, Lagging Behind Rivals, Hands Rein to a Foreigner," *Wall Street Journal,* March 7, 2005, pp. A1, A8.

6. Data and facts were adapted from the following sources: "IBM Veteran Sees Opportunity With Lenovo," *Wall Street Journal,* December 9, 2004, p. B3; "IBM Now Plans Fewer Layoffs From Offshoring," *Wall Street Journal,* July 29, 2004, p. B1+; "IBM to Buy Indian Call Center Firm," *Wall Street Journal,* April 8, 2004, p. B6; "New IBM Jobs Can Mean Fewer Jobs Elsewhere," *Wall Street Journal,* March 8, 2004, p. B1+; "Offshore Storm: The Global Razor's Edge," *Fast Company*, February 1, 2004, p. 27; "IBM Documents Give Rare Look at Sensitive Plans on 'Offshoring,'" *Wall Street Journal,* January 19, 2004, p. A1+.

Chapter

2

Assessing Industry Attractiveness and the Competitive Environment

Chapter Outline

What you will learn

- *The nature of the general environment, also known as the macroenvironment*

- *How the macroenvironment influences competition between firms*

- *The nature of the industry environment, also known as the competitive environment*

- *The five forces that make up the industry environment: barriers to entry, supplier power, buyer power, the availability of substitutes, and rivalry among firms*

- *The concept of strategic groups*

- *Changes in the way we view and think about industries over time*

- *Techniques companies use to monitor changes in the environment*

Strategic
Snapshot

The Personal Computer Industry in 2004[1]

Ever since its introduction to the public in 1981, the personal computer (PC) has become a mainstay in the office, laboratory, factory floor, home, our briefcases, and now even our cars. The omnipresence of the PC in many ways symbolizes our full arrival in the information or cyberspace age, where the convenience, low cost, versatility, power, speed, and infinitely growing applications of computing power are taken for granted. In fact, even though many analysts still claim that the PC's days are numbered, its power and appeal remains largely unchallenged. It remains the dominant computing device that most people will use in their day-to-day lives for the foreseeable future. However, the inner workings and technological capabilities of the PC have continued to evolve in ways that make each new generation so much more unimaginably versatile and powerful.

Let us consider what the PC offered back in the early to mid-1990s. Back then, the average PC had very little memory (sixteen megabits of RAM), little in the way of sound or video playback quality, and no CD-ROM. Hard drives contained approximately 100 megabits (a tiny fraction of today's standard sixty- to eighty-gigabit hard drive capacities), and most people stored their data on 5.25- or 3.5-inch floppy disks. Only around 1992–1993 did PCs begin to widely incorporate a mouse driver that helped users circumvent the difficulties of relying solely on a keyboard to enter instructions. Users physically had to type in commands to make their computers work. Equally important, PCs were stand-alone devices—for all practical purposes, the Internet did not exist for the public, and the word *modem* remained foreign

to most people. What modems that did exist were extremely slow by today's standards, and e-mail had yet to become the popular messaging system that it is today. Most people thought that the word *windows* referred to glass that you could see through in buildings. A highly advanced machine, including monitor and extra disk drive space, would cost consumers close to $3,000.

By mid-2005, the PC had metamorphosed to such an extent that, for under $500, a person could buy a sophisticated machine that runs Windows XP, has an ultrafast Intel Pentium 4 or AMD Athlon processor, and is preloaded with 512 megabits of RAM (memory), standard CD-burner DVD drive, and fast, easy connections to the Internet. Since 2000, each new generation of PC packs significantly more versatility than its predecessor. The latest PCs offer DVD recording capabilities, wireless connections to the Internet using "Wi-Fi" technology, and six to eight USB (Universal Serial Bus) ports that vastly expands the number of different appliances than can be attached. Some of the latest machines contain microprocessors that run on "multi-core technology." This refers to a new microprocessor design that enables the PC to run several simultaneous tasks without compromising speed or performance. Aesthetically, some of the latest PCs are now designed to look like avant-garde furniture. More important, laptop PC sales are overtaking desktop PCs. Each new generation of PC hits the store shelves or websites approximately every twelve to eighteen months.

Today's PC versatility to perform a wide array of functions (for example, standard computing, e-mail, music downloading, photo finishing,

Internet access, video games, home monitoring systems, video and audio entertainment, moviemaking, CD burning, DVD recording, desktop publishing) could potentially trigger another vast set of new capabilities for tomorrow. Already, many firms envision the PC to serve as the epicenter of a digital home—managing everything from refrigerators to washing machines and certainly the living room. Future televisions will connect to the PC so that viewers will be able to download movies over the Internet for immediate viewing. Future video games may even be integrated with television shows. Certainly, all forms of communication—e-mail, voice, and video—will be integrated in one easy-to-use format. Even home appliance makers are now designing their washers, dryers, and refrigerators to respond to a user's command through PCs and other wireless devices.

More powerful microprocessors (Intel's line of Pentium 4 and Centrino chips, Motorola's G5 Processor, AMD's Athlon and Opteron lines) and software operating systems (Microsoft's Windows 98/2000/XP and Apple's Macintosh system) developed through the years have made it possible for almost anyone of any age and background to learn to use the PC in a matter of hours. Learning the PC has become so much easier because many of the latest software advances no longer require customers to engage in mind-numbing installation and programming of their machines using hard-to-read, cumbersome instruction manuals. Even the most rudimentary PC sold today (for under $300) can surf the Internet, do your taxes, transmit e-mail, play video games, do spreadsheets, and even allow you to download MP3 files. At the same time, however, the average price of personal computers has continued to drop 10 to 20 percent every year. Since 2002, the biggest growth of PCs has occurred in models selling for under $600 (the previous benchmark was $1,000 in 1998).

The growing power and popularity of PCs, however, are testament to how fast an industry can develop and change over ever-shorter periods. Xerox Corporation conceived the first "true" personal computer, according to most analysts, during the mid-1960s. It was hard to use, designed for scientific applications, and certainly not as user-friendly or versatile as we expect today. However, not until companies such as Apple Computer, IBM, Compaq Computer, and others entered the market did the PC become the taken-for-granted product that it is today. The arrival of the Intel microprocessor—the "brains" of the PC—and powerful operating system software (from Apple Computer and Microsoft) triggered the PC explosion that has redefined our lives for over twenty years. Let us examine some of the factors that have dramatically shaped the PC industry over the past ten years and continue to do so.

Intensely Fierce Competition

By early-2005, there were primarily four big makers of PCs: Dell Computer, Hewlett-Packard, Gateway, and Apple Computer. IBM still sells PCs over its website, but exited their manufacture in 2002 and has negotiated to sell its entire PC business to Lenovo Group, a Chinese computer firm. Little-known eMachines became the third best-selling brand in the United States until Gateway acquired it in February 2004. Early industry innovator Compaq Computer merged with Hewlett-Packard in September 2002. For all practical purposes, all of these companies (with the exception of Apple) are known as "box makers" or assemblers in the industry—they incorporate leading-edge microprocessors made by either Intel or Advanced Micro Devices (AMD) and Microsoft software into a plastic or metal casing, and then they ship them out to buyers or directly to consumers. Other suppliers undertake most of the remaining manufacturing activities.

Among PC box makers, price-based competition is extremely fierce, and PC makers are doing whatever they can to squeeze out ever-thinner margins in order to survive. As margins continue to shrink and the industry slows down, Dell Computer appears to be enlarging its lead over other PC makers. Hewlett-Packard, after its 2002 merger with Compaq, appears to be focused on enhancing the technology content of its machines. HP is also more oriented toward commercial buyers. Gateway was reeling from major losses and purchased eMachines to solidify its base in the home market. In September 2004, Gateway announced the closure of all its signature retailing outlets and that it would focus on building large retail accounts such as Best Buy. Apple Computer is a lone standout in this industry; it writes and develops its own software (the Macintosh system) to compete with Microsoft, and it tries to become the design trendsetter for the industry. Although the company is profitable, its share of the total market continues to decline, because its software is incompatible with the vast majority of PCs that use the Microsoft Windows operating system. Apple continues to earn praise for its leading-edge, avant-garde designs. Apple users tend to be fiercely loyal to their machines and the company. Apple has pushed its design expertise from PCs to produce the wildly popular iPod digital music player that has won wide praise from customers of all ages.

However, this industry is one in which companies can easily enter and disappear just as quickly. Numerous firms once populated the industry, but have exited in the wake of fierce competition and consolidation (for example, AST Research, Acer, Packard Bell, Zenith Electronics, Texas Instruments, Tandy, Commodore, Micron Electronics). By 2005, the top PC names—Dell Computer, Hewlett-Packard, Gateway, and IBM—continued to command more than 60 percent of the U.S. market, after having squeezed out many of the players mentioned above after years of competition. However, two small but increasingly important players are making their presence felt in the industry—VoodooPC and Alienware Corporation. Both of these companies offer "bleeding-edge" machines that are designed for extremely intensive use of graphics and imaging. Buyers of PCs from VoodooPC and Alienware are typically very demanding video game players or professional designers and copy editors that need vivid colors and imagery. VoodooPC only builds extremely customized, tailor-made machines using the latest technologies at prices that often exceed $5,000. Alienware also builds custom, made-to-order machines with the latest technology at comparable prices, although some machines can be purchased through Best Buy.

Dueling but Consolidating Standards.

The PC industry currently has two competing software operating system standards. One operating system, backed by Apple Computer, is known as the Macintosh operating system. It is extremely user-friendly and runs on proprietary software, which means that the software for an Apple PC will not run on any other computer. The "brains" of the Apple PC is a family of PowerPC microprocessors made by Motorola (and uses some key technology from IBM). For several years, Apple's highly distinctive Macintosh system commanded premium prices, but its exclusive nature sharply limited Apple's total market share to about 2.5 percent by mid-2004, a decline from nearly 10 percent in 1994.

The other PC camp (and certainly the more dominant industry standard) is based on Microsoft's Windows operating system. The Windows operating system uses an alternative set of software instructions and icons that allow for significant ease of use and efficient organization of the PC's functions. In many ways, the tremendous growth of the PC industry throughout the past decade can be traced to several versions of the Windows operating system (3.0, 3.1, Windows 95, Windows 98, 2000, XP) that have greatly eased the way consumers can operate their machines. Windows makes it possible for users to load a variety of different programs into their PCs with fast speed and a high level of convenience. However, a big drawback of the Windows operating system is that its highly complex design needs continuous modification over time to remedy flaws that are hard to discover during development. Because of the tremendous popularity of Microsoft's Windows operating system, literally thousands of different broad-based software applications (for example, word processing, spreadsheet, photo manipulation, Internet access) have been designed to use Microsoft's format to make the computer more versatile. Moreover, Microsoft, in sharp contrast to Apple, freely licenses its Windows operating system (and its earlier DOS operating system) to any other PC maker willing to pay a royalty fee. This licensing policy attracted scores of new computer manufacturers and software designers seeking to capture early profits generated by the popularity of Microsoft's various operating systems. Thus, the popularity of Microsoft's operating systems became overwhelming and now represents well over 90 percent of the PC market.

Ease of Entry and Manufacture. PCs are easy to manufacture (assembly of premade parts), although some of the highest-quality machines will use customized, made-to-order parts. For example, the "average" PC requires only an Intel or AMD microprocessor as its central processing unit, a hard disk drive (which provides long-term storage of programs and data), a CD-RW/DVD drive (for CD-burning, video play, and downloads of extremely memory-intensive software programs), a few printed circuit boards, a keyboard, and a monitor. In effect, these six hardware components are so easy to source and assemble that PC manufacture has become almost a cottage industry. With the exception of the microprocessor and the software (which is protected), all other PC components are standard, off-the-shelf items that almost anyone can purchase and assemble.

Still, it is tough to distinguish one firm's machine from that of another. Driving down costs in PC assembly are significant, and the availability of manufacturing capacity and standardized, off-the-shelf technology makes assembly easy and inexpensive. Aside from the microprocessors and the software operating systems (both of which can be readily purchased or licensed), few proprietary technologies or techniques are involved in PC manufacture or distribution. What may keep even more firms from entering the PC industry is the brand recognition (for example, IBM, Hewlett-Packard, Dell) and access to distribution channels (for example, HP, eMachines) that existing firms already enjoy.

Distribution Channels. PCs can be purchased from almost any large consumer electronics retailer. Customers can more easily purchase PCs through the Internet. Dell Computer thrives in this industry through its creative marketing campaigns that offer custom-built PCs that can be ordered through the telephone or the Internet. In fact, Dell Computer got its start in the business by offering computers for sale through an 800 number. Ordering through the Internet has become standard practice, as customers can contact Gateway, IBM, Hewlett-Packard, and others directly through their websites. Even Amazon.com offers PCs for sale through its online cybermall. In fact, the growth of the Internet as an alternative distribution channel has made it possible for Gateway and HP to begin imitating Dell's strategy of delivering custom-made machines for individual customers according to their need for speed, power, number of different peripherals (for example, scanners, printers, Wi-fi capabilities, DVD, video cards), and price range. All three of these companies are using the Internet to branch out and begin selling other products as well, such as digital cameras, printers, and even flat-screen television sets.

Strong Buyers

The PC industry is full of knowledgeable and powerful buyers. With hundreds of suppliers to choose from, customers are ruthless in their search for higher value and better quality. Until about 1990, the majority of PC buyers were large and small businesses that used the machines to increase their productivity. Now, the weight of buyers is shifting toward people purchasing PCs for the home, with many families looking to purchase a second or even third PC for entertainment or dedicated Internet use. Regardless of what the PC is used for, the consumer is demanding and savvy. Technical vocabulary to describe computer parts and functions is no longer the domain of engineers or specialized salespeople. Customers are fully aware of what options they need and how much those features should cost. Because most PCs have a minimum standard of quality, power, speed, and memory, competition turns largely on price. To many customers, brand name has become less important over time. A key issue for the industry is that customers have become conditioned to think and to expect that PC prices will drop dramatically from one year to the next.

Knowledgeable buyers also mean that some customers will not base their purchase decision solely on price. This is particularly true for business and corporate buyers, who often want superior maintenance, software upgrades, repair service, and integration with other business-driven networks. In most cases, businesses will purchase either directly from large PC manufacturers (Dell, Hewlett-Packard, IBM) or from value-added resellers who will perform much of the maintenance, warranty work, and system upgrades when new technologies or software applications enter the market. Thus, there are opportunities for some PC makers to stake out important market niches with customers who seek additional security and fast service for their machines.

Strong Suppliers

Microchips. Some of the most important suppliers to the PC industry are the manufacturers of microprocessors, memory and graphics chips, and printed circuit boards, which represent the guts of the machine. For the most part, however, Intel (nearly 80 percent market share) and AMD (the remaining 20 percent) vie with one another to outdesign and outsell ever-faster microprocessors to PC manufacturers. The race between Intel and AMD to outperform each other's chips provides much of the fuel to power more versatile PCs. A larger number of firms supply the basic memory chips (DRAMs) needed for PCs (for example, Micron Technology, Samsung Electronics, Toshiba, NEC, Hynix Semiconductor). Specialized graphics chips makers, such as Nvidia and ATI Technologies, supply the vast majority of the video chips needed for brilliant imagery.

Computer Peripherals. Computer peripherals broadly include all hardware components and add-ons necessary to make the PC more complete and fully versatile. These include such important components as disk drives, monitors, scanners, printers, CD-RW drives (to burn and play music or to download software), DVD (digital video discs that play movies or store data), video cards (that make full-motion video possible on the screen), and even digital cameras (to take pictures that do not require conventional film). These peripheral components have become increasingly vital to how customers use their PCs to move beyond standard computing tasks. In fact, adding ever more powerful peripherals is an important way for PC makers to distinguish their machines from rivals and to attempt to slow down price-based competition. However, the prices of many peripherals (especially scanners, monitors, and printers) are themselves dropping 20 percent or more every year as well. Although PC makers traditionally have not focused much effort on peripherals, all of them are steadily putting more emphasis on selling and distributing them as part of their strategy to move into faster-growing businesses.

Important disk drive suppliers to the PC industry have included companies such as Seagate, Quantum, Western Digital, Applied Magnetics, and Read-Rite. IBM is also a leading supplier of key technologies and peripherals. It also has a special agreement to manufacture key components for Dell Computer. Major manufacturers of printers include Hewlett-Packard, Canon, Seiko-Epson, and Lexmark (who in turn supplies Dell with printers)—all of whom continue to design new features and technologies in this business. The traditional names in consumer electronics—Sony, Sanyo, Hitachi, Philips, Matsushita, and others—are key players that make many of the CD-RW and DVD components. In sum, suppliers of all key PC components, from chips to circuit boards to hardware components, are large and have the technological prowess to enter the industry should they choose to do so.

A Budding Potential for Substitutes

Although few direct substitutes currently exist for standardized PCs at today's low prices, the potential clearly exists for new products and technologies to redefine and reshape the way PCs are designed, made, sold, and used. However, the real growth in substitute products may occur from a number of different technological paths. The most natural substitute possibility is the growing availability of handheld, palm-top computers or personal digital assistants (PDAs) that can perform many PC functions without a keyboard (for example, BlackBerry products from Research in Motion). These handheld machines, including those from longtime leader Palm, may very well signify the rise of new types of wireless network appliances that eventually replace or "morph" with other devices such as the cellular phone, the pager, and even the laptop itself over time.

Other potential substitutes include the video game consoles made by Nintendo, Sony, and even Microsoft. Today's leading-edge video game consoles already come with Internet connectivity, Intel-class microprocessors, massive hard drives, extremely sophisticated graphics chips, and DVD drives. Some analysts have speculated that video game consoles may become the primary electronic appliances that young children and adolescents will use in their most formative years. Thus, these future buyers will likely demand that future PCs or other electronic devices are as simple to operate as their game consoles.

Core technological breakthroughs that can radically change the PC include voice recognition software (thus eliminating the need for keyboards), portable hard drives and software that connect to a variety of different electronic devices (thus blending the distinction among appliances and PCs), wireless (Wi-Max) broadband access (thus giving full-motion video capabilities to next-generation PDAs), and even televisions that offer computing capabilities. Yet, it may be possible that these same technologies could further extend the life and capabilities of a completely redesigned PC to perform many of the same tasks we now take for granted with separate electronic appliances and handheld devices.

Introduction

A firm's **environment** represents all external forces, factors, or conditions that exert some degree of impact on the strategies, decisions, and actions taken by the firm. This chapter focuses on the task of environmental analysis and its pivotal role in strategy formulation.

Every firm exists in an environment defined by the need to compete in its industry. Although the specific types of environmental forces and conditions vary from industry to industry, a number of broad environmental forces exert an impact on the strategies of every firm. In this chapter, we focus on two types of external environments: the broader macroenvironment and the industry-specific, competitive environment. In the first section, we selectively examine several key factors and conditions that make up the broader macroenvironment and discuss how they relate to all firms, regardless of industry. In the second section, we analyze a more industry-specific type of environment, the firm's competitive environment. The competitive environment refers to the forces and conditions directly relevant to the industry in which a firm competes. In other words, the competitive environment focuses on the particular factors that define a specific industry setting. We then examine the concept of strategic groups. Strategic groups help reveal specific differences in competitive behavior among firms within an industry. In the last section, we discuss techniques that firms can use to monitor their external environments to formulate their strategies.

environment:
All external forces, factors, or conditions that exert some degree of impact on the strategies, decisions, and actions taken by the firm.

The Macroenvironment

The **macroenvironment,** also known as the **general environment,** includes all of those environmental forces and conditions that have an impact on every firm and organization within the economy. As such, the macro- or general environment represents the broad collection of factors that directly or indirectly influence every firm in every industry. Consider, for example, such general environmental developments as the aging workforce, the rising trend toward greater health consciousness, changing cost of capital or interest rates, the growing use of technology in all types of products and services, declining birthrates, the impact of terrorism, the expansion of financial regulations, considerations regarding domestic security, and growing foreign competition. These factors shape the long-term environment in which all firms must operate. Some factors represent long-term shifts, such as the aging of the U.S. population, the incorporation of new technology to transform products, homeland security issues, and the growing prevalence of foreign competition. Other factors have shorter-term impact, such as interest rates, changes in household purchasing power, and exchange rates.

Of course, firms cannot control the macroenvironment. Moreover, these factors are often difficult to predict with any real precision. Although numerous factors make up the general environment, we focus on a few key developments that will impact all firms in some way in the twenty-first century. Specifically, we will consider developments in the demographic environment, the political environment, the social/cultural environment, the technological environment, and the global environment.

The Demographic Environment

Demographics describe the broad characteristics of people that make up any geographic unit of analysis, such as nation, state or region, or county/prefecture. The importance of changes in demographics lies in their influence on the eventual makeup of each firm's workforce, on human resource practices, on marketing, and on the growth of the firm. Let us examine some key demographic trends that are now redefining the United States.

One of the most important changes taking shape during this decade is the rise of the "sandwich generation." The sandwich generation refers to those baby boomers (and younger adults) who are now caught in the squeeze of raising their own children and managing their own careers, while also taking on the additional role of caring for aging parents. The sandwich generation is becoming especially important in redefining human resource and workplace policies at a growing number of U.S. firms. Members of this generation are looking for greater flexibility in their schedules so that they can juggle the multiple sets of responsibilities on their shoulders. As a result, many companies are offering revised employee benefit plans or special allowances that enable workers to cover some of the costs of providing care to elder parents.

Certainly one of the most significant and enduring changes in the United States has been the steady arrival and participation by women in the workforce. Already, women make up close to half of the workforce, and their numbers are expected to continue to grow as they find ways to balance the pursuit of a professional career with choices about raising families. Clearly, women have made substantial gains in numerous professions once dominated by males, such as law, accounting, management consulting, engineering, and other high-paying occupations. However, they continue to remain extremely underrepresented at the highest level of management in the vast majority of companies today, and they still encounter significant pay disparities when compared with their male counterparts.

Women have begun to make their presence felt on boards of directors and the ranks of chief executive officers (CEOs) of large U.S. firms. For example, in early 2005, such companies as Avon Products, Xerox Corporation, eBay, Sara Lee, and Lucent Technologies had women as CEOs. Anne Mulcahy, CEO of Xerox Corporation, hopes that in the future all women will be able to break through the "glass ceiling" that appears to limit how far women can advance within their firms, no matter how capable they are. Women from all types of industries and firms are increasingly forming their own professional networks to provide mentoring, career advice, and new career opportunities to one another. Still, despite the substantial gains made in the late 1990s, women still are confronted with decisions about careers and families that their male counterparts have not typically faced. Many companies recognize the enormous talent and contribution of their female managers and workforces and have begun instituting new types of family-friendly programs (for example, child care, flexible leaves, new types of employee benefits) that are designed to support and retain this vast reservoir of talent. Firms such as IBM, Johnson & Johnson, Procter & Gamble, Eastman Kodak, and Ford Motor Company are just a few of leading U.S. companies taking concrete steps to offer real opportunities for their female managers to grow.

Another important demographic factor is the changing racial composition of the United States. A major ongoing challenge for managers of minority descent is to create sustainable personal networks that allow them to interact with people inside and outside the firm. By creating a strong network, a manager is better able to leverage his or her knowledge, experience, and personal relationships to open up new opportunities for advancement.[2] On a broader theme, America is becoming much more diverse. By promoting diversity throughout their organizations, firms can promote the exchange of differing ideas and perspectives that may lead to new ways of developing products or entering markets.[3] For example, the Hispanic population is growing much faster than other racial groups and represents nearly one-third of the local population in many states such as California, Arizona, New York, and Texas. Asian Americans also make up a growing percentage of the U.S. population.[4] Although the United States has confronted and benefited from rising tides of immigration in previous decades (for example, 1840–1860; 1890–1910; 1970s), the massive influx of people from different ethnic and religious backgrounds also presents a new set of imperatives for U.S. companies. Certainly, immigration brings enormous positive benefits to the entire U.S. economy. For example, with the rising numbers of immigrants from South and Southeast Asia, many U.S. firms are capturing the enormous engineering and software design skills of highly trained professionals and scientists who are looking for a better life in this country. Companies located in California's Silicon Valley in particular are hotbeds of innovation—some of the newest ideas and technologies in recent years have come from new immigrants who are taking great risks to create new businesses. Immigrants have also helped spearhead the creation of many vibrantly creative companies in biotechnology, software design, semiconductors, and other vital growth industries. At the same time, however, rising tides of immigration, particularly those involving illegal entry into the United States, pose another set of challenges for the U.S. economy. Many illegal immigrants provide an important source of low-cost labor in construction and service-based industries. However, there is a continuing belief that large numbers of illegal immigrants may also siphon away employment opportunities for less affluent long-term residents and citizens.

The average age of the U.S. population is steadily rising. The combination of declining birthrates and longer life expectancy—made possible by improved health conditions—is a trend that will have direct impact on the availability of labor within the U.S. economy. An aging population means that more resources will likely be devoted to health care and medical expenses. Because many senior citizens in the United States tend to be relatively affluent, an aging population implies that more people will have more discretionary income to spend on vacations, resorts, and hobbies. Aging directly benefits industries such as pharmaceuticals, medical devices, and implants. In the restaurant industry, rising health consciousness means a shift away from fast food and more toward smaller portions or sit-down meals at restaurants whose menus offer a wide selection of healthy foods.

Unfortunately, an aging population also means that some elderly people who are less well off will spend a significant portion of their lives worried about their financial means. In particular, the rising population of senior citizens has also placed significant pressures on the pharmaceutical industry to rein in the prices of some key drugs that help treat cardiovascular and other diseases. In recent years, there has been growing debate about the government-imposed price controls on pharmaceuticals, as well as removing restrictions on reimporting drugs from Canada. Already, legions of senior citizens are purchasing their medications in Canada where fixed price controls have created wide distortions in retail prices of prescription drugs. The U.S. government has begun to cover the partial cost of prescriptions in a major revision to the Medicare program. Although price controls will likely devastate the profitability of the pharmaceutical industry, they will also suppress innovation as drug companies retreat from expensive research and development (R&D) expenditures that they may not be able to recoup. All of the drug companies are listening to what their customers and the government are saying, and a number of them are offering specially designed pricing to help senior citizens purchase prescription drugs through new discount programs targeted to them. For example, GlaxoSmithKline, Pfizer, and Novartis began to institute significantly lower prices for senior citizens who earn below certain income thresholds.

The Political Environment

Within the United States, the political environment affects business in many ways. For example, in recent years, the government has significantly increased a variety of regulatory requirements on firms operating in the United States. This is a major reversal of deregulatory trends that were in place for much of the 1980s and 1990s. For example, the telecommunications and airline industries witnessed the entry of many new competitors because of deregulation. Deregulation has facilitated greater customer choice for new products and services, thus significantly changing the nature and profitability of many of these industries. Yet, with numerous scandals regarding corporate malfeasance and accounting irregularities, government regulations are now having a significant impact on U.S. firms. The Sarbanes-Oxley Act of 2002, for example, mandates that CEOs sign off on the accuracy of their firms' accounting. Many analysts believe that this law will greatly increase the cost and complexity of financial monitoring and reporting. Already, some smaller and midsized companies are seeking to go private in order to avoid the costly impact of this law. This law has also influenced many foreign-based companies to refrain from listing their stock on the New York Stock Exchange for fear of running afoul of U.S. regulations.

The American public at large supports increased regulation because of such events as the bankruptcies of Enron Corporation (November 2001) and WorldCom (April 2002); misappropriation of corporate funds for personal use at Tyco Corporation (trial in April 2004); accounting irregularities at large firms (for example, Nortel Networks, Computer Associates); insider and illegal forms of trading at dozens of mutual funds (for example, Janus Capital, Scudder Funds); improper disclosures of impending deals to executives and insiders (for example, Frank Quattrone at CSFB's Silicon Valley unit); and high-profile trials of well-known executives (for example, Martha Stewart in March 2004; Enron criminal trial in September 2004; HealthSouth criminal trial in January 2005). The Enron debacle, in particular, has struck a raw nerve in the national conscience. Once listed in the top ten of Fortune 500 companies in 2000, Enron's fortunes began to unwind as the company engaged in many dubious accounting and business practices that were designed to hide the losses and risks that it was taking. By apparently concealing losses and certain projects in the form of limited partnerships, Enron gave the impression that it was profitable, despite the fact that many of its far-flung investments exposed the firm to a variety of risks. Many of the company's finances were hidden in "off-balance sheet" statements that were difficult to understand, even for Wall Street investors and analysts. To make matters worse, Enron's accounting auditors from Arthur Andersen destroyed key documents in order to eliminate the "paper trail" that showed what the oil and gas giant was doing. As the company's stock price dropped from a peak of $90 a share to less than a dollar in several months, Enron's middle managers and employees were prevented from selling their shares at the same time that senior executives were able to sell their stock positions. The disaster surrounding Enron opened numerous investigations by Congress, the Securities and Exchange Commission, and law enforcement agencies. Even as investigations by the federal government began in earnest in spring 2002, Enron continued to blatantly shred documents in ways that defied adherence to the law. The government has indicted top Enron officers, including CEO Kenneth Lay, President Jeffrey Skilling, and numerous others. Several top officers such as Skilling and Lea Fastow were sentenced to short prison sentences. Thus, government regulation can directly shape the way firms conduct their business across many industries.[5]

A major regulatory trend affecting all U.S. businesses is the renewed emphasis on protecting the environment. With greater debate about global warming taking place, more U.S. companies are embracing environmental protection as a crucial part of their long-term strategies, not just an afterthought. For example, many automobile makers (such as General Motors), appliance manufacturers (such as Whirlpool, Maytag, General Electric), and chemical makers (such as DuPont and Dow Chemical) are placing a major emphasis on developing more energy-efficient and environmentally friendly technologies. More companies are including environmental sustainability as a key part of their product and technology planning. DaimlerChrysler, for example, is looking for ways to build a car entirely out of recyclable plastics and metals. Ford Motor Company, in fact, diverted over 27 million square feet of carpet from landfills for use in making plastic auto parts in 2003. Semiconductor manufacturers such as Intel, Texas Instruments, Lucent Technologies, and IBM are spending more money on devising new ways to recycle the pollutants that are produced when making microchips. Many steel and utility companies are adopting new types of clean-air manufacturing technologies that prevent contaminants and noxious odors from even entering the air.

At the same time, the costs of many regulations have become so burdensome in some industries that some companies are beginning to close down mines and factories in order to save costs. These closures, in turn, have put many people out of work, leaving them with few economic opportunities. Many companies have decided to relocate their manufacturing facilities outside the United States, partially because of the rising costs and burdens of complying with new forms of regulations. This trend has been especially notable in traditional, "heavy" industries that use significant amounts of fossil fuels, petroleum, and other natural resources to create products for consumer and industrial end markets (for example, plastics, chemicals, synthetic fibers, steel, aluminum). The renewed public and governmental concern with protecting the environment is challenging U.S. businesses to incorporate environmentally friendly strategies as part of their long-term planning.[6]

A new political development confronting the United States is the growing risk that the country faces from military and terrorist actions on American soil. On September 11, 2001, a group of terrorists of Middle Eastern origin orchestrated an attack on America that resulted in the destruction of the Twin Towers of the World Trade Center, as well as an attack on the Pentagon in Washington, D.C. After hijacking four commercial jets operated by American Airlines and United Airlines, the terrorists inflicted a huge loss of life and economic damage on the United States by using the planes as missiles to attack their targets. A planned simultaneous attack on the White House was foiled after the passengers on the fourth jet overpowered the hijackers, resulting in the plane's crash in western Pennsylvania. As the United States enters this new decade, the risk of terrorist actions will likely continue to grow as terrorists and their supporters look for ways to hurt American interests around the world.

Domestically, the terrorist attack already has fundamentally changed the way many industries operate. Security has become a primary business concern for almost every U.S. enterprise. At a minimum, companies are increasing the scrutiny of people entering their premises and conducting even more extensive background checks of prospective employees. Security has also compelled the transportation industry to rethink how best to protect passengers, freight shipments, and other property in the wake of potential terrorism. Nowhere has the impact of terrorism and increased security requirements had a more profound effect than on the U.S. airline industry shortly after 9/11. Within a few months, the six major U.S. airline companies (American Airlines, United Airlines, Continental Airlines, Delta Airlines, Northwest Airlines, and US Airways Group) collectively laid off a hundred thousand employees. The losses endured by the airlines were so severe that the Bush administration and Congress worked together to offer an emergency financial rescue package to help the airlines get back on their feet. United Airlines and US Airways Group were forced into bankruptcy in order to restructure their operations. By September 2004, US Airways entered into bankruptcy for a second time, and Delta Airlines was considering the move in the wake of ever-escalating fuel costs.[7] Total industry losses for the past five years have escalated into several billions of dollars.

Security concerns will increase the economic prospects for a variety of companies, including private investigation firms and manufacturers of high-technology monitoring devices. One particular beneficiary has been Taser International, which has developed a new type of stun gun that can be used to disable criminals. For financial service companies, security means that people must provide more verifiable forms of documentation and identification to conduct transactions as a result of the U.S. Patriot Act. For railroad and trucking companies, security means devising new procedures to reduce the risk that terrorists will use these means of transport as a lethal weapon.

The Social/Cultural Environment

The social/cultural environment represents the set of values, ideals, and other characteristics that distinguish members of one group from those of another. Firms need to be aware of how social and cultural factors can directly affect the way they manage their operations, particularly human resources and marketing. For example, managers need to be increasingly aware of and sensitive to the values and ideas of people from different upbringings and backgrounds.

One of the most important developments in the social/cultural environment is the need for greater diversity awareness and training. With the rapidly changing composition of the U.S. workforce, managers and employees must understand how to manage an increasingly heterogeneous work environment. The need for programs that help managers think about diversity issues becomes especially important as a greater number of women and racial minorities enter the workforce. Several progressive companies are leading the way in using diversity as an explicit part of their long-term strategy to bring different mindsets and cultures into their planning processes.[8]

Another key development in the social environment is the apparently steady erosion of the U.S. educational system. Particularly in inner cities, many students are floundering and thus becoming less employable in U.S. businesses. This trend is alarming, not only because there are fewer young people in the U.S. population as a result of demographic changes, but also because these new employees often are underskilled, which places a greater burden on business to offer remedial training to help young people learn the skills they need to become productive employees. Recently, the Bush administration passed a new set of legislation through Congress that is designed to tighten educational standards for schools. Also, this same legislation will compel annual testing of student competency in many grade levels so that parents and teachers can see how their children are progressing in educational achievement.

Finally, a key issue all companies will increasingly face over the next few years is the growing demand by managers and employees for more flexible working arrangements. In a related vein, many working parents need a more flexible schedule to enable them to take care of children or parents during off-school or other unusual hours. This development alone has prompted many companies, such as AT&T, IBM, and Xerox, to offer either corporate day care facilities or increased employee benefits that enable managers and employees to better cope with child care needs. As a growing number of women enter and advance in the workforce, the issue of providing child care will become an increasing challenge for all U.S. businesses.[9]

Technological Developments

New technologies are dramatically reshaping the way American business competes. In just the last few years, for example, several new technologies have begun to transform the workplace and the home once again. The rise of such new offerings as Internet services, faster semiconductors, digital video disc (DVD) recorders, voice recognition, new types of wireless phones, new biotech-based drugs, and even more efficient automotive engine designs present U.S. companies with a plethora of opportunities to grow their businesses. At the same time that new technology brings forth new products and services, existing products become obsolete and dated even faster. Consider the rapid obsolescence of cellular phones, pagers, digital cameras, personal digital assistants (PDAs), and DVD players—products that were considered state-of-the-art in 1998 are now so commonplace that companies have moved to develop new generations of products with features that far transcend their predecessors. Communications technology, in particular, is making it possible for people to relate to each other in ways that make the traditional notions of distance and geography potentially obsolete. In fact, it is likely that all electronic goods in the near future (for example, appliances, televisions, automobiles) will have a wireless transmission capability designed into them. Behind the economic curtain, new manufacturing technologies in the factory are improving product quality, accelerating turnaround time, reducing inventory costs, and giving firms unprecedented flexibility. In a broader context, new technologies are now making themselves felt in many routine activities, such as video-enabled e-mail, more secure and versatile online transactions, and computers that recognize handwriting and voice.

The explosive growth of new technologies has redefined the U.S. business landscape and presented many opportunities for both entrepreneurs and established firms to create new products for new markets. The rise of new technologies has also spawned entirely new industries within the U.S. economy, such as biotechnology, genomics, specialty semiconductors, voice recognition software, biodegradable plastics, digital media, genetically engineered seeds, factory automation, Internet services, and artificial intelligence. Few of these industries were considered commercially viable even as recently as 1995. Many scientists and analysts envision that developments in nanotechnology will spawn an entirely new range of industries. Nanotechnology attempts to build electronic and even organic-based devices at the molecular and atomic levels of matter. Molecular-sized machines and chips will use new forms of current transmission by harnessing scientific disciplines at the subatomic, enzymatic, or protein level. Nanotechnology devices may even displace the use of silicon-based semiconductors in the future; they are seen as especially important tools to help design ultratiny medical devices and instruments that can treat diseased arteries and other organs. One goal of nanotechnology is to produce micromotors and robots small enough to fit within human blood vessels. These micromotor-powered robots can then be inserted into the human body to help control bleeding or to remove plaque from arteries. On a larger scale, nanotechnology may produce new generations of robots that can wash windows on skyscrapers, scrape rust and barnacles off ships, remove toxic waste materials from hazardous or contaminated sites, and even engage in deep-sea, ocean-based mining or tunneling. U.S. scientists have already developed molecular logic circuits that represent a form of "organic transistors."[10]

The rapid rise of new technologies also presents many significant challenges. For example, technology can threaten to make some people's jobs obsolete, as happened in scores of manufacturing industries during the 1990s. Growing levels of factory automation displace unskilled and semiskilled labor from once high-paying jobs. The technological challenge is present even in high-paying white-collar positions. Technology is a mixed blessing for people in the professions. Computer programs, advanced software, and Internet-enabled communications are transforming the work of accountants, consultants, engineers, and even architects. As a result, technology is accelerating the pace of outsourcing in the United States. **Outsourcing** is the shifting of work and business activities that were once performed within the firm to external providers. Over the past few years, U.S. firms have outsourced tens of thousands of jobs in high-technology and service-based industries to offshore locations in India, China, and elsewhere. Outsourcing is likely to accelerate in many industries as companies take advantage of lower-cost labor in developing countries; this practice has also become a major source of controversy and debate in all realms of U.S. politics and society.

outsourcing:
The use of external suppliers to perform activities that were once conducted within the firm.

These technological developments challenge the U.S. economy to become more productive and creative in its use of resources. The rapid pace of technological change is likely to continue, as both entrepreneurs and existing firms find new ways to use technology to improve their products and competitiveness. Constant and intense innovation of new products, services, production processes, and distribution capabilities increasingly will become the basis for future growth in the United States and elsewhere. At the same time, other countries will seek to use technology to do so the same, prompting a new form of nation-based competition across a broad spectrum of high-technology industries. Technological developments represent a real opportunity for firms with the skills to understand and apply them; they simultaneously represent genuine threats for those firms that are slow and cannot adjust to new advances. Throughout this book, we will show how different types of technologies offer new opportunities and challenges to firms in various industries.

The Global Environment

Firms in every industry are facing the rising tide of globalization. Put simply, the world is becoming a smaller place each day, and U.S. businesses need to think about selling and producing goods for customers, no matter where they may be located. Globalization presents an exciting opportunity for many companies, as firms such as Coca-Cola, General Electric, Intel, Cisco Systems, Caterpillar, Boeing, Citigroup, American Express, AT&T, IBM, and Colgate-Palmolive have learned. These companies have developed thriving operations outside the United States and now derive an increasingly high proportion of their revenues from these operations. The

Balancing Stakeholders: The Outsourcing Wave[11]

Over the past few years, a growing discussion about the merits and costs of outsourcing has become a topic of hot debate across every industry in the United States. When a firm engages in outsourcing, it relies on external suppliers to perform work that it once did in-house. Many of these suppliers are increasingly located in countries where the cost of labor is substantially lower. Outsourcing has thus become an issue of national importance, as government leaders, politicians of all stripes, businesspeople, and union representatives make their voices heard.

Declining trade barriers, advances in new technology, and the massive influx of increasingly skilled workers into the global labor force are pushing U.S. companies into a period of unprecedented change. To compete with new rivals around the world, U.S. manufacturers are forced to become ever more productive and cost-efficient. In practice, American firms have long outsourced much of their work to suppliers in foreign countries for the past three decades. Firms in the apparel, automotive, electronics, furniture, power tool, toy, and other industries have established numerous factories in the Far East and Southeast Asia to take advantage of increasingly skilled and less expensive labor. As American consumers benefited from less expensive, imported products, American workers lost their jobs by the millions. A substantial proportion of these workers, however, were able to find jobs in other fields, although in many cases, they paid less than what workers earned previously.

Now, the outsourcing trend has clearly expanded to upper-end services-based jobs and high-technology fields—two sectors that U.S. managers and employees have long believed would be insulated from such cataclysmic change. Still, the outsourcing of back-office operations and services is not an entirely new concept. During the 1980s, for example, American Airlines shifted some of its ticket-based operations to lower-cost Barbados before the airline (and the industry) went to a paperless system. The rise of the Internet and lower-cost telecommunications has dramatically accelerated the outsourcing of many skilled jobs to lower-cost regions. Many analysts describe this process as *offshoring*. For example, Dell Computer, General Electric, IBM, Microsoft, Oracle, and Citigroup are just a few of the hundreds of U.S. companies that have established service and technical operations in China, India, and other regions. General Electric alone has established over a dozen laboratories in China to take advantage of the country's abundant science and engineering talent. In addition to China and India, Hewlett-Packard is operating in Poland, Costa Rica, and the Philippines. These companies have trained thousands of employees to operate call centers that field customer service requests from anywhere in the world. A college student, housewife, or dentist with a computer problem or a billing dispute would call an 800 number and be immediately routed to a call center in India, where a trained customer support staff would provide assistance. Yet, this type of outsourcing is not limited to fairly simple or routine tasks; professional services firms such as Accenture, Electronic Data Systems (EDS), Deloitte and Touche, and other consulting firms have begun moving highly complex work to India and China as the labor force becomes increasingly skilled and competitive. Outsourcing is transforming software design, tax preparation, architecture, and even computer-chip design. In financial services, J. P. Morgan Chase hired forty junior research analysts and a thousand support staff in Bombay in 2003. Finance specialists, for example, earn $1,000 per month in India, compared with $7,000 in the United States.

Outsourcing has created an entirely new class of Indian competitors in many professional services fields. Rivals such as Infosys Technologies, Wipro Technologies, and Satyan Computers are fast becoming global competitors to such firms as IBM, EDS, Computer Associates, and Hewlett-Packard to provide companies with new software-based platforms. These Indian competitors, in turn, have ironically begun outsourcing some of their own work to even lower-cost China!

What are the merits of outsourcing and offshoring? U.S. consumers certainly receive major benefits in terms of less expensive products and services. U.S. companies can significantly increase their productivity as they rely on less costly labor and suppliers. Investors potentially receive higher returns as firms become more profitable. Capital is freed up to more productive uses. Smaller, more entrepreneurial firms may be able to use outsourcing to focus their effort on activities they can perform best. Ironically, outsourcing and offshoring may speed up the creation of an entirely new middle-class set of consumers in once poor nations. These consumers could well become important customers of U.S. firms in the future.

What are some of the costs of outsourcing? Entire U.S. industries (for example, consumer electronics, flat-screen displays, semiconductors, machine tools, auto parts, power tools) are "hollowed out" as firms decide to become entirely dependent on foreign suppliers. This may limit the ability of U.S. companies to preserve vital skills that may be important for national defense and other uses. Millions of managers and workers are displaced from their jobs, and the trend will likely continue. Although many of them will find newer and better opportunities, many will also never recover the level of income they once enjoyed. The AFL-CIO, one of America's largest unions, is pushing for government policy changes that will better protect U.S. manufacturing jobs through retraining programs. Local

(*continued*)

communities that once housed large call centers, as well as factory and service operations, face continued erosion.

Within the firm, senior management must consider a variety of stakeholder needs as it deals with outsourcing. The pressure to become more productive and profitable clashes with the aspirations of midlevel managers and employees. The commitment to shareholders clashes with the commitment to the local community. Many U.S. high-technology firms are currently in the midst of just such an internal debate. IBM, for example, announced in February 2004 that it would significantly increase company-wide employment. However, many of the company's newest jobs will be located outside the United States. At the same time, IBM is compelling senior workers and technical specialists to train their more junior counterparts to perform the work they once did. After training their replacements, many of these senior workers and specialists are then laid off.

rise of new markets outside the United States means many more jobs for U.S. exporters such as General Electric, Boeing, Caterpillar, and Merck. More prosperity and growth in places such as Brazil, China, India, Russia, and Eastern Europe mean more jobs for U.S. employees and greater opportunities for U.S. firms willing to serve those markets.[12]

At the same time, globalization presents many challenges, of course. As markets become more open, many U.S. industries will feel fierce competitive pressures from more efficient manufacturers abroad. Already, several U.S. industries have diminished greatly in size and profitability from the onslaught of global competition, including shipbuilding, textiles and apparel, electronic assembly, toys, and steel. Even high-technology U.S. industries such as semiconductors, telecommunication equipment, software, biotechnology, office equipment, and fiber optics are facing significant challenges from competitors abroad.

Globalization can accelerate changes within and across industries. In the auto industry, for example, the unrelenting pressure from Japanese automakers has contributed to the steady decline of market share by U.S. manufacturers over the past two decades. Now, both Japanese and U.S. automakers face growing pressures from reinvigorated Korean manufacturers who have begun to make steady inroads into the U.S. market. At the same time, General Motors, Ford, and the Chrysler unit of DaimlerChrysler face rising difficulties trying to hold onto their U.S. market shares as the lower cost of foreign currencies make imports more competitive in the United States. Consequently, numerous American autoworkers have been laid off during the past decade, and the trend continues unabated now.

Not only the automakers but also other companies in the steel, aluminum, and aircraft industries face the constant need to restructure their operations to meet the challenge of intensified global competition. Likewise, the suppliers to these industries face similar challenges. Companies that supply glass, rubber, steel, and other automobile parts have also been forced to become more efficient and quality conscious or close their doors. In sum, foreign competition has compelled the U.S. automotive and other industries to make better products without large employment increases and adjustment costs.

Globalization may lead to additional financial risks for U.S. corporations when local economies suffer recessions or major political changes. Throughout the late 1990s, recessions abroad led to a marked downturn of Far Eastern and Southeast Asian economies. In this decade, economic growth in Europe has remained sluggish at best. On the other hand, growth is ballooning in India and China. These broad macro trends have generated a massive shift in how American companies are planning global operations, particularly for those firms selling high-technology products. More investments abroad in factories and distribution facilities by U.S. firms expose them to increased financial risks stemming from volatile foreign exchange rates, currency devaluations, and difficult government regulations and mandates. At the same time, these investments enable U.S. firms to get closer to a fast-growing group of customers that increasingly have middle-class tastes and aspirations.

On top of these changes, many sectors of U.S. industry are becoming more global in their own right. Consider again the automotive sector. Chrysler merged with German giant Daimler-Benz in a huge transatlantic merger in July 1998 to form DaimlerChrysler. This transaction spurred other acquisitions by Ford (for example, Volvo's automobile unit, Land Rover) and by General Motors (for example, Saab of Sweden, higher equity stakes in Japan's Isuzu, Suzuki, and Fuji Industries) throughout Europe and Asia. Elsewhere, the financial services industry witnessed the cross-Atlantic mergers of many banking and insurance firms that are looking to expand operations in both regions. For example, Dutch, French, and British insurance firms are looking to merge with their U.S. counterparts as well as with banks in order to expand their presence in the United States and to lower the cost of their capital. Even the telecommunications and publishing industries have become more global, as European and American firms form cross-border ties that include alliances as well as outright mergers.

Many countries and regions of the world seek to consolidate their national markets into larger trading blocs in which member countries receive preference for imports and purchases. This development presents difficulties for firms operating outside those blocs. For example, the rise of the European Economic Community (EEC) raises difficulties for U.S. firms in such critical industries as commercial aircraft, automobiles, chemicals, computers, agriculture, and electronics. The rise of the Euro as a common European currency to be shared among the majority of European nations also presents an indirect challenge to the U.S. economy, as it enables European firms to achieve greater critical mass and currency stability in their operations back home. Countries such as France, Germany, Italy, and the United Kingdom have begun to think about economic battle plans that facilitate greater coordination of activities among their countries' large industrial firms to counter feared U.S. economic dominance, especially in certain high-tech markets such as aerospace, defense, automotive, communications, and high-technology arenas.

Interest in economic consolidation of markets is also growing in the Western Hemisphere. In the mid-1990s, the United States and every other country in the Western Hemisphere (except Cuba) began working on a plan to create a free-trade zone that would extend from Alaska to Argentina by 2005. Already, the United States has offered Chile an opportunity to join the newly created North American Free Trade Agreement. NAFTA was inaugurated in 1994 to create a free-trade zone between Canada, the United States, and Mexico. Some of these discussions to expand free trade zones now face new hurdles. For example Argentina recently faced enormous difficulties in meeting its foreign debt obligations and its economy is regarded as volatile. In December 2001, Argentina defaulted on its sovereign debt and faced numerous rioters in the street who were protesting the economic downturn in that country. Neighboring country Brazil, under President Lula da Silva, faces its own set of economic issues as high taxes and regulations slow down domestic growth. Still, several Far Eastern and Southeastern Asian countries have moved forward in similar discussions designed to create free-trade zones among such economic dynamos as Singapore, Indonesia, Thailand, and other Asian countries.

The global environment is so important to U.S. business that we will devote an entire chapter to analyzing different types of strategies that U.S. firms can adopt to compete more effectively in an increasingly borderless world.

Assessing the Impact of the General Environment

Firms need to be aware of developments in the general environment as both opportunities and threats. For example, the same environmental trend or development can have dramatically different implications for different industries. Consider the rising consciousness of the need to protect the environment. For industrial companies, meeting the need may add to their costs of doing business. For manufacturers of steel, aluminum, and copper—such as Nucor, Alcoa, and Phelps-Dodge—meeting this need means formulating new strategies and designing new processes that will protect the environment while these companies deliver products vital to the economy. On the other hand, companies such as Waste Management and Hewlett-Packard are more likely to view rising environmental consciousness as an opportunity rather than as a threat. It will likely provide Waste Management an upturn in demand for its efficient waste removal services, while high-tech electronics instrument maker Hewlett-Packard will feel an indirect rise in demand for its measurement products, because laboratory and diagnostic equipment will be needed to track wastes and to find new ways to remove them safely. Thus, the same environmental trend can exert different effects on firms in different industries.

Developments in the general environment can also have a differential effect on competitors within a single industry. For example, the deregulation and convergence of financial services now enables securities firms, such as Merrill Lynch and Fidelity Investments, to offer services similar to those of banks. Deregulation of the trucking and airline industries accelerated a "shakeout" of less efficient firms in favor of more efficient ones. Combined with large financial losses, deregulation decreased the number of full-service airlines in the United States, but increased the entry of deep-discount carriers. However, increased regulation in the health care field, for example, the Health Insurance Portability and Accountability Act of 1997 or HIPAA has prompted the growth of software and consulting firms that assist hospitals in implementing new rules and procedures to protect patient privacy.

Therefore, developments in the general environment can have intended and unintended effects on firms within and across different industries. The general macroenvironment can be regarded as a large pond in which hundreds of different firms live. When a stone is tossed into the pond, it creates ripple effects that all firms will feel. Either directly or indirectly, these ripple effects benefit some firms while hurting others.

The Competitive Environment

competitive environment:
The immediate economic factors—customers, competitors, suppliers, buyers, and potential substitutes—of direct relevance to a firm in a given industry (also known as industry environment).

industry attractiveness:
The potential for profitability when competing in a given industry. An attractive industry has high profit potential; an unattractive industry has low profit potential.

The general environment contains forces and developments that affect all firms within the economy. In addition to these forces, managers must also deal with forces whose effects are limited to their more immediate competitive environment. In this section, we examine the critical dimensions of the competitive environment. The **competitive environment** includes the key forces shaping competition in an industry. Analysis of the competitive environment for any given firm is concerned with assessing how these forces affect the attractiveness of the industry. **Industry attractiveness** refers to the potential for profitability that firms attempt to capture from competing in that industry. Each industry's attractiveness, or profitability potential, is a direct function of the interaction of various environmental forces that determine the nature of competition.

The Five Forces Model of Industry Attractiveness

The competitive state of an industry exerts a strong influence on how firms develop their strategies to earn profits over time. Although all industries are competitive, the nature of this competition can differ significantly among industries. For example, competition in the airline industry is somewhat cutthroat and occurs by way of price wars, whereas firms in printer and imaging industries often compete through enhanced product features and new models.

Competition within an industry is determined by its own particular structure. **Industry structure** refers to the interrelationship among five different forces that drive the behavior of firms competing in that industry. How firms compete with one another in any given industry is directly related to the interaction of these five key forces. As initially developed by Michael Porter, these five forces are as follows:

- The threat of new entrants into the industry
- The bargaining power of customers
- The bargaining power of suppliers
- The intensity of the rivalry among firms within the industry
- The potential for substitute products or services

Porter's five forces model is one of the most effective and enduring conceptual frameworks used to assess the nature of the competitive environment and to describe an industry's structure. This chapter draws heavily from his work on competitive industry analysis.[13] Exhibit 2-1 on the next page shows how these five forces interrelate to determine an industry's attractiveness. A highly attractive industry is one in which it is comparatively easy to make profits; an unattractive industry is one where profitability is frequently low or consistently depressed. The interrelationships among these five forces give each industry its own particular competitive environment.

To perform well, managers need to know how to identify and analyze the five forces that determine the competitive structure of their industries. By applying Porter's five forces model of industry attractiveness to their own industries, managers can gauge their own firm's strengths, weaknesses, and future opportunities.

industry structure:
The interrelationship among the factors in a firm's competitive or industry environment; configuration of economic forces and factors that interrelate to affect the behavior of firms competing in that industry.

Threat of New Entrants

A firm's profitability will tend to be higher when other firms are blocked from entering the industry. New entrants can reduce industry profitability because they add new production capacity and can substantially erode existing firms' market share positions. To discourage new entrants, existing firms can try to raise barriers to entry. **Barriers to entry** represent economic forces (or "hurdles") that slow down or impede entry by other firms. Common barriers to entry include (1) capital requirements, (2) economies of scale, (3) product differentiation, (4) switching costs, (5) brand identity, (6) access to distribution channels, and (7) promise of aggressive retaliation.

barriers to entry:
Economic forces that slow down or prevent entry into an industry.

Capital Requirements. When a large amount of capital is required to enter an industry, firms lacking funds are effectively barred from entry, thus enhancing the profitability of existing firms in the industry. For example, large investments are needed to build plants or establish brand awareness among customers of existing firms in the personal care products industry. Few firms have sufficient resources to sustain this kind of investment; as a result, entry has been limited in the past several years. Lack of vigorous entry is one reason why industry-wide profitability for pharmaceuticals, personal care products, and software tends to remain fairly high. On the other hand, the situation is quite different for the restaurant, trucking, and laundry/dry-cleaning industry in which anyone with sufficient funds can enter. In part because little capital is required for entry, numerous competitors are thus able to enter the industry with relative ease.

Economies of Scale. Many industries are characterized by economic activities driven by economies of scale. **Economies of scale** refer to the decline in the per-unit cost of production (or other activity) as volume grows. A large firm that enjoys economies of scale can produce high volumes of goods at successively lower costs than a smaller rival. Knowledge of this

economies of scale:
The declines in per-unit cost of production or any activity as volume grows.

Exhibit 2-1   *Porter's Five Forces Model of Industry Attractiveness*

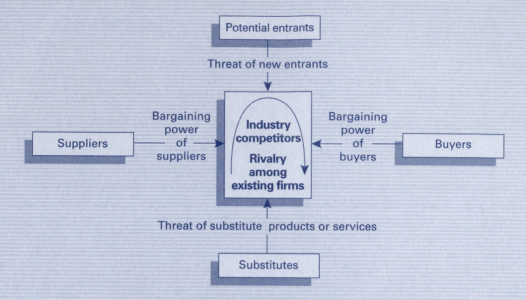

Barriers to Entry

- Economies of scale
- Proprietary product differences
- Brand identity
- Switching costs
- Capital requirements
- Access to distribution channels
- Absolute cost advantages
- Proprietary learning curve
- Access to necessary inputs
- Government policy
- Expected retaliation

Determinants of Rivalry

- Industry growth
- Fixed (or storage) cost/Value added
- Intermittent overcapacity
- Product differences
- Brand identity
- Switching costs
- Concentration and balance
- Informational complexity
- Diversity of competitors
- Exit barriers

Determinants of Substitution Threat

- Relative price/Performance of substitutes
- Switching costs
- Buyer propensity to substitute

Determinants of Supplier Power

- Differentiation of inputs
- Switching costs of suppliers and firms in the industry
- Presence of substitute inputs
- Supplier concentration
- Importance of volume to supplier
- Cost relative to total purchases in the industry
- Impact of inputs on cost or differentiation
- Threat of forward integration relative to threat of backward integration by firms in the industry

Determinants of Buyer Power

- Bargaining leverage
- Buyer concentration vs. firm concentration
- Buyer volume
- Buyer switching costs relative to firm switching costs
- Buyer information
- Ability to backward integrate
- Substitute products
- Pull-through
- Price sensitivity
- Price/Total purchases
- Product differences
- Brand identity
- Impact on quality/Performance
- Buyer profits
- Decision makers' incentives

fact tends to discourage new entrants. Consider, for example, the semiconductor industry. Larger companies, such as IBM, Infineon Technologies, Intel, Samsung, and Texas Instruments, enjoy substantial economies of scale in the production of advanced microprocessors, communication chips, and integrated circuits that power most consumer electronics, personal computers (PCs), and cellular phones. This cost advantage deters entry of most other firms seeking to produce these chips.

Product Differentiation. Product differentiation is another factor that limits entry into an industry. **Product differentiation** refers to the physical or perceptual differences, or enhancements, that make a product special or unique in the eyes of customers. Firms in the personal care products and cosmetics industries actively engage in product differentiation to enhance their products' features. Generous service and warranty provisions for luxury automobiles are important product differentiation tools for leading automobile dealerships. They enable dealerships to "lock in" customer loyalty to their products. Differentiation works to reinforce entry barriers because the cost of overcoming existing customers' buying preferences and loyalties and genuine product differences may be too high for new entrants.

product differentiation:
The physical or perceptual differences that make a product special or unique in the eyes of the customer.

Switching Costs. To succeed in an industry, new entrants must be able to persuade existing customers to switch from current providers. To make a switch, buyers may need to test a new firm's product, negotiate new purchase contracts, train personnel to use the equipment, or modify facilities for product use. Buyers often incur substantial financial (and psychological) costs in switching between firms. When such switching costs are high, buyers are often reluctant to change. For example, the software industry enjoys significant profitability in large measure because of the enormous difficulties in switching from one type of computer operating software to another. High switching costs in moving away from Microsoft's Windows operating systems used in personal computers and corporate servers powered the company's stunning growth over the past decade in the software industry.

Brand Identity. The brand identity of products or services offered by existing firms can serve as another entry barrier. Brand identity is particularly important for infrequently purchased products that carry a high dollar cost to the buyer. Oftentimes, a brand will signify in the customer's mind that the product is reliable and worth the value paid (for example, Gillette in razors, Hewlett-Packard in printers, Bosch power tools). New entrants often encounter significant difficulties in building up brand identity, because to do so they must commit substantial resources over a long period. Consider the history of the Japanese automobile industry in the United States. During the 1970s, companies such as Toyota, Nissan, and Honda had to spend huge sums on advertising and new product development to overcome the American consumers' preference for domestic cars. Only by doing so could these manufacturers gain market share against the Big Three's existing dominance. These Japanese firms have spent close to three decades trying to earn the loyalty of American buyers through superior product quality and frequent advertising. Now, the sway of such brands as Lexus, Infiniti, and Acura has given Japanese automakers considerable power in the automobile industry by virtue of these strong brands. American consumers have shown their preference for these brands by giving them high marks in annual surveys of automobile quality conducted by numerous market research firms, such as J. D. Power and Associates.

Access to Distribution Channels. The unavailability of distribution channels for new entrants poses another significant entry barrier. Despite the growing power of the Internet, many firms continue to rely on their control of physical distribution channels to sustain a key barrier to entry to other rivals. Oftentimes, existing firms have significant influence over a market's distribution channels and can retard or impede their use by new firms. For example, consumer packaged goods and personal care products companies depend on using their distribution-based clout to capture the market share and mind share of consumers. For example, Procter & Gamble fills its distribution channels with a broad range of products (such as Tide, Crest, Folger's, Pampers, Charmin) and spends considerable resources to keeping store shelves well stocked. This distribution strength enables P&G to sustain strong profit growth in most of its product categories. New entrants faced with this entrenched distribution expertise must offer aggressive promotions that ultimately are extremely expensive. The fewer the distribution channels available for any given product, the higher is the cost of entry for a new entrant. Conversely, the enormous difficulties facing U.S. manufacturers seeking to enter the Japanese and other Far East markets shows how limited access to distribution can effectively shut out new entrants.

Promise of Aggressive Retaliation. Sometimes, the mere threat of aggressive retaliation by incumbents can deter entry by other firms into an existing industry. For example, when Dr Pepper (now a unit of Cadbury-Schweppes) attempted to go national during the 1960s and 1970s, aggressive retaliation by both Coca-Cola and PepsiCo kept it from penetrating many markets outside its Texas home base. Dr Pepper found itself defending its own markets in the South from Coke and Pepsi, which retaliated because of Dr Pepper's entry into their midwestern and northern markets. Entry by firms in other industries, such as photographic film, tax preparation services, hospital supplies, and motor oil, is often deterred by the threat of aggressive, massive retaliation.

Bargaining Power of Buyers

Buyers of an industry's products or services can sometimes exert considerable pressure on existing firms to secure lower prices or better service. This leverage is particularly evident when (1) buyers are knowledgeable, (2) they spend a lot of money on the industry's products, (3) the industry's product is not perceived as critical to the buyers' needs and, (4) buyers are more concentrated than firms supplying the product. Buyers are also strong when the industry's product tends to be undifferentiated or has few switching costs and when they can enter the supplying industry fairly easily themselves.

Buyer Knowledge. Buyers lacking knowledge about the true quality or efficacy of a product are handicapped when bargaining with product suppliers. A skilled supplier can sometimes convince buyers to pay a high price, even for a product that may not be too different from those of its competitors. Suppliers selling to unsophisticated buyers thus can command higher profits over time.

In the software and electronics instruments industries, for example, these products are often so complex that users have little ability or time to compare them to competitive offerings. Companies such as Agilent Technologies, Perkin-Elmer, and Keithley Instruments, for example, have developed a highly specialized base of knowledge and experience in designing sophisticated laboratory and testing instruments that are sold to universities, government agencies, and other firms that conduct their own research endeavors. Likewise, in the software industry, consumers often rely on the advice of engineers, distributors, and specialized technical service firms to assess their particular needs. For these and other reasons (including switching costs, specialized skills, and patents), software and electronics instruments firms can sustain strong profitability.

Conversely, when buyers have sufficient knowledge and information to evaluate competitive offerings, their bargaining power grows. Competitors then have less ability to charge premium prices, and industry profitability is lower. Airline passengers, for example, can easily evaluate airline service and offerings, especially through Internet websites such as Travelocity, Orbitz and Priceline. For all practical purposes, most travelers regard any given airline as a substitute for another. Because computerized reservation systems are now linked directly with travel agents and with customers through the Internet, pricing information is freely available for customers to compare. This means that every airline must begin to match competitive discounts offered by other airlines or risk the possibility that it would lose more business from unsold seats. As a result, no airline can raise fares without experiencing a drop in traffic, which helps explain a major factor as to why its industry profitability typically has suffered.

Purchase Size. Buyers have less incentive to pressure suppliers for a low price when a small purchase is involved, because even a large percentage reduction in price has little impact on total purchase cost. Smokers, for example, pay less than $3 for a pack of cigarettes. As a result, many are relatively unconcerned with price. This circumstance enables cigarette producers such as Altria (formerly known as Philip Morris) to charge high prices on brand products, which leads to consistently high profitability for the tobacco industry. Rapid growth of lower-priced cigarette brands, extremely high health consciousness, government intervention, and ongoing legislative actions and lawsuits, however, strongly suggest that industry-wide profitability will decline significantly over the next several years in the United States.

Firms have somewhat less ability to charge a premium price when they produce big-ticket items, because even a small reduction or increase in price then has a big impact on total purchase cost. Refrigerators and dishwashers, for example, involve a large dollar outlay, so buyers often shop hard to find the best deal. This fact helps explain why the appliance industry's profitability has remained comparatively low, because competitors (for example, Maytag, Whirlpool, General Electric, LG, Electrolux) fight hard for every sale to a customer.

Product Function. When products serve a critical function, buyers will pay premium prices to obtain them. The pharmaceutical industry is a case in point. When people are sick or injured, the price of pharmaceuticals means little to them. This attitude is particularly evident when patients have health insurance that protects them from paying the full price for medications. In effect, prescription and over-the-counter drugs are important to people's health and are likely to command high prices because of their necessity. This fact contributes heavily to the drug industry's comparatively high profitability over the past two decades. Over time, however, the growing threat of price controls, government intervention, and health care reform legislation could reduce industry-wide profitability.

Concentration of Buyers. When buyers are more concentrated than firms supplying the product, suppliers often have alternatives when seeking buyers. Buyers can then often obtain better terms on price and service. For example, large firms in the computer and automobile industries have traditionally been able to bargain heavily with key suppliers to these industries because they are more concentrated than their suppliers. Computer and automobile firms can also command better prices because they offer the prospect of large-volume purchases from their suppliers. In many cases, automotive firms can even compel their suppliers to invest in new factories closer to automotive assembly plants to reduce shipping time and inventory-holding costs. A concentration of buyers over suppliers is also found in the agricultural sector. Firms such as Archer Daniels Midland (ADM), Corn Products International, and Cargill can command strong bargaining power over farmers and the farm cooperatives that supply them with corn and wheat. In the health care industry today, many firms are banding together to establish health insurance purchasing cooperatives. These cooperatives enable firms to purchase health insurance for their employees on better terms than individual firms could command.

Undifferentiated Products. Buyers also tend to have strong bargaining power when they purchase standardized, undifferentiated products from their suppliers. They can easily change suppliers without incurring significant switching costs. This phenomenon raises their bargaining power. Consider, for example, the purchase of memory chips by personal computer and cell phone makers. For the most part, memory chips remain an undifferentiated commodity, even those that are state-of-the-art. Thus, Dell, Hewlett-Packard, Nokia, and Motorola can easily obtain massive discounts from their suppliers.

Buyer Entry into the Industry. Buyers' bargaining power is increased if they can potentially enter the industry from which they are currently buying. If buyers decide to make those items for themselves that they now purchase, they can exert strong bargaining power over the supplying industry. This method is known as backward integration (and will be discussed at length in a later chapter).

Planning and Administration: Agile Supply Chains[14]

One of the most important business developments that has reshaped almost every industry is the implementation of new initiatives to help firms better manage their inventory costs and become more responsive to their customers' needs. Better known as supply chain management, these efforts link together a firm's inventory management and ordering systems with those of their suppliers through advanced computer technologies. Supply chain management brings together transportation and logistics providers (for example, airfreight, railroad companies, trucking companies, and package delivery firms) to create an online, on-time inventory replenishment system that keeps factories, distribution centers, and store shelves running at optimal levels. Using software, the best supply chains enable a firm to order precisely the amount of components, parts, or even merchandise according to what it needs on a daily or weekly basis. As a result, the firm no longer needs to order and stockpile a large amount of goods that tie up its cash and increase its inventory-holding costs.

The art and science of supply chain management depends on a firm's selecting its core suppliers and tying them together with its own ordering system. The goal is to achieve fast responsiveness with reduction in business operating costs. In the grocery, convenience store, and restaurant industries, suppliers work with their customers to ensure that fresh products are delivered on time wherever they are needed to minimize wastage due to perishability. Oftentimes, the suppliers themselves (for example, Frito-Lay, Anheuser-Busch, Coca-Cola, bakery firms) will physically stock the grocery chains' shelves and manage the inventory for them on a daily basis. In Japan, 7-Eleven's operations in that country emphasize absolute food freshness that is measured in *hours*. Because Japanese consumers frequently eat sushi (a raw fish delicacy) at different hours during the day, 7-Eleven has developed a highly intricate and extremely effective system to ensure the safety of its prepared foods. In the automotive, aerospace, electronics, and semiconductor industries, supply chain management emphasizes the coordination of hundreds of different suppliers and distributors that must work on ever-shortening design cycles for leading-edge, complex products and components. The cost of these inputs is very high, and buyers do not want to be caught with costly inventories. For example, personal computer (PC) firms prefer to buy as many memory chips and other components precisely when they are needed. If they order too many memory chips, they are stuck with inventory that cannot be easily used elsewhere and prices tend to be highly cyclical. If they order too few components, they run the risk of losing market share to their competitors. Aerospace, automotive, and electronics suppliers often span multiple countries and continents, so bringing them together is like conducting an orchestra across twenty-four time zones. Suppliers and buyers in these industries closely coordinate their production and ordering decisions, because so much capital and knowledge is invested in very specific types of product and process technologies. Absolute adherence to technical specifications and quality manufacturing are vital. In the fashion and retailing industries, clothing designers must work in tandem with apparel and garment manufacturers who are likely to be located in countries with large labor pools and lower wages. Garment manufacturers must receive the latest fashion designs (now by Internet, previously by fax or secure, overnight package delivery), manufacture the clothing in large lots, and ship them to their final destination. This process often takes months, and that is why retailers must often choose and "bet" on which seasonal clothing styles will likely sell several months in advance. Of course, quality workmanship is essential in every part of the process.

Supply chains deliver greatly improved business results when they are responsive and can adjust rapidly to changes in demand. Highly "agile" supply chains depend on the daily, if not hourly, flow of information from retailer to distributor, transportation firm, manufacturer, and including his/her suppliers. In other words, information about product sales and demand patterns should flow along the entire supply chain or web—from the point-of-purchase all the way up to manufacturers and their suppliers. Central to managing this information web is a common set of ordering systems and software tools that let each participant in the system know what is going on. Wal-Mart Stores has become dominant in U.S. retailing by virtue of its decade-long investment and improvement of its own vast supply chain system. Using a process known as "cross-docking," Wal-Mart works with its suppliers to ensure that products are delivered to each store according to specific customer buying patterns. Wal-Mart shares its customer data with all of its suppliers and compels them to use a common Internet-based ordering system so that each supplier can also see what other suppliers are doing as well. Suppliers can track how well their products are selling in individual stores also. Large suppliers, such as Procter & Gamble and Newell Rubbermaid, maintain permanent supply chain staff members at Wal-Mart's Bentonville, Arkansas, headquarters. With extremely thin profit margins in retailing, Wal-Mart and its suppliers are looking for new ways to send and receive daily purchasing and ordering data through the Internet. Suppliers are finding that saving even a few days' worth of inventory can translate into several thousand dollars a month of improved profits. Wal-Mart is now leading a nationwide effort to use radio-frequency identification device (RFID) tags to track the purchase, inventory, movement, and sale of *each individual product* in its stores. RFID tags are essentially "smart" bar codes that send out a wireless signal that allows each individual product or package to communicate with computers in stores, warehouses, distributors, and factories. Ultimately, Wal-Mart wants to use these tags to reduce inventory-holding costs even more. Other manufacturers and retailers will likely begin using RFID tags in their operations as well.

Agile supply chains are becoming especially important in the fashion industry, where designers are looking to slice down product development time from months to weeks. To eliminate imitation of leading-edge clothing designs by lesser-known companies, designers such as Ferragamo are using new software-based systems to speed up their production cycle. Ferragamo is now able to deliver a fashion concept to final product in the store in ten weeks, as opposed to requiring three months a few years ago. At J. C. Penney stores, a customer's purchase of a particular shirt is immediately tracked into a company-wide database that automatically sends a signal to Far Eastern suppliers and garment makers to make and ship another identical replacement shirt for delivery back to a specific store. Hong Kong-based TAL Apparel Limited is helping manage all of J. C. Penney's dress-shirt inventory throughout the United States and has enabled Penney to dramatically slice its costs. Penney is better able to respond to customer demand by not missing sales of popular styles through its continuous inventory replenishment system. Now, TAL even designs new shirt styles for Penney. Using computer modeling, TAL estimates the amount of inventory each store will need. TAL also forecasts the specific styles, colors, and sizes for each store, thus enabling Penney to keep half as much in stock as it needed before. TAL also supplies clothing to other U.S. firms, such as Calvin Klein, Banana Republic (a unit of Gap Stores), Tommy Hilfiger, and Brooks Brothers. The future of fashion and retailing is moving toward a zero-inventory system.

Bargaining Power of Suppliers

Conversely, suppliers can influence the profitability of an industry in a number of ways. Suppliers can command bargaining power over an industry when (1) their products are crucial to a buyer, (2) they can erect high switching costs, and (3) they are more concentrated than buyers. Suppliers also possess a certain amount of power over an industry when they can potentially enter it themselves.

Products Crucial to Buyer. If suppliers provide crucial products or inputs to buyers, then their bargaining power is likely to be high. Consider, for example, the semiconductor industry's supply relationship with firms making PCs. Because microprocessors and other specialized chips are critical to PC operation, chip suppliers can often pass on increases in chip prices to PC makers. For example, Intel has consistently been able to reap huge (but recently declining) profits from the sale of its Pentium and Xeon line of microprocessors to Dell Computer, Hewlett-Packard, and IBM. Because the microprocessor remains the central brain of the PC, Intel is able to capitalize on its strong supply position. Likewise, Charles River Laboratories, the world's largest breeder and distributor of genetically modified rats, has been able to grow its margins significantly from its unique role as a huge supplier of lab rats needed for medical experiments. Charles River breeds pedigreed rats that meet each lab's customized medical testing needs.

Products with High Switching Costs. When buyers incur a high cost for switching from one supplier to another, then suppliers will possess high bargaining power over buyers. For example, software providers possess bargaining power over the firms that need their operating systems to run computers and other applications. Switching from one software provider to another will often require buyers to undergo expensive modification of their computer systems.

In the heavy machinery and machine tool industry, product specifications and tolerances for different kinds of machinery make it difficult to switch from one supplier to another. This difficulty often means that the buying firm has to shut down an entire factory before it can install another machine made by another supplier—an extremely costly proposition. Suppliers of these products and components therefore enjoy high bargaining power over buying firms.

High Supplier Concentration. When suppliers are more concentrated than buyers, they tend to be in a better bargaining position over prices. As shown in the personal computer industry example, the comparatively few suppliers of chips relative to the number of PC makers means that PC makers are consistently absorbing the price increases passed on by their suppliers. The pharmaceutical industry is another case in which comparatively few firms produce each specific type or class of drug. This supplier concentration gives drug producers considerable bargaining power over physicians, wholesalers, and hospitals.

The poultry industry, as another example, has a high supplier concentration in relation to buyers such as restaurants and food distributors. A comparatively few number of firms are in the chicken-processing business, such as Pilgrim's Pride, Tyson Foods, and Perdue Chickens. These firms can pass on price increases to buyers, such as Yum! Brands' KFC unit, Popeye's, Church's, other restaurants, food companies, and grocery stores.

Suppliers' Ability to Enter the Buying Industry. When suppliers can fairly easily enter the industry they are supplying, their bargaining power is increased. Buyers are then reluctant to bargain too hard for price reduction because they may cause suppliers to enter the industry. For example, if chip makers such as Intel or AMD decided to make PCs, their entrance into the PC market would even further depress the profitability of the PC industry. The ability to move into a buyer's industry thus helps maintain high profitability for suppliers. This action of moving into a buyer's industry is known as forward integration (and will be discussed extensively in a later chapter).

The Nature of Rivalry in the Industry

The intensity of rivalry in an industry is a significant determinant of industry attractiveness and profitability. The intensity of the rivalry can influence the costs of supplies, distribution, and attracting customers and thus directly affect profitability. The more intensive the rivalry, the less attractive is the industry. Rivalry among competitors tends to be cutthroat and industry profitability low when (1) an industry has no clear leader, (2) competitors in the industry are numerous, (3) competitors operate with high fixed costs, (4) competitors face high exit barriers, (5) competitors have little opportunity to differentiate their offerings, and (6) the industry faces slow or diminished growth.

Industry Leader. A strong industry leader can discourage price wars by disciplining initiators of such activity. A primary tool for exercising such discipline is a retaliatory price reduction by the leader itself. Because of its greater financial resources, a leader can generally outlast smaller rivals in a price war. Knowing this, smaller rivals often avoid initiating such a contest. The comparatively high profitability of the personal care products industry is due in part to the strong price leadership exercised by giant Procter & Gamble. Likewise, Caterpillar has been able to exercise considerable industry leadership in the construction equipment industry. Caterpillar's low-cost manufacturing enables it to cut prices drastically (and still make a profit) to deter its rivals (for example, Komatsu, Hitachi) from engaging in price wars. If an industry has no leader, price wars are more likely and industry profitability generally lower. The historically low profitability of the steel, paper, memory chip, aluminum, and waste management industries is due in part to the absence of a clear leader in these industries.

Number of Competitors. Even when an industry leader exists, the leader's ability to exert pricing discipline diminishes as the number of rivals in the industry increases as communicating expectations to players becomes more difficult. Also, an industry with many players is more likely to contain mavericks whose ideas about how to compete may not reflect industry norms and expectations. Such firms are often determined to go their own way in spite of persuasion or signaling by an industry leader. For these reasons, industry profitability tends to fall as the number of competitors grows. The trucking industry's historically low profitability can be attributed in part to the large number of firms operating in the industry.

Fixed Costs. When rivals operate with high fixed costs, they feel strong motivation to utilize their capacity and therefore are inclined to cut prices when they have excess capacity. Price-cutting causes profitability to fall for all firms in the industry as firms seek to produce more to cover costs that must be paid regardless of industry demand. For this reason, profitability tends to be lower in industries (for example, airlines, telecommunications) characterized by high fixed costs.

The profitability of the metals industry (for example, steel, aluminum, copper, iron) is depressed in part from this cause. Most costs of operating highly integrated steel mills—plant setup, equipment, smelting, casting, and fabrication—are essentially fixed because of the nature of the conversion and heating process. In the steel, copper, iron, and aluminum industries, cost efficiency is highly dependent on full-capacity utilization. Moreover, the plant and equipment used to produce steel and aluminum are extremely expensive. Steel companies are therefore prone to use price reductions in order to keep their plants at full utilization, because capacity shortfalls mean they must bear the entire weight of their high fixed cost. Once one firm begins to cut prices, others generally must follow suit. The resulting price wars have depressed industry profitability for many years in the past. Profitability improved in 2003 and 2004 largely because the U.S. economic recovery coincided with enormous steel demand from China.

The airline industry is another arena where competitors face very high fixed costs. Aircraft, terminals, maintenance facilities, long-term lease agreements, and other assets cannot be added or deleted quickly to adjust to short-term demand fluctuations. Thus, airlines often must engage in extensive price-cutting behavior to amortize their fixed costs, regardless of how many passengers and planes are used at any given point in time.

Exit Barriers. Rivalry among competitors declines if some competitors leave an industry. Firms wanting to leave may be restrained from doing so by barriers to exit, however. Profitability therefore tends to be higher in industries with few exit barriers. Exit barriers come in many forms. Assets of a firm considering exit may be highly specialized and therefore of little value to any other firm. Such a firm can thus find no buyer for its assets. This discourages exit. A firm may be obliged to honor existing labor agreements or to maintain spare parts for products already in the field. In addition, discontinuing the activities of one business may adversely affect a firm's other businesses that share common facilities. When barriers to exit such as these are powerful, competitors desiring exit may refrain from leaving. Their continued presence in an industry exerts downward pressure on the profitability of all competitors.

High exit barriers have contributed to the low profitability of integrated steel producers. Profitability of such producers in recent years has been significantly below that of many industries. Their profitability has been low in part because many integrated producers are controlled by national governments, particularly in Europe. Government owners are notoriously reluctant to liquidate unprofitable facilities because doing so results in bigger transfer payments (to support unemployed workers), voter dissatisfaction, and political unrest. To avoid these difficulties, government owners often keep mills operating even when doing so has meant selling output at prices below cost. Such behavior has depressed profitability for all integrated producers worldwide. Even in 2002, the U.S. steel industry faced continuing challenges from foreign steelmakers, many of which continue to receive government aid in some form to promote production and employment at home.

Product Differentiation. Firms can sometimes insulate themselves from price wars by differentiating their products from those of rivals. As a consequence, profitability tends to be higher in industries that offer opportunity for differentiation. The high profitability of the software, pharmaceutical, sporting equipment, personal care products, and medical supplies industries results in part from the many opportunities these fields offer for product differentiation. Profitability tends to be lower in industries involving undifferentiated commodities such as textiles, memory chips, natural resources, processed metals, and railroads.

Slow Growth. Industries whose growth is slowing tend to face more intense rivalry. Slower rates of growth pervade many industries, including automobiles, telecommunications, insurance, broadcasting, advertising, retail financial services, condiments, and personal computers. As industry growth slows, rivals must often fight harder to grow or even to keep their existing market share. The resulting intensive rivalry tends to reduce profitability for all.

Threat of Substitutes

A final force that can influence industry profitability is the availability of substitutes for an industry's product. To predict profit pressure from this source, firms must search for products that perform the same, or nearly the same, function as their existing products. In some cases this search is quite straightforward. Real estate, insurance, bonds, and bank deposits, for example, are clear substitutes for common stocks, because they represent alternate ways to invest funds. Identifying substitutes for a ski resort presents more difficulty, however, because services as diverse as gambling casinos, cruise ships, and foreign travel are potential substitutes.

Consider the massive use of e-mail as a substitute for the U.S. Post Office and other overnight delivery services such as FedEx's Federal Express unit and United Parcel Service (UPS). The growing spread of the Internet, private computer intranets, and other forms of increasingly secure, digital communications that allow users to communicate and to conduct business with one another has a direct substitution effect on the mail and overnight package business. The threat of substitutes is great in many high-tech industries as well. For example, the digital filmless camera represents a direct substitute threat that could substantially erode market shares of Eastman Kodak and Fuji Film. Wireless digital phones are a substitute threat for conventional, landline telephones. Likewise, pagers have largely disappeared as a result of being substituted by more capable digital phones. Personal computers have displaced dedicated word-processing machines, which in turn eliminated the need for typewriters many years ago. New forms of engine technology (for example, advanced fuel cells, hydrogen power) may become potent substitutes for existing combustion engines in tomorrow's automotive industry. Today, steel and aluminum vie with each other to become the primary metal of choice in cars; plastics, in turn, is a potential substitute material for both metals. In the long term, advances in biotechnology will likely create substitutes for many drugs currently used to treat disease.

Having identified substitutes for an industry's product, firms must then judge their potential to depress industry profitability. As a general rule, a substitute will threaten industry profitability if it can perform the function of an industry's product at a lower cost or perform the same function better at no increase in cost. Particularly worrisome are substitutes whose price or performance characteristics are improving over time. Digital cell phones currently pose this kind of threat to landline telecommunications firms. The price of cell phone service continues to decline in most large metropolitan markets, and customers are now using more versatile digital phones for voice, video, and e-mail forms of communication. Local and long-distance calling costs the same for cell phone users. To compound matters for telecom firms, more customers are making long-distance and international calls through their PCs by harnessing new Internet-enabled technologies.[15] One can easily imagine how the software features of Internet browsers will allow customers to communicate with other people through voice and e-mail formats. Both wireless digital phones and advanced browsers threaten the very foundation of the long-distance businesses of many telecommunications firms. The continuing refinement of today's "Wi-Fi" technology that enables PC users to access the web through a wireless connection will certainly transform tomorrow's telecom industries also. As Wi-Fi capabilities grow, it will be possible for PC users to access the Internet through a wireless link that could have a range as far as thirty miles in the next two years. This technology, known as "Wi-Max," will likely evolve in much the same way that cell phones did over the past twenty years. In short, as cell phones fundamentally threaten the existence of the long-distance, wireline business, Wi-Max will likely render today's DSL and cable connections rapidly obsolete tomorrow.

Strategic Groups and the Industry Environment

Up to this point, our focus has been on analyzing the forces that drive industry-wide profitability. As we have seen, Porter's five forces model is extremely powerful in helping us understand the specific economic forces and conditions that determine industry profitability. Yet, managers often need a more detailed analysis and information of an industry. To develop effective competitive strategies, managers need to understand how their own firm's particular strategic posture will relate to building or maintaining profitability within the industry. Within any given industry, each firm's particular competitive strategies and behaviors are likely to be different than those of its rivals. In other words, even though companies in the same industry may face similar pressures from suppliers, buyers, and substitutes, in practice they may actually behave differently in reaction to these forces. Competitors within a single industry may be quite dissimilar. Firms within a single industry could differ in terms of their product attributes, emphasis on product quality, type of technology used, type of distribution channel used, type of buyer sought, and other characteristics. Thus, firms are likely to respond to environmental forces in ways that best fit their own individual strategic postures and competitive strategy.

strategic groups:
The distribution or grouping of firms that pursue similar strategies in response to environmental forces within an industry. Firms within the same strategic group will tend to compete more vigorously with one another than with firms from other strategic groups.

The focus of this section is to examine the concept of strategic groups.[16] **Strategic groups** are groups of firms that pursue similar types of strategies within the same industry. Management may find benefit in being able to classify firms within an industry into strategic groups. Such analysis can aid them in understanding which firms pursue similar types of strategies. Strategic groups exist because of strong economic forces acting within an industry that constrain firms from easily switching from one competitive posture or position to another. Generally, firms within a strategic group face similar economic and competitive conditions. These conditions are different for firms located in other strategic groups.

Strategic groups are important because they represent a valuable link between studying the behavior of an entire industry and the behavior of individual firms that compose the industry. To study the characteristics of every firm within the industry can be arduous and time-consuming. The use of strategic groups enables managers to aggregate firms into more compact, identifiable clusters of companies that display similar characteristics. It is therefore a useful tool to help managers understand and compare their own firm's strategic postures and actions with their rivals.

Defining the Strategic Group

Most industries can be decomposed into several different strategic groups. Firms within each strategic group might be similar to one another in terms of any number of different key attributes, such as (1) product line breadth, (2) type of technology used, (3) type of buyer served, (4) relative emphasis on product quality, (5) type of distribution channels used, and (6) number of markets served. Thus, many different attributes or dimensions can be used to classify firms into a strategic group. Most important, managers must choose those dimensions that are most salient and relevant to their own particular industry. Some competitive dimensions (such as type of distribution channel used and product line breadth) may be more salient for some industries (such as packaged foods, soft drinks, beer, cereals, and personal care products), whereas other dimensions (such as product function and type of technology used) may be more useful in other industries (such as semiconductors, medical equipment, and sporting goods). Thus, constructing meaningful strategic groups that effectively capture different firms' strategic postures requires a careful selection of those dimensions that best describe their industry's environment. Choosing the right dimensions depends on both industry knowledge and managerial experience in dealing with customers and competitors. Thus, managers may experiment with a number of different dimensions to assess properly the strategic groups in their competitive environment.

Strategic Groups in the Personal Computer Industry

Exhibit 2-2 portrays one way of defining the strategic groups within the PC industry. The dimensions chosen for this particular analysis include (1) emphasis on leading-edge technology/power and (2) speed of customization/delivery to customer. We could have examined the PC industry using other dimensions, such as level of product quality versus price, or customer support versus price. Using technology/power and customization/speed for dimensions in our analysis, five strategic groups appear within the PC industry.

Strategic Groups in the Personal Computer Industry | Exhibit 2-2

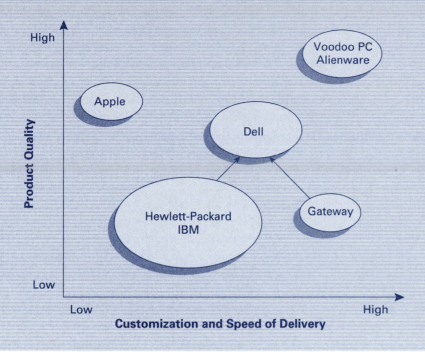

The first group, composed of one company, is Apple Computer. That Apple Computer makes up its own group is not surprising, given its high user-friendly nature, the sophistication of its distinct Macintosh operating system quality, and its high aesthetic appeal. Later product generations of Apple's computer line, such as the recently introduced cube-shaped and lantern-shaped iMac models, have continued to reinforce customers' perceptions of Apple's high quality. However, Apple's models are not available directly from the manufacturer but must be purchased through a value-added reseller or electronics retailer. As a result, it is comparatively difficult to add custom features to Apple's product line. Apple's use of a different operating system from that used by other PC makers helps insulate it from fierce rivalry; at the same time, it also limits how much market share Apple can stake out in this industry (approximately 2 to 3 percent). Yet, for any given product generation, Apple's computers tend to offer faster processors and more standard technological features than Windows-based PCs. Apple's cutting-edge models still attract a very loyal audience who use the firm's latest technologies to create digital movies and a host of other applications (for example, desktop publishing, photo finishing) that have been described as easier to use than those in Windows-based PCs.

The second group, defined by Dell Computer, captures the firm's long-standing and distinctive practice of making computers only when an order is received. Dell excels at custom-building machines to each individual's specifications and can offer a broad range of technologies within each PC. Both corporate and personal buyers flock to Dell's website to purchase fast, powerful machines at very competitive prices. In fact, Dell's strategy of combining strong product offerings with speed of customization has been so successful that every other firm has sought ways to duplicate Dell's manufacturing and distribution system. However, Dell has been able to distinguish itself from its competitors by keeping its production system and inventories exceptionally lean. It simultaneously works with key suppliers to incorporate the latest advances in chips, peripherals, and other components that drive product quality higher. Yet, even though Dell offers a broad range of customization opportunities, analysts believe that most of Dell's shipments contain leading-edge, but widely available, standardized components. Moreover, Dell keeps its distribution costs low by encouraging customers to order their computers through a toll-free number or directly through the Internet. This enables Dell to avoid the higher cost of selling through department stores, electronics retailers, and other types of resellers.

Hewlett-Packard (HP) and IBM offer high-performance, but largely standardized machines. HP sells to both corporate buyers and personal consumers. However, HP still relies heavily on selling its products through electronics stores and to business customers through value-added resellers who perform much of the final stages of customizing the product according to each individual customer's specifications (usually for corporate buyers). HP's dependence on retailers means that it cannot move as quickly as Dell to respond to price changes; it often takes weeks for retailers to place their ads in newspapers. Although HP does offer direct sales to customers through toll-free numbers and via the Internet, HP cannot move as quickly as Dell in pursuing this strategy for fear it will alienate their current distribution partners who help them perform product upgrades and other services. Recently, HP appeared to be shifting toward including more advanced technology into its machines to help distinguish itself further from Dell and IBM. HP began offering AMD's latest Opteron line of microprocessors to sell more powerful machines to scientists and graphic designers. However, only about 20 percent of HP's machines are build-to-order. IBM is still a formidable player in the PC business and targets the same group of corporate customers that HP does. However, IBM has exited from the retail consumer channel and sells to personal consumers exclusively through its website. Because IBM's primary focus remains corporate buyers, many of its PCs are sold as part of a larger "bundle of solutions" that often involve other products or services. Both HP and IBM compete for corporate buyers with innovative means of financing, maintenance, and selling related products. IBM has contracted out the assembly of its personal computer line to Sanmina-SCI, a leading contract electronics manufacturer. In December 2004, IBM took the final step of formally exiting from the PC industry by selling this business to Lenovo Group, a Chinese firm. IBM will still offer PCs to corporate and individual customers; however, it will not engage in the design and production of these machines. Ironically, IBM profitably manufactures many of the semiconductors, displays, disk drives, and power supplies that go into its line of PCs, and serves as a vital supplier of key parts for Dell!

Gateway constitutes a fourth strategic group. Combined with its recently acquired eMachines unit, Gateway markets PCs for the home market. Gateway is in the midst of an important strategic transition. Over the past two years, Gateway has outsourced all computer manufacturing and sales support. It attempted to catch up with industry leader Dell Computer by adopting a lean production process in which key suppliers build and ship components as they are ordered. It recently shut down all of its Gateway retail outlets in order to stem major financial losses. Gateway's presence in the business market is more limited, largely because its customer service center is focused on serving the individual market. With the acquisition of eMachines, Gateway has committed itself even further to selling to the home market. Before its purchase by Gateway, eMachines was known for making extremely cheap PCs that did not use the latest microprocessors or other peripherals. Its PCs aimed squarely for those consumers who wanted to spend $600 or less for an entry-level machine. Under the leadership of Wayne Inouye (who now leads all of Gateway), eMachines became the third-best-selling brand of desktop PCs in the United States behind Dell and HP in late 2003. Now, CEO Inouye wants Gateway to focus on building large retail accounts at CompUSA and Best Buy to continue much of eMachines' earlier strategy, while also maintaining Gateway's earlier build-to-order, direct sales model.[17]

A fifth strategic group effectively targets the extreme upper end of PCs. Composed of VoodooPC and Alienware Corp., the two firms vie with one another to build customized machines that are especially popular with die-hard video gamers. Graphic artists and engineers also use PCs made by both companies, but video gamers represent the largest group of customers. Using hard-to-find, "bleeding-edge" technology, these PCs often include special peripherals and graphics chips that would never be found on PCs designed for the mainstream corporate or home market. As a result, PCs made by VoodooPC and Alienware easily top $5,000 for a tailor-made machine with generous support. Lower-end Alienware machines can be found at Best Buy retailers as well.

Implications of Strategic Group Analysis

Strategic groups are useful in describing the competitive behavior of firms within an industry. The first thing to note is that competition *within* a strategic group is often more heated than that *between* strategic groups. In other words, firms that are similar to one another, and thus placed in the same strategic group, generally compete against one another more intensely than against firms residing in different strategic groups. Largely, this phenomenon results from the fact that firms within the same strategic group display similar product characteristics and target the same customers. As a result, it is difficult for rivals to distinguish themselves easily from one another. Oftentimes, they are compelled to use price wars to steal market share from their competitors.

For example, Hewlett-Packard and IBM compete fiercely against one another in the same type of distribution channel. Both firms try to capture corporate buyers by selling PCs with maintenance and service agreements, as well as special financing arrangements. HP and IBM also pitch other products in conjunction with PCs to provide a "total solution." Even after significant investment, they are still playing "catch-up" to Dell Computer in offering custom-built machines to customers over the Internet. Likewise, VoodooPC and Alienware tend to regard each other as the more immediate "enemy." Both high-end PC makers aim for the same dedicated video game-playing customer. Also, both emphasize building custom-made PCs with "bleeding-edge" if not "exotic" technologies that ordinarily would not be found in mainstream, but up-to-date machines. Part of the reason why firms within the same strategic group tend to compete more fiercely with each other is that their similarity of offerings leaves little room for maneuver. Consequently, members within a strategic group are likely to pursue a similar competitive strategy to attract the same targeted group of buyers.

Strategic groups can shift over time, so managers must continue to be aware of how firms may differ in their future competitive postures and strategies. Although not depicted in Exhibit 2-2, an entire strategic group has effectively disappeared, as AST Research, Tandy, and Packard Bell exited the industry during the 1990s. Strategic groups appear to be shifting again in this business, as Hewlett-Packard focuses ever more intently on displacing Dell, and IBM exits the business. However, Dell appears to have become even more dominant because it is able to engage in price wars and yet remain profitable through its lean production/supply system and online distribution. HP still cannot replicate Dell's efficiency and build-to-order emphasis. Compaq Computer and Hewlett-Packard merged in October 2002 as both companies sought to gain greater size advantages to compete in the PC and other businesses. IBM continues its PC sales emphasis on corporate customers, but has withdrawn from actively manufacturing the PC itself.

Apple is beginning to reassume the role that it pioneered for itself in the early 1980s—developing trendy and fashionable PCs that stand out from the crowd. More recently, Apple further reinforced its distinction by selling its wildly popular iPod portable music player, which hooks up to its iMac PCs. Apple has also entered online music retailing through its iTunes music store. Apple believes that many of its loyal customers will continue to buy its machines not only for their high quality but because they wish to make a "fashion statement" as well. The company's most loyal customers are typically publishers, graphic designers, and creative artists who love the feel of Apple's unique designs and the versatility of its Macintosh operating system. Apple also developed a new operating system that enables users to switch back and forth between the Macintosh and Microsoft's Windows operating systems. Although this innovation makes Apple's product even more distinctive and of higher quality in the eyes of consumers, it could potentially change how Apple competes against other Windows-formatted PC firms.

As mentioned before, Gateway is in the midst of a critical strategic transition. If it pursues its traditional strategy of selling made-to-order PCs online, Gateway will be on a direct collision course with the much larger and more profitable Dell Computer. If Gateway focuses on building its large retailer accounts, its strategy may begin to resemble that of its eMachines unit that it purchased in February 2004. Regardless of which direction it pursues, if Gateway faces continuing difficulties in executing its chosen strategy, it will likely confront staggering losses in the future.

What are some broader lessons about strategic group analysis that can apply to a variety of different industry conditions? Let us examine how changes in the environment can have a marked impact on the evolution of strategic groups and the firms that compose them.

- First, strategic groups can shift over time as the needs of customers or different technologies evolve in the marketplace. For example, HP has tried to move toward adopting some of the strategies that have made Dell Computer so successful in years past. However, only 20 percent of HP's machines are made-to-order. As HP cuts prices on standard PCs, IBM will feel the most immediate impact, but Dell will also suffer. Likewise, as Dell moves to steadily increase its sales to corporate buyers, it will clash even more frequently with HP and IBM. Thus, rivalry will intensify (as is the case when firms become more similar to one another), and therefore managers should not assume that membership in a particular strategic group permanently locks the firm into a fixed strategy. With sufficient resources and focus, firms can take steps to enter and exit strategic groups over time. Customers typically benefit when this occurs, because of the likely ensuing price competition.
- Second, entire strategic groups and the firms that compose them can emerge or disappear over time. An earlier strategic group composed of firms that built low- to midrange PCs eventually fell by the wayside. In the future, we might expect that Gateway could face a similar fate if it is not successful in its strategic transition. Gateway must find some way to insulate itself from both HP (in the retailer channel) and Dell (build-to-order). Thus, as the environment changes, the competitive conditions that define a strategic group may work against an entire collection of firms, resulting in the group's long-term decline if competitive conditions intensify.
- In recent years, one of the more enduring trends that have defined a growing number of industries is the hastening pace of consolidation. Competitors are now seeking to buy or merge with their rivals to limit the effects of fierce price wars that negatively impact profitability. HP's merger with Compaq Computer was designed to help the combined entity become more profitable. Consider, for example, the financial services industry. Companies such as J. P. Morgan Chase, Bank of America, Citigroup, Wachovia, Wells Fargo, and Morgan Stanley have been buying up their immediate competitors, as well as firms that once operated in completely different strategic groups. J. P. Morgan Chase merged with Bank One in August 2004; the

current Wachovia also includes its once-rival First Union. Bank of America itself is the result of numerous mergers and acquisitions, including NationsBank, FleetBoston, and so on. In addition, as commercial bank firms acquire companies in the investment banking and insurance arenas, strategic groups are becoming larger and more complex. Although groups may appear to be stable for the short term, competition will likely increase as bigger rivals muscle in on the turf of other like-minded firms. Thus, consolidation within and among industries can also markedly redefine the underlying stability and membership of strategic groups.

- Finally, the personal computer industry illustrates an important strategic lesson that will be examined in great detail throughout the balance of this book. As the Dell Computer example reveals, a firm can build and sustain competitive advantage (and profitability) only to the extent that it remains distinctive from its rivals. Competitive advantage and profitability are a direct function of distinctiveness. Or, put in another way, to the extent that customers begin to view each firm's offerings as interchangeable with that of other firms, the growing lack of distinctiveness directly means that profitability will likely suffer as well.

Strategic Application of Five Forces Analysis to the Personal Computer Industry

Let us now use the five forces model to analyze the structure and attractiveness (profitability) of the PC industry. To illustrate the potency of these five forces, let us apply these concepts to examine how the PC industry has evolved in recent years. What profitability pressures would these five forces exert on firms operating in this market?

New Entrants

Barriers to entry in the PC industry are low. Entry into this market would be fairly easy for several reasons. First, capital requirements for PC assembly are modest. Second, customers face few switching costs when changing suppliers and probably would not hesitate to buy a Windows-formatted operating system PC from a new supplier if the price were right. This makes competition very intense. In fact, some Internet start-up firms in 1998 and 1999 offered stripped-down PCs free to customers who subscribed to an Internet service provider for an extended multiyear contract. These entrants deployed many of the same strategies that cellular telephone companies implemented during the 1990s: give away the hardware for free in exchange for long-term customer commitment to purchasing a service for several time periods. Third, product differentiation is elusive in this industry. Numerous small firms can easily and quickly enter this business through subassembly and subcontracting their manufacturing activities. The presence of so many competitors in this market would thus depress profitability.

Direct Competitors

PC firms have engaged in cutthroat pricing to maintain and even grow their market shares in the past few years, especially as the sagging economy deterred consumers from buying more expensive models. Also, PC assembly involves few exit barriers, so competitors experiencing profit problems could exit fairly quickly. Yet, product differentiation is much less favorable. Product differentiation is likely to be increasingly difficult to achieve as mainstream PCs become more and more like a commodity. Potential opportunities for differentiation do exist to the extent that PC makers target markets with very different or unique needs. This is what Voodoo PC and Alienware have done by focusing on die-hard video gamers. For its part, Apple Computer has relied on innovative designs, software, and now online music retailing to stand out successfully from the crowd. Still, broader opportunities for differentiation are fleeting, because manufacturers of components and peripherals freely sell such add-ons to any PC manufacturer willing to pay for them. Thus, competition among PC firms has increasingly turned on price (even for those midrange, built-to-order machines packed with added-on features), exerting enormous downward pressure on profitability.

Buyers

Users are increasingly knowledgeable about PCs and increasingly inclined to regard them as a commodity. Many buyers (especially individuals and families) are starting to purchase second and third PCs for the home, in much the same way that they purchased multiple color television sets for home entertainment use in earlier years. These characteristics will lead buyers to be increasingly price conscious when shopping for PCs. This sensitivity to price, in turn, will exert strong downward pressure on the profitability of PC producers.

Suppliers

Suppliers of memory chips, microprocessors, integrated circuits, and other key peripherals and components are comparatively few and concentrated. Intel and AMD dominate the microprocessor side of the business and have used their strong bargaining power to capture much of the profits in the PC business. Likewise, Microsoft's dominant position in software, and the fierce protection of its intellectual property, allows it to capture a large share of the profit as well. For these reasons, suppliers are in a good position to negotiate effectively with PC producers, thereby exerting strong downward pressure on their profitability.

Substitutes

More recently, the emergence of smaller, handheld personal digital assistants (PDAs) has attracted some interest among leading-edge PC users, but their high cost and limited software applications contribute to a limited market presence. However, the rise of new handheld personal computers that can recognize handwriting and even voice commands may become important substitutes in the near future. This technology could become a real threat to the current PC industry if PDAs are thought of as advanced consumer electronics products that combine Internet access with other new communication features. Already, the latest offerings from Palm, Research in Motion, and even Nokia provide many of these functions.[18] Internet service providers, wireless phone companies, and even video game firms are developing capabilities and products to provide Internet access through non-PC consumer electronic devices. For example, Microsoft's Xbox game system, Sony's PlayStation series of video game consoles, as well as Nintendo's GameCube, are starting to display computing, software, communication, storage, and video capabilities that mimic those of many new PCs.

In summary, these developments do not bode well for sustained high profitability in the PC industry. Many of these have already materialized and have caused a number of competitors to exit the industry. In summary, the PC industry is rapidly becoming less attractive over time, especially because customers have begun to view the PC as a commodity. Equally important, competitors appear to be mimicking each other's strategies, thus strongly suggesting that it is becoming even harder to maintain distinctiveness in this industry.

Alternative Ways to Examine Industry Structure and Dynamics

In our discussion of the PC industry, we have focused solely on the how the PC "box makers" compete with one another to produce ever faster machines. Our use of Porter's five forces model analyzed the underlying attractiveness of the PC industry. Yet, a focus solely on the PC itself ignores some of the broader product and customer trends that have been reshaping the larger high-technology sector. In other words, the PC industry is delineated by a group of firms offering a similar type of product to a well-defined set of customers based on similar value-adding processes. However, a narrow view of the PC industry alone may blind us from uncovering and understanding a larger set of customer needs and value-adding processes that might share some commonalities with other industries. Let us examine some of the evolving high-technology trends and relationships that impact not only the personal computer, but also other electronic devices, to understand how customers' needs are changing in today's environment.

Exhibit 2-3 presents an overview of what might be described as the broader multimedia arena that includes a variety of different industries. In this exhibit, we consider each industry as its own strategic group. How do the personal computer, digital cell phone, flat-screen television, portable music player, and video game console industries interrelate and impact one another? We chose two dimensions to capture the complexity and evolution of this relationship: multifunctionality and portability. Multifunctionality describes the extent to which products from a focal industry allow the user to engage in multiple uses or applications.

Strategic Groups in the Broader Multimedia Arena   Exhibit 2-3

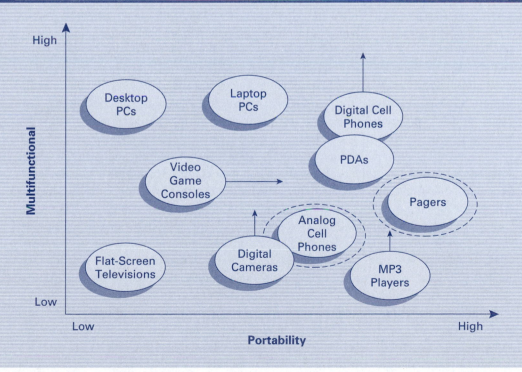

Portability refers to whether the products from a focal industry allow themselves to be moved around easily during use. As we can see, flat-screen televisions are currently not very multi-functional (not easy for most users to connect to the Internet, no ability to make voice-based phone calls), and not portable (heavy and fixed in a location). However, digital cell phones embody high levels of both dimensions. They are certainly portable by their very design and nature, and increasingly perform many functions (MP3 player, Internet access, digital cameras, and even online gaming).

Why should practitioners of strategy take a broader view of the industry they are studying? Major technology improvements or changes in customer demand that occur in one industry often exert "ripple effects" on other industries that may begin to share similar charac-teristics. For example, as laptop computers steadily gain sales within the PC industry, customers looking for new PC models will increasingly demand lighter weight and faster wireless Inter-net access. Over the past two years, almost all laptop PCs have begun offering wireless Internet access as advanced microprocessors (for example, Intel's Centrino line) incorporate this feature. At the same time, many companies and individuals have begun using new Internet-powered technology to make long-distance and international phone calls. As the latest laptops offer easy wireless connections and become ever thinner, buyers may begin to make voice-based calls through their PCs using the same headsets that currently hook up with today's digital cell phones. In other words, as laptops offer easier wireless connections that facilitate voice-based phone calls in the future, buyers may begin to think about their laptops as a potential substitute to digital cell phones. Because laptops offer a rising level of portability as they get lighter and thinner, prospective buyers of laptop models may begin to think about them in the same way they think about their digital cell phones.

Conversely, customers looking to purchase next-generation digital cell phones may begin to expect greater multifunctionality from them as well. Next-generation phones are likely to come with a dizzying array of new features; many already have larger storage capacity for phone numbers, offer the ability to play video games (some even offer online gaming), play MP3s, ac-cess the Internet, and even perform limited officelike functions (for example, scheduling calen-dars). As digital cell phones become more multifunctional, they are likely to offer an increasing number of features and capabilities that have long been associated with the PC. Already, digital cell phones have displaced the need for an entire class of products (and their respective indus-tries) as well. Pagers, for example, have all but disappeared as cell phones became dominant in this space. Analog cell phones have already become obsolete. Also, digital cell phones may well render portable MP3 music players obsolete in the future as their storage capacity and audio fidelity improve.

Thus, managers should examine the competitive environment from multiple angles. First, it is natural to think about the firm's product and how it compares with that offered by rivals. A firm can only achieve profitability to the extent it distinguishes itself from its rivals. This on-going race to achieve distinction is at the heart of all industry-based competition. However, managers need to ask questions about their products and services from the perspective of serv-ing not only existing customers, but also likely future customers as well. As new technologies work to blur the distinction between once-separate products, managers need to redefine their "industry" from a broader context of how many different types of customers they are likely to serve in the future. Customers who buy products in other industries often have valuable insights and product expectations that are not readily apparent to managers focused only on their im-mediate markets. The purchasing patterns and behavior of customers provide much more in-sight into the future. Finally, managers should also ask how their firm (and its industry) fits within a larger competitive environment that may include a host of different industries. These other industries may be the source of future competitors. New products or technologies spawned in one industry may turn out to have a major impact on another industry sometime in the future.

Techniques to Monitor the Environment

To keep abreast of rapid environmental changes, firms need to monitor their environment continually. **Environmental scanning** refers to gathering information about external conditions for use in formulating the firm's strategies. Scanning is an important ongoing activity because it helps managers understand and oversee potential changes in market demand, industry rivalry patterns, the rise of potential substitute products, and general macroenvironmental forces that may have long-term effects on the firm.

environmental scanning:
The gathering of information about external conditions for use in formulating strategies.

Scanning can occur at several levels. Broad-based scanning focuses on spotting new trends or changes in the general macroenvironment. For example, PC makers examine the potential growth of new markets outside the United States to develop and sell computers. Industry-level scanning is often much more specific in intent and scope. Managers and technical personnel from rival firms frequently visit their competitors, buy their products, and then break them down to see what progress competitors have made in such areas as product quality and new product features. In another example, airline personnel often take trips on competing airlines to assess service quality, timeliness of departure, and general maintenance. Managers from different department stores, hotels, banks, and other service establishments perform similar types of monitoring activities to gauge their competitors' strengths, skill levels, and focus. This type of scanning effort is also known as **competitor intelligence gathering**. Competitor intelligence gathering includes getting information on potential products under development, new technologies that may be incorporated in existing products, new markets to enter, service quality, and responsiveness. In other words, competitor intelligence gathering seeks to acquire as much information as can be found legitimately to help firms better track, understand, and deal with their competitors. Continuous scanning and intelligence gathering can help firms better understand their environments and their competitors to identify new opportunities for future improvements as well as possible threats to a firm's existing competitive position.

competitor intelligence gathering:
Scanning specifically targeted or directed toward a firm's rivals; often focuses on a competitor's products, technologies, and other important information.

Firms can gather huge amounts of information about their competitors from numerous public sources. For example, newspaper interviews and stories, trade magazines, and research results published in journals all can be valuable sources of information about competing firms. Broader economic or industry-level data can be found through many computer databases, such as Gartner Group, Compustat, Bloomberg, WSJ.com, CNNfn, and Valueline, which provide financial data for individual firms and their industries. Trade shows and conventions often represent opportunities for firms to display their best products and thus can be useful sources of information for their rivals as well.

Ethical Dimensions

This chapter shows how a firm can improve profitability by careful selection of the industry and strategic groups in which it competes. Careful positioning can enable it to charge higher prices and limit rivalry. But are these objectives really proper? Should firms charge as high a price as the market will bear? Are there limits to the means firms should take to limit competition? These questions have ethical ramifications too complex to discuss in detail here.

However, in closing this chapter, we reflect briefly on two critical ethical issues: legal requirements and long-run consequences of preserving industry-wide profitability.

Legal Requirements

Society enacts laws constraining the actions firms can take to limit competition, gouge customers, or otherwise take advantage of stakeholders. The United States, for example, has a vast network of regulations governing the claims firms can make about their products, the actions they can take to limit supply, and their ability to collude with competitors. At the very least, all firms must satisfy these legal requirements. Unfortunately, legislation is often so complex that meeting its mandate is difficult in practice.

Long-Run Consequences

When building barriers to entry in the areas discussed earlier, firms must look beyond the present to the long-run consequences of their actions. As an example, consider a decision to charge what the market will bear. Such a policy may boost a firm's profitability in the short run but at the same time alienate customers so that they defect as soon as an alternate source of supply becomes available. Price gouging can seriously injure a firm's long-run position. For example, a number of consumer groups have accused oil companies of engaging in price-gouging behavior when gasoline was in short supply during the summers of 2000 and 2001. Behavior not in society's best interest can have another kind of adverse long-run consequence: it can invite additional government regulation. Indeed, most laws currently on the books in a wide range of areas (financial disclosure, product safety, food and drug safety, contract requirements, and advertising claims) were enacted to eliminate abuses that were widespread at the time. To head off imposition of additional legal restrictions, managers must avoid abusive behavior giving rise to them.

Whether a particular behavior is abusive is sometimes difficult to determine, however. To explain the high prices charged by pharmaceutical firms, for example, managers claim that these high drug prices are needed to generate funds for further drug development. However, an increasing number of those who pay the bill—employers, state and local governments, and the public at large—are objecting to high pharmaceutical prices in the face of large profits. Negative sentiment is now so strong that some sort of legislation is likely. If enacted, it may be also be counterproductive to the point that drug companies have fewer incentives to invest in exploring and developing new treatments. Drug price levels, reimportation, drug safety review processes at the FDA, and the complexity of the prescription drug benefit under Medicare will likely remain important political issues for the balance of this decade.

Summary

- Analysis of the external environment is vital for firms to identify opportunities and threats. The external environment may be examined from two different levels of analysis: the general macroenvironment and the more specific industry-level, competitive environment.
- The general macroenvironment describes those forces and conditions likely to affect all firms in the economy. The general environment includes such forces as the demographic environment, the political environment, the social/cultural environment, technological developments, and the global environment. These forces can have a stronger impact on some firms than on others.
- The competitive environment describes those forces and factors that characterize the specific industry conditions in which a firm competes. These forces often have an immediate and direct effect on the firms in an industry.

- Porter's five forces model describes the key factors that influence an industry's environment. These forces include (1) the threat of new entrants, (2) the bargaining power of buyers, (3) the bargaining power of suppliers, (4) the intensity of rivalry, and (5) the potential threat of substitutes.
- Industry attractiveness defines the potential for profitability from competing in that industry. An attractive industry is one in which a high potential for earning profits exists. An unattractive industry is one with few opportunities to earn high profits.
- Strategic groups consist of those firms with similar strategic postures and competitive characteristics within an industry.
- Strategic group analysis helps managers develop competitive strategies for their firms within the context of the industry.
- Intensity of rivalry is often stronger among firms within a strategic group than among firms from different strategic groups.
- Environmental scanning is a set of techniques that allows managers to better understand and to track developments within the environment. An important scanning technique is that of competitor intelligence gathering.

Exercises and Discussion Questions

1. After the United States suffered through its worst attack on home soil on September 11, 2001, how do you think most companies will begin thinking about and planning to protect their people? What will the impact of September 11 be on firms that supply the commercial airline, hotel, gaming, and travel industries? If you were a supplier, what would be some things that you are likely to consider doing?

2. Around the world, people in many nations have not yet felt or realized the benefits of instituting economic policies that promote free enterprise at home and less restrictive trade abroad. If foreign governments increasingly turn away from these policies, what will likely be the impact on American companies? If you were the CEO of McDonald's, what strategies and actions would you consider taking? On the other hand, if you were Caterpillar, Ford Motor Company, or IBM, what would you be doing also?

3. Clearly, the personal computer industry is beginning to slow down dramatically after twenty years of phenomenal growth. What other industries do you see sharing similar characteristics with the PC industry? Do you think Palm and Handspring are likely to face the issues that now confront Compaq Computer, Hewlett-Packard, and Gateway? Are the changes taking placing in the personal computer industry likely to occur in the same way in other industries, such as consumer packaged goods or processed foods? What are some important differences between the PC industry and the consumer packaged goods industry?

4. As customers become ever more knowledgeable about the products they buy, they become more demanding about what they want from companies. How do you think companies should plan for the eventuality that customers become smarter and more savvy over time? Which firms appear to have a good grasp on how to understand their customers' evolving needs over time?

Endnotes

1. Data and facts for the personal computer industry were adapted from the following sources: "BlackBerry: Born Again for the Mass Market," *BusinessWeek,* September 20, 2004, p. 26; "Gateway CEO Presses Restart: Back to PCs," *Wall Street Journal,*

September 13, 2004, p. B1; Alienware Targets CE Retailers with High End Gear," *Warren's Consumer Electronics Daily,* July 29, 2004; Companies Craft Specialty PCs in Pursuit of Profits," *USA Today,* June 21, 2004, p. B1; "Picking a Big Fight with Dell, H-P Cuts PC Profits Razor-Thin," *Wall Street Journal,* May 12, 2004, pp. A1, A10; "Voodoo Rage," *PC Magazine,* February 20, 2004; "Dell to Unveil Powerful New PCs Aimed at Game-Playing Market," *Wall Street Journal,* February 12, 2004, p. B6; "Gateway Buys eMachines to Boost Its Own Electronics Sales," *Wall Street Journal,* February 2, 2004, pp. B1, B4; "Slowing PC Sales Drive Computer Firms' Push to Consumer Gadgets," *Investor's Business Daily,* October 8, 2003, pp. A1, A6; "Microsoft Takes On Consumer Electronics with New PC," *Wall Street Journal,* September 30, 2003, pp. B1, B6; "As Apple Stalls, Steve Jobs Looks to Digital Entertainment," *Wall Street Journal,* April 25, 2003, pp. A1, A5; "The Case of the Incredibly Shrinking PCs," *PC World,* February 1, 2003, p. 70; "Dell Does Domination," *Fortune,* January 21, 2002, pp. 71–75; "On to the Living Room! Can Microsoft Control the Digital Home?" *BusinessWeek,* January 21, 2002, pp. 68–72; "As PC Industry Slumps, IBM Hands Off Manufacturing of Desktops," *Wall Street Journal,* January 9, 2002, pp. B1, B4; "Dell Soars Above Rival Amid Slump in Market for PCs," *Wall Street Journal,* January 18, 2002, p. B4; "Apple's 21st Century Walkman," *Fortune,* November 12, 2001, pp. 213–220; "Technology Grows Up," *Wall Street Journal,* October 25, 2001, pp. B1, B3; "Handspring Plans Line of Hybrid Devices," *Wall Street Journal,* October 15, 2001, p. B7; "Nokia Expects New 5510 Mobile Phone to Boost Popularity of Mobile Internet," *Wall Street Journal,* October 15, 2001, p. B7; "The New Computer Landscape," *Wall Street Journal,* September 6, 2001, pp. B1, B8; "Windows XP Pricing Looks Good for Consumers," *Wall Street Journal,* September 6, 2001, p. B4; "H-P's Deal for Compaq Has Doubters as Value of Plan Falls to $20.52 Billion," *Wall Street Journal,* September 5, 2001, pp. A3, A14; "Hewlett Packard Deal Will Hurt Component Suppliers," *Wall Street Journal,* September 5, 2001, p. B6; "As More Buyers Suffer From Upgrade Fatigue, PC Sales Are Falling," *Wall Street Journal,* August 24, 2001, pp. A1, A4; "Compaq to Give AOL Edge on XP PCs," *Wall Street Journal,* July 27, 2001, p. B2; "How Dell Fine-Tunes Its PC Pricing to Gain Edge in a Slow Market," *Wall Street Journal,* June 8, 2001, pp. A1, A8; "Dell Dethrones Compaq as Global PC Sales Leader," *Investor's Business Daily,* April 23, 2001, p. A6; "No Cartwheels for Handspring," *BusinessWeek,* April 2, 2001, pp. 56–58; "Price War Squeezes PC Makers," *Wall Street Journal,* March 26, 2001, pp. B1, B3; "IBM Turns Around Its PC Unit, Though Skeptics Still Call It a Drag," *Wall Street Journal,* February 15, 2001, pp. B1, B4; "Market for Hand-Held Computers Doubled in 2000," *Wall Street Journal,* January 25, 2001, p. B6; "Market Declines for PCs," *Dallas Morning News,* January 20, 2001, p. 3F; "Domestic Growth in PC Market Hits Slowest Rate in 7 Years," *Wall Street Journal,* January 19, 2001, p. B3; "Chips Designed to Prod PC Sales," *Investor's Business Daily,* January 18, 2001, p. A4; "Palm, Microsoft Extend Rivalry to Wireless Arena," *Investor's Business Daily,* November 20, 2000, p. A6.

2. See, for example, "Isolation at Top Hurts Minorities When Layoffs Hit," *Wall Street Journal,* January 29, 2002, pp. B1, B8.

3. See D. A. Thomas, "Diversity as Strategy," *Harvard Business Review* (September 2004): 98–108.

4. See, for example, W. B. Johnston, "Global Work Force 2000: The New World Labor Market," *Harvard Business Review* (March–April 1991): 115–127.

5. See "Enron Collapse Has Congress Backing off Deregulation," *Wall Street Journal,* January 29, 2002, p. A22.

6. See, for example, A. J. Stern, "The Case of the Environmental Impasse," *Harvard Business Review* 69 (May–June 1991): 14–29. For an overview of how companies can formulate a strategic framework to think about environmental issues, see F. L. Reinhardt, "Bringing the Environment Down to Earth," *Harvard Business Review* 77, no. 4 (July–August 1999): 149–157.

7. See "Northwest, US Airways Continue Industry's Losing Streak," *Wall Street Journal,* January 18, 2002, p. B6; "American Air, Continental Report Losses Totalling Almost $1 Billion," *Wall Street Journal,* January 17, 2002, p. A4.

8. See D. A. Thomas, "Diversity as Strategy," *Harvard Business Review* 82 (September 2004), pp. 98–108.

9. See B. Avishai, "What Is Business's Social Compact?" *Harvard Business Review* 72 (January–February 1994): 38–48.

10. See, for example, "Scientists Build Molecular Logic Circuits," *Wall Street Journal,* November 9, 2001, p. B3.

11. Data and facts were adapted from the following sources: "Outsourcing Booms, Although Quietly Amid Political Heat," *Wall Street Journal,* October 18, 2004, pp. B1, B2; "GE Plans to Sell Call-Center Unit Based in India," *Wall Street Journal,* September 17, 2004, pp. C1, C13; "Nortel Will Sell to Flextronics Most Manufacturing Operations," *Wall Street Journal,* June 30, 2004, p. B4; "Big Three's Outsourcing Plan: Make Parts Suppliers Do It," *Wall Street Journal,* June 10, 2004, pp. A1, A6; "IBM to Buy Indian Call-Center Firm," *Wall Street Journal,* April 8, 2004, p. B6; "Where Are the Jobs?" *BusinessWeek,* March 22, 2004, pp. 35–55; "New IBM Jobs Can Mean Fewer Jobs Elsewhere," *Wall Street Journal,* March 8, 2004, pp. B1, B11; "Software: Will Outsourcing Hurt America's Supremacy?" *BusinessWeek,* March 1, 2004, pp. 84–95; "H-P Outsourcing: Beyond China," *Wall Street Journal,* February 23, 2004, p. A14; "Scrambling to Stem India's Onslaught," *BusinessWeek,* January 10, 2004, pp. 81–82; "Skilled Workers Mount Opposition to Free Trade, Swaying Politicians," *Wall Street Journal,* October 10, 2003, pp. A1, A11; "Giant Sucking Sound," *Forbes,* September 29, 2003, pp. 58–60; "Move Over, India," *BusinessWeek,* August 11, 2003, pp. 42–43; "AOL's Tech Center in India is Money-Saver," *Wall Street Journal,* August 7, 2003, p. B4; "Is Your Job Next?" *BusinessWeek,* February 3, 2003, pp. 50–59.

12. See S. A. Zahra, "The Changing Rules of Global Competitiveness in the 21st Century," *Academy of Management Executive* 13, no. 1 (1999): 36–42.

13. See, for example, M. E. Porter, *Competitive Strategy* (New York: Free Press, 1980); M. E. Porter, Competitive Advantage (New York: Free Press, 1985); and M. E. Porter, "Towards a Dynamic Theory of Strategy," *Strategic Management Journal* 12 (Winter 1991): 95–117.

14. Data and facts were adapted from the following sources: "Suppliers Struggle with Wal-Mart ID-Tag Plan," *Wall Street Journal,* November 18, 2004, pp. B4, B5; "Making Labels for Less," *Wall Street Journal,* August 13, 2004, pp. B1, B3; "Just Two Words: Plastic Chips," *BusinessWeek,* May 10, 2004, pp. 109–110; "China Moves Up in World of Leather," *Wall Street Journal,* April 7, 2004, p. B2B; "Making Fashion Faster," *Wall Street Journal,* February 24, 2004, pp. B1, B6; "To Sell Goods to Wal-Mart, Get on the Net," *Wall Street Journal,* November 21, 2003, pp. B1, B6; "Is Wal-Mart Too Powerful?" *BusinessWeek,* October 6, 2003, pp. 100–110; "Made to Measure: Invisible Supplier Has Penney's Shirts All Buttoned Up," *Wall Street Journal,* September 11, 2003, pp. A1, A8; "Price War in Aisle 3," *Wall Street Journal,* May 27, 2003, pp. B1, B6; "At 7-Eleven, Fresh-Food Fix Is Focus," *Wall Street Journal,* August 21, 2002, p. B3A. An excellent article that summarizes the principles of supply chain management is H. L. Lee, "The Triple-A Supply Chain," *Harvard Business Review,* Volume 82 (10), October 2004, pp. 102–112. Also see in the same issue R. E. Slone, "Leading a Supply Chain Turnaround," *Harvard Business Review,* October 2004, pp. 114–121.

15. See "PC Users Can Now Make Long-Distance Calls for Free," *Wall Street Journal,* October 9, 2003, p. D2.

16. Early discussion of strategic groups is included in M. E. Porter, *Competitive Strategy* (New York: Free Press, 1980), chap. 7. Some of the most recent empirical work examining strategic groups include the select following: A. Fiegenbaum and H. Thomas, "Strategic Groups and Performance: The U.S. Insurance Industry, 1970–1984," *Strategic Management Journal* 11 (March 1990): 197–215; A. Fiegenbaum,

D. Sudharshan, and H. Thomas, "Strategic Time Periods and Strategic Groups Research: Concepts and Empirical Examples," *Journal of Management Studies* 27 (March 1990): 133–148; W. C. Bogner and H. Thomas, "The Role of Competitive Groups in Strategy Formulation: A Dynamic Integration of Two Competing Models," *Journal of Management Studies* 30 (January 1993): 51–68; R. E. Caves and P. Ghemawat, "Identifying Mobility Barriers," *Strategic Management Journal* 13 (January 1992): 1–13; M. J. Tang and H. Thomas, "The Concept of Strategic Groups: Theoretical Construct or Analytical Convenience?" *Managerial and Decision Economics* 13, no. 4 (1993): 323–330; K. O. Cool and I. Dierickx, "Rivalry, Strategic Groups and Firm Profitability," *Strategic Management Journal* 14, no. 1 (1993): 47–59; M. A. Peteraf, "Intraindustry Structure and Response Towards Rivals," *Journal of Managerial and Decision Economics* 14 (1993): 519–528; R. Wiggins and T. Ruefli, "Necessary Conditions for the Predictive Validity of Strategic Groups: Analysis Without Reliance on Clustering Techniques," *Academy of Management Journal* 38 (1995): 1635–1655; R. K. Reger and A. Huff, "Managerial Categorization of Competitors: Using Old Maps to Navigate New Environments," *Organization Science* 7 (1996): 22–39; D. Nath and T. S. Gruca, "Convergence Across Alternative Methods for Forming Strategic Groups," *Strategic Management Journal* 18, no. 9 (1997): 745–760; M. Peteraf and M. Shanley, "Getting to Know You: A Theory of Strategic Group Identity," *Strategic Management Journal* 18, Special Issue (1997): 165–186; D. Dranove, M. A. Peteraf, and M. Shanley, "Do Strategic Groups Exist? An Economic Framework for Analysis," *Strategic Management Journal* 19, no. 11 (1998): 1029–1044.

Recent work on strategic groups has continued to examine their relationship with other measures of performance. See, for example, G. McNamara, D. L. Deephouse, and R. A. Luce, "Competitive Positioning Within and Across a Strategic Group Structure: The Performance of Core, Secondary and Solitary Firms," *Strategic Management Journal* 24, no. 2 (2003): 161–181; J. D. Osborne, C. I. Stubbart, and A. Ramaprasad, "Strategic Groups and Competitive Enactment: A Study of Dynamic Relationships Between Mental Models and Performance," *Strategic Management Journal* 22, no. 5 (2001): 435–454; A Nair and S. Kotha, "Does Group Membership Matter? Evidence From the Japanese Steel Industry," *Strategic Management Journal* 22, no. 3 (2001): 221–235; T. D. Ferguson, D. L. Deephouse, and W. L. Ferguson, "Do Strategic Groups Differ in Reputation?" *Strategic Management Journal* 21, no. 12 (2000): 1195–1214.

17. See "Gateway CEO Presses Restart: Back to PCs," *Wall Street Journal,* September 13, 2004, p. B1; "The McDonald's of Computers," *Forbes,* November 24, 2003, pp. 170–172; Powering up at eMachines," *Business Week,* November 17, 2003, pp. 77–79.

18. See "Palm Device Sorts E-Mail in Real Time," *Wall Street Journal,* January 28, 2002, p. B6.

Chapter 3

Matching Firm Capabilities with Opportunities

Chapter Outline

What you will learn

- *The strategic tool known as the value chain*
- *The use of the value chain in evaluating an organization's internal strengths and weaknesses*
- *The differences between primary and supporting value-adding activities*
- *How the value chain relates to firm-based capabilities*
- *The concept of distinctive competence*
- *Some important economic sources of competitive advantage*

Pizza Hut and Domino's Pizza[1]

Pizza Hut, a division of Yum! Brands, is one of the largest and most established pizza sellers in the world. Beginning as a single-unit restaurant in Wichita, Kansas, in the 1950s, it mushroomed into a nationwide chain of pizza restaurants during its fast-growth days throughout the 1960s and 1970s. Pizza Hut was able to build important sources of competitive advantage. Although new competitors have clearly made significant market share gains in the restaurant industry, Pizza Hut remains an important player. Among some of the key advantages Pizza Hut enjoys as a result of its strong position are the following:

- **Location:** As the first competitor to establish a facility in many high-traffic areas, it has been able to preempt some of the most desirable restaurant locations.
- **Reputation:** Pizza Hut has expanded rapidly throughout the United States. In addition, it offers new types of pizza combinations in different markets. This allows Pizza Hut to maintain a high level of brand awareness.
- **Purchase discounts:** Its large-scale purchase of advertising time and food ingredients enables it to enjoy quantity discounts not available to smaller competitors.
- **Interrelationships:** Its interrelationships with other units of Yum! Brands, including KFC (formerly Kentucky Fried Chicken), Taco Bell, A&W All-American Food Restaurants, and Long John Silver's, enable Pizza Hut to gain significant negotiation leverage with advertising firms to conduct jointly

sponsored marketing campaigns. These advantages are often less available to smaller rivals operating as single-business firms.

Even with these many strengths, Pizza Hut's ability to maintain a dominant market share has repeatedly faced numerous challenges. Perhaps most important was the massive growth of Domino's Pizza in the early 1980s, which pioneered the concept of pizza delivery in 1965 under founder Thomas Monaghan. Taking advantage of this opportunity to serve customers in a new way, Domino's seized the initiative in redefining how customers can order and receive pizzas from their home or workplace. As a result, Domino's has been able to challenge Pizza Hut's long-standing position and capture significant market share over the years. It is now the number two pizza chain behind Pizza Hut, but it is the leader in pizza delivery. Some major advantages that Domino's enjoys include:

- **First-mover advantage:** Domino's focused its entire business on delivering freshly cooked pizza to customers who called in their orders, rather than open sit-down restaurants. This focus on delivery enabled Domino's to seize the initiative in this previously underserved segment.
- **Reputation:** Domino's fast growth and innovative marketing gave it strong brand awareness among customers who preferred the convenience of delivered pizza. Over time, many people came to associate pizza delivery with Domino's.
- **Location advantage:** Because Domino's did not offer any sit-down

restaurants, it could lease or build pizza preparation and delivery facilities in less costly locations than Pizza Hut could.

As a result, two very different modes of competing in the pizza restaurant segment emerged, with Pizza Hut and Domino's pursuing very different routes to building competitive advantage. Pizza Hut eventually decided to offer home delivery and played catch-up to Domino's for a long time. Nevertheless, the fierce rivalry between Pizza Hut and Domino's Pizza has not prevented other companies such as Papa John's International, Little Caesar's, and others from joining the fray.

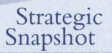

Strategic Snapshot

General Motors Corporation[2]

Over the past few years, General Motors (GM) has made tremendous strides to improve its competitive position as the world's largest automotive manufacturer. Although GM continues to face a variety of strategic and organizational challenges, it has made considerable headway toward improving the productivity of its factories, the cost of its operations, and the quality of its vehicles. Under CEO Rick Wagoner, GM has focused on achieving operational improvements in every aspect of its business. By slashing costs and closing aging factories, GM is now closing in on Japan's Honda Motor Company and Toyota Motor in productivity, and has overtaken rival Ford Motor Company to dominate the U.S. truck segment. Although the company is attempting to "reinvent itself" by offering highly advanced vehicles, developing new hybrid technologies, and creating sleeker car designs, General Motors is still trying to recover from decades of flat productivity, difficult relations with workers, obsolete production facilities, and organizational practices that impede major improvements in product quality.

General Motors' productivity gains over the past few years have been remarkable, given how large the company is. How well a firm improves its productivity determines its long-term competitiveness vis-à-vis its rivals. Simply put, productivity is a measure of how much labor and capital is required to produce a given unit of output. Over time, successful companies should be able to either steadily produce more output with the same level of labor or capital or find ways to reduce some of their labor and capital costs. GM's relentless focus on improving the productivity of its operations has enabled it to nearly reach the highly vaunted levels of Toyota and Honda, and it already beat Ford on this critical measure back in 2001. The key to achieving productivity gains is to design, develop, manufacture, and distribute a new car in less time.

- **Design:** In the past, GM designed a new car model from the ground up, using a "clean sheet of paper" to redo all aspects of the car. This often means that components that were successfully used in an earlier line of cars are often not reused in a new one. This approach to product design often required five years before a car actually reached the dealer's showroom. Now, following the lead of

Japanese manufacturers, GM (and its U.S. and European rivals) is attempting to design a car in less than twenty months. If proven components work from year to year, they are incorporated in new cars, thus saving the manufacturer from spending large sums to test a new part.

- **Operations:** When building a new factory, GM spends prodigiously on new robots, computer-aided technology, ultraclean paint rooms, and other "hardware" that make up the backbone of the factory. However, it often takes a long time to make sure that all parts of the factory are working together in a coordinated, synchronized manner. To make sure that this happens, GM needs to cultivate the knowledge and skills of its workers and technical personnel. However, GM's history of difficult labor relations has made workers fearful that the new technology is ultimately designed to replace them. The decades-old practice and mind-set whereby GM would view the United Auto Workers (UAW) as the "enemy" rather than as a partner continues to sorely test and aggravate labor relations.

- **Inbound and outbound logistics:** GM is working much more closely with the major railroads and distribution companies to speed up the shipment and delivery of parts needed for its nationwide network of factories. By attempting to emulate Toyota's "just-in-time" inventory system, GM seeks to dramatically cut the cost of holding inventory that sits in its warehouses. Using advanced tracking technology, GM hopes to be able to ship parts from its suppliers to the right factory when they are needed on the same day. Once vehicles are produced, GM wants to ship them to its dealerships in much less time than in the past. GM has already instituted a web-based, online ordering system so that dealers can send their vehicle requests directly to the factory for confirmation.

- **Procurement initiatives:** GM is undertaking a massive program to reduce the cost, effort, and time required to work with suppliers to order materials, parts, and components. Until recently, purchase orders were filled out in triplicate and often signed and countersigned to ensure approval at different ranks or locations in the company. GM spends over $85 billion a year to order and work with a base of some thirty thousand suppliers. Documentation costs make up a significant portion of the overhead costs in building a car. Overhauling the management of this vast network is now a top priority for GM, which is investing heavily in the Internet as a means of streamlining its ordering practices. However, getting approval from all parts of the company to use the Internet to accelerate orders, lower costs, and build online relationships with suppliers requires "buy-in" and a change in mind-set from managers that will likely take a long time. GM is also asking its suppliers to take on more of the work involved in designing, producing, and testing many of the key components that are assembled into the vehicle. Suppliers are increasingly required to tie their own operations more closely with those of GM through the Internet. By working more closely with its suppliers, GM hopes to reduce its internal fixed costs even more. Until recently, GM traditionally made more (and bought less) of the components it uses to assemble cars than its rivals. GM must therefore spend more on factories, plants, and equipment than its competitors to build these components. The high cost of capital spending directly contributed to lower productivity gains.

Because of its large size, GM experiences greater difficulty making and implementing decisions than smaller competitors such as Nissan or Honda. In the past, GM's large size slowed its adaptation to important changes in the industry environment. For example, GM lagged behind Japanese rivals in seizing new opportunities to

incorporate electronics and new computerized
engine management technologies to improve fuel
efficiency and performance during the early 1990s.
Now, GM is orchestrating its worldwide network
of engineers and suppliers to work together to deliver even greater productivity gains. Already, GM
engineers in the United States, Sweden, and
Germany are sharing a common "platform" to
build different lines of cars for each market. For example, the Chevy Malibu, the Opel Vectra, and the
Saab 9-3 midsize sedans use many of the same parts
and components. GM's legendary Saturn unit is
also receiving a needed makeover by using designs
and components from GM's German Opel unit.
This sharing of expertise and parts throughout the
company has cut engineering costs by a third.

Introduction

To identify opportunities and to neutralize threats in the external environment, managers
must thoroughly evaluate their firm's potential capabilities to compete. A vital part of successful
strategy formulation depends on a careful assessment of the firm's strengths and weaknesses. This
task requires each firm to conduct an internal analysis to determine those activities it can perform better than its competitors. Finding those activities that allow the firm to perform in ways
that other competitors cannot do as well is key to competitive success. Even though numerous
rivals may compete in the same industry environment, some firms are likely to perform some
activities better than others.

This chapter examines the concept of firm capabilities and internal analysis of strengths
and weaknesses. Developing effective strategies requires managers to understand how each
firm's strengths and weaknesses may differ from those of competitors. These differences lay the
foundation on which each firm bases its own strategy in the competitive environment.

We begin by examining the concept of the value chain. The value chain is an analytical
tool that helps firms understand how their primary and supporting activities can be used to
create value. It is the starting point to help firms identify their strengths and weaknesses. We will
then apply the value chain analysis tool to examine the types of activities that occur in two
different industries: pizzas and automobiles. In a later section, we discuss other issues related to
developing firm capabilities outside the value chain, such as financial analysis and internal
organization.

The Value Chain

To understand how a firm builds its capabilities to compete, one must identify the
specific types of activities that make up the firm's competitive posture. Every firm engages in
numerous activities that, in sum, determine its competitiveness in serving customers in the
marketplace. These activities create economic value. A useful analytical tool for portraying and
analyzing these activities is the value chain shown in Exhibit 3-1.[3] The **value chain** describes
all of the activities that make up the economic performance and capabilities of the firm. It
portrays activities required to create value for customers of a given product or service. As such,
the value chain is an excellent framework by which managers can determine the strengths and
weaknesses of each activity vis-à-vis the firm's competitors.

value chain:
*An analytical tool that
describes all activities that
make up the economic
performance and capabilities
of the firm; used to analyze
and examine activities that
create value for a given firm.*

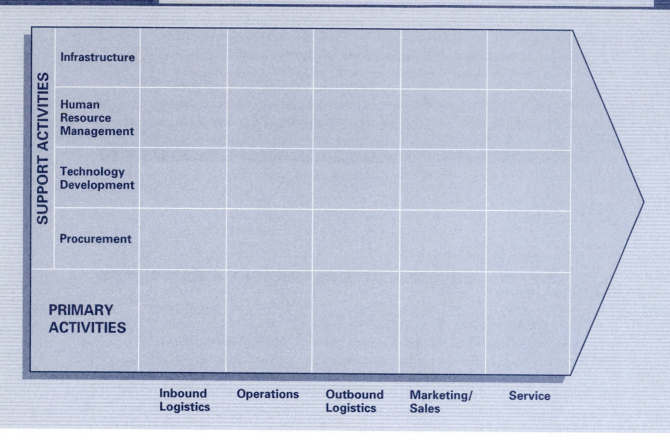

Exhibit 3-1   The Value Chain

SUPPORT ACTIVITIES					
Infrastructure					
Human Resource Management					
Technology Development					
Procurement					
PRIMARY ACTIVITIES					
Inbound Logistics	Operations	Outbound Logistics	Marketing/ Sales	Service	

primary activities:
Economic activities that relate directly to the actual creation, manufacture, distribution, and sale of a product or service to the firm's customer (see support activities).

support activities:
Economic activities that assist the firm's primary activities (see primary activities).

upstream activities:
Economic activities that occur close to the firm's suppliers but far away from the consumer. Examples include inbound logistics, procurement, manufacturing, and operations (see also downstream activities).

The value chain classifies each firm's activities into two broad categories: primary activities and support activities. **Primary activities** relate directly to the actual creation, development, manufacture, distribution, sale, and servicing of the product or service offered to the firm's customer. These activities represent the key tasks a firm performs to produce and deliver a product or service to a customer. **Support activities** refer to those tasks that contribute to or assist the firm's primary activities. In other words, support activities work to enhance or to help the functioning of primary value-adding activities. The combination of both primary and support activities determines the firm's basis for adding value. By breaking up the firm's value chain into discrete, isolated centers of activity, managers can assess whether they are performing each activity in ways that are better than that of their competitors (for example, lower cost, better quality, faster delivery). In other words, it is not enough to say that one firm is better than another in some overall way; the value chain allows managers to compare their firm's specific activities with the same activities performed by competitors. Thus, comparing a firm's chain with that of competitors can provide valuable insight into each firm's individual strengths and weaknesses.

Activities in the value chain can be characterized as being upstream or downstream. **Upstream activities** occur far away from the consumer, closer to the firm's suppliers. In other words, upstream activities are performed in the early stages of the value-adding process.

Downstream activities occur closer to the firm's buyers. Downstream activities add value to those inputs that were processed through earlier upstream value-adding activities.

downstream activities: *Economic activities that occur close to the customer but far away from the firm's suppliers. Examples include outbound logistics, distribution, marketing, sales, and service (see also upstream activities).*

Primary Activities

The sequence of activities through which raw materials are transformed into benefits enjoyed by customers is called primary activities. These activities are shown along the bottom row of Exhibit 3-1. Five major activities make up this sequence: inbound logistics, operations, outbound logistics, marketing/sales, and service. Working together, these five activities determine the key operational tasks surrounding the product or service.

- Inbound logistics: In most industries, the transformation process begins with conveyance or delivery of raw materials to a firm's manufacturing (or service) facilities.
- Operations: Inputs are transformed into products.
- Outbound logistics: Products are shipped to distributors or to final users.
- Marketing/sales: Users are informed about products and encouraged to buy them.
- Service: Once in the customers' hands, products are installed, repaired, and maintained.

Let us now examine more closely the specific tasks and operational procedures that make up these five primary activities.

Inbound Logistics. As the words imply, inbound logistics deal with the handling of materials and inventory received from the firm's suppliers. The typical operational procedures and tasks surrounding inbound logistics include warehousing, storage, and control of raw materials or managing component flows from different suppliers. Inbound logistics are considered a primary activity because they represent the beginning of the firm's value-adding conversion of inputs. Inbound logistics represent a major source of direct costs to the firm; thus, new techniques and improvements in inventory control, storage, and materials handling can dramatically improve a firm's cost position in this activity. For example, a reduction in inventory and storage costs over time can have a major positive impact on a firm's cost position. Differences in storage and inventory costs relative to one's competitors can add up to a significant competitive strength or weakness.

In many firms, inbound logistics require significant capital investment. The location and management of warehouses, and the inventory held in them, are important areas in which to focus cost control and efficiency. Many manufacturers around the world have taken numerous steps in recent years to improve the efficiency and reduce costs involved with inbound logistics activities. At General Electric, for example, the huge major appliances (dishwashers, refrigerators) plant at Louisville, Kentucky, uses highly automated bar coding, sorting, and inventory checking systems that enable GE to move components and parts quickly from the railhead to its factory. Parts and components do not sit idle in warehouses for long. Fast movement of components and inventory greatly reduces the operating costs for the entire Major Home Appliance Group business. Now, firms in every industry from home appliances to consumer staples are striving to dramatically improve the efficiency and timeliness of their inbound logistics operations. Continuous improvements and developments in new ordering systems are transforming the way that companies track and monitor the shipment of their inputs and finished products.[4]

Improvements in inbound logistics activities are not confined to manufacturing firms. For example, both United Parcel Service (UPS) and Federal Express (now a unit of FedEx Corporation) have built strong competitive positions by using techniques that promote superefficient, time-responsive sorting of packages and overnight mail. Both firms expect their business to grow substantially with the rise of online ordering and delivery through the Internet and e-commerce. Likewise, hospitals depend on smooth, well-honed ordering and delivery systems to ensure that critical supplies of pharmaceuticals, medical supplies, and surgical instruments are available on a daily basis. Even restaurants, grocery stores, and convenience store chains are harnessing new technologies to ensure timely delivery of products on a daily, and sometimes, hourly basis. Banks and financial service firms depend on extremely automated, real-time, and efficient inbound, computer-driven logistics to manage, coordinate, and track the flow of payments and funds that enter their systems for different purposes such as check clearance, credit card payments, investments, and cash management.

Inbound logistics has become a major focus of cost savings for companies in every industry. New "supply chain" technologies and ordering systems have dramatically increased the productivity of ordering key inputs and parts from suppliers. One ongoing initiative underway is the use of Internet-enabled supply chain software to coordinate the ordering, production, and delivery of key inputs in a way that reduces or even eliminates inventory. Japanese automotive firms, such as Toyota and Honda, have spent many years fine-tuning the development of inventory-less ordering systems that substantially reduces inventory holding costs. A key to this major Japanese advantage (that also exists in consumer electronics and other industries) is the closeness with which suppliers and firms work together to share costs and ordering information so that parts are delivered on a daily basis in the exact amount needed. Many of these Japanese innovations occurred even before the Internet was widely used in business applications. Now, U.S. firms have made great strides in adopting some of the same techniques, especially by combining the Internet with leading-edge software to remove cumbersome documentation procedures and other obstacles to fast ordering and delivery. "Extended" supply chains are designed to help firms coordinate their product shipments from their suppliers through real-time Internet-based ordering, replenishment, and tracking systems. Logistics specialists such as UPS have developed their own documentation and ordering systems to help firms of all sizes become more efficient in this key activity.

Operations.   Operations are the activities and procedures that transform raw materials, components, and other inputs into finished end products. In other words, operations concerns itself with the generation, manufacture, and/or production of products and services. Specific task activities in the operations realm include stamping, machining, testing, fabrication, and assembly in manufacturing-based settings. In a broader sense, any type of processing activity that results in a product or service is the heart of the firm's operations. Operations also represents the dominant upstream activity in many firms. Operations is thus a big cost driver that overshadows many other activities. Success in managing and improving upstream operations over time represents a critical source of leverage in building or reinforcing a firm's ability to compete in a sustained manner. Differences between firms conducting similar types of operations may result from relative age of equipment, type of technology used, size of plant, economies of scale, degree of automation, productivity levels and gains, wage rates, and possible improvements resulting from longer experience.

For many service businesses, operations is concerned directly with the provisioning of a service to its customers. For telecommunications firms, operations is focused on managing and updating the vast network of routers, switches, and other gear that is the backbone of communications and the Internet. For health care providers, operations represents a multifaceted set of activities, ranging from emergency room care, to surgery, to postoperative care, and to direct personal care of patients. Operations in a financial services firm could relate to check clearing and automated teller machines (ATMs) for banks, trading securities for brokerages, and transmitting funds and clearing credit transactions for banks and credit card processors. Operations in a restaurant focuses on the actual preparation and delivery of food to customers. All of these activities are also major cost drivers for service providers. Each service provider may also exhibit varying approaches to managing its operational activities based on technology used, economies of scale, productivity levels, and potential improvements from experience.

In many ways, how a firm manages its production/transformation operations will strongly influence the entire firm's competitive posture. For example, in the chemical, oil refining, and paper industries, the dominant production mode is that of continuous flow processes. Continuous flow processes are characterized by rigid and dedicated production systems geared to the standardized production of a single or limited range of products. These capital-intensive processes are costly to operate and hard to switch between products; they represent very large fixed costs for the firm. Any disruption of a continuous flow process generates enormous downtime costs for the firm. As a result, firms in industries whose dominant production mode is that of continuous flow processes are likely to develop strategies that recognize the nature of the production process's high fixed costs, rigidity, and lack of flexibility in switching to alternative products.

The considerable focus and effort that firms have placed on implementing total quality management (TQM) in manufacturing and service spawned new technologies and practices that allow firms to improve the efficiency and quality of their operations-based activities. Consider, for example, the illustration of Nucor in the steel industry. Unlike integrated steel mills such as USX's U.S. Steel unit and AK Steel, Nucor built up a significant competitive position in the steel industry by focusing on minimills. These mills are superefficient and can produce a ton of steel of significantly better quality for less cost than older integrated mills. Investment in highly responsive and efficient minimills has enabled Nucor to sustain its profitability for many years, even when the industry moved into downturns and recessions. The focus on improving operations has certainly not been limited to the heavy manufacturing sector. Intel, the largest semiconductor company in the world, has defined state-of-the-art manufacturing improvements for this industry. Each of Intel's gargantuan chip factories is designed in the exact same way; this enables Intel to minimize variation in its manufacturing processes and capture the maximum degree of cost savings from huge economies of scale.

Outbound Logistics. Outbound logistics refers to the transfer of finished end product to the distribution channels. The focus in outbound logistics is on managing the flow and distribution of products to the firm's immediate buyers, such as wholesalers and retailers. Activities and procedures associated with outbound logistics include inventory control, warehousing, storage, and transport of finished products. As is the case with inbound logistics and operations, improvements in efficiency and responsiveness of outbound logistics can greatly aid the firm's competitive posture. Many of the same technologies and innovations used to dramatically boost the efficiency and timeliness of inbound logistics can readily apply to outbound logistics activities as well. For example, the use of Internet-based online ordering and tracking systems can help wholesalers and retailers slice the amount of inventory they must hold. Firms can build competitive strengths based on their ability to lower the costs of outbound distribution and to enhance responsiveness.

Procter & Gamble (P&G) over the past several years has made major efforts to improve the efficiency and turnaround of its outbound logistics activities. By linking up more closely with key wholesalers and retailers (for example, Wal-Mart Stores), P&G has accelerated the timely delivery of goods that retailers have trouble stocking. By making extensive use of bar-coding technology, P&G and its key buyers balance the flow of inventory and goods between P&G's warehouses and the retailers' store shelves. This responsive distribution system becomes an overwhelming competitive strength for P&G and helps the company track which products are in particularly high demand. By sharing and garnering information from Wal-Mart's sales, P&G is able to uncover new ideas for future product development, while delivering more of its current products that customers want. A close understanding of how its products are distributed and sold gives P&G a better understanding of how to work with its buyers to improve everyone's margin over time.

Outbound logistics will be a key focus for many suppliers as buyers demand even greater efficiency and cost savings from them. One key initiative underway is the use of radio-frequency identification devices (RFIDs) to track and monitor shipments to retailers. RFID technology goes beyond bar coding and enables both suppliers and retailers to track individual pallet shipments at every stage of the ordering, transport, and delivery process. RFID technology is designed to help retailers fine-tune their orders from the suppliers, who in turn know how much to ship based on previous forecasts and actual purchase histories. In its most sophisticated form, RFID technology will enable retailers to monitor a person's purchase of individual products based on RFID tags or chips that are embedded in the product. Although this new technology will generate serious privacy concerns for the individual consumer, all of the major suppliers to key retailers such as Wal-Mart Stores are working on ways to improve the technology and allow the final consumer to shut off the RFID tags or chips to preserve their individual privacy.

Marketing and Sales.

Marketing and Sales. Marketing and sales activities include advertising, promotion, product mix, pricing, specific distribution channels, working with wholesalers, and salesforce issues. Marketing is vital in helping the firm determine the competitive scope of its value-adding activities. For example, some firms may decide to concentrate their efforts on a specific market segment or niche, whereas other firms may want to pursue a more broad-line product strategy. Thus, marketing becomes a vehicle by which the firm can develop specific competitive postures and strategies to serve a variety of segments or niches within the industry. Marketing activities deal extensively with pricing issues as well. The price of a firm's product can be an important signal or indicator of the firm's value-creating capabilities; a product's price becomes a surrogate measure of what value the firm is delivering to the market. Marketing activities also represent a central part of the firm's downstream value-adding activities; planning in these activities is oriented toward meeting the needs of immediate buyers and the final consumer.

Clearly, numerous companies have built extensive competitive positions and strengths based on their superior approaches to managing marketing activities. Companies such as Coca-Cola, McDonald's, PepsiCo, Pfizer, Anheuser-Busch, Bristol-Myers Squibb, Intel, and American Express come to mind as leading corporate examples of firms that have built effective competitive strengths based on excellence in marketing activities. Pharmaceutical firms, in particular, have begun direct marketing campaigns to promote their leading-edge products, as well as to encourage customers to ask their physicians if certain types of drugs are appropriate for them.

Service.

Service. Customer service is a central value-adding activity that a firm can seek to improve over time. During the 1990s, an increasing number of companies began redefining the way they manage their customer service activities. Value is more often defined in the eyes of the customer rather than by what the firm thinks it has created. Thus, customer service has become a vital means to compete in any industry environment. Customer service includes such activities and procedures as warranty, repair, installation, customer support, product adjustment and modification, and immediate response to customer needs.

Customer service is so important as a competitive weapon because it enables a firm to create value immediately before the customer's eyes. How well the firm conducts these tasks will strongly impact the customer's preference for buying from the firm again in the future. Both FedEx and UPS thrive in the overnight delivery business because of their superior approaches to customer service. Both firms also allow and even encourage customers to track the status of their packages and deliveries through the Internet. Conversely, the U.S. Postal Service, which offers a similar overnight delivery service, has only just begun to match what FedEx and UPS can offer in terms of Internet-based tracking systems. Despite the enormous size and reach of the postal system, many business customers still prefer to rely on FedEx and UPS for managing their critical deliveries and urgent package shipments.

Companies in every industry ranging from telecommunications to hotels, industrial equipment, and hospitals are rethinking and reinventing the ways they perform customer service activities. For example, many internal reengineering efforts are devoted to improving how firms meet their customers' needs. **Reengineering** means redefining the way firms organize their operations to improve responsiveness to customer needs. For example, at most telecommunications companies, customers can now call one number and get all of the information they need about their account from one customer service representative. In the past, customers had to dial separate numbers for different requests, such as telephone installation, equipment repair, leasing, purchase, and account adjustments.

Perhaps the most important source of technological change that has transformed the very notion of fast and responsive customer service is the Internet. Internet pioneers such as Amazon.com, E*Trade, and Ameritrade used this new medium as a platform for all of their business activities. In response, many established firms soon embraced the Internet as a competitive weapon to dramatically improve their customer service operations during the late 1990s. By creating sophisticated websites, almost all large and medium-sized companies are encouraging their current and potential customers to use the Internet as a means to gather information, select their desired products, and order products through online, instantaneous transactions. In the financial services industry, for example, many securities brokerage operations (for example, Fidelity, Schwab, Merrill Lynch) have built state-of-the-art, secure Internet sites that enable customers to set up accounts, transfer funds, and invest in stocks and other investment vehicles from their computer screens. Eventually, all of their competitors have done the same to provide convenient service to customers. In fact, the rise of entirely new companies such as Ameritrade and E*Trade was a critical factor in compelling the larger securities firms to make the Internet a key part of their customer service operations.

In the most advanced form of Internet-driven customer service, companies such as IBM, Intel, Dell Computer, General Electric, and Amazon.com are using the Internet to link up directly and transfer a customer's order to their distribution centers, factories, and even suppliers for immediate processing, billing, and delivery. Dell Computer, for example, can receive and process a customer's order for a highly customized personal computer over the Internet and have it shipped and delivered in less than four days. Amazon.com, a company that did not exist as recently as 1995, has become a major retailer of books, compact discs (CDs), videos, toys, electronics, and other items through the Internet. By allowing customers to order any book or music CD in print, Amazon.com offers customers a fast, secure, and easy way to purchase these items (often at prices lower than those of existing brick-and-mortar competitors) without leaving the comforts of their home. In these firms, the Internet serves to coordinate both outbound and inbound logistics-based activities.

reengineering:
The complete rethinking, reinventing, and redesign of how a business or set of activities operates.

Support Activities

The remaining activities of the value chain are undertaken to support primary activities. They are therefore referred to as support activities. Support activities help the firm improve coordination across and achieve efficiency within the firm's primary value-adding activities. Support activities are located across the first four rows in Exhibit 3-1 and include procurement, technology development, human resource management, and firm-level infrastructure.

- Procurement: Inputs are secured for primary activities.
- Technology development: Methods of performing primary activities are improved.
- Human resource management: Employees who will carry out primary activities are recruited, trained, motivated, and supervised.
- Infrastructure: Activities such as accounting, finance, legal affairs, and regulatory compliance are carried out to provide ancillary support for primary activities.

Because each primary activity generally requires assistance in each of these four areas, the value chain includes four cells above each primary activity, one for each category of support activity. Let us examine how each of these four support activities contributes to building the firm's capabilities.

Procurement. Procurement refers to purchasing the necessary inputs, resources, or components for the firm's primary value-adding activity. The purchasing function involves specific procedures such as billing systems, methods for dealing with suppliers and vendors, and information systems about different components and parts. Even though it is a support activity, the purchasing function can significantly enhance the firm's cost position relative to its competitors. Improved procurement practices enable the firm to gain significant economies of scale and higher bargaining power over suppliers if the firm coordinates its procurement across different functions and even businesses. For example, procurement activities within the firm will focus heavily on learning and adapting new types of supply chain software to help improve documentation and ordering procedures.

Technology Development. Technology is found in every value-adding activity within the firm. Given the rapid technological changes that are present in almost every industry (for example, new forms of communications, software, Internet, security systems), this support activity has assumed enormous importance in every firm. Technology in firms today transcends the conventional wisdom that it is primarily focused on research and development (R&D). Although most firms still have engineering and R&D staffs devoted to exploring and using new sources of technology, in practice, technology is developed and used in countless ways throughout the firm. It can be the software found in computers; the standard operating procedures used to manage a factory; the human know-how employed in developing, manufacturing, and selling products; the layout of the factory; the sophisticated nature of the firm's Internet capabilities; and the laboratory equipment involved in the firm's value-adding activities. Technology is pervasive in both upstream and downstream activities of the firm.

product development:
The conception, design, and commercialization of new products.

process development:
The design and use of new procedures, technologies, techniques, and other steps to improve value-adding activities.

Technology is concerned with both product development and process development. **Product development** refers to the conception, design, and commercialization of new products. For example, the design of new aircraft, more sophisticated microchips, more effective pharmaceuticals, better-tasting potato chips, more environmentally-friendly laundry detergents, and faster-heating, microwave-oriented convenience foods all represent different types of product development. Even though the end products are completely different, they are all based on the firm's ability to conceive and design new product ideas. **Process development,** on the other hand, refers to the development and use of new procedures, practices, or equipment to improve the value-adding activity itself. For example, the development of new assembly and packaging techniques, the use of new factory layouts to reduce work-in-process (WIP), the creation of a new medium to deliver advertising, the creation of new software to manage the firm's purchases, and the improvement of inventory tracking systems represent some different ways to conduct process development. The aim of process development is to adapt new techniques or to improve existing methods of conducting value-adding activities.

Many companies have refocused efforts on technology development to improve their value-adding activities. For example, Allen–Bradley (now known as Rockwell Automation), a leading U.S. producer of motor controls, has developed new techniques to use factory automation that have dramatically reduced the unit costs of new motor components. Likewise, competitors in the pizza restaurant business are investigating new types of pizzas that they can offer their customers; they are also looking at investing in faster, state-of-the-art ovens to improve consistency. General Electric has invested large sums to introduce new forms of flexible automation and materials handling that lower the production costs and improve the quality of its dishwashers and refrigerators. In the defense industry, Boeing and Lockheed Martin have designed and implemented entirely new computer-driven design and production systems to build leading-edge fighter aircraft that incorporate stealth technology and advanced electronics. These firms are investing steadily in technology—product and process—to find new sources of competitive strength.

Human Resource Management. Human resource management refers to working with people throughout the firm. These activities focus on recruiting, hiring, compensating, and training people to perform their jobs within the firm. As with technology development, human resource management receives considerable attention from top management because of its strategic role in helping the firm learn and build new types of competitive skills. Human resource management activities thus affect every aspect of the firm's value-adding activities.

When conducted properly, human resource management enables the firm to cultivate the skills necessary for competitive success. Although managers typically tend to think of investments in terms of capital budgets and physical, durable assets, continuous investment in the firm's people represents a more enduring way to build the firm's capabilities. Managers and employees are the most flexible and capable assets firms have. By providing the right levels of training, firms can assign people to perform different tasks, thus enhancing job satisfaction, efficiency, and quality. Highly focused training efforts can produce enormous gains in productivity and customer satisfaction. At Walt Disney's theme parks, for example, the company's training programs have instituted leading-edge practices that make customer satisfaction the highest priority. Employees are taught to view and treat customers as "guests," and training even extends to methods that improve each employee's communication skills. For most firms, however, assessing the direct costs of investing in human resource activities is often difficult, because factors such as employee turnover and morale are hard to measure.

Successful human resource management is often a key factor in determining a firm's competitive strengths. As a result, hotels and restaurants need to ensure that their employees are well trained and know the correct procedures for treating guests. Direct customer service activities, in particular, require extensive training. Professional service firms, such as accounting, architecture, management consulting, and legal firms, depend heavily on the human resource function to recruit, select, and hire the right people that make up the workforce.

Firm Infrastructure. Infrastructure includes such activities as finance, accounting, legal affairs, information systems, and payroll. These activities assist all of a firm's value-adding functions, so it is difficult to put an accurate dollar figure on their worth to the firm. Because infrastructure costs are hard to isolate, they are often called overhead expenses. Certainly over the past few years, this has been an area where firms have sought significant cost reduction and improved efficiency. Although many firms seek to cut infrastructure expenses during business downturns, such activities can be important sources of competitive strength. For example, in highly regulated industry environments, such as electric utilities, telecommunications, financial services, and pharmaceuticals, the firm's legal department can be as critical to success as operations, outbound logistics, marketing, or technology development activities. Understanding legislation and government regulations may be just as important as designing new types of drugs or pricing long-distance telephone calls. Thus, infrastructure activities cannot be ignored when formulating competitive strategies.

Pizza Industry Value Chain

Let us now apply the value chain concept to a service setting, using the pizza restaurant industry as our reference point (see Exhibit 3-2).

Exhibit 3-2   *Pizza Restaurant Industry Value Chain*

		Inbound Logistics	Operations	Outbound Logistics	Marketing/Sales	Service
SUPPORT ACTIVITIES	**Infrastructure**	Acquire capital, perform accounting, legal, and administrative tasks for each activity				
	Human Resource Management	Supervise warehouse or facilities/shipping personnel	Supervise kitchen personnel/training	Supervise drivers/ensure safety	Oversee marketing personnel	Oversee service personnel/waiters
	Technology Development	Improve supply chain to lower cost for ingredients	Develop new menu items; improve oven design	Develop new ordering systems to serve customs; improve delivery time	Develop new promotional materials/media	Develop new restaurant formats/layouts
	Procurement	Lease space for restaurants or delivery facilities	Purchase ingredients and other supplies	Purchase or lease telephone or online ordering systems	Buy TV time	Purchase furniture/tableware
PRIMARY ACTIVITIES		Transport ingredients to restaurants and delivery facilities	Prepare pizzas, salads, other food items	Deliver pizzas to ordering customers	Develop advertising copy, programs, promotions	Serve food in restaurants

Primary Activities

The value chain in this industry begins with transport of foodstuffs, such as dough, cheese, and pasta, from suppliers to restaurants (inbound logistics). Materials are then sliced, cut, cooked, heated, and assembled in each restaurant's kitchen into items such as pizza and salads (operations), which are then served to customers (service) or prepared for delivery (outbound logistics). In addition, customers must be persuaded to order pizzas (marketing/sales). Outbound logistics refers to delivery of pizzas to homes or workplaces. Customer service applies mostly to restaurant facilities.

Support Activities

Let us now examine the support these activities require.

Procurement. Trucks and warehouse space must be procured to perform inbound logistics activity; ovens and foodstuffs to perform operations; TV advertising to perform marketing/sales; and tables, chairs, and silverware to provide restaurant service. Because restaurant firms do not generally produce these inputs themselves, they must procure them from outside vendors. Identification of suppliers for these inputs, evaluation of supplier offerings, and negotiation of purchase terms are major procurement activities in this industry.

Technology Development. Movement of materials to restaurant sites can be improved by streamlining warehousing methods, kitchen operations by designing better ovens, marketing/sales by devising more effective advertising copy, outbound logistics with new means to track drivers, and customer service by improving restaurant design or online and telephone ordering. Opportunities for technology development thus exist in each primary activity of the industry.

Human Resource Management. Personnel responsible for inbound logistics, operations, outbound logistics, marketing, and customer service must be hired, trained, motivated, and supervised.

Infrastructure. Finally, those involved in primary activities need financing and budgeting assistance, accounting activities, and legal affairs. These are infrastructure activities.

Automobile Industry Value Chain

To illustrate the value chain in a manufacturing context, consider the automobile industry (see Exhibit 3-3).

Primary Activities

The value chain in this industry begins with transport of components from suppliers to auto assembly facilities (inbound logistics). Components are then assembled into finished autos (operations), and the finished cars are shipped to dealers (outbound logistics). Finally, dealers sell cars to customers (marketing/sales) and maintain the products owned by customers (service).

Exhibit 3-3   *Automobile Industry Value Chain*

		Inbound Logistics	Operations	Outbound Logistics	Marketing/ Sales	Service
SUPPORT ACTIVITIES	**Infrastructure**	←——— Acquire capital, perform accounting, legal, and administrative tasks for each activity ———→				
	Human Resource Management	Oversee warehouse and transport personnel	Supervise workforce, union relations	Oversee warehouse and transport personnel	Oversee advertising and sales personnel	Supervise maintenance personnel
	Technology Development	Work with suppliers to develop more efficient means of transporting parts	Improve product design and manufacturing processes; quality programs	Work with distributors and logistics firms to improve delivery	Improve marketing programs and dealership relations	Improve auto service procedures
	Procurement	Negotiate with suppliers to lower costs and improve quality	Purchase components and factory equipment; ensure supplier quality	Negotiate with distributors to lower costs and improve quality	Hire advertising agency; buy media time	Purchase tools for maintenance personnel
	PRIMARY ACTIVITIES	Transport components to assembly facilities	Make and assemble components into autos	Transport autos to dealers	Advertise, promote, and sell autos	Maintain and repair autos

Support Activities

These primary activities require assistance in each of the support areas noted previously.

Procurement. Work with suppliers and transport firms to secure parts and warehouse space; procure machinery, equipment, parts, and components to operate factories; media advertising space to conduct marketing/sales; and specialized tools, lubricants, parts, and diagnostic machines to provide auto service. Identification of suppliers for these inputs, evaluation of supplier offerings, and negotiation of prices are procurement activities. Note that procurement does not deal with the physical movement of goods or "logistics." Rather, it focuses on identification of suppliers, evaluation of supplier offerings, and negotiation of purchase terms.

Technology Development. Inbound and outbound logistics activities in the auto industry can be improved by redesigning the flow of component and finished product inventories in warehouses and transportation facilities to improve efficiency and timeliness. These initiatives include suppliers, distributors, logistics firms, railroads, and trucking companies. Auto firms can improve their operations by simplifying product design, introducing automated manufacturing techniques, using robots and computers, and redesigning factories to make work easier and more satisfying for employees. Marketing and sales can be improved through designing better advertising copy, whereas service activity can be improved by instituting more efficient repair procedures, training service personnel to be more responsive to customer needs, and installing more sophisticated diagnostic equipment. Activities undertaken to achieve such improvement are designated technology development.

Human Resource Management. Personnel performing primary activities must be recruited, trained, developed, motivated, and supervised. Human resource management, through its activities, helps improve product quality, innovation, and productivity.

Infrastructure. Primary activities require capital budgeting, financing, accounting, legal affairs, governmental affairs, and other administrative assistance. These infrastructure activities help automakers finance expansion, communicate with shareholders, and work with the government in implementing new types of environmental and fuel efficiency regulations.

The Value Chain as Part of a Business System

So far, we have seen how different activities make up the value chain. A firm need not always perform every single activity of the value chain. Indeed, most firms do not. The subset of value chain activities that a firm actually performs is referred to as its business system.[5] To illustrate, let us return to Pizza Hut, Domino's Pizza, and General Motors.

Pizza Hut

Pizza Hut's business system includes only a portion of the activities contained in its industry's value chain (see Exhibits 3-4A and 3-4B).

Primary Activities. Suppliers deliver food ingredients and other required products to Pizza Hut's restaurants. Consequently, Pizza Hut performs little inbound logistics activity. Traditionally, Pizza Hut's restaurant business performed no outbound logistics because customers come to its restaurants to be served. However, Pizza Hut has been extensively involved in operations (food preparation), marketing/sales (mainly advertising), and service (serving restaurant customers). Once Pizza Hut started offering delivery of pizzas, outbound logistics became a core activity. These four activities are therefore integral parts of its business system.

Support Activities. Pizza Hut conducts procurement activity for each of its primary activities. For example, it procures dough, cheese, ingredients, and ovens for operations; drivers and telephone ordering systems for outbound logistics; TV advertising time for marketing/sales; and tables, chairs, and silverware for service. It also conducts technology development for most primary activities. For example, Pizza Hut devotes considerable effort to improve pizza-making procedures, to enhance advertising copy, to streamline restaurant design, and to reduce wait-time for online delivery orders. It also conducts extensive human resource management and

Exhibit 3-4A   Pizza Hut's Business System

SUPPORT ACTIVITIES	Infrastructure	◄——— Administrative, legal, and accounting tasks managed systemwide ———►			
	Human Resource Management	Performed by external suppliers	Supervise kitchen personnel/ training	Supervise drivers/ ensure safety	Oversee marketing personnel	Oversee waiters/ service personnel
	Technology Development	Outsourced to software companies	Develop new menu items; improve oven design	Develop new ordering systems to serve callers; improve delivery time	Develop new promotions on a regular basis	Develop new restaurant formats
	Procurement	Lease space for restaurants and delivery facilities	Purchase ingredients and other supplies	Purchase or lease telephone or online ordering systems	Buy TV time	Purchase furniture, tableware
PRIMARY ACTIVITIES		Performed by external suppliers	Prepare pizzas, salads, other food items	Deliver pizzas to ordering customers	Develop advertising copy, programs, promotions	Serve food in restaurants
		Inbound Logistics	Operations	Outbound Logistics	Marketing/ Sales	Service

infrastructure activities for each primary activity. These support activities are therefore integral parts of its business system.

Domino's Pizza

Primary Activities. Suppliers deliver food ingredients and other required products to Domino's Pizza food preparation facilities. As with Pizza Hut, the company performs little inbound logistics activities. Compared with Pizza Hut, Domino's offers only pizza delivery. Thus, outbound logistics is a core activity that Domino's Pizza uses to distinguish itself. Domino's is also actively involved in operations (food preparation) and marketing/sales (advertising and product promotion). Domino's offers no restaurant service.

Support Activities. Domino's Pizza engages in procurement activity for each of its primary activities. It purchases food ingredients as well as ovens for operations, drivers and telephone/online ordering systems for outbound logistics, and TV advertising time for marketing sales. The firm also conducts technology development activity for many primary activities.

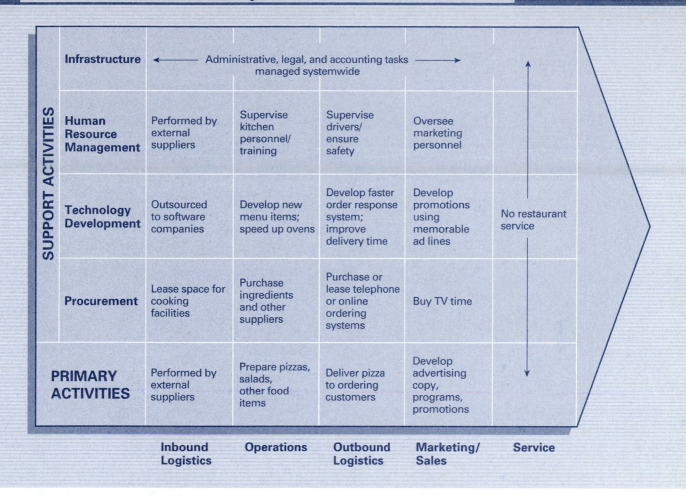

Domino's Pizza Business System — Exhibit 3-4B

		Inbound Logistics	Operations	Outbound Logistics	Marketing/Sales	Service
SUPPORT ACTIVITIES	Infrastructure	← Administrative, legal, and accounting tasks managed systemwide →				
	Human Resource Management	Performed by external suppliers	Supervise kitchen personnel/ training	Supervise drivers/ ensure safety	Oversee marketing personnel	No restaurant service
	Technology Development	Outsourced to software companies	Develop new menu items; speed up ovens	Develop faster order response system; improve delivery time	Develop promotions using memorable ad lines	
	Procurement	Lease space for cooking facilities	Purchase ingredients and other suppliers	Purchase or lease telephone or online ordering systems	Buy TV time	
	PRIMARY ACTIVITIES	Performed by external suppliers	Prepare pizzas, salads, other food items	Deliver pizza to ordering customers	Develop advertising copy, programs, promotions	

Domino's continues to refine its menu with new offerings, rolls out new marketing campaign ideas, and finds new ways to improve driver/delivery time. It also conducts extensive human resource management and infrastructure activities for each primary activity. These support activities are therefore key parts of its business system.

General Motors

General Motors' business system is shown in Exhibit 3-5. As indicated, it includes many but not all activities of the automobile industry value chain.

Primary Activities. GM purchases an increasing number of components from outside suppliers. These purchased components are generally delivered to GM's facilities by other firms, such as trucking and railroad companies. Consequently, GM depends more heavily on these firms for efficient and reliable delivery of parts to its factories (inbound logistics). It builds and assembles components into automobiles and trucks (operations). GM delivers finished autos and

Exhibit 3-5   General Motors' Business System

SUPPORT ACTIVITIES	Infrastructure	← Administrative, legal, and accounting tasks → managed systemwide				
	Human Resource Management	Oversee personnel involved in supplier management tasks	Develop new virtual teams; union relations; oversee workers	Oversee personnel involved in managing distribution	Oversee marketing personnel	
	Technology Development	Streamline turnaround time with suppliers to ship parts	Invest in new engine designs, car models; develop new factories and tooling	Streamline shipping time; web-based inventory tracking	Work with dealers to improve selling and product mix	No direct service to customers
	Procurement	Streamline documentation and ordering systems	Source parts and components; partner with key suppliers	Purchase capacity on railroads/ trucks	Buy media time; work with advertisers	
	PRIMARY ACTIVITIES	Adopt faster means to order and receive parts/ components	Make and assemble components into autos	Ship to dealers using railroads/ trucks; deliver vehicles	Advertise to promote product to public; work with dealerships	
		Inbound Logistics	Operations	Outbound Logistics	Marketing/ Sales	Service

Adapted with the permission of The Free Press, a Division of Simon & Schuster Adult Publishing Group, from *Competitive Advantage: Creating and Sustaining Superior Performance*, by Michael E. Porter. Copyright © 1980, 1998 by Michael E. Porter. All rights reserved.

trucks to dealers using railroads and its own fleet of distributors (outbound logistics). GM advertises and promotes its products but leaves the actual selling up to its dealers; it thus performs only a portion of the marketing/sales activity associated with its industry. Independently owned dealers maintain and repair GM vehicles, so GM is not significantly involved in auto service.

Support Activities. Procurement activities for GM include purchase of components for cars, factory equipment from machine tool and electronics companies, automotive paints and coatings from chemical firms, and lubricants and supplies from oil and chemical companies. Recent procurement initiatives have focused on reducing the amount of paperwork (documentation) needed to fulfill orders. General Motors devotes considerable effort to technology development for its key value-adding activities. For example, it is attempting to improve internal warehousing and factory inventory control through just-in-time (JIT) techniques. GM has invested heavily in new forms of factory automation and software to improve both product quality and the responsiveness of its factories. GM also commits substantial resources and effort to managing the human resource function. For example, it must work closely with the union leadership to create new labor contracts. Within individual plants, GM attempts to cooperate with workers to find new ways and insights to build better cars. By encouraging its workforce to look for new ways to improve quality and reduce waste, GM hopes to make continuous quality improvement an integral part of its business system. Finally, it has an extensive group of people working in legal affairs and government relations. In recent years, the company has spent considerable time working with consumer groups and government safety boards.

Capability Drivers

Once a firm's various activities have been identified using the value chain, an analyst interested in strategy must then assess the firm's capability in performing each activity. Any activity that the firm can perform more efficiently than its rivals (because fewer resources are required) or more effectively than rivals (because greater customer benefits are produced with the same resources) constitutes a strength. Similarly, activities that the firm performs less efficiently and effectively than rivals constitute weakness. The specific attributes and practices that determine efficiency and effectiveness differ markedly across industries. For example, the practices that enable the Walt Disney Company to excel in theme park operations are very different from those underpinning Intel's success in microprocessors. As a result of these differences, it is difficult to provide general guidance to a strategy analyst on what to look for when trying to assess a firm's strengths and weaknesses. However, guidance is possible at a more general level. In most industries, enduring competitive strength (that is, strength that cannot be easily duplicated or imitated by rivals) derives from a few fundamental capability drivers. **Capability drivers** represent broad routes to achieving competitive strength regardless of the particular industry setting in which a firm operates. By assessing capability drivers underlying an activity, an analyst can often gain valuable insight into whether a firm possesses strength in performing the activity. In this section, we examine four common capability drivers—first-mover status, scale, experience, and interrelationships—and consider the kinds of competitive strength provided by each.

First-Mover Status

Early entrants to an industry sometimes enjoy benefits that are not available to firms arriving later. These benefits are referred to as **first-mover advantages.**[6] Common benefits in this category are patent protection, a government license, superior location, channel access, supply access, reputation, and in some cases, organizational factors (see Exhibit 3-6). In most instances, a firm attempting to exploit a first-mover advantage must move quickly to penetrate its market and stake out its position. More often than not, first-mover advantages allow a new firm to seize the initiative early on, but the firm must be able to reinforce its position through sustained investment and continuous innovation. Because established firms have operated in the

capability drivers:
The basic economic and strategic means by which a firm builds an underlying source of competitive advantage in its market or industry. Examples of basic capability drivers include first-mover advantages, economies of scale, experience effects, and interrelationships among business units.

first-mover advantages:
The benefits that firms enjoy from being the first or earliest to compete in an industry.

Common First-Mover Advantages   Exhibit 3-6

- Patents
- License
- Location
- Channel access
- Supply access
- Reputation

competitive environment for longer periods, they often possess commanding, but not impenetrable, advantages over new entrants in these areas.

Patent Protection.

Early entrants sometimes own patents on important technology. They enjoy a strong competitive advantage over later entrants that must either circumvent the patented technology or develop a new one on their own. Xerox Corporation, for example, held early patent rights to the xerographic duplicating process. These rights gave it a strong advantage over other entrants during the long period over which the patents applied. In the pharmaceutical industry, patents are a critically important source of advantage, because they legally protect the chemical composition of a drug from unauthorized duplication by other firms. Blood pressure medications, cholesterol-lowering drugs, advanced treatments for diabetes, cancer drugs, and genetically engineered proteins are among some of the hundreds of products and technologies for which pharmaceutical companies need patents. Chemical firms also rely heavily on patents to protect the proprietary formulas that make up their key products (for example, engineered plastics and superstrong fibers) and manufacturing processes (for example, carbon fiber weaving and spinning). Patents thus represent a very strong source of competitive advantage in the pharmaceutical and other science-based industries.

Licenses.

A government license is needed to operate some businesses. Licenses are necessary, for example, to operate an airline, a radio or TV station, an electric generation facility, and a gas distribution company. Governments often limit the number of licenses they make available. Once all available licenses have been issued, new entrants may be blocked from entering an industry or, if allowed to enter, may be forced to operate at a disadvantage. Thus, early holders of licenses have a significant competitive advantage over later entrants. Most recently, the U.S. government over the past three years has auctioned off a large portion of the radio frequency spectrum that it once reserved for its own security uses. Many bidders from the telecommunications industry, particularly wireless firms such as Verizon Wireless and NextWave Communications, bought frequencies for use in their own plans to offer high-speed data and voice communications.

Firms can also create their own versions of licenses to protect their first-mover advantages. Licenses created by a firm can help protect intellectual property that includes product designs, concepts, ideas and technologies. Licenses enable firms to earn profits from their intellectual property by requiring an authorized user to pay for the use of the firm's idea. A company will often discover that its patents may have alternative uses that extend beyond the original product or process. Thus, it may offer to allow another firm to use its patent by issuing a license in exchange for a fee, access to the other firm's technology, or other consideration. 3M, for example, has thousands of patents related to its proprietary adhesive and coatings-based products and technologies. In recent years, 3M has begun to license its patents to other firms who may want to speed up their own product development ideas. In another example, software companies such as Microsoft and Oracle have spent billions developing their operating systems and network platforms for business applications. However, these companies have shrewdly used licenses not only to protect their intellectual property, but also to allow other firms to use their patented technologies and software packages for a predetermined fee or royalty. Both the Walt Disney Company and McDonald's use licensing as a way to profit from the creation of distinctive toys based on their companies' popular line of cartoon figures and personalities.

Location Sites.

In some industries, a suitable location is an important source of competitive advantage. A waterfront site, for example, may be useful to a boat dealer; a site near a busy intersection is often useful for a fast-food operator. By entering an industry early, leaders can sometimes preempt the best locations. In some industries, such as resource extraction, location can be an essential source of competitive advantage. Later entrants must often make do with less attractive sites.

Channel Access. Early entrants sometimes lock up the most desirable channels of distribution. Newer entrants or smaller existing firms then have difficulty finding outlets for their products, and they must often engage in extensive promotions and negotiations with wholesalers and retailers to obtain suitable shelf space. Once established, the early entrants can then build market share that is difficult for later entrants to challenge successfully. For example, new entrants in the packaged goods field—canned goods, beverages, breakfast cereal, diapers, personal care products—often face this challenge. The chief distribution channels for such products are supermarkets. Because of limited capacity, supermarkets often restrict the amount of shelf space they devote to each product category to just two or three brands, giving preference to well-known brands that can generate the most volume. Because of this policy, smaller firms and later entrants often experience difficulty getting their products on the shelf.

Supply Access. Early entrants can sometimes monopolize critical supplies. Later entrants then experience difficulty securing inputs for their own operations. U.S. Steel, for example, once controlled the world's richest iron ore deposits. Exclusive access to this valuable resource gave it a formidable advantage over newcomers forced to rely on more costly supplies that often required high transportation costs. Now some of the most important deposits of iron ore are found in Brazil and Australia.

Firms do not necessarily have to own a resource to enjoy exclusive access. A long-term supply contract can sometimes produce the same benefit. Large food processors, for example, sometimes dominate supply by entering into long-term contracts with groups or cooperatives of farmers in a region. In the Midwest, companies such as Pillsbury, General Mills, Kellogg, Carnation, Archer-Daniels-Midland (ADM), and Cargill are large purchasers of wheat and corn. They often buy huge amounts of wheat and corn through long-term contracts with farmers for use in making processed foods. This practice can make it difficult for a small processor to secure low-cost supplies.

Reputation. Many customers have already used products made by companies who have built important brand recognition. If satisfied, they will often seek out the same brand when making subsequent purchases. Even customers who have not yet tried an industry's product will often be familiar with a well-known brand and therefore may give it higher preference when making their first purchase. For example, customers are more likely to place a higher degree of trust with brand-name products and medications rather than "generic" versions if the price differential is not too great.

Scale of Operation

As companies grow, they produce, distribute, sell, and advertise in greater volume than smaller firms and later entrants. Their greater volume allows them to take advantage of economies of scale within many primary and supporting value-adding activities. Research has shown that as the scale of many business activities increases, the cost of carrying them out per unit of output declines.[7] This phenomenon is shown in Exhibit 3-7. Among the most

Exhibit 3-7 | *Economies of Scale*

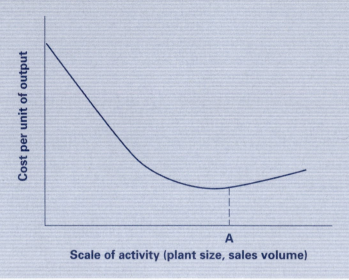

Exhibit 3-8 | *Major Contributors to Economies of Scale*

- Specialization
- Fixed-cost spreading
- Purchase discounts
- Vertical integration

important contributors to economies of scale, shown in Exhibit 3-8, are specialization, fixed-cost spreading, purchase discounts, and vertical integration.

Specialization. As the scale of an activity increases, more employees are needed to carry it out. The more employees who are involved in performing an activity, the greater are the opportunities for individuals to specialize. Because specialization fosters expertise, increasing scale often enhances productivity.

Fixed-Cost Spreading. Many fixed costs (for example, technology development and automated production equipment) do not increase proportionally as an activity expands in size. These costs can therefore be spread over a larger number of units as an activity increases, resulting in declining per-unit cost. Because large firms can operate activities on a big scale, they often have greater opportunity to spread and amortize fixed costs than smaller rivals or later entrants.

Purchase Discounts. Because large purchasers frequently enjoy high bargaining power, suppliers frequently extend them quantity discounts. Greater volume—and therefore greater profit—allows suppliers to offer large, established firms in the industry major discounts on components, inputs, and other raw materials, which may not be available to smaller rivals.

Planning and Administration: Samsung Electronics[8]

STRATEGIC COMPETENCY *in action*

In 2003 and 2004, Samsung Electronics burst onto the global marketplace with a broad range of cutting-edge products that astonished the consumer. Largely an unknown Korean-based company as recently as five years ago, Samsung is emerging as the market leader across key products and technologies, including flat-screen televisions, flash memory chips, cellular phones, DVD players, MP3 players, and microwave ovens. From $32 billion in revenues in 2002, Samsung is pushing to exceed $80 billion by 2009. This amazing transformation has pushed Samsung into the forefront of new digital technologies that offer new forms of communication, entertainment, and convenience for consumers. Samsung's most recent marketing campaigns promote the company's products with the new "Digit-All" logo that reflect both the company's technological strengths and the future direction of consumer electronics. Yet, behind Samsung's stunning success rests a series of important steps that the company has taken to bolster its value-adding activities.

Samsung relies heavily on building ever-larger plants that offer huge economies of scale. For example, Samsung spent $19 billion to construct state-of-the-art factories to produce memory chips that drive performance of many computer and consumer electronic devices. With these investments, Samsung has propelled itself into the number one maker of these chips, and has overtaken Intel in 2004 in producing flash memory chips. Unlike standard memory chips, flash memory chips retain data after power is shut down. Digital cameras, MP3 players, and cell phones consume vast amounts of flash memory chips, and Samsung continues to design and produce a new generation of flash memory devices that offer more performance at less cost. Next-generation Samsung chips will let cell phones manage twenty hours of talk time, while holding two thousand songs, eight hours of video, and play 3-D games. Samsung has also invested heavily in new factories to become a leader in producing liquid crystal displays (LCDs) that are vital for flat-screen television sets and cell phones. LCDs are becoming the basis for newly redesigned consumer appliances that offer better picture quality and resolution with less space needed. In both memory chips and LCDs, Samsung has become so efficient at producing these components that it sells vast amounts of them to other companies to incorporate in their products as well. In fact, Samsung's LCD technology is so advanced that it provides many of the flat screens that are now used in rival Sony's television sets.

Samsung also believes in strong vertical integration among its components and end products. Samsung is the world's number three producer of digital cell phones, behind Nokia and Motorola. Yet, unlike these two firms, Samsung produces all of the chips and displays that go into its phones, thus enabling it to lower costs even further. In contrast, Nokia and Motorola purchase most of the chips that power their phones. Samsung's vertical integration approach is not limited to cell phones alone; Samsung chips, displays, power supplies, and other components drive the company's major product lines. Through total control over its operational activities, Samsung has been able to develop new products quickly. For example, Samsung rolls out a new cell phone model in the United States every two weeks. It was also the first company to merge the cell phone with an MP3 player, and it will soon introduce a combination TV-cell phone. Vertical integration also allows Samsung to put its chips and displays into a new line of refrigerators, air conditioners, and microwave ovens that can be powered through a wireless home network. These leading-edge digital appliances will enable Samsung to influence future home designs that will offer greater convenience.

In those parts of the company that are weak, Samsung spares no effort to build up its competitive strengths. In the past, Samsung was best known for producing inexpensive, "me-too" products that imitated other companies' designs. Most consumers had come to expect Samsung to produce copycat products with little creativity or design flair. For example, Samsung's earlier microwave ovens were built from General Electric's original designs. Realizing that this reputation would serve as a ceiling that would limit Samsung's global aspirations, the company invested heavily in its design staff. Samsung now employs more than 350 people (double the number five years ago) to design ever-thinner LCD televisions, sleeker cell phones, and home appliances that have softer edges and ergonomic features. These efforts have paid off handsomely; in 2002, Samsung won five Industrial Design Excellence Awards for its digital appliances—a feat matched only by Apple Computer. Samsung's young design staff are given free reign to test new product concepts. They also work closely with market researchers and manufacturing engineers to ensure that innovative designs can also be produced at low cost (and sold at high prices). Samsung's emphasis on design has also changed the focus of its marketing. Samsung will no longer offer its products up for sale at discounters such as Wal-Mart and Target. Instead, the company has made a huge push to dominate the shelves of Best Buy and Circuit City where prices are often higher. Samsung's ambitions are not confined solely to consumer electronics, semiconductors, and cell phones; the company has begun working with Maytag Corporation to design and build a new line of home appliances that use advanced electronics. Samsung is also investing heavily in research, spending over $3 billion a year. It already employs over twenty thousand people in fifteen labs spread around the world.

Vertical Integration. Vertical integration refers to the expansion of the firm's value chain to include activities once performed by its suppliers and buyers. By manufacturing inputs itself, a firm can eliminate the potentially high costs associated with locating suppliers, evaluating the quality of their products, negotiating purchase contracts, and litigating disputes. A large firm is usually in a better position than a smaller one to make its own inputs, because it consumes inputs in greater volume and can therefore operate larger, more efficient facilities to produce them. Similarly, large firms are often in a superior position than smaller firms or new entrants to undertake activities that its buyers once performed. Thus, large established firms are in a better position than smaller rivals to reduce a variety of different costs by pursuing vertical integration. (Vertical integration is discussed more fully in Chapter 6.)

Experience

As an organization's experience in carrying out an activity increases, the cost of performing the activity often declines on a per-unit basis. Cost reductions of this sort are called **economies of experience.**[9] Continuous repetition of activities that allow for improvements with each successive repetition is the basis of economies of experience. Established firms have more opportunity than later entrants to make such improvements because they typically have greater experience conducting and improving their activities.

A typical experience curve, also known as a learning curve, is shown in Exhibit 3-9. Its vertical axis is the same as an economies of scale curve, cost per unit of output. Its horizontal axis is different, however; it depicts the number of units processed (that is, produced, sold, or serviced) since a firm began performing that activity. This variable is customarily referred to as **cumulative volume.** The most important processes that facilitate declining costs with growing cumulative volume are employee learning, product redesign, and process improvement (see Exhibit 3-10).

Employee Learning. As employees repeat activities, they learn how to carry them out more quickly and accurately. The net result is continuing improvement in both productivity

economies of experience:
Cost reductions that occur from continuous repetition of activities that allow for improvement with each successive act (also known as experience curve effects or learning curve effects).

cumulative volume:
The quantity that a firm has produced since the beginning of that activity, up to this point in time.

Exhibit 3-9   Economies of Experience

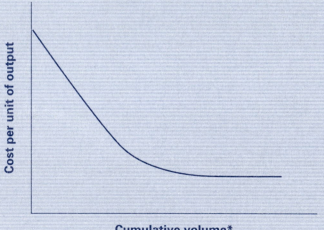

*Number of units produced (or sold, serviced, developed, etc.) since commencing an activity.

Major Contributors to Experience Benefits	Exhibit 3-10

- Employee learning
- Product redesign
- Process improvement

Creating Distinctive Value: Toyota Motor of Japan[10]

In 2003, Toyota Motor of Japan had become the world's second largest auto producer, overtaking Ford Motor Company in worldwide market share (10 percent) and is hoping to overtake General Motors by 2010. According to many analysts, Toyota has the depth of talent, financial clout, manufacturing capability, and product quality that will enable it to grow faster than its rivals to achieve global dominance of the automobile industry. In the United States alone, over the past five years, Toyota's sales have jumped over 36 percent without resorting to heavy discounting or massive use of rebates. Toyota is already in excellent position to displace DaimlerChrysler to become the third member of the Big Three in the United States. As Toyota continues to gain on its rivals, other automotive companies are seeking to adopt many of the same techniques and methods that have propelled Toyota to the top of the industry.

One of Toyota's most important competitive weapons is the practice of *kaizen*. Roughly translated, *kaizen* means the search for continuous improvement in every aspect of designing and building a car. No part of the car or the production process escapes scrutiny for potential improvement. For example, factory management, engineers, and workers on the line study each part to look for ways to reduce its manufacturing cost and/or to improve its durability or ease of assembly. Pioneered in the 1950s by Taiichi Ohno, a legendary Toyota engineer, kaizen depends heavily on cultivating each employee's ability to identify new and better ways of doing things. In the past, when Mr. Ohno trained recruits to practice kaizen, he compelled each trainee to watch a particular job or task until the person could identify ways to improve it. Legend has it that some trainees could stand there for an entire day before they could give Mr. Ohno a satisfactory answer. Over the ensuing decades, kaizen has been deeply interwoven in every aspect of Toyota's operations. Although kaizen is focused on improving both products and processes, the heart of kaizen rests in empowering employees to think for themselves. Employees are often given special rewards for isolating and fixing errors and problems on the production line. Continuous improvement of Toyota's processes and work flow enables the Japanese firm to accelerate time-to-market for new car models and to reduce its inbound logistics, operations, and outbound logistics costs.

Another central part of Toyota's famed production system is the practice of "error-proofing," or "poke-yoke" in Japanese. This practice relies heavily on using electronic sensors to help workers detect missing parts or improperly assembled components. Toyota also designed another method to eliminate errors by synchronizing the way that parts move down the assembly line. Parts are transported in shelves or buckets that match the exact vehicle they were designed for, thus ensuring that workers on the line would install the right part for the right vehicle.

Toyota's production system has long been considered far more efficient than systems found in the United States. Toyota practices "lean production," which relies heavily on suppliers to ship parts when they are needed. In the most efficient Toyota plants, the typical assembly line contains only eighty minutes' worth of parts. This "just-in-time" approach to production means that Toyota and its suppliers must ensure that parts are designed and built according to very tight quality specifications in order to avoid costly shutdowns of the assembly line. Consequently, Toyota's ability to build a car without relying on large warehouses to hold vast amounts of inventory drives down production costs. Another series of Toyota initiatives to improve its already legendary efficiency seeks to use the same set of factory tooling to assemble its cars. This step will help Toyota build a greater variety of cars in each factory without the costly downtimes required to retool the assembly line for each car model. More recently, Toyota just announced an internal program known as CCC21, which stands for Construction of Cost Competitiveness for the 21st Century. The goal of CCC21 is to dramatically cut the number of parts needed to make parts. By working jointly with its key suppliers, Toyota hopes to slice the costs of more than 170 key parts that make up 90 percent of its part costs. In 2003, Toyota removed $2.6 billion out of its $113 billion in manufacturing costs without any plant closures or layoffs. The company is attempting to replicate this performance again for 2004.

To further increase the appeal of Toyota's already popular cars, the company has been investing heavily in hybrid engine technology. The Toyota Prius, which is one of the first commercially available hybrid cars in the United States, uses a gasoline engine and an electric motor to increase fuel efficiency. A second-generation Prius incorporates many improvements to the engine that boost performance without sacrificing its thrifty fuel consumption. Toyota's Lexus division has begun to incorporate hybrid engines in its RX 330 line of sport-utility crossover vehicles as well.

Toyota also wants consumers to buy its cars because of their distinctive, sleek looks. The company's design studios in Southern California, France, and Japan are now competing with one another to push the leading edge of design so that future Toyota cars will be known for their looks as well as for their traditional quality. Toyota also organizes its design activities differently from its rivals. At Toyota, designers, engineers, product planners, and suppliers are expected to work together to brainstorm and develop new ideas. Engineers talk about the manufacturability of the design concept, while product planners assess if the new design will sell. Suppliers, in turn, provide guidance as to how best use existing components and parts to reduce costs. This process helps Toyota reduce the time needed to bring a new car concept to market. Many Toyota models are designed and produced in under two years, compared with an average three years for the rest of the industry.

and quality as employees' experience base expands. For example, workers in factories learn how to use their tools better, how to set up equipment more quickly, and when to perform equipment maintenance to avoid breakdown. This is why the know-how and insight provided by employees can become valuable "hidden" assets. Long-term technicians or employees in a factory or laboratory, for example, often "know the ropes" of how to perform their tasks with a much higher degree of efficiency than newly hired employees or outsiders. Long-term personnel also know when an operational process or activity is running correctly, and can thus detect quality problems before they occur. This source of knowledge avoids costly mistakes when designing and implementing new technologies. Equally important, this source of knowledge is difficult for rivals to imitate, and thus confers an important source of competitive advantage.

Among the first to study this phenomenon systematically were engineers at Wright-Patterson Air Force Base in Ohio. As they studied contractors building aircraft for the U.S. Air Force, they noticed that the labor time needed to assemble an aircraft of a particular type tended to decline as more and more aircraft of the same type were produced. In fact, a systematic relationship was discovered. The number of direct labor hours used in assembling each aircraft tended to decline by about 20 percent with each doubling of cumulative volume. Thus, if 3,000 direct labor hours were required to produce the first unit of an aircraft model, only about 2,400 hours $(0.80 \times 3,000)$ would be needed for the second, 1,920 hours $(0.80 \times 0.80 \times 3,000)$ for the third, and so on. Observers attributed this decline to learning on the part of employees involved. Similar declines have been observed in a wide range of manufacturing and service settings.

Product Redesign. As a firm's engineers become more familiar with the way a product is manufactured, they can often redesign components that cause problems in later assembly, reduce the number of components needed to make the product, and substitute better materials. These changes not only reduce manufacturing costs but help improve product quality as well. For example, large Japanese manufacturers of consumer electronics such as Sony, Hitachi, Matsushita, Sharp, Sanyo, and Toshiba have successfully engaged in ongoing programs of redesigning each new generation of consumer electronics (for example, televisions, DVD players, and home appliances) to use fewer but better components. Likewise, engineers at Texas Instruments, who have worked on designing and making sophisticated chips for cell phones for two decades, have been able to shrink the number of chips required to power a phone from over sixteen to just one. Nokia, Sony-Ericsson, Motorola, and Samsung are racing one another to design increasingly more versatile digital wireless phones that use fewer microchips to transmit and receive signals of all types. These same phones also incorporate digital cameras, MP3 players, and other features to enhance the device's overall functionality. Similarly, designers of videogame consoles (for example, Sony and Nintendo) are creating even more versatile devices that not only use fewer and more powerful chips, but they are also able to perform many more tasks than those from previous generations.

Process Improvement. Increasing experience also enables engineers to improve the process by which a product is manufactured through such means as changing the work flow and altering equipment design. Continuous improvements in these areas can, over time, not only reduce manufacturing cost but enhance product quality and reliability as well. For example, Intel is leading the way to develop ever-smaller microprocessors and other chips through extensive process improvement efforts. Intel spends billions every year on new chip-making equipment and process technologies to drive down the cost of making ever more powerful chips. Process improvement initiatives based on long-held experience are also important in the energy industry. Companies exploring and producing oil, for example, are now using advanced, proprietary imaging and software-driven techniques to locate more promising wells. Once these wells are discovered, oil companies can improve the efficiency or yield of a given field by injecting ceramic "cracking" agents into the ground to loosen up the oil. These steps help boost the productivity of locating and producing more oil.

Interrelationships

Competitive advantage can also come from carefully managed interrelationships with other businesses of the same firm. Interrelationships enable a firm's businesses to transfer resources and share activities among each other. We will discuss these mechanisms at length in later chapters. By way of introducing that material, let us briefly examine the chief benefits these two mechanisms can provide.

Resource Transfer. If one business possesses a resource of value to another, then transfer of the resource across the two businesses can provide a potentially valuable competitive advantage. Many different kinds of resources are potential candidates for such transfer: cash, personnel, information, and different forms of knowledge or expertise in particular.

To illustrate the value of transferring expertise between businesses, consider the interrelationships among PepsiCo's different businesses. Personnel in its soft drink and other beverage businesses are highly skilled in such activities as market research, market segmentation, consumer promotion, and TV advertising. These skills are valuable and can be transferred to PepsiCo's snack food unit, Frito-Lay. Frito-Lay, in turn, can apply these skills to its business to create new product concepts or enter new markets. By transferring expertise from its beverage businesses to its snack food unit, the Frito-Lay unit enjoys an advantage not available to rivals lacking this kind of interrelationship.

Activity Sharing. Two or more businesses can sometimes share a common activity, thereby eliminating unnecessary duplication and high activity costs. Sharing permits operation of value-adding activities on a larger, more efficient scale than would be possible for any single business acting on its own. In effect, sharing a critical resource enables the firm to exploit potentially significant cost savings among a number of businesses, or to enhance and deepen the skills needed to compete. Large, diversified firms with established market positions in several different industries or market segments share activities in numerous ways to create competitive advantage. For example, most of PepsiCo's businesses make heavy use of TV advertising. By pooling their advertising effort, they can combine multiple products within the same message, achieve quantity discounts on purchase of TV time, and create bargaining power with media firms. Similarly, 3M's overall competitive position among a number of different businesses—tapes, weather stripping, automotive finishing products, sandpaper, and specialized paints—is significantly bolstered when the company is able to share its highly proficient R&D skills and marketing to accelerate product innovation and to lower its costs. By pooling the knowledge and skills from different businesses, 3M can achieve the critical mass of talent to investigate new opportunities for innovation.

Assessing Competitive Advantage

Generally, only a few value-adding activities qualify for the advantages previously noted. Firms contemplating entry must therefore carefully examine each value-adding activity of established firms to determine where there may be opportunities to exploit any potential weaknesses or oversights. In this section, we present some considerations and guidelines for assessing firms' strengths and potential sources of competitive advantages.

First-Mover Advantages

In practice, only a few activities of the value chain generally qualify for first-mover advantages (see Exhibit 3-11). For example, in most industries only operational activities can derive much benefit from patent protection, since such protection generally applies to product design, product formulas, or manufacturing processes. Patents, however, cannot prevent competitors from attempting to do something different. Particularly in manufacturing processes, rivals and new entrants may sometimes be able to substitute a new or different process for the patented one. For example, a firm may be able to patent its discovery of a new production process to improve the quality of its integrated circuits. But that patent does not prevent another firm from discovering and exploiting an entirely new method to design an entirely different method for improving microchip production. Companies in the electronics, machinery, and medical device industries often seek to develop their own proprietary products, processes, and methods to circumvent the patents held by their rivals. Thus, for the vast majority of products, patents do not represent complete protection from imitation. Similarly, a government license is likely to be needed to perform only a few activities of the value chain. Included in this category are outbound logistics activity (for example, a radio station or a cellular telephone operator needs a license to transmit its signal), service (restaurants often need a license to process and sell food), and operations (a waste disposal company needs a license to operate a toxic waste dump). Likewise, the possession of intellectual property that enables a company to license its ideas and products to other firms will generally apply to only a few activities in the value chain, such as technology development and operations. These activities are therefore the most likely to benefit from first-mover advantage.

First-mover advantages carry their own set of disadvantages. For example, changes in technology or buying patterns can render an early-mover's advantage obsolete. During the early 1980s, minimills took advantage of major advances in steel-casting technology that made the larger, integrated steel companies' processes obsolete. First-mover advantages are particularly fleeting in high-technology industries, where the rapid pace of product and process innovation makes sustaining an early lead difficult. Companies can use a variety of different technologies and methods to create semiconductors, digital cell phones, MP3 players, and flat-screen televisions that circumvent patents held by other firms. Thus, a first-mover that invests large sums to patent a product or process may find itself "outflanked" by another firm that pursues a "fast-follower" strategy that focuses on improving upon a new or existing product design.

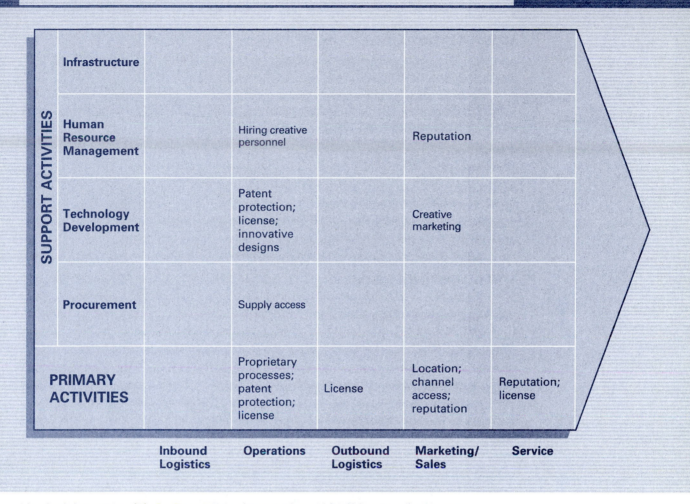

Activities Frequently Benefiting From First-Mover Advantages

Exhibit 3-11

SUPPORT ACTIVITIES		Inbound Logistics	Operations	Outbound Logistics	Marketing/ Sales	Service
Infrastructure						
Human Resource Management			Hiring creative personnel		Reputation	
Technology Development			Patent protection; license; innovative designs		Creative marketing	
Procurement			Supply access			
PRIMARY ACTIVITIES			Proprietary processes; patent protection; license	License	Location; channel access; reputation	Reputation; license

For example, Apple Computer developed the iPod digital music player that became a smashing success in 2004 and 2005. However, Sony and Microsoft are designing their own versions of a miniaturized digital music player that may soon give Apple's iPod serious competition. Apple's initial first-mover advantage may prove illusory if Sony is able to design an even more sleek and easier-to-use music player. Likewise, Netscape Communications popularized the concept of a web browser with its Netscape browser in 1995 to help people surf the web. Yet, Netscape's innovation did not provide the company with a long-term competitive advantage. Within a few years, Microsoft's Internet Explorer soon became the dominant browser as Microsoft incorporated its browser with its well-established Windows operating system. Microsoft was able to harness the power of strong interrelationships (that is, sharing technologies and marketing costs among its different software businesses) to blunt Netscape's edge.

In the broader retailing industry, large department stores such as Sears Roebuck and J. C. Penney pioneered the concept of offering a wide range of merchandise at reasonable cost to consumers for many decades. Wal-Mart Stores and other later-entrant discounters, however, seriously eroded the first-mover benefits of the larger, diversified department stores by developing new inventory-replenishment systems that enabled them to dramatically lower their operational costs. Over the past ten years, J. C. Penney was forced to undertake extremely expensive and time-consuming renovations and revamping of their merchandise mixes to win back customers they lost to other retailing entrants. Penney's was forced to close smaller stores and to develop its own inventory ordering and tracking system to lower its costs. To reverse its long-term decline, Sears Roebuck merged with Kmart Holdings in November 2004 to gain the critical mass needed to compete with Wal-Mart Stores and Target. The combined entity will begin to share merchandise and cross-sell each other products (for example, Kmart's line of Martha Stewart home accessories will be sold in Sears Stores, and Sears' line of Die-Hard batteries will be sold in some Kmart locations). Once-fierce competitors Federated Department Stores and May Department Stores are also seeking to merge their operations in order to better compete in this brutal retailing landscape. Some competitors, such as Montgomery Ward and Ames Department Stores, were eventually forced out of business because they could not readily adapt to the changing retailing environment.

Scale and Experience Advantages

To enjoy significant advantage from scale or experience, an activity must generally meet four requirements as shown in Exhibit 3-12: it must be centralized, it must be susceptible to scale or experience, it must be properly implemented, and the resulting benefits must be proprietary.

Centralization. Activities operated on a decentralized, fragmented basis cannot achieve significant critical mass; hence, they will rarely enjoy significant economies of scale. Decentralized activities will also rarely achieve significant experience curve benefits, since such benefits come from repetition of an activity by the same group of employees over many cycles. Thus, centralization of activities is generally a prerequisite before firms can reap the benefits of economies of scale and cumulative experience effects. In manufacturing activities, for example, centralization usually means consolidating the activities of many smaller factories into one larger factory.

Susceptibility. Because economies of scale are derived from such characteristics as specialization, spreading fixed costs, and quantity discounts, activities that provide opportunity for these processes to occur are particularly susceptible to producing scale advantage. In practice, value-adding activities differ widely in providing such opportunity. Manufacture of a standardized product, for example, provides considerable opportunity for these processes to occur, thus

Exhibit 3-12	**Requirements for Achieving Scale and Experience Advantage**

• Centralization	• Activity must be centralized
• Susceptibility	• Activity must be susceptible to the processes that produce scale and experience benefits
• Implementation	• Activity must be properly implemented
• Proprietary	• Benefits of scale and experience must be proprietary

promoting scale economies. Manufacture of custom-made products, on the other hand, generally offers few such opportunities, although recent developments in new technology may be relaxing this constraint. As a result, most custom-made products are significantly less susceptible to scale benefits.

One factor that complicates the assessment of scale susceptibility is the variation in scale benefits that occurs when scale of an activity increases. Consider most types of manufacturing activities, for example. They lend themselves to economies of scale as long as scale does not exceed a certain point. However, beyond this point, diseconomies of scale set in. This means further increase in scale then produces an increase rather than a decrease in unit cost. The letter *A* in Exhibit 3-7 indicates this point. Diseconomies of scale sometimes occur when the scale of an activity becomes very large, because employees involved in the activity become bored and disgruntled as their jobs become more specialized and they experience increasing communication problems as their numbers grow. Many observers suspect that GM suffered extensively from these difficulties in the recent past. It is also likely to be a primary reason why GM continues to search for ways to reduce the amount of in-house manufacturing that it performs.

Because beyond some point an increase in scale often raises rather than lowers unit cost, benefits that large firms can realize from increasing the scale of their activities are limited. However, for many activities, this point is not reached until considerable output is attained. Large, established firms are therefore often able to derive some scale advantage over smaller rivals in performing at least a few activities of the value chain.

Let us now consider susceptibility of activities to experience benefits. Processes that most likely benefit from experience-based advantage occur when there is significant employee learning, product redesign, and process improvement. These activities occur repeatedly within the firm and are hard for rivals and outsiders to learn. Manufacture of a standardized product that uses a highly sophisticated and finely-tuned production process, for example, provides ample opportunity of this sort and thus is often quite susceptible to experience benefits. Traditionally, production of custom-made products, by contrast, provided somewhat less of an opportunity for experience benefits, since employees had to use a different set of tools and methods for each product. However, even custom-made products and services now lend themselves to experience-based benefits as new technologies reduce the time and effort required to switch between product or service offerings. Consider, for example, the major advances made in laser-based eye surgeries that use state-of-the-art machines and techniques that require exceptionally high levels of skill and knowledge. Each patient that receives treatment is a "custom-job," so to speak, but the physician deepens his/her experience (and competitive advantage) with each new patient.

Effective Implementation. Although scale and experience provide firms with opportunities to develop competitive advantage, such benefits do not come automatically. Managers must work hard to achieve them through effective implementation of activities. General Motors' failure to realize scale and experience advantages despite its position as world leader of the automobile industry has resulted in part from serious implementation problems over a long period.

Proprietary Access. Established rivals can derive competitive advantage from scale and experience only if they retain proprietary access to the resulting benefits. Unfortunately, rivals can often easily imitate or develop substitutes for such benefits, thus neutralizing some of the early entrants' advantages. To illustrate, consider Pizza Hut's development of new menu items. Pizza Hut centralizes this activity to operate it on a larger scale than smaller rivals. However, rivals can easily copy or imitate new menu items as soon as Pizza Hut introduces them. Because Pizza Hut does not have proprietary access to menu innovations, it derives little competitive advantage from operating menu development activity on a large scale.

The situation is somewhat different with Pizza Hut's procurement of TV advertising time. In particular, the interrelationships that Pizza Hut can share with sister businesses KFC and Taco Bell enable Pizza Hut to enjoy significant discounts on media purchases. This benefit is more proprietary because smaller rivals cannot capture the discounts Pizza Hut receives nor duplicate them on their own. By way of its internal interrelationships, Pizza Hut thus enjoys an important scale advantage over smaller rivals in this area.

The Growth of the Internet and Competitive Advantage

The momentous rise of the Internet as a key distribution and marketing channel will redefine the basis of many firms' strategies to reach their customers in almost every industry. It is becoming clear that Internet-driven e-commerce applications will continue to expand across industries and markets. The Internet has already allowed firms in every industry to offer instantaneous service to customers and enables companies to become even closer to them. Online ordering and payment systems are extremely commonplace. Online management of suppliers and inventory levels is becoming widely practiced across a growing range of industries as well. Thus, the Internet's power is now felt along three key dimensions of competitive advantage.

Compressing the Value Chain

First and foremost, the Internet enables firms to establish direct links to almost anybody anywhere and to deliver new products and services at very low cost. The major challenge that the Internet poses to established brick-and-mortar businesses is that it enables innovative upstart firms to circumvent existing barriers to entry in many industries. Using the Internet, many companies (for example, Amazon.com, Overstock.com, TD Waterhouse, Vehix.com, Di-Tech.com) are finding they can establish a direct link to their customers and suppliers to perform transactions on a real-time basis. The Internet also enables firms to bypass many existing distribution channels (such as wholesalers, value-added resellers, and even retailers) to reach customers directly. This enables some firms to pass impressive cost savings directly to the customer (travel websites such as hotels.com, Orbitz, Travelocity, and Expedia.com). Likewise, websites such as automallusa.com, Vehix.com, and autobytel.com enable customers to preselect the type and model of car they want, the options they want to go with the car, and the dealer in a geographic area who is likely to have the lowest prices. Thus, the Internet is already serving as a giant, cyberspace-based "auction house" that compels firms to compete with one another on many price and product attributes. The result will likely be significant compression of current value chain configurations found in many industries today as firms find new ways to squeeze cost out of the system.

The Internet lends itself to immediate, real-time learning about and adjustment to customers' needs. Learning and product/service development cycles are becoming much shorter as a result. This new development compels firms to become faster in how they gather, synthesize, use, and disseminate information within the organization. Fast processing and synthesis of information to detect new market trends and emerging customer needs will become a new type of capability that firms must learn. Firms that learn the fastest and are most willing to experiment with new product and service offerings will become the best equipped to compete using the Internet. The faster a company learns, the more quickly it will be able to create new products and services for Internet customers. This in turn enables the company to capture a growing base of customers, thus allowing it to learn even more from the marketplace.[11]

A major by-product of the growth of the Internet is that it is now possible for some firms to serve customers as effectively over the computer as with an actual salesperson. Sophisticated web pages that offer customers a full array of product, service, and pricing information can perform many of the tasks that traditionally were associated with personalized selling. Thus, even the basic notion of how to sell to a customer will now come under great reexamination. For example, financial services companies' websites (such as TD Waterhouse and Fidelity Investments) provide the foundation and tools for customers to become more empowered to undertake financial planning and perform transactions on their own. In the motorcycle industry, Harley-Davidson's website enables customers to determine which type of motorcycle is best suited for their needs. Harley-Davidson's site also offers a full array of information about motorcycle accessory products, maintenance, and company-sponsored events that build a community of Harley fans.

Building Extended, Internet-Driven Supply Chains

The Internet also enables firms to work more closely with suppliers further upstream in the value chain. The automotive, aerospace, and semiconductor industries represent an area where large manufacturers (for example, General Motors, Cisco Systems, Boeing, Texas Instruments) are using the Internet to work with key suppliers to design new products and test new technologies jointly. For example, designs for new automotive parts are created at one supplier. It then forwards the design's technical specifications and other data electronically to the automotive firm through corporate intranets and extranets that prevent outsiders from eavesdropping or snooping on proprietary information. The automotive firm then uses the supplier's data to test the component in a variety of simulation exercises for different car models and driving conditions. The results of these experiments and tests are then returned to the supplier for additional improvements. The cumulative effect of using the Internet to create such "extended" supply chains greatly slices the amount of development time and resources needed to create next-generation designs. Organizing and managing these Internet-driven activities means that suppliers, firms, and customers must be able to freely exchange information, insights, and ideas to create new products and services quickly. Previously, designing and producing a new line of cars for General Motors and other U.S. firms required upwards of five years. Already, automakers are reducing the development cycle to less than twenty months by using new Internet-driven information and manufacturing technologies. GM uses the Internet to link up its vast, worldwide network of suppliers and engineers to test new design concepts before a single car is even built. The Internet's facilitation of far-reaching, "extended" supply chains enables firms to collaborate more effectively among each other to greatly cut down development time and costs. As supply chains expand in power and reach, so will the need for firms to understand how best to organize their knowledge and other value-creating activities with suppliers and customers.

Competitive Dynamics and the Internet

Broadly speaking, the Internet will cause almost every firm in every industry to rethink its relationships with distributors, retailers, and the end customer. As the Internet becomes more pervasive in every industry, the more innovative firms will seize the initiative in redefining what customers can expect in terms of value, pricing, delivery, and customization. Companies that use the Internet to listen to their customers and design products specifically for them will steadily accumulate market share from competitors that are slow to react. Over time, the number of competitors within an industry may drop as the winners continue to grab market share away from weaker firms. Although this process has always occurred in every industry for many decades, the Internet will likely hasten the process of "shaking out" weaker competitors who suffer declining market share. As the weaker firms' market shares decline, they cannot afford to invest in the newer technologies that allow them to reach and serve customers with innovative approaches. As customers steadily gravitate toward the faster-growing firms, the winners accumulate more economies of scale that, in turn, support further investments in new technologies.

Ironically, established brick-and-mortar businesses that may have not been the first to adopt the Internet but later aggressively embrace it as part of their total competitive strategy may be in the best position to benefit if and when their respective industries consolidate. First, such businesses are likely to have accumulated significant economies of scale and experience about how best to compete in their respective industry. They also likely have significant assets already in place that an upstart Internet firm will have to create from the ground up. Equally important, their brand identities are likely to offer competitive advantage and some initial defensive value, especially to customers who may be risk-averse to using the Internet. However, these preexisting advantages will dissipate over time if the established firm does not learn to compete with an Internet upstart that cleverly redesigns the industry's value chain from a novel perspective. Because the Internet dramatically changes the nature and cost of distribution and customer benefits, established firms must embrace the Internet early to help make online customer service a vital and complementary part of the way they do business. Thus, established businesses that quickly embrace and deploy the Internet can still effectively riposte new upstart firms and defend their competitive positions.

Diagnosing Pizza Hut's Capabilities

Assessing internal strengths and weaknesses is a highly complex task for several reasons. First, many firms generally perform numerous types of value-adding activities. Second, firms can derive several different kinds of advantage in performing each activity. Third, a variety of different economic or technical requirements must be satisfied before the various sources of competitive advantage can be realized.

To illustrate the complex nature of analyzing strengths and weaknesses, let us focus on Pizza Hut in an attempt to perform a summary analysis to demonstrate the power of internal analysis of strengths and weaknesses. Our objective is to identify the major advantages Pizza Hut enjoys over other rivals in each of the four areas discussed earlier. Exhibit 3-13 summarizes these advantages.

First-Mover Advantages

Many consumers have personal experience with Pizza Hut's restaurants. Even individuals who are not frequent consumers of pizza are often aware of Pizza Hut. They have become familiar with the company as a result of passing Pizza Hut units on the highway, testimonials from acquaintances, and the company's extensive TV advertising. In recent years, Pizza Hut has developed advertisements that are linked to blockbuster movies. This awareness predisposes them to consider Pizza Hut when selecting a restaurant. The firm thus enjoys a reputation advantage over other firms to a limited extent.

Pizza Hut's Sources of Competitive Advantage — Exhibit 3-13

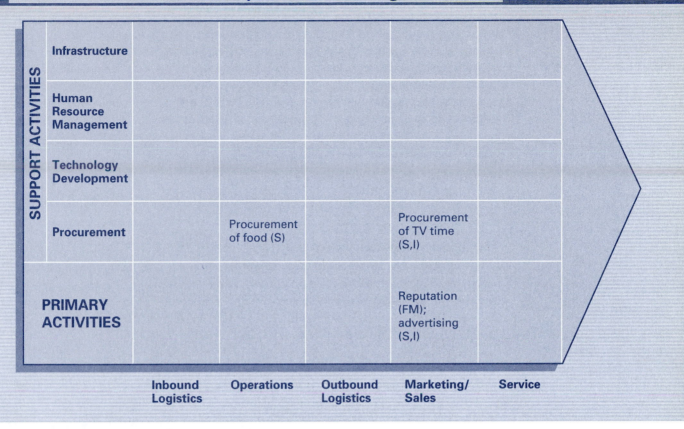

On the other hand, Pizza Hut enjoys little first-mover advantage in other value–adding activities. Possession of a license to operate, for example, means little, because any firm willing to enter the industry can easily obtain one in most areas. Consequently, Pizza Hut probably enjoys no first-mover advantage in this area. Patents are unimportant in this industry, since food-making technology and restaurant procedures are well known and easy to imitate. Pizza Hut thus enjoys no significant advantage in this area, either. Although it secured good restaurant sites initially, Pizza Hut enjoys only modest location advantage, because good alternative locations are still available in most areas. More important, other competitors such as Domino's Pizza and Papa John's International compete with Pizza Hut for new facilities in fast-growing suburban areas. Competitors can purchase from the same suppliers, so Pizza Hut enjoys no proprietary access to supplies. These considerations all point to the likelihood that this company enjoys no significant first-mover advantages except perhaps a small edge in reputation.

Scale Advantages

Pizza Hut's primary value-adding operational activity of preparing food and its service activity of serving restaurant customers are both carried out on a decentralized basis within in-dividual restaurants. Consequently, Pizza Hut derives few scale benefits in these two areas. On the other hand, it may derive some scale-based advantage from its TV advertising activity.

Advertising tends to be centralized, is highly susceptible to economies of scale (since TV advertising costs can be spread over Pizza Hut's many units), and produces benefits that are highly proprietary (since competitors cannot immediately appropriate such benefits). Pizza Hut thus enjoys a significant marketing/sales advantage over smaller or newly entering rivals.

Let us now consider support activities. Procuring food, since such activity is mostly centralized, is highly susceptible to economies of scale (because of quantity discounts) and produces benefits that are proprietary (because smaller competitors cannot achieve similar discounts). Pizza Hut's other support activities fail to satisfy one or another of the requirements for scale. Technology development is limited as an advantage because rivals easily imitate improvements resulting from it. Human resource management activities are confined within restaurants and therefore are highly decentralized, whereas infrastructure activities are not very susceptible to meaningful scale. Consequently, Pizza Hut probably enjoys few if any scale advantages outside advertising and procurement.

Experience Benefits

Many activities that Pizza Hut centralizes either are not very susceptible to experience benefits, (for example, procurement), or produce benefits that cannot be kept proprietary (for example, technology development). As a result Pizza Hut probably enjoys few significant experience advantages over smaller rivals.

Interrelationships

Pizza Hut enjoys several benefits from interrelationships with other Yum! Brands businesses, such as KFC, Taco Bell, A&W All-American Food Restaurants, and Long John Silver's. It can pool certain procurement activities—obtaining silverware, restaurant furnishings, ovens, and other materials—with those of other Yum! Brands businesses to achieve purchase discounts. It can draw on marketing expertise and expertise from these businesses as well. Pizza Hut can also negotiate advertising rates jointly with the other Yum!-based restaurant chains, thus enhancing its bargaining power and sharing advertising costs. These benefits provide it a significant marketing/sales advantage over smaller or nondiversified rivals.

Achilles' Heel of Established Firms

Thus far we have focused on potential advantages that established firms may enjoy over smaller rivals because of first-mover advantages, scale, experience, and interrelationships. These advantages do not come without trade-offs, however. Established firms tend to suffer from a distinct weakness that smaller rivals and new entrants can often avoid. Because of their large size and entrenched practices, they are often slower to respond to environmental change. Pizza Hut, for example, was late in responding to consumer demand for home delivery of pizza. In much the same way, General Motors was slow in responding to increased consumer demand for smaller automobiles.

Let us examine Pizza Hut's predicament in more detail. Consider how Domino's Pizza dramatically changed the competitive environment of the pizza industry during the mid-1980s, making substantial inroads by focusing its efforts on the one part of the industry's value chain that Pizza Hut (and everyone else) largely ignored—that of outbound logistics. Pizza Hut and other established pizza restaurants based their competitive strategies on the key assumption that customers preferred coming to restaurants to be served. Domino's Pizza redefined the competitive balance of the industry by developing a strategy based on home delivery. Domino's Pizza developed a formidable source of competitive advantage by focusing its efforts on that part of the value chain (outbound logistics) the rest of the industry ignored. By doing so, Domino's Pizza seized the initiative from Pizza Hut and was able to stake out a large market share position. To keep its effort concentrated on home delivery, Domino's did not set up restaurants, thereby minimizing its on-site customer service. This was possible because customers called from home for pizza to be delivered. The success of Domino's Pizza's business model, however, has attracted numerous other entrants seeking to develop their own delivery and carryout formats. In particular, the steady rise of Papa John's International to become the number three pizza chain in the United States reveals that Domino's must also monitor the environment for aspiring competitors. Papa John's locations offer delivery, but consumers also like the variety of pizza styles and topping choices that it offers. Papa John's also offers carryout service, which may attract customers who will order a pizza from their car and pick it up on the way to their destination. This carryout option may present a challenge to both Pizza Hut and Domino's Pizza in the future.

For General Motors, its large size has often slowed down its ability to respond quickly to new environmental developments. In particular, GM was slow to adopt new process technologies, human resource practices, and engine designs that have enabled Toyota and Honda to dominate the quality rankings. Throughout the 1980s and early 1990s, GM believed that it could "automate" its way out of rising costs and poor product quality. GM spent tens of billions on the latest robotics and other factory automation technologies, only to find that productivity gains were fleeting. However, truly sustainable gains in productivity and efficiency require a redesign of not only the car itself, but also of all the practices in each of the value chain activities involved. GM also lost numerous opportunities to develop innovative practices that would enable it to capture the benefits of employees' experience and insights to improve the quality of its vehicles. Because of its organizational size and complexity, GM faced numerous internal challenges in adapting to the faster-moving innovations and productivity gains of Japanese competition.

Although value chain analysis can help both established firms and those contemplating entry identify strengths and weaknesses, it is unfortunately static in nature. Firms often base their strategies on the assumption that current strengths and weaknesses will persist in the future. Larger firms, in particular, are often saddled with significant fixed costs, investments, and methods of operation that impede fast response to new developments. However, to make the value chain analysis meaningful on an ongoing basis, managers need to challenge such assumptions about the competitive environment. New competitors that can change the "rules" of competition in an industry (for example, growth of the Internet and electronic online commerce; the rise of new technologies that transform an industry; the unforeseen arrival of a new type of customer or need) can often make major inroads the way that Domino's Pizza did if existing firms become overreliant on existing sources of competitive advantage without challenging themselves to think about how the future may evolve.

Inflexibility and slow response in the face of environmental change is the Achilles' heel of large, established firms. This may be an important issue for many businesses to consider as new technologies, changes in market demand, the widening influence of the Internet, and new competitors take root in every industry. We will examine this weakness in more detail in later chapters.

Assessing the Financial Position of Competitors

comparative financial analysis:
The evaluation of a firm's financial condition across multiple time periods.

ratio analysis:
The use of a proportion of two figures or numbers that allow for consistent comparison of performance with other firms.

return on assets:
Net income divided by total assets.

return on equity:
Net income divided by shareholders' equity.

return on capital:
Net income divided by total capital.

return on investment:
Net income divided by total investment.

liquidity:
The ability of a firm or business to pay or meet its obligations (for example, debt payments, accounts payable) as they come due. The more liquid the firm, the easier its ability to meet these obligations.

The strategic tools and concepts presented in this chapter can only go so far in assessing a firm's strengths and weaknesses relative to competitors'. A more thorough assessment of the firm's capabilities also requires analysis of the firm's financial position. **Comparative financial analysis** compares a firm's financial condition to that of competitors for two or more time periods. The objective of comparative financial analysis is to assess a firm's financial health. Managers use income statements, balance sheets, and other financial data and projections to compare their firm's financial position with that of other firms in the same industry.

The most common approach to financial analysis is through ratio analysis. **Ratio analysis** selects two vital figures or indicators and expresses them as a proportion that allows for comparison with other firms over time.[12] Financial ratios serve as important indicators of financial health. The most common types of financial ratios focus on profitability, liquidity, activity, and leverage. Key ratios are defined in each category in Exhibit 3-14.

Profitability can be measured through any number of return-based ratios, such as **return on assets** (net income divided by total assets), **return on equity** (net income divided by shareholders' equity), and **return on capital** (net income divided by total capital). All three return ratios are common measures of **return on investment** (ROI). These return ratios are considered the most important indicators of profitability because they indicate how productively firms are using their resources.

Liquidity is an indicator of the firm's ability to make payments to suppliers and creditors. A common measure of liquidity is the **current ratio**, which is current assets divided by current liabilities. A firm with a comparatively low current ratio presents a problem for creditors who fear it may not be able to meet its short-term obligations. The firm may use variations of the current ratio that factor out inventory, because inventory often cannot be sold quickly. Inventory is less liquid than cash. High liquidity means the firm can meet all of its financial obligations.

The firm's **activity ratios** refer to efficiency in handling inventory or other assets. Many activity ratios are also known as **turnover ratios.** For example, asset turnover is calculated by

Exhibit 3-14	Comparative Financial Analysis: Key Ratios

Type	Examples	Measures	Indicators
Profitability	Return on Equity (ROE)	$\dfrac{\text{Profit after taxes}}{\text{Shareholders' Equity}}$	Productivity of firm's value-adding activities
Liquidity	Current Ratio	$\dfrac{\text{Current Assets}}{\text{Current Liabilities}}$	Measure of financial solvency
Activity	Asset Turnover	$\dfrac{\text{Sales}}{\text{Total Assets}}$	Asset use efficiency
	Inventory Turnover	$\dfrac{\text{Sales}}{\text{Inventory}}$	Turnaround of inventory
Leverage	Debt/Equity Ratio	$\dfrac{\text{Liabilities}}{\text{Shareholders' Equity}}$	Corporate financing; financial risk; default risk

dividing sales by total assets; it gives a rough measure of the firm's ability to generate sales for any given level of assets. Inventory turnover is measured by sales divided by inventory. This ratio gives a sense of how well the firm is managing its inventory.

A firm's **debt ratio** measures the firm's leverage. Debt ratios measure the extent to which the financing of the firm's activities is based on debt or equity. It measures the financing provided by creditors in relation to that provided by stockholders or owners. One of the most common measures of leverage is the ratio of debt to equity. A high ratio of debt to equity means the firm has borrowed considerable sums in relation to shareholder investment. High leverage, or high debt to equity, works to the firm's benefit if it can use the borrowed funds to produce gains (create value) that are higher than the firm's after-tax borrowing costs. Conversely, high leverage can cripple a firm if its value-adding activities generate returns that are less than the firm's after-tax cost of borrowing. Note that leverage can also increase earnings per share (EPS), but high leverage can make EPS relatively more volatile.

The use of all these ratios requires care in interpretation. For example, an excessively high ROI measure not only may mean high profitability but also could suggest that the firm is not investing sufficiently to build up its competitive strengths. Ratios have limited meaning if managers do not compare them to competitors in the same industry. Moreover, ratios must be assessed over relevant time periods to be meaningful. Cyclical or business upturns and downturns can distort an individual firm's ratios unless they are viewed within the context of the entire industry. To use ratios effectively, managers should also compare an individual firm's ratios with respect to average ratios for the industry. Each industry is likely to have its own set of historically based average ratios with which the firm can compare its own ratios.

current ratio:
A measure used to assess a firm's ability to make payments to its short-term creditors; current assets divided by current liabilities.

activity ratios:
Measures used to assess the efficiency of a firm's use of assets (for example, sales divided by assets).

turnover ratios:
Measures that assess the speed with which various assets (inventory, receivables) are converted into cash.

debt ratio:
A measure of a firm's leverage; the amount of debt it possesses divided by stockholder equity.

Ethical Issues

In this chapter, we have examined methods of analysis that enable managers to assess the strengths and weaknesses of firms competing in an industry. In closing, let us consider some of the ethical issues associated with this effort. To conduct strength and weakness analysis, managers need detailed information about how rivals operate. They must therefore exert serious effort to obtain such information. In doing so, however, they must be careful not to overstep the bounds of ethical behavior. Consider the following means that firms commonly use to learn about and appropriate their rivals' advantages.

Examining Competitors' Products

One way to gain proprietary information about a protected technology is to disassemble and carefully study each firm's new products. Since new products are generally available to all who wish to purchase them, few would object to the propriety of this practice. Most companies often will look at the quality of the components, the product's overall functionality and fit, as well as the kind of technology that is used. On a more intricate level, companies will often "benchmark" the performance of their own products versus those of rivals. "Benchmarking" enables a firm to evaluate the cost, quality, and performance of its products when compared with offerings from competitors over time.

Questioning Competitors' Employees

Another approach to obtaining proprietary information about a competitor is to talk to employees of a competitor's organization. Such questioning or "probing" can take place in many different settings—during professional meetings, on the golf course, at cocktail parties, or in other social settings. Some would argue that this kind of questioning is proper so long as those seeking information clearly identify themselves as representatives of a rival firm. But what if they do not? Is it ethical to question employees from a rival organization under some other guise—that of a curious third party, for example?

Using Consultants

Yet another approach to securing information about a competitor is to hire a consultant to gather such data. Some may feel that this method absolves a firm of blame if information is inappropriately obtained. However, if a consultant uses improper means to obtain such information, is its client wholly blameless?

Engaging in Industrial Espionage

industrial espionage:
Systematic and deliberate attempts to learn about a competitor's technologies or new products through secretive, and often illegal, ways.

Still another approach to obtaining information about a rival is to pay a fee to an employee of a rival organization to supply such information. This practice is called **industrial espionage.** Few managers would justify this practice on ethical grounds. Furthermore, the practice is illegal in most countries, including the United States, carrying significant penalties if discovered.

Nevertheless, some unscrupulous firms employ it to obtain information about competitors. In September 2001, Procter & Gamble admitted to engaging in espionage against one of its competitors, European consumer packaged goods firm Unilever. Apparently unbeknownst to Procter & Gamble's senior management, several managers and employees undertook a clandestine effort to learn about the ingredients of Unilever's shampoo. Procter & Gamble employees would search through Unilever's garbage in an effort to identify how Unilever was developing its product. To the company's credit, however, Procter & Gamble's CEO openly admitted that his company was engaging in this practice, once the issue was disclosed to him. The company then immediately informed Unilever about its own self-investigation and has offered to settle the issue outside court.[13]

The pattern of industrial espionage has assumed important international dimensions as well. In late 2002, FBI agents undertook a sting operation that involved a Chinese firm's alleged theft of intellectual property and designs from U.S. networking giant Cisco Systems. Huawei Technologies, a company that once enjoyed strong relationships with China's military, apparently copied the design for Cisco's networking products (for example, routers) to such a flagrant degree that it also incorporated the same software flaws from Cisco's products into its own. As a result of legal action, Huawei was forced to withdraw its routers from the U.S. market and admitted in court that indeed much of its software matches that of Cisco's. Despite this legal action, Huawei remains committed to becoming an important competitor in high-technology products. In fact, by October 2004, Huawei had already commanded the second largest market share for optical networking products after France's Alcatel and ahead of Canada's Nortel Networks and Lucent Technologies of the United States.[14]

"Pirating" Employees

pirating:
Hiring individuals from a competitor specifically to gain their knowledge (also known as raiding).

raiding:
Hiring individuals from a competitor specifically to gain their knowledge (also known as pirating).

Yet another method of obtaining information about rivals is to hire individuals from rival organizations who have access to such information. This practice is often referred to as employee **pirating** or **raiding.** Many argue that this practice is justifiable as long as information possessed by new hires is general in nature. However, new hires often come with specific knowledge about former employers' strategic plans, new product intentions, or other confidential information. High-level managers are particularly likely to possess such information.

This practice has becoming increasingly common in Silicon Valley, the San Jose, California, region. Silicon Valley has become proliferated with hundreds of innovative firms doing cutting-edge research and product development in the fields of semiconductors, software, Internet technology, advanced imaging, and other high-technology products. Because qualified technical and managerial talent is often short, firms will often seek to "raid" other firms, including their competitors, for the people they need to manage their operations. This kind of pirating can often result in a firm's losing its critical talent and skills to a competitor in a short period. In some industries, however, firms have required that their departing managers sign noncompete agreements that preclude them from working with their competitors for an extended period. Some of these noncompete agreements even include clauses that prohibit departing managers or employees from encouraging their colleagues to leave with them to another firm.

Conclusion

The tools described in this chapter are useful for identifying a firm's strengths and weaknesses relative to competitors. Such information is not the only input needed to formulate strategy, however. As noted in Chapter 1, strategy formulation involves finding an appropriate fit between strengths and weaknesses on the one hand and opportunities and threats on the other. To formulate an effective strategy, the opportunities and threats appearing in the firm's external environment must therefore also be first identified. How to go about making this identification and how to match a firm's strengths and weaknesses to opportunities and threats presented to it are topics explored in depth in subsequent chapters.

Summary

- Firms need to undertake a thorough analysis of their own internal strengths and weaknesses to lay the foundation for building effective strategies.
- The activities of all firms in an industry can be studied through an analytical tool known as the value chain. A value chain identifies and isolates the various economic, value-adding activities that occur in some way in every firm.
- The value chain can highlight the strengths and weaknesses of firms competing in the industry. It distinguishes between primary activities and support activities.
- Primary activities are directly concerned with the conversion of raw materials, inputs, and designs into products or services that are then sold to customers. Support activities assist primary activities in carrying out their functions and tasks. A firm's business system consists of the subset of value chain activities that it actually performs.
- A major task of the strategic management process is to match the conditions of the external environment with the firm's internal strengths and weaknesses. If a firm can perform an activity or activities particularly well relative to its competitors, it then possesses a distinctive competence. A distinctive competence enables the firm to build its own source of competitive advantage. The choice of which strategies to pursue should be based on using and exploiting the firm's competitive advantage.
- In any industry, established firms are likely to enjoy prevailing strengths as compared with firms entering later. In particular, larger established firms, and especially

industry leaders, often enjoy advantages derived from first-mover, scale, experience, or interrelationship benefits. These benefits may provide initial sources of competitive advantage; however, competitive advantage from these sources is significant only when specific requirements are met.

- Understanding the financial position of the firm is as important as knowing its value chain. The financial position of the firm can and should be measured in many different ways. Four common measures of financial position are financial ratios that examine profitability (return), liquidity, activity, and leverage. These ratios should be compared with rivals in the same industry and over the same time periods of interest.

- Companies engage in industrial espionage in an attempt to learn about competitors' strategies, products, technologies, and future plans. In most countries, this practice is illegal.

Exercises and Discussion Questions

 1. Using the Internet, visit the website for General Motors (**http://www.gm.com**). What are some initiatives that GM appears to be taking that could resuscitate its competitive advantage? In particular, how does GM want to deal with its suppliers, distributors (dealers), and final customers such as ourselves?

2. What are some fundamental trade-offs that large companies are likely to face? In particular, do economies of scale come with their own sets of costs?

3. Assume the role of an entrepreneur who has a burning desire to get into the pizza business. What value-adding activity would you focus on to build your own source of competitive advantage? How would you compete with the sit-down restaurants, as well as with the firms that focus on home delivery? Are there any other routes to building competitive advantage that have not yet been discovered?

Endnotes

1. Data for this strategic snapshot were adapted from the following sources: "Hungry for More: Sales Increase for Local Pizza Chains, but Crowded Field Intensifies Battle for Market Share," *Crain's Detroit Business,* September 13, 2004, p. 3; "Domino's IPO: Not as Tasty as It Smells," *Business Week,* July 19, 2004, p. 94; "Restaurant Companies' Good Times Slow Down," *Wall Street Journal,* July 7, 2001; "High Court Rejects Review of Pizza Hut's Lawsuit Against Rival," *Wall Street Journal,* March 21, 2001; "Raw Deal: Take-and-Bake Pizza May Not Sound Appetizing, but Papa Murphy's Undercuts Rivals by Taking Out Seats, Delivery— and Cooking," *Forbes,* December 25, 2000; "For Pizza Hut, a New Pie-in-the-Sky Ad Strategy," *Wall Street Journal,* September 30, 1999; "Pizza Hut Test-Markets Charging a Delivery Fee," *Wall Street Journal,* September 20, 1999.

2. Data for the GM Strategic Snapshot were adapted from the following sources: "Will These Rockets Rescue Saturn? *Business Week,* January 17, 2005, pp. 78-79; "General Motors Faces a Bumpy Road, And Reverberations Could Be Wide," *Wall Street Journal,* January 10, 2005, pp. C1, C5; "GM and Daimler Are Stepping On It," *Business Week,* December 27, 2004, p. 49; "Reversing 80 Years of History, GM Is Reining in Global Fiefs," *Wall Street Journal,* October 6, 2004, pp. A1–A12; Can Caddy's Driver Make GM Cool?" *Business Week,* September 20, 2004, pp. 105–106; "Chevy's Small-Car Gambit," *Wall Street Journal,* July 15, 2004, pp. B1, B2; GM to

Shift Basics of U.S. Cars to German Unit in Big Overhaul," *Wall Street Journal,* June 21, 2004, p. A6; "Can This Brand Be Saved?" *Forbes,* March 29, 2004, pp. 62–64; "Detroit Buffs Up," *Fortune,* February 9, 2004, pp. 90–96; "Detroit Tries It the Japanese Way," *BusinessWeek,* January 26, 2004, pp. 76–78; "When Flawless Isn't Enough," *BusinessWeek,* December 8, 2003, pp. 80–82; "Rick Wagoner's Game Plan," *BusinessWeek,* February 10, 2003, pp. 52–60; "GM Product Guru Prepares to Overhaul Auto Maker's Development of New Models," *Wall Street Journal,* January 28, 2002, p. A4; "Cruising for Quality," *BusinessWeek,* September 3, 2001, pp. 74–75; "GM Appoints an Industry Guru to Fix Its Lineup," *Wall Street Journal,* August 3, 2001, pp. B1, B4; "GM Tests a Web-Based Ordering System, Seeking to Slash Custom-Delivery Time," *Wall Street Journal,* November 17, 2000, p. B4; "GM Sees Internet as Means to Make It Fast and Flexible," *Investor's Business Daily,* October 27, 2000, p. A5; "How GM, Ford Think Web Can Make Splash on Factory Floor," *Wall Street Journal,* December 3, 1999, pp. A1, A8; "GM Will Connect Drivers to the World Wide Web," *Wall Street Journal,* November 3, 1999, pp. B1, B4; "Reviving GM," *BusinessWeek,* February 1, 1999, pp. 114–122.

3. For an excellent and seminal discussion of this topic, see M. E. Porter, *Competitive Advantage* (New York: Free Press, 1985), 36–61. Also see K. Cool and J. Henderson, "Power and Firm Profitability in Supply Chains: French Manufacturing Industry in 1993," *Strategic Management Journal* 19, no. 10 (1998): 909–926; C. B. Stabell and O. D. Fjeldstad, "Configuring Value for Competitive Advantage: On Chains, Shops and Networks," *Strategic Management Journal* 19, no. 5 (1998): 413–438; R. Normann and R. Ramirez, "From Value Chain to Value Constellation," *Harvard Business Review* 71, no. 4 (1993): 65–77; M. Hergert and D. Morris, "Accounting Data for Value Chain Analysis," *Strategic Management Journal* 10, no. 2 (1989): 175–188; C. G. Armistead and G. Clark, "Resource Activity Mapping: The Value Chain in Service Operation Strategy," *Service Industries Journal* 13, no. 4 (1993): 221–239.

4. See, for example, "Radio Wave of the Future," *Dallas Morning News*, February 8, 2005, pp. 1D, 12D.

5. This notion was initially developed by McKinsey & Company, management consultants.

6. See, for example, R. Kerin, R. Varadarajan, and R. Peterson, "First-Mover Advantage: A Synthesis, Conceptual Framework, and Research Propositions, *Journal of Marketing* 56, no. 4 (1992): 33–52; B. Mascarenhas, "First-Mover Effects in Multiple Dynamic Markets," *Strategic Management Journal* 13, no. 3 (1992): 237–243; M. B. Lieberman and D. B. Montgomery, "First-Mover Advantages," *Strategic Management Journal* 9 (1988): 41–58; M. Lambkin, "Order of Entry and Performance in New Markets," *Strategic Management Journal* 9: (1988): 127–140; R. Rosenbloom and M. Cusumano, "Technological Pioneering and Competitive Advantage: The Birth of the VCR Industry," *California Management Review* 29, no 4 (1987): 51–76; P. N. Golder and G. Tellis, "Pioneer Advantage: Marketing Logic or Marketing Legend?" *Journal of Marketing Research* 30 (1993): 158–170. Also see M. B. Lieberman and D. B. Montgomery, "First-Mover (Dis)Advantages: Retrospective and Link with the Resource-Based View," *Strategic Management Journal* 19, no. 12 (1998): 1111–1126; P. Vanderwerf and J. F. Mahon, "Meta-Analysis of the Impact of Research Methods on Findings of First-Mover Advantage," *Management Science* 43, no. 11 (1997): 1510–1519; C. Nehrt, "Timing and Intensity of Environmental Investments," *Strategic Management Journal* 17, no. 7 (1996): 535–547.

   Recent representative empirical work examining the first-mover effect includes K. Carow, R. Heron, and T. Saxton, "Do Early Birds Get the Returns? An Empirical Investigation of Early-Mover Advantages in Acquisitions," *Strategic Management Journal* 25, no. 6 (2004): 563–586. Also see J. Shamsie, C. Phelps, and J. Kuperman, "Better Late Than Never: A Study of Late Entrants in Household Electrical Equipment," *Strategic Management Journal* 25, no. 1 (2004): 69–84;

W. T. Robinson and J. Chiang, "Product Development Strategies for Established Market Pioneers, Early Followers, and Late Entrants," *Strategic Management Journal* 23, no. 9 (2002): 855–866.

7. See, for example, J. A. Buzacott, ed., *Scale in Production Systems* (New York: Pergamon, 1982). An excellent examination of scale and related effects in promoting competitive advantage is M. B. Lieberman, "The Learning Curve: Technological Barriers to Entry and Competitive Survival in the Chemical Processing Industries," *Strategic Management Journal* 10 (1989): 431–447. Earlier work that looks at scale and learning effects includes P. Ghemawat, "Capacity Expansion in the Titanium Dioxide Industry," *Journal of Industrial Economics* 33 (December 1984): 145–163; M. E. McGrath and R. W. Hoole, "Manufacturing's New Economies of Scale," *Harvard Business Review* (May–June 1992): 94–102; B. J. Seldon and S. H. Bullard, "Input Substitution, Economies of Scale and Productivity Growth in the U.S. Upholstered Furniture Industry," *Applied Economics* 24 (September 1992): 1017–1026; S. C. Kumbhakar, "A Reexamination of Returns to Scale, Density and Technical Progress in U.S. Airlines," *Southern Economic Journal* 57 (October 1990): 425–443; M. J. Farrell, "Industry Characteristics and Scale Economies as Sources of Intra-Industry Trade," *Journal of Economic Studies* 18 (November 1991): 36–58; A. Seth, "Sources of Value Creation in Acquisitions: An Empirical Investigation," *Strategic Management Journal* 11 (1990): 431–446; G. Forestieri, "Economies of Scale and Scope in the Financial Services Industry: A Review of Recent Literature," *Financial Conglomerates, Organization for Economic Cooperation and Development* (1993): 63–124.

8. Data and facts for Samsung were adapted from the following sources: "Samsung Design," *BusinessWeek,* December 6, 2004, pp. 88–96; "Samsung's Next Act," *Forbes,* July 26, 2004, pp. 102–108; "Rivals Samsung, Sony Unite in Flat-Screen-TV Venture," *Wall Street Journal,* July 15, 2004, pp. B1, B5; "Samsung Net More Than Doubles on Cellphone Sales," *Wall Street Journal,* April 16, 2004, p. A10; "Samsung is Aiming to Make the Jetsons' World a Reality," *Wall Street Journal,* September 16, 2003, pp. B1, B15; "Samsung Closes Flash-Chip Gap with Intel," *Wall Street Journal,* September 11, 2003, pp. B6, B7; "The Samsung Way," *BusinessWeek,* June 16, 2003, pp. 56–64.

9. The landmark work that first examined the effects of cumulative learning and experience curve effects within large firms is found in The Boston Consulting Group, *Perspectives on Experience* (Boston: Author, 1972). Examples of research that empirically tested this phenomenon include A. Spence, "The Learning Curve and Competition," *Bell Journal of Economics* 12 (1981): 49–70; R. J. Gilbert and R. G. Harris, "Investment Decisions with Economies of Scale and Learning," *American Economic Review* 71 (May 1981): 172–177; M. B. Lieberman, "The Learning Curve, Diffusion and Competitive Strategy," *Strategic Management Journal* 8 (1987): 441–452; R. H. Hayes, S. C. Wheelwright, and K. B. Clark, *Dynamic Manufacturing: Creating the Learning Organization* (New York: Free Press, 1988); L. Argote and D. Epple, "Learning Curves in Manufacturing," *Science* 247 (February 23, 1990): 920–925; P. S. Adler and K. Clark, "Behind the Learning Curve: A Sketch of the Learning Process," *Management Science* 37 (March 1991): 267–282; C. Koulamas, "Quality Improvement Through Product Redesign and the Learning Curve," *Omega* 20 (March 1992): 161–168; F. Malerba, "Learning by Firms and Incremental Technical Change," *Economic Journal* 102 (July 1992): 845–860; H. Gruber, "The Learning Curve in the Production of Semiconductor Memory Chips," *Applied Economics* 24 (August 1992): 885–895; B. Bahk and M. Gort, "Decomposing Learning by Doing in New Plants," *Journal of Political Economy* 101 (August 1993): 561–584.

10. Data and facts for Toyota were adapted from the following sources: "Full Speed Ahead," *Fortune*, February 7, 2005, pp. 79–84; "Toyota Aims to Rival GM

Production," *Wall Street Journal,* November 2, 2004, pp. A3, A12; "Can Anyone Stop Toyota?" *Barron's Online,* September 13, 2004; "Toyota's Secret Weapon," *Fortune,* August 23, 2004, pp. 60–66; "As Toyota Closes In on GM, Quality Concerns Also Grow," *Wall Street Journal,* August 4, 2004, pp. A1, A8; "The Americanization of Toyota," *Fortune,* December 8, 2003, pp. 165–170; "Can Anything Stop Toyota?" *BusinessWeek,* November 17, 2003, pp. 114–122; "The Americanization of Toyota," *BusinessWeek,* April 15, 2002, pp. 52–54.

11. See, for example, D. B. Yoffie and M. A. Cusumano, "Judo Strategy: The Competitive Dynamics of Internet Time," *Harvard Business Review* 77 (January–February 1999): 70–82; J. F. Rayport and J. J. Sviokla, "Exploiting the Virtual Value Chain," *Harvard Business Review* 73 (November–December 1995). Also see "The e-Corporation," *Fortune,* December 7, 1998, pp. 80–102.

12. See, for example, S. Eilon, "Analysis of Corporate Performance," *Business and Economic Review* (Summer 1987): 20–29; and L. J. Gitman, *Basic Managerial Finance* (New York: HarperCollins, 1992).

13. See "P&G's Covert Operation," *Fortune,* September 17, 2001, pp. 42–44; also see "The Prying Game," *Fortune,* September 17, 2001, p. 235.

14. See "U.S. Businesses Urge China To Rein in Piracy," *Wall Street Journal,* September 17, 2004; "The New Weapon in China's Arsenal: Private Contractors," *Wall Street Journal,* July 16, 2004, pp. A1, A6; "Sting Operation Led Cisco to Sue Chinese Rival," *Wall Street Journal,* April 4, 2003, pp. B1, B2.

Building Competitive Advantage through Distinction

What you will learn

- *The three types of "generic" competitive strategies that can be used to build competitive advantage, including low-cost leadership, differentiation, and focus*

- *The benefits and costs of pursuing each type of generic strategy*

- *The rise of mass customization as a new strategy*

- *How the Internet reshapes business strategy and customer expectations about value and service*

- *How the evolution of the product life cycle impacts business strategy*

Strategic
Snapshot

Nordstrom, Inc.[1]

Competition among firms in the retailing industry has always been fierce. Within the department store segment, large nationwide chains such as J. C. Penney, Sears, May Department Stores, and Federated Department Stores have strengthened their presence in ever-expanding malls throughout the country. May Department Stores and Federated, in particular, operate a collection of different store brands, many of which were acquired over the past two decades as a wave of consolidation reshaped the department store landscape.[2] All of these firms operate large stores that offer a wide merchandise selection where they can leverage their distribution strengths. With the growth of computerized, real-time inventory tracking systems, many of these chains have invested in new technologies that enable them to keep track of customer demand patterns while lowering their inventory costs through streamlined ordering systems. By capturing significant economies of scale in their procurement and distribution activities, the large consolidated chains have been able to steadily accumulate cost savings, some of which are passed on to their customers.

Although consolidation has dominated the landscape of the retailing industry in recent years, a number of retailers have attempted to compete by offering superior service and emphasizing upscale, high-quality products. These include such smaller firms as Neiman Marcus Group and Saks Fifth Avenue. However, there is one firm that every competitor sought to imitate when learning how best to provide customer service. Considered one of the finest retailers in the United States, Nordstrom has always prided itself on the exceptional customer service that it offers to its customers. In fact, the very name Nordstrom has become synonymous with quality, intimate service, and personal charm. Throughout the company's history, family management led the company over the past hundred years to set the standards for the finest possible customer service that could be delivered in person.

With deep roots in Seattle, Washington, Nordstrom originally began its operations as a shoe retailer in 1901. For the first sixty-seven years of its history, Nordstrom sold only shoes throughout the Pacific Northwest. In 1968, the family began to add women's fashions and other clothing lines to its merchandise assortment. The company began to expand nationally during the 1990s, with over ninety full-line stores in every region. It also operates fifty outlet stores (Nordstrom Rack) in about twenty-five states. In 2003, Nordstrom rang up sales of $5.9 billion, earning $90 million in net profit.

The defining hallmark of Nordstrom's approach to retailing has been its obsessive focus on customer service. In fact, the vast majority of the company's managers all started their careers by working on the sales floor where they learned and refined the fine art of delivering highly personalized service. Sales associates always put the needs of their customers first. In fact, they are expected to notify customers of impending sales events and special offers through personal phone calls or notes in the mail. These loyal customers frequently return to make future purchases of an expanding line of fashions, shoes, accessories, and maternity wear. In turn, Nordstrom rewards its sales associates with compensation that is often significantly higher than what competitors offer; more important, Nordstrom follows a policy of promoting from within its own ranks. The company believes that it can preserve and improve its distinctive customer service only by ensuring that its managers have fully embraced the concept through personal sales experience. In addition, Nordstrom is known for its caring human resources practices. Many Nordstrom employees turn customer service and sales work into a full-time, well-paid career. Experienced Nordstrom employees can make upwards of $60,000 per year, compared with the $8 per hour that many Wal-Mart employees receive. It offers a generous family leave program for future mothers and allows time off for employees to care for other family members as well. See Exhibit 4-1 for these defining characteristics of Nordstrom's service-driven strategy.

Nordstrom's singular focus on customer service enabled the firm to vault over its competitors in customer loyalty, sales per square foot, and earnings growth during the 1980s and early 1990s. However, the changing retailing environment posed significant challenges for Nordstrom, especially with the recession of 2001. Many of Nordstrom's stores have become bigger as it offers

Nordstrom's Differentiation from Department Store Chains — Exhibit 4-1

SUPPORT ACTIVITIES		Inbound Logistics	Operations	Outbound Logistics	Marketing/ Sales	Service
	Infrastructure		Strong legacy of family emphasis on service			
	Human Resource Management		Promotion from within for managers; caring practices		Development of service culture	Training on service expectations; service rewarded
	Technology Development	Perpetual inventory replenishment	Development of new ordering systems		Customer loyalty programs; Internet sales	Make Internet as user-friendly as possible
	Procurement	Emphasis on high fashion labels				
PRIMARY ACTIVITIES			Smaller stores; higher store density; narrower product line		Higher prices; emphasis on classic designs	Personalized, friendly, customer-first policy

a broader line of merchandise in new regions of the country. Although the company has invested considerable resources to expand nationally, it is encountering new operational challenges as its competitors begin to invest heavily in new computer-driven ordering and distribution technologies. Most important, some these new in-store technologies have begun to erode Nordstrom's competitive edge. Even as the company expanded rapidly, family management at Nordstrom believed that it could replicate its intimate customer service strategy at each store to compete effectively.

Until recently, Nordstrom operated over twelve different buying centers to procure merchandise for its stores. This often meant that each region would place its own separate orders, thus losing any potential scale benefits from shared buying. Also, the firm has lagged behind its competitors in installing real-time inventory tracking systems that enable the firm to automatically reorder merchandise where needed. Equally important, Nordstrom's dispersed buying and ordering systems meant that buyers could not communicate with one another about what particular market trends were taking shape, nor could they fine-tune the right mix of fashionable offerings for increasingly savvy customers. Fragmented buying, in turn, led to higher costs for inventory and difficulties in matching what local customers in each region wanted.

To counter some of these difficulties, Nordstrom attempted to combine both contemporary clothing (lots of color, trendy prints) with classical styles and brand names across its departments. This meant that high-fashion labels were sold alongside house brands and other less well-known labels in the same clothing category. Over time, customers became confused with what Nordstrom was offering, because the merchandise mix appeared to be diluted and offered mixed messages, rather than promoting its traditional upscale, classical taste. When interviewed by market research firms, some customer groups felt that Nordstrom had become overly formal (store piano players often wear tuxedos) while lagging behind other stores in offering cutting-edge fashions. In recent years, Nordstrom

was also perceived as overemphasizing its reach toward younger customers (loud hip-hop music in many stores) at the expense of its more loyal, baby-boomer shoppers.

As Nordstrom seeks to enhance its top-notch service even further, the firm is in the midst of investing in many of the same technologies that have enabled its competitors to better track and order inventory. For the past three years, Nordstrom has invested $185 million in new perpetual inventory and point-of-sale (POS) systems. Perpetual inventory systems are designed to help Nordstrom immediately reorder items that have been sold, thus minimizing out-of-stock items in its stores. POS systems are integrated with technologically advanced and faster registers that enable customers to complete their sales at twice the speed as before. Nordstrom believes that it must speed up these transactions, especially during busy periods, in order to make the shopping experience even more enjoyable and convenient for customers. At the same time, Nordstrom continues to focus on offering superior customer service, even as it begins to provide merchandise designed for middle-income shoppers. Nordstrom believes that customers represent long-term relationships, and that these relationships can form the basis for an emotional connection that goes beyond frequent buyers points or loyalty cards. Still, Nordstrom's legendary promote-from-within policy has also come under question from some analysts, who believe that the company's obsessive focus on superior service may have limited the kind of professional backgrounds and experience that could flourish in the company's ranks. In fact, Neiman Marcus, Saks Fifth Avenue, and Talbot's have made serious inroads into Nordstrom's customer base, as these competitors offer similar classic merchandise with an emphasis on top-notch service. Saks, in particular, is seeking to retool itself as a more potent competitor to Nordstrom as it seeks to reverse its recent trend of attempting to broaden its market reach to more middle-market customers. Saks also faced some of the same difficulties that confronted Nordstrom, such as allowing regional stores to conduct their own procurement initiatives. For all luxury retailers, many upscale customers prefer discounts to highly pampered service, espe-cially during times of economic uncertainty.

To counter some of these challenges, Nord-strom has begun to consolidate its catalog and Internet business into one unit called Nordstrom Direct. The company's website continues a strong emphasis on shoes—the same line of merchandise that was the foundation for the company's early growth. In March 2004, Nordstrom began offering home furnishings and accessories. Such products include ceramic tableware, bedding, lighting, and rugs to complement its fine line of gifts and crystal. However, Nordstrom's family management still asserts that superior customer service will re-main the ultimate trump card over its competitors. As the company moves into a new competitive era, it will have to balance its traditional focus on customer service with alternative approaches to capture new customers who may want something beyond personalized service.

Introduction

In Chapter 3, we presented an overview of some of the generalized sources of competitive advantage that established firms within an industry are likely to possess. Although first-mover, scale, experience, and interrelationship advantages are important, especially for large firms, in practice companies of all sizes need to build their own specific sources of competitive advantage based on their distinctive competences. Each firm is likely to possess its own set of distinct strengths and weaknesses among its set of value-adding activities. Developing a distinctive com-petence that builds on a firm's strengths while minimizing its weaknesses enables a firm to lay the foundation for a sustainable competitive advantage. In this chapter, we explore the opportunities and routes available for firms to build competitive advantage over their rivals.

We begin by examining the concept of competitive advantage as it applies to specific value-adding activities performed by the firm. Competitive advantage arises when a firm can perform an activity that is distinct or different from that of its rivals. Superior earnings can only come from distinction. Therefore, a strategy is only as useful as it is distinctive. Generally speak-ing, there are three sources of competitive advantage: low-cost, differentiation, and focus. How-ever, other emerging sources of competitive advantage have also surfaced for firms that seek to provide improved customer value through customization of product and service offerings.

We also analyze the advantages and disadvantages that accompany each approach to building competitive advantage. We explore each of these "generic" strategies in separate sec-tions and point out the benefits and costs associated with each one. In the last section, we in-vestigate how competitive strategy depends significantly on the product life cycle. We consider how sources of competitive advantage may shift over the span of the product life cycle as well.

Routes to Building Competitive Advantage

Competitive strategies must be based on some source of competitive advantage to be suc-cessful. Companies build competitive advantage when they take steps that enable them to gain an edge over their rivals in attracting buyers. These steps vary: for example, making the highest-quality product, providing the best customer service, producing at the lowest cost, or focusing resources on a specific segment or niche of the industry. Regardless of which avenue to build-ing competitive advantage the firm selects, customers must receive superior value than that

Exhibit 4-2 — Generic Strategic Approaches to Build Competitive Advantage

Competitive Advantage

		Defined by Cost	Defined by Distinctiveness
Target Market	Industry-wide (Broad)	**Low-cost leadership**	**Differentiation**
	Specific Niche or Segment (Narrow)	**Cost-based focus**	**Differentiation-based focus**

Adapted with the permission of The Free Press, a Division of Simon & Schuster Adult Publishing Group, from *Competitive Advantage: Creating and Sustaining Superior Performance*, by Michael E. Porter. Copyright © 1980, 1998 by Michael E. Porter. All rights reserved.

offered by its rivals. Providing superior value to customers also translates into superior financial performance for the firm. Numerous studies consistently demonstrate that firms providing superior value in the form of lower-cost products or services or distinctive, high-quality products are able to sustain high profitability and competitive advantage.[3]

Competitive advantage is developed at the industry or business level of analysis. Recall that business-level strategy focuses on how to compete in a given business or industry with its different types of competitors aiming to sell to the same or similar group of customers. In practice, competitors within an industry may be companies with no other lines of business (single-business firms) or business units belonging to larger, diversified companies that operate across many industries. Analysis at the *business or industry level* is the basis for building competitive advantage.

Firms have long attempted to build competitive advantage through an infinite number of strategies. Competitive strategies are designed to help firms deploy their value chains and other strengths to build competitive advantage. Thus, in practice, each company formulates its specific competitive strategy according to its own analysis of internal strengths and weaknesses, the value it can provide, the competitive environment, and the needs of its customers.

generic strategies:
The broad types of competitive strategies— low-cost leadership, differentiation, and focus— that firms use to build competitive advantage (see low-cost leadership; differentiation; focus strategies).

Although there are as many different specific competitive strategies as there are firms competing, three underlying approaches to building competitive advantage appear to exist at the broadest level. They are (1) low-cost leadership strategies, (2) differentiation strategies, and (3) focus strategies. These strategies are depicted in Exhibit 4-2. These three broad types of competitive strategies have also been labeled **generic strategies.** All three generic strategies are designed to achieve distinction relative to a rival.[4] Let us now examine how each generic type of competitive strategy can build competitive advantage.

Low-Cost Leadership Strategies

low-cost leadership:
A competitive strategy based on the firm's ability to provide products or services at lower cost than its rivals.

Low-cost leadership strategies are based on a firm's ability to provide a product or service at a lower cost than its rivals. The basic operating assumption behind a low-cost leadership strategy is to acquire a substantial cost advantage over other competitors that can be passed on to consumers to gain a large market share. A low-cost strategy then produces a competitive advantage when the firm can earn a higher profit margin that results from selling products at current market prices. In many cases, firms attempting to execute low-cost strategies aim to sell a product that appeals to a broad target market. Oftentimes, these products or services are highly standardized and not customized to an individual customer's tastes, needs, or desires.

A central premise of the low-cost leadership strategy is the following: By making products with as few modifications as possible, the firm can exploit the cost reduction benefits that accrue from economies of scale and experience effects. Low-cost leadership strategies can flourish in service businesses as well. In these arenas, firms attempt to capture economies of scale in information systems, procurement, logistics, and even marketing.

Examples of firms that have successfully used a low-cost leadership strategy to build competitive advantage include Whirlpool in washers and dryers, Black & Decker in power tools, BIC in ballpoint pens, Wal-Mart Stores in retailing, Tyson Foods in processed and packaged meat products, Gillette in razor blades, Texas Instruments and Intel in semiconductors, Samsung in digital cell phones, Sharp in flat-panel screens and LCD technology, Citigroup in credit card services, Vanguard Group in mutual funds, Emerson Electric in power drives and tools, and DuPont in nylon and other synthetic fibers.

Building a Low-Cost Advantage

The low-cost leadership strategy is based on locating and leveraging every possible source of cost advantage in a firm's value chain of activities. As Exhibit 4-3 shows, numerous opportunities are available for firms seeking to build cost-based advantages among their primary and supporting value-adding activities. Once a firm pursuing a low-cost leadership strategy has discovered an important source of cost improvement and reduction, however, it must then seek new ways to lower its activity costs even further over time. The sources of low-cost advantage are not enduring or sustainable without continuous improvement and ongoing searches for improved process yields, streamlined product design, or more efficient means of delivering a service.

Building a cost-based advantage thus requires the firm to find and exploit all the potential cost drivers that allow for greater efficiency in each value-adding activity. A **cost driver** is an economic or technological factor that determines the cost of performing some activity. Important cost drivers that shape the low-cost leadership strategy include (1) economies of scale, (2) experience or learning curve effects, (3) degree of vertical integration, and even (4) location of activity performance. Firms can tailor their use of these cost drivers to build low-cost leadership across different value-adding activities.

In pursuing a cost-based advantage, no firm can obviously ignore such product attributes as quality, service, and reliability. If it does, its offering will become so unacceptable that consumers will refuse to buy it. A firm pursuing a cost-based advantage must therefore strive to achieve some degree of quality parity with other firms that have defined the standards of product quality valued by customers.[5]

cost driver:
A technological or economic factor that determines the cost of performing some activity.

Economies of Scale and Experience Effects. Economies of scale and experience curve effects (as initially discussed in Chapter 3) enable firms to successively lower their unit costs as both capacity and experience grow. Economies of scale and experience curve effects are particularly significant in the inbound logistics, operations, outbound logistics, procurement, and technology development activities of the value chain. For example, large factories (such as steel mills and semiconductor plants) and service delivery centers (such as overnight delivery facilities, database management, centralized reservation systems, and call centers) often have operating systems characterized by high fixed costs and capital-intensive processes that are sensitive to economies of scale. Experience effects are important in these activities, too, because employees have opportunities to become more proficient in performing their tasks over time.

Exhibit 4-3   Competitive Advantage Based on Low-Cost Leadership

SUPPORT ACTIVITIES		
Infrastructure	Centralized cost controls	
Human Resource Management	Intensive training to emphasize cost saving means; encourage employees to look for new ways to improve methods	
Technology Development	Economies of scale of R&D and technology development; learning and experience amortized over large volume	
Procurement	Purchasing from numerous sources; strong bargaining power with suppliers	

PRIMARY ACTIVITIES	Large shipments; massive warehouses	Economies of scale in plants; experience effects	Bulk or large order shipment	Mass marketing; mass distribution; national ad campaigns	Centralized service facilities in region
	Inbound Logistics	**Operations**	**Outbound Logistics**	**Marketing/ Sales**	**Service**

Reprinted/Adapted with the permission of The Free Press, a division of Simon & Schuster, Inc., from *Competitive Advantage: Creating and Sustaining Superior Performance,* by Michael E. Porter. Copyright © 1985 by Michael E. Porter.

For example, workers in a factory or scientists in a laboratory setting often become better accustomed to performing their work over time so that output yield rises with greater familiarity. In another vein, procurement and technology development costs can also be shared and spread among a variety of different products and activities. For instance, improvements in the coatings used to create weather stripping and tape products can help create new adhesives for automotive and aerospace applications. All of these activities are based on significant scale or experience drivers that lower unit costs. Firms that are able to build a low-cost strategy on both scale and experience effects can thus reap higher returns for products sold at market prices.

Vertical Integration. Vertical integration is an economic concept that refers to the degree of control a firm exerts over the supply of its inputs and the purchase of its outputs. For example, when an automobile manufacturer acquires a steelmaker (a key supplier of crucial materials needed to produce cars), it is pursuing one form of vertical integration. Here, the car company is attempting to control a supply source. Similarly, when the automobile manufacturer purchases a car rental firm, it is pursuing another form of vertical integration. In this case, the automobile company is extending its control over an important buyer of its products. Extending control over sources of supply (upstream operations) or buyers (downstream operations) is vertical integration.

Firms may find that different approaches to vertical integration enable them to produce at low costs, although the nature of this relationship requires some explanation. Vertical integration can be an important cost driver, depending on the nature of the firm's product, the degree of technological change, the relative strength of buyers and suppliers in that industry, and other external factors. How it contributes to building cost-based competitive advantage depends on the specific situations facing the firm.

High levels of vertical integration help firms control all of the inputs, supplies, and equipment needed to convert raw materials into the final end product. In many instances, a high degree of vertical integration allows the firm to leverage scale and experience effects from one activity to another. For example, vertical integration is prominent in the oil refining, paper, and steel industries, where the firm is better able to control costs and potentially reduce total costs for all of the firm's activities by bringing many production or conversion activities in-house. For oil, paper, and steel companies, the transaction costs of dealing with numerous external suppliers and buyers are removed, which often results in large cost savings, greater predictability of supplies, and greater production efficiency. **Transaction costs** refer to the costs of finding, negotiating, selling, buying, and resolving disputes with other firms in the open market. Thus, high vertical integration is a significant cost driver when products and technologies tend to remain fairly stable over long periods. For example, Matsushita Electric Industrial of Japan is highly vertically integrated in the manufacture of televisions, VCRs, DVD players, office equipment, and medical equipment. Matsushita makes the circuit boards, switches, semiconductors, controls, wiring harnesses, plastic casings, and power supplies that become important components for its end products (for example, consumer electronics products). By performing most of these activities in-house, Matsushita can reap substantial cost advantages through numerous value-adding activities of components and activities that directly "feed" into its final products. Similarly, in the U.S. food processing industry, pork and poultry production lends itself to high vertical integration. There is considerable economies of scale and opportunities to share costs when breeding, raising, administering medications, and processing certain types of meat and egg products. Companies perform many of the activities in highly centralized facilities that yield substantial cost savings over time.

In other situations, firms can sometimes achieve a strong cost advantage by having very little vertical integration. By deliberately choosing not to perform certain activities in-house, a firm avoids the start-up and fixed costs that often accompany high integration. Firms can thus seek to lower their costs by buying more than they make. This approach is broadly known as outsourcing. **Outsourcing** is the reliance upon external suppliers to perform value-adding activities that were once conducted in-house. By outsourcing some of its activities, the firm may avoid high fixed-cost capital investments in key parts of its value chain. Outsourcing is particularly well suited for firms in rapidly evolving industries. When products and technologies change quickly, firms seek to outsource their activities, rather than bring them in-house, since there is considerable risk in investing in production facilities and/or methods that may become out of date. Firms do not seek to invest in those product technologies or production processes that could become obsolete in such a short time that they cannot recoup their investment. Many companies in high-technology industries (for example, personal computers, cell phones, memory chips, flat-panel displays, communication products) rely increasingly on outsourcing to avoid the fixed costs that accompany vertical integration. More important, because product and process technologies evolve so quickly, these firms can lower their investment risks and operating costs by purchasing key components rather than making them. These savings translate directly into enhanced profitability margins.[6]

For example, low levels of vertical integration have served Dell Computer well in the fast-changing personal computer (PC) industry. By devoting its effort to assembling and distributing PCs, Dell avoids many of the fixed costs that accompany R&D, manufacturing, and other

transaction costs:
Economic costs of finding, negotiating, selling, buying, and resolving disputes with other firms (for example, suppliers and customers) in the open market.

outsourcing:
The reliance upon external suppliers to perform value-adding activities that were once conducted in-house.

activities had it pursued a higher degree of vertical integration. Instead, Dell purchases key computer parts from a number of different key suppliers to limit its inventory and production costs. This enables Dell to concentrate on what it does best—taking orders from customers and assembling computers for fast delivery. Dell has become so efficient and lean in its production approach that it has consistently been more profitable and more agile than Hewlett-Packard and IBM in producing personal computers over the past several years. Dell has also recently begun selling computer printers made by Lexmark International to complement its PC offerings. This same lean business model now enables Dell to begin offering flat-screen televisions at prices much lower than those of Sony or Samsung. Whereas these two companies design and make their own parts, Dell purchases components from a number of different suppliers and passes much of the cost savings on to customers.[7]

Location of Activities. The actual location where a value-added activity is performed may be a significant cost driver in determining a firm's cost advantage. Perhaps one of the best examples of how location can be used to build cost-based competitive advantage is Toyota's strategy for dealing with its suppliers in the automobile industry. To keep inventory costs minimal and quality of parts high, Toyota works with key suppliers to build their component factories near its own assembly plants. By having suppliers' factories close to its own assembly plants, Toyota can implement just-in-time (JIT) inventory management. This means that Toyota can receive the parts it needs almost immediately without the costs of holding inventory. This "lean production" strategy enables Toyota to further reduce the costs of building and assembling cars. Moreover, lean production and just-in-time inventory practices enable both Toyota and its key suppliers to continuously improve the quality of their products. In addition, all of the components must be of the highest production quality standard, because neither Toyota nor its suppliers can afford a shutdown because of defects or missing parts. Inbound logistics costs at Toyota are thus reduced substantially, because little inventory sits in the warehouse. In addition, operations run more efficiently and seldom experience a shutdown due to unscheduled deliveries or poor-quality components or parts. Toyota practices its lean production approach in both Japan and the United States, where it has begun large-scale production of midsized automobiles and pickup trucks for the American market over the past decade.[8]

In a similar vein, location is a vital strategic cost driver for Federal Express, a unit of FedEx Corporation. By centralizing all inbound and outbound logistics or distribution activities near its Memphis headquarters, FedEx can achieve tremendous economies of scale and experience in sorting the overnight packages and letters that are key to its business. Because Memphis is centrally located in the United States, FedEx can use its location-based strategy to develop its low-cost, highly efficient air-flying routes across its entire system.

STRATEGIC COMPETENCY *in action*

A Vision of Industry Dominance: Nike[9]

Nike is the world's largest shoemaker and controls over 20 percent of the U.S. athletic footwear market. Led by Chairman, CEO, and Cofounder Phil Knight, the company was founded with track coach Bill Bowerman in 1962 and eventually became Nike in 1972. Nike takes its name from the Greek goddess of victory. The $12.2 billion-dollar giant (2003 figures) distinguishes itself from its competitors (for example, Adidas, Reebok, Puma, K-Swiss) through aggressive "celebrity marketing" and by associating itself with college athletic teams, Olympic teams, and major professional sporting events throughout the world. Regardless of

the type of shoe or apparel that Nike offers, the underlying vision behind the company is its relentless drive for high-performance products. Although Nike's aggressive marketing campaigns have brought us "The Swoosh" and the famous marketing slogan, "Just Do It," there are many sources of Nike's powerful competitive advantage including its R&D capabilities, extensive worldwide production and sourcing network, cross-selling products, and funding of various community-based programs.

Nike possesses strong in-house R&D capabilities that have led to a number of important innovations. At its corporate labs, Nike's scientists work in such disciplines as biomechanics, exercise physiology, materials engineering, and industrial design. Nike even forms research committees and advisory boards composed of athletes, coaches, trainers, equipment managers, orthopedists, and podiatrists who work with Nike to review designs, materials, and new product concepts. An early Nike innovation is its Shox technology that features a special shoe cushion system that is especially designed for runners and can now be found in basketball shoes as well. One of the most important developments that Nike has recently pioneered is its made-to-order shoe system known as NikeID. This technical advance combines state-of-the-art design software and advanced manufacturing to offer customers a personalized shoe with all of their desired features at an affordable price. At the company's website (Nike.com), customers can envision what their personalized shoe will look like by clicking through eighteen different color options, three sole choices, and two cushioning systems. There is also the capability to print your name or slogan on the shoe as well.

The backbone of Nike is its huge global production and sourcing network. Nike is able to command huge economies of scale in purchasing raw materials and in capturing low-cost suppliers around the world. Much of its shoe production occurs in the Far East, and Nike relies heavily on independent contractors to perform all of the key steps in shoe manufacture. Nike has also invested $400 million to install a new supply chain system that links shoe orders more closely with its contractors to reduce inventory costs. In past years, Nike's heavy reliance on third-party contractors generated significant controversy, especially when it was discovered that workers in many of these plants faced extremely difficult working conditions for a subsistence wage. However, Nike has taken major steps to compel its network of independent contractors to undertake important reforms.

Sponsoring athletic teams, events, or individual celebrities serves as the foundation for Nike's effective marketing programs. "Nike Teams" exist in virtually all athletic events. In particular, Nike targets professional athletes such as Lebron James and Lance Armstrong to lead the company's marketing efforts in a particular line of business. Stars such as Michael Jordan, who reach the pinnacle of recognition, are even given their own division and symbol (for example, Air Jordan shoes). Nike's relationship with Tiger Woods has sparked the development of Nike golf clubs and a Tiger Woods line of apparel. Even though this strategy has been extremely successful for Nike, the risk of public scandal (for example, Kobe Bryant in 2004) or perceived poor quality (Tiger Woods's initial set of golf clubs) has the potential to tarnish the company's image. Nike is trying to duplicate its successful U.S. marketing approach in overseas markets. For example, it has established a relationship with Manchester United, by some accounts the world's most popular soccer team. Soccer will likely continue to drive Nike's sales, especially in Europe. In 2004, Nike's market share for soccer shoes edged past 35 percent, which is 4 percent higher than that of rival Adidas.

Nike has broadened the line of footwear, apparel, and even sporting equipment that it offers. In recent years, Nike has acquired Cole Haan, Converse, Hurley International, Bauer Italia S.p.A., and Official Starter. Cole Haan enables Nike to sell dress shoes, whereas Hurley designs and distributes a line of action sportswear for surfing and skateboarding. The Hurley brand also gives Nike better exposure to the youth lifestyle market. In July 2003, Nike acquired Converse to broaden its portfolio of alternative and athletic footwear. Converse is best known for its line of Chuck Taylor All-Star sneakers that have been a key competitor to Nike. Nike's acquisition of Bauer gives it a new avenue to sell ice skates, in-line roller skates, protective gear, and hockey equipment. These acquisitions help Nike engage in greater cross-labeling and selling to reach every possible athletic segment. The company also operates its Niketown shoe and sporting apparel stores, as well as Nike Factory Outlets and Nike Women shops.

Nike has also funded various community outreach programs to foster more active forms of recreation among youth. Nike has partnered with the Boys & Girls Clubs and Positive Coaching Alliance to help at-risk teens to benefit from competitive sports and to build self-esteem. NikeGO helps install and refurbish sporting facilities and courts throughout the United States with recycled materials (including used footwear!) to support physical education classes in less prosperous urban areas.

Benefits and Costs of Low-Cost Leadership Strategies

Low-cost leadership strategies carry their own set of advantages and disadvantages to firms that practice them. Many of the advantages associated with low-cost leadership strategies are based on the relatively large size of the companies pursuing them. However, the disadvantages of low-cost leadership strategies may outweigh some of the benefits.

Advantages of Low-Cost Strategies. The appeal of the low-cost leadership strategy is based on the strong relationship that appears to exist between high market share and high profitability. Numerous studies have found that firms with high market share, for various reasons, can command above-average industry profitability over extended periods.[10] Some of the empirical findings that appear to explain, at least partially, the relationship between high market share and profitability include economies of scale, risk avoidance by customers, strong market presence, and focused management.[11]

Risk avoidance by customers means that buyers who are currently familiar with the low-cost leader's products are unlikely to switch to a competing brand of a similar product, unless that brand has something very different or unique to offer. Thus, low-cost producers that achieve a dominant market share position may induce risk aversion on the part of the industry's buyers. Customers often prefer to buy from well-known, dominant-share companies because they feel these firms will be around a long time after their purchase. This reasoning is particularly true for products that are costly or require after-sales service, such as electrical products, computers, and appliances. Emerson Electric, a leading firm in developing a broad range of electrical motors, drives, tooling, and other components, has built a commanding market position in these products. Emerson's emphasis on being the "best-cost producer" in any given category means that it invests in state-of-the-art manufacturing processes to strive for ever-higher efficiencies. At the same time, industrial customers that use Emerson's products feel the company's commitment to its businesses and know that components and after-sales service will be available.

Strong market presence means that low-cost firms are sometimes able to "convince" their competitors not to start price wars within the industry. This means that low-cost firms can set the stage for pricing discipline within the industry. In turn, prices are kept stable enough over time to ensure that all firms in the industry maintain some degree of profitability. The arrival of intense global competition, however, has made this type of discipline difficult to enforce in most manufacturing industries today.

Low-cost firms are often able to keep potential competitors out of the industry through their price-cutting power, which can generate substantial obstacles to firms contemplating entry into the industry. In other words, low-cost leadership strategies, when effectively implemented and understood by potential entrants, constitute a very effective barrier to entry that governs industry rivalry. For example, Intel currently dominates the production of microprocessors that serve as the "brains" for personal computers. By investing heavily in the latest generation of new technologies and processes, Intel has become the lowest-cost producer of these microprocessors. Its cutting-edge manufacturing skills complement its fast product development cycles. Other competitors (for example, Transmeta) may think about entering the microprocessor business, but Intel has enormous power to lower the prices of its Pentium, Xeon, and Itanium to deter entry. Intel's price-cutting power and manufacturing skill thus slow down the ability of other chipmakers to grab significant market share from Intel. However, even Intel must continually remain vigilant as a reinvigorated AMD continues to chip away at Intel's market share in not only the lowest-priced segments but also some midrange microprocessor segments.[12]

Low-cost firms also have the advantage of being able to sustain price increases passed on by their suppliers. By operating at more cost-efficient levels of production, low-cost firms can more easily absorb increases in the prices of components or ingredients used in their products. For example, Hershey Foods, a low-cost producer of chocolates and candies, is probably in a better position to absorb increases in cocoa prices than other smaller chocolate and candy manufacturers.

Disadvantages of Low-Cost Strategies. Cost-based strategies are not without their disadvantages, some of them rather extreme. The biggest disadvantage associated with low-cost leadership is the high level of asset commitment and capital-intensive activities that often accompanies this strategy. To produce or deliver services at low cost, firms often invest

considerable sums of resources into rigid, inflexible assets and production or distribution technologies that are difficult to switch to other products or uses. Thus, firms can find themselves
locked in to a given process or technology that could rapidly become obsolete. Such was the
case with Motorola during the late 1990s when the company was the low-cost producer of
analog-based cell phones. When more advanced digital cell phones became popular in 1998,
Motorola was so committed to its analog-based technology that it could not respond to the
changing market.

A huge disadvantage facing low-cost firms is that cost reduction methods are easily
imitated or copied by other firms. Cost advantages, particularly in standardized production or
service delivery processes, are often short-lived and fleeting. U.S. steelmakers were caught in this
situation during the 1970s when they faced the rising tide of cheaper Japanese steel imports. In
fact, many Japanese steelmakers were able to leapfrog ahead of U.S. companies by innovating an
even more advanced manufacturing process called continuous casting that made U.S. processes
using open-hearth furnaces obsolete. Japanese steelmakers were able to forge better-quality
steel at lower costs than comparable U.S. plants. What made the situation even worse for U.S.
companies was their failure to reinvest in new technologies; companies such as U.S. Steel,
Bethlehem Steel, and National Steel believed their low-cost production was a long-standing,
enduring advantage. Now, Korean steelmakers are adopting more innovative steel fabrication
technologies to undercut even their Japanese competitors. Korean steel companies, such as
Posco, have found new techniques to lower steel production costs even further, thus making it
difficult for even Japanese firms now to respond effectively.[13] The shift towards even lower-cost
sources of steel production continues to intensify in the Far East. New Chinese steelmakers,
such as Baosteel of Shanghai, have recently completed the construction of ever larger integrated
mills to supply a fast-growing domestic market. However, they are also beginning to export
significant quantities of standard-grade steel to many markets, especially in Asia. As Chinese
steelmakers continue to ramp up operations and gain experience, they will likely become
potent rivals to Korean and Japanese steel companies later this decade.

More important, companies fixated on cost reduction may blind themselves to other
changes evolving in the market, such as growing customer demand for different types of products, better quality, higher levels of service, competitor offerings, and even declining customer
sensitivity to low prices. Since 2001, many U.S. companies in the airline, telecommunications,
retail, and health care industries have greatly cut back on providing customer service in order to
cut costs relentlessly. As a result, customers now face longer waiting times, frustrating attempts
to resolve billing issues, and more complicated, tortuous procedures to order new products. For
example, Sprint and several other telecom firms have forced customers to migrate through a
dizzying array of automated menu choices when they call for customer services. This automated, cost-cutting approach to providing service has earned many cell phone service companies some of the worst reputations for poor customer service. Likewise, in the airline business,
American Airlines and Northwest Airlines attempted to charge customers higher ticket prices
for reservations not booked on their websites. When customers called in for personal service,
they had to pay for higher ticket prices. Shortages of key staff (for example, pharmacists, nurses)
and slow implementation of new technologies (for example, digital patient records, automated
inventory tracking) in hospitals and other facilities have become a long-standing part of the
health care landscape. Faced with declining reimbursements, hospitals continue to search for
ways to pare down their costs.

In practice, a low-cost leadership strategy usually allows room for only one firm to pursue this strategy effectively. When numerous firms compete with one another to become the
low-cost producer, the result is outright warfare in which everyone in the industry bleeds. In a
short period, rivals build enormous amounts of excess capacity that depress industry-wide

profitability. This situation now confronts firms in the automotive, airline, food processing, retailing, and telecommunications industries. In the airline industry, for example, customers have become accustomed to searching for the lowest fares on the Internet. Fewer and fewer people pay for higher-priced tickets, even when flying in business and first-class seats. Faced with ever-higher fuel costs, every U.S.-based carrier has already cut wages and benefits significantly since the disaster of September 11, 2001. Total industry losses have exceeded $5 billion in the past four years alone. Even with these massive restructuring efforts, it is expected that more carriers will seek bankruptcy protection (often on multiple occasions, such as US Airways Group), and some even face the prospect of liquidation. More mergers and consolidations are likely for this industry, especially as it grapples with the enormous losses of 2001, and the worrisome trend is spreading outside the United States.[14]

Likewise, in the telecom industry, the industry-wide losses have been so profound that MCI (previously known as WorldCom) filed for bankruptcy in 2002, and AT&T announced in July 2004 that it would no longer provide long-distance service for new consumers as the firm contemplates a full withdrawal from this business. Consolidation is already occurring in the telecom industry, as SBC Communications (formerly Southwestern Bell) announced a $16 billion dollar merger with AT&T in January 2005. Both Verizon Communications and Qwest are seeking to purchase other long-distance phone companies. Likewise, the mergers of Sprint with Nextel Communications and Cingular Wireless with AT&T Wireless during 2004 have hastened the consolidation of cell phone service providers as well. In turn, the shrinking number of service providers will likely give rise to a faster consolidation and mergers of firms that supply telecom equipment, such as Lucent Technologies, Nortel Networks, JDS Uniphae, Alcatel, Ciena, Tellabs, and other key players in this space.[15]

Differentiation Strategies

differentiation:

Competitive strategy based on providing buyers with something special or unique that makes the firm's product or service distinctive.

Another strategic approach to building competitive advantage is that of pursuing differentiation strategies. **Differentiation** strategies are based on providing buyers with something that is different or unique, that makes the company's product or service distinct from that of its rivals. The key assumption behind a differentiation strategy is that customers are willing to pay a higher price for a product that is distinct (or at least perceived as such) in some important way. Superior value is created because the product is of higher quality, is technically superior in some way, comes with superior service, or has a special appeal in some perceived way. In effect, differentiation builds competitive advantage by making customers more loyal—and less price sensitive—to a given firm's product. Additionally, customers are less likely to search for other alternative products once they are satisfied.

Differentiation may be achieved in a number of ways. The product may incorporate a more innovative design, may be produced using advanced materials or quality processes, or may be sold and serviced in some special way. Often, customers will pay a higher price if the product or service offers a distinctive or special value or "feel" to it. Differentiation strategies offer high profitability when the price premium exceeds the costs of distinguishing the product or service. The essential idea behind differentiation is to offer the customer an important *enhancement* of the product or service. Examples of companies that have successfully pursued differentiation strategies include Prince in tennis rackets, Callaway in golf clubs, Mercedes and BMW in automobiles, Sony in consumer electronics, Coors and Heineken in beer, Beretta in guns, Brooks Brothers and Paul Stuart in classic-cut clothing, Diners Club/Carte Blanche in credit cards, Bose in stereo speakers, American Express in travel services, J. P. Morgan Chase in investment banking, Krups in coffee makers and small kitchen appliances, and Benetton in sweaters and light fashions.

Building a Differentiation-Based Advantage

Firms practicing differentiation seek to design and produce highly distinctive or unique product or service attributes that create high value for their customers. Within the firm, differentiation-based sources of competitive advantage in value-adding activities can be built through a number of methods. Exhibit 4-4 portrays some sources of competitive advantage that a differentiation strategy can provide.

An important strategic consideration managers must recognize is that differentiation through product or service enhancements does not mean the firm can neglect its cost structure. Although low unit cost is less important than distinctive product features to firms practicing differentiation, the firm's total cost structure is still important. In other words, the costs of pursuing differentiation cannot be so high that they completely erode the price premium the firm

Competitive Advantage Based on Differentiation	**Exhibit 4-4**

SUPPORT ACTIVITIES		Inbound Logistics	Operations	Outbound Logistics	Marketing/ Sales	Service
	Infrastructure	Try to coordinate activities tightly among functions; build quality into organizational practices				
	Human Resource Management	Treat employees as special team members; emphasize reward systems that promote innovation or quality				
	Technology Development	Heavy R&D expenditures to make distinctive or even unique products; refinement of high quality manufacturing and technology processes; emphasis on excellence, world class quality				
	Procurement	Selective purchasing from best or world class suppliers				
	PRIMARY ACTIVITIES	Use of best materials, parts, and components	Extremely fine quality manufactured workmanship emphasized	Fast delivery to distributors; extra care in packaging and transport	Special, distinctive ads; Technical sales and know-how	High emphasis on treating customer as special individual; Fast and courteous special service

can charge. Firms pursuing differentiation must still control expenses to balance somewhat higher costs with a distinctive edge in key activities. The cost structure of a firm or business pursuing a differentiation strategy still needs to be carefully managed, although attaining low-unit costs is not the overriding priority. A firm selecting differentiation must therefore aim at achieving cost parity or, at the very least, cost proximity relative to competitors by keeping costs low in areas not related to differentiation and by not spending too much to achieve differentiation. Thus, the cost structure of a firm practicing differentiation cannot be that far above the industry average. Also, differentiation is not an end in itself; companies must continue to search for new ways to improve the distinctiveness or uniqueness of their products and services.

7-Eleven (formerly Southland Corporation) has practiced differentiation to avoid direct competition with large supermarket chains. It offers consumers greater convenience in the form of nearby location, shorter shopping time, and quicker checkout. It achieves these benefits by designing a business system within the value chain that is different from that of supermarket chains in several key respects: smaller stores, more store locations, narrower product line, and much faster inventory turnover. Its approach is higher cost than that of supermarket chains, so 7-Eleven must ordinarily charge higher prices to achieve profitability. However, customers are generally willing to pay a premium in exchange for the greater convenience that 7-Eleven provides. 7-Eleven still strives for cost parity, however, by buying some nonperishable items in bulk and keeping close control of inventory. Its current management team is placing renewed emphasis on turning inventory even faster so that customers purchase the freshest possible products, especially sandwiches and other food items. The company is installing a new computer system that automatically tracks and reorders the best-selling items and removes the slow-moving items from store shelves. For example, freshly made sandwiches at many 7-Eleven locations are tracked and sold on an hourly basis.[16]

Starbucks Coffee has grown at an annual rate exceeding 30 percent during the 1990s. Even now, the company continues to marvel investors with revenue growth rates exceeding 20 percent a year. Once a Seattle-based coffee-bean retailer that pioneered the concept of uniquely blended coffees, Starbucks has grown to almost 7,500 outlets throughout the country and is currently opening up a new location almost every day. Starbucks draws over 33 million customers worldwide into its stores each week. Total revenues exceeded $11.5 billion for 2003. For the unique flavor of Starbucks' premium coffees and ice coffee drinks, the company can charge upwards of $2.50 per serving. It recently increased prices slightly in September 2004, the first price increase since August 2000, to pay for higher rent costs. To remain ahead of other competitors such as Dunkin' Donuts and even smaller specialized coffee chains, Starbucks has begun to roll out an increasing number of different types of beverages that capture and retain its premium image. It has also begun to test the idea of offering hot breakfast items in some of its locations as part of its strategy to branch out beyond coffee. And Starbucks has begun selling music at many of its locations as well. Starbucks recently initiated a program to help coffee growers improve their crops to meet the firm's exacting quality standards. By choosing not to franchise its operations (like McDonald's), Starbucks is in a much better position to monitor quality in its store operations. Starbucks keeps employee morale high by offering health care benefits and stock options to all those who work more than twenty hours a week. According to *Fortune* magazine, Starbucks may be the most dynamic new brand and retailer created over the past decade.[17]

Maytag Corporation has practiced differentiation successfully to distinguish itself from such larger rivals as General Electric and Whirlpool in the major home appliance industry. The company offers a full line of washers, dryers, stoves, and refrigerators that is bolstered by ongoing efforts at continuous improvement and new product development. In 2004, Maytag's line of washers and dryers represented the industry's premium brand. Its famous television commercials feature a Maytag repairman who often has nothing to do while on call. Maytag seeks to attract customers at the higher end of the appliance market with superior quality and value offered to buyers. Maytag's strong ability to differentiate its products stems from its focus on innovation and quality. Innovative new products are launched every year, and it strives to make its products flexible, convenient, and even customized for individual users. One of its most recently introduced new products is an extremely energy-efficient washing machine known as the Neptune, which has begun to generate high margins in an industry characterized by fierce rivalry and discounting to major wholesalers and retailers. Later versions of the Neptune are using state-of-the-art "smart" technology to self-diagnose potential mechanical problems before a costly repair is needed. Future versions of the Neptune are believed to incorporate Internet-access technology that will automatically place a service call once a problem is detected. Although early versions of Maytag's Neptune line of appliances were plagued with technological glitches, the Neptune initiative has lead all major appliance makers to accelerate their own versions of the product. Because of the company's focus on new product development, continuous quality improvement, and premium pricing, Maytag's margins rose during the late 1990s, and so far it has been able to insulate itself from General Electric and Whirlpool's scale-based advantages.[18]

In almost all differentiation strategies, attention to product quality and service represents the dominant routes for firms to build competitive advantage. For example, firms may improve a product's quality or performance characteristics to make it more distinctive in the customer's eyes, as Lexus does with its sleek line of automobiles or Tiffany & Co. does with its broad line of jewelry and gift items. The product or service can also embody a distinctive design or offering that is hard to duplicate, thus conveying an image of unique quality, as with Krups coffee and espresso makers or with American Express in travel services and charge cards. After-sales service, convenience, and quality are important means to achieve differentiation for numerous firms, such as for IBM in computer and electronic commerce technology or Hewlett-Packard in desktop printers and digital imaging technologies.

It is not unusual for firms practicing differentiation to invest in production processes that use specially designed equipment that makes it hard for rivals to imitate the product's quality. Canon's line of fast digital cameras is one example. Canon's distinctive skills in fine optics, semiconductors, precision manufacturing, and focused R&D have enabled the company to become many customers' preferred brand for a wide line of cameras, including the professional Digital Rebel line, that command premium prices. Canon also chooses to make most of the components for its camera line in-house to preserve its quality edge. For its massive copier and printer operations, Canon also continues to invest heavily in state-of-the-art automation to speed up development times and improve product quality. By automating domestic production lines in Japan, Canon also protects and reinforces its expertise in precision engineering and advanced optics from rapid competitor imitation.[19]

Any potential source of increased buyer value represents an opportunity to pursue a differentiation strategy.[20] Buyer value can be increased or made more distinctive through several approaches, including (1) lowering the buyer's cost of using the product, (2) increasing buyer satisfaction with the product, and (3) modifying the buyer's perception of value. Of course, these three approaches to increasing buyer value are not mutually exclusive; a distinctive product or service that lowers buyers' direct costs can certainly increase their level of satisfaction as well. Nevertheless, increasing buyer value on any dimension usually means a need to reconfigure or to improve other activities within the firm's value chain.

Lowering Buyer Cost. One important means of lowering the buyer's cost to attain differentiation is through designing products that require less time, energy, or other physical, emotional, or financial costs on the part of the customer. Companies serving other industrial buyers are constantly seeking ways to lower the costs to users of their services, components, or parts. For example, Canon, Ricoh, and Sharp of Japan have built extremely reliable and durable photocopying machines that do not require lengthy and costly downtime to service. By using better-designed and better-quality components, the Japanese copier companies made substantial inroads into Xerox's market share in the United States. These machines enabled customers to save considerable sums in repair and downtime costs. Canon, in particular, has been able to turn Xerox's recent weaknesses into its advantage by offering cutting-edge color copying technologies and printers that are easy to service and expandable according to the user's needs. Since 2001, Canon has continued to strengthen its market share gains in the newest line of digital copiers and other office automation products.

In the consumer market, major appliances such as air conditioners, refrigerators, and washers and dryers are made more energy-efficient each year, thus reducing the consumer's energy costs. The introduction of electronic controls also enables customers to reduce the cost of these appliances' use, as sophisticated sensors regulate the amount of energy, hot water, and detergent needed to achieve a desired effect. For example, increasingly better and higher energy-efficient and reliable appliances are what allow Maytag to pursue a successful differentiation-based strategy, despite heavy competition from Whirlpool and General Electric. In general, one can expect that major appliances and consumer electronics products will significantly increase their use of "smart technology," which provides self-diagnostic routines and even warns the user of impending failure.

Lowering costs for buyers is a significant competitive advantage for firms that can redesign their products that simplify the number of steps involved in their use. Reducing the costs of inconvenience and other "hassle" factors can raise a product's appeal. For example, flexible contact lenses produced by Johnson & Johnson's Vistakon division are designed for long-term use without the need for daily removal and washing. By designing ultrathin contact lenses that are flexible and less irritating, Vistakon can charge a premium price because customers are saved from the "aggravation" costs that come with daily washing and rinsing.

Increasing Buyer Satisfaction. Another way to achieve differentiation is to increase the satisfaction of the buyer consistently, which usually means increasing the performance and quality characteristics of a product over those of a rival's. For example, manufacturers of tennis rackets, such as Head, Prince, and Wilson, race each other in providing better, more powerful, lightweight rackets based on new composite materials such as graphite and even titanium. Players using these rackets can deliver more forceful volleys than with older and heavier steel or wood rackets. Sporting equipment—bicycles, protective gear, tennis rackets, golf clubs— incorporating advanced materials do not reduce the buyer's costs in using the product; instead, the higher performance of the product enhances buyer satisfaction. For example, a number of companies in the golf equipment business (such as Karsten Manufacturing) are making their mark in customers' minds by offering clubs with new designs (for example, Ping) that enable even an average or occasional player to enjoy the game more.

In the food industry, companies continuously search for new ways to increase buyer satisfaction. Mustards, mayonnaise, steak sauces, ketchup, teas, coffee creamers, and soft drinks are frequently reformulated, redesigned, and repackaged to serve every possible niche segment that may exist. The rising popularity of newly introduced ethnic foods makes differentiation a natural strategy for companies such as H. J. Heinz, ConAgra, Unilever, Campbell Soup, and Del Monte to pursue. Reaching out with distinctive tastes and new brands enables these firms to bypass direct pricing competition with each other while enhancing a new appealing food category to customers in different markets. For example, differentiation enables firms to target their offerings to different niches according to regional tastes and preferences. Certain customers prefer their food preparations with a distinctive "kick" or spice level; others prefer a milder version. ConAgra's Hebrew National business, for example, proclaims the fact that its line of hot dogs is made entirely of natural meat products and does not have the same fillers that are found in other companies' offerings. This emphasis on wholesome, natural products not only helps Hebrew National hot dogs remain popular with its traditional kosher-oriented market but also makes inroads into other market segments as well. Regardless of the actual market segment, meeting these needs provides further opportunity to enhance differentiation. These products do not serve to lower the buyer's costs but do increase buyer satisfaction by meeting some need.

In another powerful example of how differentiation can create new products and the basis for future innovation, 3M's enormous success in the coatings, adhesives, and office supplies markets is based on designing innovative products that solve needs that future customers have not even articulated. For example, 3M's Post-It notes, flexible weather-stripping products, Scotch tapes, glass sealants, carpet cleaners, and other products are designed to solve many customers' practical office and household needs. The success of 3M's products is based on fulfilling a need that in many cases customers had not even anticipated. The firm's ability to successfully leverage its powerful differentiation strategy has also enabled the firm to pioneer many new coatings-driven technologies for the electronics and health care industries.

Increasing Buyer's Perceived Value. Finally, firms may find opportunities for differentiation by increasing the buyer's perceived value of the product or service. This task is much trickier, because the firm must attempt to "manage" how customers perceive its product. Differentiation strategies based on perceived value alone are extremely difficult to carry out. For example, Burger King continues to blitz the airwaves with television advertisements designed to promote the better value and better-tasting food it offers as compared with McDonald's and other fast-food restaurants. A recent promotion in summer 2004 proclaimed that Burger King would begin using better-quality Angus beef for its larger, premium sandwiches. However, such a move is easy for McDonald's and other hamburger chains to respond to with their own offerings.

On the other hand, American Express (AMEX) has been successful in expanding and growing its travel-related services business through carefully shaping the public's perception of value and security that it receives from AMEX. Security and peace of mind are defining themes that AMEX has used to heighten differentiation of its travelers' checks and other products. The company reinforces the security theme by showing how travelers abroad will always feel safer when using American Express travelers' checks and through familiar television advertisements that feature vacationers caught in exotic locales with competitors' travelers' checks that cannot be easily cashed or replaced. American Express is even implementing a personal security-based differentiation strategy as it embraces the Internet to serve its customers better. Through the company's website, card members can get preferred access to sporting and other entertainment events. More important, American Express recognizes the high level of importance that customers place on their financial privacy. The company has invested in state-of-the-art technology that now allows customers to access their accounts and to surf the Internet without revealing who they are.

Perceived value is often directly related to the lack or incompleteness of information possessed by consumers. Consumers without sufficient knowledge of the product or competing offerings eventually become smarter over time, so perceptions of value alone are unlikely to sustain a higher price premium. For example, people selling antiques often encountered a wide degree of price variance and acceptance by consumers before the advent of the Internet and online auction systems. Differentiation strategies based on increasing perceived value alone will not endow the firm with durable competitive advantage, because rivals can easily match and even exceed what the firm attempts to do. Of course, firms able to produce truly distinctive products that lower the buyer's costs or improve product performance have an easier time increasing perceived value.

Toyota's strategy for differentiating the Lexus automobile is based on all three aspects of increasing buyer value. First, because of their exceptional quality of manufacturing and use of the latest technologies, Lexus automobiles have high resale value, low service needs, and comparatively high fuel economy for luxury cars. These attributes reduce both the direct costs of ownership and the "aggravation" costs to consumers of frequent servicing. Second, Lexus automobiles directly increase buyer satisfaction through the use of genuine wood paneling, advanced sound systems, leather seats, easy-to-access controls, numerous safety features, and high engine performance. The latest Lexus models even offer a number of standard, integrated electronic applications that allow drivers to use a satellite-assisted technology to help them navigate unfamiliar surroundings. Even more advanced features include Internet access, smart headlights that highlight a curve in the road, and DVD-assisted navigation systems that cover the entire country. Smart technology also tracks the maintenance of each Lexus vehicle to anticipate and diagnose potential mechanical problems before they occur, thus saving drivers the stressful experience of breakdowns in traffic or in unsafe areas. Finally, Lexus has continued to produce an ongoing series of distinctive and memorable ads that, in one of the earliest examples, feature a Lexus car moving at speeds in excess of 120 miles per hour on a test platform, with no champagne glasses falling from an arrangement placed on the hood of the car. Newer ad campaigns focus on Lexus cars' ultrafast responsiveness to sudden obstacles and events that occur on the road. These ads reinforce the perception of how stable and well built Lexus cars are. These frequent advertisements, in combination with high annual customer satisfaction ratings, increase both the actual and perceived value of the car.[21]

Benefits and Costs of Differentiation Strategies

Differentiation strategies, when carried out successfully, reduce buyers' price sensitivity, increase their loyalty, and reduce the extent to which they search for alternative products. Compared with firms pursuing low-cost leadership strategies, firms practicing differentiation strategies are willing to accept a lower share of the market in return for higher customer loyalty. Yet, differentiation strategies come with their own set of advantages and disadvantages.

Advantages of Differentiation. A big advantage behind the differentiation strategy is that it allows firms to insulate themselves partially from competitive rivalry in the industry. When firms produce highly sought-after, distinctive products, they do not have to engage in destructive price wars with their competitors. In effect, successful pursuit of high differentiation along some key product attribute or buyer need may allow a firm to carve its own strategic group within the industry. This has been particularly the case in the food preparations industry, where large manufacturers try to avoid direct price-based competition with one another through frequent product differentiation and new product introductions.

A major advantage behind differentiation is that customers of differentiated products are less sensitive to prices. In practice, this attitude means that firms may be able to pass along price increases to their customers. Although the price of Lexus automobiles has risen steadily over the past several years, demand for these cars also continues to rise, as does buyer loyalty. The high degree of customer satisfaction with Lexus cars has translated over to the sport utility vehicle segment, where vehicles command a far higher price and profit. Buyer loyalty means that successful firms may see a substantial increase in repeat purchases for the firm's products.

Another advantage is that strategies based on high quality may, up to a point, actually increase the potential market share that a firm can gain. One landmark study noted, in fact, that competitive strategies based on high product quality actually increased market share over time. The combination of both high quality and higher market share resulted in significantly increased profitability. Product quality often leads to higher reputation and demand that translate into higher market share.[22]

Finally, differentiation poses substantial loyalty barriers that firms contemplating entry must overcome. Highly distinctive or unique products make it difficult for new entrants to compete with the reputation and skills that existing firms already possess. Nordstrom's ability to woo and retain customers in the cutthroat fashion and clothing retailing industry enabled the leading-edge store chain to anticipate its customers' needs and to offer them special promotions before they became available to the general buying public. Nordstrom's focus on superior customer service has, until recently, allowed the firm to sell top-of-the-line brands that offer a much higher margin than brands targeted to the middle market.

Disadvantages of Differentiation. A big disadvantage associated with differentiation is that other firms may attempt to "outdifferentiate" firms that already have distinctive products by providing a similar or better product. Thus, differentiation strategies, although effective in generating customer loyalty and higher prices, do not completely seal off the market from other entrants. Consider the market for steak sauces in the food industry. Once a competitor develops a particular flavor of steak sauce, its rivals can easily meet that challenge with their own offerings. In fact, excessive product proliferation can even hurt a firm's attempt to differentiate, because customers may become confused with the wide variety of offerings. For example, H. J. Heinz's recent moves to offer ketchup with different colors may have backfired, as some buyers are turned off by the prospect of putting purple or green ketchup on their French fries. The attempt to outdifferentiate another rival's moves occurs frequently in the radio broadcasting industry. Often, a station will adopt a format that emphasizes a particular theme: oldies, light rock, rock from the 1970s, pop, easy listening, country, or Top 40. However, the initial gains that any given station makes are difficult to sustain, because competing stations can dilute this message with their own variation of a theme. Most recently, some radio stations are attempting to reach a previously underserved market segment, such as the growing Hispanic or African American audience. Companies such as Radio One are buying stations in different parts of the country that have a strong African American presence. Radio One hopes that its distinctive music offerings and programs will enable it to capture a disproportionate share of advertising dollars of products that target the African American market.[23] Differentiation may be difficult for all radio stations over time, especially as new forms of satellite-based systems come into play. For example, new rivals Sirius Satellite Radio and XM Satellite Radio offer no commercials and unlimited music for a monthly subscription fee. Thus, unless differentiation is based on the possession of some truly proprietary technology, expertise, skill, service, patent, or specialized asset, a firm runs the risk of being outmaneuvered by an even shrewder competitor.

Another disadvantage of differentiation is the difficulty in sustaining a price premium as a product becomes more familiar to the market. As a product becomes more mature, customers become smarter about what they want, what genuine value is, and what they are willing to pay. Price premiums become difficult to justify as customers gain more knowledge about the product. The comparatively high-cost structure of a firm practicing differentiation could become a real weakness when lower-cost product imitations or substitutes hit the market. Consider, for example, the recent travails that beset Callaway Golf. Despite the enormous popularity of its Big Bertha golf club design that made swinging and hitting the ball easier, Callaway Golf was unable to sustain a huge market share position in the golf equipment business because other competitors eventually followed with similar, but somewhat different, designs or variations on the same theme. Even existing golf equipment providers, such as Wilson, innovated their own sets of large-head golf clubs that eroded Callaway's once-distinctive identity in the marketplace. Callaway's differentiation strategy yielded fewer benefits as new entrants seized the initiative away from the innovator and started producing similar clubs at lower cost. In the retailing arena, Starbucks may be feeling the heat of intensified competition from other coffee and latte providers, especially those rivals seeking to capture customers who may be turned off by Starbucks' comparatively high price. Although Starbucks has established itself as a premium brand, the rising cost of coffee ingredients makes it difficult for Starbucks to continue remain highly profitable if other entrants are willing to endure much lower margins or use less premium-grade ingredients to enter the coffee retailing business.

Differentiation also leaves a firm vulnerable to the eventual "commoditization" of its product, service offering, or value concept when new competitors enter the market or when customers become more knowledgeable about what is available. Over time, firms that are unable to sustain their initial differentiation-based lead with future product innovations, service enhancements, or other features will find themselves at a significant, if not dangerous, cost disadvantage when large numbers of customers eventually gravitate to those firms that can produce a similar product or service at lower cost. This trend is beginning to impact the pricing and differentiation-based strategies of companies selling flat-screen televisions in the United States. Although Samsung, Sony, Sharp, and others jockey with one another to produce a bigger, flatter, and better picture using their proprietary technologies (for a higher price), Dell Computer, Hewlett-Packard, and other firms are beginning to offer similar flat-screen televisions at much lower prices to customers who are not swayed by the cachet of more famous brand names. Sony, in particular, has been hit hard by its higher-cost structure and its slower response time to create even more leading-edge televisions that command premium prices.[24] Thus, differentiation requires firms to remain on the cutting edge of innovation and quality to accelerate new product development and to stay in touch with customer's needs and market trends.

Finally, firms also face a risk of overdoing differentiation that may overtax or overextend the firm's resources. For example, Nissan Motor of Japan during the past decade became so obsessed with finding new ways to differentiate its cars that it produced more than thirty types of steering wheels for its line of cars and a broad line of engines, all of which eventually confused customers and made manufacturing costly. Nissan recently announced a sharp reduction in the number of steering wheel sizes, optional accessories, and other features in its cars to lower its operating costs. In 2000, Nissan reduced the number of core automobile platforms to seven in order to reduce the high cost of overlap and design.[25] Excessive differentiation can seriously erode the competitive advantage and profitability of firms as rising operating costs eat into price premiums that customers are willing to pay.

focus strategies:
Competitive strategies based on targeting a specific niche within an industry. Focus strategies can occur in two forms: cost-based focus and differentiation-based focus.

Focus Strategies

The third generic strategy is known as a focus strategy. **Focus strategies** are designed to help a firm target a specific niche within an industry. Unlike both low-cost leadership and differentiation strategies that are designed to target a broader or industry-wide market, focus strategies aim at a specific and typically small niche. These niches could be a particular buyer group, a narrow segment of a given product line, a geographic or regional market, or a niche with distinctive, special tastes and preferences. The basic idea behind a focus strategy is to specialize the firm's activities in ways that other broader-line (low-cost or differentiation) firms cannot perform as well. Superior value, and thus higher profitability, is generated when other broader-line firms cannot specialize or conduct their activities as well as a focused firm. If a niche or segment has characteristics that are distinctive and lasting, then a firm can develop its own set of barriers to entry in much the same way that large established firms do in broader markets.

A major assumption of focus strategies is that the firm can attract a growing number of new customers and/or continue to attract repeat buyers. Expanding the firm's reach to new customers helps give the firm greater exposure about its offerings. Repeat buyers, however, are especially important for firms pursuing focus strategies, because they are knowledgeable about the firm's offerings and are less likely to be price sensitive. Moreover, repeat buyers in some cases may be extremely committed or enthralled with the firm's product or service, particularly if the product design, service concept, or technology is extremely hard to imitate.

Building a Focus-Based Advantage

Firms can build a focus in one of two ways. They can adopt a cost-based focus in serving a particular niche or segment of the market, or they can adopt a differentiation-based focus. As previously shown in Exhibit 4-2, focus strategies are different from low-cost leadership and differentiation strategies in terms of the scope of the target market. Within a particular targeted market or niche, however, a focused firm can pursue many of the same characteristics as the broader low-cost or differentiation approaches to building competitive advantage. Thus, many of the sources of competitive advantage discussed earlier for cost and differentiation also apply to focus strategies at the niche or segment level. It is important to remember that focus strategies attempt to pursue low cost or differentiation with respect to a much narrower targeted market niche or product segment. Thus, the resources and skills that the firm or business uses must be specialized as well.

What do Blue Bell Creameries, Solectron, Magna International, Guitar Center, Bang and Olufsen, Nucor, Chaparral Steel, and Patek Philippe have in common? These firms have adopted a well-defined focus/specialization strategy that has enabled them to earn high profits in industries that are fundamentally unattractive or fast changing. All of these companies have reconfigured their focus-driven value chain to emphasize either differentiation or cost-based sources of competitive advantage. Each of these companies has targeted a particular type of buyer or product segment that other broader-line competitors cannot serve as well. In effect, firms with highly refined focus/specialization strategies have developed a distinctive competence in defending their niches from larger firms that have difficulty understanding or serving their target customers.[26]

Blue Bell is the third-largest branded ice cream in the United States. Named after a beautiful Texas flower that sprouts in April, Blue Bell offers an extremely rich, textured ice cream that commands close to 60 percent market share in Texas and Louisiana. The company maintains an extremely tight control over production and distribution operations, with no one but the drivers stocking retail freezer shelves. The ice cream is so popular that the company does not have to negotiate with grocery store chains that are anxious to stock the product. Blue Bell also enjoys a high degree of employee and family ownership that enables the company to grow slowly without resorting to discounts and other financial inducements to groceries and convenience stores.[27]

Solectron is a highly specialized manufacturer of circuit boards used in personal computers and other electronic devices. It has followed a focused strategy of building low-cost, but well-manufactured, circuit boards for other PC manufacturers and assemblers that have decided to outsource this particular operation. In effect, Solectron has built a commanding presence in a particular cost activity of the personal computer industry value chain that other larger firms cannot perform as well. This strategy has won it many admirers and customers who prefer not to undertake some of the more mundane manufacturing tasks that are required for components and peripherals to fill out their product needs. Recently, Solectron has begun expanding contract manufacturing operations to meet the needs of firms in the cellular phone and personal digital assistant (PDA) industries as well. Solectron operates lean and extremely efficient manufacturing facilities that build circuit boards according to the designs provided by such personal computer firms as Gateway, IBM, and others. In effect, contract manufacturing enables Solectron to carve a highly defensible niche from broader-line players with significantly higher cost structures.

In a remarkable turnaround for American manufacturing, Mitsubishi Electric and Sony of Japan announced that they also would utilize Solectron's well-honed manufacturing skills to outsource production of components for cellular phones and even video game consoles. In the past, large Japanese companies such as Mitsubishi and Sony would have never even considered using the manufacturing services of an American company.[28] In recent years, however, Solectron has begun to face growing competitive pressures from similar contract manufacturers such as Flextronics, Sanmina-SCI, and Celestica—all of which have begun to offer manufacturing services to large firms in different high-technology industries.

In the automobile industry, outsourcing has become an important trend in which the Big Three (DaimlerChrysler, Ford, and General Motors) manufacturers have delegated an increasing amount of manufacturing work to more specialized firms that have the expertise to design, produce, and supply an entire component or subassembly. Magna International, one of the world's largest and probably lesser-known firms in the automobile component business, makes the bumpers and fascias that are found on many of General Motors' and DaimlerChrysler's cars. Today's bumpers and front grilles are much more sophisticated than those of previous decades, since these components are made with advanced engineered plastics that require specialized molding and shaping technology. Magna's distinctive competence is its ability to work with a range of different types of engineered plastics and other advanced materials to make fashionable, low-cost, and safe bumpers for large automakers that will in turn assemble them into their cars. Some analysts believe that Magna International will eventually be able to design and develop an ever more sophisticated range of automotive subassemblies for manufacturers throughout the North American market.

The Guitar Center offers another look at a well-orchestrated focus strategy. Tapping into the demand for self-generated music, Guitar Center provides equipment for home and professional recording. Although traditionally known for selling music equipment to professional groups, Guitar Center has begun selling digital recording software that helps aspiring performers to improve their sound. By selling more recording gear, Guitar Center is an excellent position to also provide microphones, mixers, synthesizers, and other equipment. Home recording has become a major growth market for Guitar Center as legions of new and untested artists hope to create their own digitally recorded music (which is later converted into MP3 form for Internet distribution).[29]

Bang and Olufsen is an innovative Danish designer and manufacturer of stereo systems. These stereo systems have a distinctive flat shape, silver color, and design flair that looks ultramodern. These expensive stereo systems are sold to music and stereo hobbyists who prefer to avoid the more mass-produced look of Japanese equipment. Bang and Olufsen has carved out a defensible niche through its innovative designs that allow it to stand on its own against fierce Japanese consumer electronics companies.

Founded in 1839 by a Polish aristocrat and a French watchmaker, Patek Philippe is one of the world's finest brands for luxury watches. In the highly competitive watch industry, Patek Philippe is one of the few companies that have been able to withstand the forces of consolidation. The company's lowest-priced watch starts at $3,000, and prices can easily climb into the millions. Production is limited to just thirty thousand per year, and the company closely guards its reputation to protect it from counterfeiters. A watch owner is encouraged to contact the company to check on the historical archives and production data to determine the origin of his or her timepiece. Patek Philippe's newest watch, the Star Caliber set, has over eleven hundred parts fitted into a watch case that is no bigger than three inches in diameter and a little over an inch high. Both faces of the double-sided watch are adorned with filigree and jewels. The company spent over seven years and dedicated ten of its 180 watchmakers to design the Star Caliber since 1993.[30]

The number of examples of companies finding and building niche-based focus strategies is growing. For example, in many parts of the United States, an increasing number of microbreweries have begun operations. These small breweries are designed to brew beer in limited quantities and cater to a specific taste or regional market. Although these breweries represent no real threat to national breweries such as Anheuser-Busch and Miller (now a unit of SAB Breweries of South Africa) they could carve out a significant local market presence in cities such as Seattle and San Francisco.

Benefits and Costs of Focus Strategies

By finding and serving a narrow market niche, firms that practice focus strategies often can remain highly profitable, even when the broader industry appears to be unattractive. Firms that practice focus/specialization strategies look for a niche and avoid deviating from it. Concentration of resources and effort to serve and defend a niche makes the focused/specialized firm less vulnerable to major changes in the industry's competitive environment. Yet, even a focus/specialization strategy brings its own set of advantages and disadvantages.

Advantages of Focus Strategies. The biggest advantage of a focus strategy is that the firm is able to carve a market niche against larger, broader-line competitors. Some firms pursuing this strategy have even been able to locate niches within niches (for example, handcrafted, Oriental musical instruments), thus further insulating themselves from the attention and efforts of larger industry-wide players that cannot serve the niche as well. Thus, defensibility and avoidance of direct, price-based competition are big advantages that accrue to a focus/specialization strategy.[31]

In many cases, a focus/specialization strategy enables a firm to improve other sources of value-adding activities that contribute to cost or differentiation. Consider, for example, the case of McIlhenny Company. Its expertise with Tabasco sauces gives it some ability and detailed knowledge of how to make Bloody Mary mixes as well. Thus, focus/specialization strategies may enable firms to use their specialized distinctive competence or set of assets to create new niches. Solectron's growing expertise with electronics-based manufacturing from work outsourced by larger firms has given the firm valuable experience and even critical mass to take on larger projects that move beyond the personal computer industry and into other electronics segments, such as cellular phones and telecommunications equipment. Magna International's growing experience with bumpers and front-end systems has given it the capability to design entirely new subsystems and assemblies at costs and quality levels that are by some measures superior to that of in-house production by the Big Three automakers.

Sometimes, a firm's focused product or service may attract a "cultlike" following among very committed buyers. For example, it is not unusual for customers to wait for as long as two hours for a table at a Cheesecake Factory restaurant, where the ambience, exceptionally rich desserts, and fresh ingredients have made the firm a standout in the restaurant industry. Likewise, for over two decades, Krispy Kreme Doughnuts was able to create a cultlike group of customers who are willing to stand in line at 5:00 A.M. for high-priced, fresh-from-the-oven doughnuts. Blue Bell ice cream also has a special appeal to customers in Texas, who will load up on a particular flavor when it is seasonally available.

Disadvantages of Focus Strategies. The biggest disadvantage facing the focus/ specialization strategy is the risk that the underlying market niche may gradually shift more toward characteristics of the broader market. Distinctive tastes and product characteristics may blur over time, thus reducing the defensibility of the niche. This may be particularly the case when tastes and preferences, once considered exotic or nouveau at an earlier period, become more widely accepted and even imitated by larger market segments. As mentioned earlier, a central assumption of focus strategies is that the firm can attract a high frequency of repeat buyers. Customers must love the firm's offerings so much that they become long-term buyers of its products or services. However, customers can just as quickly fall out of love with a product if perceptions about it change. Likewise, if a company tried to broaden the appeal of its product, it may alienate its core group of buyers. For example, Krispy Kreme Doughnuts has fallen on hard times recently as the company began selling its doughnuts in gas stations, grocery store chains, and other more accessible locations. By expanding the number of locations where its doughnuts can be purchased, Krispy Kreme may have grown too rapidly and diluted the cult status of its doughnuts.[32] Likewise, outsourcing has become so widespread as a common business practice that Solectron now faces a broad array of competitors in the contract electronics manufacturing field. Companies such as Flextronics International and Sanmina-SCI have become important rivals to Solectron by offering their own manufacturing services to large electronics companies that have chosen to steadily outsource more of their manufacturing activities.

A related risk is the potential for broad-line competitors to develop new technological innovations or product features that may redefine the buying preferences of the niche. For example, the growing use of flexible, advanced manufacturing technology makes it possible for larger firms to produce ever-smaller quantities of products that could be used to serve a variety of market niches or segments. Speed and flexibility, in addition to low-cost scale economies, are becoming important competitive requirements in a growing number of industries. This is also already happening in the designer and leather clothing market, in which Levi Strauss is now using cutting-edge computer-aided design (CAD) technologies, once relegated to industrial and engineering applications, to create new one-of-a-kind clothing patterns and designs according to each individual customer's tastes. Also, larger broad-line competitors could become swifter and faster in responding to market changes, thus enabling them to practice some variation of a focus/specialization strategy as well. All of the large U.S. home builders (for example, Pulte Homes, Toll Brothers, Centex) are beginning to invest in new technologies that allow customers to create their own home designs using a mixture of customized and standardized building materials and components.

Strategic Application to Nordstrom

One of Nordstrom's current strategic challenges is how best to maintain its superb customer service, while deciding how best to reduce its cost structure through better inventory and distribution cost controls. Thus, Nordstrom must carefully balance its traditional intimate service approach with improved operations to attain cost parity with its rivals. Also, despite Nordstrom's reputation for superior service, some younger customers have felt that the stores are too formal in their appearance and often lack the kind of cutting-edge fashions that ordinarily do not mix well with Nordstrom's traditional line of classic-cut clothing.

To attract these younger customers, Nordstrom in recent years began to tone down the formality of its displays and interior store décor, and it started selling fashions targeted specifically for a much younger crowd. The attempt to win over this new audience may have seriously diluted Nordstrom's reputation for top-of-the-line quality, as customers became confused about what Nordstrom was offering in recent years. Even more nimble competitors such as Neiman Marcus Group and Saks are beginning to make serious inroads into Nordstrom's traditional market base, as the boomer market becomes turned off from some of the avant-garde fashions designed for the twenty-something segment. However, it is the boomer market that provides the vast majority of Nordstrom's current revenues.

Nordstrom has attempted to broaden its opportunities for renewed growth by offering home furnishings with the same level of personalized service for the first time. The company hopes that it can find the right mix of lighting, bedding, tableware, and other offerings that will make Nordstrom a destination for home accessories in the same way that it has become a place for apparel and shoes.

A greater long-term threat to Nordstrom, though, is the renewed emphasis by larger retailing chains to provide better levels of customer service through buyer affiliation and reward programs, as well as improved training of sales personnel to enhance personal attention to customers. The larger chains are able to implement these steps as they continue to reap the benefits of cutting-edge computer-based inventory management systems that allow them to respond quickly to changing fashions and market needs. This emphasis on using advanced technology to lower inventory and distribution costs will serve the large retailing chains well, especially in economic downturns. As the larger chains adopt strategies that emphasize cost reduction, they will need to attract a larger number of customers in order to pay down the fixed costs of making such technology investments. To counter some of these developments, Nordstrom has invested heavily in new types of inventory replenishment and point-of-sales (POS) technologies that greatly speed up the time required to service customers. These new POS systems enable a store associate to check on inventories and speed the customer through the checkout counter with much greater ease and accuracy.

Ultimately, Nordstrom must preserve the top-notch service that its customers have been accustomed to receiving, and yet continue to invest in new technologies that transform the relationship between the sales staff and the customer. All the major retailing chains have invested in their own inventory replenishment and POS systems in the past few years, so technology by itself will not confer an enduring advantage. However, Nordstrom is continuing to look at using technology to serve increasingly choosy customers. Nordstrom is hoping to use the technology to create a strong emotional tie with its customers. For example, Nordstrom could use new technology to send customers information about new product launches, special sales, or even a personal series of interactions with individual customers to make them feel special. Another possible technology development is the creation of wireless networks that "unplug the store." Using wireless devices to automatically track inventory and sales will help sales people interact directly with their customers, instead of being reliant on a traditional register location. This may help Nordstrom sales associates to spend even more time helping their customers personally.

As growing numbers of people seek better value from their purchases, even the larger, consolidated chains such as May Department Stores and Federated will attract customers that once predominantly shopped at Nordstrom. Thus, differentiation strategies do not allow a firm to endure a "war of attrition" for a long period, especially when the firm's costs are significantly higher than those of its rivals.

An Emerging View of Strategy: Mass Customization for Best Value

Increasingly, companies in every industry and from every part of the world need to find new ways to satisfy their customers' quest for ever-increased value and performance. Although each of the basic generic strategies—low-cost leadership, differentiation, and focus—provides the basis for building a source of competitive advantage, the long-term viability of any single approach rests on a firm's ability to provide new sources of value continuously. As an industry evolves and innovation flourishes, firms must provide more value to their customers while controlling costs and even perhaps lowering their prices over the long term. Firms will have to devise new, innovative solutions to create and deliver value and productivity in each and every stage of their business system. Finding new ways to accelerate the creation and delivery of improving value will become the next battleground for firms in all industries. Ideally, companies will begin to formulate and execute those business strategies that enable them to deliver unique sources of value and solutions to their customers quicker and faster, rather than simply a product or service that can be readily imitated or copied. Ultimately, speed and flexibility will become as important as economies of scale. The way firms create and deliver a product or service will become just as important as the offering itself.

An interesting example of how low-cost, differentiation, and focus are coming together to redefine both customers' expectations of flawless service and the leading-edge technologies required to innovate new offerings is the phenomenal growth of refractive eye surgery. During the late 1980s and 1990s, eye specialists (ophthalmologists) steadily developed new software and laser-based surgical techniques that offered patients the ability to dramatically improve their vision. By measuring how the cornea, lens, and other eye tissues interact among themselves, scientists were able to isolate the specific refractive flaws that are at the source of nearsightedness and farsightedness in most patients. In 1995, the FDA approved another generation of corrective laser eye surgery known as LASIK. The price of LASIK surgery has dropped from as much $4,000 in 1996 to as low as $500 today. However, even LASIK today is giving way to another innovation known as wavefront-guided LASIK. Wavefront technology goes beyond traditional LASIK to create a three-dimensional image of the eye that offers surgeons an even more precise angle to correct visual flaws. Surgeons create a unique three-dimensional map for each patient. In turn, the laser automatically adjusts to the contour and eye shape that is unique to each individual patient. Of patients who have received wavefront-based surgery, 94 percent report 20/20 or better vision. By 2006, it is estimated that more than half of all refractive surgeries will use this method. As the technology improves and more physicians offer it, one can expect that the price of wavefront-based surgery will also decline steadily over time.[33]

What is the purpose of introducing our eye-surgery example in this chapter? We believe that the advances in LASIK and wavefront technology represent the spearhead of product and service innovation that will eventually define many other industries as well. LASIK is designed to offer each individual patient dramatically improved, and in most cases, perfect vision. Its cost has declined dramatically over the past several years, while newer techniques are developed simultaneously. At its core, LASIK symbolizes the *personalization* of value creation and value delivery. Our perspective is that reliance on any single, generic strategy (low-cost, differentiation, or focus) in itself will not endow the firm with a sustained capability to innovate new sources of value more quickly and more efficiently over time. Speed, rapid response, customized offerings, low cost, and innovation can no longer be trade-offs when formulating competitive strategy. Firms will need to provide quality products and services in a way that targets customers as if they were "market segments of one." Companies are now compelled to compete on the basis of *both* cost efficiency and customer-defined quality. **Customer-defined quality** represents the best value a firm can put into its products and services for the different market segments and niches it serves. In effect, competitive advantage will increasingly require firms to offer fast response and best source of value to each market segment or customer targeted. In its most sophisticated form, customer-defined quality leads to personalized offerings for each individual. However, each generic strategy by itself imposes a set of limitations and constraints that make it difficult for firms to respond rapidly along some key dimension: enhancement, cost, or variety. Instead, we believe that other types of business strategies will likely emerge that will come close to delivering a new, fast-response, value-driven concept of competitive advantage: mass customization that ultimately leads to mass personalization.[34]

Mass customization is an evolving strategic capability that allows firms to produce an increasing variety of products or services while simultaneously lowering unit costs. At its best, mass customization seeks to combine the positive benefits of low-cost and differentiation strategies while reducing the negative effects. Mass customization, when understood and exploited, provides the basis for fast response, creation of best-value solutions, and a high degree of flexibility to serve new customers and segments with future innovations. In effect, a business strategy based on mass customization enables firms to reconcile and even remove some of the trade-offs that are conventionally associated with pursuing each generic strategy alone.[35]

The principle behind mass customization rests on a growing set of advanced technological, distribution, and marketing capabilities that enable firms to produce products or deliver services to smaller and smaller segments while simultaneously lowering their unit costs. Traditional manufacturing and service operations typically confronted an economic trade-off in which lower unit costs required a high degree of product or service standardization. Conversely, differentiation strategies often left the firm competitively vulnerable to rivals that could provide a comparable bundle of value at lower costs. However, mass customization is an increasingly viable way to avoid these trade-offs. Some of the most important economic drivers that facilitate the potential of mass customization strategies include (1) the rise of advanced manufacturing technology, (2) the rapid use of modular product design techniques, (3) the growth of the Internet as a distribution channel, and (4) market segmentation tools and techniques (for example, data mining) that enable firms to locate and uncover previously unserved customer needs and market niches.

Advanced Manufacturing Technology

State-of-the-art advances in manufacturing technology, such as the introduction of computers into product design and factory work, have made it possible to substantially reduce the amount of time it takes to commercialize a new product from the lab to the market. Moreover,

customer-defined quality:
The best value a firm can put into its products and services for the market segments it serves. Customer-defined quality is more important to competitive strategy than what the firm thinks its quality should be.

mass customization:
The capability to produce a growing variety or range of products at reduced unit costs. Mass customization is a strategic competitive weapon that helps firms to expand the range of their product offerings and modifications without incurring the high costs of variety.

computers in manufacturing have also boosted quality significantly, as machines and processes are integrated through common databases and routines that simplify procedures and reduce the scope and potential of human error. Perhaps the most significant contribution of advanced manufacturing technologies to mass customization strategies is their ability to produce a wider scope, or envelope, of variety using the same design and production equipment to serve a growing number of market segments and differentiated needs. In effect, advanced manufacturing systems provide the basis to transfer the benefits of low-cost production (once confined to extremely standardized product designs) to an expanded range of product offerings and families. Thus, firms have the technical capability to produce more quantities in more ways that previously were not possible.

Levi Strauss has successfully used CAD systems to help design customized, one-of-a-kind leather outfits for its customers. Using an engineering workstation and advanced software, Levi Strauss can measure a customer's specific contours, body shape, weight, and preferences to create a customized pattern that becomes the basis for a perfectly fitting leather suit or dress in a short time. A customer's color and style preferences, as well as his or her body measurements, are then directly input into a computer that is electronically linked to a highly flexible stitching and finishing operation. Currently, most Levi Strauss outlets carry somewhere between eighty to one hundred different varieties of jeans and outfits. With the use of its new manufacturing and customization capability, the company feels that it will have somewhere between four hundred and five hundred different variations out on the shelves in the near future. Levi Strauss can thus provide the customer an individual, personalized sense of best value, while preserving a relatively low cost of operations.

Levi Strauss, however, has an important rival offering custom-made jeans, pants, and other clothing as well. The Interactive Custom Clothes Company (IC3D.com) uses advanced software to create customized clothing from measures taken from a three-dimensional (3-D) body scan. The company was founded in May 1996 to solve the "fit" problem that plagues the apparel industry. IC3D is expanding into dresses and even fashion accessories. The company is located near the Fashion Institute of Technology in New York, and it hopes to become the design leader of all types of clothing that enables customers to have their clothing just the way they want.

Other examples where advanced manufacturing techniques can create customized solutions include Footmaxx in orthopedic shoes and Paris-Miki in individual eyewear. Footmaxx used advanced three-dimensional modeling techniques to create individualized shoe implants that help the patient walk better. Traditional molds of a patient's foot are often made from plastic or Styrofoam, but these approaches cannot capture the impact of walking and normal foot movement. Footmaxx uses advanced computer-aided design modeling to generate a dynamic view of the patient's foot by taking over nine hundred different measurements. An electronic version of the mold is then used to design the best possible insoles that are worn in the shoes. Paris-Miki is an innovative provider of individualized glasses and eyewear. Using artificial intelligence and modeling software to capture the specific contours of a person's face, Paris-Miki makes eyewear that is tailor-made to each individual. The best-shaping lenses and frames are designed according to both the customer's physical features as well as what the customer wants his or her glasses to express in a personal way.

Modular Product Designs

modularity:
An element of product design that allows for the mixing and matching of different components and parts that all share the same interface or means of connecting with one another. A product exhibits modularity if its constituent parts can be rearranged among themselves or with additional parts that share the same pattern of linkage.

In many industries, the design and manufacturing of products (and even services) have taken on a new concept—that of modularity. **Modularity** refers to the capability of mixing and matching different components and product features together to create a customized offering. The key to successful modularity in product design is to ensure that the individual components that make up the final end product can be rearranged in any number of ways so as to increase variety. However, modularity requires that the underlying components and product features share a common set of design interfaces, or "protocols," to guarantee that they can be mixed and matched without costly retooling or extensive modification. Compatibility among different parts is key.[36]

Modularity has become a key driver that shaped product design in many segments of the electronics industry. For example, the proliferation of USB (Universal Standard Bus) ports in most personal computers (PCs), digital cameras, memory sticks, MP3 players, printers, and other devices makes it much easier for consumers to "plug and play" different devices with little hassle. Modularity has enabled companies to begin offering "bundles" of products to create even more value for customers. In fact, many of the "building blocks" used to build computers and other devices are standard, off-the-shelf components that share common design interfaces. For example, this growing modularity of product and component design enables Dell to apply its fast-turnaround manufacturing capability across a growing number of electronics products. Dell has always generated substantial revenues and profits from its ability to mix and match personal computer components according to what each individual customer wants. Parts are delivered on demand from nearby warehouses, and assembled according to customer specifications. In effect, by maintaining a very flexible supply and manufacturing system, Dell can custom-build each computer and price it according to what the customer wants. All of the standardized components are made by key suppliers who design these parts according to computer industry specifications. These common standards allow for full interoperability across manufacturers and user applications (for example, memory cards, USB ports). Models change continuously as new technology evolves. Through a common USB port, digital cameras and color printers enable consumers to use their PCs to shoot and develop their own pictures. Now, Dell wants to apply its same fast-turnaround strategy to provide computer printers, digital cameras, and even flat-panel television sets using the same strategic approach. Dell hopes to become a major player in these industries as well by harnessing modularity to sell a broader range of products.

One company that has taken modularity as a core design competence is Mattel in the fiercely competitive toy industry. The company envisions that its young female customers will soon be able to custom-design their own dolls (for example, Barbie) and other toys through modular choices of clothing, hair coloring, skin texture, and other desired attributes. Already, Mattel has produced large numbers of custom-ordered Barbies for major retailers that have special accounts with the firm (for example, Toys "R" Us and organizations that want the doll for their own promotion packages). Mattel has also moved the design of its major toy categories online so that virtual models can be produced and sent electronically to the company's factories. This step has cut development time 20 percent.[37]

A leading home furnishings company that has used modularity to enhance the elegant functionality of its products is IKEA. Swedish-based IKEA offers a line of chairs, futons, bookcases, and other home furnishings that enable a consumer to mix and match the furniture to best fit the specific amount of space available. One of IKEA's modular design concepts is the "Kubist" approach to building bookcases and shelves. "Kubist" uses wood construction to create highly functional, sturdy, and inexpensive cubes that the consumer can rearrange in any number of ways to maximize storage space in the home.

Modularity is a concept that can apply to other products as well. In the fashion industry, women are beginning to mix and match clothes in a way that suits their own personal style. This trend toward choosing one's own style is forcing retailers to move away from the cookie-cutter approach of offering a single line of clothing introduced by a fashion design house such as Gucci or Prada. Instead, these designers must now produce a broader range of dresses, shirts, blouses, and pants that enable finicky customers to create their own unique sense of style. Nordstrom, for example, has begun training its personal shoppers to help customers navigate through the dizzying array of options that hit the store shelves every season. Likewise, Gap Stores, which used to be well known for its khakis and T-shirts, must now stock tweed jackets, corduroy pants, and striped tops to capture this new type of customer who prefers a "modular" approach to individual style.[38]

Internet-Driven Distribution Systems

The rise of the Internet as a powerful distribution channel over the past several years testifies to the enormous leverage that customers have over firms in choosing and purchasing their products and services. The growth and spread of the Internet means that customers can become much closer to their firms and expect from them a level of speed and response that was previously not possible. For example, firms in the airline, travel services, financial services, music distribution, and book retailing businesses are now facing new rivals that are using the Internet to circumvent preexisting barriers to entry to reach new customers.

The Internet is a powerful economic driver that is now compelling firms to link up their product and service offerings more closely with their customers. Because customers effectively face very little switching costs (see Chapter 2) when they surf the web to find alternative product or service providers, it is incumbent upon firms to significantly upgrade and improve their distribution capabilities to exploit this new "real-time" virtual marketplace. The Internet has transformed the marketplace into a "marketspace" in which customers can freely select and demand the best possible value bundle or value solution from firms willing to tailor and modify their offering according to individual taste.

Service industries have been the first to adopt the Internet as a key vehicle to provide for mass customization strategies, but product-based firms are increasingly using the Internet to get a better feel for what their customers want. In fact, some firms are moving ahead to use the Internet to provide custom-ordered coupons for individuals who sign up for company-sponsored services. Procter & Gamble and many store chains offer special coupons and promotional discounts to customers through the Internet. Toy firm Mattel is even using the Internet to encourage young children to custom-order the toys and dolls they want according to their unique preferences. The data gathered from the Internet are then directly fed into Mattel's manufacturing and supply operations. Thus, the growing use of the Internet to capture each customer's individual preferences, combined with advanced manufacturing and modular product designs, create new possibilities for making mass customization strategies a reality for the next century.

New Market Segmentation Techniques

New statistical techniques developed by market research firms and computer software companies are now allowing marketers to identify previously hidden market segments and customer needs that were not easily found through traditional research techniques. For example, a new artificial intelligence program, known as data mining, enables firms to search for new market segments and latent demand for product and service offerings that have not yet been developed or are in testing stages. Data mining allows companies to search for patterns through massive amounts of research data to find correlations and results that the human mind and more rigorous hypothesis testing previously excluded.

The use of computers, bar coding, and later-generation radio-frequency identification devices (RFID) technology has made it much easier now to further identify segments within established segments. In other words, groups of consumers sharing similar purchasing and buying habits can be further defined and isolated into even smaller subgroups for the purposes of better identifying and capturing new ways to provide value. Through the use of new segmentation techniques, companies are no longer compelled to design a product that fits "an average customer" (as was the case with low-cost leadership strategies) but can now customize product attributes and features more aligned or in sync with the needs of much smaller market segments.

The Internet's Impact on Cost and Responsiveness to Customer Needs

The growth of the Internet has the potential to transform competitive strategy across a wide spectrum of industries.[39] In short, the Internet has a particularly strong impact on certain types of businesses. These businesses include those that (1) offer a wide product selection, (2) are well understood by customers, and (3) exhibit fluctuating product availability.

Wide Product Selection

When there is a wide selection of products, the Internet often becomes an important medium to reach customers. For example, the enormous number of books and CDs makes it difficult for individual stores, even the large chains, to stock all that customers may want to purchase. Shelf space is very limited for most retailers. The costs of purchasing and holding such a large inventory becomes prohibitive, even for the largest chains such as Borders and Barnes & Noble. More important, traditional retailing chains may only stock the books and music that are the most popular (and therefore most likely to sell), thus leaving many selections unavailable for customers. On the other hand, it is easy for Amazon.com to offer books and music through the Internet because it ships products to customers only when the company has received a firm order. Customers are purchasing an increasing number of other products such as toys and videos for much the same reason. In a similar vein, automobile dealers will participate in such Internet-based initiatives as autobytel.com, cars.com, and automallusa.com in order to reach a broader base of customers. At the same time, prospective car buyers use these sites to reduce the effort required to search for the car they want to buy at the right price.

However, products that require personal customer trial also do not lend themselves to easy online sales. This explains why it is difficult to sell clothing and shoes over the Internet, because sizes may vary across manufacturers. Customers also prefer speaking directly with informed salespeople when buying materials or products for highly complex activities, such as installing new kitchen appliances or building a swimming pool. In these situations, customers will probably feel comfortable receiving advice from more experienced professionals, rather than attempting to explain something over the Internet or even the telephone.

Well-Understood Products

The Internet is a powerful driver of competition in those industries where customers understand the nature of the product. For example, airline tickets, hotel rooms, office supplies, and pet supplies lend themselves to sales over the Internet because buyers know what they are purchasing. Often, these products are not complex and do not require extensive trial by customers. Moreover, these products do not change over time and typically are highly mature. In the case of the pet food industry, many retailers have sprung up over the past few years to supply customers with products with which they are already familiar. Petopia.com and Petsmart.com offer frequent shoppers additional discounts for the foods and supplies that their pets consume on a regular basis. Purchasers like the fact that they can order their pet care products from these sites without much hassle and receive a discount as well. Likewise, online travel service companies such as Priceline.com, Expedia, and Travelocity offer a wide array of airline tickets and hotel rooms through the Internet, and customers do not hesitate buying from these firms because they know what they are receiving.

On the other hand, certain types of products and services cannot be easily sold or provided over the Internet. Products that require extensive after-sales support, such as sophisticated electronic or medical equipment, are often sold face-to-face. Buyers will often have numerous technical questions and will usually request demonstrations on-site.

Fluctuating Product Availability

The Internet is well suited to sales of products whose availability changes rapidly, even on a day-to-day basis. For example, customers will frequently use the Internet to browse different online retailers and auction sites to search for hard-to-find toys and video games during the December holiday season. Also, customers can use the Internet to search for out-of-print books that traditional book retailers are unlikely to carry. Business customers frequently use the Internet to purchase hard-to-locate products or inputs that they need for their own operations. For example, automotive manufacturers will frequently use the Internet to widen their search for vendors of specialty plastics or electronics that may not be readily available from their established suppliers. Often, industrial buyers who face highly fluctuating availability of components will use the Internet to scour the world for other suppliers that can provide an immediate shipment or an alternative, backup source of supply. For example, Owens & Minor, a leading provider of health care products and services to hospitals, has introduced a web-based service that lets hospitals track purchases they make with hundreds of competing medical suppliers. The system allows hospitals to identify pricing discrepancies for similar items, thus helping hospitals take advantage of prenegotiated discounts with their suppliers. Hospitals are better able to keep track of their costs, which have been cut an average 2 to 3 percent.[40]

In brief, the Internet provides a new medium by which companies can meet and support customers' needs regardless of distance and time. By using new technology to generate and transmit vast amounts of information, the Internet is now linking together customers, suppliers, employees, transportation companies, and other economic entities to provide real-time information on products and services, pricing, and availability.[41] In fact, the Internet provides such enormous cost reduction opportunities that Wal-Mart Stores made it an official policy in August 2002 that all of its suppliers would have to receive and send data over the Internet. By November 2003, more than 98 percent of Wal-Mart's suppliers were connected to the retailing giant through a Wal-Mart-designed software package. An advanced version of this software enables a Wal-Mart supplier to connect to the retailer as well as to a hundred different other Wal-Mart suppliers to coordinate their deliveries. This system enables Wal-Mart to receive custom orders and shipments for each store. Wal-Mart is now pushing all of its suppliers to use advanced RFID technology to track their shipments by 2005.[42]

In short, the Internet is forcing companies to simultaneously lower their costs and improve their customer responsiveness as the following developments take place:

- It can establish a direct link to customers and suppliers that lowers the cost of not only products and services but of activities required to support the transaction. The Internet also speeds up the transaction.

- It lets companies reduce the number of middlemen involved in order to reach the customer. In short, the Internet allows companies to bypass other firms that are in the value chain.
- It enables companies to access new customers in new markets in ways that were not possible with traditional distribution channels.
- It can help companies develop new products and services in ways that better match specific customers' needs.
- It gives companies more opportunities to identify and create customer-specific solutions based on their likely buying patterns. The Internet can help firms design or offer products and services to meet customers' needs faster.

A recent corporate study undertaken by J. C. Penney uncovers preliminary findings that customers who shop in stores, catalogs, and on the Internet actually tend to purchase more than traditional customers who shop in the store only. Contrary to popular fears that the Internet would displace the need for in-store shopping, this study notes that customers who "window-shop" online are far more likely to spend more overall than customers who shop only in stores. Consultants believe that the study's results show that retailers need to discover more opportunities to blend all three distribution channels together. This could mean encouraging customers to shop online but then pick up purchases in the stores. Likewise, it means that stores should also provide direct ordering systems and web access within the store so that customers can still purchase the item if it becomes out of stock.[43]

Leveraging Technology: Reinventing Amazon.com[44]

Ever since its beginning in 1994, Amazon.com has been considered the leading online retailer. Over the past seven years, Amazon has grown by leaps and bounds to become one of the biggest sellers of books, compact discs (CDs), videos, gifts, and even electronic products on the Internet. Founded by Jeff Bezos, Amazon.com initially started selling books by offering over a million titles that included most of the English titles in print. Amazon offered book customers a significant discount to list price, and it was able in most cases to ship books out within a day or two upon receiving the order. By the end of 2003, Amazon.com posted its first full-year profit, and it is on track to hit more than $7 billion in sales. Amazon is one of the few web-based companies (including eBay, Yahoo!, and WebMD) that survived the massive Internet bust of 2000–2001. In the process, Amazon.com has morphed from an online retailer to a very sophisticated technology company.

Amazon first sold books in the summer of 1995 by offering customers a selection of over a million titles (books in print). This selection of available titles was far greater than any traditional book retailer (for example, Barnes & Noble, Borders Group, Waldenbooks) was able to provide at the time; even the largest conventional bookstores carry about 150,000 titles in stock. Amazon attracted a huge customer following as readers loved the enormous array of titles, the discounted pricing, and the ease with which people can search for their titles and order securely over the Internet. Of growing importance, Amazon even allowed readers to communicate their thoughts and reviews about a book on the company's website. For each title that is available on Amazon's site, customers have the opportunity to provide their comments. Thus, any given reader is free to provide his or her thoughts about the book and other prospective customers can read those reviews.

Amazon also provides an extremely responsive service for its virtual customers. Every book that Amazon carries also shows the expected delivery time, ranging from one to two days to four to six weeks, depending on how readily available the item is. More important, Amazon offers a high degree of convenience and security for customers. It was one of the first companies to offer credit card transactions over the Internet and explains in great detail the lengths the company will go to in order to preserve security. Once a customer is ready to check out, he or she enters an e-mail address and creates a personal password. First-time customers need to enter their billing and credit card information, shipping address, and other items to create a personal profile. Each time the customer revisits Amazon.com, the website then retrieves the customer's personal profile in order to expedite the ordering process. Once an order is entered and verified by the customer, Amazon sends an e-mail back to the customer confirming what the customer ordered. Later, as Amazon ships the order out, it will then send another e-mail indicating how long to expect delivery and what items might be back-ordered.

Over the past few years, Amazon has attempted to reinvent itself on several occasions. In late 1998, it began the process of steadily expanding the array of merchandise

(*continued*)

available through its website to include toys, CDs, DVDs, consumer electronics, sporting goods, and even clothing. Its popularity grew so rapidly with customers that by April 2001, Amazon even took over rival Borders Group's online retailing operations. More profoundly, Amazon is in the processing of transforming itself into a "virtual storefront platform." Amazon is converting the powerful web-based innovations that it used for itself as a service for other merchants. In some ways, Amazon.com envisions itself becoming an omnipresent virtual mall. By connecting into Amazon's e-commerce system, many well-known "brick-and-mortar" retailers are selling through Amazon's site, including Lands' End, Target Stores, Toys "R" Us, J&R Music & Computer World, Golfsmith, as well as legions of smaller mom-and-pop operations. Amazon runs each of these companies' websites and handles the packaging of products for delivery; retailers ensure that the merchandise is available. In November 2002, Amazon launched a huge virtual apparel department, where all of the clothing is sold by third-party companies. Yet, Amazon serves only as a virtual platform; the clothing retailers control and stock their own inventory. Many analysts now believe that other large retailers will begin using Amazon's web technology and expertise to sell on its site. By the end of the decade, it is very possible that these third-party retailers could account for more than half of the products sold on Amazon's site. Already, the *Wall Street Journal* reports that Amazon's 25 percent gross margin is double that of Costco and three points higher than that of Wal-Mart Stores. Ultimately, Amazon may become a technology and web services company that provides an onsite platform for other retailers, rather an online retailer itself. It poses a rising challenge to much larger eBay, whose $20 billion in sales has so far dominated e-commerce with its wildly popular and increasingly global online auction site. At the same time, Amazon may be feeling growing competitive pressure from rival websites, such as Overstock.com, which also sells a wide line of books, videos and many other products. To continue its growth in cyberspace,

Amazon may transform itself into a website where anyone, anywhere, anytime could buy and sell to anyone else. Amazon has even introduced a new Internet-based search engine that allows users to personalize how they want to view search results. Developed by Amazon's A9 unit, this new search engine will let users search the web, bookmarks, images, movie-information databases, and even digital versions of books sold on Amazon's website. This new technology allows Amazon to challenge both Yahoo! and Google to dominate new cyber technologies.

To fulfill customers' expectations of speedy and accurate delivery of their orders, Amazon has invested huge sums into new technology and warehouses that can now handle triple the volume of four years ago. These same technology investments allow the warehouses to run like Dell's build-to-order factories and have actually lowered Amazon's costs of operations dramatically. Amazon is squeezing out inefficiencies and finding new ways to lower costs through consolidating orders and rewarding its employees to devise creative solutions to manage its warehouses better. Amazon's management is also employing "Six Sigma" techniques to reduce error rates throughout its warehousing and delivery operations.

Amazon's ambitions to sell an even wider range of merchandise on its website have begun to generate some important competitive issues for the firm. Many companies fear partnering with Amazon because customers will increasingly demand even deeper discounts for their products. Some top-name golfing equipment firms have hesitated to partner with Amazon, because they fear that their premium pricing and image will become diluted. More recently, one of its long-standing partners, Toys "R" Us, filed suit against Amazon in May 2004. Toys "R" Us believes that it has an exclusive arrangement with Amazon to sell toys on its website; however, the toy giant discovered thousands of items from competing rivals as well. As Amazon's web presence strengthens even further, its relationships with other retailers will likely produce important questions as well.

Strategy and Competitive Advantage over the Life Cycle

The strategy a firm selects depends on both the industry environment and its own distinctive competences and strengths. Yet, the evolution of the industry environment can have a marked impact on how firms build different sources of competitive advantage.[45] In this section, we examine the impact of the product life cycle on formulating competitive strategies.

The product life cycle exerts significant influences on both the competitive dynamics of the industry environment and the sources of competitive advantage that may be most effective in designing a competitive strategy.[46] As products (and their markets) move from introductory stages, through growth and maturity, and then into the decline stage, the strategic setting for competing within the industry changes. Exhibit 4-5 portrays the impact of each life cycle stage

Exhibit 4-5   The Impact of the Product Life Cycle on Sources of Competitive Advantage

Stage	Introductory	Growth	Mature	Decline
Nature of competitive rivalry	Limited focus on competitors; product is center of attention	Firms stake out key positions in market	Firms try to survive shakeout; many exit or fail	Remaining firms seek to reduce intensity of competition
Nature of entry	Pioneering firms define industry	Large-scale entry by firms seeking profits	Growth slows and entry is less attractive	Few, if any, entrants
Product technology	Emerging, untried technology; no dominant design is set in most cases	Competing designs hope to set industry standard	Dominant design for industry, few modifications	No real product change
Process technology	General purpose equipment and tools for flexibility	Growing investment in specialized tools/assets	Emphasis on efficiency and volume production; high automation	Processes do not change; may become exit barrier if rigid or capital intensive
Marketing emphasis	Focus on innovators; volatile prices that have no set level	Build growing product and brand awareness; prices begin to decline	Promote to as many segments as possible; prices are more stable	Marketing emphasis changes to preserving existing share position; prices steady or declining
Investment intensity	Very high—needed to build business	Massive expenditures to reinforce position	Deemphasis on adding new capacity	Begin gradual exit and even divest activities
Profitability levels	Generally unprofitable, lots of cash needed	Moving to higher profits; cash flow negative or uneven	Peak profits; cash is high	Profits decline; cash flow declining rapidly

TIME →

As the industry environment approaches maturity and decline stages, cost efficiency becomes important. It is generally difficult to find new opportunities for differentiation.

on strategic considerations and policies facing the firm. Note that as the industry environment progresses toward maturity and decline, the industry experiences a growing tendency to consolidate and shake out some of the weaker competitors. Also, each generic strategy will impose a different set of strategic requirements on firms as they evolve through the life cycle. Let us now briefly examine the impact of each life cycle stage on developing competitive strategies.

Introductory Stage

This early or emerging stage of the product's life cycle is often characterized by pioneering firms attempting to get their innovative products accepted by the market. A key strategic task facing the firm is to create product awareness within the market. In many cases, pioneering firms are able to establish important sources of competitive advantage based on their first-mover status.[47] First-movers often gain market share rapidly and early over the competition and thus can build initial competitive advantage as the product concept begins to penetrate the market. Many strong sources of competitive advantage are derived from patents and other proprietary technologies. However, first-mover status by itself does not mean that the firm will always retain its advantage; firms possessing first-mover status must continue to invest in product designs and ultimately in cutting-edge process technologies to sustain advantage as the life cycle evolves.

In many industries, pioneering firms are often more focused on their products than on the processes. This stage is characterized by an enormous degree of uncertainty over the technology to be used in the product; the nature, number, and type of future competitors; as well as the risk aversion and lack of awareness by potential customers. Competing product designs and prototypes are likely to proliferate as firms jockey with one another to define a future industry or technical standard for customer use and adoption. Buyers of products in the introductory phase of the life cycle must be convinced of the new product's merits. Therefore, firms search for new types of buyers and regions to become early adopters. In many cases, the new product offers the prospect of a substitute for an existing product or way of doing things.

Consider the development of software for personal computers. Each time a new software product comes out (word-processing software, spreadsheets, graphics, statistics) it becomes a substitute for a preexisting method or product (calculators, adding machines, copy print, mainframe computers) performing the same function. Thus, buyers must feel that the new product offers significant value in substituting or complementing what they are already doing. The same economic logic also drove the innovation and eventual proliferation of DVD players in the market during the late 1990s. DVD players are regarded as not only a substitute for traditional VCRs but also a component that can be readily used with personal and laptop computers. The stunning clarity of DVD players' images, plus their ability to play traditional compact discs, makes these devices especially appealing to the market.[48] By 2004, many portable electronic devices even began to include DVD-recording devices that offer even greater product functionality. The same logic is likely to apply to new types of digital cell phones that include a digital camera, MP3 player, FM radio, and in some cases, online gaming capabilities since the beginning of 2002. These hybrid, multifunctional phones will, in turn, likely reduce the demand for stand-alone MP3 players as their storage capacity grows over time.

Some of the strategic problems facing firms in the introductory phase include (1) difficulty in accessing and obtaining resources or raw materials, (2) challenge in defining quality controls, (3) uncertainty in articulating a standard or set of value-providing features that customers will clearly accept, (4) high initial production and marketing costs, and (5) the potential response of established firms. Certainly, capital cost and availability remain pressing issues.

The development of new products or services often requires new skills, technologies, and raw materials that may be difficult to obtain. For example, advanced composite materials for building graphite tennis rackets and golf clubs were initially scarce; much of this material was high priced and went to government defense projects.

A major technical and marketing problem facing pioneering firms is also defining and producing a high-quality product. For example, new software or video games with unforeseen "bugs" or glitches can easily destroy the value of the firm's innovations if buyers are turned off. This was the series of events that plagued the introduction of first-generation personal digital assistants by Apple and Sharp in 1993. Both companies' offerings, the Apple Newton and the Sharp Wizard, were difficult to operate and the software was slow. Not until the advent of the Palm operating system and smaller versions of PDAs did the market really blossom. In almost all industries, initial entrants face high production, development, and marketing costs. Unit costs will be high until fixed costs of production can be spread over greater volume. Economies of scale and cumulative experience effects do not usually decrease costs until after considerable volume is produced.

Articulating a set of technical standards or features that customers will come to accept is a major challenge for any firm developing early products or services. Although pioneering firms may have the initial advantage of defining what the product or service should provide, it is in no way guaranteed that customers will be satisfied with what they are offered. In practice, firms will find that they will have to devote considerable resources and expenses to change and modify their original prototypes and designs to fit more in line with what their customers will want. What complicates this matter is that other competing firms will likely do the same thing, with the end result being that the product design ultimately accepted by the market may very well be quite different (and thus require different skills) from that originated by a pioneering firm. Pioneering firms, in turn, are likely to devote a considerable amount of resources to developing the concept, only to find that the product ultimately evolved along a very different path. Established firms, in particular, may adopt "fast-follower" strategies that allow them to learn from the pioneer's missteps, or improve the product's features or cost. This is a major reason why pioneering firms are often unable to sustain an early advantage as the product, service, or technology unfolds.[49]

This series of difficulties appear to be a significant factor in slowing down Palm, Inc.'s growth as its handheld digital assistants become more widely accepted in the marketplace. Although the size of the original Palm Pilot has remained fairly constant over the past several years, customers have been demanding that the company add new features to make the device more versatile. New-generation Palm Pilot machines include expansion slots for additional memory, as well as potential link-ups with digital cellular phones. However, the widespread popularity of handheld computer operating systems and hardware has attracted the interest of Microsoft, which has significant ambitions to further extend its own Pocket PC technology to challenge Palm more directly in the marketplace. Microsoft's size and relationships with established customers (for example, Hewlett-Packard) make it a formidable threat to Palm.[50] Newer versions of handheld computers from a variety of vendors are expected to have many of the same features as those produced by Palm. In particular, the new line of "BlackBerry" models from Research In Motion has become wildly popular over the past two years. The latest versions of BlackBerry offer greater functionality than those from Palm, and some models even incorporate cell phone capabilities. Ultimately, many of these devices will likely "morph" or converge into a technological platform that more closely resembles a cell phone.[51]

Finally, a huge uncertainty hanging over these firms is the potential reaction of established firms facing the prospect of substitute products. New industries, such as biotechnology, represent a long-term threat to established pharmaceutical and other life-science companies. Thus, biotechnology firms must gauge the response and potential impact of countermoves by established players. In the automobile industry, a high level of uncertainty faces firms that are developing and pioneering electric cars that operate on batteries and other alternative, advanced fuel cell technologies. Batteries and long-lasting fuel cells threaten to replace many of the current electrical and even drive-train components found in today's cars.

Growth Stage

The growth stage of the life cycle is characterized by an increasing level and intensity of competitive rivalry. More firms seek to enter the industry because they believe the new product will be a commercial success. The new product or service is generally taking off, and industry growth surges. Profitability also dramatically increases, but competing businesses will consume vast amounts of cash to build new factories, to serve new customers, and to refine the product's features and quality.

In the growth stage of the life cycle, numerous firms emerge, each trying to establish its own design or format as the industry standard. Firms will try to stake out and expand key portions of the market by offering what they believe is the best-valued product or service for their customers. In fact, the demand for the product may be growing so fast that it causes a shortfall of capacity. As firms invest in new factories, plants, and equipment, the process technology will become increasingly specialized and dedicated to producing a given type of design or format. However, increased specialization is expensive and requires large volumes to justify its cost.

In many industries such as video games, pharmaceuticals, cosmetic skin treatments, teeth-whitening products, advanced telecommunications systems, and even new pet food products, firms will spend prodigiously to build brand awareness. In fact, the growth stage offers some of the best opportunities for firms to formulate differentiation-based strategies. Sufficient growth and profitability enable firms to look for new ways to avoid direct, head-to-head competition. Quality becomes a key driver in attracting and retaining customers and distinguishing rivals from one another. As profitability grows, however, many firms will be inclined to begin charging a premium price for their products. Rising prices, high industry profitability, and the rapid entry of new competitors set the stage for an eventual "shakeout" of many weaker firms. Some of the strategic problems confronting firms in the growth stage of the life cycle include (1) the need to deal with potential excess capacity, (2) the search for new product applications, and (3) rising buyer power.

Firms in the growth phase are likely to spend large sums on new capital equipment and factories. High market growth rates and demand create a tendency for many firms to overinvest in capital equipment. When growth eventually begins to slow, industry-wide overcapacity eventually hurts the entire industry. For any one firm, however, overinvestment in capital equipment represents a major and possibly continuing drain on cash. Each firm needs to judge carefully the timing of its own capacity additions and to calculate the potential capacity expansion made by rivals. High growth may actually set the stage for a much less attractive industry resulting from overcapacity. This series of developments provided the backdrop for the massive collapse of the telecom sector during the late 1990s. Now, the large number of firms producing and selling different types of digital cell phones, DVD players, video game consoles, and flat-screen televisions signals the growing possibility of excess capacity that will plague these industries. Already many producers of flat-screen televisions and their components have begun to feel the impact of slower market growth, and subsequently reduced profitability.[52]

Firms also must deal with the growing challenge of finding and developing alternative applications for the new product. The costs associated with finding new product applications—engaging in more R&D and testing activities for a smarter and well-established market—are likely to rise. Instead, firms perhaps should consider devoting more R&D effort and resources toward improving product quality and the cost efficiency of their production processes.

The growth stage is also the period during which buyers become increasingly more knowledgeable about the different designs, standards, and formats of a product. Thus, buyer power is likely to rise just as growth begins to level off. Because the product is no longer truly new or novel, buyers will pay more attention to brands and images. Strong buyer power means that firms will have to spend more effort and resources in marketing and promotional activities that maintain differentiation.

Sometimes, firms wait too long before they recognize the strength of buyers' power and delay their response to rivals' price cuts. This points to a significant potential weakness for those firms hoping to extend their differentiation-based strategies and advantages over the product's life cycle. As a product or service concept evolves through the growth phase and enters the mature phase, the viability of sustaining differentiation-based advantages begins to require ever more effort, because cost control and more focused, process-driven management issues will begin to predominate. As the Nordstrom example reveals, firms engaged in differentiation strategies need to ensure that they have a sufficient degree of effort dedicated to cost control in order to reach at least a strategic cost parity with those firms already executing a low-cost leadership strategy. For those firms practicing low-cost leadership strategies, stronger buyer power is a signal that they need to become more cost conscious about their operations and seek new ways to create and extend value solutions without compromising their internal operational efficiencies. In the electronics industry, for example, companies such as Sony, Sharp, Philips Electronics, Toshiba, Pioneer Electronics, and Samsung Electronics must now figure out new ways to continue their fast product innovation, while at the same time taking steps to manage their costs carefully.[53]

Mature Stage

The mature stage of the cycle is where the majority of U.S. businesses are located. Market growth is slow in the mature stage. A dominant design or industry standard defines the product technology in the industry, and buyers are knowledgeable about the product. Process technologies at this time become highly specialized, and cost efficiency becomes extremely important in determining profitability. Other key characteristics of maturity include a stronger emphasis placed on competition based on cost and price, difficulty in finding new opportunities for differentiation, a "shakeout" of weaker competitors, and more predictable offerings. Opportunities for differentiation still exist, but they are more difficult to pursue because buyers are familiar with competing firms' products. Declining differences between products of competing firms generally means an increased similarity in pricing.[54] Strategic issues and problems facing firms competing in mature industries include (1) excessively emphasizing price wars to utilize capacity and gain small market share and (2) finding new markets for mature products.

Many mature industries, such as airlines, automobiles, aluminum, packaged foods, personal care products, diapers, and industrial equipment, are characterized by occasionally fierce fights among existing rivals to gain additional market share. Because the prospect for actual market growth of the industry is virtually nil, an increase in one firm's market share must ordinarily come at the expense of another firm. Thus, firms competing in mature industries must monitor and prepare for occasional, if not frequent, price wars between existing firms. Oftentimes, the end result of such price wars is a lowering of the entire industry's overall profitability.

Some firms will initiate a price war to dislodge potentially weaker rivals; others need to lower prices to sell more products to use existing production capacity. For example, airfare wars are becoming increasingly common as stronger major airlines seek to dislodge weaker carriers from the industry. In the semiconductor and steel industries, firms cut their prices to continue operating at near capacity. The high-capital intensity of these industries means that firms continue to produce as long as they can meet their variable costs. Paradoxically, long-term profitability for all the firms involved in the industry will likely suffer. A big strategic issue facing most mature businesses is how best to deal with dedicated and rigid production processes or technologies that have few alternative uses.

Firms in mature industries need to engage in efforts to locate other faster-growing markets for their products. Expanding into new markets abroad represents a useful option for many firms that face the prospect of maturity in their home markets. For example, companies such as Merrill Lynch and Wal-Mart Stores are exploring further opportunities to expand beyond the United States as the domestic market becomes replete with new competitors. In another case, Crown Cork and Seal, a leading firm in the metal can industry, faces an extremely unattractive industry environment in the United States because of overcapacity and slow growth. However, it prospered because its specialized technology enables it to create bottle caps and other containers in ways that other companies could not. The firm has remained profitable for a long time because of its differentiation-based strategy, and it has begun selling in new markets overseas.

The example of Crown Cork and Seal also shows that firms can still manage to execute - differentiation-based strategies in a mature life cycle stage, but they need to be careful in managing their costs and search for new opportunities to extend their sources of competitive advantage to new arenas. Many other firms, such as Corning, 3M, Cisco Systems, PepsiCo, Procter & Gamble, and General Electric, are shifting their strategic focus to overseas markets that are rapidly growing and where maturity is a long time away. Even small regional firms, such as bakeries, are moving into Mexico and other developing markets to take advantage of rapid growth to complement mature operations back in the United States.[55] Thus, global expansion offers many mature businesses the opportunity to continue their operations and to increase profitability.

Decline Stage

Every product at some point in time reaches the decline stage of the life cycle. Decline results when demand for the product drops, when the number of substitute products increases, and when customer needs shift or change. Many entire products and industries have disappeared over past decades as a result of declining markets such as buggy whips, nonelectric typewriters, wooden agricultural plows, mechanical automobile brakes, rotary dial telephones, and black-and-white televisions in the United States. Other industries that are clearly approaching decline in the United States include shipbuilding, clock manufacture, textiles, and brass implements.[56] Products that currently appear to be on a fast decline include VCRs, floppy disks, and chemical-based photography film. The decision of whether to continue competing in a declining industry should be based on an objective assessment of the firm's viability and what returns the owners of the firm or business can gain from a sale.

Most firms cannot survive profitably in a declining industry. Not only is the industry structure deteriorating, but also rivals are confronted with numerous potential exit barriers that make smooth exit difficult. Exit barriers can result from earlier excessive investment in a specialized process technology that has yet to be paid for, emotional commitment by managers to a given business, and natural resistance by workers, managers, and the society in which they reside to shutting down plants. The presence of strong exit barriers means that firms will continue to compete fiercely with one another for a declining share of the market. In this environment, firms must consider several different strategic options: immediate divestiture or sale of the business, harvesting, or focusing on some niche.

Divestiture and sale of the business to other owners is often more difficult than it appears. Exit barriers often make leaving quickly difficult. More important, many firms are unable to sell assets at a price high enough to recoup some of the residual investment value. Attempts to divest and sell the business quickly often encounter resistance from workers and political pressure from communities intent on saving jobs. Thus, divestiture and sale, although viable economic options, may not be entirely easy steps. Many firms currently seeking to exit the defense industry, for example, face great pressures from communities concerned with preserving jobs in a declining market.

Harvesting means gradually "disinvesting" in the business. In other words, management deliberately and calculatingly runs the business into the ground so as to maximize the cash flows that can be extracted from future product sales in a declining market. Investment is stopped, maintenance is reduced, and employees are gradually let go. Harvesting strategies, however, are not without their downside. As might be expected, businesses that harvest often suffer from extremely poor employee morale. It is usually better to sell off the business (even when there are exit barriers) rather than to engage in extended harvesting.

Finally, a declining business could search for some niche in which to survive. This option, too, is highly problematic, since by nature a niche affords only enough room for one firm or business to serve it. Motorola has pursued a declining niche strategy in deciding to stick with the basic transistor business. Because integrated circuits and advanced semiconductors have long replaced basic transistors in most electronic applications, many of the original firms producing basic transistors have finally exited. Motorola is now the last niche producer of basic transistors that still have a tiny market (mostly hobbyists) in the United States.

Life Cycle Dynamics and Competitive Advantage

Firms can use the life cycle concept as an approximate basis for planning the next generation of technology and products that the market will likely need and use. However, truly reliable forecasting is extremely difficult. Future product concepts, designs, and competitors can evolve in unanticipated ways. Yet, despite these uncertainties, some general patterns do apply that help provide a roadmap as to which sources of competitive advantage are likely to be more prominent across the life cycle. Technology can sometimes rejuvenate an old product idea into a newly redefined concept.

Toward the early stage of a given product's life cycle, factors such as creativity, design expertise, flexibility, product innovation, and agility are important sources of competitive advantage. New ways of thinking about a product, a "clean-sheet" approach to design, and the ability to adapt quickly to changing product formats are important drivers of innovation and competitive advantage early on.

As the product evolves and matures, however, the relative importance of design elegance, creativity, and product innovation tends to become less significant as the primary drivers of competitive advantage. Instead, manufacturing expertise, process technology improvements, cost reduction, and yield management become the dominant technological and cost drivers that define subsequent sources of competitive advantage. As a given product concept or design matures, the mastery of advanced manufacturing techniques tends to become much more important, since cost, experience, and volume-based advantages become the basis for competing in maturing markets. By the time any given product design enters the latter part of the mature stage and into decline, firms will have already begun working on introducing and commercializing the next generation of product.

Consequently, firms in different industries need to consider how their distinctive competence can be harnessed to build competitive advantage according to life cycle dynamics. Yet, it is also important to note that within each industry, there may be a variation in the kinds of drivers that define competitive advantage across the cycle. In the video game industry, for example, Microsoft, Sony, and Nintendo have been strong competitors in designing wildly popular games. After they design their games, both companies leverage their marketing and distribution strengths to reach every possible electronics outlet, department store, and toy shop. Creativity is a driver of competitive advantage early on, but mass-marketing techniques become vital to high profitability as a game approaches maturity. To capitalize on some new technologies, Sony's entrance into the video game industry through its series of technologically advanced PlayStation systems enables Sony to leverage its quality and differentiation-based skills to become a major force in new-generation games that are sufficiently different from what Nintendo and other PC-based game companies have to offer. Sony's ability to leverage its marketing and new technology was crucial to stimulating buyers' potential interest in new game formats such as the PlayStation series of consoles. Yet, Sony must remain vigilant and focused in its effort to promote innovation of new games and video consoles, while monitoring its own costs and competitor developments.

Life cycle dynamics, however, should not serve as a substitute for effective strategy formulation. Companies should not use the life cycle concept as a road map to predict how broader industry or technological changes are likely to evolve. In fact, excessive devotion to life cycle thinking can lead a firm down dangerous paths. For example, U.S. consumer electronics manufacturers during the early 1970s, such as General Electric, Motorola, RCA, Sylvania, and Zenith, believed that the radio and color television set were highly mature products that had little future. These U.S. companies thought that the future of consumer electronics was largely predictable and unprofitable; in turn, they shut down their factories and sold off many of their operations. Sony, on the other hand, took a different view. It redesigned the basic transistor radio to incorporate a sleeker, more elegant design that consumers could use when walking, exercising, or performing other routine tasks. This product became known as the Walkman, and Sony was able to jump-start and regenerate an entirely new product life cycle in the consumer electronics industry. Therefore, firms should be aware of life cycle dynamics in their own industries but not use them as a substitute for strategy.

Ethical Dimension

In this chapter, we have examined how firms can formulate different types of competitive strategies to build competitive advantage. Competitive advantage and high profitability come from delivering superior value to customers through desirable products. Regardless of the individual competitive strategy it selects, a firm must ensure that its products and services are sold with integrity. Thus, the competitive strategy a firm ultimately adopts must also satisfy ethical criteria. Ethical standards differ from society to society and among individuals within a particular society. They also evolve over time. Consequently, generalizations are difficult. However, most U.S. managers operating today would agree that, at the very least, a firm should strive to satisfy a worthy customer need, to supply a safe product, and to provide honest information about its offering.

Worthy Need

Some consumer desires may be less worthy of satisfaction than others. Consequently, even highly profitable businesses may be hard to justify on an ethical basis. Most managers would judge businesses involving illegal narcotics, illegal gambling, falsely labeled nutritional products, deliberately shoddy products, and financial scams as part of this category. In other cases, judging worthiness is not so straightforward. For example, many record label and film production companies appear comfortable operating businesses that produce violent films and music (a source of major controversy and parent concern in the late 1990s); other managers would be uncomfortable in this kind of business. Likewise, a variety of different companies find themselves involved in the distribution of pornography. Companies in the satellite television, hotel chains, cable television operators, and Internet service providers are major purveyors of pornography through their distribution systems. Yet, many of these same companies strive to maintain a clean image in the community as well. Because of these differences, management may be unable to specify precisely which consumer needs constitute ethically worthy targets deserving of attention. Rather, each management group must consult its own collective conscience to arrive at a sound judgment.

Safe Product

All firms have an obligation to provide safe products to customers. Companies that fail to meet this requirement often face serious consequences. Consider, for example, that several pharmaceutical companies during the past several years were the targets of class-action lawsuits alleging that their drugs were unsafe. American Home Products (now known as Wyeth) faced considerable litigation in 1998 over the potential side effects that resulted from its Redux diet drug (also known as Fen-phen). In 2001, Bayer AG of Germany withdrew its Baycol cholesterol-lowering drug after noting that a disproportionate number of deaths accompanied its use. The government and a variety of consumer interest groups are now pushing drug companies to release the test results of all of their drugs, even extending to proprietary research that may show unintentional side effects. For example, the New York Attorney General's office filed suit against GlaxoSmithKline for failing to disclose the negative impact of its antidepressant drug Paxil when used in children. Glaxo settled the suit in September 2001 and agreed to post the results of all its clinical drug tests for drugs marketed after 2000 on its website.[57] In a similar vein, Merck in August 2004 faced inquiries as to whether its Vioxx anti-arthritis drug may cause unsafe reactions in patients suffering from heart disease. In October 2004, Merck announced the voluntary recall of all Vioxx drugs from pharmacy shelves and promised to reimburse patients for any that had not been consumed. Although Merck took this step to prevent further patient endangerment, this step is not likely to prevent litigators from filing class-action lawsuits against the firm. A similar series of questions may be confronting Pfizer as it also sells a competing line of pain medications (for example, Celebrex, Bextra) that may produce side effects in certain patients as well.[58]

The issue of product safety has become especially significant in the wake of a massive recall by Ford Motor Company in 2001 to replace the Firestone tires that equip its popular line of Explorer SUVs. Over two hundred people are believed to have died from accidents that resulted from either potentially faulty tires made by Bridgestone/Firestone or potential design flaws in the Ford Explorer. Although Ford has been aggressive to recall any Explorer using Firestone tires, Bridgestone/Firestone has been somewhat slower to react to the market's outcry over its potentially defective tires. The company has acknowledged that manufacturing problems in its Decatur, Illinois, plant did result in some tires losing their treads, but it feels that a significant portion of the responsibility belongs with the Ford Explorer design.

Ample Information

All firms have an obligation to provide customers with ample information about new products or services. In some industries, this requirement is codified into law. Manufacturers of packaged foods, for example, must provide a full list of ingredients on their package labels, whereas issuers of common stock must warn investors in a detailed written prospectus about potential risks associated with an offering. Procter & Gamble managed this issue of ample information carefully by informing consumers of the potential risk that its new fat substitute product, Olestra, may introduce. For some people, Olestra (as used in potato chips and other foods) may cause digestive distress.

The obligation to inform customers about products does not end with legal requirements, however. Where customer ignorance about a product is high and the potential damage that a product can inflict on customers is large, firms must often go beyond legal requirements. Failure to fully inform customers under such conditions constitutes a serious ethical lapse that can cause damage to a firm's reputation as well as considerable expense. This reasoning is the basis for heightened pressures on pharmaceutical companies to provide more information on both the efficacy and safety of their drugs.

Summary

- Competitive strategies must be based on some source of competitive advantage for success. A company must possess an advantage that enables it to perform an activity(ies) or task(s) better than its competitors. Every part of the value chain should be examined for opportunities to build competitive advantage.
- All firms compete with other rivals for customers at the industry or business level. Competitors may be small entrepreneurial start-ups, established single-business firms, or business units of a larger, diversified corporation.
- Competitive strategies may be analyzed from three generic categories: low-cost leadership, differentiation, and focus/specialization. Each type of strategy is designed to build competitive advantage in a different way.
- Low-cost leadership strategies are based on producing a product or service at a lower cost than that of rivals. A low-cost strategy builds competitive advantage through economies of scale, experience curve effects, and other factors to gain a large share of the market.
- Differentiation is based on enhancing the distinctiveness or uniqueness of a product or service. Differentiation builds competitive advantage by making customers more loyal, less price sensitive, and less willing to consider other product alternatives.
- Focus strategies aim to sell products or services to a narrow or specific target market, niche, or segment. Focus builds competitive advantage through high specialization and concentration of resources in a given niche.
- In the future, firms will be compelled to offer improved sources of value to their customers faster, better, and at lower cost. Mass customization enables firms to use new technologies (manufacturing, Internet, modular product designs, and market segmentation) to respond faster to customers' needs and to provide new sources of value continuously. The combination of all four emerging technologies will make mass customization a new strategy to serve individual customers. Mass personalization may become the ultimate standard of service.
- The Internet is compelling firms of all types and sizes to compete on the basis of both lower cost and faster response to customer needs. The Internet makes itself particularly felt in those industries where there is (1) wide product selection, (2) well-understood products, and (3) fluctuating product availability.
- The product life cycle is an important factor that influences how firms develop their competitive strategies. Each stage of the life cycle presents different issues with which the firm must deal. As a product progresses through the life cycle, certain skills and competences play a more important role than others in building competitive advantage, depending on the life cycle stage and the nature of the industry.

Exercises and Discussion Questions

1. What kind of trade-offs does a firm face when it chooses a particular type of generic strategy (low-cost leadership, differentiation, or focus)? How does the choice of a generic strategy ultimately affect the kind of people the firm would hire for its management team? What kind of skills would be needed for a firm pursuing low-cost leadership? Are these skills different from those needed to support a differentiation or focus strategy?

2. What are some disadvantages that come from large size? What are some industries in which large firms have encountered difficulties competing with smaller firms?

3. How do you see the product life cycle affecting the nature of competition within an industry? What types of competitive actions seem to be most important at each life cycle stage? Use the current evolution of DVD players as the basis for your discussion. What do you think DVD players will look like in five years?

 4. Using the Internet, look up the website for Starbucks Coffee. How would you evaluate Starbucks' position in the product life cycle for specialized coffees? Do you believe Starbucks is well positioned to compete as this market continues to evolve? What are some things that this firm needs to think about as it continues to grow at the pace that it has in recent years?

5. Using the LASIK example as an analogy for mass customization and mass personalization, what other industries do you think will face a similar trend? What should the affected companies in these focal industries do to remain competitive or to build new sources of competitive advantage?

6. Amazon has become synonymous with online retailing in many people's minds. What do you see are some challenges and threats facing Amazon's business model? How is selling books and videos different from selling toys and electronics?

Endnotes

1. Data for the Nordstrom Strategic Snapshot were adopted from the following sources: "Saks Inc. Mulls Splitting Units, Possible Sale," *Wall Street Journal,* February 9, 2005, pp. B1, B9; "A New Wrinkle: Beauty Stocks Are Looking Attractive Again," *Wall Street Journal,* March 3, 2004; "Is Nordstrom Still Relevant?" *OC Metro,* March 4, 2004, p. 82; "Nordstrom Is Adding Home to Its Wardrobe," *HFN,* March 1, 2004, p. 1; "Catering to the Luxury Customer," *Women's Wear Daily,* January 9, 2004, p. 20; "Nordstroms Had the Right Fit," *Investor's Business Daily,* October 21, 2003, p. A4; "Can Nordstroms Find the Right Style?" *Business Week,* July 30, 2001; "Nordstrom Cites Slowing Economy for Drop in Profit," *Wall Street Journal,* February 23, 2001; "Slaughter in the Aisles," *Forbes,* January 8, 2001; "The 100 Best Companies to Work For," *Fortune,* January 8, 2001; "In Return to Power, the Nordstrom Family Finds a Pile of Problems," *Wall Street Journal,* September 8, 2000; "Nordstrom Cleans Out Its Closets," *Business Week,* May 22, 2000; "In Retailing, Bricks Beats Bytes," *Wall Street Journal,* January 6, 2000; "Heard in the Northwest: Nordstrom Sags as Analysts Fault Store Merchandise," *Wall Street Journal,* December 15, 1999; "Filling Big Shoes," *Forbes,* November 15, 1999; "Nordstrom to Start Web Unit with Cash From Two Venture Capital Concerns," *Wall Street Journal,* August 25, 1999; "Nordstrom Tries to Cut Costs While Maintaining Service," *Wall Street Journal,* April 8, 1999.

2. Several store chains affiliated with May Department Stores include Foley's, Strawbridge's Kaufmann's, Hecht's, and Lord & Taylor. Federated Department Stores includes Macy's, Bloomingdale's, Rich's, and Goldsmith's. In January 2005, Federated and May announced that they would seek a merger to combine both firms into a

larger retailing entity. In November 2004, Kmart Holding announced that it would merge with Sears, Roebuck & Co. to form the nation's third largest retailer at the time.

3. See, for example, W. K. Hall, "Survival Strategies in a Hostile Environment," *Harvard Business Review* (September–October 1980): 75–85. A good discussion of the antecedents of high performance can be found in R. E. Caves, B. T. Gale, and M. E. Porter, "Interfirm Profitability Differences," *Quarterly Journal of Economics* (November 1977): 667–675; C. S. Galbraith and C. H. Stiles, "Firm Profitability and Relative Firm Power," *Strategic Management Journal* 4 (1983): 237–249; G. S. Day, "Strategic Market Analysis and Definition: An Integrated Approach," *Strategic Management Journal* 2 (1981): 281–299. Also, the use of firm-specific assets and resources to capture higher profitability can be found in K. Cool and I. Dierickx, "Rivalry, Strategic Group and Firm Performance," *Strategic Management Journal* 14 (1993): 47–59; M. J. Chen and D. Miller, "Competitive Attack, Retaliation and Performance: An Expected-Valency Framework," *Strategic Management Journal* 15 (1994): 85–102.

   Some of the more recent work examining this area includes the following sample pieces: T. J. Douglas and J. A. Ryman, "Understanding Competitive Advantage in the General Hospital Industry: Evaluating Strategic Competencies," *Strategic Management Journal,* 24 (2003): 333–348; C. Lee, K. Lee, and J. M. Pennings, "Internal Capabilities, External Networks, and Performance: A Study on Technology-Based Ventures," *Strategic Management Journal* 22, issues 6–7 (2001): 615–640; J. Gimeno and C. Y. Woo, "Multimarket Contact, Economies of Scope, and Firm Performance," *Academy of Management Journal* 42, no. 3 (1999): 239–259; W. J. Ferrier, K. G. Smith, and C. M. Grimm, "The Role of Competitive Action in Market Share Erosion and Industry Dethronement: A Study of Industry Leaders and Challengers," *Academy of Management Journal* 42, no. 4 (1999): 372–388; K. Smith, C. M. Grimm, G. Young, and S. Wally, "Strategic Groups and Rivalrous Firm Behavior: Towards a Reconciliation," *Strategic Management Journal* 18 (1997): 149–157; M. Chen, "Competitor Analysis and Inter-Firm Rivalry: Toward a Theoretical Integration," *Academy of Management Journal* 21 (1999): 100–134; J. A. Baum and J. J. Korn, "Competitive Dynamics of Interfirm Rivalry," *Academy of Management Journal* 39 (1996): 255–291. A more detailed review of the academic literature can be found in the next endnote, which more specifically covers the topic of generic strategies.

4. This section draws heavily on the excellent treatment of generic strategies by M. E. Porter, *Competitive Strategy* (New York: Free Press, 1980), and his second work, *Competitive Advantage* (New York: Free Press, 1985), chaps. 1, 3, and 4. An excellent academic treatment of generic strategies may be found in C. W. L. Hill, "Differentiation Versus Low Cost or Differentiation and Low Cost: A Contingency Framework," *Academy of Management Review* 13, no. 3 (1988): 401–412. Empirical tests of generic strategies have been an important research area. Some sample works include R. Amit, "Cost Leadership Strategy and Experience Curves," *Strategic Management Journal* 7 (1986): 281–292; G. G. Dess and P. S. Davis, "Porter's Generic Strategies as Determinants of Strategic Group Membership and Organizational Performance," *Academy of Management Journal* 27 (1984): 467–488; R. E. White, "Generic Business Strategies, Organizational Context and Performance," *Strategic Management Journal* 7 (1986): 217–231; L. Kim and Y. Lim, "Environment, Generic Strategies, and Performance in a Rapidly Developing Country: A Taxonomic Approach," *Academy of Management Journal* 31 (1988): 802–827; E. J. Zajac and S. M. Shortell, "Changing Generic Strategies: Likelihood, Direction and Performance Implications," *Strategic Management Journal* 10 (1989): 413–430; V. A. Zeithaml, A. Parasuranam, and L. L. Berry, *Delivering Quality Service* (New York: Free Press, 1990); J. Beath and Y. Katsoulacos, *The Economic Theory of Product Differentiation* (Cambridge: Cambridge University Press, 1991); E. Mosakowski, "A Resource-Based Perspective

on the Dynamic Strategy-Performance Relationship: An Empirical Examination of the Focus and Differentiation Strategies in Entrepreneurial Firms," *Journal of Management* 19, no. 4 (1993): 819–839.

5. See Porter, *Competitive Advantage.*

6. See, for example, K. R. Harrigan, *Strategies for Vertical Integration* (Lexington, MA: Heath, 1983). An excellent literature review of vertical integration can be found in J. T. Mahoney, "The Choice of Organizational Form: Vertical Financial Ownership Versus Other Methods of Vertical Integration," *Strategic Management Journal* 13 (1992): 559–584.

7. See "New Flat-Panel TVs Give Consumers Cheaper Option," *Wall Street Journal,* August 31, 2004, p. D1.

8. See "As Toyota Closes In on GM, Quality Concerns Also Grow," *Wall Street Journal,* August 4, 2004, pp. A1, A8.

9. Data and facts for Nike, Inc. were adapted from the following sources: "The New Nike," *BusinessWeek,* September 20, 2004, pp. 78–86; "Nike Introduces Latest Line of Triax Running Watches," *BusinessWorld,* September 8, 2004, p. 19; "Nike Goes Digital and Splashes City with Speed Theme," *Media,* August 27, 2004; "Nike Buys Sports-Gear Maker Starter for $43 Million," *Associated Press Newswires,* August 11, 2004; "Nike Inc.: Net Income and Revenue Surge Amid Olympics Preparations," *Wall Street Journal,* June 25, 2004, p. B6; "Nike, Serena Williams Partner Up," *Wall Street Journal,* December 12, 2003, p. B2; "The Web Smart 50," *BusinessWeek,* November 24, 2003, p. 98; "Nike's New Advice? Just Strut It," *BusinessWeek,* November 3, 2003; "The Real Nike Is Happening Abroad," *BusinessWeek,* July 21, 2003, p. 30; "Nike Goes Old School," *Fortune,* August 11, 2003, p. 150; "Leading the News: Nike to Swoosh Up Old-Line Converse for $305 Million," *Wall Street Journal,* July 10, 2003, p. A3; "Sneakers' Savile Row: Custom Running Shoes Are Gaining a Footing," *Wall Street Journal,* August 22, 2002, p. D1.

   The author would also like to acknowledge the assistance of former students Pablo Fernandez, Susan Foley, Matthew Jurecky, and Amada Keith for their insightful contributions.

10. Some of the landmark academic pieces on this topic include S. Schoeffler, R. D. Buzzell, and D. F. Heany, "Impact of Strategic Planning on Performance," *Harvard Business Review* (March–April 1974): 137–145; R. D. Buzzell, B. T. Gale, and R. Sultan, "Market Share—A Key to Profitability," *Harvard Business Review* (January–February 1975): 97–106. An excellent overview of the research literature documenting the different relationships between market share and various levels of profitability can be found in R. D. Buzzell and B. T. Gale, *The PIMS Principles: Linking Strategy to Performance* (New York: Free Press, 1987). These authors present an overview of the research findings that attempt to explain the relationship between share and industry profitability. Also see J. E. Prescott, A. K. Kohli, and N. Venkatraman, "The Market Share—Profitability Relationship: An Empirical Assessment of Major Assertions and Contradictions," *Strategic Management Journal* 7 (1986): 377–394; N. Varaiya, R. Kerin, and D. Weeks, "The Relationship Between Growth, Profitability, and Firm Value," *Strategic Management Journal* 8 (1987): 487–497 and N. Capon, J. Farley, and S. Hoenig, "Determinants of Financial Performance: A Meta-Analysis," *Management Science* 36, no. 10 (1990): 1143–1159.

    Later work addressing this issue includes the following: S. Davies and P. Geroski, "Changes in Concentration, Turbulence, and the Dynamics of Market Shares," *Review of Economics and Statistics* 79 (1997): 383–391; C. Banbury and W. Mitchell, "The Effect of Introducing Important Incremental Innovations on Market Share and Business Survival," *Strategic Management Journal* 16 (1995): 161–182.

11. See Buzzell and Gale, *The PIMS Principles.*

12. See "Intel Hastens Delivery of Chips Amid Increasing Competition," *Wall Street Journal,* February 8, 2005, p. B3; "Rewiring Intel," *Wall Street Journal,* January 12,

2005, pp. B1, B4; "How Its Missteps Let Rival AMD Catch Up," *Wall Street Journal,* January 12, 2005, pp. B1, B4.

13. See "Posco: One Sharp Steelmaker," *BusinessWeek,* August 30, 2004, pp. 66–67.

14. See, for example, "United Airlines Seeks Payroll Cuts as Way to Survive," *Wall Street Journal,* September 1, 2004, p. A2; "Alitalia CEO Wants to Cut Jobs by a Third," *Wall Street Journal,* August 26, 2004, p. B3; "Big Airlines Face Pressure to Simplify Pricing as Low-Cost Carriers Expand," *Wall Street Journal,* August 26, 2004, p. B1; "US Air Seeks Wavers on Pension; ATA Posts Loss, Issues Warning," *Wall Street Journal,* August 17, 2004, p. B3; "How Discount Airlines Profited From Their Bigger Rivals' Woes," *Wall Street Journal,* August 12, 2004, pp. A1, A2; "Can Delta Carry Song's Tune?" *BusinessWeek,* August 2, 2004, pp. 80–81.

15. See "Telecom-Gear Mergers May Start to Heat Up," *Wall Street Journal,* February 11, 2005, pp. C1, C4; "SBC Reaches Tentative Pact To Acquire AT&T for $16 Billion," *Wall Street Journal,* January 31, 2005, pp. A1, A12; "AT&T Retreats From Long-Distance Battle," *Dallas Morning News,* July 23, 2004, pp. 1D, 3D.

16. See "Good to Go? 7-Eleven Shops for the Latest in Convenience Items," *Dallas Morning News,* November 30, 2003, pp. 1D, 2D.

17. See "Starbucks Brews Broader Menu," *Wall Street Journal,* February 9, 2005, p. B9; "Lattte Letdown: Starbucks Set to Raise Prices," *Wall Street Journal,* September 2, 2004, p. B1; "Hot Starbucks," *Fortune,* January 26, 2004, pp. 60–74.

18. "Company's Try-Before-You-Buy Stores Allows Customers to Eliminate Suspicions Before Purchasing Appliances," *Houston Chronicle,* August 15, 2004, p. 9; "Maytag Stores Let Shoppers Try Before They Buy," *USA Today,* June 7, 2004; "Maytag Dishwasher Plant Wins Award," *Appliance,* May 1, 2004; Maytag Releases Campaign for Neptune Drying Center," *Adnews Online,* March 17, 2004.

19. See "Canon Inc.: Automation of Japanese Plants to Help Streamline Operations," *Wall Street Journal,* November 23, 2004, p. B3; "Canon to Build Research Center," *Wall Street Journal,* September 14, 2004, p. A15; "Canon Manufacturing Strategy Pays Off with Strong Earnings," *Wall Street Journal,* January 30, 2004, p. B3.

20. I. C. MacMillan and R. G. McGrath, "Discovering New Points of Differentiation," *Harvard Business Review* (July–August 1997): 133–145.

21. See "Lexus Sports a New Look," *The Advertiser,* August 28, 2004; Toyota Imports Ideas for Lexus," *Nikkei Weekly,* August 23, 2004; "Lexus Takes a Hard Look at Selling Superluxury," *Automotive News,* July 26, 2004; "Why You Can Call Lexus Mr. Reliable," *The Advertiser,* July 24, 2004; "The Lexus Nexus," *Forbes,* June 21, 2004; "Selling Lexus Is Tough Slog on Mercedes, BMW Home Turf," *Wall Street Journal,* December 4, 2003, pp. B1, B4; "Lexus' Big Test: Can It Keep Its Cachet—and Appeal to the Young?" *BusinessWeek,* March 24, 2003, p. 48; "Why Toyota Wins Such High Marks on Quality Surveys," *Wall Street Journal,* March 15, 2001, pp. A1, A11.

22. See L. W. Philips, D. R. Chang, and R. D. Buzzell, "Product Quality, Cost Position and Business Performance: A Test of Some Key Hypotheses," *Journal of Marketing* 47 (Spring 1983): 26–43.

23. See "Radio One Deploys an Urban Beat to Make Revenue Jump," *Wall Street Journal,* August 29, 2001.

24. See, for example, "Videogame Whiz Reprograms Sony After 10-Year Funk," *Wall Street Journal,* September 2, 2004, pp. A1, A10; "Sony TVs Take Sibling Tips," *Wall Street Journal,* August 20, 2004, p. B3; "Once a Footnote, Flat Screens Grow into Huge Industry," *Wall Street Journal,* August 30, 2004, pp. A1, A8; "New Sony TV Chips Give Viewers Control; Can 'Pan and Scan,'" *Wall Street Journal,* August 12, 2004, pp. B1, B2.

25. See "Nissan: The Squeaks Get Louder," *BusinessWeek,* May 17, 2004, p. 44; "Nissan Shines as Spotlight Hits Japan Car Makers," *Wall Street Journal,* May 12, 2004, p. B4B.

26. See "Specialized Firms Stick to the Straight and Very Narrow," *Wall Street Journal,* May 19, 1989, p. B2.

27. See "How Sweet It Is," *Forbes,* March 1, 2004, pp. 90–92.

28. "Why Some Sony Gear Is Made in Japan—By Another Company," *Wall Street Journal,* June 14, 2001, pp. A1, A10; "Solectron Becomes a Force in Stealth Manufacturing," *Wall Street Journal,* August 18, 1998, p. B4; "Solectron to Take Over Manufacturing of Some Mitsubishi Electric Products," *Wall Street Journal,* July 30, 1998, p. A6.

29. See "Guitar Center Strikes a Chord with Home-Recording Gear," *Wall Street Journal,* February 4, 2004, p. B3B.

30. See "Patek Philippe Is Luxuriating in Independence," *Wall Street Journal,* December 11, 2000, p. B18.

31. See, for example, C. Y. Woo and A. C. Cooper. "The Surprising Case for Low Market Share," *Harvard Business Review* (November–December 1982): 106–113; and R. G. Hammermesh, M. J. Anderson, and J. E. Harris, "Strategies for Low Market Share Businesses," *Harvard Business Review* (May–June 1978): 95–102. Also see C. Y. Woo, "Market-Share Leadership—Not Always So Good," *Harvard Business Review* (January–February 1984): 2–4; M. J. Chen and D. C. Hambrick, "Speed, Stealth and Selective Attack: How Small Firms Differ From Large Firms in Competitive Behavior," *Academy of Management Journal* 38, no. 2 (1995): 453–482; and A. Fiegenbaum and A. Karnani, "Output Flexibility—A Competitive Advantage for Small Firms," *Strategic Management Journal* 12 (1991): 101–114.

32. See "Ovens Are Cooling at Krispy Kreme as Woes Multiply," *Wall Street Journal,* September 3, 2004, pp. A1, A5; "A Hole in Krispy Kreme's Story," *Fortune,* June 14, 2004, p. 40.

33. See "Why Settle for 20/20?" *BusinessWeek,* Mach 17, 2003, pp. 95–96.

34. Mass customization is a term that has become well-defined and accepted in the academic and practitioner fields. We introduce the notion of "mass personalization" as an emerging concept that may enable customers to directly participate in the design and creation of products and services in tandem with firms. Some of these ideas can be found in D. Lei and C. R. Greer, "The Empathetic Organization," *Organizational Dynamics* 32, no. 2 (2003): 142–164.

    See also "Have It Your Way," *Forbes,* February 14, 2005, pp. 78–86 for a very quick look at how some companies are using their customers to create new products.

35. The concept of mass customization has become more popular as the basis for rethinking some of Porter's unidimensional, generic strategies. For example, see B. J. Pine, B. Victor, and A. C. Boynton, "Making Mass Customization Work," *Harvard Business Review* (September–October 1993): 108–121, for an early introduction to the concept. The use of advanced manufacturing technologies to undertake mass customization and integrated low-cost/differentiation strategies is explained in D. Lei, M. A. Hitt, and J. D. Goldhar, "Advanced Manufacturing Technology: Organization Design and Strategic Flexibility," *Organization Studies* 17, no. 3 (1996): 501–523.

    A recent empirical piece that examines the growing role of customer involvement in the firm's production process is B. C. Skaggs and M. Youndt, "Strategic Positioning, Human Capital, and Performance in Service Organizations: A Customer Interaction Approach," *Strategic Management Journal* 25, no. 1 (2004): 85–99. Also see B. C. Skaggs and T. R. Huffman, "A Customer Interaction Approach to Strategy and Production Complexity Alignment in Service Firms," *Academy of Management Journal* 46, no. 4 (2003): 775–786.

    A conceptual look at customer involvement can be found in D. Lei and C. R. Greer, "The Empathetic Organization," *Organizational Dynamics* 32, no. 2 (2003): 142–164. Also see S. Nambisan, "Designing Virtual Customer Environments for New Product Development: Toward a Theory," *Academy of Management Review* 27, no. 3 (2002): 392–413; C. K. Prahalad and V. Ramaswamy, "Co-opting Customer Competence," *Harvard Business Review* (January–February 2000): 79–90; M. A. Kaulio,

"Customer, Consumer, and User Involvement in Product Development: A Framework and a Review of Selected Models," *Total Quality Management* 9 (1998): 141–149.

36. See N. Worren, K. Moore, and P. Cardona, "Modularity, Strategic Flexibility and Firm Performance: A Study of the Home Appliance Industry," *Strategic Management Journal* 23, no. 12 (2002): 1123–1140; M. A. Schilling, "Toward a General Modular Systems Theory and Its Application to Interfirm Product Modularity," *Academy of Management Review* 25, no. 2 (2000): 312–334; C. Baldwin and K. Clark," Managing in an Age of Modularity," *Harvard Business Review* 75 (September–October 1997): 84–93; R. Sanchez and J. Mahoney, "Modularity, Flexibility, and Knowledge Management in Product and Organizational Design," *Strategic Management Journal* 17 (1996): 63–76; R. Langlois and P. Robertson, "Networks and Innovation in a Modular System: Lessons From the Microcomputer and Stereo Component Industries," *Research Policy* 21 (1992): 297–313.

37. See "The Web Smart 50," *Business Week,* November 24, 2003, p. 84; "The Customized, Digitized, Have-It-Your-Way Economy," *Fortune,* September 28, 1998, pp. 114–124.

38. See "As Consumers Mix and Match, Fashion Industry Begins to Fray," *Wall Street Journal,* September 8, 2004, p. A1.

39. See "E-Biz Strikes Again," *Business Week,* May 10, 2004, pp. 80–90; "Renaissance in Cyberspace," *Wall Street Journal,* November 20, 2003, pp. B1, B13; "The E-Biz Surprise," *Business Week,* May 12, 2003, pp. 60–68; "The Price is Really Right," *Business Week,* March 31, 2003, pp. 61–67.

40. See "The Web Smart 50," *Business Week,* November 24, 2003, p. 92.

41. An enormous amount of information about the Internet has sprung up in recent years. A new category of business publications focuses exclusively on the Internet, including such magazines as *Fast Company, E-Company, Red Herring,* and *Wired.* Some of the more recent academic pieces on the advent of the Internet include the following representative works: R. Amit and C. Zott, "Value Creation in E-Business," *Strategic Management Journal* 22, Special Issue (2001): 493–520; S. Zaheer and A. Zaheer, "Market Microstructure in a Global B2B Network," *Strategic Management Journal* 22, no. 9 (2001): 859–873; P. M. Lee, "What's in a Name.com? The Effects of '.com' Name Changes on Stock Prices and Trading Activity," *Strategic Management Journal* 22, no. 8, (2001); R. Wise and D. Morrison, "Beyond the Exchange: The Future of B2B," *Harvard Business Review* 78 (November–December 2000): 86–98; D. Kenny and J. F. Marshall, "Contextual Marketing: The Real Business of the Internet," *Harvard Business Review* 78 (November–December 2000): 119–130; F. F. Reichheld and P. Schefter, "E-Loyalty: Your Secret Weapon on the Web," *Harvard Business Review* 78 (July–August 2000): 105–114; S. Kaplan and M. Sawhney, "E-Hubs: The New B2B Marketplaces," *Harvard Business Review* 78 (May–June 2000): 97–103; P. Evans and T Wurster, *Blown to Bits: How the New Economics of Information Transforms Strategy* (Boston: Harvard Business School Press, 1999); W. C. Kim and R. Mauborgne, "Creating New Market Space," *Harvard Business Review* 77 (January–February 1999): 83–94; R. Kraut, C. Steinfield, A. Chan, B. Butler and A. Hoag, "Coordination and Virtualization: The Role of Electronic Networks and Personal Relationships," *Organization Science* 10, no. 6 (1999): 722–740; P. Evans and T. Wurster, "Getting Real About Virtual Commerce," *Harvard Business Review* 77 (November–December 1999): 84–94; S. Ghosh, "Making Business Sense of the Internet," *Harvard Business Review* 76 (March–April 1998): 125–135.

42. See "To Sell Goods to Wal-Mart, Get on the Net," *Wall Street Journal,* November 21, 2003, pp. B1, B6.

43. See "Shoppers Who Blend Store, Catalog and Web Spend More," *Wall Street Journal,* September 3, 2004, pp. A7, A8.

44. Facts and data for Amazon.com were adapted from the following sources: "Overstock's Chief Restates View that Market Favors Amazon," *Wall Street Journal,* February 9, 2005, p. C5; "Amazon Squeezed by Online Rivals," *Wall Street Journal,*

February 3, 2005, p. A3; "Amazon's Search Engine Unit Expands with New Features," *Wall Street Journal,* September 15, 2004, p. D12; "Inside the Mind of Jeff Bezos," *Fast Company,* August 2004, pp. 52–58; "Amazon Reports Profit, Raises Forecast for Year," *Wall Street Journal,* July 23, 2004, p. A2; "Amazon's eBay Challenge," *Wall Street Journal,* June 3, 2004, p. B1; "Amazon Goes for Gold with Discount Jewelry," *Wall Street Journal,* April 22, 2004, p. B1; "Reprogramming Amazon," *BusinessWeek,* December 22, 2003; "Amazon Plans a Search Service to Drive Sales," *Wall Street Journal,* September 25, 2003, p. B1; "New Chapter: In Latest Strategy Shift, Amazon is Offering a Home to Retailers," *Wall Street Journal,* September 24, 2003, p. A1; "Amazon.com Inc.: Outsourcing Pact with Target Is Extended to August 2008," *Wall Street Journal,* August 13, 2003; "Survival Strategy: Amazon Takes Page From Wal-Mart to Prosper on Web," *Wall Street Journal,* November 22, 2002, p. A1; "Leading the News: Amazon to Sell Clothing Online in Partnership with Retailers," *Wall Street Journal,* October 30, 2002, p. A3; "Amazon + Wal-Mart = Win-Win," *BusinessWeek,* March 19, 2001; "Amazon and Wal-Mart Have Discussed an Alliance, but No Deal Is Likely Soon," *Wall Street Journal,* March 7, 2001; "Diving into Amazon," *Forbes,* January 22, 2001; "Amazon: Cheaper—But Cheap Enough?" *BusinessWeek,* December 4, 2000; "Amazon.com, Toys 'R' Us Agree to Combine Online Toy Stores," *Wall Street Journal,* August 11, 2000; "Amazon vs. Everybody," *Fortune,* November 8, 1999; "Amazon.com Throws Open the Doors," *BusinessWeek,* October 11, 1999.

45. See, for example, C. R. Anderson and C. P. Zeithaml, "Stage of the Product Life Cycle, Business Strategy, and Business Performance," *Academy of Management Journal* 27 (1984): 5–24; J. G. Covin and D. P. Slevin, "New Venture Strategic Posture, Structure, and Performance: An Industry Life Cycle Analysis," *Journal of Business Venturing* 5 (1990): 123–135.

46. See R. A. Thietart and R. Vivas, "An Empirical Investigation of Success Strategies for Businesses Along the Product Life Cycle," *Management Science* 30 (December 1984): 1405–1423. Also see D. C. Hambrick and D. Lei, "Towards an Empirical Prioritization of Contingency Variables for Business Strategy," *Academy of Management Journal* 28 (1985): 763–788; and C. Hofer, "Towards a Contingency Theory of Business Strategy," *Academy of Management Journal* 18 (1975): 784–810.

47. A landmark work in this area is R. A. Kerin, P. R. Varadarajan, and R. A. Peterson, "First-Mover Advantage: A Synthesis, Conceptual Framework and Research Propositions," *Journal of Marketing* 56 (October 1992): 33–52. Also see R. Makadok, "Can First-Mover and Early-Mover Advantages Be Sustained in an Industry with Low Barriers to Entry/Imitation?" *Strategic Management Journal* 19, no. 7 (1998): 683–696; C. Brown and J. Lattin, "Investigating the Relationship Between Time in Market and Pioneering Advantage," *Management Science* 40, no. 10 (1994): 1361–1369; L. Huff and W. Robinson, "The Impact of Leadtime and Years of Competitive Rivalry on Pioneer Market Share Advantages," *Management Science* 40, no. 10 (1994): 1370–1377; P. Golder and G. Tellis, "Pioneer Advantage: Marketing Logic or Marketing Legend," *Journal of Marketing Research* 30 (1993): 158–170; M. B. Lieberman and D. B. Montgomery, "First-Mover Advantages," *Strategic Management Journal* 9 (1988): 41–58; and M. Lambkin, "Order of Entry and Performance in New Markets," *Strategic Management Journal* 9 (1988): 127–140.

48. See "Technology Titans Battle over Format Of DVD Successor," *Wall Street Journal,* March 15 2004, pp. A1, A8; "DVD-Standard Panel Approves Format Backed by Toshiba, NEC," *Wall Street Journal,* February 26, 2004, p. B6; "Tsunami of Digital Devices Heads for U.S. Shores," *Wall Street Journal,* October 20, 2003, pp. B1, B4; "Hollywood Heist," *BusinessWeek,* July 14, 2003, pp. 75–82; "DVD Gains on Tape, but Economics Have Hollywood in a Tizzy," *Wall Street Journal,* February 5, 2002, pp. A1, A6; "For Now, at Least, DVD Sales Are Soaring as Prices Drop," *Wall Street Journal,* September 11, 2001, p. B4.

49. See, for example, "When Being First Doesn't Make You No. 1," *Wall Street Journal,* August 12, 2004, pp. B1, B2.

50. See "How Palm Tumbled From Star of Tech to Target of Microsoft," *Wall Street Journal,* September 7, 2001, pp. A1, A4.

51. See "Cellphones Become 'Swiss Army Knives' As Technology Blurs," *Wall Street Journal,* January 4, 2005, p. B1.

52. See "Flat Panel Consolidation," *Wall Street Journal,* February 8, 2005, p. B2.

53. See "Profit Squeeze Bodes Shakeout in Electronics," *Wall Street Journal,* January 27, 2005, pp. B1, B2.

54. See, for example, D. C. Hambrick, "High Profit Strategies in Mature Capital Goods Businesses: A Contingency Approach," *Academy of Management Journal* 26 (1983): 687–707; and D. C. Hambrick, "An Empirical Typology of Mature Industrial-Product Environments," *Academy of Management Journal* 26 (1983): 213–230.

55. See "Bakers Find Acquisition Is Now the Recipe for Growth," *Wall Street Journal,* June 16, 1994, p. B4.

56. See, for example, K. R. Harrigan, *Strategies for Declining Industries* (Lexington, MA: Heath, 1985).

57. See "GlaxoSmithKline Posts First Drug Trial Studies Online," *Wall Street Journal,* September 1, 2004.

58. See "Vioxx Recall Raises Questions on FDA's Safety Monitoring," *Wall Street Journal,* October 4, 2004, p. B1; "Merck Pulls Vioxx From Market After Link to Heart Problems," *Wall Street Journal,* October 1, 2004, pp. A1, A14; "Merck Dealt Setback by Zocor Study," *Wall Street Journal,* August 31, 2004, p. A3.

Chapter 5

Responding to Shifts in Competitive Advantage

What you will learn

- *How and why a firm's competitive advantage can change over time*

- *Some important sources or triggers of environmental change*

- *Strategies that firms can undertake to respond to change*

Delivery of Online Music[1]

The growth of the Internet has brought significant change to a variety of different industries in the United States and globally. One of the industries most profoundly affected by the Internet is the music industry, as customers now have the opportunity to purchase music online rather than through traditional retailing channels. Thus, the delivery of online music (through a variety of formats) represents a tectonic shift in how record label companies deal with new technology and new methods of distribution that threaten to challenge how music is created, packaged, delivered, and sold to customers. Some doomsayers in 2000 went as far as to predict that the availability of online music would eventually spell the death of conventional CDs sold by the record companies.

Physical Capture of Music

Throughout the music industry's history, record label companies such as Universal Music, Warner Music (a unit of Time Warner), EMI Group, Sony Music (a unit of Sony), and Bertelsmann AG have built strong market positions by selling and publishing all genres of music to customers through a physical storage medium of some type. In earlier years, music was stored and played in prerecorded formats, such as vinyl records (LPs) and magnetic tapes (for example, eight-track and cassettes). In 1982, Sony and Philips Electronics jointly introduced a new format of music storage known as the compact disc (CD), thus delivering stunning clarity and audio fidelity. The advent of the CD, however, also meant that music was now recorded and stored in digital form, where each and every sound in a given audio track was converted into binary form (using 0s and 1s) as a means to improve fidelity and to reduce background noise. The biggest impact of the CD during the late 1980s and early 1990s was that sales of traditional vinyl records and cassette tapes plummeted dramatically over the succeeding years. In fact, most music retailers today do not carry vinyl records in any form, and sales of cassette tapes are relegated to a small corner of the store, if at all.

The "digitization" of music, however, also triggered a series of important changes in other related industries as well. New consumer electronic devices such as CD players began to displace sales of phonographs and tape players. More important, digitization of music meant that record label companies needed to invest in a whole new set of skills and technologies in order to ensure that customers were able to get the highest-quality music possible. Many of the skills and technologies involved are computer related, thus compelling the record label companies to invest in state-of-the-art manufacturing facilities that can process millions of CDs in a "clean room," highly automated environment. For consumers, digitization also heralded potentially significant changes in how people listened to music. As technology evolved to the point where CD players could be hooked into personal computers by way of CD-ROM drivers, consumers could also listen to music while they were engaged in other computer-based activities, either at home or on the job. Thus, people could begin to enjoy music when working on their PCs, in addition to driving, reading, exercising, or doing other tasks.

The fact that music was recorded and stored in physical form only by the record label companies helps to explain much of the music industry's relatively high profitability—until now. To secure a steady "pipeline" of music to reach its customers, record label companies would sign contracts with a large number of promising artists and performers in exchange for royalties paid to them. More important, artists and performers often sign long-term contracts with the record label companies, often for a period of years at a time. This means that a very popular performing group or artist (for example, The Beatles, Elton John, Mariah Carey, Gloria Estefan, Garth Brooks, Brittany Spears, Beyonce) will produce a very rich stream of income for the record company. Predicting which type of music or which performing group will become a success in the future, however, is almost an impossible task. In fact, for many record labels, 80 percent of the recordings made do not make money. To protect themselves from excessive financial losses, the record label companies hedge their financial risk by deducting production and marketing costs from the artists' and performers' initial royalties. If the record company is unable to sell a sufficient number of recordings to recoup this up-front cost, the artists and performers will receive no payment. If the recording turns out to be a real winner, the royalties paid to artists and performers will grow correspondingly.

For consumers, the physical storage of music on a CD format also highlights a major strength of the record label companies. These firms are able to predetermine which selections of recorded music that consumers can buy on any given CD; also, they are able to roll out future CDs of popular artists and performers according to the companies' marketing timetable. Artists and performers typically record a stream of different performances and hits, and the record companies then disperse the most popular tracks among a number of different CDs. This means that consumers will very often pay the full price for a CD with a dozen or more tracks of prerecorded music, when, in fact, what attracted consumers to buy the CD was only one or two of the most popular tracks.

The Arrival of Web-Based Music

The massive growth of online, web-distributed music over the past few years actually has its roots in a series of important technical achievements that began in the early 1990s. The digitization of music into CDs during the previous decade also made possible the "compression" of music into computer files. In 1992, the Motion Picture Experts Group (also known as MPEG) developed a standard for condensing audio into a well-defined computer format. This standard ultimately became known as MP3 (which refers to the layer 3 of MPEG1 code). Three years later, a company that would become better known as RealNetworks pioneered a new type of software that made it possible to engage in "audio streaming." Streaming is the process by which listeners can hear music one digital bit at a time. In practice, streaming re-creates music or other audio by stringing together the series of binary 0s and 1s (digital computer form) into audible form. This technology dramatically took off around 1996–1997 as the Internet became more widely accessible to personal computers. However, Internet connections were often haphazard, especially with dial-up modems that have been the predominant basis of how most people access the net. Downloading an entire two-minute song in MP3 required six minutes using a traditional phone modem and thus became impractical to most people. Because Internet transmission speeds were relatively slow during that time, streaming-based technology made it impossible for listeners to hear music without consuming a vast amount of computer memory and processing time to store downloaded music on their own PCs. By early 1998, however, faster and more reliable Internet transmission speeds made it possible for listeners to download entire music and audio files (in MP3 format) onto their PCs. Downloading an entire song now became much easier and faster to do.

The strategic situation facing record companies became increasingly more complex and challenging by 1999. First, a series of new developments in the consumer electronics industry made it possible for music listeners to store and hear music without relying entirely on conventional CDs. For example, MP3 players made by consumer electronics and PC firms, and even cellular phone makers, allowed users to download and carry MP3 music files anywhere they wanted. Second, new companies created a variety of different software to download music and to open up the compressed digital file. Internet users could in fact download most of these "digital players" for free, including Real Audio, Liquid Audio, and Microsoft's Media Player. Third, more technologically advanced PCs were now equipped with CD drives that write files as well. Thus, consumers were able to create and "burn" their own custom-made CDs on their computers. In fact, consumers can now store music in digital MP3 format by using their PCs as a giant "digital jukebox," and they can then copy whatever files they choose directly onto blank CDs for replay in the car or in traditional CD players. Finally, because MP3 music is stored in digital form, it was now possible for listeners to literally send music files by e-mail to their friends and other listeners. (See Exhibit 5-1 for a contrast of how traditional CD music differs from web-based forms.)

The cumulative effect of all these new developments was that music, for all practical purposes, was becoming a free good that was distributed over the Internet without any restrictions or controls imposed by the record label companies. In the very worst case, listeners received music free through many websites, including one of the most popular requested ones—Napster, which was seen as offering "pirated" music for free to listeners around the world. Napster became synonymous with the "Wild West" quality of the Internet—impossible to provide a sense of law and order or economic stability. Napster (and subsequent other file-sharing systems) enabled MP3 files to be copied repeatedly with no degradation of audio quality. Record label companies lost billions of dollars in royalties as MP3 files were beamed across the Internet, and very few listeners may have actually paid for what they received. The massive use of Napster by college students to access and to trade music, for example, contributed to a surge in Internet use during 1999. Even more foreboding to the record companies was the development of even more sophisticated downloading software, such as Gnutella, Kazaa, and other "peer-to-peer" sharing formats that do not use central computer servers for storage. In fact, continuing improvements of all types of technology presented a real challenge for record companies. MP3 players are rapidly falling in price. PC hard drives and other storage devices are sold for a mere pittance when compared with earlier-generation products. Even PC companies are taking advantage of online music to design compact but ever more powerful MP3 players, such as the iPod by Apple and competing offerings from Sanyo, Sony, and increasingly, Microsoft. Even

Exhibit 5-1   *The Rise of New Music Platforms*

Early CD-Based

- Captured in disc form
- Dependent on retailers to sell
- Companies determine/select offerings on CD
- Requires advanced manufacturing to produce discs
- Pricing set by label company
- Marketing and promotion drive disc sales

MP3-Variants

- Completely portable in digital code form
- Downloadable directly through the Internet
- Listener chooses what he or she wants to pay for
- Listener able to "burn" discs through PC/other device
- Pricing varies by demand/popularity
- Music "communities" may evolve over chat rooms on web

Nokia, Motorola, and all of the cellular phone makers are incorporating MP3 capabilities in their latest phones. New wireless forms of Internet transmission now even make it possible to download and hear MP3 files in cars and elsewhere. Moreover, the real issue for record label companies is that it has become much more difficult for them to decide when and where listeners are able to purchase and enjoy the music they actually want to hear. Music is no longer encapsulated in a physical form (CD or tape) whose tracks are preselected and determined by the record companies.

By 2004, a number of start-up firms were engaged in a variety of strategies to dominate online music delivery. A legal online music service known as Rhapsody began offering customers the right to copy and burn songs onto their own blank CDs for as little as 49 cents per song. Customers can burn as many songs as they want. In turn, customers can transfer these songs into an MP3 format that can be played on computers or portable music players. Even more recent start-ups such as Magnatune and Weed are also experimenting with pricing as low as 50 cents per song or five dollars per album. Dozens of other non-U.S.-based services have entered into the industry, often using the same type of file-sharing or peer-to-peer networks that made Napster illegal a few years back.

Response Initiatives

All of the record label companies realized the threat that online music represented to sales of conventional CDs. More important, the rampant piracy of copyrighted music threatened to erode their future profitability as listeners became further emboldened to download a blossoming list of MP3 files using a variety of different devices. On the one hand, the record companies need to protect their copyrights and intellectual property. Yet, these companies recognize that music storage and distribution have changed to an irreversible degree.

Recognizing this development, all of the major record label companies (Universal Music, Sony, EMI Group, Warner Music, and Bertelsmann AG), as well as a host of different technology companies (for example, software), came together to form the Secure Digital Music Initiative (SDMI) to devise new technology standards that would enable digital distribution of music but continue to protect copyrights. To protect their intellectual property even further, several record label companies and a number of different performers in 1999 sued MP3.com and Napster in federal courts, charging them with copyright piracy. In several cases that were brought to trial in 2000, both MP3.com and Napster lost a series of important court decisions. Later in 2000, a federal judge ordered Napster to shut down its operations permanently until it could figure out a way to charge customers for each music track downloaded. Now, a newly reconfigured (and legal) version of Napster is back in operation, under the ownership of Roxio, a leading provider of CD-burning software over the Internet. Roxio is managing Napster as a music subscription/purchase business.

Although all of the record companies engaged in extensive litigation to bring the piracy problem under control, a number of them began to undertake steps to incorporate the new technology into their own business models. The music industry has essentially formulated two different models for selling music over the Internet: (1) a subscription program, whereby users pay a fixed monthly fee to download a set amount of music per month, and (2) a pay-per-download system, in which a customer pays for one song or CD at a time.

For example, three major record companies—Warner Music, EMI Group, and Bertelsmann AG—joined together with RealNetworks to license their music offerings using RealNetworks' digital technology. Forming a subscription service called MusicNet, the venture will act as a distributor of digital music files to other companies wanting to sell music over the Internet. Universal Music (a unit of Vivendi), in turn, inked a deal with Sony Music to form Pressplay, a competing digital subscription service that is designed to match MusicNet.

The pay-per-download format received a significant boost in June 2002, when both Universal and Sony began to charge 99 cents per song to customers who did not want to join their Pressplay subscription service. Using technology provided by Liquid Audio, Universal wants to make its music affordable enough to deter music listeners from engaging in piracy. At the same time, this pay-per-download technology helps Universal compete with the subscription-based services, including its own Pressplay venture with Sony. These deals are especially significant for the industry, since they reveal the extent to which the record companies are beginning to use digital distribution in their own plans to expand their music offerings over the Internet. Eventually, both Sony and Universal Music sold their interests in Pressplay to Roxio, the same company that now runs a legal version of Napster. Roxio has its own big ambitions for Napster. Sony and Universal believe that Pressplay represented a "stepping stone" on the way to the truly digital, nonsubscription forms of music that are now proliferating.

A huge boulder in that technology "stepping stone" has been the arrival of the extremely popular iPod digital music player from Apple Computer in early 2002. The iPod's elegant design, sleek looks, and huge hard drive made it the market leader for portable music storage players. Later in 2002, Apple ensured that the iPod would become compatible with Windows-based PCs, thus avoiding the risk of marginalizing the product to only users of Apple computers. By April 2003, CEO Steve Jobs convinced the major record label companies to begin offering music downloads to the iPod for as low as 99 cents per song through Apple's iTunes online music store, boosting demand even further. CEO Jobs persuaded the major record label companies that the iPod's technology would not allow for unlimited music transfers through file sharing and other methods that promote piracy. Moreover, the iPod and the iTunes music store would make it much easier to sell legally protected music downloads without a lot of technology hassle. By mid-2004, Apple had sold upwards of 3 million iPods at a cost of around $300 each. In January 2004, Apple signed a deal that allows Hewlett-Packard to resell the iPod, thus turning a potential rival into a partner with huge distribution and marketing reach. By June 2004, Apple's iTunes online music store accounted for 70 percent of all legal music downloads. By September 2004, other entrants offering their own variation of digital online music included Microsoft, Yahoo!, MTV, Sony, and even Virgin Group. Microsoft emphasizes the compatibility of its service with a wide range of music players from different electronics manufacturers. Apple's iTunes service, however, only works with its proprietary iPod system—a feature that may ultimately limit the reach of Apple's service.

In September 2003, the Recording Industry Association of America (RIIA) filed 261 lawsuits against individuals who used file-sharing software to amass and distribute vast numbers of copyrighted music online. These suits are designed to send a message that the record label companies will no longer tolerate piracy, and the companies have gone as far as to sue Internet service providers for the names of people who download music illegally. In that same month, Universal slashed prices on CDs in a bid to resuscitate sales that had declined rapidly over the past few years. The price cut meant that in many cases the price of a CD would drop to under ten dollars or less, although none of Universal's competitors had aggressively matched the reduced prices. Some analysts believe that Universal's move to discount CDs means that it will be much more difficult to raise prices ever again.

Now, all of the record companies are beginning to sell digital files of their music, as either whole albums or individual tracks, in a downloadable format to listeners. At the same time, record label companies are strengthening their efforts to work together to prevent piracy and to jointly coordinate their legal strategies to protect their copyrights. The RIIA continues to remain active on the legal front, with ongoing suits to stop the spread of new types of file-sharing systems (for example, Morpheus).

Strategic Snapshot

Eastman Kodak and Digital Photography[2]

As we enter the next century, consumer photography is also undergoing a revolutionary technological change. Eastman Kodak is a global leader in developing chemical-based film. Even though its biggest competitor, Fuji Photo of Japan, sells lower-priced film, as recently as 1996, Kodak commanded upwards of 60 percent of the U.S. market for all makes of consumer film. Kodak's shares are even higher in the industrial and medical film segments. Yet throughout the late-1990s, double-digit growth in the chemical-based film market slowed dramatically, leaving Eastman Kodak in a real struggle to redefine its core technologies and products in the wake of technological change, revitalized competitors, the advent of the Internet, and different customer tastes.

Kodak must now deal with the major challenge presented by the arrival of new competitors who are accelerating the transition of chemical-based imaging to new electronic and digital imaging techniques that will change the way consumers use their cameras. This technological change also redefines how manufacturers link up the camera with other product platforms and applications. Although Kodak still holds a large number of patents that protect both its core, proprietary silver-halide film coatings technology and some of its own advances in digital imaging, the company now faces challenges from emerging technologies that threaten its chemical-based investments over the past century. Ironically, Kodak invented the first digital camera prototype in 1976!

Semiconductors and Digital Imaging

Two particular agents of change threaten Kodak's traditional technology. The first is the growing use of semiconductors to create digital cameras. In particular, the rise of so-called flash memory has become a direct substitute for chemical-based film. Flash memories serve to store a series of images on a disc or memory card that is then easily inserted into a personal computer for long-term storage, imaging manipulation, and eventual printing. Cameras that incorporate these and other state-of-the-art chips allow weekend photography amateurs to match the quality of professional photographers. By the end of 2004, digital cameras were able to produce images with stunning clarity and resolution, and their prices continued to drop. The number of tiny dots in a digital image—known as pixels—in any square area determines the clarity of the image. The greater the number of pixels, the finer is the resolution. For example, 4-megapixel cameras sold for under $300, and even more powerful versions were already on the market. Prices for these cameras have steadily dropped as much as 20 percent a year, even as performance dramatically improves. A 4-megapixel camera allows a user to create a photographic image of stunning clarity that will fit within an 8 × 11-inch frame.

The second development facing Kodak is the rise of new photograph manipulation software. An example of such software is Adobe Systems' line of Photoshop digital imaging tools. Offerings from Adobe, Microsoft, and Hewlett-Packard enable customers to manipulate images for clearer pictures, accentuate shadows or lines, and even make wholesale changes to the picture's background. These expensive digital imaging tools that previously only magazine publishers and artists bought for professional purposes are now

Exhibit 5-2   *Transformation of Imaging at Eastman Kodak*

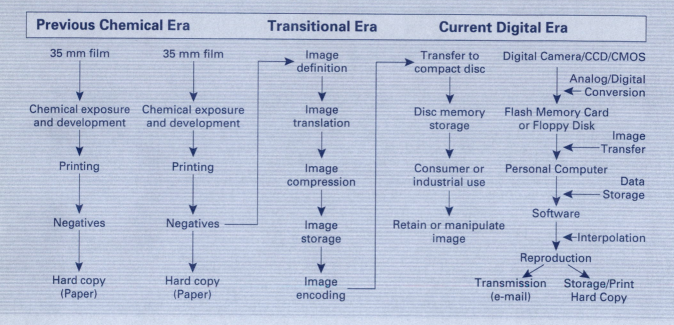

much cheaper. They enable everyday users to use photographic images in new ways. In fact, many of these digital images cannot only be stored on a computer or optical disc but can also be downloaded and shared through the Internet. The power to edit photographs on a computer or television screen, for example, means that photographers can custom-build and assemble their own set of pictures; only the user's imagination defines how far the technology can be applied. Camera buffs, advertisers, copy editors, medical diagnosticians, and other industrial users will find many new uses for digital imaging methods to capture, store, and manipulate images. In particular, the rapid ability to digitize an image and send it through the Internet allows for fast capture and translation of images for medical applications (second opinions), insurance claims, real estate (virtual sales), and other forms of video transmission. Consequently, the production and use of cameras and film development methods are becoming more similar to the technologies used to make compact discs, optical discs, semiconductors, and even software techniques for image manipulation.

These technologies defined the evolution of the personal computer, consumer electronics, and computer peripherals industry. This transformation of imaging at Eastman Kodak from chemical-based to digital, electronic-based methods is depicted in Exhibit 5-2.

Impact of New Technology on Kodak

The full magnitude of continuous improvement in digital camera technology weighs heavily on Kodak. The company must now learn new semiconductor and digital-based imaging technologies that depart from its chemistry background and traditional technology. In the most extreme case of this threat, consumers can completely bypass all of Kodak's traditional film business offerings.

Many of Kodak's rivals are fierce Japanese competitors such as Canon, Nikon, Sony, Epson, and Sharp. Sony actually created the first commercially available digital camera known as the Mavica in 1984, but it was ahead of its time. All of these firms have camera designs that enable a user to insert the flash memory card into a PC or portable printer for immediate image capture. South Korean competitor Samsung is also a major contender in this business, since it has ambitions to dominate all types of digital appliances. Yet, the threat to Kodak does not stop with makers of digital cameras alone. Even cell phone companies such as Nokia, Motorola, LG Electronics, and Samsung have been integrating a digital camera as a standard feature on advanced wireless phones. In fact, a majority of cell phones sold by 2006 will likely have some type of digital camera capability. Other potential rivals have included Hewlett-Packard and Intel, both of which have strong semiconductor and/or imaging technologies in their own right. Hewlett-Packard's advanced software and controller chips are already used in state-of-the-art laser and ink-jet printers, whereas Intel's flash memory and microprocessor businesses are natural potential entrants into the digital imaging industry. Either way, Kodak faces both domestic and foreign competitors who have mastered and utilized advanced digital imaging techniques learned from their own respective core businesses. People may even ask if Eastman Kodak is even relevant anymore in the photography field.

Searching for an Effective Response

Kodak's first response to the digital threat in 1994 was an early product known as Photo-CD. It allowed customers to transfer their film negatives onto optical discs that could then be seen on a television set. However, this initial effort faltered as the process was cumbersome and the technology slow. Customers griped at the fact they had to buy a VCR/DVD-sized appliance in order to look at their photos on the television set. Moreover, Photo-CD meant that customers still had to use conventional chemical-based film in order to capture the images they wanted.

Toward the late 1990s, Kodak developed an Internet site that allowed customers to drop off their film at a finishing lab, only to have the pictures available to them on the Internet through a special web account with Kodak. This online service, known as PhotoNet, enables customers to develop their film cartridges or have negatives scanned into the system to be available the next day on the Internet. Customers can then download these net-based images into their PCs or send them to friends and family through e-mail. Even this effort did not help Kodak significantly.

To help learn how better to compete in the semiconductor and digital-imaging arenas, Kodak formed a joint venture with Intel in May 1998 to codevelop new flash memories specifically for digital imaging applications. It also simultaneously worked with Motorola to develop superior flash memory technology. These flash memory cards have enabled Kodak to begin learning about new core technologies. However, competitors are not standing still. Sony, Samsung, Canon, Nikon and others are investing in even more versatile digital cameras. Flash memory companies such as SanDisk are also ramping up production of ever more sophisticated memory chips. To keep abreast of these developments, Kodak also entered into an array of relationships with Microsoft, Adobe Systems, Hewlett-Packard, and even a few Silicon Valley start-ups (for example, Live Picture) to better understand how these new technologies will evolve. With Microsoft, Hewlett-Packard, and even arch rival Fuji Photo of Japan, Kodak helped create a network of more uniform standards to make it easier for customers to print their digital images. These standards are designed to let users send their images via the Internet for printing at local retailers—in much the same way that a person uses an ATM to get cash. Kodak has also begun to work with Cisco Systems and Motorola to produce a new wireless communications standard that will be able to support high-speed Internet transmission.

Sales for chemical-based film peaked in 1999 at $14 billion, and declined to $13.3 by 2003. Since 1999, Kodak has successfully undertaken innovations in some new areas, such as next-generation technology for digital displays, including a new format called organic light-emitting diodes (OLEDs), which are brighter and thinner than conventional transistor-based displays. In September 2003, Kodak announced a huge initiative to enter the market for ink-jet printers, a sector that it had ignored for a long time. Most customers now produce their digital images through a PC-to-printer connection, and Kodak is hoping to create a new line of printers where consumers can dock their cameras directly to the printer. Even in this area, however, Kodak is behind the curve compared to faster-moving rivals, especially Canon. Also in September, Kodak slashed its dividend in order to amass some $3 billion needed for acquisitions and internal investments to be made through 2006. By the end of 2003, digital cameras outsold film cameras for the first time in the United States. In January 2004, Kodak announced that it would no longer sell film cameras anymore. Even though Kodak never made much money on selling cameras, the company continued selling them in order to drive film sales. In March 2004, Kodak sued Sony over alleged patent violations concerning different aspects of digital technology.

Kodak remains committed to learning and applying the latest digital imaging technology. In August 2004, Kodak signed a deal with National Semiconductor to acquire that firm's chip imaging unit. Kodak plans to open up a digital imaging office in Silicon Valley that will be staffed by former National Semiconductor technicians. The acquisition is expected to help Kodak strengthen its image sensor design skills. In September 2004, Kodak began working with IBM to design and manufacture image sensors for both digital cameras and camera phones. IBM's technology behind the image sensors will enable Kodak to mass-produce these devices in large volumes for the consumer market.

Introduction

As we have seen in the previous examples, the structure and nature of competition in industries can change quickly. New developments in the environment can threaten a firm's competitive advantage if it does not or cannot respond to change. Determining when and how to respond to environmental change is the subject of this chapter. We begin by examining different triggers of change that can seriously erode a firm's distinctive competence and sources of competitive advantage. Then, we explore the options available to firms in their response to these changes. Finally, we consider the factors that influence the selection of these options.

New Developments Affecting Competitive Advantage

Changes in the industry environment can have dramatic effects on firms' sources of competitive advantage. New developments represent triggers that can redefine the way that firms compete. In some instances, the developments are industry-wide and substantially alter the nature of competition and the long-term structure of the industry. Changes in government regulations (for example, deregulation in electric utilities, airlines, health care, and telecommunications) can have major intended and unintended effects on the industry. Other developments may be "spillover" effects resulting from changes that result from innovations and new products that occur in other industries (such as the impact of digital imaging and new microchips on chemical-based film). Developments or triggers that frequently change the nature of competition and sources of competitive advantage include (1) new technology, (2) new distribution channels, (3) shifts in economic variables, (4) changes in related industries, and (5) changes in government regulation.

New Technology

In any industry, a firm invests considerable resources in the technologies used in its value-adding activities. The choice of technology determines the materials, designs, methods, processes, and equipment used to carry out its activities. Technology shapes the firm's knowledge base. Over time, a firm learns and builds a considerable base of expertise in dealing with the technologies that directly impact its value chain configuration (business system). Technological change impacts both products and processes. The emergence of a new or superior product or process technology can undermine a firm's existing distinctive competence.

On a general level, all firms face the potential threat of obsolescence. This problem is especially salient, however, for established firms that compete along a given technology format or product standard for an extended time. When new technologies threaten to undermine or replace existing product designs or process technology, they are known as competence-changing technologies. **Competence-changing technologies** redefine an industry's structure and the dominant technological format used by competing firms. In many situations, competence-changing technologies represent substitutes for existing industry processes, methods, and materials. Another way to think about competence-changing technologies is that they are "disruptive innovations." Disruptive innovations unleash a process of "creative destruction" that enables new products and technologies to replace older ones.[3]

In the automobile industry, for example, ceramic-based engines and even sophisticated hybrid fuel cells, as well as battery-powered systems, promise the possibility of markedly improved efficiencies and performance than internal combustion engines. They represent disruptive, competence-changing technologies for all established automotive industry participants that build gasoline and diesel technologies.

Both Kodak and record label firms such as Universal Music, Sony, EMI Group, Time Warner, and Bertelsmann AG faced threats of disruptive, competence-changing technologies in the 1990s and 2000s, respectively. As noted in the opening examples, these firms built their original business models around older technologies that now face immediate substitute threats. They achieved distinctive competence and substantial competitive advantage in these areas. Digital-based technologies promise to change the way images are created, transferred, stored, manipulated, and even transmitted along today's information media. New music formats such as MP3 and other variants promise to make music freely available over a wide range of Internet-driven media and new devices.

Other sources of disruptive technological change can stem from the use of new materials in products, as well as new process-based technologies that dramatically improve manufacturing performance. Thus, older skills and methods become less useful to compete.

competence-changing technology:
A technology that markedly changes or redefines the structure of an industry; often new processes or innovations that disrupt and erode the market for existing products.

New Materials. Advances in materials sciences have accelerated "disruptive innovations" in a number of industries. Fiber-optic cable made of glass is rapidly replacing copper as a medium for transmitting telecommunication signals. This development enabled new competitors such as Corning Incorporated and Lucent Technologies to enter the telecommunications supply field in a major way in the late 1990s. These new materials created opportunities for both Corning and Lucent to redefine the capacity and offerings that telecommunications companies can provide to their customers. In another example, newly engineered plastics are replacing steel and other metal parts in automobiles and heavy machinery. Composite body panels, doors, and dashboards made of synthetic fibers and plastics, for example, can be found in almost all cars. These materials help reduce the weight and cost of automobiles. Their development creates important opportunities for chemical manufacturers that produce these plastics and for the firms that use them. Some of the most exciting developments in new materials include the use of "smart technology," which enables hybrid alloys to deflect stresses and fractures that would cause failure in traditional metals.

New Manufacturing Techniques. In the steel industry, minimills use an alternative technology to make steel, rather than the traditional open hearth method. Using this low-cost manufacturing technology, smaller firms such as Nucor and Chaparral Steel have achieved spectacular success over the past two decades. By using scrap iron and metal, minimills avoid the high fixed costs of more traditional, integrated steelmakers, such as U.S. Steel, to produce steel wires, rods, and beams used in the construction and road-building industries. Larger steel firms depend on much bigger mills and higher ore-based processing costs. In another case, many firms in the plastics industry are using new types of liquid-injection molding technologies to produce plastic products. These machines inject hot plastic liquids into molds directly to make parts, components, and toys more quickly and efficiently than past methods. This development provides new entrants to the industry a valuable opportunity for technology differentiation.

The automotive, steel, plastics, music recording, and film industries are not the only settings to have experienced this kind of technological change. As shown in Exhibit 5–3, superior technology has emerged in a wide range of settings. In each of the industries shown, a new technology eventually surpassed the traditional one in terms of market acceptance. Firms unable (or unwilling) to develop a new source of expertise to embrace the technology face erosion and, in some instances, extinction of their market positions.

New Distribution Channels

Established firms must also look for potential threats to their distribution methods and channels to reach customers. Changes in distribution often mean that the customer can gain access to a product or service through some other means—more conveniently, faster, and usually at lower cost. A new method of distribution also indicates that a competitor has unlocked and penetrated a barrier to entry that no longer shields the established firm. *In many instances, a new distribution channel or method often signals the arrival of an entirely new type of competitor.* Certainly, for Barnes & Noble and Borders Group, the arrival of Amazon.com on the Internet signified a dangerous threat because Amazon can sell to anybody who has access to the Internet. The arrival of

Exhibit 5-3	*Emergence of New Technology*	
Industry	**Old Technology**	**New Technology**
Electronics	Transistors	Integrated circuits
Shoe materials	Leather	Engineered polymers
Appliances	Discrete controls	Fuzzy logic
Airframes	Steel, Metal	Composite materials
Automobile engines	Aluminum	Ceramics
Automobile body frames	Welded pieces	Unibody, single piece construction
Computers	Mainframes	Personal computers Networked systems
Medical equipment	Stand-alone X-ray	CAT scans, MRI
TV manufacturing	Handcrafted	Automated insertion tools
Cameras	Silver-halide film	Flash memory cards

each new type of distribution channel will likely bring with it a new set of entrants. These entrants will probably use an entirely different business model and value proposition to win over customers.

Internet-Powered Methods. A company can better scan its environment for new products ideas, service opportunities, and customer needs by developing a broad understanding of how alternative distribution systems evolve. Perhaps the single greatest change in distribution channels now affecting every industry and organization is the growing use of the Internet to provide online ordering, distribution, sales, logistics, billing, payment options, and even customer service. In just the past five years, the Internet has forced existing firms in the real estate, financial services, office supplies, and airline industries to rethink how best to reconfigure their distribution and marketing systems to serve their customers. In one of the most extreme examples of "creative destruction," Internet-based distribution models have spawned such powerful travel service companies as Orbitz, Travelocity, Priceline.com, and hotels.com. In turn, hundreds of travel agencies have gone by the wayside as customers flock to these new services.

Pitney Bowes, a company best known for making postage machines, has confronted a similar type of challenge from the rise of the Internet. For over seventy years, Pitney Bowes has provided a valuable service to many businesses through the durable machines that allow them to issue the right amount of postage needed to mail letters and packages on their own. Companies traditionally have prepurchased the amount of postage they want from the U.S. Postal Service. In turn, the Postal Service gives each customer's postage machine an assigned number that designates permission to issue postage on the customer's outgoing mail. However, by late 1998, new upstarts using the Internet had begun to challenge Pitney Bowes' long-held dominance in the postage machine market. Companies such as E-Stamp, StampMaster, and others attempted to design websites that enable customers to pay for postage over the Internet, download a customer-specific set of coded data into their computers, and then print it out on mailing labels and envelopes. In effect, the Internet, with the permission of the U.S. Postal Service, now allows customers to print their own stamps. In turn, Pitney Bowes has introduced its own version of user-friendly, Internet-based software to help customers order prepaid postage with greater ease. The web-based auctioneer eBay now contracts with Pitney Bowes to offer online postage for its buyers and sellers. Now, millions of users on eBay's website download postage and print it out, with Pitney Bowes capturing a small fee each time.[4]

From the online music example, many record label companies were initially unaware of how new distribution channels (besides the Internet) actually helped pave the way for the arrival of new competitors. The record label companies did not at first realize that telecommunications firms (which manage much of the Internet), as well as consumer electronic firms that develop and sell digital phones and other electronic devices, were highly influential in promoting the use of personal computers, cell phones, MP3 players, and handheld computers as alternative distributors of music. These new platforms do not require the use of compact discs as the sole means to store music. Record companies did not realize that customers wanted to listen to music anytime and anywhere—the compact disc was no longer the driver of customer value.

Kodak has struggled to adapt the Internet to enable customers to use their digital cameras and PCs to instantaneously transmit images. Its original version of PhotoNet technology required that customers drop off their film cartridges at Kodak-affiliated outlets (drugstore chains, grocery chains, camera outlets, and convenience stores) and receive the images on the web. Once the images are available to customers, they can choose which ones to download to their own PCs or to send to other people through e-mail. America Online and PictureVision were two firms that helped Kodak in its initial Internet-based venture. Yet, PhotoNet represented a transitional technology that gave way to wireless digital cameras that come preconfigured with a phone and Internet service as well.

Cheaper Distribution Methods. Firms in many other industries have faced threats from the arrival of new distribution methods and channels, even those that are not specifically Internet driven. Brokerage houses such as Merrill Lynch have been hurt by the growth of discount brokers. Discount brokers such as Fidelity Investments and Charles Schwab have eroded the once-dominant position of established, full-service brokers by offering lower-cost commissions on stock and bond trades. These discount brokers, in turn, face the problem of dealing with online brokerage firms, such as Ameritrade, E*Trade, TD Waterhouse, and other upstarts, that offer customers even lower commission rates, free research, and low account maintenance fees. In addition, because they tend to have small research departments (if any); their overhead costs are lower, and they can pass these savings on to consumers.

Competing Channel Approaches. In a similar vein, broadcast leaders such as Disney's Capital Cities/ABC unit, Viacom's CBS unit, and GE's NBC Universal television unit now face even more intense threats from cable, pay-per-view, and digital video recorders (DVRs) that shrink the potential audience that broadcasters hope to reach. Unlike other industries where distribution has shown signs of consolidating around a new technology format, method, or channel approach, broadcasting is actually beginning to fragment in unanticipated ways. Viewers have many more options to watch shows, learn about news events, and will soon have the technology to access digital video. Broadcasting will now have to compete with "Netcasting" as an alternative medium. Broadcasting will face renewed technological challenges in the next few years as the FCC compels networks to complete the transition from analog (over the airwave) transmission to digital television standards. For the networks and affiliated television stations, this challenge means investing large sums into new technologies that will also change their fundamental business models and the types of programming they offer. As a result, NBC is rethinking its current approach and business model in the broadcasting industry to preempt some of these threats.[5]

Department stores must now build on new "brick-and-click" business models to reach out to customers that want to shop from the convenience of their homes or elsewhere. Companies such as Target, Wal-Mart Stores, Sears, Home Depot, and Lowe's must now offer customers the speed of the Internet and the convenience of easily returning items they do not want. This means they must bridge two different retailing models (retail stores and websites) within the same firm—a difficult task that places enormous strain on their procurement, customer ordering, inventory, logistics, and billing systems.

More recently, Blockbuster's nationwide franchises in videotape and DVD rentals have faced a number of simultaneous challenges. The first challenge has been the steady evolution of pay-per-view services offered by cable companies. The second challenge is that as DVDs get cheaper, many customers have simply preferred to buy the DVD and keep it for their personal library—often at a cost comparable to renting a movie for two days. The third challenge is from a competitor known as Netflix, which offers customers a subscription service for cheaper DVD rentals and the convenience of mail-based returns. Ultimately, the most potent challenge looming over the horizon will be the availability of films over the Internet once legal and technological issues are resolved. Even if legal issues are not solved, it is likely that the film production industry will undergo the same kind of piracy and file-sharing technology assaults that characterized music recording. Improvements in bandwidth and transmission speeds over telecom and Internet lines will only hasten the likely arrival of this challenge.[6] All of this means that customers have even fewer reasons to visit a Blockbuster outlet.

Economic Shifts

Changes in the basic economic parameters or structure of an industry can dramatically shift the nature of competitive advantage. Consider the current difficulties facing Japanese automobile and electronics manufacturers, for example. Their highly advanced, quality-driven, Japan-based manufacturing facilities once enjoyed an enormous cost advantage over U.S. factories and competitors. Rising wages of Japanese workers, a dramatic slowdown in the domestic economy, and severe fluctuations in the value of its currency (the yen) have combined to undermine many Japanese firms' advantage substantially over the past decade. Now Japanese manufacturers are taking aggressive steps to reduce costs through such means as automation, outsourcing, reduced number of product variations, and shifting manufacturing to facilities outside of Japan, particularly through aggressive investments in Southeast Asia. In fact, Japanese investment in this region has grown so dramatically that economic downturns and recessions in many Southeast Asian economies (for example, Indonesia, Thailand, Malaysia, Singapore) in the late 1990s affected the profitability of Japanese firms. The same developments have strengthened the market and cost positions of General Motors, Ford, and DaimlerChrysler—both in the United States and in other export markets. Thus, sharp swings or changes in the exchange rate, domestic demand, commodity prices, oil prices, or even the receptivity of trade partners can dramatically alter the competitive advantage of firms across many industries.

Changes in Related or Neighboring Industries

Sometimes, shifts in one industry's competitive environment may be precipitated or triggered by changes in a neighboring or related industry. A **related industry** is one that shares many of the same economic, technological, production, or market-based drivers or characteristics. For example, consumer electronics and personal computers may be thought of as related, because these two industries often rely on the same type of mass market distribution channel, incorporate many of the same electronic components, and even manufacture key components or peripherals in the same factories. Increasingly, the telephone, Internet, and computer-networking industries are becoming more related since they share the same basic telecommunications architecture and are growing more linked together through the use of common information transfer technologies (for example, routers, bridges, and packet switches). Even the cable TV business is becoming more similar to the telecommunications industry as well. Cable providers are now jockeying with phone companies to provide telephone and other Internet services.

For example, the rise of new Voice over Internet Protocol (VoIP) technology means customers can now place phone calls over the Internet. This means that for all practical purposes, local, long-distance, and international calls are essentially the same—and they are also becoming exceptionally inexpensive. Improvements in methods to route Internet traffic have facilitated the creation of new software that makes traditional phone calls using dedicated landlines and closed switch technology obsolete. As a result of these cascading changes, long distance phone companies such as AT&T and MCI have lost customers steadily over the past few years. AT&T, one of America's greatest technology companies, no longer exists as it merges with SBC Communications. The same fate may befall MCI as well.

Let us consider a hypothetical example of how changes in one industry can trigger changes in another. Take the relationship between leather shoes, the tanning industry, and chemicals. Countries such as Italy and Brazil have large and profitable shoe industries because their manufacturers often can purchase large quantities of high-quality, processed leather from long-standing tanning firms. The high quality and output of Brazilian and Italian shoes are based not

related industry:
An industry that shares many of the same economic, technological, or market-based drivers or characteristics as another.

only on the economies of scale and experience effects that established shoe firms have built up, but also on the close relationships they have developed with tanning firms. Innovations in tanning leather are likely to have been passed on to shoe makers; conversely, shoe firms have probably suggested ways to improve the tanning process. However, if a chemical firm were to develop a cheaper, alternative material (for example, a new type of soft vinyl) that could be used to make more durable and comfortable shoes, then growing use of this new material could dramatically change the competitiveness of the Brazilian and Italian shoe industries. First, the arrival of a substitute material would reduce the amount of leather that Brazilian and Italian shoe factories purchase from tanning firms over time. Thus, tanning firms would face an enormous amount of new competition and a sharp drop-off in business. Second, a new chemical material might be used in new ways to make even less costly shoes. If the chemical material lends itself to more efficient or perhaps automated means of production, then this material would threaten the existing cost advantages and investment in equipment by Brazilian and Italian firms. The growing availability of the new chemical-based material might also encourage entry by other shoe firms into the niches currently served by the existing firms, since cheaper shoe materials would lower the cost of differentiation. Thus, technological, economic, or other developments in a related industry can trigger marked changes and shifts in sources of competitive advantage in another industry.[7]

Changes in Government Regulation

Actions taken by the government can markedly shift or threaten the sources of advantage needed to compete in an industry. For example, the U.S. government's imposition of high tariffs on Japanese motorcycle imports in the 1970s damaged the competitive position of Japanese manufacturers such as Kawasaki, Honda, and Yamaha. More recently, quotas imposed in the early 1990s on Japanese auto imports, especially minivans, threatened Honda, Toyota, and Nissan, forcing them to increase U.S. manufacturing capacity more rapidly to remain competitive in this country. Likewise, the Clean Air Act of 1990 threatened to render obsolete many U.S. oil refinery operations because of the extremely high costs required to meet new regulations. The proposed global Kyoto Accord that committed national signatories to reduce their emissions and use of carbon-based fuels is a regulation of such magnitude that it is expected to cause considerable financial distress to companies in many industries; this is one reason why the United States has not been a signatory to this agreement.

Changes in antitrust regulations can alter the competitive dynamics in an industry. For example, the recent sparring and court battles between Microsoft and the U.S. Department of Justice and the European Union have reduced Microsoft's dominance over the PC software industry, especially as it relates to Internet search engines. This agreement makes it easier for personal computer manufacturers to use Internet search engines software made by other firms. Moreover, PC makers are not required to pay as much in royalties to Microsoft as in the past. Even though the U.S. government has not sought to break up Microsoft into a series of smaller companies, European regulators were considering more stringent and punitive measures in late 2004 to constrain Microsoft's market power in Europe. These government actions will likely stimulate the interest of competing software firms to design new forms of PC operating systems. By early 2005, Microsoft agreed to comply with the EU's requirement that the company separate its Media Player from its Windows operating system.

A significant degree of deregulation was occurring in many industries within the United States during the late 1990s. For example, deregulation of the telecommunications industry, through the Telecommunications Act of 1996, makes it legally possible for local phone companies (for example, Regional Bell Operating Companies such as SBC Communications, Verizon Communications, and Bell South) to enter the long-distance market once held solely by larger interexchange carriers that are the heart of the national telephone system (such as AT&T, Sprint, and MCI). Likewise, the same act enables cable television companies (for example, Cox Communications, Comcast, Cablevision) to enter the telephone and data transmission markets directly as well. Deregulation of this industry has already unleashed enormous pressures to lower costs and to consolidate the number of competitors. For example, Bell Atlantic merged with GTE to form Verizon Communications, whereas Qwest Communications International bought US West (both deals completed in 2000). Other Regional Bell Operating Companies (RBOCs) are now in the midst of their own consolidation, with SBC Communications (formerly known as Southwestern Bell) purchasing West Coast giant Pacific Telesis and Ameritech (completed in 1999). Consolidation in the telecom industry continues at an unrelenting pace as traditional long-distance companies become less relevant in today's competitive arena.[8]

Response Options

Firms can respond to environmental developments in three fundamentally different ways: by prospecting, defending, or harvesting (see Exhibit 5-4). Each approach aims at a specific objective, requires specific adjustments, and has varying advantages and drawbacks.

Prospecting

The most aggressive approach a firm can adopt to deal with environmental change is to strive to be the first to accommodate it. Because the objective is to acknowledge and embrace the new development first, we refer to it as **prospecting**.[9] The actions required of a prospector vary depending on the nature of the environmental development involved. Consider the emergence of new, potentially superior product technology—the kind of change that Kodak faced in the mid-1990s. A prospector experiencing this kind of development must strive to be the first competitor to launch a product incorporating the new technology. To achieve this end, it will need to undertake a series of initiatives. These include conducting research into the new technology, designing prototypes that incorporate the new approach, retooling manufacturing equipment to produce the new design, and promoting finished products once they are ready for market.

prospecting:
An activity designed to help the firm search, understand, and accommodate environmental change; a proactive attempt by a firm to make an environmental change favorable to itself (see defending).

Implementing Strategic Response		Exhibit 5-4

Response Option	Typical Implementing Actions
Prospect	Develop new distinctive competence
	Initiate R&D in new technology
	Learn new manufacturing processes
	Learn how to design and promote new product
Defend	Preserve existing distinctive competence
	Reduce price on existing product
	Increase promotion of existing product
	Intensify R&D in existing technology

From a historical perspective, consider the issues facing Timex Watch Company, a leading U.S. watch company during the 1970s. Timex faced enormous competitive pressures from new competitors using electronic and digital-based technologies. These technologies represent substitute offerings that steadily displaced mechanical watches, the heart of Timex's product line. One response option for Timex was to engage in prospecting. A prospecting strategy designed to penetrate and secure a portion of the electronic watch market would involve significantly higher levels of investment in learning new forms of electronics and in adopting highly automated tooling processes. These tools would fabricate and assemble quartz and light-emitting diode (LED) components. Eventually, they would displace standard mechanical parts of levers, winding gears, spring wheels, and turning movements. Understanding the new product, learning the new process technologies, and designing a new promotional campaign would represent significant changes in both managerial attention and focus. Prospecting would also cause Timex's existing distinctive competence in mechanical watches to become less relevant over time. Equally important, Timex would have to make capital expenditures in many high fixed-cost investments before uncertainties surrounding the electronic watch would be resolved. Thus, Timex would have to reinvent its entire set of knowledge and skills to compete.

In the currently fast-changing semiconductor industry, many firms in the late 1990s and the early part of this decade have attempted to become prospectors. Numerous companies are racing to develop new types of advanced breakthrough materials that enhance the power of microchips (for example, germanium, silicon-on-insulator (SOI) techniques). If these companies' efforts are successful, then next-generation microchips will be much more powerful and capable of performing even more tasks, thus giving the smaller firms important headway in refocusing the industry's R&D efforts. Equally important, these breakthroughs would help the smaller firms escape some of the enormous pressures of competing with much larger companies. Firms such as Applied Micro Circuits and Transmeta are beginning to challenge larger companies (for example Intel, Motorola) through prospector-type strategies by offering new microprocessor designs that provide "system-on-a-chip" capabilities. These chips incorporate many more functions on a single sliver of silicon than those from previous generations.

Sony exhibited many characteristics of a prospector when it developed the first consumer-oriented digital camera in 1984. Known as the Mavica, Sony hoped that it could redefine the entire consumer photography industry by enabling customers to capture and develop pictures quickly without using chemical-based film. Although the Mavica was considered a technological marvel, few customers were attracted to it—largely because it produced grainy images. Yet, Sony regarded this setback as the initial cost of learning a new technology and continued to push ahead. Now, Sony's digital cameras are among some of the most popular and versatile models, including its recent T1 model that sold briskly for much of 2004. The company has ramped up production and expects to grow 20 to 30 percent a year.[10] Investing in digital camera skills has also helped Sony to develop next-generation portable digital videodisc recorders (DVRs).

When formulated and implemented effectively, prospecting enables a firm to gain a head start in exploiting a new development or market trend, thereby securing first-mover, surprise, and timing advantages over later entrants. Prospecting therefore could help a firm preserve its industry position that might erode if it failed to respond. However, prospecting is not without substantial risks and requires persistence to pay off, as shown by Sony's digital camera investment. If an anticipated change or development never materializes, if it evolves in an unanticipated direction, or if the product or service conceived is inadequate, the investment made by a prospector could be partially or wholly lost.

Planning and Administration: Prospecting at Texas Instruments[11]

Texas Instruments (TI) is one of the world's leading producers of semiconductors (or microchips) that are best known for their use in digital cell phones, and increasingly, in flat-screen television sets. As recently as 1996, however, many people believed that TI was losing its edge as a technology leader. Spread out over a broad range of disparate businesses, TI lost the battle with archrival Intel to provide the microprocessors for PCs, and much of TI's earnings came from the highly volatile and commoditized memory chip business. Under the leadership of Tom Engibous, TI shed all of its defense, memory chip, and other marginal businesses to focus on a core technology known as digital signal processing chips (or DSP for short). DSP chips convert analog signals (such as audio and video) into digital format that computers can understand and use. In short, TI placed a bet that it could find new applications of DSP technology to reinvigorate its growth and claim to technological leadership. By prospecting for new commercial applications for its technology, TI began the process of searching for higher-growth markets.

In 1997, TI began working with Nokia to implant its DSP chips into the Finnish giant's phones. Nokia itself needed a leading-edge product that would break Motorola's hold over the cell phone market, which at the time was based almost entirely on analog technology. TI designed its DSP chips to work with Nokia's unique software specifications, and Nokia's phone sales took off. Sound quality was much better, and digital technology laid the foundation for the cell phone to take on other functions as well. DSP technology transformed the architecture of the cell phone, and today half of all of the world's 460 million cell phones use TI's chips. TI's latest DSP chip for cell phones now enables manufacturers to shrink the number of physical components from 185 to 25. This allows cell phone companies to greatly cut the cost of designing and assembling next-generation phones. They also greatly increase the phones' functionality. By 2004, the vast majority of digital cell phones began to include a digital camera and wireless Internet capability.

TI's DSP-driven efforts did not stop with the cell phone. In fact, under its newest CEO, Rich Templeton, TI is betting that it can dramatically shrink the size of its DSP chips to become the brains of all types of devices—digital cameras, broadband modems, advanced forms of Wi-Fi and Wi-Max technology, and handheld computers. Some of the latest gadgets to use TI's DSP chips include a wristwatch that can receive e-mails and surf the Internet, and a ballpoint pen that can take photos and transmit them wirelessly. TI is investigating new techniques that reduce the number of other supporting chips in a phone or other electronic appliance. The ultimate goal is to have a multifunctional cell phone operate with a single TI chip. Although TI's competitors (for example, Qualcomm, Intel, STMicroelectronics) are not standing still, TI is seeking to broaden its customer base and share its technical standards with other companies so they remain committed to using TI technology in future generation products.

TI is betting that next-generation television sets will offer it the same opportunity that Intel found with PCs. TI is hoping to dominate digital television sets with a dual emphasis on both technology and marketing that worked so well for Intel. One of TI's oldest innovations is a digital light processor (DLP) chip that uses a million or more mirrors to magnify and reflect images. Developed in the mid-1990s, this DLP technology floundered for a long time until TI regained its focus. DLP was primarily used for large conference room projectors and did not seem to offer many growth prospects. Now, CEO Templeton is seeking to make TI's DLP chip the brains of all future flat-screen television sets that will offer sharper images and much higher resolution. In January 2001, TI approached Samsung of Korea with a plan to use DLP technology in Samsung's television sets. Although Samsung had growing digital skills and manufacturing strengths, the company lacked the brand equity of other companies such as Sony or Panasonic. Samsung needed a breakthrough product that would help it make major inroads into the U.S. market, and TI's DLP chip offered significant benefits in image quality and production cost that were superior to that of other competing technologies (for example, plasma and liquid crystal displays [LCDs]). After extensive product testing, Samsung committed itself to using TI's DLP chip in much the same way that Nokia did with TI's DSP chip for cell phones. In 2003, Samsung sold more than one hundred thousand television sets powered by TI's DLP chip. Costs for the DLP-powered televisions are dropping from over $5,000 to under $3,000. Moreover, Samsung also now advertises its televisions as driven by digital light processing technology in a tribute to TI. Samsung's market share of digital television sets rose from 5 to 15 percent, and the company is ramping up production to sell more than half a million by 2004. TI recently signed up Thomson of France and Toshiba of Japan to use DLP technology in their flat-screen television sets. TI, however, is not relying on Samsung or other companies alone to herald its DLP technology. Samsung, for its part, continues to develop other flat-screen alternatives, such as LCD technology, while continuing to use TI's DLP chip. Texas Instruments has persuaded set makers to put a DLP logo on the face of every television set—a strategy that resembles its competitor's "Intel Inside" campaign that worked so well for PCs.

TI's prospecting efforts continue to yield new customers for the company's line of chips. It has begun partnering with European giant STMicroelectronics to standardize chip designs for next generation video and multimedia applications. The company believes it can become the dominant supplier of superchips for tomorrow's products that are still unimaginable today.

Defending

Another approach to dealing with an environmental change is to make a deliberate choice not to accommodate it. Instead, the firm seeks to defend its traditional business from the development's potentially adverse effects. The chief objective in **defending** is to protect a firm's traditional business from direct or collateral damage brought about by a new development.[12] One of the most common actions to defend a business's current position is a price cut. By lowering price, an established firm can sometimes sustain sales of its traditional product despite stiff competition from a new product or substitute. Recently, Altria (formerly known as Philip Morris) engaged in a series of massive price cuts in its premier Marlboro brand of cigarettes to counter the effects of lower-priced generic and off-brand cigarettes that were beginning to erode its margins. By cutting prices aggressively, Altria had hoped to slow down the inroads of generic cigarette makers who must themselves lower their own margins to capture new buyers. Price warfare is also extremely common among consumer nondurable products such as soft drinks, snacks, and other food products. Established firms hope to protect their core market positions and brand recognition from inroads by other firms or new entrants practicing their own form of prospecting in a given segment. PepsiCo's unit Frito-Lay, for example, is now aggressively defending its market position in salt-based snack foods through "value pricing" that enables it to slow the prospecting efforts of generic products made by other food companies.

Another common defensive move is increased promotion. By beefing up its advertising outlay, a defender can delay consumer acceptance of a new approach. One firm that has relied extensively on increased promotion is Blockbuster in the video rental industry. Blockbuster's promotional and price-cutting efforts are designed to slow down the number of customers who instead might choose to use Netflix's mail-based return of DVDs. Traditional broadcasting networks, such as NBC in television and Clear Channel Communications in radio, are aggressively increasing promotion of their offerings, stars, and new shows to ward off the potential erosion brought about by new digital mediums and satellite/Internet transmission technology.

Upgrading an existing technology can also help defend an established firm's position by enhancing the attractiveness of its traditional product. Intel's move in 2003 to incorporate wireless connectivity into all of its microprocessors demonstrated strong defender-like behavior. As Intel began to lose market share for its chips used in PCs, it designed its laptop-oriented microprocessors with a capability to access the Internet through "Wi-Fi" technology. Wi-Fi allows a laptop user to connect to the Internet through a wireless modem that searches for an available access point, which many restaurants, airports, and bookstores are offering as a convenience to their customers. In addition, Intel also promoted the chip heavily, introducing it as the Centrino line of microprocessors. Intel has attempted to make Centrino synonymous with mobile laptop computers that can access the Internet from anywhere without cumbersome wires.

Although defending enables a firm to avoid the prospecting risks already described, it subjects the firm to risk of another kind. Some environmental developments and changes are so powerful that even the most vigorous defense cannot thwart them. This result is particularly likely if the defending firm faces a radical shift in competence-changing technology or new distribution channels. For example, traditional vinyl records and cassette tapes could not withstand the popularity of CDs in the music industry. Likewise, hospitals and doctors switched away from using glass syringes to those made from plastic in order to cut costs, improve safety, and enhance convenience. Low-cost, disposable plastic syringes dramatically increased the safety of administering drugs to patients. Many retailing firms are facing this kind of threat from Internet-driven commercial firms that seek to gain access to new customers without investing in the traditional "brick-and-mortar" infrastructures and costs. Travel agencies, in particular, face enormous competition from Internet-based airline, hotel, and car-rental reservation sites. Certainly, bookstores and brokerage firms have been affected in a major way also. Now, pharmacies and drugstores are facing a new threat in the Internet space with the arrival of new health care websites that promise low prices and speedy delivery. This trend has accelerated as many U.S. consumers search for cheaper prescription drugs on Canadian pharmacy websites. Likewise, drugstore chains such as CVS and Walgreen face continued erosion of pharmacy-driven sales as large corporations begin to compel their employees to order their prescriptions through lower-cost mail-order services. Thus, new technologies or Internet distribution systems threaten to render obsolete the firm's initial investment in its distinctive competences, brand names, market positions, and other sources of competitive advantage. Defending against such major shifts can lead to serious loss of competitive position, regardless of later steps taken to reorient the firm's strategy.

From the current perspective of the music industry, prerecorded CDs will likely face even steeper sales declines as customers become more familiar with new ways to download music over the Internet. As customers can now create their own personalized CDs cheaper and faster, many music retailers (for example, Sam Goody's, Musicland, Wherehouse Music) have shut down store locations and streamlined their operations around the country. Similarly, it is only a matter of time before VCRs fade before advances in digital videodisc recording (DVR) technology. When these new devices allow users to record their music and video on advanced DVD-R systems in the next few years, the market for existing VCR systems, videotapes, and even playback-only DVD machines will likely plummet. Customers' growing expectations will likely accelerate the rapid adoption and diffusion of this new technological standard in both home and commercial settings as the price of DVR technology drops. Thus, the advent of new, more versatile DVD technology means that both VCRs and existing CD formats are likely to fade rapidly in the near future. Defending strategies to ward off the advances of DVR technologies are likely to be futile in the long run.

Harvesting

A third general option for a firm facing an environmental shift is to harvest its business while it still has time to do so. The objective of **harvesting** is to generate as much cash from a business as possible before the adverse consequences of an environmental threat materialize. One key difficulty associated with harvesting is high exit barriers facing the firm. Exit barriers usually exist in the form of dedicated production equipment, specialized assets, and other sunk costs, some of which may have not been completely paid for (amortized). As a result of such barriers, the processing of exiting often costs as much as investing in new equipment to serve another possible niche or segment.

harvesting:
The systematic removal of cash and other assets from a slow-growth or declining business; may be thought of as "milking" a business before it loses all its value.

To harvest a business, a leader must take actions opposite of those described for defending: increase the price of its products and reduce expenditures for such things as research, maintenance, and advertising. Westinghouse Electric during the late 1980s and early 1990s pursued a modified version of this harvesting strategy by selling factories gradually to Asea-Brown-Boveri (ABB) in the power distribution business. Believing that power distribution represents a declining industry, Westinghouse has gradually sold off the businesses that produced heavy-duty transformers and power relays used for high-voltage grids. The completion of Westinghouse's harvesting process occurred in 1999 when the company merged with CBS. The remaining Westinghouse assets were subsequently sold or carved out into independent companies.

Despite its availability as a response option, gradually harvesting a business is generally a poor strategic approach to managing change. Usually, selling assets to a willing buyer if possible is better, because other owners and managers may be able to derive additional value out of assets that would otherwise be "stripped" in harvesting. This situation confronted the Sylvania division of GTE (now part of Verizon Communications) during the early 1980s, when GTE decided investment in consumer electronics represented a major distraction from its core telephone businesses. Eventually, GTE sold its Sylvania line of color televisions to a competitor.

Harvesting also means that the firm must devote considerable managerial effort to a declining business when that effort could be better spent looking for more attractive businesses. To focus on its faster-growing core businesses, General Electric in 1989 decided against harvesting its consumer electronics group by selling the entire business outright to Thomson, S.A. of France (now known as Thales, S.A.), in exchange for the French firm's medical electronics business and a large cash infusion. GE was able to gain considerable economies of scale by integrating Thomson's medical operations with its own. As the market for traditional color television continued to decline, Thomson in 2004 sold its consumer electronics business to China's TCL, which has great ambitions to enter and revitalize the television business with new technology. Likewise, Siemens of Germany in 2005 decided that harvesting was a poor strategy to exit from the fast moving cell phone industry. Instead, Siemens has put its cell phone business on the block for potential sale to other interested parties. In the United States currently, domestic cigarette and traditional long-distance telephone companies have begun to implement harvesting-type strategies in order to slowly reduce the investment and resources needed to sustain these businesses.

Generic Change Situations

A key pillar of strategic management is that managers have the ability to make adjustments to their firms' strategies following an environmental change. In reality, constraints imposed by the competitive environment, the needs of different stakeholders, and the organization itself may limit senior management's degree of "maneuvering room" needed to undertake rapid adjustments. Nevertheless, adjusting to environmental change demands considerable managerial skill and judgment to decide on the best response option. In selecting one of three response options—prospecting, defending, or harvesting—a firm must balance two critical factors: the magnitude of the threat posed by an environmental development and a firm's ability to adjust.

Magnitude of Threat

Some environmental developments have only modest impact on a firm's core business. Growth of a small specialty niche within an industry is a case in point. Such a development may cause defection of only a few of the established firms' traditional customers. When new niches remain small and confined, the need to adapt is relatively minor. For example, the rise of Polaroid in instant photography resulted in limited inroads into Kodak's business. Although customers were initially fascinated with the concept of instant photography that did not require long waiting times for film development, the poor picture quality of Polaroid's instant photography technology limited its appeal to a wide base of Kodak customers. On the other hand, this situation is unlike one in which a development threatens the very foundation of an established firm's business and sources of competitive advantage. Failure to adjust can then bring about rapid and severe loss of market position.

Ability to Adjust

Adjusting to an external development compels a firm to learn and build new skills and competences. To offer customers new ways of sampling and purchasing music, for example, the record label companies need to develop a new competence in digital security, encryption, and telecom-based skills that allow for fast downloads and easy use. Similarly, Eastman Kodak will need significantly greater investment, competence, and experience with semiconductors, display technologies, and digital imaging techniques to make a successful transition to new forms of digital photography. Before attempting such an adjustment, however, firms must assess their ability to develop the necessary new competence and skill set.

New types of distinctive competences and skills required to adapt to an environmental shift can come in many forms. For example, skills in software engineering and mathematical algorithms would help record label companies better understand and manage the complexity of offering music over the Internet. Likewise, record label companies need to develop new types of marketing programs to cater to Internet-driven and satellite-driven listeners who can select programming that carry no commercials. In the consumer electronics industry, a strong capability in flat-screen technology would help an electronics manufacturer quickly adjust to developing laptop and notebook computers, as well as state-of-the-art televisions and even medical equipment. Experience and competence in applied chemistry and blending techniques can be valuable skills for a consumer nondurables firm to make new types of laundry detergent or stain removers (as is the case for Procter & Gamble, Unilever, Henkel, as well as Clorox).

In assessing the capability for adjustment, a firm must often reconfigure its entire value chain or business system to develop a broad range of new skills. Finding and building a new distinctive competence is extremely difficult, because significant resistance to change is likely to occur within the organization. In particular, established firms may experience more difficulty in creating an entirely new distinctive competence than would a new entrant. Established firms are likely to have their own managerial practices and ways of thinking that can complicate the adjustment to a new technology, distribution channel, or other shift. This difficulty that established firms may face in implementing change is known as **inertia.** Inertia is an important factor that inhibits fast response to environmental developments, especially for large, well-established firms in mature industries facing new types of technologies and competitors. Sometimes, the best approach to developing a new distinctive competence required for adjustment is a clean sheet of paper that "frees" management from the cognitive maps and mental constraints imposed by long experience with an existing technology or distribution setup.[13] In other words, the existence of older distinctive competences and sources of competitive advantage may erect real cognitive and economic adjustment barriers to learning new ones. Pre-existing distinctive competencies can ironically lead to significant difficulties in embracing new technologies, skills, and insights.

inertia:
The difficulty that established firms face when trying to adjust to change; inhibits fast response to new developments in the environment.

The underlying tone of our discussion so far has implied that an environmental development or shift usually poses a threat to existing sources of competitive advantage. On the other hand, new developments can also represent opportunities for firms willing and able to recognize and adjust to them. Established firms that already possess many of the skills needed to make the adjustment may find that the new development opens up markets previously unavailable to them. In other words, adjustment efforts could pave the way for unforeseen prospecting opportunities. For example, the rise of digital-based, multimedia technologies that transform the design and manufacture of consumer electronics poses a dual threat and opportunity for companies such as Sony, Hewlett-Packard, Motorola, IBM, Cisco Systems, Nokia, Samsung, and Philips Electronics. On the one hand, those firms with a strong base of experience and skills in semiconductors and computers, such as IBM and Motorola, may find that they have many of the ingredients and "raw materials" necessary to participate and compete in a redefined consumer electronics industry. As a result, this new development could represent an opening to serve markets that previously did not exist. Similarly, Samsung, Sony, and Philips Electronics possess many of the distinctive competences, brand-name recognition, and market insights needed to design products that would appeal to a broad array of global markets. The manufacturing and marketing "muscle" of these three firms could push the acceptance of digital products into many new markets. Finally, Cisco Systems' exceptionally strong position in designing computer networks makes it a potential player to provide the technologies that connect next-generation electronic appliances to the Internet to better serve customers' needs (for example, for online gaming, distance education). Thus, even though the rise of digital multimedia formats represents a potential threat to each of these players in terms of shifting technologies, their arrival also means an opportunity for each of the firms to apply their existing distinctive competences and skills to participate in this emerging arena. Certainly, each firm's current sources of competitive advantage would need some adjustment to enable the firm to compete fully and effectively in the emerging industry. However, successful learning of new competences and skills in addition to existing skills would enable each of these firms to prospect in a completely new, related, or potentially redefined industry.

Common Change Situations

Let us now combine these two dimensions—ability to adjust and magnitude of threat—to form the matrix shown in Exhibit 5-5. The figure depicts four generic change situations distinguished on the basis of the magnitude of the opportunity or threat posed by environmental change and the ability of a firm to deal with developments brought about by change. An established firm facing environmental change will generally need to respond differently to each of these situations.

Cell 1. A firm in this kind of situation faces a serious environmental development. The development could result in permanent loss of competitive position if the firm fails to respond. However, the firm possesses the ability to respond. When these two conditions are present, then

Exhibit 5-5   *Major Response Options*

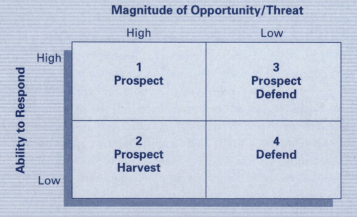

	Magnitude of Opportunity/Threat	
	High	Low
High	**1** **Prospect**	**3** **Prospect** **Defend**
Low	**2** **Prospect** **Harvest**	**4** **Defend**

(Ability to Respond)

a firm should try to establish itself quickly in the new area, meaning it should prospect. Any other approach would enable rivals to gain the lead in responding to the development by giving them the first-mover, experience, and scale advantages that a hesitant or late-responding firm would have trouble matching.

For the past seven years, Intel has faced this predicament when designing microprocessors for PCs that continue to decline in price. If Intel failed to respond to develop newer microprocessor technologies that reduced power consumption and simultaneously boosted computer performance, Intel would likely face diminished demand for personal computers developed with its existing line of semiconductor technology. To counter this threat, Intel has invested heavily in new chip-making techniques that enable the firm to build two or more microprocessor "cores" onto one piece of silicon. This "multi-core" approach to chip design will dramatically increase the power, speed, and versatility of PCs beginning in 2006.[14]

Microsoft is now forced to deal with open-source software that, in many cases, is available free over the Internet. The most popular variant is known as Linux. This operating system allows small and medium-sized firms to capture many of the same benefits that they used to obtain from Microsoft's proprietary Windows-based systems. Customers have increasingly demanded new forms of software that can work across products from different vendors, cost less to purchase and operate, and offer easily upgraded capabilities. Already, Microsoft's initially sluggish response to confront the Linux-based threat has left the company somewhat vulnerable to other new entrants and established firms that have developed more sophisticated versions of Linux, such as IBM. Microsoft's current Windows NT product lines are designed to allow machines from different manufacturers—IBM, Hewlett-Packard, and Sun Microsystems—to "talk" with one another. More recently, Windows Pocket PC, as adopted by such manufacturers as Hewlett-Packard and Casio, has given rise to new digital network appliances that work across and link up with copiers, computers, personal digital assistants, network devices, telephones, and other office equipment through a common software language using a streamlined version of Windows. Yet, Microsoft's size may actually work against the company in the short term as more agile competitors seize the initiative to design bold new products more nimbly (for example, Research in Motion). To regain the initiative, Microsoft is heading a consortium of twenty different companies (including software, computer, and office equipment manufacturers) to design their hardware offerings around variants of Microsoft's proprietary software language codes. This step helps Microsoft's corporate customers gain access to new products first, and it slows down other software providers.[15]

In the aerospace industry, Boeing confronts a situation similar to those facing Intel and Microsoft. The advent of a powerful competitor in Europe, Airbus Industries, has challenged Boeing with new types of commercial jet aircraft. An emerging technological development and challenge also exist. The rise of new technologies, such as fly-by-wire controls (replacing hydraulics) and advanced avionics, threaten Boeing's skills in its current line of aircraft designs and manufacturing skills. After some ongoing difficulties, Boeing has learned and applied these new electronics-driven technologies for use in its new line of 777 and 7E7 aircraft. With competition between Boeing and Airbus now intensifying, Boeing is now planning to develop a whole new line of advanced aircraft that promise to greatly slice down the amount of fuel that is consumed.

Cell 2. The most difficult situation confronting an established firm occurs when an environmental development or shift poses a major threat to its sources of competitive advantage, but the firm lacks the ability to respond. Timex faced this kind of situation when the electronic revolution swept through its industry in the 1970s. The new technology threatened to revolutionize manufacture of low-priced watches. Consequently, if Timex failed to respond, it risked serious loss of competitive position. Timex possessed little electronic capability, and thus it lacked the ability to make an effective response.

During the 1970s and 1980s many integrated U.S. steelmakers (such as U.S. Steel, Inland, National, Armco, LTV, and Bethlehem) suffered from two types of shifts. First, domestic minimills used nonunion labor and cheaper scrap metal to gain market share. They produced lower-cost steel and responded more quickly to customer changes in demand, because they tended to operate closer to their customers. Second, more efficient and modernized plants in Korea and Japan eroded U.S. technological leadership. The U.S. steel industry failed to invest consistently in new oxygen-based furnaces and continuous casting processes. On the other hand, Japanese and Korean producers spent large sums on R&D to improve the steel-making process by introducing new forms of temperature controls and quality improvement techniques. The U.S. steel industry fell behind when its open-hearth furnace technology could not produce the high-quality steel demanded by its key customers. Auto and appliance makers then began to buy the improved steel needed in making cars, motors, components, and appliance frames from ultramodern Korean and Japanese plants.

An industry currently undergoing massive changes is the U.S. health care system. The U.S. hospital industry continues to face many of the environmental shifts that signify a cell 2 predicament. Overcapacity and investment in high-technology equipment have forced many U.S. hospitals, both private and public, to operate with large losses. In addition, hospitals also face wrenching demands for lower costs, improved efficiency, and quality care made by managed care firms, traditional insurance companies, doctors, patients, and the federal government. Even worse, reimbursements for hospital care have been declining so fast over the past several years that many hospitals are close to bankruptcy. This kind of pressure for cost containment and technological improvement are also impacting physicians and other care providers in a major way, as the U.S. health care system adjusts to the demands of managed care systems and markedly fewer hospitals in existence. Already, many doctors are performing specialized or rapid-recovery medical services and care in facilities outside traditional hospitals. Known as carve-outs, these physician-owned and physician-managed facilities are beginning to compete with hospitals for the more lucrative lines of care (for example, cardiology, ophthalmology, oncology, radiology, diagnostic testing). Moving these activities out of the hospital helps lower the costs for patients and managed care firms. In this way, patients receive care and managed care or insurance providers do not incur the high costs of using traditional hospital facilities. Medical procedures that are now performed routinely outside of the hospital include cataract, corrective vision (such as LASIK), and minor skin surgeries.

These trends have been devastating to hospital finances. To deal with this development, many hospital chains (particularly those managed by Columbia HCA and Tenet) have restructured, consolidated, and even merged their operations. Columbia HCA's noteworthy acquisition and restructuring moves of many hospitals around the country during the 1990s were designed to reposition hospitals so they can gradually slim down their operations, gain economies of scale in key activities (particularly information processing, pharmaceutical purchases, and government reimbursement of Medicare fees), and thus lower their fixed costs. In fact, competing hospitals in all the major U.S. cities have begun merging their care centers together so that they can better compete with these new providers.

One approach for a firm in this kind of situation is harvesting—extracting cash from a business before adverse consequences take full effect. Harvesting represents an extreme and generally undesirable solution, since it deliberately and methodically reduces a once-healthy business to extinction. Moreover, environmental developments and shifts often proceed so rapidly that harvesting yields only a limited amount of cash, potentially far less than if the business were sold outright.

The only viable solution is to begin prospecting. This is extremely difficult, since the firm lacks the necessary skills and resources. More important, firms must always be on the lookout for major changes in customer needs or technological breakthroughs. Oftentimes, the firm will have to look beyond its immediate, focal industry to spot emerging trends. To succeed, it must begin searching for new ways to adapt and to learn, long before adverse developments threatening its businesses fully materialize, as Barnes & Noble and Borders Group tried to do in the wake of Amazon.com's challenge. Concentration of effort is essential. Unfortunately, in many cases, senior management may resist these moves. Prospecting almost always means commitment of resources to some uncertain endeavor—resources that are in demand by other areas within the organization. As a result, serious organizational obstacles often impede this sort of initiative, as was the case with the domestic steel industry during the 1980s and with many hospital systems in the late 1990s. All too often, firms that are either unwilling or unable to recognize the need for early prospecting find themselves unable to handle serious competitive challenges later.

A firm facing the need to prospect quickly can sometimes shorten the time required to develop new competences and skills by teaming up with a partner who already possesses new skills. For example, in an earlier period Timex might have obtained the electronic-based technologies it needed by working with an electronic component manufacturer such as Texas Instruments or Motorola (with which it now has a joint technology development relationship). It would then have had instant access to the new forms of skills or technologies needed to make the adjustment. Conversely, Timex potentially could have licensed existing electronic technologies from other firms that were either unaware or uninterested in entering the watch market. Today, Kodak's relationships with Microsoft, Hewlett-Packard, and other firms help the firm gain access to important new digital-related skills related to software, printing, and distribution. In addition, Kodak's arrangements with Intel and Microsoft give the firm important exposure to developments in the microchip industry. By working together with other firms who possess valuable digital expertise, Kodak can begin the process of attempting to reinvent itself.

Cell 3. A firm in this situation has the capability to respond to an environmental change, so prospecting is a fully viable option. Prospecting is not immediately urgent, however, because not doing so will not result in serious erosion of the firm's competitive advantage. Defending to reinforce a firm's current distinctive competences and skills is an equally viable option. Merrill Lynch's decision to avoid excessive commitment to the LBO (leveraged buyout) sector during the 1980s is a cell 3 response. In the wake of massive corporate restructurings, powerful LBO firms, such as KKR (Kohlberg, Kravis and Roberts), carved up this market. Merrill Lynch instead reinforced its core brokerage business and its expertise in the consumer market for financial planning and investments. It invested in new computer technologies and expanded its traditional product offerings in the stock and bond markets. Merrill also maintains a host of smaller positions in asset management, mutual funds, and other lines of businesses. Merrill's strong brokerage franchise, wide consumer recognition, and computer-based investments allow it to enter many new financial service areas without facing undue environmental risk from existing competitors. Eventually Merrill was confronted with a different technological development—setting up operations on the Internet.

Firms in cell 3 will often rely on working with other firms. This is an effective strategy that enables a company to prospect and defend at the same time. For example, many companies in a given industrial sector have joined together to create websites that enable them to learn how best to harness the Internet for online ordering and distribution activities. Websites dedicated to a particular industry—steel, chemicals, plastics—allow customers to place orders directly with the appropriate manufacturer who has the right mix or products, pricing, and capacity to meet the customer's needs. By working together, they share the costs and risks of using the web to learn and incorporate new technologies into their business systems (limited form of prospecting). At the same time, experience with using the web helps reduce ordering complexity and lowers costs (defending an existing business). In a similar vein, airline companies have joined together to form Orbitz, an online virtual travel agency that offers customers the ability to make air, hotel, and car reservations from anywhere they have an Internet connection. By working together, the major airline companies can better improve their web-based technologies, while solidifying their joint efforts to discourage customers from using other vendors (such as Travelocity, priceline.com, and hotels.com).

In the automotive industry, Ford undertook an important prospecting initiative by forming a technology-sharing partnership with Toyota Motor of Japan in 2003. Ford wanted to learn from Toyota how to better design and manufacture hybrid cars that offer significantly better fuel economy. Even though Ford has the knowledge and labs to design hybrid motors, working with Toyota helps Ford overcome product development and manufacturing delays that accompany new technologies. Although hybrid cars do not yet threaten traditional combustion engines in a major way, Ford believes that it must act now to improve its own design skills that will be important for future car models. Already, Ford has designed hybrid versions of both smaller compact vehicles (the Focus), and midsized SUVs (the Escape) for sale in the United States. For its part, Toyota is also selling a version of its hybrid technology to Nissan as well. General Motors and DaimlerChrysler have their own array of internal projects and technology partnerships that are structured to help both companies adapt to the needs of this new technology. In January 2005, both GM and DaimlerChrysler dedicated even more resources to their joint effort to work on gasoline-hybrid engines. Even this venture may face an uphill battle, as Toyota is already working on a second-generation hybrid engine, and GM-Daimler's technology will not be available until 2007. [16]

Even though the Big Three automotive manufacturers can still easily defend their market positions with current technologies and aggressive price discounting, they all realize that a combination of prospecting and defending is needed to build new sources of competitive advantage for the long term. Customers are demanding more fuel-efficient engines; governments are enforcing more strict pollution controls; and the cost of oil is volatile. All of the automakers realize that they must pursue new technologies to develop new vehicles while maintaining their existing market shares and popular lines of cars. On the one hand, prospecting efforts help all three companies gain experience with new types of energy and power storage technologies (for example, advanced motors, long-life batteries) that will lay the foundation for even more leading-edge concepts (such as hydrogen and fusion systems). The cost of designing hybrids now provides the necessary experience and insight to think about even greater scientific breakthroughs later. Yet, developing hybrid cars helps the Big Three defend their market shares from other rivals. Hybrids made by GM, Ford, and DaimlerChrysler attract customers who ordinarily might have purchased an imported model in the belief that U.S. automakers are behind the curve in environmentally friendly technologies. European and Japanese car makers have been investing in hybrid technologies for a longer time because of high gasoline costs in their markets. If GM, Ford, and DaimlerChrysler are successfully able to design and build hybrid cars in large numbers, they might be able to stem the erosion of their market share. Over time, as buyer interest in hybrids and other environmentally friendly technologies increases, we should expect to see the automakers increase their prospecting efforts and investments substantially (that is, move from cell 3 to cell 1).

Cell 4. A firm in this situation lacks the capability to respond to an environmental development, but the development poses only a modest threat to its position. A strong emphasis on defending the firm's current market position makes considerable sense in the short term. In theory, firms in cell 4 face little need to engage in large-scale prospecting because changes in technology or customer needs are slow in coming. Large-scale prospecting may be impractical to carry out for both economic and organizational reasons. Economically speaking, large-scale prospecting means that the firm will have to place "big bets" on what it sees as the future direction of the industry. This certainly involves large risks if the company is wrong in its prediction. Organizationally, large-scale prospecting will encounter significant resistance, as resources are devoted to more pressing, immediate needs within the defending business. In practice, however, all organizations in any industry need to engage in some form of limited prospecting, even if it means small-scale projects or teaming up with a partner to learn new skills.

A cell 4 situation faces the big food processors—Archer Daniels Midland (ADM), Bunge, Cargill, and ConAgra—in their continued production and use of corn fructose syrup as a key sweetener. Although a variety of new substitute sweeteners are becoming more readily available (for example, Splenda), they are not expected to completely displace natural sources of sugar for a number of years. Corn processing and milling are highly stable technologies that produce vast amounts of fructose at extremely low cost. Because of their higher cost, substitute sweeteners have so far not captured significant market share. However, as people in developed nations become increasingly attracted to nonsugar or fructose-based forms of sweetener, market demand will likely pick up (especially given the high personal and medical costs associated with obesity). Corn and food processors will eventually have to step up their prospecting efforts to learn about new types of substitute products, and even new types of value-creating activities that may be very different from what they are accustomed to now. At the same time, the grain and food processing companies may well discover alternative uses for corn, such as advanced fibers and even an alternative source of energy.

Uncertainty

Thus far, we have generally ignored the issue of uncertainty associated with environmental change. In reality, environmental change and responding to it are usually fraught with great uncertainty. The changing situations in digital music distribution and Eastman Kodak capture the uncertainty that established firms face when confronted with new developments. Uncertainty surrounds the impact of new developments on a firm's existing sources of competitive advantage and on its ability to learn new skills and competences.

Impact of Environmental Development

From our current perspective, anyone could surmise that consumer acceptance of new formats of digital music ultimately depended on the speed of Internet connections, convenience and ease of use, and the cost relative to conventional CDs. Even though technology continues to progress, a fair degree of uncertainty still surrounds both Internet speed and the cost of incorporating new types of electronics to make this media more easily accepted by the broader marketplace. In addition, some performing artists may feel the Internet can potentially result in the mass piracy of their performances.

Consider first the issue of Internet speed. As downloading music files becomes faster and easier, the growth of digital music will surge. Second, the acceptance of digital music will likely depend on how fast the cost for MP3 players, CD burners, and other new forms of consumer electronics will decline in the next few years. If history is any indication, these "hardware" products typically follow steep price curves wherein they become less expensive over time as the devices mature. The enormous popularity of Apple's iPod digital music player demonstrates the critical role of easy-to-use technology that fits in a sleek design. As a result, Apple now dominates much of the legal music download business through both the iPod player and its iTunes online music store. However, Apple's iTunes online store only works with its iPod music player—a feature that may work against Apple in the long run. Customers who paid a premium to acquire the iPod may eventually resent the fact that portable music players from other firms will likely be much less costly, because they can operate on a variety of other technical formats as well. As Microsoft, Sony, and other rivals begin to offer digital online music storefronts that are compatible with a broad range of music players, Apple will confront a much more intensely competitive environment. Even such rivals as Yahoo!, MTV, and even Wal-Mart Stores are thinking of getting into the market even further.

Finally, with respect to performing artists, the Internet is a double-edged sword. On the one hand, it allows customers to sample their music and bring the performing artist much greater awareness by the public. On the other hand, the proliferation of the Internet means that performing artists (and their record companies) now must compete for a share of cyberspace that is always growing. It is possible to envision hundreds of thousands of music tracks on the Internet. This means that even popular bands and upcoming songs could become overwhelmed by the sheer amount of music available over the net. Unless there are new ways to sift through all the information and music samples that are out there, some consumers may feel that searching for Internet-based music may not be worth the trouble.

Now, Eastman Kodak faces a parallel set of uncertainties concerning the rise of digital photography. As flash memory and other semiconductors become cheaper, their influence over digital camera performance will continue to grow. Steep price declines also characterize this industry. Leading-edge cameras introduced in one year become commodity-like products in the following year. However, consumer acceptance of next-generation technology formats and equipment designs will likely remain open questions. Product acceptance ultimately depends on how customers feel about the new technology, its versatility, and its cost, thus introducing significant uncertainty into the planning process. Advances by Kodak rivals compound the situation, as Canon, Sony, Samsung, Epson, and Nokia take different routes to pushing their versions of digital photography using different consumer products as platforms. For example, Nokia's push to incorporate a digital camera in every cell phone could actually propel the company to be the world's leading producer of such devices. The combination of digital camera with cell phone and MP3 player could propel Nokia and other cell phone manufacturers to become important competitors to Kodak and other companies who focus on cameras alone. Yet, digital camera firms are attempting to further enhance and differentiate their product to appeal to more professional users. For example, Canon's introduction of newer removable lenses that greatly magnify the focus and clarity of digital pictures makes the firm a leading contender to dominate the professional segment (for example, Canon's Digital Rebel). Thus, competitor dynamics introduces a wide range of uncertainties as to how Kodak should best respond and position itself to capture new customers. Even though Kodak remains committed to developing and applying new types of digital imaging-based skills to its future products, it must still learn how to produce digital cameras in sufficient volumes to lower their costs and reach a critical mass of the market.

Ability to Adjust

If the record companies decide to embrace new digital music formats fully, they can initially benefit from their well-known brand names, sponsorship of popular bands, creation of videos, promotion of concerts, relationships with existing distribution channels, worldwide distribution network, and sophisticated promotional abilities. These sources of competitive advantage would not guarantee success in the new field, however. To become a potent competitor or leader in digital music formats, Universal Music, Sony, Bertelsmann AG, and Warner Music would need skills in areas such as encryption, digital compression techniques, and telecom-based skills. As noted in the initial example, MusicNet and Pressplay represent transitional initiatives by the music companies to learn how to compete on the Internet. Sony, in particular, has other businesses within the same firm that could offer some of these technical skills. However, the development of the iPod music player by Apple Computer perhaps represents a real turning point in this industry so far. Apple has promised to protect the intellectual property of music companies through its iTunes online music store, and it has designed the iPod to prevent music from being e-mailed from one person to another. These steps have done much to assuage many music executives' concern about rampant piracy, characterized by such terms as "rip, mix, and burn." Yet, despite Apple's growing dominance of this business, other firms that specialize in these areas are developing their own business models through subscription services that are becoming cheaper (for example, RealNetworks' Rhapsody unit). By forming new distribution relationships with such firms, music companies might be better able to extend their reach to new customers.

Eastman Kodak today confronts a similar set of questions concerning its adjustment ability. One of Kodak's key problems is that its current competence in digital imaging technology is not significantly better than that possessed by many of its rivals. These firms have major sources of competitive advantage in their brand names, production skills, and faster innovation. They also compete fiercely in semiconductor, software, consumer electronics, office equipment, and other imaging industries. Firms competing in these related or neighboring industries are likely to develop new product designs, technical standards, and manufacturing processes that could eventually be applied to digital imaging. Because Eastman Kodak is not a significant player in any of these industries, it has little potential to transfer or share skills to its imaging unit, despite its current command and ownership of many digital imaging patents. As a result, Kodak is intensifying its efforts to learn a broad range of digital imaging technologies, as reflected by its deal to acquire National Semiconductor's image sensor unit. Still, Kodak continues to deal with the strategic dilemma of learning how to apply uncertain technologies for next-generation consumer photography and imaging, without betting on the wrong format or technical standard that customers do not want. This dilemma is a major source of organizational uncertainty.

If significant uncertainty surrounds a new development, the best initial course may be simply to investigate the development to learn more about it. Investigating involves learning about developments in related or neighboring industries, finding out what other competitors are doing, studying technology research, developing prototypes of new products, and conducting market research. Investigating enables firms to avoid making a large investment that may ultimately be unsuccessful. However, simply investigating poses another kind of risk: a firm that spends too much time investigating a new development risks losing the lead to more aggressive competitors.

Another potentially better approach is to allocate small resources to establishing "skunk works" whose sole purpose is to better understand new technology. A term that originated in the defense and high-technology industries, skunk works are laboratories and test sites that are dedicated to experimenting and developing cutting-edge technologies, often away from corporate headquarters. These skunk works would thus engage in a variety of R&D activities, as well as reverse engineering, active searching for new product development approaches, and streamlining existing technologies to improve upon a competitor's development. For these efforts to work effectively, managers and technical personnel in skunk works or other sites need to be kept separate from existing business units. Also, these people should report directly to the CEO, and not through the regular chains of command or reporting structures. Managers in existing units (often adopting a defender-like strategy) are unlikely to understand the nature of new technologies and their potential impact, and thus are often highly skeptical of skunk works and similar types of efforts.

Firms can sometimes establish small divisions or business units whose sole purpose is to prospect and experiment with new technologies with the hope that they can capture some new insights and develop a new product, service, process, or distribution channel within enough time to recover from a competitor's moves. An even more novel approach would be to form a direct relationship with competitors to learn jointly the potential benefits of emerging core technologies. This strategy would be particularly useful for a company in a substantially weaker position, since it has little to lose and much to gain. For example, General Motors is now working with its archrival DaimlerChrysler to share the costs and risks of developing hybrid engines. At the same time, GM works with a number of small, innovative companies that are developing advanced types of batteries and fuel cells. A further alternative approach is to undertake a small acquisition of a firm that possesses promising core technology. For example, Eastman Kodak's acquisition of National Semiconductor's imaging unit may provide important insight and skills that complement Kodak's internal efforts to apply and learn new technologies. Likewise, Universal Music acquired MP3.com to gain a better perspective on how to distribute and market online music offerings.

Creating Distinctive Value: Whole Foods Market[17]

Whole Foods Market, Inc. is the world's premier natural foods chain and pioneered the concept of selling organic and health foods in a distinctive supermarket model. The company operates 155 stores in twenty-six states and has recently begun expanding in Canada. Founded in 1978 by CEO John Mackey in Austin, Texas, with a ten-thousand-dollar loan from his father, Whole Foods has grown rapidly by building new stores and acquiring smaller chains in the New England, Mid-Atlantic, and Los Angeles regions. In 2003, Whole Foods generated sales that topped $3 billion with net income of over $100 million. Whole Foods plans to open another ten stores in 2004 and another fifteen to twenty in 2005. CEO Mackey hopes to grow revenues to $10 billion by 2010. As the company continues to grow, Whole Foods is now enjoying considerable success for a number of reasons.

First, Whole Foods has successfully tapped into the baby boomers' growing interest in health, longevity, and total well-being as they age. Moreover, consumer interest in safe, pesticide-free foods has grown markedly in recent years as people seek more naturally grown vegetables and other items. This interest in healthy foods has produced an even stronger interest in "nutraceuticals," which are foods that produce pharmaceutical-like benefits through naturally occurring enzymes. Organic and natural foods are no longer a small niche, but rather the fastest growing market segment in the grocery industry. As a result, Whole Foods avoids selling food that contains pesticides, chemicals, preservatives, and sweeteners, even though most products are conventionally grown. Whole Foods has even pledged that it will become the first grocery chain to adopt humane animal treatment standards. These policies enable Whole Foods to gain strong brand recognition and high repeat purchases. Through the store's wide assortment of natural and organic foods, many customers even attribute Whole Foods as a lifestyle brand. Whole Foods has even been able to gain market share and customers at a time when most of the major grocery store chains are rapidly losing ground to low-price Wal-Mart Stores and other deep discounters.

Second, Whole Foods has excelled in providing superb service to its customers. Knowledgeable, but unobtrusive, service is available at every counter or department. Also, product quality is extremely high, as only the freshest fruits and vegetables are sold. Thus, the company can enjoy a higher markup on prices of natural foods compared to those of regular grocery stores. Although Whole Foods earned its reputation offering organic foods free of preservatives, it also offers wide array of conventionally grown foods as well. Whole Foods is hoping that customers will continue to shop at its locations for all of their food purchases, not just for preservative-free items. To make its higher-priced items more appealing, Whole Foods competes by offering freshness and novelty in many food categories. In other parts of the same store, customers can purchase freshly prepared hot foods, as well as a variety of natural herbs, teas, and other vitamin supplements. Whole Foods also tries to model each store to best fit the community it serves. Unlike larger grocery store chains that strive for a consistent, national look, Whole Foods tries to blend and customize its exteriors to match each market. By striving to work the storefront's exterior into the fabric of each community, Whole Foods generates considerable goodwill. Inside the stores, Whole Foods tries to offer the right mix of ingredients that match local market conditions and tastes. For example, in a California store that is located near a small Buddhist sect, the local Whole Foods posts signs that direct potential customers to foods that contain none of the ingredients that may offend Buddhists. Whole Foods' new Manhattan location, on the other hand, has been called a "temple to culinary obsession." Forbes magazine reports that the deli in this 59,000 square foot location's serves over 850 sandwiches a day.

Third, Whole Foods devotes considerable effort and time to promoting environmentally sustainable growth. Its recently launched Green Mission program introduces recycling and composting into all of its stores. Each store will convert wasted food, cardboard, and other biodegradable products into compost that will be sold for under $2 per bag. Across the entire company, Whole Foods recycles more than two million pounds of glass, plastic, and aluminum. Management seeks to build new stores using recycled and sustainable building materials. Whole Foods has formed partnerships with the Marine Stewardship Council, the World Wildlife Fund, and the Alaska Seafood Marketing Institute to promote sustainable seafood harvesting practices. Whole Foods tries to sell seafood that comes from fishing practices that allow the fish population to grow and replenish itself, rather than be depleted. In its New England and Mid-Atlantic stores, Whole Foods contracted with a local utility that will provide up to 10 percent of its stores' electricity needs through wind generation. The electricity will help power fifty-four stores and distribution facilities in nine states. Although Whole Foods will pay a 5 percent premium on wind-generated electricity, the company believes it can help popularize the concept with other businesses so that more people can see the environmentally clean benefits offered. If more and larger businesses were to use wind power, the cost of this service would ultimately come down as well.

CEO John Mackey is extremely modest about his company's achievements. A committed vegan (someone who does not eat animal or animal by-products), Mackey prefers to avoid publicity. He shuns business suits and communicates with employees and staff informally. He believes that Whole Foods represents not only a solid business idea, but also a philosophy. In November 2003, consulting firm Ernst & Young proclaimed John Mackey its Entrepreneur of the Year.

Future Scenarios and Applications—Distributing Films on the Internet

Clearly, the enormous growth of online music distribution has an emerging parallel story in Hollywood. Film production executives are justifiably worried that another version of Napster lurks around the corner that threatens to distribute movies illegally over the Internet, thus promoting video piracy on a rampant scale. However, unlike music companies, the film studios and production companies should have a better understanding of the technological drivers of change that will impact their industry. New software, faster computers, and ever-bigger hard drives can now compress movies into much less space. A two-hour film currently takes less than one gigabyte (1G) of storage. That is equivalent to several hundred songs in digital form. At the same time, broadband connections are becoming more common and cheaper for consumers. Even newer technology enables a movie to download itself in less time than it takes to watch it. This means that consumers can begin watching Internet-delivered films as immediately as they can with conventional television shows.

All of this presents a challenge to film production companies, who must now take steps to simultaneously prospect and defend. Prospecting would involve investments and partnerships to learn about new kinds of technologies that could be included in future movies, such as virtual reality and even direct participation by the viewer into the film. Although film production companies have considerable experience with special effects software, moving to virtual reality will likely require another set of technical skills and software. This would make future films approximate a holistic entertainment experience, rather than a passive experience as they are now. At the same time, film companies need to prospect to understand and apply the latest digital technologies that converge with computers and software so that Internet-powered film distribution moves move away from the personal computer and toward the television set. Currently, downloaded movies can only be seen on PCs, unless the user has the expertise (and the right ports and connections) to hook it up to the television set. Even this step is full of technological complexity and hassles for the average consumer. Thus, a likely prospecting move could include the creation of technical standards among all of the film production companies that offer easier-to-use multimedia formats and compatibility. Defending-based strategies are also important. These could include industry-wide consortia to support and initiate legal actions against companies or individuals that promote illegal file sharing. For example, the Motion Picture Association of America plans to file lawsuits against individuals who trade illegal digital copies of films online—a move that parallels what the music industry is doing to shut down illegal file sharing.[18] Film production companies can take active steps to share the costs of preempting and combating piracy where it occurs. Lobbying to protect their intellectual property would be a natural defensive strategy. More active defending measures include protecting digital films with software encryption codes that slow down or even impede transfers between computers and other devices.

The impact of digital movie downloads has already begun to affect the video rental industry. Blockbuster announced in August 2004 that it would begin offering an online DVD rental service to catch up with its arch rival Netflix, which has offered this service for over five years. Blockbuster also sought to merge with its rival Hollywood Entertainment to defend its existing video franchise. However, Netflix announced that it would also offer direct digital downloads (without the need to return a DVD) as a subscription service to customers beginning sometime in 2005. Yet, even Netflix may not possess any meaningful first-move advantages, because companies such as Movielink and CinemaNow have already started offering a limited number of movies to customers. Still, all companies face a major challenge in this emerging business— consumers still prefer to watch movies on television and not on their PC. Until a technology arrives that offers either easy movie transfers from PCs and other digital devices to televisions, or a digital television set with direct access to the Internet, demand in this business will likely to remain somewhat constrained. In addition, more homes would need to upgrade their telecom and Internet access to faster speed, broadband hook-ups to make film-downloading a practical alternative to current viewing formats. In other words, the digital film business needs its own version of a "video iPod" that makes the downloading experience much easier and legally accepted.[19]

Shareholder Considerations and Ethical Dilemmas

What balance should top managers strike between the alternative objectives of prospecting, defending, or harvesting? Should top managers seek to "get ahead of the curve" and sell a currently prosperous business before being confronted with the decision to harvest? How much should senior management tilt their judgment toward prospecting versus defending? Clearly, no single answer is applicable to firms in different types of change situations. The decision to prospect or to defend hinges heavily on the nature of the environmental development, the firm's ability to adjust, and the extent to which the firm or business can devote sufficient resources to make the adjustment. Unfortunately, senior management in many firms starts addressing and acting upon these issues only when their backs are against the wall. Nevertheless, the decision to prospect, defend, or harvest depends significantly on the degree of uncertainty and risk that senior management feels that the firm can bear.

Many prospecting efforts involve considerable short- to medium-term risk. Sufficient funds must be devoted to exploring and investing in new technologies, skills, distribution channels, and other future sources of competitive advantage that may not bear fruit for several years. However, failure to respond to an environmental development will often subject the firm to another kind of long-term risk—the risk that the firm will eventually lose all of its existing sources of competitive advantage and never recover. Regardless of which strategic option is invoked, the balance between risk and return inherent within each of these response options should also factor in the needs of different stakeholders.

The task of reconciling stakeholder needs with respect to risk and return is complicated by the fact that top managers are one stakeholder group whose interests are factored into this equation. Unfortunately, their needs sometimes conflict with those of other stakeholder groups, particularly with those of shareholders. Managers are sometimes tempted to give their own needs undue weight when making a decision.[20] Succumbing to this temptation raises potentially serious ethical questions, since managers have a fiduciary responsibility to act on behalf of shareholders. To understand the nature of this problem, let us briefly contrast the risk and reward preferences of top managers and shareholders.

Risk Preference

Institutions—pension plans, mutual funds, and insurance companies—hold a majority of shares of public companies. Let us therefore put ourselves in the place of an institutional shareholder. The holdings of institutions are generally widely diversified. For example, a mutual fund commonly holds shares in more than a hundred different firms. Because their holdings are so diverse, institutions stand to suffer only minor loss if an effort to prospect or to enter a new market undertaken by one of the companies in their portfolio ultimately fails. Institutions can thus tolerate considerable prospecting risk.

Now let us consider managers of companies owned by institutions. They are often held accountable when new ventures fail. Such failure can result in termination of their employment, problems securing employment with other firms, and severe psychological hardship. Managers thus stand to suffer serious professional and personal hardship from failure of ventures for which they are responsible. Consequently, they may be inclined to be more risk averse over the short to medium term and therefore avoid large-scale prospecting efforts.

Return Preference

The payoff from success of high-risk prospecting efforts is also generally different for managers and shareholders. Top managers of most public companies own only a small portion of the equity of the firms they oversee. As a result, their reward from successful new ventures is limited mainly to such things as enhanced compensation and improved career prospects. These benefits are important. However, they pale next to those that shareholders can derive from new venture success. These considerations suggest that managers often have more to lose and less to gain from high-risk, high-return ventures than shareholders. As a consequence, managers are often tempted to forego such projects in favor of lower-risk, lower-return efforts. In other words, defending becomes a natural outcome or response because of the way senior management is itself rewarded. Requests by lower-level managers to engage in prospecting initiatives often meet significant resistance and must be justified by the presence of a direct and immediate threat. The status quo becomes preferable, because operating the firm on "cruise control" is much easier. Managers who succumb to this temptation often end up putting their own interests above those of shareholders, thereby potentially sidestepping their fiduciary duty to shareholders. The extent to which risk avoidance may inhibit top managers of public companies from exploiting potentially lucrative opportunities is difficult to judge.

The issue of harvesting a business also presents another ethically related dilemma in the sense that this particular response option can be demoralizing to lower-level managers and employees in the firm. Harvesting involves the gradual dissolution of the business, which inevitably results in people losing their jobs over time. Selling the business outright may offer some of the affected managers and employees at least some potential for continued employment with another owner who could better identify valuable uses for the underlying assets. Also from a shareholder perspective, harvesting is usually less desirable than selling the firm or business. Selling the business, even with associated exit barriers, releases existing capital from increasingly less productive uses.

Summary

- Environmental change and developments can significantly alter an industry's competitive environment. Moreover, new developments or shifts can sometimes dramatically affect the value and threaten existing sources of competitive advantage.
- Competence-changing technologies are advances that could redefine an industry's structure and technological format.
- The growth of the Internet as a new distribution system has fundamentally changed the way firms in both product and service industries can now reach and meet their customers' needs. The Internet will likely become an important competitor to firms in many existing industries as customers face fewer switching costs, greater convenience, and easy access to competitors' offerings.
- Environmental changes or developments in related or neighboring industries can eventually make themselves felt in any given industry. Oftentimes, technological, distribution, or demand changes in one industry can have ripple effects that ultimately require a shift in a firm's strategy, resource allocation, and sources of competitive advantage in another.
- Firms facing new developments or shifts can respond in three fundamentally different ways: prospecting, defending, or harvesting.
- Selection of the appropriate response option should be based on the magnitude of the opportunity or threat that the change presents and the firm's ability to adjust.
- High levels of uncertainty accompany environmental developments. When uncertainty is extremely high, it is sometimes preferable to investigate the change first until a clearer picture emerges. Spending an excessive amount of time investigating, however, can result in costly response delay.

Exercises and Discussion Questions

 1. The rise of digital photography remains an ongoing challenge for Eastman Kodak. Look up Kodak's website and describe some of the investments that it has made recently in learning how to compete in this era. How would you describe Kodak's strategy in this emerging digital photography arena? In what areas does the website suggest that Kodak is prospecting? What are some different approaches that Kodak has used in its prospecting strategy?

@ **2.** Visit the websites of E-Stamp and the U.S. Postal Service. What other services would you recommend that these two entrants provide to broaden the appeal of their strategy? Now look up Pitney Bowes on the web. What should this company do to help it compete against the new entrants?

3. Which type of firm appears to be better able to carry out a prospecting strategy—large or small? What are some key attributes that prospectors need to have, regardless of size?

4. Imagine yourself as the CEO of a large consumer electronics company. You are confronted with the opportunity to acquire a small software company that offers new technology that can dramatically improve the quality and features of your product. You do not see any immediate threats from the current environment that would negatively impact your product line. What might be some reasons you would want to acquire this company, especially if the acquisition will not cost very much?

5. As a mid-level manager that has worked for many years at a large manufacturing company, are you more likely to support or a resist an attempt by the company to introduce an entirely new production process into the firm? What might be some factors that would influence your decision? Conversely, as a newly hired employee or manager, are you more likely to support or resist this same move? What might be some factors that you would consider?

Endnotes

1. Facts and data for examining this strategy snapshot were adapted from the following sources: "Not Much to Sing About," *Wall Street Journal,* January 31, 2005, p. R5; "Music Industry Fears Bad Tidings in Slowing CD Sales," *Wall Street Journal,* November 19, 2004, pp. B1, B2; "Apple Wants Japanese Music Service," *Wall Street Journal,* November 19, 2004, p. A10; "Microsoft, the Entertainer?" *Business Week,* September 13, 2004, pp. 96–100; "The Song Remains the Same," *Forbes,* September 6, 2004, pp. 54–55; "Microsoft Gets Ready to Rock," *Dallas Morning News,* August 31, 2004, p. 2D; "Online Music's Latest Tune," *Wall Street Journal,* August 27, 2004, pp. B1, B2; "H-P to Sing Apple's Songs," *Wall Street Journal,* August 27, 2004, pp. B1, B2; "Downloads: The Next Generation," *Business Week,* February 16, 2004, p. 64; "The Big Squeeze," *Forbes,* January 12, 2004, pp. 178–181; "Music Industry Presses 'Play' on Plan to Save Its Business," *Wall Street Journal,* September 9, 2003, p. B1; "The High Cost of Sharing," *Wall Street Journal,* September 9, 2003, p. B1, B8; "Roxio Looks to Resurrect 'Napster,'" *Wall Street Journal,* May 20, 2003, p. B7; "Clear Channel Will Offer Data on Internet Music," *Wall Street Journal,* March 14, 2003, p. B2; "Music Industry Faces New Threats on Web," *Wall Street Journal,* February 21, 2003, pp. B1, B4; "Rhapsody Lets You Burn CDs Online at 49 Cents a Song," *Wall Street Journal,* February 13, 2003, p. B1; "Legalize It," *Forbes,* February 17, 2003, pp. 99–100; "Vivendi, Sony Set Music-Service Prices," *Wall Street Journal,* June 13, 2002, p. D10; "Dysfunctional Discs," *Dallas Morning News,* February 21, 2002, p. 3D; "Vivendi Seeks Respect From U.S. Investors," *Wall Street Journal,* February 12, 2002, pp. A12, A14; "Universal Music Prospers in Hard Times for Media Firms," *Wall Street Journal,* December 18, 2001, p. B8; "Entertainment Industry Sues to Curtail Web Music-Sharing System Morpheus," *Wall Street Journal,* October 4, 2001, p. B9; "Vivendi to Begin Releasing CDs Equipped with Technology to Deter Digital Piracy," *Wall Street Journal,* September 26, 2001, p. B2; "Online Music: Can't Get No . . . ," *Business Week,* September 3, 2001, pp. 78–80; "Sony, Warner to Back Protection Standard," *Wall Street Journal,* July 17, 2001, p. B7; "Sony to Unveil Online Music Studio," *Wall Street Journal,* June 18, 2001, p. B8; "Universal Music Is Betting on Future of Wireless Movies and Music," *Wall Street Journal,* May 24, 2001, pp. B1,

B4; "Universal Music to Buy MP3.com for $372 Million in Cash and Stock," *Wall Street Journal,* May 21, 2001, pp. A3, A12; "Plugging into the Web Is a Jarring Experience for the Music Industry," *Wall Street Journal,* April 12, 2001, pp. A1, A10; "Music Companies Plan to Team Up with RealNetworks," *Wall Street Journal,* April 3, 2001, p. B8; "Download, Downshift and Go: MP3 Takes to the Road," *Wall Street Journal,* February 27, 2001, pp. B1, B4; "Tech Firms to Announce Improvements in Delivery of Internet Audio and Video," *Wall Street Journal,* December 11, 2000, p. B12; "Napster Alliance Boosts Prospects for Encryption," *Wall Street Journal,* November 2, 2000, p. B1, B20; "Bertelsmann Deal Marks Alternative Web Strategy," *Wall Street Journal,* September 25, 2000, p. A20; "Warner Music Will Join Digital-Download Market," *Wall Street Journal,* September 11, 2000, p. B14; "Bertelsmann, in Online Play, to Buy CDNow," *Wall Street Journal,* July 20, 2000, pp. B1, B4; "Now the Napsterization of Movies," *Wall Street Journal,* July 17, 2000, pp. B1, B7; "AOL Agrees to Use Software Made by RealNetworks," *Wall Street Journal,* July 13, 2000, p. B14; "Making Music Together on Web Becomes Reality," *Wall Street Journal,* July 6, 2000, pp. B1, B10; "Can the Record Industry Beat Free Web Music?" *Wall Street Journal,* June 20, 2000, pp. B1, B4; "MP3.com Plans to Store CD Copies on Web Site," *Wall Street Journal,* January 13, 2000, p. B11.

2. Facts and data for Eastman Kodak were adapted from the following sources: "A Price War Hits Digital Photos," *Wall Street Journal,* March 17, 2005, pp. D1, D6; "Kodak Urges Camera-Phone Progress," *Wall Street Journal,* March 15, 2005, p. B4; "As Cameras Go Digital, a Race to Shape Habits of Consumers," *Wall Street Journal,* November 19, 2004, pp. A1, A10; "Kodak Teams Up with IBM to Develop Image Sensors," *Wall Street Journal,* September 16, 2004; "Kodak Buys Imaging Unit From National Semiconductor," *Wall Street Journal,* August 25, 2004, p. B8; "No Excuse Not to Succeed," *BusinessWeek,* May 10, 2004, pp. 96–98; "Kodak Sues Sony in Patent Dispute," *Wall Street Journal,* March 10, 2004, p. B4; "As Kodak Eyes Digital Future, Big Partner Starts to Fade," *Wall Street Journal,* January 23, 2004, pp. A1, A8; "Kodak to Cut Staff up to 21%, amid Digital Push," *Wall Street Journal,* January 22, 2004, pp. A1, A7; "Ending Era, Kodak Will Stop Selling Most Film Cameras," *Wall Street Journal,* January 14, 2004, pp. B1, B4; "Investors Seek to Rewind Kodak," *Wall Street Journal,* October 21, 2003, pp. C1, C3; "Kodak Shifts Focus From Film, Betting Future on Digital Lines," *Wall Street Journal,* September 12, 2003, pp. A1, A12; "Kodak Answers Digital Siren," *Wall Street Journal,* August 22, 2003, p. B4; "Kodak Wants to Ease Digital-Photo Printing," *Wall Street Journal,* June 19, 2002, p. B12; "Kodak Advances in Market Share of Digital Cameras," *Wall Street Journal,* December 21, 2001, p. B2; "Price Wars, Shift to Digital Photos Leaving Kodak Out of the Picture," *Investor's Business Daily,* March 19, 2001, p. A1; "Y Factor: A Camera That Tapes and Plays," *Washington Post,* March 24, 2001, pp. E1, E8; "Kodak Streamlines Units to Be Nimbler in Digital Age, and Names Coyne to Post," *Wall Street Journal,* October 24, 2000, p. A3; "Kodak Hires Web Guru to Develop Its Digital Plans," *Wall Street Journal,* October 9, 2000, pp. B1, B6; "Kodak's Digital Moment," *Forbes,* August 21, 2000, pp. 106–111.

3. The effects of new technologies on firm capabilities have received significant treatment in the research literature. The following sample research pieces are representative of some of the work undertaken in recent years. See N. Jones, "Competing After Radical Technological Change: The Significance of Product Line Management Strategy," *Strategic Management Journal* 24, no. 13 (2003): 1265–1288; C. W. L. Hill and F. T. Rothaermel, "The Performance of Incumbent Firms in the Face of Radical Technological Innovation," *Academy of Management Review* 28 (2003): 257–274; F. T. Rothaermel, "Incumbent's Advantage Through Exploiting Complementary Assets via Interfirm Cooperation," *Strategic Management Journal* 22, nos. 6–7 (2001): 687–700; M. Song and M. M. Montoya-Weiss, "The Effect of Perceived Technological Uncertainty on Japanese New Product Development,"

Academy of Management Journal 44, no. 1 (2001): 61–80; C. E. Helfat and R. S. Raubitschek, "Product Sequencing: Co-evolution of Knowledge, Capabilities and Products," *Strategic Management Journal* 21, nos. 10–11 (2000): 961–980; R. S. Rosenbloom, "Leadership, Capabilities and Technological Change: The Transformation of NCR in the Electronic Era," *Strategic Management Journal* 21, nos. 10–11 (2000): 1083–1105; W. J. Orlikowski, "Using Technology and Constituting Structures: A Practice Lens for Studying Technology in Organizations," *Organization Science* 11, no. 4 (2000): 404–428; M. Tripsas and G. Gavetti, "Capabilities, Cognition, and Inertia: Evidence from Digital Imaging," *Strategic Management Journal* 21, nos. 10–11 (2000): 1147–1162; C. M. Christensen, "Will Disruptive Innovations Cure Health Care?" *Harvard Business Review* 78 (September–October 2000): 102–117; C. M. Christensen and M. Overdorf, "Meeting the Challenge of Disruptive Change," *Harvard Business Review* 78 (March–April 2000): 66–77; "B. Dyer and X. M. Song, "Innovation Strategy and Sanctioned Conflict: A New Edge in Innovation," *Journal of Product Innovation Management* 15 (1998): 505–519; L. Kim, "Crisis Construction and Organizational Learning: Capability Building in Catching-Up at Hyundai Motor," *Organization Science* 9, no. 4 (1998): 506–521; C. M. Christensen, *The Innovator's Dilemma* (Boston: Harvard Business School Press, 1997); S. L. Brown and K. M. Eisenhardt, "The Art of Continuous Change: Linking Complexity Theory and Time-Paced Evolution in Relentlessly Shifting Organizations," *Administrative Science Quarterly* 42, no. 1 (1997): 1–34; M. W. Lawless and P. Anderson, "Generational Technological Change: Effects of Innovation and Local Rivalry on Performance," *Academy of Management Journal* 39, no. 5 (1996): 1185–1127; D. Dougherty and C. Hardy, "Sustained Product Innovation in Large, Mature Organizations: Overcoming Innovation-to-Organization Problems," *Academy of Management Journal* 39, no. 5 (1997): 1120–1153; D. Dougherty and T. Heller, "The Illegitimacy of Successful New Products in Large Firms," *Organization Science* 3 (1994): 200–218; K. M. Eisenhardt and B. M. Tabrizi, "Accelerating Adaptive Processes: Product Innovation in the Global Computer Industry," *Administrative Science Quarterly* 40 (1995): 84–110; J. L. Bower and C. M. Christensen, "Disruptive Technologies: Catching the Wave," *Harvard Business Review* (January–February 1995): 43–53; C. J. G. Gersick, "Pacing Strategic Change: The Case of a New Venture," *Academy of Management Journal* 37 (1994): 9–45; T. Amburgey, D. Kelley, and W. Barnett, "Resetting the Clock: The Dynamics of Organizational Change and Failure," *Administrative Science Quarterly* 38 (1993): 51–73; H. Haveman, "Between a Rock and a Hard Place: Organizational Change and Performance Under Conditions of Fundamental Environmental Transformation," *Administrative Science Quarterly* 37 (1992): 48–75; R. Henderson and K. Clark, "Architectural Innovation: The Reconfiguration of Existing Product Technologies and the Failure of Established Firms," *Administrative Science Quarterly* 35 (1990): 9–30; W. Mitchell, "Whether and When: Probability and Timing of Incumbents' Entry into Emerging Industrial Subfields," *Administrative Science Quarterly* 34 (1989): 208–230. Additional work on technological change and sources of competitive advantage can be found in D. Lei, "Competence-Building, Technology Fusion and Competitive Advantage: The Key Roles of Organizational Learning and Strategic Alliances," *International Journal of Technology Management* 14, no. 2 (1997): 208–237; G. Dosi, "Technological Paradigms and Technological Trajectories," *Research Policy* 11 (1982): 147–162; J. Galbraith, "Designing the Innovating Organization," *Organizational Dynamics* 10, no. 3 (1982): 5–25.

4. See "Meet eBay's New Postman," *Business 2.0,* September 2004, pp. 52–54; "It's Digital, It's Encrypted—It's Postage," *Wall Street Journal,* September 21, 1998, pp. B1, B6.

5. "Reinventing CBS," *BusinessWeek,* April 5, 1999, pp. 74–82; "GE's NBC Unit Is Seeking to Expand in Cable as Broadcast Economics Soften," *Wall Street Journal,*

July 17, 1998, p. B3; "As Viacom Ponders a Breakup, Industry Rethinks Old Notions," *Wall Street Journal,* March 17, 2005, pp. A1, A9.

6. See "Hollywood's Burning Issue," *Wall Street Journal,* September 18, 2003, pp. B1, B4.

7. Shifts in the sources of competitive advantage in one industry can occur rapidly, particularly if changes are triggered by a related or adjacent industry. See M. E. Porter, *Competitive Strategy* (New York: Free Press, 1980), for a discussion of neighboring industries. To examine the ramifications of change across industries and their impact on entire national economies, see M. E. Porter, *The Competitive Advantage of Nations* (New York: Free Press, 1991).

8. See "Curtain Rises for WiMax Broadband," *Wall Street Journal,* February 2, 2005, p. B2C; "Internet and Phone Companies Plot Wireless-Broadband Push," *Wall Street Journal,* January 20, 2005, pp. A1, A10.

9. This term was originally used by R. E. Miles and C. C. Snow in their groundbreaking study of the way businesses deal with environmental change: *Organizational Strategy, Structure and Process* (New York: McGraw-Hill, 1978). Some of the more recent research studies that have tested and used the Miles and Snow typology include the following: S. F. Slater and E. M. Olson, "Strategy Type and Performance: The Influence of Sales Force Management," *Strategic Management Journal* 21, no. 8 (2001): 813–830; C. Homburg, H. Krohmer, and J. Workman, "Strategic Consensus and Performance: The Role of Strategy Type and Market-Related Dynamism," *Strategic Management Journal* 20, no. 4 (1999): 339–358; W. James and K. Hatten, "Further Evidence on the Validity of the Self-Typing Paragraph Approach: Miles and Snow Strategic Archetypes in Banking," *Strategic Management Journal* 16, no. 2 (1995): 161–168; S. F. Slater and J. Narver, "Product-Market Strategy and Performance: An Analysis of the Miles and Snow Typology Types," *European Journal of Marketing* 27, no. 10 (1993): 33–51; D. Dvir, E. Segev, and A. Shenhar, "Technology's Varying Impact on the Success of Strategic Business Units Within the Miles and Snow Typology," *Strategic Management Journal* 14, no. 2 (1993): 155–161; S. Zahra and J. Pearce, "Research Evidence on the Miles-Snow Typology," *Journal of Management* 16, no. 4 (1990): 751–768; J. Conant, M. Mokwa, and P. R. Varadarajan, "Strategic Type, Distinctive Marketing Competencies, and Organizational Performance: A Multiple Measures-Based Study," *Strategic Management Journal* 11, no. 5 (1990): 365–383; S. W. McDaniel and J. Kolari, "Marketing Strategy Implications of the Miles and Snow Strategic Typology," *Journal of Marketing* 51, no. 4 (1987): 19–30.

10. See "Sony Sees Jump Next Fiscal Year of Up to 30% in Digital Cameras," *Wall Street Journal,* August 18, 2004, p. B8.

11. Data and facts for the Texas Instruments competency were adapted from the following: "Don't Mess with Texas Instruments," *Business 2.0,* September 2004, pp. 47–49; "For Every Gizmo, a TI Chip; Texas Instruments CEO Rich Templeton Is Looking Way Beyond Cell Phones," *BusinessWeek,* August 16, 2004, pp. 52–55; "High Definition via Mirrors," *Wall Street Journal,* February 5, 2004, pp. B1, B8; "Is the Price Right? HD-Set Prices Are Falling, and an Increased Supply of LCD Screens Will Force Down Plasma-Set Prices, Too," *Forbes,* March 1, 2004, p. 80; "Vonage, TI Plan a Web-Phone Deal," *Wall Street Journal,* January 9, 2004, p. A8; "Mirror, Mirror," *Forbes,* May 12, 2003, p. 128; "TI Unveils Fastest Chip for Cellphones," *Dallas Morning News,* May 5, 2003, p. 3D; "Dawn of the Superchip," *BusinessWeek,* November 4, 2002, p. 128A.

12. This term is also one developed by Miles and Snow in *Organizational Strategy, Structure and Process.*

13. See G. Hamel and C. K. Prahalad, "Strategic Intent," *Harvard Business Review* (May–June 1989): 63–76.

14. See "Intel, AMD Lay Out Strategies to Boost Sales, Spur Growth," *Wall Street Journal,* August 29, 2001, p. B4; "Intel Chip Is Cited in AMD Price Cut, Rambus Stock Rise," *Wall Street Journal,* August 28, 2001, p. B4; "Intel Researchers Build Tiny

Transistors That Could Sharply Boost Chips' Speed," *Wall Street Journal,* June 11, 2001, p. B2; "Intel Aims New Chips at High-End Market," *Wall Street Journal,* May 21, 2001, p. A9.

15. See "With Growth Slowing, Microsoft Plans Cost-Cutting, Profit Push," *Wall Street Journal,* July 7, 2004, p. A1; "Microsoft Struggled to Set Strategy," *Wall Street Journal,* June 25, 2004, p. B6; "The Linux Uprising," *BusinessWeek,* March 3, 2003, pp. 78–85.

16. See "GM and Daimler Are Stepping On It," *BusinessWeek,* December 27, 2004, p. 49; "Revolution Under the Hood," *Wall Street Journal,* May 12, 2004, pp. B1, B2; "Ford Ratchets Up Hybrid-Car Effort as Gas Price Rises," *Wall Street Journal,* April 8, 2004, p. A3; "Hybrid Autos May Proliferate but at a Price," *Wall Street Journal,* August 22, 2003, pp. B1, B4; "Dude, Where's My Hybrid?" *Fortune,* April 28, 2003, pp. 112–118.

17. Data and facts for the Whole Foods Market competency were adapted from the following sources: "Whole Foods: Food Porn," *Forbes,* February 14, 2005, pp. 102-112; "Whole Foods CEO Expecting Year of 'Solid Growth' in 2005," *Dow Jones News Service,* July 28, 2004; "His Nutritious 15 Minutes—Whole Foods CEO Accepts Fame Reluctantly as He Pursues Mission of Saving the World," *Austin American-Statesman,* July 4, 2004, p. 5; "Whole Foods Market Sets Example for Sustainable Environmental Initiatives," *Business Wire,* June 10, 2004; "Whole Foods Transcends Grocery Shopping Experience," *DSN Retailing Today,* June 7, 2004, p. 17; "Whole Foods Markets to Use Wind to Generate Some of the Electricity for Stores," *Providence Journal,* June 3, 2004; "Fitting In," *Chain Store Age,* June 1, 2004, p. 70; "Whole Foods Market Inc.: U.K. Organic-Food Retailer to Be Acquired for $38 Million," *Wall Street Journal,* January 19, 2004, B4; "No Preservatives, No Unions, Lots of Dough," *Fortune,* September 15, 2003, pp. 127-130.

18. See "Film Industry Vows Crackdown on Online Movie Thieves," *Wall Street Journal,* November 5, 2004, pp. B1, B3.

19. See, for example, "TiVo Setbacks Raise Doubt About Its Future," *Wall Street Journal,* February 2, 2005, pp. B1, B3; "Comcast, TiVo Are Discussing A Partnership," *Wall Street Journal,* March 15, 2005, pp. B1, B4; "Netflix to Try New Online Sales Avenue," *Wall Street Journal,* August 25, 2004; "The Big Squeeze," *Forbes,* January 12, 2004, pp. 178–181; "Hollywood's Burning Issue," *Wall Street Journal,* September 18, 2003, pp. B1, B4.

20. See an excellent discussion of this problem by T. Goss, R. Pascale, and A. Athos, "The Reinvention Roller Coaster: Risking the Present for a Powerful Future," *Harvard Business Review* (November–December 1993): 97–108.

Extending Competitive Advantage

Corporate Strategy: Leveraging Resources

What you will learn

- *The concept of corporate strategy*

- *The notion of a "resource-based view" of corporate strategy*

- *How effective corporate strategy can be used to extend and leverage a firm's distinctive competence*

- *The broad types of corporate strategy, including vertical integration, related diversification, and unrelated diversification*

- *Economic forces that motivate the pursuit of different corporate strategies*

- *How to balance the benefits and costs of diversification*

- *Benefits of sharing and leveraging resources among businesses or activities*

- *Costs accompanying diversification and the limitations of sharing*

- *How companies undertake corporate restructuring to boost shareholder value*

- *How spin-offs and divestitures represent a form of restructuring designed to regain focus and renewed competitiveness*

The Kellogg Company[1]

Perhaps one of the best-known companies in the United States, the Kellogg Company has begun to shift its focus away from being the country's largest producer of ready-to-eat cereals and other breakfast food items that have traditionally been synonymous with the company. The company has a long history, having got its start in Battle Creek, Michigan, where Dr. John Harvey Kellogg originally pioneered the cereal flake as a way to provide grain-based foods to cure indigestion. His brother, Will Keith Kellogg, developed innovative packaging that would preserve cereal flakes for a long period. This enabled the company to begin shipping prepackaged cereal on a nationwide basis. In turn, this spawned the growth of a tremendous cereal empire, in which Kellogg would dominate this market for many decades.

By the late 1990s, however, times had changed for Kellogg. Although the company remains highly profitable, Kellogg has faced numerous strategic challenges. The company earned $843 million in net income on $9.05 billion in revenues for 2003. Even with such highly recognized brands as Kellogg's Corn Flakes, Frosted Flakes, Special K, Raisin Bran, Rice Krispies, Eggo waffles, Pop-Tarts toaster pastries, and Nutri-Grain cereal bars, the company has faced increasingly tough competition from other packaged foods producers such as General Mills, PespiCo's Quaker Oats line of cereals, Kraft Foods (Post line of cereals), and Ralcorp Holdings (a big manufacturer of private-label, generic brands). More important, eating cereal at breakfast is no longer an important part of many Americans' lives when they wake up in the morning. As a result, in the past decade,

Kellogg has watched its earnings growth slow down, while its market share in cereals dropped from 37 percent to 31 percent in late 2003. Other food items such as croissants, bagels, yogurt, and energy bars have made serious inroads into the market for cereals; in fact, one in five Americans now does not even eat breakfast. When people do eat breakfast, only 35 percent eat cereal, whereas many prefer to consume hot breakfast items at such fast-food restaurants as McDonald's and Burger King. To the extent that people are eating cereal, many of them are switching to cheaper, private-label or generic alternatives.

Many of the challenges facing Kellogg, however, resulted from breakfast consumption trends that slowly took shape over the past decade. Traditionally, Kellogg would introduce a new line of cereal or breakfast food item with an expensive marketing promotion that would emphasize the newness or novelty of the product. Unlike its competitors, Kellogg generally prefers not to compete on the basis of price. Although consumers sometimes enthusiastically greet Kellogg's new cereal products (for example, Raisin Bran Crunch), they often care more about the price of the product, rather than who made it. However, the company is beginning to significantly change its long-standing approach to product development and marketing. In January 1999, Kellogg promoted Carlos Gutierrez as its new CEO to resuscitate the company's profitability and to lead the company into new directions. A Cuban-born émigré who believes that Kellogg needs to become more innovative, Gutierrez has sought to inject faster growth into the company.

Moving into Vegetarian and Alternative Foods

One of Gutierrez's earliest moves in 1999 was to purchase Worthington Foods for $307 million, a leading natural foods company that develops soy-based products and other vegetarian foods. Other products made by Worthington Foods include veggie burgers and soy-based hot dogs and corn dogs. Worthington's best-known brand is Morningstar Farms, which holds over 50 percent market share of vegetarian and nonmeat alternative food products in U.S. supermarkets. With the acquisition of Worthington, Kellogg is now able to participate in the fast-growing organic and natural foods segment, which has grown at a 20 to 25 percent clip in recent years.

The purchase of Worthington Foods by Carlos Gutierrez shows how he intends to find growth for Kellogg in noncereal foods products. Worthington's skills in developing vegetarian foods, as well as its strong supermarket position, will help Kellogg accelerate the creation of its own line of new health food products. Some of these ideas include dry pasta, fiber-coated potato chips, and even a line of frozen entrées. Many of these food products will be vitamin enhanced or fiber enriched to help lower blood cholesterol levels.

Finding Growth Through Snack Foods

Perhaps the biggest and most important acquisition to date is Kellogg's purchase of Keebler Foods for $3.86 billion in October 2000. Keebler is one of the largest snack food companies in the United States, making such well-known products as Cheez-It crackers, Club crackers, and a broad line of cookies (for example, Chips Deluxe, Fudge Shoppe). The company is also highly recognized through its famous television advertisements that feature its Keebler Elves making and delivering fresh cookies. Kellogg's acquisition of Keebler has transformed the combined entity into a $10 billion breakfast and snack food company. With Keebler's product lines, Kellogg will now derive only 40 percent of its sales from breakfast cereals, as opposed to 75 percent from just a few years ago. More important, Keebler brings to Kellogg not only the potential for much higher earnings growth, but also a new set of product development and distribution skills that can help the company breathe new life into its existing brands.

Under Keebler's CEO Sam Reed, the company proved itself to be very successful in finding ways to jump-start growth for many of its cookie and cracker products. For example, Keebler was able to grow sales of Cheez-It by 81 percent since 1996 by modifying serving sizes and by offering it through new means of distribution. Keebler has also led the food industry in offering cookies and other snack foods in smaller single-serving portions. These smaller portion sizes may be more profitable than larger-sized boxed cookies and crackers, since Keebler can stock some of its cookies near the candy displays at the grocery checkout lines. Customers often make these purchases impulsively, often when they are in the checkout line, and are less likely to think about comparing the prices to other competitors' offerings.

Kellogg is also hoping to acquire a new set of distribution skills from its acquisition of Keebler Foods. In particular, Keebler excels in a different type of packaged-foods distribution system than what Kellogg has traditionally relied on. For many decades, Kellogg has relied heavily on selling its breakfast cereals through wholesalers and food brokers, who in turn would serve supermarket chains. Because brokers and store personnel would be responsible for shelving the products and handling merchandising issues (for example, displays, in-store promotions, location of products along aisles), it often takes anywhere from six to eight weeks before a new Kellogg breakfast product would reach supermarket shelves. This lengthy and time-consuming process would often allow competitors, such as General Mills, Kraft Foods, and Ralcorp Holdings, to gain valuable time and insight into what Kellogg would be offering. Even worse, General Mills would be able to rapidly develop its own line of competing products that would take away the initial product enthusiasm and momentum from Kellogg.

Keebler Foods, on the other hand, has developed its own direct-to-store distribution system that bypasses wholesalers and food brokers. Keebler's method of distribution speeds its products on trucks directly to the store. Equally important, Keebler's food representatives handle in-store shelving of products and other merchandising issues. Thus, Keebler brings to Kellogg a new way of managing the distribution of food products, especially for those items that have short shelf lives (spoils easily) or are sold in smaller single-serve portions (for example, crackers and cookies). In particular, Keebler has begun using its distribution system to serve other channels besides supermarkets, including vending machines and convenience stores, where single-serve portions are most likely to be sold. In addition, customers shopping at convenience and gasoline stores are less likely to be as price sensitive as they are in traditional supermarkets.

As part of the larger Kellogg Company, both Worthington Foods and Keebler Foods will bring the potential for new growth and opportunities to broaden the scope and depth of Kellogg's distribution system. Already, Keebler is managing the distribution of such traditional Kellogg products as Rice Krispies Treats and Nutri-Grain snack bars. Even before acquiring Keebler, the company had already begun introducing single-serve portions of these and other food products to reignite sales. Keebler, on the other hand, will now be able to better handle and sell these existing Kellogg products through its own direct-to-store distribution system. Morningstar Farms, the leading brand that comes from Worthington Foods, remains the leader in vegetarian, nonmeat foods. Kellogg, on the other hand, offers both Worthington and Keebler much in the way of new product R&D capabilities and the use of its advanced $75 million development facility near headquarters. Already, new product development is accelerating as Kellogg begins to introduce a new product for the market each month. Some of the most recent innovations include peanut butter and chocolate Rice Krispies, Pop-Tarts that are divided into small pieces for toddlers, and muffins in the shape of

bread slices so that they can be toasted like traditional Pop-Tarts. Kellogg will continue to look for ways to make its other products more vitamin enhanced, while continuing to expand the Morningstar Farms line of healthier products to the fast-growing organic foods market segment.

Even after these two major acquisitions, Kellogg continues to search for new high-growth opportunities. In November 1999, Kellogg sold its Lender's Bagels business to Aurora Foods for $275 million. Acquired originally in 1996, Lender's Bagels turned out to be a difficult acquisition for Kellogg, since fewer people ate frozen or refrigerated bagels. Instead, most consumers would purchase them at bagel shops that sold them fresh. Kellogg had originally hoped to acquire a bagel business in the belief that it could capture that segment's fast growth during the early 1990s. In June 2000, Kellogg acquired Kashi Company, a maker of breakfast cereals that use natural ingredients without sugar or artificial products. Kellogg believes that Kashi can help reinforce the company's new product strategy for the natural foods business and is an important complement to its Worthington acquisition. Kashi may prove even more valuable for Kellogg as the firm considers developing new products that take advantage of many consumers' desire for a lower-carbohydrate diet that incorporates more whole grained foods.

Accelerating Internal Product Development

Kellogg has recently put greater emphasis on accelerating its time-to-market of new products. During much of the 1990s, Kellogg's new product launches were comparatively scarce, with the exception of Nutri-Grain bars and Raisin Bran Crunch. Today, about 100 scientists work in a modern R&D center in Battle Creek to discover new types of food recipes. This laboratory also includes a 9,000 square-foot test kitchen and a scaled-down factory. In the first seven months of 2004, Kellogg introduced over 100 new products, compared with just 68 in all of 1999. Kellogg's scientists are working on new ways to enhance the freshness of ingredients inside the cereal box, especially fruits and other natural products. The benefits of Kellogg's product development efforts are spilling over to Keebler's products as well. For example, Cheez-It Twisters, introduced in 2003, are made with a new technology that twists the dough into a light and airy snack. Keebler did not possess this capability before its merger with Kellogg; Kellogg originally developed the technology to enhance its Fruit Loops cereal. To promote the value of its brands, Kellogg has also commenced a series of marketing programs to enhance the public's awareness of its most famous brands. For example, Kellogg is now working with a leading fashion designer to develop a line of women's apparel based on the Special K consumer. Also, Kellogg has begun looking for new ways to license its Tony the Tiger and other Kellogg characters for use in a new line of toys. The success of Carlos Gutierrez's leadership in revitalizing Kellogg has not gone unnoticed. In December 2004, President George W. Bush asked Mr. Gutierrez to serve as the U.S. Secretary of Commerce beginning in January 2005. Mr. Gutierrez, one of America's most prominent business leaders of Hispanic origin, has left a legacy of faster innovation at a much reinvigorated Kellogg Company.

Introduction

Thus far, most of our examination of competitive advantage has been from the standpoint of a firm operating a single business within an industry. We are now ready to broaden our view. A firm can develop new capabilities by expanding into other segments, businesses, or industries. Such expansion is guided by corporate strategy. **Corporate strategy** in this book refers to the identification of opportunities and the allocation of resources to develop and extend the firm's competitive advantage to other activities or lines of businesses. In its most powerful application, corporate strategy is more than the sum of the firm's individual business unit strategies; it seeks to leverage the firm's distinctive competence from one business to new areas of activity. The issues surrounding corporate strategy are different and significantly more complex than those for a firm operating a single business in one industry. Corporate strategy requires managers to establish a coherent, well-defined direction that guides the allocation of resources into new areas of activity.

Corporate strategy is an important but often misunderstood area of management. An overwhelming number of the Fortune 500 companies operate more than one line of business. In fact, recent research shows that the average Fortune 500 company has positioned itself in about ten different businesses. Such expansion, however, is not easy. One early landmark study found that more than half of all acquisitions made by thirty-three large corporations before 1975 were subsequently divested by 1985.[2] Moreover, many of the large Fortune 500 companies that have attempted to enter new lines of businesses (General Electric, Citigroup, Time Warner, IBM, General Mills, Sears, American Express, and AT&T) have encountered serious difficulties in building and extending their competitive strengths even to businesses and industries that they knew well. The key issue of corporate expansion into new activities or businesses may be viewed as follows: *Is a firm's competitive advantage in one business or area of activity strengthened by the firm's presence in another?* Identifying activities or businesses that satisfy this requirement is the focus in this chapter.

First, we examine the concept of what resources are important to formulating a coherent corporate strategy. Ideally, well-formulated corporate strategies are based on utilizing and

corporate strategy:
Plans and actions that firms need to formulate and implement when managing a portfolio of businesses; an especially critical issue when firms seek to diversify from their initial activities or operations into new areas. Corporate strategy issues are key to extending the firm's competitive advantage from one business to another.

leveraging resources that enable the firm to create distinctive sources of value and advantage over a long time period. Managers need to build their corporate strategies on those resources—assets, skills, and capabilities—that are hard for other firms to duplicate. Second, we consider the various routes to expanding the number of businesses a firm operates. Third, we look at specific types of corporate strategies that enable firms to leverage their resources and skills to extend their competitive advantage to new areas of activity. We focus our attention on the issue of diversification in particular. Fourth, we then consider the chief benefits and costs associated with each type of expansion, especially as it concerns diversification. Finally, we offer guidelines to help firms achieve the benefits of expansion into new areas while avoiding its costs.

The Concept of Resources in Corporate Strategy

resource-based view of the firm:
An evolving set of strategic management ideas that place considerable emphasis on the firm's ability to distinguish itself from its rivals by means of investing in hard-to-imitate and specific resources (for example, technologies, skills, capabilities, assets, management approaches).

Corporate success in extending sources of competitive advantage to new arenas—products, businesses, and market segments—depends heavily on how well firms have created a set of distinctive competences and resources that are significantly different from those of its competitors. Successful corporate strategy is based on identifying those resources that enable a firm to build *systemwide advantage among its businesses in ways that other firms cannot readily imitate or duplicate.* During the 1990s, this **resource-based view of the firm** became more important to understanding corporate strategy.[3] From this perspective, corporate strategy will be successful only to the extent that the firm possesses and leverages those resources (assets, skills, technologies, and capabilities) that share a number of important characteristics.

First, a firm's resources should ideally be so distinctive that they *are hard for competitors to imitate or duplicate.* The more distinctive or hard to imitate the resource, the less likely there will be direct competition in that arena. If a resource (skill, technology, or capability) is hard to imitate, then any future profit stream and competitive advantage is likely to be more enduring and sustainable. Conversely, those resources that are easy to imitate will generate only temporary value, since other firms can readily copy that skill. Over the long term, however, few corporate resources will sustain their hard-to-imitate qualities unless firms continue to invest and upgrade them at a rate faster than what other competitors can do. For example, an organizational capability for fast innovation such as that found at 3M, Johnson & Johnson, Sony, or Procter & Gamble might be considered a valuable resource that is hard to imitate.

Second, a firm's resources should also be *highly specialized and durable.* Highly specialized assets and skills can enable a firm to lower the cost of entry into new businesses. Examples of highly specialized and durable resources include such assets as brand names and patents. Brand names such as Walt Disney, Procter & Gamble, 3M, Sony, Nokia, IBM, Frito-Lay, Honda, American Express, Intel, and Microsoft provide these firms with a durable, lasting degree of staying power and freedom to maneuver, even when their respective markets may be fast moving. Patents, especially those in the pharmaceutical and chemical industries, are another way in which specialized and durable resources can be readily harnessed, protected, and reused to build and leverage new sources of competitive advantage.

Third, firms need to monitor the environment so that their corporate resources do not suffer from easy substitution from other competitive providers of similar value-adding activities. Even when a firm's set of resources is hard to imitate and highly durable, senior managers need to remain aware of potential substitute threats from firms in other industries that may bring to bear an entirely different set of assets, skills, technologies, and capabilities to the current industry or arena. Over the long term, however, emerging products, services, or technologies that could serve as substitutes are likely to surface in any industry. Successful corporate strategy mandates that firms *learn and apply new sets of skills and capabilities* to help them neutralize or even embrace the substitute threat. For example, until 1994, Microsoft had not really developed a well-thought-out strategy for dealing with such pioneering upstarts as Netscape Communications and others who were riding the first wave of the Internet. By late 1995, realizing the potential threat that Netscape's web-browser products could eventually provide powerful substitutes for many of its existing stand-alone, desktop applications, Microsoft completely shifted its strategy and made the Internet a central part of its corporate strategy to extend its software design and applications skills to learning and building new businesses.

Using many of these resource-based perspectives, we now begin to examine how firms can develop various types of corporate strategies for leveraging their sources of competitive advantage into new arenas.

Alternative Routes of Corporate Strategy

Firms usually begin their existence serving just one or a few niches. At some point during their evolution, many expand beyond their initial base or core business.[4] Such expansion increases the diversity of customers a firm serves, the number of products it produces, and the technologies it must learn and manage. This pattern is therefore broadly referred to as expanding the scope of operations. **Scope of operations** refers to the extent of a firm's operations across different activities, products, and markets. Corporate strategy is concerned with selecting the products, markets, and industries in which to extend the firm's distinctive competence.

Expansion into other activity areas is considered successful when the firm's distinctive competence is strengthened by moving into new areas.[5] Distinctive competence is rooted in such attributes as a core technology, resource, expertise, or skill that the firm uses to create and add value. From the perspective of corporate strategy, if a firm can successfully apply and extend its distinctive competence to new activities, products, or markets, then it can develop competitive advantage across multiple businesses. The most common routes to enlarging the firm's scope of operations are expansion into new stages of the industry value chain and expansion into new businesses and industries (see Exhibit 6-1).

scope of operations:
The extent of a firm's involvement in different activities, products, and markets.

Common Avenues to Enlarging the Firm's Scope of Operations	Exhibit 6-1

- Entrance into new stages of activity (i.e., vertical integration)
- Entrance into new businesses/industries (i.e., industry-based diversification)

New Stages

Firms may expand their scope of operations to include different stages or levels of value-adding activity within the same industry. Expansion into an earlier or later stage of a firm's base industry is referred to as vertical integration. We briefly discussed **vertical integration** in previous chapters as a source of competitive advantage for a single-business firm. Yet, vertical integration is also a corporate strategy issue, since it involves enlarging the scope of what the firm does to include other value-creating activities. It can take two basic forms: backward integration and forward integration. **Backward integration** moves the firm into an activity currently carried out by a supplier. In other words, backward integration occurs when the firm performs those activities that it used to receive from a supplier. **Forward integration** moves the firm closer to its customers.[6]

Consider the recent investments that Tiffany & Co. has made in Canadian diamond mines. This move represents backward integration since the jewelry firm wants to secure a key supply source for its diamond-based jewelry offerings. By investing in Canadian mines, Tiffany's hopes to protect itself from supply instability from mines that are located in more dangerous parts of the world.

Now let us examine the strategies that many U.S. automakers pursued during the early 1990s. By purchasing car rental firms such as Hertz, Avis, and Dollar, the Big Three acquired their largest immediate buyers. This move represents forward integration. The Big Three hoped to capture a secure, stable source of demand. However, these moves eventually floundered as the automakers lacked the management skills required to manage these operations.

New Businesses and Industries

Backward and forward integration do not take a firm beyond its initial industry, often represented by a line of business within the firm. **Diversification** does, however. Diversification involves entry into fields where both products and markets are significantly different from those of a firm's initial base.[7] There are two basic types of diversification: related and unrelated.[8]

Related diversification occurs when a firm expands into businesses similar to its initial business in terms of at least one major function (manufacturing, marketing, engineering) or type of skill used (for example, fast product development, microelectronics, packaging, distribution, surface coatings, thin-film technologies, display screens). Related diversification is thus concerned with extending the firm's distinctive competence to other lines of business.

Unrelated diversification is expansion into fields that do not share any functional or skill-based interrelationship with a firm's initial business. Unrelated diversification therefore involves entry into new industries that share no distinctive competence with the firm's initial business. For example, when an electric utility company becomes involved in the automobile parts business, that would represent unrelated diversification.

To illustrate related diversification, consider Microsoft's recent expansion into the video game industry with the introduction of its Xbox game console. Software and video games are different products used by different customers, so this strategy represents industry diversification. The two businesses, however, do share similar skills in software technologies (generating computer programs and codes to run on machines), similar product research and development skills (the need for fast innovation in both industries), and even similar technological platforms (ensuring that future video games work on a range of different electronic appliances). These characteristics thus make Microsoft's strategy more like related diversification. In a similar vein, Kellogg's acquisition of Worthington Foods and Keebler Foods also represents a form of related diversification. Health-oriented, soybean-based vegetarian foods, crackers, and cookies are products often consumed by different customers, although they are still food products. Cereal and breakfast food items, vegetarian products, and snack foods share a similar set of distribution requirements (managing wholesaler channels and working with supermarkets and other retail outlets), similar skills in product development (finding better-tasting foods), and similar skills in marketing (engaging in market research, cross-promotional activities, developing advertising). For Kellogg, these activities represent key aspects of a related strategy. Related diversification seeks to build on activities or skills that share a high degree of similiarity. Even when a firm engages in related diversification to broaden its scope of business operations, it still does not guarantee that the company will succeed in boosting shareholder value and long-term competitive advantage. Related diversification lays the foundation for expansion into new arenas, but does not assure enduring advantage.

On the other hand, consider Intel's earlier moves to establish a web-hosting business. During the late 1990s, Intel hoped to dominate a market where small and midsized businesses would outsource their websites and Internet networks to a third-party company. A web-hosting business requires a company to manage a vast telecommunications network that links companies' websites with other companies, customers, suppliers, and people using the Internet. Building data centers and "server farms" (groupings of thousands of computers to manage Internet data flows) took Intel far from its semiconductor manufacturing expertise. The value chain configuration required to manage web-hosting activities is very different from those involved in semiconductor manufacturing. Managing a web-hosting business requires Intel to operate a business that is more similar to a telecommunications company, rather than a fast-moving, highly precise manufacturing business. Thus, Intel's move into this area constitutes unrelated diversification.[9] Unrelated diversification also generates its own set of strategic and organizational issues. Firms that engage in unrelated diversification risk doing too many things in too many places that they may not fully understand.

A New Corporate Vision: Transforming DuPont[10]

As one of America's leading chemical firms, DuPont is now looking at ways to reinvigorate its growth. DuPont is best known for its wide range of chemical-driven innovations that have transformed the way we live: Nylon, Lycra, and Dacron (polyester fibers); Mylar (space-age materials); Kevlar (armored, bulletproof vests); and Tyvek (superstrong fibers). In 2003, DuPont earned $1 billion on $27 billion in revenues. Now DuPont realizes that it must transform itself as it strives to discover new innovations, enter new businesses, and exit older ones. Many of DuPont's traditional businesses (for example, textiles, fibers, paints, commodity chemicals, pigments) are growing slowly. These businesses also face the prospect of growing government regulation in the future as concern over environmental pollution and greenhouse emissions grows. Under CEO Charles (Chad) Holliday, DuPont is hoping to transform itself with a vision on leading-edge products based on expertise in both biotechnology and chemistry. In fact, DuPont wants to be a leader in pushing U.S. industry to reduce its reliance on petroleum and other pollution-intensive resources. The company wants up to 25 percent of its revenues to come from renewable resources (up from the current 14 percent) by 2010.

For most of its history, DuPont has invented products that became huge world-class leaders in their respective categories. Nylon and Lycra made it possible, for example, to produce clothes and fibers at much lower cost. Other industries started incorporating Nylon into their products, including carpets (for example, DuPont's Stainmaster brand), tires, industrial belts, and even cassette tapes. Moreover, these fibers also helped the automotive industry develop new types of interiors (for example,

dashboards) that are both stronger and lighter weight than previous materials of the same size. Yet, DuPont's brilliant laboratories were often slow in translating their discoveries into new products. Over the past several years, however, CEO Holliday has realized that it needs to invest more in new product R&D. The company now focuses its efforts on those core seventy-five products that have the highest revenue potential. In the process, DuPont has been banking heavily on such promising innovations as advanced miniaturized fuel cells to power automobiles, new types of organic materials to power flat-screen televisions, and the latest advances in biotechnology to substitute corn and other materials for oil-based ingredients. DuPont's newest line of fiber-based products will be based on Sorona, which will use corn to produce materials that are stronger, more stretchable, and stain-resistant. One of the potential uses for Sorona is to create new clothing materials that offer much greater comfort. DuPont hopes Sorona will become a future blockbuster product the way that Nylon was during the 1930s. In its large paint business, DuPont has created an environmentally friendly class of paints called Super Solids. Automotive companies can spray and apply these paints to new cars without discharging toxic materials into the air. DuPont's electronics labs are now devising ways to print electronic circuits onto plastics, rather than silicon-based materials. Ultimately, these breakthroughs will lead to advanced technology products that offer much higher performance with lower production costs.

DuPont is now in the midst of a multiyear transition to redefine its core businesses. The one area that DuPont has *(continued)* placed the biggest emphasis is agriculture-based biotechnology. In 1999, DuPont spent nearly $7.5 billion to purchase Pioneer Hi-Bred International, a leading genetic seed producer. In late 1997, DuPont also purchased a biotechnology unit from Ralston-Purina, hoping to position itself where it can create an entirely new way of improving food production. Many analysts criticized DuPont for these moves because of the high acquisition costs, as well as the long development time needed for successful new products. Yet, DuPont hopes to make further strides with derivatives of soy-based proteins for new types of food ingredients and additives. In late 2003, DuPont and the Department of Energy began working together to create a new type of "bio-refinery" that would make new types of corn-based fuels at competitive costs. At the same time, DuPont has also aggressively shed some once-sacred business units. In 1999, DuPont spun off its Conoco petroleum business. In 2001,

DuPont sold its pharmaceuticals business to Bristol-Myers Squibb for nearly $8 billion. In November 2003, it announced that it is selling its textiles and fibers unit to privately held Koch Industries for $4.4 billion. This unit, which once represented over 25 percent of the company's revenues, faced the slowest growth prospects for all of DuPont's businesses. The sale will also help DuPont significantly reduce its debt and make the company more nimble to compete better in the future. These sales also reduce DuPont's dependence on petroleum as a key input to its businesses.

The ongoing challenge for DuPont is to continue its transformation. Although many of DuPont's newest products have great promise, they still represent a small proportion of the company's revenues compared to older chemical-based businesses. Managing this transition to higher-growth businesses will continue to test DuPont's senior management on an ongoing basis.

Broad Types of Corporate Strategies

These three expansion routes lead to three broad types of corporate strategies. In this section, we examine in detail these three types of corporate strategies: (1) vertical integration, (2) related diversification, and (3) unrelated diversification. These strategies provide very different opportunities to extend distinctive competence. Each is based on a specific economic motive as it relates to enlarging the firm's scope of operations. Each has different implications for the way that companies can extend their distinctive competence into new areas of activity.

Vertical Integration

Vertical integration allows the firm to enlarge its scope of operations within the same overall industry. Vertical integration is characterized by the firm's expansion into other parts of the industry value chain directly related to the design, production, distribution, and/or marketing of the firm's existing set of products or services. Vertical integration focuses on gaining operational control over key functional activities that have an impact on the creation of products and services. Many companies practice vertical integration in some way. Companies engage in vertical integration primarily to strengthen their hold on resources deemed critical to their competitive advantage. Vertical integration is an important strategy for firms that face great uncertainty, especially as it concerns their sources of supply or future buyers of their products. Moreover, vertical integration enables the firm to reduce the external transaction costs of working with numerous suppliers and customers. These costs include finding, buying, selling, negotiating, and overseeing activities with other firms in the open market. Lower transaction costs are especially important for firms when high economic uncertainties make external long-term contracts costly.[11]

full integration:
Vertical integration that seeks to control every activity in the value chain. In full integration, firms bring all activities required to design, develop, produce, and market a product in-house (see partial integration).

Full versus Partial Integration. Firms can vertically integrate in varying degrees. Some firms may attempt full integration. **Full integration** occurs when the firm seeks to control all stages of the value chain related to the final end product or service. In the automobile industry, a potential example of full integration would be Ford Motor Company's owning everything from the coal mines used to make steel; the steel mills that make body panels, doors, engines, and car frames; the glass used in windshields; all the way to the dealerships that finance and sell cars to customers.

On the other hand, firms can also attempt a limited form of vertical integration known as partial integration. **Partial integration** refers to a selective choice of those value-adding stages that are brought in-house. For example, Ford Motor Company could achieve partial integration (and does so) by owning the engine, powertrain, and assembly operations necessary for making cars but selling off the coal mines and steel mills to other firms that may be more efficient than Ford in managing those operations. In the past few years, Ford has gradually sold off its parts-making operation to focus on product design, assembly, and core engine-manufacturing operations. Firms exhibit some degree of partial integration when they attempt to control strategically important or valuable activities but rely on external providers to outsource activities that do not match their competitive strengths.

partial integration:
Vertical integration that is selective about which areas of activity the firm will choose to undertake. In partial integration, firms do not control every activity required to design, develop, produce, and market a product (see full integration).

Backward Integration. The direction of vertical integration may be as important as its degree. Backward integration can allow firms to convert a previously external supplier into an internal profit center. Backward integration is particularly common in industries where low cost and certainty of supply are vital to maintaining the firm's competitive advantage in its end markets. For example, drug companies often exhibit high levels of backward integration to ensure supply of necessary chemical ingredients for their pharmaceuticals. On the other hand, firms competing in industries defined by rapid product and technological change are likely to avoid extensive backward integration, fearing that the high fixed capital costs associated with backward integration will reduce the flexibility needed to respond to rapid change. This is a major reason why Dell has become such a vibrant competitor in the personal computer industry. Dell performs only the assembly of the PC and avoids manufacturing any of its fast-changing components.

Forward Integration. Forward integration is designed to help the firm capture more of the value added in the product or service offered to the customer. For example, when American Express sells travelers' checks and other financial services through its travel agencies, it is seeking to capture those customers who might otherwise buy their travelers' checks and insurance from banks and other firms. Likewise, when Samsung Electronics, a big chip manufacturer, decided to make cell phones using its own chips, it engaged in forward integration also. By starting to produce products that use Samsung's chips, the company hopes to capture more of the value added that would have otherwise gone to another cell phone manufacturer that has closer contact and understanding of end customers.

Thus, vertical integration strategies extend the firm's scope of operations to other activities within the same industry. Basically, all vertical integration strategies are motivated to some extent by (1) accessing vital resources, both backward toward suppliers and forward toward customers, (2) extending the firm's control over critical value-adding activities that have a direct impact on its core products or services, (3) reducing uncertainty of relying on external suppliers or buyers, (4) ensuring a more stable or efficient flow of value-adding activities within its own operations and key processes, and (5) capturing profits that might otherwise leave the firm. The cumulative potential benefit of vertical integration strategies is that they tend to reduce the economic uncertainties and transaction costs facing the firm, at least in the short term.

Costs of Vertical Integration. Vertical integration strategies are not without their disadvantages, however. Some of these costs can be quite significant. They can sometimes lead a firm to overcommit scarce resources to a given technology, production process, or other activity that could then lock the firm into eventual obsolescence. Once a firm overcommits to a given way of performing key activities, it is much more vulnerable to technological changes that emanate from the external environment. In addition, excessive vertical integration may also weigh down the firm with significantly high fixed costs, leaving it even more vulnerable to an industry downturn. Vertical integration can especially pose problems of meshing different capabilities and skill sets. For example, at Tiffany & Co., combining distinctive retailing skills with a detailed understanding of how best to engage in diamond mining represent two different skill sets that require different mindsets as well.

During the 1990s, large U.S. drug companies such as Merck and Eli Lilly did not realize that acquiring and managing extensive drug distribution channels would require a very different set of skills as compared to pharmaceutical R&D and marketing. Merck and Lilly found that their respective drug distribution businesses, Medco Containment Services and PCS, were big drags on their financial performance. Lilly subsequently sold its PCS unit, which later merged with Advanced Paradigm to form Advance PCS. In a similar move that spanned much of 2002 and 2003, Merck divested itself of Medco Containment. Merck hoped to gain renewed focus by accelerating its drug development initiatives, particularly as many of leading drugs face patent expirations later in the decade. It ultimately realized the two businesses' requirements for success were very different.[12]

Likewise, vertical integration can also pose problems of balancing capacity and throughput in the firm's operations. These disadvantages are particularly amplified for those firms attempting full integration. For example, if Ford Motor Company were to attempt to own its own set of coal mines, steel mills, assembly plants, and dealerships to a much greater degree than rival DaimlerChrysler, then an economic recession would have much more devastating effects on Ford than it would on DaimlerChrysler. Ford's higher level of fixed costs threaten to keep Ford in the red longer than DaimlerChrysler, which would not be as burdened with excess capacity and other problems. On the other hand, for many companies in the petroleum and other resource-extractive industries, the benefits of full integration outweigh the disadvantages. For companies such as ExxonMobil, ChevronTexaco, ConocoPhillips, and Royal Dutch/Shell Group, control over all stages of oil exploration, drilling, production, refining, and marketing is important. Any significant disruption in supply or distribution would send shock waves throughout the entire company.[13]

Related Diversification

Related diversification is perhaps the most important corporate strategy discussed in this chapter for a number of reasons. First, related diversification is an increasingly common corporate strategy found in large companies worldwide. Many Fortune 500 firms are pursuing some variant of related diversification, and interest in this strategy is growing in Europe and the Far East. In particular, many companies outside the United States are seeking to realign their operations in such a way as to achieve greater focus and more productive use of their assets. For example, German and Japanese companies such as Siemens, NEC, Hitachi, Fujitsu, and Toshiba are attempting to shed businesses and activities that do not support a renewed focus on their core competences.

Second, related diversification is directly concerned with extending the firm's distinctive competence or set of firm-specific resources into new lines of business and industry, as opposed to limiting the firm's scope of operations to within the same industry. Related diversification offers firms the potential to extend and leverage their distinctive competences and resources into new industries that share common characteristics.

Third, related diversification poses a highly complex set of issues for managers, since the resources and skills used to guide related diversification strategies are often the key to obtaining corporate synergy and increased shareholder value. **Synergy** exists when the whole of the company is greater than the sum of its parts. Synergy enables the firm to build a *corporate-wide advantage* based on applying a distinctive competence among multiple businesses. Corporate-level advantage occurs when value is created both in a firm's individual business units and systemwide across the firm's businesses. This corporate-level advantage makes it difficult for other rivals to imitate. In turn, this corporate-level advantage creates value for the shareholder as well. For these reasons, achieving related diversification remains the single most important trend defining current corporate strategy today. To attain the benefits of synergy, related diversification generally involves (1) a focus on internal development, (2) building mutually reinforcing businesses, (3) making the distinctive competence hard to imitate and durable, and (4) ensuring managerial fit.

synergy:
An economic effect in which the different parts of the company contribute a unique source of heightened value to the firm when managed as a single, unified entity.

Focus on Internal Development. Firms can attempt related diversification through various channels. For example, firms could (1) identify and exploit an underlying technology or skill that defines the way a set of products is designed or manufactured; (2) start up new products or services where key value-adding activities can be shared across a wider base of activities; (3) develop and commercialize new products that leverage the firm's brand-name recognition, manufacturing prowess, or R&D capability; or (4) acquire new businesses that closely match and complement the firm's existing strengths or distinctive competence in its original activity. Note that the most common steps to achieve synergy are through internal development as opposed to acquiring other firms or businesses. Internal development seeks to share or transfer the firm's resources and skills to other business units.

Numerous examples of related diversification can be found in every industry. In particular, many firms competing in different sectors of high technology practice related diversification. For example, Sharp Corporation of Japan pursues related diversification when it develops and produces a broad line of calculators, desktop copiers, television sets, and video camcorders. Sharp's set of distinctive resources includes its highly specialized competence in precision manufacturing skills, expertise with liquid crystal display (LCD) technology, flat-screen technology, miniaturization, and an organizational capability for fast product development. All of Sharp's product groups share a common need and access to these distinctive resources. By extending its manufacturing skills from calculators to camcorders, Sharp expands its manufacturing base and experience to new products. Sharp's CEO Katsuhiko Machida believes the company should always seek ways to create something new, something different. In turn, Sharp creates value by being able to lower its manufacturing costs even further by spreading them over a wider base of products. As Sharp faces intense competition from new Chinese, Taiwanese, and Korean entrants in the flat-screen television business, Machida wants to discover new ways and products where Sharp's distinctive LCD skills be used in innovative ways. Over the past five years, Sharp has become Japan's most profitable electronics company. Sharp's products are not only similar in using related LCD and flat-screen technologies, but they also lend themselves well to similar marketing by way of mass distribution channels, such as Best Buy, Circuit City, and other electronic superstores.[14]

Procter & Gamble also successfully pursues a related diversification strategy. Some of P&G's best known products include Tide detergent, Ivory Soap, Folger's coffee, Pringles potato chips, Crest toothpaste and whitestrips, Charmin bathroom tissue, Oil of Olay facial cleanser, as well as a broad line of hair conditioning, shampoo, and cosmetics products. Over the past several years, P&G has redirected its efforts to innovating new products faster. P&G excels in such key skills as managing distribution channels, market research, and product innovation. In particular, P&G has developed a highly refined understanding of women's tastes, especially in developing new hair-care and cosmetics products. When P&G develops a new series of Oil of Olay products, it can learn how best to market them by sharing marketing research, knowledge, and distribution skills from its cosmetics and hair-care units. P&G also excels in many aspects of scientific research, especially in the fields of surfactants, emulsifiers and softeners. Skills and experience with these fields help P&G develop new versions of Liquid Tide, Febreze, and other products that require and use sophisticated blending technologies. In turn, knowledge gained from working on advanced surfactants used in detergents can help lay the foundation for more powerful dishwashing liquids. As a company, the broad array of P&G's products, and the depth of its distribution skills and marketing knowledge, helps the firm negotiate from a much stronger position with key customer accounts, such as Wal-Mart Stores and Target Corporation.[15]

Building Mutually Reinforcing Businesses.

The first step in building synergy is identifying the potential for close fit among the firm's different businesses. For example, in the case of Sharp, the precision manufacturing skills, flat-screen display technologies, and innovative R&D used in making wall-thin television sets, microwave ovens, DVD players, and notebook computers also apply to office and industrial equipment (for example, copiers and solar panels, respectively). Related diversification also requires a close integration of business unit strategy around a core technology or marketing approach. In the case of SBC Communications, this company's future telecom service offerings are based on recent investments in advanced transmission networks, Internet services, electronic commerce applications, and even data transmission and networking for commercial buyers. By leveraging and combining skills from one business to another, SBC has been able to offer its customers a full range of telecommunications and electronic-commerce applications. In January 2005, SBC Communications announced that it would acquire AT&T Corporation for $16 billion, thus completing its transition to a full-service telecommunications provider.[16]

Finding a close fit to build synergies is not easy. Oftentimes companies will discover that their distinctive competences do not lend themselves well to application in other industries or markets. For example, Marriott Corporation found that its expertise in providing high-quality food in its family-oriented restaurants, cafeterias, and hotels did not give it much capability to compete in top-of-the-line gourmet restaurants. As a result, Marriott has refocused its efforts on improving the service, appearance, and comfort of its hotel rooms. Similarly, Black & Decker's excellent reputation for high-quality appliances and tools designed for do-it-yourselfers did not automatically translate into higher sales of power tools aimed at professional contractors and construction firms. It took several years and a modified marketing approach for Black & Decker to gain success with its DeWalt brand of tools that are aimed at the professional contractor market. Thus, a crucial first step for managers undertaking related diversification is to assess how well the firm's distinctive competence lends itself to direct application to other markets or industries. The firm's distinctive competence should be leveraged for competitive advantage across all of its business units.

Making the Competence Hard to Imitate and Durable.

The third step in building synergy is to make the firm's distinctive competence and resources (assets, technologies, capabilities, and skills) as distinctive as possible from the competition and enduring over a long period. A truly distinctive skill or competence will enable the firm to lower costs, enhance differentiation, or accelerate learning in ways faster or better than its competitors.

Related diversification works best when firms can build a competence that is so distinctive and utilized systemwide that it is nearly impossible for competitors to duplicate it. Durable, specialized assets or skills are a key pillar in attaining successful related diversification. In the case of 3M, its proprietary and durable skills in applied chemistry, coatings, adhesives, and thin-film technologies make it difficult for competitors to imitate the quality of 3M's products; yet these same skills allow 3M to develop future sets of related products with greater ease and lower cost. For example, few people ordinarily know that all of the transdermal medical delivery products (for example, NicoDerm or "patches" that are applied to the skin) are actually made by 3M for drug companies. Transdermal medical products share the same technologies that 3M uses to develop specialized coatings and adhesive products for other industries. Likewise, in the Sharp and Procter & Gamble examples, few companies could have easily mustered or quickly copied the precision manufacturing or product development skills of both companies. An organizational capability for continuous product innovation or highly-refined manufacturing is hard to imitate and constitutes a specialized and durable resource that lasts over many product generations and life cycles. Firms with very distinctive competences are well positioned to create potentially new sources of value and competitive advantage across their businesses that will be difficult for competitors to imitate and copy.

Ensuring Managerial Fit.   Finally, a strong fit among the different managers that run the underlying businesses is important. Managers with similar levels of entrepreneurial qualities, technical knowledge, marketing savvy, or engineering backgrounds provide an important foundation for building synergies. A convergence of managerial mind-sets can reduce the coordination costs among the businesses. Transfer or rotation of managers across different business units can help solidify the firm's management fit. Shared managerial experiences can produce outlooks that also help reduce the effort and time needed to communicate and coordinate activities and expectations among business units. The more closely fitting and related the various business units are, the more important a tight managerial fit becomes. This fit helps management understand both the characteristics of individual businesses and the overarching distinctive competence of the firm. Value creation at both business and corporate levels becomes easier when managers work jointly to develop ways to extend the firm's distinctive competence across businesses. For example, managers at PepsiCo often rotate their positions throughout the company in order to learn how other PepsiCo businesses function. Corporate management believes that transferring and rotating managers among various business units will help provide a new set of insights and a "total view" of the entire company's operations.

Thus, related diversification strategies are designed to extend the firm's distinctive competence and corporate resources to other products, businesses, and industries. Related diversification aims to create synergy, whereby the firm leverages its distinctive competence to achieve a mutually reinforcing, tight fit among its businesses. When pursued successfully, related diversification enables the firm to (1) *lower its costs across a wider base of activities;* (2) *increase or heighten the differentiation of its businesses;* and (3) *accelerate learning and transfer of new technologies, skills, or other capabilities at a rate faster than if the business units remained separate.*

Unrelated Diversification

Although the majority of Fortune 500 firms are now emphasizing related diversification, many firms during earlier periods engaged in a corporate strategy of unrelated diversification. Unrelated diversification occurs when a firm seeks to enter new industries without relying on a distinctive competence to link up business units. These firms were popularly known as conglomerates. **Conglomerates** are firms that practice unrelated diversification. Unlike related

conglomerates:
Firms that practice unrelated diversification (see unrelated diversification; holding company structure).

diversification, unrelated diversification is not based on any distinctive competence or central set of hard-to-imitate corporate resources. Consider, for example, the case of Allegheny-Teledyne, a large conglomerate that grew by acquiring numerous businesses across different industries. Until its recent restructuring, Allegheny-Teledyne possessed extensive defense electronics businesses, financial services, stainless steel industrial products, consumer goods (such as Water Pik toothbrushes), and machinery. The company did not attempt to share an underlying technology or skill among these various businesses.

During the 1970s, the list of unrelated diversified firms or conglomerates was long and included such names as Teledyne, Textron, Litton Industries, Gulf and Western (now part of Paramount Communications, a unit of Viacom), American Can (now Primerica, which has recently merged with financial services firm Citigroup), and ITT. Although some of these firms are still found in the Fortune 500 listings, their proportional representation of large U.S. companies has declined significantly in the past fifteen years. In particular, conglomerate firms have largely divested themselves of many disparate businesses over the past twenty years so that comparatively few exist.[17]

Unrelated diversification, or conglomerate-based strategies, became popular during the 1960s and 1970s. Conglomerates grew by way of acquiring other companies, instead of developing core skills internally. Because unrelated diversification does not rely on a distinctive competence, companies are free to purchase existing firms with already established market positions. Some of the highlights of unrelated diversification include (1) an emphasis on acquisitions over internal development and (2) attempting to beat the market in the search for higher returns. Note that these methods do not attempt to identify and to extend a distinctive competence from one business unit to another. The primary corporate resource used among these subunits is financial leverage. In addition, the only linkage between newly acquired and preexisting business units is that of financial sharing and budgeting, as opposed to technological or skill-based resources. Over time, the strategies undertaken by these firms have often produced unintended consequences, such as the rise of a "conglomerate discount."

Acquisitions over Internal Development.   The unrelated diversification strategies of conglomerates are designed to acquire, hold, and sell businesses in various industries without the benefit or guide of an underlying distinctive competence. Unrelated, or conglomerate-based, diversification is based entirely on acquiring and selling different parts of the firm to maximize corporate profitability. When compared with related diversified firms, unrelated firms grow and contract primarily through asset acquisitions and divestitures. These firms often rely on a series of acquisitions and divestitures to keep corporate-level profitability high. Unrelated diversification presents little opportunity to grow by developing new businesses internally. Senior management is not focused on identifying and extending a distinctive competence that can be leveraged across businesses.

Perhaps the most preeminent example of unrelated diversification as practiced in more recent years is that of Tyco International. Although Tyco is now seeking renewed focus, the recent wide span of Tyco's operations involved such businesses as a large fiber-optic network crossing the Atlantic, sewage and water treatments plants around the world, burglar alarm and fire security systems throughout the United States, and a wide array of medical products, including surgical gloves, sutures, and vascular care products. Tyco International's acquisition of over 200 different companies and businesses from 1992 to 2002 positioned the company into several broad lines of business. These included medical products, electronics products, and security systems. Each business, in turn, sought continued growth and dominant market share in the segment that it serves, usually by pursuing a low-cost leadership strategy. This emphasis on attaining a dominant market position has been the underpinning of Tyco's search for acquisitions. Until recently, Tyco looked at over a thousand different acquisition candidates each year, with each one assessed on how fast it could contribute to the company's earnings immediately. Often these acquisition candidates possessed underperforming assets or were cash poor.

However, Tyco and its previous CEO have faced significant controversy over the past few years. Facing renewed pressures for better accounting transparency, the company has begun to reverse its aggressive acquisition strategy and has even begun selling parts of itself to other firms. Tyco has acknowledged growing difficulties in capturing synergies from operating in so many different businesses. More stunning, former CEO Dennis Kozlowski in 2002 was indicted for misuse of corporate resources and for extremely lavish spending that included social parties that cost well into the millions of dollars. Kozlowski's trial for different types of corporate malfeasance continued through 2005.

Another legendary company that still practices unrelated diversification is Textron. At the height of its diversification posture, some of Textron's most well-known businesses included business jets (Cessna), helicopters (Bell Helicopter), golf carts and sporting equipment (E-Z-GO), chain saws (Homelite), lawn mowers (Jacobsen), watch bands (Speidel), disability insurance (Paul Revere), consumer finance (Avco), aircraft parts (Accustar), tank and aircraft engines (Lycoming), and industrial fasteners. In 1998, Textron sold its Avco insurance and consumer finance subsidiaries to Associates First Capital, a financial powerhouse that was recently part of Ford Motor Company. Associates First Capital, now itself part of Citigroup, bought Avco Financial Services because it represented a complementary fit to its own commercial and credit card financial services businesses. Textron subsequently allocated some $1 billion to buy new businesses, mostly on the industrial side, that are clearly dominant in their industries.[18]

Attempting to Beat the Market. These examples also point out some of the problems in pursuing an unrelated diversification strategy. All of these companies thought they could make informed bets that they could purchase fast-growing, highly profitable businesses for the long term. However, senior management cannot always accurately predict how each individual business is likely to perform in the future. Also, senior management cannot effectively formulate the specific competitive strategies required for each business and market. The economic motive of unrelated diversification is that the corporation creates value to the extent that it is able to identify attractive acquisition or new business opportunities faster than the market can. Trying to even out the business cycle swings across different industries requires precise resource allocation and timing to ensure that the value acquired from new businesses justifies their acquisition costs. This task is difficult to accomplish at best.

Rise of a Conglomerate Discount. Unrelated diversification strategies assume that senior management can predict which businesses will do well over time. In other words, the economic rationale for conglomerates is based on the financial market's acceptance of senior management's judgment and selection of acquisition candidates that appear to be attractive for the future. The basic source of value in a conglomerate is senior management's ability to time the market to buy and sell businesses. This task generally proves to be difficult to perform consistently, because senior management cannot stay abreast of day-to-day operations in each individual business. In addition, throughout the 1990s, many conglomerate firms suffered because of the high debt costs incurred to buy businesses.

Several researchers have pointed out the existence of a so-called conglomerate discount, whereby the sum of the individual parts is greater than the value of the whole.[19] In fact, poorly managed conglomerate firms appear to provide negative synergy, in which individual businesses may actually be worth more on their own rather than when placed under a larger corporate umbrella with other unrelated units. In other words, unrelated diversification strategies can actually destroy value instead of creating it. In most instances, managers perform a disservice to investors when they engage in unrelated diversification. Senior management often cannot lower costs, enhance differentiation, or accelerate learning in the conglomerate's vast array of businesses.

During the 1990s, however, senior management at many conglomerate firms began to recognize the strong tendency by the market to discount these firms' values. To counter this tendency, many firms, such as Litton Industries and Textron, have dramatically reduced the scope of their diversification by selling off their businesses. Consider the case of Tenneco. Some of Tenneco's disparate businesses at the beginning of that decade included farm and construction equipment (J. I. Case), natural gas pipelines, shipbuilding (Newport News Shipbuilding), chemicals and materials (Albright and Wilson), automotive parts, and containers/packaging (Packaging Corporation of America). Tenneco acquired these businesses in the belief that diversity brought stability of earnings. The farm equipment business, for example, operates on a cycle different from the shipbuilding or packaging businesses. During a recession, for example, farm equipment sales plummet, while automotive parts go up (mostly because people keep their older cars longer). However, this strategy did not help Tenneco improve its earnings significantly. Throughout the 1990s, the company reversed course and sold off the majority of its businesses to other firms (for example, Northrop Grumman bought Newport News Shipbuilding in 2001; New Holland N.V. purchased the remaining stake of J. I. Case in 1999).[20] Packaging Corporation of America is now a very key player in the paperboard and plastic container businesses, whereas Tenneco Automotive will likely become an acquisition candidate for other auto parts companies seeking to consolidate their position in this industry.[21]

Unrelated Diversification in Limited Form. Although full-blown conglomerate strategies have continued to fade in popularity, there are occasional instances where firms will still pursue a milder form of unrelated diversification. Even these limited moves have caused the acquiring firm significant difficulties. Consider, for example, the case of Schlumberger Ltd., one of the world's largest and best-known oil services firms. Schlumberger specializes in developing the technologies that are required to help oil exploration companies discover, exploit, and manage the wells that are drilled in the search for petroleum. Some of Schlumberger's advanced products include electronic wireline monitoring systems (used for well measurement and control); bits, muds, and packs (used for drilling); and seismic technologies (used to calibrate geological surveys and to test for well stability). In February 2001, Schlumberger purchased Sema PLC, an Anglo-French software, outsourcing, and systems integration firm, for $5.2 billion. Schlumberger thought that its acquisition of Sema would help the oil services giant use the Internet to manage the complex process of gathering critical information to monitor oil drilling and well-management operations. Schlumberger also believed that Sema could help it develop a new line of "smart cards" that can store all kinds of information for consumer and commercial uses. Smart cards are plastic cards that have microchips embedded within them. Ultimately, the acquisition proved to be a costly mistake. The company sold its Sema unit to another French software company, Atos Origin S.A., in September 2003. As a result of this disastrous acquisition, Schlumberger was forced to write off almost $3 billion in goodwill charges.[22]

Corporate Strategies Compared

So far, we have examined three different types of corporate strategies: vertical integration, related diversification, and unrelated diversification. The basic differences between these three strategies are important enough to reiterate. Vertical integration is based on extending the firm's scope of operations to other value-adding activities within the same industry. Unlike related or unrelated diversification, vertical integration is concerned primarily with improving efficiency and the core operations of the firm's existing activities. It does not extend the firm's distinctive competence to activities in other industries or businesses.

Related and unrelated diversification represents two corporate strategies that do extend the firm's scope of operations beyond the initial industry. Both of these diversification strategies move the firm into new areas of activity that represent different competitive conditions, products, and markets. Related diversification is based on extending the firm's distinctive competence among closely fitting businesses. Firms pursuing this strategy seek to use their existing resources (assets, skills, capabilities, and expertise) as a way to build corporate-wide advantage. Unrelated diversification also takes the firm beyond the initial industry. However, it does not require a distinctive competence to identify and select new areas of activity. Acquiring and selling businesses remains the dominant focus of the unrelated diversification strategy.

Diversification is directly concerned with extending the firm beyond its original industry. The next section considers the three major benefits that diversification can provide: (1) more attractive terrain, (2) access to key resources, and (3) opportunity to share activities among businesses (see Exhibit 6-2).

More Attractive Terrain

New terrain may be more attractive than that of a firm's base business for several reasons (see Exhibit 6-2A).

Growth

New terrain may be growing more rapidly, thus providing opportunity for more rapid expansion, economies of scale, and learning new skills. Entry into high-growth areas gives the firm access to potential new sources of technologies and skills. In time, these resources could become the basis for future industries. This search for growth by way of extending technologies into new products and markets is particularly appropriate for related diversification strategies.

Kellogg's concern about the declining margins it was facing in its traditional breakfast cereals business motivated the firm to consider its most recent diversification moves. As

Benefits of Diversification	**Exhibit 6-2**

A. More attractive terrain

- Faster growth
- Higher profitability
- Greater stability

B. Access to resources

- Physical assets and access to markets
- Technologies and skills
- Expertise

C. Sharing of activities

(any business system activity)

competition heated up in the cereals business, Kellogg also found that fewer Americans were eating cereal as part of their breakfast regimen. This prompted Kellogg to move into other food products that could help compensate for its sluggish growth in breakfast foods. The same growth logic also applied to McDonald's decision in 1999 to spend $325 million for the Boston Market, Donato Pizza, and Chipotle restaurant chains. McDonald's senior management realized that customers were moving away from traditional fast-food offerings. To bolster its growth prospects, McDonald's believed it needed to invest in alternative restaurant formats (freshly cooked chicken, pizzas, and Mexican offerings) to counter the highly mature state of hamburger chains.

Companies such as IBM, DuPont, Toshiba, and Hitachi are also diversifying their core operations to search for newer growth opportunities. In the case of IBM, the slow growth of revenues from its core mainframe business means that IBM must carefully identify and select new emerging product and market opportunities in which to invest (such as semiconductors, networking systems, servers, IT consulting, electronic commerce, software platforms, Internet-related businesses). For example, IBM has steadily grown its consulting business in the past few years to move beyond the selling of computer hardware.[23] Japanese electronics giants Toshiba and Hitachi are seeking to revitalize their growth by diversifying away from their mature core power generation, memory chip, and mainframe computer businesses. The growth in these businesses has slowed considerably in recent years, and several of these firms, including Hitachi and Fujitsu, have decided to exit the mainframe business.

Profitability

The desire for higher profitability also leads firms to search for new terrain. New terrain may be less competitive, thereby enabling a firm to earn a higher rate of return. Fewer competitors mean that firms often have "breathing room" to improve their profitability and to innovate new, related products. Consider the following examples. The cost of developing ever-faster microprocessors is becoming an extremely costly endeavor, even for Intel, which has traditionally led the semiconductor industry. Competition from Advanced Micro Devices, Transmeta, and other smaller firms has recently taken a significant toll on Intel's earnings. At the same time, Intel believes that there are new opportunities to use its semiconductor technology and skills that are more profitable, such as building communications chips for Internet and consumer applications. This motivation explains why Intel has purchased over twenty companies in the past few years as it searches for a more attractive market in which to compete. By diversifying into new fields, Intel hopes to resuscitate its profitability and to capture new market segments.

Despite its wide range of successful consumer products, Procter & Gamble continues to feel strong competition from such companies as Colgate-Palmolive, Clorox, Unilever, and other firms in its traditional consumer packaged and personal care products businesses. Unrelenting pressure to cut costs, accelerate product development, and streamline operations has taken a toll on P&G's earnings in recent years, despite the company's legendary record of product innovation. This explains why P&G at one point seriously considered acquiring a large pharmaceutical company to diversify its earnings, even entering the bidding process to purchase Warner-Lambert Company, before Pfizer finally acquired the firm. In August 1999, P&G purchased Iams Company, a leading pet foods maker that has a fiercely loyal customer base. P&G hopes to use its formidable distribution skills and base to help sell Iams in other channels besides those of pet supply stores and veterinarians' offices. Throughout 2000–2003, P&G also acquired a number of companies involved in the hair-coloring business (e.g., Clairol, Wella). In perhaps the biggest acquisition designed to enhance P&G's market reach and distribution strength, CEO

A.G. Lafley announced a $54 billion deal to acquire Gillette, the leading maker of razors, such as the Mach 3 and the Braun line of shavers. Many analysts laud the combination of the two companies, since Gillette brings fast product development and innovation skills that complement those of P&G. Gillette's long-term focus has been to continuously improve longstanding products with new technologies using state-of-the-art manufacturing and engineering methods. As Gillette introduces new razors every few years, it also raises the prices of older models so that customers become more willing to try the costlier, newer product.[24]

In another example, Japanese producers of DVD players and television sets are beginning to feel low-cost pressure from Korean firms (Samsung, LG Electronics) in their core consumer electronics businesses. This pressure is prompting firms such as Sharp, Sony, Canon, and Matsushita to develop new technologies that allow them to enter higher profit areas, including office equipment, factory automation, electronic instruments, semiconductors, and household appliances (related diversification). Movement into these new areas gives the Japanese firms an opportunity to sidestep some of the fierce competition that characterizes many segments of the consumer electronics industry.

Stability

Finally, new terrain may be more stable than a firm's base business in terms of the cyclical nature and fluctuations of output. Firms sometimes face huge price swings in their core business, which lead to distortions in both production planning and pricing of the firm's product. Diversification into businesses with different industry cycles may allow a firm to generate more predictable levels of sales and profits. Entering other businesses to counterbalance the core business's output swings can even out the company's total revenue and profit picture. By expanding into a field with more stable characteristics, a firm can sometimes move away from problems in its core business. This rationale explains why many chemical companies (for example, Dow Chemical, DuPont, BASF, ICI) have often diversified into other lines of business, such as plastics, fertilizer, synthetic fibers, and other advanced materials. In July 2004, Bayer AG of Germany sought to purchase the consumer drug line of Swiss firm Roche Holding for $2 billion. Bayer hopes to balance its portfolio of businesses that include pesticides and seeds, health care, and advanced plastics.[25] Unrelated diversification is particularly concerned with stability of earnings from different businesses. Both Textron and Tyco appear to be practicing it today for this reason as well. Other smaller U.S. companies, such as Temple-Inland and Allete, appear to be focused on achieving earnings stability as well in their unrelated diversification strategies.

Access to Resources

A second common motive for diversification is a desire to secure access to resources. By acquiring a firm that possesses a scarce resource or market position, a firm can significantly improve its own competitive position. Similarly, a firm that possesses a critical resource can often improve the position of another business by acquiring and transferring the resource to it. Resources frequently acquired and transferred in this way are physical assets, technologies, and expertise (see Exhibit 6-2B).

Scarce Assets

Diversification can be prompted by firms seeking access to scarce or underutilized assets. Firms will often buy another company because it can manage the assets better, or because of the scarcity or uniqueness of the assets involved. Scarce assets can include well-known brand names, patents on drugs or technologies, and even prime real estate locations. For example, Sony of Japan acquired U.S. entertainment assets during the late 1980s (Columbia Pictures and CBS Records). Part of the reason for these acquisitions was the Japanese giant's desire to secure the large film libraries whose values were likely to grow in the future. Films and television shows made by Columbia Pictures represented important assets because they are becoming critical pieces of the emerging multimedia and cable television industries. Under this strategic conception, the films, television shows, and documentaries possessed by movie studios represent the "content" or "software" that could potentially flow along the Internet and reach interactive television sets. General Electric was similarly attracted to the entertainment assets of Vivendi Universal, which include an advanced television production facility, a massive library of movies and television shows, theme park operations, and attractive cable properties. In September 2003, GE paid $14 billion to acquire an 80 percent stake of these assets. GE hopes to link up the Vivendi Universal properties with its own NBC broadcasting network assets. GE has also reorganized and renamed its NBC unit to become NBC Universal in its bid to produce hot television shows in its own studios.[26]

Technologies

Technological advances provide the underlying basis for innovating and commercializing new products. Developments in new technologies, such as robotics, display screens, microelectronics, software, genetic engineering, and advanced composite materials, represent the building blocks of future industries. Diversification is an important way for firms to learn, extend, or acquire new technological resources that could have serious future impact on their businesses, especially for firms practicing related diversification.

Many industries are becoming more related because of the sheer intensity and use of technology involved. For example, United Technologies, a leading provider of jet engines (Pratt & Whitney), elevators (Otis), flight systems and helicopters (Hamilton Sundstrand and Sikorsky), building systems (Carrier), and microelectronics, is facing a growing technological convergence among its businesses. All of these individual businesses are becoming more related because of the growing degree that microelectronics, hydraulics, and control systems play in making UTC's products function. The control technology used to develop avionics and aircraft cockpits is similar to those in the air-conditioning, heating, lighting, and security systems found in many modern office buildings. Thus, technology developed in one core business can often be leveraged and extended to other fields far beyond the original industry. Also, by offering a variety of different products as one combined set of "technology solutions" to its aerospace customers, UTC can provide a full array of skills in ways that other less diversified companies cannot do so as efficiently. UTC, in fact, has found that diversification also helps the company maintain a strong market position in businesses that have robust cash flows that come from selling spare parts and advanced services.[27]

Cisco Systems is another example of a firm that has obtained needed technologies through diversification. Ever since the firm went public in 1990, Cisco Systems has strengthened its leading technological and market position in providing network equipment solutions to firms in the telecommunications and Internet-related industries. Over the past ten years, Cisco has made over a hundred acquisitions of firms that possess a proprietary technology or capability in the fields of bridges, hubs, routers, and software-management tools that allow data to be transmitted throughout the world along fiber-optic Internet networks. In 2000 alone, Cisco acquired some twenty companies in the fields of wireless Internet technologies and optical networking. All of these firms have developed critical computer networking technologies that enable Cisco to blend its offerings with those of the acquired firms to provide customers with a full array of technologies and advanced products. Cisco's growth strategy has been so successful that it is now able to offer telecommunications carriers many products and technologies that were once developed by other companies such as Lucent Technologies, Nortel Networks, and Alcatel.[28]

Medtronic, Inc. is one of the world's leading manufacturers of medical devices, cardiac defibrillators, and heart pacemakers. The company has also diversified in recent years to gain access to new technologies to develop state-of-the-art surgical and disease treatment products. For example, some of its acquisitions include Xomed (ear/nose/throat surgery products), Sofamor Danek (spinal surgery tools), and Arterial Vascular Engineering (cardiac stents). All of these products complement the kind of specialized R&D and quality-driven manufacturing that Medtronic has been refining for many years. In the future, Medtronic believes that its next-generation pacemakers and defibrillator devices will employ advanced information-based technologies to warn a patient's doctor of an impending heart attack or dangerously irregular heartbeat patterns. Medtronic is developing pacemakers that incorporate state-of-the-art wireless telecommunications chips that automatically either dial 911 or use the Internet to contact a patient's physician in case the patient's heart develops some type of abnormality—a major improvement in ongoing treatment of chronic diseases that can save lives before heart attacks or other syndromes become too serious to be treated easily. Thus, Medtronic is devoting a high proportion of its R&D to learning and building on new types of technologies to strengthen and leverage its existing competitive position. In addition, Medtronic has also developed its own line of products designed to treat Parkinson's disease with electrical brain-stimulation devices. In May 2001, Medtronic spent $3.7 billion to acquire MiniMed Inc. and Medical Research Group, two companies that have developed innovative new insulin pumps to help diabetic patients regulate the flow of insulin. Both MiniMed and Medical Research Group will help Medtronic strengthen its market position by harnessing new electronic and mechanical-based technologies to assist patients to better treat their chronic disease conditions.[29]

Creating Distinctive Value: The 3M Company[30]

Perhaps one of the best-known companies in the United States, 3M has long prided itself on its capability for fast innovation and the creation of many new technologies. Customers all around the world value 3M's broad array of such top-quality products as Scotch tape, Post-It Notes, weather-stripping products, medical masks, and a broad array of technical products for the chemical, paint, automotive, and electronics industries. By the end of 2003, 3M produced revenues of $18.2 billion, and earned $2.04 billion in profits. Over its long history, 3M had pioneered over a hundred different core technologies that spawned tens of thousands of highly innovative products. Most recently, 3M has even produced some core breakthroughs that are found even in fiber-optic networks, optical discs, advanced displays, and new medical applications. 3M's ability to create new products quickly has become so legendary that the company is frequently seen as a model of corporate innovation.

Under the direction of William McKnight, the man most often credited with helping 3M to grow in its formative years, the company built its own laboratory to generate ideas and

new techniques to improve the quality of sandpaper. Improvements in the design and production of sandpaper resulted in new types of sandpaper (for example, coarse-grained, medium-grained, fine-grained) that could be used for a variety of different products (for example, woods, metals, porcelains). Customers in different industries began to use 3M's sandpaper for a variety of different uses. Feedback from customers also helped 3M to develop ideas for new products. Within a few years, scientists at 3M's lab created masking tape, Scotch tape, and other innovative products that were soon to power the company's fast growth. All of these abrasive and tape products laid the foundation for 3M's growing technical and marketing expertise with adhesives and coatings.

3M instituted some key policies that were designed to promote innovation and creative thinking. McKnight and his management team genuinely believed that 3M needed to foster and promote innovation on a continuous basis. Innovation led to new opportunities for both personal and corporate growth. In

(continued)

the late 1930s, 3M created a Central Research Laboratory whose purpose was to stimulate creative thinking and experimentation that would help the company grow. More important, 3M's organization encouraged people from all parts of the expanding company to communicate with one another on a frequent basis. Scientists working on different projects were encouraged to share their knowledge through group meetings as well as through company-sponsored technology forums that promoted free-flowing discussions. As the company grew and more labs were created, management wanted to ensure that scientists working on one project could communicate with their counterparts working on different projects. The continuous exchange of knowledge produced an intellectual ferment at 3M. By sharing knowledge and viewing the work of his or her colleagues, a scientist could gain new insights into how a technology might be developed or better refined. More important, by expanding his or her horizon, a scientist might be able to discover a technical idea or breakthrough that might not have otherwise occurred. 3M continuously praised its scientists' personal achievements, and promoted communications and informal idea exchanges. The company actively encouraged scientists to communicate with people from marketing and manufacturing to discuss new product designs, manufacturing feasibility, customer needs, and the like. Over time, 3M's salespeople provided critical data and product feedback to technical personnel in design and manufacturing; in turn, 3M's scientists often visited customers to see how their products were working.

One of 3M's earliest strategies could be summarized as "unintentionally discovering new niches." To ensure that 3M could sustain such a high level of individual creativity and innovation-driven growth, 3M became one of the first companies to form business units that could devise their own strategies to grow as they saw fit. In fact, within a few decades, 3M had spawned dozens of different business units, each of which possessed its own laboratory, manufacturing operation, and salesforce. This policy of spawning new divisions at one point resulted in several dozen 3M divisions, with each one working on its own product and market ideas. At the same time, however, senior management insisted that the entire company be able to freely share core technologies and breakthroughs that were developed in any part of 3M. For example, one division's development of advanced thin-film adhesives that ultimately proved to be a failure for high-stress industrial applications later became the basis for 3M's wildly popular Post-It Notes in another division. Conversely, fiber technologies that lay the foundation for 3M's mask products also created opportunities to develop specialized filters and membranes in another division. Thus, individual creativity and innovation, when combined with active sharing of core technologies and knowledge throughout 3M, powered the company's annual double-digit growth rate for many years until the 1980s.

3M was able to sustain its legendary growth throughout the 1970s and 1980s as its products became synonymous with innovation and high quality. Yet, growth eventually slowed down throughout much of the 1990s as the company became extremely large. Although 3M continued to foster individual creativity and innovation, revenue and earnings growth became more difficult as the company expanded into many new areas and markets. Under its current CEO, James McNerney (who took over in January 2001), 3M is striving to recreate its days of fast growth. A former GE top executive, he takes great pride in 3M's creativity, claiming, "I was handed a pretty good deck of cards here." As a result, McNerney has not pushed 3M into a radically different direction. Instead, he implemented a new company-wide program known as 3M Acceleration to speed up the creativity, innovation, and commercialization of new products. Much of the impetus of this new program has been implemented to boost 3M's health care and electronics units, where promising new ideas have already hit the market from the company's labs. Already, according to McNerney, 3M was able to increase operating income by more than $400 million through this initiative. 3M is now encouraging its customers to visit the company more frequently and to even provide ideas for 3M's legendary labs. By working more closely with customers, 3M hopes its product pipeline will exceed over $5 billion in new sales over the next several years, up from an estimate of $3.5 billion just a few years ago.

Expertise

Expertise possessed by a business in the form of information, knowledge, or skill has already been paid for. It therefore represents an essentially free good and invaluable resource to another business that can utilize it. If two such businesses merge, expertise possessed by one can be transferred to the other, producing potentially important economic benefits, especially if the expertise is highly specialized, durable, and hard to imitate. This extension of knowledge and expertise between companies forms a vital ingredient of the synergy behind diversification. In many ways, knowledge and expertise represent the best types of resources on which to build and extend new sources of competitive advantage. Knowledge and expertise are increasingly intangible (nonphysical) and based in organizational capabilities, meaning that they cannot easily be copied or imitated by competitors. Over time, competitors can learn the secrets behind new manufacturing plants and distribution channels, but it is much more difficult to imitate a competitor with distinctive knowledge or expertise. Knowledge-based assets, such as reputation, marketing know-how, brand names, patents, quality improvement skills, scientific testing, and fast product development teams, take time to accumulate and to grow. They are also highly specialized and tend to last a long time. This time requirement makes these characteristics especially distinctive, perhaps even unique, to the firm possessing them. Firms with such knowledge and expertise-based resources are well situated to extend their own distinctive competences into new areas of activity, since the uniqueness of such knowledge makes it hard for competitors to follow rapidly.

In the pharmaceutical industry, many leading drug firms are beginning to purchase small, vibrant biotechnology companies to supplement their own R&D efforts. Many small biotechnology companies, such as Amgen, Genentech, Immune Response, and others, were originally formed by small groups of scientists. They were specially trained and skilled in new cutting-edge technologies, such as genetic and molecular engineering. Large pharmaceutical firms' interests in acquiring many of the smaller biotechnology firms are based on the latter's distinctive knowledge and skills, which are essential to developing drugs against cancer, AIDS, hereditary diseases, and other ailments.[31] Companies such as Eli Lilly, Pfizer, Merck, and Johnson & Johnson are continuing to investigate new biotechnology developments in order to develop safer and more effective drugs, especially those for cancer, diabetes, and other hard-to-treat conditions.[32] Several biotechnology firms have become important established firms in their own right, such as Genentech and Amgen. Amgen, for example, has become the market leader in developing new forms of biotech-based treatments that help combat blood sepsis and clot formation during heart attacks. It is also a leader in inflammation and soft-tissue repair drugs.

General Motors' acquisition of Electronic Data Systems (EDS) in 1986 was motivated by a similar technology transfer consideration. EDS's core competence is data processing and systems integration. Systems integration helps computers, software, and machines from different vendors "talk" to one another. GM planned to introduce EDS's computer systems integration technology to make GM's factories work more smoothly and more compatibly, thereby making GM's factories more responsive and cost-efficient when changing car models or tooling. GM reasoned that EDS's expertise in systems integration would make its factories more flexible and computer driven. However, the potential synergies between the two companies never really materialized. Ultimately, General Motors sold off its EDS unit to the public in a complex transaction spanning 1995 and 1996.

In the financial services industry, the purchase by American Express of Shearson, Lehman Brothers, IDS, and other financial firms during the 1980s stemmed from its need for expertise in investment and merchant banking. American Express's core business was that of providing high-quality travel and limited financial services to an upscale customer base. By expanding and acquiring Shearson, Lehman Brothers, and E. F. Hutton during the 1980s, American Express instantly transformed itself into a leading Wall Street financial powerhouse. In 1998, Travelers merged with Citibank to form a giant financial services powerhouse that combines banking, insurance, brokerage, asset management, and other operations. The combination of the two firms, known as Citigroup, allows for transfer of expertise and knowledge of financial services, distribution, and other businesses that are increasingly technological and knowledge based. Citigroup itself is now looking for new acquisition candidates to help it become even bigger in key financial service segments. For example, it acquired Associates First Capital to enter the commercial financing and leasing industry in late 1999. With diversified interests across a wide array of businesses, Citigroup now competes with megabanks (such as J. P. Morgan Chase, Bank of America), brokerages (such as Merrill Lynch, Morgan Stanley), and even some insurance firms (such as Prudential, Metropolitan Life, Manulife) to provide financial services. Yet, even Citigroup has begun to feel the difficulties of managing such a broad line of financial service activities after undertaking so many acquisitions of seemingly similar businesses; in January 2005, Citigroup sold many of the life-insurance and annuity businesses of its former Travelers unit to MetLife Inc. for $11.5 billion. On the other hand, it continues to build greater strength by sharing expertise among its commercial leasing, investment banking, and consumer units.[33]

New product expertise, such as genetic engineering techniques, EDS's system integration skills, or American Express's investment banking skills, is not the only kind of expertise that can be usefully transferred from one business to another. Resources in virtually any functional area (R&D, production, marketing, distribution) or core skill (surface coatings, miniaturization, brand management, fast product development, packaging) are candidates for this kind of transfer. These skills ideally should be highly specialized, durable, and applicable to reinforcing the firm's distinctive competences. Many of these functional area or core skills represent the basic building blocks of each firm's distinctive competence. Examples of successful diversification involving transfer of expertise are shown in Exhibit 6-3.

Sharing Activities

A third common motive for diversification is a desire to share one or more value chain activities among businesses. Such sharing avoids unnecessary duplication. It also enables businesses to operate activities on a larger scale than would be possible for any single business

Exhibit 6-3   *Sharing Expertise Among Businesses*

Company	Partial List of Businesses	Shared Expertise
Hewlett-Packard	Computers/workstations Laser printers Digital imaging Engineering systems Microprocessors	• Engineering skills • Rapid product development • Distinctive manufacturing quality • Leverage design skills
Sharp Corp.	LCD Technology Office Equipment Flat Screen Technology Calculators	• Precision manufacturing • Flat-screen technology • Miniaturization • Fast innovation
PepsiCo	Soft drinks (Pepsi, Mountain Dew) Snack food (Frito-Lay) Gatorade (Quaker Oats) Tropicana juices	• Distribution systems • Marketing research • Segmentation skills • Consumer advertising • Brand development • Advertising
Medtronic	Heart devices Insulin pumps Spinal surgery Nervous system disorders	• Shared R&D skills • Wireless initiatives • Advanced technologies for less invasive treatments

operating on its own. Sharing an activity produces greater economies of scale and thus lowers total costs. Equally important, sharing also offers the prospect for faster learning and application of new skills and technologies. Effective sharing of key resources among business units lays the foundation for building strong, highly inimitable core competences.

To illustrate, consider Kellogg's acquisition of Keebler Foods. Keebler's direct-to-store distribution system provides an important skill that could benefit Kellogg's endeavors to sell its ready-to-eat products and single-serve products more quickly and with less cost. At the same time, Keebler benefits from Kellogg's internal R&D and strong supermarket distribution channels. Both companies offer skills that allow for considerable sharing, which in turn helps Keebler to sell more of its products in Kellogg's traditional supermarket channels, whereas Kellogg is now able to learn how to compete in direct distribution systems. By diversifying into snack foods, Kellogg added a business that could share the expense of this important activity. Joint conduct of distribution helps both the cereals and snack foods businesses in two ways. First, it avoids unnecessary duplication. Second, it enables the two businesses to mount a more concerted distribution effort than would be possible for either business acting alone.

Sharing remains a vital part of 3M Corporation's diversification strategy, especially of technologies and product applications that utilize skills based on coatings and adhesives. Production and R&D skills and insights gained from making superstrong adhesives are likely to be effective in developing more popular products, such as Post-It Notes. Also, 3M's R&D laboratories encourage scientists to work on a broad array of projects that have potential application to future lines of products that combine insights from a number of different disciplines. Technology is freely shared throughout the company, whereas businesses are free to pursue those opportunities that best fit their own marketing plans. Moreover, 3M scientists are encouraged to share their insights and breakthroughs and even to lead in new product development activities using their ideas. This approach to product development makes it difficult for competitors to imitate. Thus, technology sharing at 3M reduces the costs of entering related businesses that borrow and build on an underlying coatings, adhesive, or thin-film competence.

Sharing becomes a vital part of diversification when skills learned in one business can be transferred to others. Virtually any activity in the value chain is a potential candidate for such sharing. Exhibit 6-4 provides several illustrative examples. Firms that can learn new skills or technologies and then share activities among businesses can reinforce their competitive advantage. Because sharing has its own challenges, it will be covered in a later chapter devoted to building and managing interrelationships.

Costs of Diversification

Thus far we have considered only the benefits of diversification. Let us now turn to its costs. Diversification often imposes costs arising from (1) ignorance about newly entered fields, (2) neglect of a diversifier's core businesses, and (3) effort exerted to coordinate the businesses that result from diversification (see Exhibit 6-5).

Cost of Ignorance

A firm that diversifies into a new area generally knows less about the new field than competitors. It is therefore less able to articulate consumer needs, predict technology developments, and foresee environmental shifts. This deficiency puts it at a disadvantage when compared with more experienced competitors, increasing the likelihood that it will miss important opportunities and make costly errors.

Exhibit 6-4	Sharing Activities Among Businesses	

Firm	Partial List of Businesses	Key Shared Activity
3M	Sandpaper, tapes, fabric treatments, sealants, weather stripping, Post-It Notes, medical patches, signs	Technology development: coatings adhesives, thin-film substrates, advanced membranes
Altria	Cigarettes, packaged foods, consumer nondurables	Marketing: distribution, advertising, market research, promotion
IBM	Semiconductors, computers, network systems, disk drives, software, electronic commerce	Technology: silicon etching, systems integration, advanced materials, miniaturization. Marketing: distribution, Internet, salesforce, consulting
Fidelity Investments	Mutual funds, brokerage, securities, annuities, institutional services, retirement plans	Operations: network management, telecommunications, internal logistics. Marketing: distribution, sales, service, Internet, e-commerce

Consider for example Sony's purchase of Columbia Pictures in 1989. As a giant electronics firm with a strong engineering flavor to its corporate culture, Sony was unable to manage effectively its newly acquired U.S. entertainment unit for several years because it was a completely different kind of business. Competitive advantage in entertainment depends much more on relationship building and fostering creativity, whereas success in electronics mandates tight quality control, focused product development, and product–driven sources of innovation that do not readily transfer to businesses that promote experiences and visual images. Many analysts now feel that General Electric may face these same kinds of issues as it seeks to integrate its recently acquired Vivendi Universal entertainment assets into its NBC operations. GE has typically emphasized squeezing costs out of its acquisitions to improve profitability, whereas Universal Pictures' current leadership has encouraged a strong creative flair and wide autonomy for its movie production staff.[34]

Cost of Neglect

To carry out a diversification program, a firm's senior managers must deal with a host of issues. They must first decide that diversification is desirable. Because this is a critical decision, they

Exhibit 6-5	Costs of Diversification

- Ignorance (about newly entered fields)
- Neglect (of core business)
- Coordination
  - communication
  - compromise
  - accountability

must work with key individuals inside and outside the firm before reaching a conclusion. Consultants and investment bankers are outsiders who can advise top management in diversification issues. This effort takes time and can potentially distract attention from core businesses.

Once a decision to diversify has been made, top managers must decide how to enter the new area. If entry is by way of internal development, they must find managers to head up the new business. If acquisition is the route, they must identify suitable targets for purchase. Top managers must then integrate and manage the new unit after purchase. These activities significantly reduce the effort they can devote to a firm's original business. These problems are especially likely to occur in firms that engage in unrelated diversification into new industries. Consider the following two situations.

To some extent, McDonald's has faced this issue from 1999 to 2003 as it sought to integrate and learn how to compete in different restaurant businesses. Its 1999 acquisition of the Boston Market, Donato Pizza, and Chipotle chains consumed a disproportionate amount of senior management's time and efforts. As McDonald's later discovered, the firm allowed its core hamburger unit to deteriorate. Product quality, service, and the creation of new product concepts all suffered. The situation had gotten so bad that many franchisees wanted out of the system. In 2003, new management decided to go back to the basics of improving product and service quality.[35]

To some extent, even Sony must now face the costs of neglect that have hurt the firm's leadership position in the consumer electronics industry. Long considered a cutting-edge innovator of new types of televisions, CD players, Walkmans, and other hotly desired products, Sony lost its technological edge in designing flat-screen television sets to other competitors such as Samsung, Sharp, and LG Philips LCD. As Sony's senior management spent an increasing amount of time on learning the complexities of the entertainment business, it unwittingly allowed its dominance in technology slip. Now Sony must relearn how to design and build flat-screen technologies with Samsung of South Korea.[36]

Costs of Cooperation

To share a common resource, two businesses must cooperate with each other. Achieving cooperation often entails substantial costs. This issue is especially important to senior managers in firms engaged in related diversification. Among the most significant costs are those of (1) communication, (2) compromise, and (3) accountability.

Cost of Communication. To share an activity, businesses must reach agreement on such issues as objectives for the activity, resources to be allocated to it, scheduling of new products, assignment of personnel to use, and a reporting structure for personnel. These vital issues can significantly affect the performance of each business. Managers in the businesses need to communicate, perhaps extensively, to resolve these issues. The time devoted to such communication is a cost that businesses must incur to share an activity.

To illustrate, consider the sharing of resources between Kellogg's breakfast foods and its recently acquired vegetarian foods and snack foods businesses. These three businesses must determine what types of product development, marketing, and distribution the firm will pursue jointly. Scheduling of different product testing and marketing initiatives needs to be resolved among the businesses to determine priorities. The three businesses must also decide from which division product and marketing specialists will come and how to divide the expenses.

To illustrate further, consider General Electric's Major Home Appliance Group. It uses plastics and motors produced by other GE divisions. The scheduling of plastics and motors production must be closely coordinated with the assembly of dishwashers. Motors must sometimes be customized to the particular speeds of dishwashers, whereas plastic tubs that go into dishwashers may need additional coatings and other protection from harsh dishwashing liquids. The businesses involved must communicate extensively about these issues.

Northrop Grumman has become one of America's leading defense contractors by purchasing many other smaller defense firms over the past ten years. Some of these firms include Litton Industries, Vought Aircraft, Newport News Shipbuilding, TRW, and Westinghouse Electric's former defense business. Northrop's former CEO, Kent Kresa, calls Northrop a company of "corporate immigrants," since the vast majority of the firm's people have arrived with the company's aggressive acquisition policy. Each of these acquired businesses brings with it different ways of thinking, different ways of doing business, and different priorities when it comes to designing and integrating new types of weapon systems. Thus, a key management challenge for Northrop is to ensure that its people can effectively communicate with one another and think of themselves as belonging to a larger Northrop Grumman corporation.[37]

Many Japanese firms, currently suffering in the wake of a domestic recession and slow growth throughout Southeast Asia, are now finding that a significant cost accompanying their broad-based diversification strategies is the need for frequent and extensive communication among managers from many businesses. Companies such as Toshiba, Mitsubishi, Mitsui, and Sumitomo have been slow to respond to changing environments and new sets of customer needs in part because of their internal need to communicate, often at great length, among managers. Even as many Japanese firms currently struggle with their ongoing efforts to slim down their operations, they have proved very reluctant to abandon entire lines of businesses to improve their focus. Only recently have several major Japanese firms decided to exit such tough businesses as memory chips, mainframe computers, and even some types of consumer electronics.[38]

Cost of Compromise. Businesses involved in coordination will sometimes place different priorities on development projects. Decisions ultimately reached may therefore involve compromises that do not fully satisfy the needs of one or both businesses. Compromises can result in political frictions and reduced strategic flexibility for both businesses. For example, designing and making a particular line of dishwashers might be more time-consuming if plastics and motors provided by other GE units are used than if components are purchased from outside suppliers. Fine-tuning and calibrating dishwasher motors may require additional time and testing, especially if the motors were originally designed for other purposes. Internally supplied plastic dishwasher tubs may need an additional sealant and may cost more. On the other hand, outside suppliers might be faster, more responsive, or more skilled in making dishwasher components. Oftentimes, external suppliers will offer key products and components at a deep discount with the hope of capturing more business in the future. For managers at GE's Major Home Appliances Group, obtaining components internally would then involve a compromise for GE's dishwasher businesses.

IBM currently faces important issues and costs that result from the need to find the right balance of compromise and coordination among its many different businesses. IBM's most recent strategy is to become a full-service provider of all types of computer, electronic-commerce, and technology solutions to firms in every industry. However, the pace of product development within IBM often moves at different speeds. IBM Microelectronics, for example, leads the semiconductor industry in developing new types of microchips that use copper-based technologies that speed up processing speed at lower cost. IBM's software group excels in creating new middleware—electronic-commerce platforms that integrate supply chain, procurement, and logistics management across different parts of a client company's operations. These businesses typically move at a rapid pace because they must respond to fast-changing environmental developments within their respective industries. However, other IBM businesses, such as mainframe computers, may not move so quickly, since these products' architectures and standards tend to have long life cycles. Managers in these units often think in terms of years, rather than months, to design next-generation products. This means that IBM managers must spend a great deal of time to coordinate the product development efforts of multiple units and technologies to ensure that IBM's products enter the market at the right time. Compromises among the different businesses are often required to ensure that each unit understands the timing and strategic imperatives facing the others. Thus, to be able to provide customers with a full range of solutions, IBM managers must often try to coordinate the product development, production, and sales activities of their many units to ensure that customers receive the best mix of products at a price they are willing to pay. Managers must also speak and negotiate with one another about pricing and sharing costs. This is a complex organizational task that occasionally gives the impression that IBM is slow to respond to customers' needs. Sometimes, IBM managers may be compelled to use products from competitors if customers demand them to do so.[39]

Cost of Accountability. When a business operates independently, its managers can be held accountable for results. Accountability is reduced if a business is asked to cooperate with other units, since its performance will then be influenced, perhaps to a large degree, by compromises it makes to work with other units. Also, the help it receives from them will affect its results. For example, if GE's Major Home Appliance Group uses plastics and materials from other GE units, then the costs of goods sold for dishwashers are mostly based on internal prices that may be different from market prices. A manager's performance can then no longer be strictly equated with financial results of the business's operations; instead, performance must be judged in part on other subjective factors. Such evaluations complicate the job of senior managers by requiring them to consider these subjective factors when measuring a manager's performance. Subjective evaluations in turn can create motivational problems, since subordinates will sometimes disagree with evaluations made at higher levels. This disparity can lower morale and reduce motivation to perform.

Maximizing Benefits, Minimizing Costs

Diversification thus involves a series of important trade-offs (see Exhibit 6-6). It can sometimes produce important benefits due to more attractive terrain, resource transfers, and activity sharing. However, it also imposes potentially formidable costs stemming from ignorance,

---

Balancing the Benefits and Costs of Diversification   **Exhibit 6-6**

Diversification Benefits ⟷	Diversification Costs
● More attractive terrain	● Ignorance
● Access to key resources	● Neglect
● Sharing resources	● Coordination

neglect, and reduced accountability. To achieve a favorable balance between these opposing elements, top managers charged with diversification must try to maximize benefits while minimizing costs.

Achieving Powerful Diversification Benefits

Let us now consider the conditions leading to powerful advantages for each kind of diversification benefit discussed previously (see Exhibit 6-7).

More Favorable Terrain.   Some stakeholders may derive important benefits from a firm's expansion into more favorable terrain. Consider, for example, workers of a firm currently operating in a declining industry saddled with high fixed costs and underutilized capacity, such as coal mining or sugar refining. Unless such a firm can increase its market share, its employees will be laid off as the level of activity declines over time. Expansion into a more rapidly growing field enables a firm to avoid this situation by providing employment opportunities for workers no longer needed in its core business. Managers can also benefit from expansion, since it brings them expanded responsibility, greater career challenge, and higher compensation.

Shareholders are much less likely to benefit from diversification designed solely to improve terrain, however. Shareholders can improve terrain on their own simply by purchasing shares in other firms already operating in desirable new areas. *To help shareholders, diversification must produce benefits that they cannot achieve by diversifying their own portfolios.* Again, the key issue underscoring diversification's performance is the following question: Does a company reinforce and improve its distinctive competence by entering another area? Only if the answer is yes can diversification benefit shareholders. Diversification undertaken solely to improve terrain is thus a mixed bag, producing benefits for some stakeholders, but not for others (Exhibit 6-7A). Indeed, diversification with this sole objective in mind will often be a losing proposition for shareholders, because it imposes various costs—ignorance, neglect, reduced accountability—without providing offsetting benefits that shareholders cannot achieve on their own. Whether top managers should proceed with diversification despite this potentially unfavorable trade-off will depend on the relative importance they attach to shareholder needs relative to those of other stakeholder groups. This issue is complicated by the fact that top managers are one of the groups that most benefits from diversification. Therefore, they are often least able to make an objective decision.

Exhibit 6-7	Conditions Leading to Powerful Diversification Benefits

A. Achieving more attractive terrain
(This is rarely a source of powerful benefits for all stakeholders.)

B. Transferring resources which are . . .
- competitively important to receiving businesses
- difficult for receiving businesses to duplicate on their own
- hard for competitors to imitate

C. Shared activities must be . . .
- large in dollar terms
- susceptible to economies of scale and experience

Resource Transfers. Diversification that transfers resources between two businesses can provide important benefits to shareholders, since shareholders cannot reproduce resource transfers simply by diversifying their own portfolios. These benefits will tend to be large when three conditions are present (Exhibit 6-7B). First, a transferred resource must be competitively important to the receiving business. It can be competitively important by either significantly reducing the receiving business's costs or by enhancing its uniqueness in some important way. Also, a transferred resource must be difficult to duplicate by the receiving business acting on its own, meaning that the receiving business could not develop the resource by itself because of high cost, time, lack of skills, or other factors. Finally, the resource should be sufficiently specialized and durable to produce value over long time periods.

Whether these three conditions are satisfied in any particular instance is often difficult to assess. Consider General Motors' acquisition of EDS in 1986, for example. GM's managers expected that EDS's highly specialized skills in managing technology and computers would significantly improve GM's ability to automate its factories, and thus build better-quality cars using advanced robotics. Their expectation went unmet, however. EDS's computer-oriented skill set proved to be of little use to General Motors, mainly because of its high cost and limited applicability to factory automation systems. The resource was not valuable in enhancing GM's cost, differentiation, or capability to generate new knowledge. Resources transferred between GM and EDS therefore had little beneficial impact on either company's competitive position.

Often diversifiers learn only through trial and error what capabilities may be useful to other businesses. Consider the evolution of Viacom over the past decade. It is one of the nation's leading diversified media firms. Some of its best-known businesses include Paramount Pictures, CBS, MTV, Nickelodeon, and Infinity Broadcasting. Viacom also owns 80 percent of Blockbuster, Inc., the largest video-rental giant in the United States. Viacom believed that Blockbuster would be instrumental in boosting the popularity and rental revenues of the many movies produced by its Paramount Pictures unit. However, Viacom discovered that its film production and television broadcasting skills were not suited to managing what is essentially a retailing operation. As a result, Viacom possessed little expertise that it could transfer to Blockbuster. In 2004, Viacom continued to work on plans to divest itself of Blockbuster completely. Viacom, on the other hand, experienced a much bigger success with its Comedy Central business. A fast-growing network, Comedy Central's audience has jumped nearly 50 percent over the past five years. Viacom's ability to create and manage networks, such as MTV, VH1, and Nickelodeon, provides much needed expertise that can help Comedy Central reach an even larger audience. These skills are highly specialized and useful in developing new media distribution channels.[40] Now, Viacom is pondering realigning and even separating some of the assets it acquired during the late 1990s, such as CBS and Infinity Broadcasting. New media technologies are changing the way customers watch television and listen to commercial radio.

Activity Sharing. The sharing of an activity between two or more businesses will produce a powerful benefit when two distinct conditions are satisfied (Exhibit 6-7C). First, the activity being shared must involve a large dollar outlay. Without this prerequisite, even a major reduction in the activity's cost will have little impact on total business expense. Most staff-related, nonoperational activities (accounting, legal, finance) fail to meet this requirement. Sharing them among businesses therefore rarely produces powerful benefits. This is a big reason why conglomerate-type diversification tends to produce little lasting value or competitive advantage. By contrast, activities such as operations, sales, advertising, procurement, and technology development often involve substantial financial outlays. Thus, even a small percentage reduction in their cost can have a major impact on total business expense.

Second, a shared activity must also be susceptible to economies of scale and experience. Only through this susceptibility will sharing the activity among businesses produce significant benefits for the businesses involved. Recall that the susceptibility of a firm's activities to economies of scale and experience varies greatly. For example, key manufacturing tasks such as automated tooling, molding, die-casting, fabrication, and managing information networks are activities that typically display high economies of scale. Likewise, managing and coordinating distribution activities using advanced online tracking systems also favors high economies of scale. On the other hand, gourmet cooking, construction of new buildings, and interior décor are activities that often depend upon meeting a customer's exact specifications, thus limiting the potential to capture significant economies of scale.

Limiting Diversification Costs

In addition to trying to maximize diversification benefits, diversifiers must also attempt to limit diversification costs. A diversifier can take certain steps to contain each of the diversification costs noted earlier in the chapter (see Exhibit 6-8).

Exhibit 6-8	*Limiting Diversification Costs*

Limit Costs of Ignorance by . . .
- entering familiar fields
- centering new areas internally rather than by acquisition

Limit Costs of Neglect by . . .
- ensuring new businesses fit easily with existing ones
- leveraging a distinctive competence systemwide

Limit Costs of Cooperation by . . .
- carefully managing the sharing of activities
- designing organizational support systems that promote interrelationships

Cost of Ignorance. One way to limit the cost of ignorance is to confine diversification to familiar fields, which are areas close to a firm's base business. New segments or new stages of a firm's core industry generally satisfy this requirement, since they usually involve products, technologies, and a general environment similar to those of a firm's original business. Carefully implemented related diversification also satisfies this requirement.

Entering new areas through internal development rather than by acquisition can also limit costs of ignorance. This step is an important key to the success of the related diversification strategy. Internal entry provides a firm with opportunities to build up its investment gradually in a new area, thereby limiting risk in early stages when ignorance is the greatest. By the time an investment reaches a critical mass, a firm using internal entry will often have learned enough about a new business to avoid serious missteps. Diversification by acquisition, however, often requires a firm to make a substantial investment up front, before it has had time to learn much about a new field. In this situation, acquiring relatively small firms can limit some of the difficulties involved in learning and gaining experience with a new field. Large acquisitions in a familiar field can especially pose significant management and integration problems for firms. This happened to many companies in the managed care, airline, broadcasting, financial services, railroad, and telecommunications industries during the late 1990s, even as they pursued related diversification. For example, Citigroup's acquisition and management of its Travelers' insurance unit resulted in significant organizational difficulties as the fit between investment banking and insurance became less tenable over time. Likewise, the massive acquisition strategies undertaken by megarailroads Union Pacific, Burlington Northern, and CSX to purchase similar sized railroads resulted in massive organizational upheaval, persistent difficulties in meshing different work practices, and major customer dissatisfaction with shipment delays during the late 1990s. A strategy that relies heavily on acquisitions will raise significant organizational issues, such as how best to integrate different corporate cultures, reward systems, performance evaluation systems, and other internal practices. In particular, balancing the capital needs and resource allocation decisions among various business units is a big challenge that often confronts managers pursuing an unrelated diversification strategy. The cost of miscalculation can then be much greater and harder to reverse.[41]

For example, GE has experienced significant success when it has confined its acquisitions to businesses that it already knows. In the medical field, GE acquired Data Critical, a key manufacturer of wireless and Internet-driven systems for transmitting health care data, in July 2001. This acquisition will help GE make much of its medical equipment Internet-ready so that technicians and medical personnel can then transfer patient findings and data with fewer steps and greater ease. In late 2003, GE also acquired Amersham and Instrumentarium, two large medical companies that complement GE's growing presence in the health care industry. Amersham, a British firm, is well known for its distinctive skills in contrast agents and other technologies that help provide superior imaging of the body with MRI, CT, and other medical scanning techniques. GE's acquisition of Finnish company Instrumentarium helps the firm develop better instruments that monitor a patient's vital signs when in the hospital. This deal complements GE's larger health care initiative to provide new ways of transmitting medical information and delivering better patient care.[42]

Cost of Neglect. A diversifier's core business is most likely to be neglected when crises occur in one or more of its newly entered businesses. This situation occurred with Eastman Kodak when problems arose in its Sterling Drug acquisition in 1988. Kodak discovered that skills required for researching and producing pharmaceuticals were substantially different from those used to develop new films. Kodak's efforts to improve Sterling Drug's performance caused it to neglect important aspects of its film business, especially new product development. Eventually, Kodak sold its wide-ranging pharmaceutical operations in a number of different transactions in 1994 and 1995. These moves represented a serious strategic distraction for Kodak. Kodak's acquisitions also cost the company valuable time and resources that could have been devoted to learning about digital technologies, something that was already available as far back as the mid-1980s. Instead, Kodak hoped to use its acquisitions as a way to compensate for the steadily declining earnings of its traditional film business.

Sony's purchase of Columbia Pictures in 1989 resulted in senior managers refocusing their time and commitment to integrate the newly acquired entertainment unit within Sony's corporate umbrella of operations. However, the significant effort required to learn about how the entertainment business operates resulted in neglect of the firm's core electronics operations. Capital once allocated to new product development and process improvements in consumer electronics was siphoned off to produce blockbuster movies, many of which were financial failures during the 1990s. Realizing the potential effects of neglect on its core operations, Sony refocused its investment and managerial priorities on learning new forms of digital electronics, PlayStation video game consoles, and Internet-driven technologies needed for consumer electronics. These moves, by contrast, have been more successful, since they are based on harnessing Sony's creative and fast product development skills in electronics, a more familiar field. Yet, despite a renewed focus on electronics, Sony now finds itself lagging in flat-screen technology, a key requirement for next-generation television sets.

Intel's move to enter the web-hosting and consumer electronics businesses during the late 1990s resulted in significant difficulties for the company's core semiconductor business. As Intel tried to build its web-hosting business for corporate customers, it became distracted from the significant progress that its archrival AMD was making. By the end of 2001, AMD had seized upwards of 20 percent of the microprocessor market, and appeared to be gaining on Intel in the more lucrative market for corporate servers as well. At the same time, Intel tried to compete in the consumer electronics business by designing such gadgets as digital cameras, home networking devices, and even MP3 digital music players. By October 2001, Intel announced that it would retreat from consumer electronics to concentrate on its core semiconductor business. To further strengthen its core semiconductor competence, Intel also withdrew from the web-hosting business as well.[43]

To avoid neglect of their core businesses, top managers must take steps to reduce the likelihood of new crises in their newly entered businesses. Crises in newly entered businesses will tend to be fewer and of smaller magnitude when diversification is confined to familiar fields and achieved through internal entry rather than by acquisition. Thus, diversifying firms can avoid costs of neglect and ignorance by following the same two guidelines.

Cost of Cooperation.   To transfer resources and share activities, businesses must cooperate with each other. Some cooperation costs therefore inevitably accompany these benefits. Such costs can be minimized, however, by careful design of a diversifier's administrative systems. We will focus on this subject in later chapters that examine the role of various organizational structures.

Alternatives to Diversification: Corporate Restructurings

Diversification is one potentially useful remedy available to a firm operating in a troubled industry. However, it is not the only remedy. In fact, diversification for its own sake can produce significant managerial difficulties, destruction of shareholder value, dilution of corporate resources and distinction, and long-term problems in recovering firm competitiveness. The difficulties that confronted such firms as American Express, Aetna, Citigroup, Sears, Sony, Intel, McDonald's, General Motors, Merck, Union Pacific, and others in recent years testify to the significant managerial challenges posed by complex or overly ambitious diversification strategies. When diversification is likely to produce fewer benefits (in the form of resource transfers and activity sharing) than costs (from ignorance, neglect, and cooperation), then some other solution to industry decline should be pursued. Equally important, when diversification has failed to produce sustainable increases in long-term shareholder value and new ways to use the firm's set of distinctive competences and resources, action is needed to induce a renewed focus on the firm's core business.

corporate restructurings:

Steps designed to change the corporate portfolio of businesses to achieve greater focus and efficiency among businesses; often involve selling off businesses that do not fit a core technology or are a drag on earnings.

Fortunately, alternatives and remedies for excessive diversification exist. Many of these efforts can be broadly described as corporate restructurings. **Corporate restructurings** involve changing the firm's portfolio or mix of businesses to become more efficient and focused in key activity areas.[44] Particularly worthy of consideration are (1) selective focus and (2) divestitures and spin-offs of noncore units (see Exhibit 6-9). Both forms of corporate restructurings are designed to help senior managers rebuild sources of competitive advantage in their core businesses. Simultaneously, restructurings help shareholders (the firm's owners) gain improved value and financial performance from a tighter focus.

| Steps in Corporate Restructuring | Exhibit 6-9 |

- Selective focus on carefully chosen activities or niches
- Divestitures and spin-offs

Selective Focus

By carefully targeting new segments, a firm may be able to expand its market share even though the industry in which it operates is in decline. The ease of increasing market share will depend on the tenacity of competitors. If competitors are tough, as often occurs when fixed costs are high, market share will be difficult to gain. However, if competitors have lost interest in an industry, as is often the case in maturing or declining industries, gains in market share are more feasible. Selective focus also fits a careful acquisition strategy.

Perhaps the one firm that best exemplifies a strategy of carefully identifying and targeting new market segments is Southwest Airlines. From its original core base in the Southwest and California markets, Southwest overcame the worst problems of an airline by targeting new short-haul routes in the Northeast where it could make a sustainable penetration of airports or metropolitan areas that were previously underserved. After completing its acquisition of Morris Air to reach the Rocky Mountain region in 1994, Southwest began to duplicate its successful short-haul strategy in the dense metropolitan cities of the East. For example, in 1996, Southwest entered the East Coast market by establishing a base area in Baltimore, a city often bypassed by other larger carriers. Later, Southwest moved into Providence, Rhode Island, to use that facility as a way of avoiding direct competition with larger established carriers that use Boston's Logan Airport as their core hub. Now, Southwest has begun to challenge the major airlines in the New York area by offering service from a small airport in Long Island, and it has also become a major player in the Philadelphia airport.

Acquisitions of smaller firms in market niches that complement a firm's existing core business interests may help build the kind of critical mass needed to overcome problems of a declining industry. By focusing on specialized segments in its existing industry, a firm can sometimes maintain steady sales and profitability despite overall industry decline. Crown Cork & Seal has taken this approach in the metal can industry. Industry sales have declined in recent decades as a result of inroads made by substitute packaging materials, such as plastic, paper, and glass. Crown Cork & Seal continued to dedicate itself entirely to metal containers for a long period. It concentrated its product development efforts on those segments unaffected by substitute materials, such as bottle caps and crowns. Crown Cork & Seal's selective focus also includes hard-to-hold applications, such as aerosols, and customers in developing countries where the newer materials have not yet penetrated. This selective focus has enabled Crown Cork & Seal to far outperform American Can and Continental Can, whose diversification programs have had disastrous results.

WellPoint Health Networks has successfully grown through careful internal development and acquisition of small managed care firms throughout the country during the 1990s. Now based in Indianapolis with major operations in California, WellPoint works to develop good relations with hospitals, physicians, employers, and patients who use its managed care HMO and PPO networks. Under CEO Leonard Schaeffer, WellPoint has become a leader in offering innovative health insurance solutions to large and small businesses, and has gained important market share in its newly acquired territories in many parts of the United States. It announced a deal in 2004 where it merged with Anthem, another leading managed care firm. The combined entity, now known as WellPoint, serves over 28 million members as the United States' largest managed care firm.[45]

In contrast, growth for its own sake can produce enormous difficulties and massive destruction of shareholder value. In late 1996, for example, managed care firm Aetna purchased U.S. Healthcare, a leading health maintenance organization (HMO) provider. The combination of the two firms was designed to give both critical mass as well as the ability to create new products and services for customers in different health plans around the nation. Aetna has even acquired other managed care firms, such as New York Life's NYLCare unit and Prudential's health care unit (after divesting certain regions for competitive reasons). However, it became readily apparent that Aetna seriously overextended its strategy. Integrating NYLCare and Prudential HealthCare proved especially daunting, and costs ballooned in ways that management never predicted. Employers and other customers of Aetna's health plans began to balk at the insurance firm's poor coordination of activities, while doctors revolted against the firm's lower reimbursement rates for patient care. In 2001, Aetna actually fell behind such other competitors as UnitedHealth Care, WellPoint Health Networks, and CIGNA in the race to win over new customers in the fast-consolidating managed care industry. Now Aetna is the midst of a multiyear program to turn around its operations and to exit those markets where it cannot compete effectively. By early 2005, many of Aetna's restructuring efforts succeeded in turning around a beleaguered managed care firm into a much more potent and vibrant competitor.[46]

Divestitures and Spin-offs

spinning off:
A form of corporate restructuring that sells businesses or parts of a company that no longer contribute to the firm's earnings or distinctive competence.

Yet another powerful and increasingly used means of corporate restructuring for a firm confronting the challenges of diversification is that of divesting or "spinning off" parts of the company. **Spinning off** businesses means selling those units or parts of a business that no longer contribute to or fit the firm's distinctive competence. Spin-offs can involve sales of assets to another firm or to the public in the form of a new stock offering, often known as an initial public offering (IPO). The major purpose of a spin-off or divestiture is to unlock the hidden value of assets or businesses that floundered with excessive diversification and reduced corporate focus. By the time a company decides to spin off a business unit, it has already lost significant competitive advantage to rivals in key markets. Spin-offs are designed to reverse "diversification creep" that may have ensued over an extended period of time. In recent years, literally hundreds of firms across a wide array of industries have undertaken major corporate spin-offs of noncore or maturing assets in order to increase shareholder value and renew focus. Exhibit 6–10 presents some of the more prominent spin-offs over the past few years in different industries.

Exhibit 6-10 **Key Corporate Spin-offs in Recent Years**

Firm	Spun-off Unit	Industry/Intent
Baxter Healthcare	• Allegiance	• Divest low margin, mature medical supply unit
AT&T	• Lucent Technologies	• Separate telecom equipment maker from telecommunications service firm
PepsiCo	• Tricon Global Restaurants Yum! Brands	• Free up KFC, Taco Bell, Pizza Hut into new unit

Key Corporate Spin-offs in Recent Years (continued)
Exhibit 6-10

Firm	Spun-off Unit	Industry/Intent
Ralston-Purina	• Ralston Ralcorp.	• Separate animal feed business cereals business
Ford	• Associates First Capital	• Divest commercial lending unit to focus on automobile business
	• Visteon Corp.	• Divest of part-making unit
Monsanto	• Solutia	Frees up Monsanto to focus on biotechnology
DuPont	• Conoco	• Use cash from spin-off to focus on life sciences
ICI	• Zeneca	• Separation of commodity chemical and agribusiness units
Motorola	• Freescale	• Separation of chip-making unit from cell phone manufacturing unit
Marriott International	• Host Marriott	• Separation of hotel management and real estate businesses
General Mills	• Darden Group	• Divest restaurant unit to focus on core foods business
Sears	• Allstate Insurance • Coldwell Banker • Dean Witter • Discover	• Divest four financial services units to focus on retailing
American Express	• Lehman Brothers	• Separation of brokerage/ underwriting unit from travel services
Eastman Kodak	• Eastman Chemical	• Focus on digital photography and imaging
CBS	• Westinghouse industrial businesses	• Renew focus to become a pure play media company
AT&T	• AT&T Broadband	• Focus on core long-distance business
Tyco International	• Four business units	• Increase transparency to shareholders
Citigroup	• Travelers unit	• Divest of some noncore property/casualty business
Lucent Technologies	• Agere Systems	• Divest of chipmaking unit to focus on wireless and optical segments
Merck	• Medco Containment	• Focus on core drug development activities
H. J. Heinz	• Weight Watchers unit	• Focus on condiment and flavorings business
Hewlett-Packard	• Agilent Technologies	• Focus on printing, digital imaging, and computing systems
AMR Corp.	• The Sabre Group	• Divest of software and reservations systems
Altria	• Kraft Foods	• Unlock food value unit
General Motors	• Delphi Automotive Systems	• Divest of auto part-making unit

Spinning off businesses and other assets can help the firm regain a stronger sense of focus and unlock critical funds by divesting assets whose value has plateaued or declined as a result of ignorance or neglect. Firms can utilize the cash generated from spin-offs to invest in emerging or future technologies that better leverage or revitalize their distinctive competences. For example, Procter & Gamble in October 2001 announced that it would divest its Jif peanut butter and Crisco cooking oil units by selling them to the family-run J. M. Smucker Company for $810 million. This move allows P&G to concentrate its resources on those businesses that it believes to have greater growth potential, while allowing J. M. Smucker to gain critical market share in the peanut butter and shortening businesses. In addition, J. M. Smucker will be able to devise new marketing programs that combine its strong positions in the jellies and jams with its peanut butter offerings. At the same time, P&G has focused on speeding up its own product development process. It is solidifying its position in consumer personal care products and is now formulating a new line of cosmetics based on ideas conceived from its Japanese operations. It has also begun to limit its efforts to engage in full-scale diversification into the pharmaceutical industry; instead, P&G will now focus on marketing and promoting various over-the-counter drugs, such as Prilosec OTC with drug partner AstraZeneca.[47]

Spin-offs enable firms to reverse their diversification postures that may have resulted in reduced corporate focus or dilution of their distinctive competences. These corporate restructurings enable firms to "downscope" the wide degree of diversification that became unwieldy and cumbersome over time. When firms can no longer generate value from acquired or internally developed businesses, spinning off these units is preferable to retaining underutilized assets. Consider, for example, the following recent major corporate spin-offs of the past few years.

In 1997, PepsiCo spun off its $10 billion restaurant unit (including KFC, Taco Bell, and Pizza Hut) as a new company known as Yum! Brands. Pepsi's senior management realized that competing in restaurants would become a highly capital-intensive endeavor, with more money being diverted away from its core beverages and Frito-Lay snack food businesses. The highly profitable and cash flow–rich earnings from Frito-Lay were being diverted to a restaurant unit that faced a higher cost of capital and significantly tougher competition from revitalized pizza chains (such as Domino's Pizza, Papa John's International, Little Caesar), ethnic food chains (such as Taco Bueno), and even from small players in the fiercely competitive chicken market (such as Popeye's, La Madeleine). Moreover, the restaurant business was slowing as the entire industry entered a period of slow-growth maturity. In addition, coordination and communication between the restaurant group with the rest of PepsiCo's operations were difficult at best. More important, other restaurant chains were reluctant to purchase Pepsi beverages (in the highly lucrative fountain business) because they felt that they would be indirectly helping their competitors (KFC, Taco Bell, and Pizza Hut). Thus, PepsiCo's ability to create further value in the restaurant unit, and vice versa, deteriorated and no longer provided a rationale for its earlier diversification strategy. Yum! Brands has become a fierce competitor in the fast-food restaurant business, and it has even grown aggressively by acquiring the A&W and Long John Silver's restaurant chains. Now, PepsiCo is focusing more closely on its beverage businesses, especially after its most recent large acquisition of Quaker Oats, which Pepsi bought in December 2001 for $14 billion. PepsiCo is hoping to use Quaker's Gatorade brand of sports drinks to push further into the noncarbonated beverage market.[48]

One of the biggest corporate restructurings in late 1999 was Hewlett-Packard's spin-off of Agilent Technologies to divest itself of its traditional electronic instruments businesses. Hewlett-Packard believed that it needed to sharpen its focus on developing next-generation Internet-oriented technologies, such as electronic commerce solutions, digital imaging, and advanced computer solutions. In addition, HP felt that it needed to concentrate its resources on continuing to build state-of-the-art laser and inkjet printers, as well as committing to its personal computer business. By June 2000, Hewlett-Packard completed its spin-off of Agilent into a fully independent company with forty-three thousand employees. Agilent Technologies is a recognized world leader in such fields as semiconductor test equipment, measurement instruments, fiber-optic components, and even tools used in the biotechnology field. The skills required for developing these innovative products are quite different from those used for laser printers and networking applications for the Internet. Agilent's DNA microarray technology offers leading-edge solutions that enable scientists to accelerate the development of new genetically engineered drugs. DNA microarray technology is also an important tool that is used to isolate genes in living organisms in order to determine how disease processes and mutations are initiated. Some of Agilent's other promising R&D activities include new "bubble technology" that improves the speed and productivity of fiber optics–based communication systems. Agilent's bubble technology is seen as an important competitor to Corning Incorporated's photonics products that will power next-generation telecommunications networks.[49]

Hewlett-Packard itself has become the focus of enormous investor interest as the company has failed to gain much synergy from its 2002 acquisition of Compaq Computer. Undertaken by then-CEO Carly Fiorina, Hewlett-Packard believed that it could gain significant economies of scale by combining the two companies' personal computer (PC) businesses to better compete with IBM and Dell Computer. However, despite enormous time and resources devoted to integrating the two companies, many senior managers became demoralized with the effort. Many senior HP engineers left the company, taking their valuable knowledge with them. In fact, the board of HP compelled Fiorina to submit her resignation in February 2005, signaling that important changes in HP's corporate strategy will ensue. Some of these changes may involve asset sales and spin-offs of selected business units.[50]

Other firms in the late 1990s that have spun off businesses to renew their focus include Ralston-Purina (Ralcorp Holdings—private-label cereals, Protein Technologies—biotechnology applications, and AgriBrands International—animal feed businesses), Monsanto (its Solutia commodity chemicals business), Rockwell International (automotive, industrial, and semiconductor units), Ford Motor Company (Associates First Capital financial services unit), Sears Roebuck (financial services units Allstate, Coldwell Banker, and Discover), General Mills (its restaurant unit known as the Darden Group), DuPont (Conoco oil unit), American Express (Lehman Brothers financial brokerage unit), H. J. Heinz (pet food business), ITT (automotive, Rayonier forestry and paper products, hotels, and entertainment units), General Motors (Delphi Automotive Systems), Ford Motor Company (Visteon Corporation), AMR (The Sabre Group), Motorola (its semiconductor unit), Citigroup (Travelers insurance unit) and Dun & Bradstreet (financial publishing and database businesses). In the vast majority of these transactions, these spin-offs enabled both the remaining core business and the newly independent spin-off or sold unit to compete better in the marketplace. The high costs of diversification (ignorance, neglect, compromise, and communication) had seriously outweighed the benefits of competing across multiple businesses and industries.

Strategic Application to Kellogg

To what extent do Kellogg's corporate strategies support our prescriptions? Although Kellogg's entire corporate strategy and diversification experiences over its long history is not analyzed here, a brief look at a single instance for each will highlight some of the ongoing dilemmas and issues surrounding diversification.

Let us first consider some of the recent moves undertaken by the Kellogg Company. By acquiring Keebler Foods, Kellogg has diversified into new food businesses that share several characteristics with its core breakfast food business. As such, Kellogg is engaging in related diversification. This move took Kellogg into new areas where the company could learn new skills and develop new products to reverse the declining earnings and market share position of its traditional cereal products. On the other hand, acquiring Keebler did not really move Kellogg too far into new or completely unfamiliar terrain, since Kellogg has considerable experience in developing and marketing prepackaged food products. This acquisition opens up opportunities for Kellogg to learn new skills from Keebler. Keebler's renowned skills in reinvigorating growth in mature brands (such as its 1996 experience with Cheez-It) will greatly assist Kellogg as it tries to devise new product mixes and marketing programs to boost the sales of both existing and newly created cereals. In addition, Keebler offers Kellogg considerable expertise in the area of direct-to-store distribution systems, especially for convenience stores and gas stations where Kellogg has virtually no presence. Keebler already handles many of Kellogg's smaller single-serve portions of such traditional branded products as Nutri-Grain granola bars that are often sold in the same way that candy bars are. Thus, Keebler's direct-to-store distribution system has considerable potential to complement Kellogg's traditional wholesaler and brokerage-based distribution methods. However, meshing two types of distribution systems within the same company will cause Kellogg to deal with the costs of coordination and compromise. Kellogg will need to take special care not to alienate its traditional wholesale channels as it begins to deploy Keebler's direct-to-store systems. One way for Kellogg to do this is to initially limit Keebler's skills toward those nonsupermarket channels that are already accustomed to this type of arrangement. Over time, however, Kellogg will eventually have to work with supermarket chains and its wholesalers in order to slowly introduce the direct-to-store system so that it can sell newer and fresher products without generating considerable inventory. At the same time, Kellogg offers Keebler a much bigger R&D platform in which to experiment and to develop new types of recipes for future packaged goods. Both units of the company can now share a modern lab to share the costs of developing new food products based on both existing and new food-processing technologies. Already, Keebler's newest Cheez-It Twisters product line has been a big beneficiary of cereal-making technology that Kellogg has long used for its own products. Such transfer of expertise and knowledge helps Kellogg find new uses for its R&D and manufacturing skills that have long been paid for.

With Worthington Foods, Kellogg enters fairly new terrain—that of vegetarian and soy-based products with which it has little experience. In addition, customers who purchase vegetarian products are likely to be different from those who purchase Kellogg's traditional breakfast products. This means that opportunities to closely share and coordinate marketing programs may be more difficult than initially presumed. More important, Kellogg needs to work closely with Worthington's management to learn how to sell to health-conscious customers, who may have different demographics and marketing requirements. Since Kellogg's acquisition of Worthington Foods is comparatively large, there is inherently more risk and cost associated with making the deal work. On the other hand, Kellogg will be able to transfer important R&D and marketing skills to help Worthington develop new products for its Morningstar Farms brand. These skills are clearly valuable to Worthington and difficult for it to develop on its own quickly. However, if Kellogg's R&D and marketing skills are not completely applicable, then the costs with such diversification may prove too high. For example, Kellogg acquired Lender's Bagels in 1996 for $400 million, only to sell it three years later for $275 million. Lender's Bagels required a different set of marketing skills, especially since customers were beginning to eat freshly baked bagels offered by doughnut and specialty bagel shops. Kellogg's acquisition of the

Kashi Company, on the other hand, holds the seeds for potentially much more successful related diversification, since Kashi is a small company and already makes different types of natural-grain cereal products, a better fit with Kellogg's traditional core business. Kashi also enables Kellogg to mitigate some of the effects of the current dieting trend that avoids high levels of carbohydrates and other high-sugar products.

In the past few years, Kellogg has made major strides to speed up its internal product development programs. Despite moves to diversify outside of cereal, Kellogg has renewed its focus on innovating new cereal and snack food concepts. Kellogg is now reaping the benefits of its internal R&D as its share of sales from new products has leaped beyond that of the overall cereal industry. The company strives to innovate new variants of its most famous cereal products, including a recent Special K Red Berries cereal mix that contains freeze-dried berries. Kellogg has also licensed from the Walt Disney Company the use of names for products such as Mickey's Magix and Mud & Bugs to develop more kid-oriented cereals. As Kellogg emphasizes more premium-style products, the firm is trying new ways to boost the value of its cereal business even as long-term growth in this industry will likely remain slow.

Summary

- Corporate strategy deals with the issue of enlarging the firm's scope of operations to new areas of activity or businesses.
- The most important issue behind corporate strategy is this question: Does a firm improve its competitive advantage by entering new areas of activity?
- Successful diversification requires firms to utilize distinctive competences and resources in new ways. Resources (such as skills, assets, technologies, capabilities) should be hard to imitate, specialized, and durable to produce value and profits over a long period.
- A firm can enlarge the scope of its operations by entering new segments, new stages, new product areas, and new industries. Scope enlargement can be accomplished by vertical integration, related diversification, and unrelated diversification.
- Vertical integration may occur through partial or full integration. Backward integration moves the firm closer to its sources of supply. Forward integration moves the firm closer to its customers.
- Related diversification extends the firm's distinctive competence into new industries that are similar to the firm's original business.
- Unrelated diversification is not based on the firm's underlying distinctive competence.
- Diversification enables a firm to secure more attractive terrain, access resources not otherwise available, and share activities on a potentially economical basis.
- Diversification imposes costs. These costs arise because diversifiers are often ignorant about newly entered fields, neglect their base businesses, and must expend cooperative effort to transfer resources and share activities among businesses.
- Diversification will be fruitful only when the benefits generated by diversification outweigh the related costs.
- Transferring a resource between two businesses will produce a significant benefit if the resource is competitively important to the receiving business and is difficult for the receiving business to develop on its own.
- Sharing an activity between two or more businesses will produce a significant benefit when the activity involves a large dollar expenditure and is highly susceptible to economies of scale and experience.
- A diversifier can sometimes contain diversification costs by confining diversification to familiar fields and by diversifying internally rather than by acquisition.

- When analysis reveals that diversification will most likely produce greater costs than benefits, a firm operating in a troubled industry should undertake corporate restructurings.
- Possibilities include increasing market share and selective focus, as well as divesting and spinning off noncore operations or businesses.
- Spinning off noncore or less related businesses helps produce renewed focus on remaining core operations. It also helps shareholders capture the full value of assets being used by management.

Exercises and Discussion Questions

 1. Using the Internet, look up the website for General Electric. How many different businesses does General Electric have? What appears to be the underlying basis for General Electric's strength in many of its business units? What type of diversification strategy would you say General Electric is pursuing? Which GE businesses appear to be doing the most acquiring?

 2. Look up the website for Viacom Corporation and find its most recent annual report. What is CEO Sumner Redstone attempting to accomplish with Viacom's position in the entertainment and multimedia industries? How does Viacom's strategy of spinning off Blockbuster Entertainment help with its new strategy?

3. Throughout this chapter, we noted that unrelated diversification, or conglomerates, appear to be declining in popularity throughout the United States. On the other hand, this particular type of diversification strategy appears to be extremely widespread in Mexico, Brazil, South Korea, Japan, and even some countries throughout Europe. In Mexico, companies are organized along a "Grupo" structure. Why do you think unrelated diversification and the proliferation of conglomerate-type companies are so prevalent in Mexico, Brazil, and other nations? What does the presence of so many conglomerates seem to say about the nation's underlying financial institutions and the role of shareholders in the management of these companies? What is the real contribution of senior management in conglomerate-type firms in Mexico and elsewhere?

4. When managers within a firm share activities to achieve related diversification, they must also compromise on some issues in order to make the sharing successful. What issues, in particular, appear to be the basis for making sharing successful in a related diversified firm? How can these same issues cause a potentially successful strategy to slip?

Endnotes

1. Data for the Kellogg Company case were adapted from the following sources: "The Man Who Fixed Kellogg," *Fortune,* September 6, 2004, pp. 218–226; "Recipes Without Borders?" *Wall Street Journal,* August 18, 2004, pp. B1, B6; "Some Food Makers Trim Low-Carb Plans as Trend Slows," *Wall Street Journal,* July 12, 2004, pp. B1, B4; "Kellogg's Quarterly Net Rose 34% Despite Switch to Low-Carb Diets," *Wall Street Journal,* April 23, 2004, p. B4; "Kellogg's Chief Takes Firm From Shaky to Gr-r-reat," *Dallas Morning News,* April 7, 2004, p. 3D; "Thinking Outside the Cereal Box: General Mill's Far-Flung Search for Efficiency Ideas," *BusinessWeek,* July 28, 2003, pp. 74–75; "Honey, I Shrank the Box," *Wall Street Journal,* November 10, 2003, p. 82; "Kellogg Co.: Expanded Licensing Program to Use Apparel, Entertainment," *Wall Street Journal,* June 12, 2003, p. B10; "My Cookies Are Crumbled," *Wall Street Journal,* August 27, 2002, p. D1; "Snap, Crackle, Plop: Cereal Is a Sore Subject in Battle

Creek, Michigan," *Wall Street Journal,* August 27, 2001; "How to Make a Frozen Lasagna (with Just $250 Million)," *Fortune,* April 30, 2001; "Kellogg, General Mills Battle over Bars," *Wall Street Journal,* March 27, 2001; "Thinking Out of the Cereal Box," *BusinessWeek,* January 15, 2001; "Keebler Acquisition Trims Near-Term Profit Forecast," *Wall Street Journal,* November 29, 2000; "Kellogg to Buy Keebler Foods for $3.86 Billion," *Wall Street Journal,* October 27, 2000; "Keebler Auction Is Said to Draw Interest From Kellogg, Danone," *Wall Street Journal,* October 17, 2000; "Kellogg Spurts into Lead," *BusinessWeek,* October 9, 2000; "Kellogg Agrees to Buy Kashi Co.," *Wall Street Journal,* June 30, 2000; "Kellogg Promotion Creates Corn Flakes Craze," *Wall Street Journal,* May 17, 2000; "Kellogg, Salton Form Alliance," *Wall Street Journal,* April 25, 2000; "Why the Cereal Business Is So Soggy," *Fortune,* March 6, 2000; "Kellogg's Net Surges Despite Slight Decline in Its Sales of Cereal," *Wall Street Journal,* January 28, 2000; "Granola Hits the Big Time," *BusinessWeek,* January 10, 2000; "General Mills Passes Kellogg Co. as Leader Based on Cereal Volume," *Wall Street Journal,* December 30, 1999; "Kellogg to Buy Mondo Baking," *Wall Street Journal,* December 21, 1999; "Kellogg Completes Acquisition," *Wall Street Journal,* November 24, 1999; "Kellogg Company: Ensemble Line of Foods Axed Because of Poor Results," *Wall Street Journal,* November 22, 1999; "Kellogg Posts Third-Quarter Net Loss, but Results From Operations Improved," *Wall Street Journal,* October 29, 1999; "Food Firms to Tout Health Benefits of Soybeans," *Wall Street Journal,* October 26, 1999; "Kellogg Plans to Go Vegetarian in Deal for Worthington," *Wall Street Journal,* October 4, 1999; "Breakfast King Agrees to Sell Bagel Business," *Wall Street Journal,* September 28, 1999; "Food Makers, amid Bland Performance, Are Facing Heat to Cook Up Mergers," *Wall Street Journal,* September 13, 1999; "Kellogg Profit Jumps 7.7% as Growth in Convenience Foods Offsets Cereal Woes," *Wall Street Journal,* July 30, 1999; "Kellogg Cranks Up Its Idea Machine to Grow," *Fortune,* July 5, 1999; "Kellogg May Close Part of Cereal Plant, Cut Jobs in Michigan," *Wall Street Journal,* June 18, 1999; "Outside the Box: Kellogg's New Boss, Carlos Gutierrez," *Forbes,* June 14, 1999.

2. See, for example, M. E. Porter, "From Competitive Advantage to Corporate Strategy," *Harvard Business Review* 66 (May–June 1987): 43–59. Another study by D. J. Ravenscraft and F. M. Scherer, *Mergers, Selloffs and Economic Efficiency* (Washington, D.C.: Brookings Institution, 1987), found comparable results.

3. An excellent discussion of the underpinnings of the resource-based view of the firm may be found in B. Wernerfelt, "A Resource-Based View of the Firm," *Strategic Management Journal* (September–October 1984): 171–180; J. B. Barney, "Firm Resources and the Theory of Competitive Advantage," *Journal of Management* 17 (1991): 99–120; K. R. Conner, "A Historical Comparison of Resource-Based Theory and Five Schools of Thought Within Industrial Organization Economics: Do We Have a New Theory of the Firm?" *Journal of Management* 17, no. 1 (1991): 121–154; R. M. Grant, "The Resource-Based Theory of Competitive Advantage," *California Management Review* 33, no. 3 (1991): 114–135; I. Dierickx and K. Cool, "Asset Stock Accumulation and Sustainability of Competitive Advantage," *Management Science* (December 1989): 1504–1511; R. Hall, "The Strategic Analysis of Intangible Resources," *Strategic Management Journal* 13 (1992): 135–144; R. Amit and P. Schoemaker, "Strategic Assets and Organizational Rent," *Strategic Management Journal* (January 1993): 33; M. A. Peteraf, "The Cornerstones of Competitive Advantage: A Resource-Based View," *Strategic Management Journal* (March 1993): 179; J. A. Black and K. B. Boal, "Strategic Resources: Traits, Configurations and Paths to Sustainable Competitive Advantage," *Strategic Management Journal* 15 (1994): 131–148; D. J. Collis and C. A. Montgomery, "Competing on Resources: Strategy in the 1990s," *Harvard Business Review* (July–August 1995): 118–125; J. A. Robins and M. Wiersema, "A Resource-Based Approach to the Multibusiness Firm," *Strategic Management Journal* 16 (1995): 277–299.

The development of additional theories surrounding the concept of resources has progressed markedly over the past several years. Examples of academic pieces that have furthered knowledge in this area include the following sample works: G. Ahuja and R. Katila, "Where Do Resources Come From? The Role of Idiosyncratic Situations," *Strategic Management Journal* 25, no. 8–9 (2004): 887–908; G. Ray, J. B. Barney, and W. Muhanna, "Capabilities, Business Processes, and Competitive Advantage: Choosing the Dependent Variable in Empirical Tests of the Resource-based View," *Strategic Management Journal* 25, no. 1 (2004): 23–38; S. A. Lippman and R. Rumelt, "A Bargaining Perspective on Resource Advantage," *Strategic Management Journal* 24, no. 11 (2003): 1069–1086; C. E. Helfat and M. A. Peteraf, "The Dynamic Resource-based View: Capability Lifecycles," *Strategic Management Journal* 24, no. 10 (2003): 997–1010; S. Winter, "Understanding Dynamic Capabilities," *Strategic Management Journal* 24, no. 10 (2003): 991–996; R. Makadok, "Toward a Synthesis of the Resource-Based and Dynamic Capability Views of Rent Creation," *Strategic Management Journal* 22, no. 5 (2001): 387–402; S. D. Hunt, *A General Theory of Competition: Resources, Competences, Productivity, Economic Growth* (Thousand Oaks, CA: Sage, 2000); J. G. Combs and D. J. Ketchen, "Explaining Interfirm Cooperation and Performance: Toward a Reconciliation of Predictions From the Resource-Based View and Organizational Economics," *Strategic Management Journal* 20 (1999): 768–888; T. C. Powell, "Information Technology as Competitive Advantage: The Role of Human, Business and Technology Resources," *Strategic Management Journal* 18, no. 5 (1997): 375–405; C. Oliver, "Sustainable Competitive Advantage: Combining Institutional and Resource-Based Views," *Strategic Management Journal* 18 (1997): 607–713; C. Helfat, "Know-how and Asset Complementarity and Dynamic Capability Accumulation: The Case of R&D," *Strategic Management Journal* 18 (1997): 339–360; K. R. Conner and C. K. Prahalad, "A Resource-Based Theory of the Firm: Knowledge versus Opportunism," *Organization Science* 7 (1996): 477–501; J. A. Black and K. B. Boal, "Strategic Resources: Traits, Configurations and Paths to Sustainable Competitive Advantage," *Strategic Management Journal* 15 (1994): 131–148.

An interesting debate about the validity of the resource-based view of the firm can be found in the following: R. L. Priem and J. E. Butler, "Is the Resource-Based View a Useful Perspective for Strategic Management Research?" *Academy of Management Review* 26, no. 1 (2001): 22–40; J. Barney, "Is the Resource-Based View a Useful Perspective for Strategic Management Research? Yes," *Academy of Management Review* 26, no. 1 (2001): 41–56; R. L. Priem and J. E. Butler, "Tautology in the Resource-Based View and the Implications of Externally Determined Resource Value: Further Comments," *Academy of Management Review* 26, no. 1 (2001): 57–66.

Some empirical research pieces that have utilized or tested the resource-based view include the following representative sample works: M. H. Hansen, L. T. Perry, and C. S. Reese, "A Bayesian Operationalization of the Resource-based View," *Strategic Management Journal* 25, no. 13 (2004): 1279–1295; Y. E. Spanos and S. Lioukas, "An Examination into the Causal Logic of Rent Generation: Contrasting Porter's Competitive Strategy Framework and the Resource-Based Perspective," *Strategic Management Journal* 22, no. 10 (2001): 907–934; M. A. Hitt, L. Bierman, K. Shimizu, and R. Kochhar, "Direct and Moderating Effects of Human Capital on Strategy and Performance in Professional Service Firms: A Resource-Based Perspective," *Academy of Management Journal* 44, no. 1 (2001): 13–28; P. L. Yeoh and K. Roth, "An Empirical Analysis of Sustained Advantage in the U.S. Pharmaceutical Industry: Impact of Firm Resources and Competition," *Strategic Management Journal* 20, no. 7 (1999): 637–753; E. Mosakowski, "Managerial Prescriptions Under the Resource-Based View of Strategy: The Example of Motivational Techniques," *Strategic Management Journal* 19 (1998): 1169–1182; M. V. Russo and P. A. Fouts, "A Resource-Based Perspective on Corporate Environmental Performance and Responsibility,"

Academy of Management Journal 40 (1997): 534–559; A. Madhok and S. Tallman, "Resources, Transactions and Rents: Managing Value Through Interfirm Collaborative Relationships," *Organization Science* 9, no. 3 (1998): 326–339; M. V. Russo and P. A. Fouts, "A Resource-Based Perspective on Corporate Environmental Performance and Profitability," *Academy of Management Journal* 40, no. 3 (1997): 534–559; K. M. Eisenhardt and C. B. Schoonhoven, "Resource-Based View of Strategic Alliance Formation: Strategic and Social Effects in Entrepreneurial Firms," *Organization Science* 7, no. 2 (1996): 136–150; D. Miller and J. Shamise, "The Resource-Based View of the Firm in Two Environments: The Hollywood Film Studios from 1936 to 1965," *Academy of Management Journal* 39, no. 3 (1996): 519–543; S. Maijoor and A. Van Witteloostujin, "An Empirical Test of the Resource-Based Theory: Strategic Regulation in the Dutch Audit Industry," *Strategic Management Journal* 17, no. 7 (1996): 549–569; J. Robbins and M. F. Wiersema, "A Resource-Based Approach to the Multibusiness Firm: Empirical Analysis of Portfolio Interrelationships and Corporate Financial Responsibility," *Strategic Management Journal* 16 (1995): 277–299.

4. One of the first to systematically examine this phenomenon was Alfred D. Chandler's *Strategy and Structure* (Cambridge, MA: MIT Press, 1962). His later work also examines the benefits of garnering additional economies of scale, scope, and efficiencies in A. D. Chandler, *Scale and Scope: The Dynamics of Industrial Capitalism* (Cambridge, MA: Harvard University Press, 1990). Also see R. Rumelt, *Strategy, Structure and Economic Performance* (Cambridge, MA: Harvard University Press, 1974).

5. The concept of distinctive and core competences has begun to redefine the way researchers and practitioners look at their corporate diversification strategies. Further excellent reading on this subject may be found in C. K. Prahalad and G. Hamel, "The Core Competence of the Corporation," *Harvard Business Review* (May–June 1990): 79–93; G. Hamel and C. K. Prahalad, "Corporate Imagination and Expeditionary Marketing," *Harvard Business Review* (July–August 1991): 81–92; A. A. Lado, N. G. Boyd, and P. Wright, "A Competency Model of Sustained Competitive Advantage," *Journal of Management* 18 (1992): 77–91; and G. Hamel and C. K. Prahalad, "Strategy as Stretch and Leverage," *Harvard Business Review* (March–April 1993): 75–85. Prahalad and Hamel's numerous articles on the topic can be found in their summarized book version entitled *Competing for the Future* (Boston: Harvard Business School Press, 1994).

The notion of core competence, distinctive competence, and core skills can also be found in a landmark work by K. Andrews, *The Concept of Corporate Strategy* (Homewood, IL: Dow Jones-Irwin, 1971). Core competences can also be dynamic; see, for example, D. Lei, M. A. Hitt, and R. A. Bettis, "Dynamic Core Competences Through Meta-learning and Strategic Context," *Journal of Management* 22, no. 4 (1996): 549–569. Also see D. J. Teece, G. Pisano, and A. Shuen, "Firm Capabilities, Resources and the Concept of Strategy," working paper, University of California at Berkeley, no. 90-9, 1990; G. Stalk, P. Evans, and L. E. Shulman, "Competing on Capabilities: The New Rules of Corporate Strategy," *Harvard Business Review* (March–April 1992): 57–69; and M. A. Peteraf, "The Cornerstones of Competitive Advantage: A Resource-Based View," *Strategic Management Journal* 14 (1993): 179–191. An excellent treatment of core skills and competences may be found in H. Itami, *Mobilizing Invisible Assets* (Cambridge, MA: Harvard University Press, 1987). An excellent piece that discusses and empirically tests the notion of distinctive competence is R. Makadok and G. Walker, "Identifying a Distinctive Competence: Forecasting Ability in the Money Fund Industry," *Strategic Management Journal* 21, no. 8 (2000): 853–864.

Also see the following theoretical and empirical research pieces examining different aspects of core competences and firm capabilities: D. J. Miller, "Firms' Technological Resources and the Performance Effects of Diversification: A Longitudinal Study," *Strategic Management Journal* 25, no. 11 (2004): 1097–1120;

C. Zott, "Dynamic Capabilities and the Emergence of Intraindustry Differential Firm Performance: Insights From a Simulation Study," *Strategic Management Journal* 24, no. 2 (2003): 97–126; M. Zollo and S. Winter, "Deliberate Learning and Dynamic Capabilities," *Organization Science* 13, no. 3 (2002): 339–351; S. A. Zahra and A. P. Nielsen, "Sources of Capabilities, Integration and Technology Commercialization," *Strategic Management Journal* 23, no. 5 (2002): 377–398; E. Danneels, "The Dynamics of Product Innovation and Firm Competences," *Strategic Management Journal* 23, no. 12 (2002): 1095–1122; A. Wilcox King and C. P. Zeithaml, "Competencies and Firm Performance: Examining the Causal Ambiguity Paradox," *Strategic Management Journal* 22, no. 1 (2001): 75–98; C. E. Helfat and R. S. Raubitschek, "Product Sequencing: Co-evolution of Knowledge, Capabilities, and Products," *Strategic Management Journal* 21, issues 10–11: 961–979; D. C. Galunic and S. Rodan, "Resource Recombinations in the Firm: Knowledge Structures and the Potential for Schumpeterian Innovation," *Strategic Management Journal* 19, no. 12 (1998): 1193–1201; W. J. Duncan, P. M. Ginter, and L. E. Swayne, "Competitive Advantage and Internal Organizational Assessment," *Academy of Management Executive* 12 (1998): 6–17; D. J. Teece, G. Pisano, and A. Shuen, "Dynamic Capabilities and Strategic Management," *Strategic Management Journal* 18, no. 7 (1997): 509–533; D. Lei, M. A. Hitt, and R. Bettis, "Dynamic Core Competences Through Meta-Learning and Strategic Context," *Journal of Management* 22, no. 4 (1996): 549–569; R. M. Grant, "Prospering in Dynamically Competitive Environments: Organizational Capability as Knowledge Integration," *Organization Science* 7 (1996): 375–387; J. P. Liebeskind, "Knowledge, Strategy, and the Theory of the Firm," *Strategic Management Journal* 17, Special Issue (1996): 93–107; R. Henderson and I. Cockburn, "Measuring Competence: Exploring Firm-Effects in Pharmaceutical Research," *Strategic Management Journal* 15 (1994): 63–84; G. Pisano, "Knowledge, Integration, and the Locus of Learning: An Empirical Analysis of Process Development," *Strategic Management Journal* 15, Special Issue (1994): 85–100; R. Reed and R. J. DeFillippi, "Causal Ambiguity, Barriers to Imitation, and Sustainable Competitive Advantage," *Academy of Management Review* 15 (1990): 88–102; M. A. Hitt and R. D. Ireland, "Relationships Among Corporate Level Distinctive Competencies, Diversification Strategy, Corporate Structure and Performance," *Journal of Management Studies* 23 (1986): 401–416; M. A. Hitt and R. D. Ireland, "Corporate Distinctive Competence, Strategy, Industry and Performance," *Strategic Management Journal* 6 (1985): 273–293.

6. An excellent treatment of this subject appears in K. R. Harrigan, "Formulating Vertical Integration Strategies," *Academy of Management Review* 9, no. 4 (1984): 638–652. The strengths and weaknesses of different vertical integration approaches may also be found in K. R. Harrigan, "Matching Vertical Integration Strategies to Competitive Conditions," *Strategic Management Journal* 7 (1986): 535–555; O. E. Williamson, *The Economic Institutions of Capitalism* (New York: Free Press, 1985); S. Balakrishnan and B. Wernerfelt, "Technical Change, Competition and Vertical Integration," *Strategic Management Journal* 7 (1986): 347–359; R. E. Caves and R. M. Bradbury, "The Empirical Determinants of Vertical Integration," *Journal of Economic Behavior and Organization* 9 (1988): 265–279; M. B. Lieberman, "Determinants of Vertical Integration: An Empirical Test," *Journal of Industrial Economics* 39 (1991): 451–466. Also see R. G. Buzzell, "Is Vertical Integration Profitable?" *Harvard Business Review* (January–February 1983): 92–102; M. E. McGrath and R. W. Hoole, "Manufacturing's New Economies of Scale," *Harvard Business Review* (May–June 1992): 94–103, to see how technological changes can make different forms of manufacturing-based integration possible; as well as R. Normann and R. Ramirez, "From Value Chain to Value Constellation: Designing Interactive Strategy," *Harvard Business Review* (July–August 1993): 65–77.

The relationship between vertical integration and external dependence is discussed by J. M. Pennings, D. C. Hambrick, and I. C. MacMillan in "Interorganizational

Dependence and Forward Integration," *Organization Studies* 5 (1984): 307–326. An outstanding overview of the relationship between vertical integration and internal firm costs is R. D'Aveni and D. J. Ravenscraft, "Economies of Integration versus Bureaucracy Costs: Does Vertical Integration Improve Performance?" *Academy of Management Journal* 37, no. 5 (1994): 1167–1206; G. Walker and D. Weber, "Supplier Competition, Uncertainty, and Make-or-Buy Decisions," *Academy of Management Journal* 30 (1987): 589–596; G. Walker, "Strategic Sourcing, Vertical Integration, and Transaction Costs," *Interfaces* 18, no. 3 (1988): 62–73; R. J. Maddigan and J. K. Zaima, "The Profitability of Vertical Integration," *Managerial and Decision Economics* 6 (1985): 178–179; A. R. Burgess, "Vertical Integration in Pharmaceuticals: The Concept and Its Measurement," *Long Range Planning* 16, no. 4 (1983): 55–60.

　　　　Also see S. White, "Competition, Capabilities, and the Make, Buy, or Ally Decisions of Chinese State-Owned Firms," *Academy of Management Journal* 43, no. 3 (2000): 324–341; L. Poppo and T. Zenger, "Testing Alternative Theories of the Firm: Transaction Cost, Knowledge-Based, and Measurement Explanations for Make-or-Buy Decisions in Information Services," *Strategic Management Journal* 19 (1998): 853–877; T. Robertson and H. Gatignon, "Technology Development Mode: A Transaction Cost Explanation," *Strategic Management Journal* 18 (1997): 515–531.

7. During the 1980s and 1990s, a plethora of research literature has covered the diversification issue. Excellent reviews can be found in R. A. Johnson, "Antecedents and Outcomes of Corporate Refocusing," *Journal of Management* 22 (1996): 437–481; R. E. Hoskisson and M. A. Hitt, "Antecedents and Performance Outcomes of Diversification: A Review and Critique of Theoretical Perspectives," *Journal of Management* 16, no. 2 (1990): 461–509; R. E. Hoskisson, M. A. Hitt, and C. W. L. Hill, "Managerial Risk Taking in Diversified Firms: An Evolutionary Perspective," *Organization Science* 2 (1991): 296–314; V. Ramanujam and P. Varadarajan, "Research on Corporate Diversification: A Synthesis," *Strategic Management Journal* 10 (1989): 523–552. A meta-analysis that examines the diversification–performance relationship is L. E. Palich, L. B. Cardinal, and C. Miller, "Curvilinearity in the Diversification-Performance Linkage: An Examination of Over Three Decades of Research," *Strategic Management Journal* 21, no 2 (2000): 155–174.

　　　　The strategic management research literature is replete with studies examining the impact of diversification on corporate performance and innovation. Some representative works include the following: M. Zollo and H. Singh, "Deliberate Learning in Corporate Acquisitions: Post-acquisition Strategies and Integration Capability in U.S. Bank Mergers," *Strategic Management Journal* 25, no. 13 (2004): 1233–1256; H. Kim, R. E. Hoskisson, and W. P. Wan, "Power Dependence, Diversification Strategy, and Performance in Keiretsu Member Firms," *Strategic Management Journal* 25, no. 7 (2004): 613–636; W. P. Wan and R. E. Hoskisson, "Home Country Environments, Corporate Diversification Strategies, and Firm Performance," *Academy of Management Journal* 46, no. 1 (2003): 27–45; M. L. Hayward, "When Do Firms Learn From Their Acquisition Experience?" *Strategic Management Journal* 23, no. 1 (2002): 21–39; M. Lubatkin, W. S. Schulze, A. Mainkar, and R. W. Cotterill, "Ecological Investigation of Firm-Effects in Horizontal Mergers," *Strategic Management Journal* 22, no. 4 (2001): 335–358; G. Ahuja and R. Katila, "Technological Acquisitions and the Innovation Performance of Acquiring Firms: A Longitudinal Study," *Strategic Management Journal* 22, no. 3 (2001): 197–220; J. M. Geringer, S. Tallman, and D. M. Olsen, "Product and International Diversification Among Japanese Firms," *Strategic Management Journal* 21, no. 1 (2000): 51–80; L. Capron, "The Long-Term Performance of Horizontal Acquisitions," *Strategic Management Journal* 20, no. 11 (1999): 987–1018; Y. Amihud and B. Lev, "Does Corporate Ownership Structure Affect Its Strategy Towards Diversification?" *Strategic Management Journal* 20, no. 11 (1999): 1063–1070; D. J. Denis, D. K. Denis, and A. Sarin, "Agency Theory and the Influence of Equity Ownership Structure on

Corporate Diversification Strategies," *Strategic Management Journal* 20, no. 11 (1999): 1071–1076; M. A. Hitt, R. E. Hoskisson, and H. Kim, "International Diversification: Effects on Innovation and Firm Performance in Product-Diversified Firms," *Academy of Management Journal* 40, no. 4 (1997): 767–798; M. A. Hitt, R. E. Hoskisson, R. A. Johnson, and D. D. Moesel, "The Market for Corporate Control and Firm Innovation," *Academy of Management Journal* 39, no. 5 (1996): 1084–1119; R. E. Hoskisson, M. A. Hitt, and C. W. L. Hill, "Managerial Incentives and Investment in R&D in Large Multiproduct Firms," *Organization Science* 4 (1993): 325–341; M. A. Hitt, R. E. Hoskisson, R. D. Ireland, and J. S. Harrison, "The Effects of Acquisitions on R&D Inputs and Outputs," *Academy of Management Journal* 34 (1991): 693–706; P. G. Simmonds, "The Combined Diversification Breadth and Mode Dimensions and the Performance of Large Diversified Firms," *Strategic Management Journal* 11 (1990): 399–410.

8. One of the earliest to use these terms was R. Rumelt, *Strategy, Structure and Economic Performance* (Cambridge, MA: Harvard University Press, 1974). A vast literature has ensued over the past twenty years examining the impact of different related and unrelated diversification strategies on performance. Some of the representative works include R. A. Bettis, "Performance Differences in Related and Unrelated Diversified Firms," *Strategic Management Journal* 2 (1981): 406–415; B. Baysinger and R. E. Hoskisson, "Diversification Strategy and R&D Intensity in Large Multiproduct Firms," *Academy of Management Journal* 32 (1989): 310–332; A. Lemelin, "Relatedness in the Patterns of Interindustry Diversification," *Review of Economics and Statistics* 64 (1982): 646–657; K. Palepu, "Diversification Strategy, Profit Performance and the Entropy Measure," *Strategic Management Journal* 6 (1985): 239–255; C. K. Prahalad and R. A. Bettis, "The Dominant Logic: A New Linkage between Diversity and Performance," *Strategic Management Journal* 7 (1986): 485–501; C. A. Montgomery, "Product-Market Diversification and Market Power," *Academy of Management Journal* 28 (1985): 789–798; M. Lubatkin and R. C. Rodgers, "Diversification, Systematic Risk and Shareholder Return: A Capital Market Extension of Rumelt's 1974 Study," *Academy of Management Journal* 33 (1989): 454–465; H. Singh and C. A. Montgomery, "Corporate Acquisition Strategies and Economic Performance," *Strategic Management Journal* 8 (1987): 377–386; D. J. Teece, R. Rumelt, G. Dosi, and S. Winter, "Understanding Corporate Coherence: Theory and Evidence," working paper, University of California at Berkeley, July 1992; P. R. Nayyar, "On the Measurement of Corporate Diversification Strategy: Evidence From Large U.S. Service Firms," *Strategic Management Journal* 13, no. 3 (1992): 219–235; R. E. Hoskisson and R. A. Johnson, "Corporate Restructuring and Strategic Change: The Effect on Diversification Strategy and R&D Intensity," *Strategic Management Journal* 13 (1992): 625–634; C. W. L. Hill, M. A. Hitt, and R. E. Hoskisson, "Cooperative versus Competitive Structures in Related and Unrelated Diversified Firms," *Organization Science* 3 (1992): 501–521; R. E. Hoskisson, M. A. Hitt, R. A. Johnson, and D. Moesel, "Construct Validity of an Objective (Entropy) Categorical Measure of Diversification Strategy," *Strategic Management Journal* 14 (1993): 215–235; C. A. Montgomery, "Corporate Diversification," *Journal of Economic Perspectives* 8 (1994): 623–632; R. E. Hoskisson, R. A. Johnson, and D. D. Moesel, "Corporate Divestiture Intensity in Restructuring Firms: Effects of Governance, Strategy, and Performance," *Academy of Management Journal* 37 (1994): 1207–1251; P. J. Lane, A. A. Cannella, Jr., M. H. Lubatkin, "Agency Problems as Antecedents to Unrelated Mergers and Diversification: Amihud and Lev Reconsidered," *Strategic Management Journal* 19, no. 7 (1998): 555–578; M. Farjoun, "The Independent and Joint Effects of the Skill and Physical Bases of Relatedness in Diversification," *Strategic Management Journal* 19, no. 7 (1998): 611–630; R. Kochhar and M. A. Hitt, "Linking Corporate Strategy to Capital Structure: Diversification Strategy, Type, and Source of Financing," *Strategic Management Journal* 19, no. 6 (1988): 601–610; D. D. Bergh and M. W. Lawless,

"Portfolio Restructuring and Limits to Hierarchical Governance: The Effects of Environmental Uncertainty and Diversification Strategy," *Organization Science* 9, no. 1 (1998): 87–102; J. E. Bethel and J. P. Liebeskind, "Diversification and the Legal Organization of the Firm," *Organization Science* 9, no. 1 (1998): 49–67.

Recent works that continue to investigate the concept of related diversification include: C. E. Helfat and K. M. Eisenhardt, "Inter-temporal Economies of Scope, Organizational Modularity, and the Dynamics of Diversification," *Strategic Management Journal* 25, no. 13 (2004): 1217–1232; C. Park, "Prior Performance Characteristics of Related and Unrelated Acquirers," *Strategic Management Journal* 24, no. 5 (2003): 471–480; J. A. Robins and M. F. Wiersema, "The Measurement of Corporate Portfolio Strategy: Analysis of the Content Validity of Related Diversification Indexes," *Strategic Management Journal* 24, no. 1 (2003): 39–60; J. Fan and L. Lang, "The Measurement of Relatedness: An Application to Corporate Diversification," *Journal of Business* 73, no. 4 (2000): 629–660.

9. See, for example, "Intel Unleashes Its Internal Attila," *Fortune,* October 15 (2001): 168–184; "Intel: Can Craig Barrett Reverse the Slide?" *BusinessWeek,* October 15 (2001): 80–90.

10. Data and facts were adapted from the following sources: "One Word of Advice: Now It's Corn," *Wall Street Journal,* October 12, 2004, p. B1; "DuPont Co.: Maxygen Plant-Sciences Unit to Be Bought for $64 Million," *Wall Street Journal,* June 4, 2004, p. B4; "DuPont to Sell Textiles Unit to Koch," *Wall Street Journal,* November 2, 2003, p. A6; "Developments to Watch: Up From the Farm—and the Seas," *BusinessWeek,* October 27, 2003, p. 82; "Is a Low-Fiber DuPont More Appetizing?" *BusinessWeek,* September 8, 2003, p. 118; "Tree Huggers, Soy Lovers and Profits," *Fortune,* June 23, 2003, p. 98; "The Greenhouse Effect," *Forbes,* February 3, 2003, pp. 54–60; "DuPont Tries to Unclog a Pipeline," *BusinessWeek,* January 27, 2003, p. 103; "DuPont Cajoles Independent Units to Talk to One Another," *Wall Street Journal,* February 5, 2002, p. B4; "Bristol-Myers Reaches Agreement to Buy DuPont Drug Business for $7.8 Billion," *Wall Street Journal,* June 8, 2001; "DuPont Plans Sale of Unit Developing Pharmaceuticals," *Wall Street Journal,* December 15, 2000; "DuPont Co.: Apparel, Fiber Businesses to Be Combined into Unit," *Wall Street Journal,* October 31, 2000; "Flat DuPont Needs to Find Right Mix of Businesses," *Wall Street Journal,* May 8, 2000; "DuPont Returns to More-Reliable Chemical Business—Plans for Biotech, Drug Divisions Fizzle as Mergers Change Landscape," *Wall Street Journal,* February 23, 2000; "Teijin to Form a Venture to Produce Polyester Film," *Wall Street Journal,* February 4, 1999; "DuPont's Pioneer Hi-Bred Stake," *Wall Street Journal,* September 19, 1997; "DuPont to Buy Ralston-Purina Unit in Building Dirt-to-Dinner Biotech Line," *Wall Street Journal,* August 25, 1997, p. A8.

11. A solid discussion of transaction costs in corporate strategy may be found in G. R. Jones and C. W. L. Hill, "Transaction Cost Analysis of Strategy-Structure Choice," *Strategic Management Journal* 9 (1988): 159–172.

12. See "Merck's Man in the Hot Seat," *Fortune,* February 23, 2004, pp. 111–114; "Merck Plans to Spin Off Medco Unit," *Wall Street Journal,* April 23, 2003, p. A5; "Merck to Shed Medco, Its Drug-Benefits Unit, in Bid to Boost Stock," *Wall Street Journal,* January 22, 2002, pp. A1, A8; "Lilly Rides a Mood Elevator," *BusinessWeek,* November 11, 1996, p. 63.

13. See "Merger to Leave Much Room for Chevron Texaco to Grow," *Wall Street Journal,* October 9, 2001, p. B14.

14. See "How Sharp Stays on the Cutting Edge," *BusinessWeek,* October 18, 2004, p. 56.

15. See P&G's Gillette Edge: The Playbook It Honed at Wal-Mart," *Wall Street Journal,* January 31, 2005, pp. A1, A12.

16. See, for example, "SBC Reaches Tentative Pact To Acquire AT&T for $16 Billion," Wall Street Journal, January 31, 2005, pp. A1, A12; "SBC Making Some Connections," *Investor's Business Daily,* April 26, 2001, p. A5.

17. Despite their steadily declining numbers, interest in conglomerates has taken a new turn. See, for example, "A New Mix: Conglomerates Make a Surprising Comeback—with a '90s Twist," *Wall Street Journal,* March 1, 1994, pp. A1, A6; J. R. Williams, B. L. Paez, and L. Sanders, "Conglomerates Revisited," *Strategic Management Journal* 9, no. 5 (1988): 403–414.

    An interesting academic study that has examined the decline of conglomerate-type firms is D. D. Bergh, "Predicting Divestiture of Unrelated Acquisitions: An Integrative Model of Ex Ante Conditions," *Strategic Management Journal* 18, no. 9 (1997): 715–731; G. F. Davis, K. A. Diekmann, and C. H. Tinsley, "The Decline and Fall of the Conglomerate Firm in the 1980s: The Deinstitutionalization of an Organization Form," *American Sociological Review* 59 (1991): 547–570. One of the first pieces to examine the nature of conglomerate firms is Y. Amihud and B. Lev, "Risk Reduction as a Managerial Motive for Conglomerate Mergers," *Bell Journal of Economics* 12 (1981): 605–617. Also see J. R. Williams, B. Paez, and L. Sanders, "Conglomerates Revisited," *Strategic Management Journal* 9 (1988): 404–414.

    Also see B. Villalonga, "Diversification Discount or Premium? New Evidence From the Business Information Tracking Series," *Journal of Finance* 59 (2004): 479–506; V. Maksimovic and G. Phillips, "Do Conglomerate Firms Allocate Resources Inefficiently Across Industries?" *Journal of Finance* 57 (2002): 721–767; R. Rajan, H. Servaes, and L. Zingales, "The Cost of Diversity: The Diversification Discount and Inefficient Investment," *Journal of Finance* 55, no. 1 (2000): 35–80.

18. "Acquiring by the Book," *CFO* (February 1999): 25–26; "Textron Gives Henkel No. 2 Job, Putting Him in Line for CEO Post," *Wall Street Journal,* July 23, 1998, p. B10.

19. See, for example, M. C. Jensen and R. C. Ruback, "The Market for Corporate Control: The Scientific Evidence," *Journal of Financial Economics* (April 1983): 7–23.

20. See "Newport News Says It Will Reconsider Bid From Northrop," *Wall Street Journal,* October 8, 2001, p. A4.

21. Data adapted from "Adding Up All of Tenneco's Many Parts," *Wall Street Journal,* August 9, 1991, p. A4; "Tenneco Restructuring Is Over, but Doubts Remain," *Wall Street Journal,* September 8, 1992, p. B4; "Tenneco Plans to Sell 35% of Case Unit to Public, on Revival in Agriculture," *Wall Street Journal,* April 27, 1994, p. A2; "Tenneco Packaging Subsidiary Weighs Making Acquisitions as Big as $1 Billion," *Wall Street Journal,* October 11, 1994, p. B10; "Tenneco Plans to Divide Operations; As Many as Three Concerns to Result," *Wall Street Journal,* July 22, 1998, p. A6.

22. See "Atos to Acquire Schlumberger Unit," *Wall Street Journal,* September 23, 2003, p. B5; "Schlumberger to Find Out If Oil and High Tech Mix," *Wall Street Journal,* February 15, 2001, p. B4.

23. See "IBM Expands Technology R&D," *Wall Street Journal,* January 6, 2005, p. A13.

24. See "Branding: Five New Lessons," *Business Week,* February 14, 2005, pp. 26–28; "When Beauty Met Sweaty," *Wall Street Journal,* January 31, 2005, pp. B1, B7; "Deal Brings 'Proctoids' to 'Plywood Ranch,'" *Wall Street Journal,* January 31, 2005, pp. B1, B7; "Warm and Fuzzy Won't Save Procter & Gamble," *Business Week,* June 26, 2000; "After Gobbling Up Iams, P&G Finds People Who Have Bones to Pick," *Wall Street Journal,* June 14, 2000; "P&G Is Out to Fetch Distribution Gains for Iams Pet Food," *Wall Street Journal,* January 6, 2000, p. B4; "Stirring Giant: P&G Is on the Move," *Wall Street Journal,* January 24, 2000; "P&G to Buy Iams: Will Pet-Food Fight Follow?" *Wall Street Journal,* August 12, 1999.

25. See "Bayer Enters Talks to Acquire Roche's Consumer-Drug Line," *Wall Street Journal,* June 29, 2004, p. B3.

26. See "The Unlikely Mogul," *Fortune,* September 29, 2003, pp. 82–90; "Will GE Be Enjoying the Movie?" *Wall Street Journal,* September 3, 2003, pp. C1, C3.

27. See "The Unsung CEO," *Business Week,* October 25, 2004, pp. 74–84; "United Technologies Looks to Lift Image, Stock," *Wall Street Journal,* October 14, 2003, pp. C1, C3; "The Thinker: The Next Big Challenge for United Technologies,"

Forbes, March 3, 2003, p. 62; "United Technologies' Otis, Carrier Units Gain Importance amid Aviation Crisis," *Wall Street Journal,* September 28, 2001, p. B6.

28. See "What Makes Cisco Run," *Forbes,* July 26, 2004, pp. 66–74.

29. See "Medtronic to Buy MiniMed and Medical Research," *Wall Street Journal,* May 31, 2001, pp. A3, A4.

30. A variety of data sources were used for the 3M Corporation, including the following: "3M Co.: FDA Approves Aldara Cream for Treatment of Skin Cancer," *Wall Street Journal,* July 16, 2004, p. A6; "3M's Rising Star," *Business Week,* April 12, 2004, pp. 60–74; "Prescription for Growth," *Forbes,* February 17, 2003, pp. 65–66; "3M + General Electric = ?," *Fortune,* August 12, 2002, p. 127; "3M: A Lab for Growth," *Business Week,* January 21, 2002, pp. 50–51; "At Minnesota Mining and Manufacturing, Hope Grows for a Payoff in Health Care," *Wall Street Journal,* December 10, 2001, p. B7B; "Eli Lilly, 3M Sign Deal on Herpes Treatment in Advanced Trials Phase," *Wall Street Journal,* October 9, 2001; "3M Cuts Back Earnings Forecast Again, Cites Slow Growth Abroad," *Wall Street Journal,* July 3, 2001, p. A3; "Spreading the GE Gospel—As 3M Chief, McNerney Wastes No Time," *Wall Street Journal,* June 5, 2001, pp. A1, A6; "McNerney: A Short Jump From GE to 3M," *Business Week,* December 18, 2000; "3M's Next Chief Plans to Fortify Results with Discipline He Learned at GE," *Wall Street Journal,* December 6, 2000; "Minnesota Mining & Catchall: 3M Has Sexy Technology and Sleepy Earnings," *Forbes,* September 4, 2000.

   In addition, An excellent overview of how 3M currently formulates strategies at the business unit level is found in G. Shaw, R. Brown, and P. Bromiley, "How 3M Is Rewriting Business Planning," *Harvard Business Review* 76, no. 3 (May–June 1998): 41–50.

31. See, for example, "SmithKline Beecham Enters Genetic-Diagnostics Race," *Wall Street Journal,* September 3, 1997, p. B4; "Biotech Companies Abandon Go-It-Alone Approach," *Wall Street Journal,* November 21, 1995, p. B4.

32. See "Growing Against the Grain," *Fortune,* May 23, 2004, pp. 144–156; "Drug Industry's Big Push into Technology Falls Short," *Wall Street Journal,* February 24, 2004, pp. A1, A8; "How Genentech Got It," *Fortune,* June 9, 2003, pp. 81–88; "Biotech's Billion Dollar Breakthrough," *Fortune,* May 26, 2003, pp. 96–101; "The $10 Billion Pill," *Fortune,* January 20, 2003, pp. 58–68;

33. See "Citi: A Whole New Playbook," *Business Week,* February 14, 2005, pp. 72–75.

34. See "At Universal Pictures, a Tight-Knit Ensemble Awaits NBC," *Wall Street Journal,* September 5, 2003, pp. B1, B4; "Behind GE's Interest in Vivendi: A Changing Media Landscape," August 29, 2003, pp. A1, A5.

35. See "Hamburger Hell," *Business Week,* March 3, 2003, pp. 104–107.

36. See "Rivals Samsung, Sony Unit in Flat-Screen TV Venture," *Wall Street Journal,* July 15, 2004, p. B1.

37. "See "Northrop's Heavy Artillery," *Business Week,* March 8, 2004, pp. 52–54; "We See You, Saddam," *Forbes,* January 6, 2003, pp. 102–107.

38. See, for example, "Sony and NEC, Slow to Eliminate Weak Lines, Cut Profit Forecasts," *Wall Street Journal,* October 1, 2001, p. A18. Also see "Japanese Chip Makers End Love Affair with the D-RAM," *Financial Times,* August 13, 2001, p. 22; "Turnaround at Mitsubishi Motors Could Prove Difficult," *Wall Street Journal,* March 6, 2001, p. A14; "How Japan's Toshiba Got Its Focus Back," *Wall Street Journal,* December 28, 2000, A6, A7.

39. See, for example, "Content Management is Top Goal of IBM," *Wall Street Journal,* October 1, 2001, p. B4; "IBM Plans Energy-Efficient Chip to Counter High Electricity Costs," *Wall Street Journal,* October 1, 2001, p. B4.

40. See "Under Viacom, Comedy Central Finds Its Groove," *Wall Street Journal,* June 23, 2004, pp. B1, B10; "As Viacom Ponders a Breakup, Industry Rethinks Old Notions," *Wall Street Journal,* March 17, 2005, pp. A1, A9; "Paramount's New Mantra: Risk Is Healthy," *Wall Street Journal,* March 18, 2004, pp. B1, B2; "Viacom Nearing Decision

on Divesting Blockbuster," *Wall Street Journal,* December 2, 2003, pp. A1, A15; "After Living on Rented Time, Blockbuster Plunges into Sales," *Wall Street Journal,* February 13, 2003, pp. A1, A8.

41. See, for example, "More and More, Mergers of 90's Are Becoming Today's Spinoffs," *Wall Street Journal,* February 6, 2002, pp. C1, C7; "Big Mergers of '90s Prove Disappointing to Shareholders," *Wall Street Journal,* October 30, 2000, pp. C1, C21.

42. See "GE Breaks the Mold to Spur Innovation," *Business Week,* April 26, 2004, pp. 88–89; "Will Jeff Immelt's New Push Pay Off for GE?" *Business Week,* October 13, 2003, pp. 94–98; "GE Makes Overture to Buy Amersham," *Wall Street Journal,* October 9, 2003, pp. A3, A14; "GE's Deal for Instrumentarium Finally Is Cleared by EU Panel," *Wall Street Journal,* September 3, 2003, p. A8; "Merger Machine: Can GE Keep Growing Through Deals?" *Wall Street Journal,* July 31, 2001, pp. C1, C2.

43. See "Intel Plans to Pull Back Diversification Effort," *Wall Street Journal,* October 22, 2001, p. B5.

44. A number of studies have addressed the issue of restructuring and the impact on competitive advantage. Some of the following works are representative of the recent studies examining this topic: L. Capron, W. Mitchell, and A Swaminathan, "Asset Divestiture Following Horizontal Acquisitions: A Dynamic View," *Strategic Management Journal* 22, no. 9 (2001): 817–844; S. Chang and H. Singh, "The Impact of Modes of Entry and Resource Fit on Modes of Exit by Multibusiness Firms," *Strategic Management Journal* 20, no. 11 (1999): 1019–1036; R. L. DeWitt, "Firm, Industry, and Strategy Influences on Choice of Downsizing Approach," *Strategic Management Journal* 19, no. 1 (1998): 59–80; J. L. Stimpert and I. M. Duhaime, "Seeing the Big Picture: The Influence of Industry, Diversification, and Business Strategy on Performance," *Academy of Management Journal* 40, no. 3 (1997): 560–583; S. J. Chang, "An Evolutionary Perspective on Diversification and Corporate Restructuring: Entry, Exit, and Economic Performance During 1981–1989," *Strategic Management Journal* 17, no. 11 (1996): 587–611; C. C. Markides, "Diversification, Restructuring and Economic Performance," *Strategic Management Journal* 16, no. 2 (1995): 101–118; M. A. Hitt, B. W. Keats, H. F. Harback, and R. D. Nixon, "Rightsizing: Building and Maintaining Strategic Leadership and Long-Term Competitiveness," *Organizational Dynamics* 23, no. 2 (1994): 18–32; R. E. Hoskisson, R. A. Johnson, and D. D. Moesel, "Corporate Divestiture Intensity in Restructuring Firms: Effects of Governance, Strategy and Performance," *Academy of Management Journal* 37, no. 5 (1994): 1207–1251; E. H. Bowman and H. Singh, "Corporate Restructuring: Reconfiguring the Firm," *Strategic Management Journal* 14, Special Issue (1993): 5–14; P. A. Gibbes, "Determinants of Corporate Restructuring: The Relative Importance of Corporate Governance, Takeover Threat and Free Cash Flow," *Strategic Management Journal* 14, Special Issue (1993): 51–68; J. E. Bethel and J. Liebeskind, "The Effects of Ownership Structure on Corporate Restructuring," *Strategic Management Journal* 14, Special Issue (1993): 15–32; M. A. Hitt and R. E. Hoskisson, "Strategic Competitiveness," in *Applied Business Strategy,* ed. L. Foster (Greenwich, CT: JAI, 1991), 1–36; F. R. Lichtenberg, "Industrial De-Diversification and Its Consequences for Productivity," *Journal of Economic Behavior and Organization* 18 (1992): 427–438; H. O'Neill, "Turnaround and Recovery: What Strategy Do You Need?" *Long Range Planning* 19, no. 1 (1986): 80–88; M. A. Hitt and B. W. Keats, "Strategic Leadership and Restructuring: A Reciprocal Interdependence," in *Strategic Leadership: A Multiorganization-Level Perspective,* eds. R. Phillips and J. G. Hunt (New York: Quorum, 1992), 45–61.

45. See, for example, "WellPoint Agrees to Buy RightChoice for Cash, Stock, Totaling $1.3 Billion," *Wall Street Journal,* October 19, 2001, p. B8.

46. See "Behind Aetna's Turnaround: Small Steps to Pare Cost of Care," *Wall Street Journal,* August 13, 2004, pp. A1, A6; "The Volcano Behind Aetna," *Business Week,* June 9, 2003, pp. 98–102.

47. See "P&G: Teaching an Old Dog New Tricks," *Fortune,* May 31, 2004, pp. 167–184; "Kid Nabbing," *Forbes,* February 2, 2004, pp. 84–89; "P&G: New and Improved," *Business Week,* July 7, 2003, pp. 52–63; "Aisle 9 to Saks: P&G Brings Its $130 Skin Treatment to U.S.," *Wall Street Journal,* March 12, 2004, pp. B1, B3; "Prilosec OTC: P&G's Blitz Is New Drug Foray," *Wall Street Journal,* September 12, 2003, pp. B1, B4; "It's a Natural: P&G Sells Jif to J. M. Smucker," *Wall Street Journal,* October 11, 2001, pp. B1, B12.

48. See, for example, "A Touch of Indigestion," *Business Week,* March 4, 2002, pp. 66–68; "PepsiCo Inc. Gains in Soda Market as Coca-Cola's Shares and Sales Slip," *Wall Street Journal,* March 1, 2002, p. B5; "Pepsi Names Chief of New Bottling Unit," *Wall Street Journal,* September 25, 1998, p. A3; "Revamped PepsiCo Still Needs to Conquer Wall Street," *Wall Street Journal,* July 27, 1998, p. B3; "PepsiCo Looks at a Spinoff for Bottling," *Wall Street Journal,* July 24, 1998, p. A3.

49. See "H-P's Agilent Spinoff Greeted Warmly on Wall Street, as Stock Climbs 41%," *Wall Street Journal,* November 19, 1999; "The Secret's Out: It's Agilent Technologies," *Semiconductor International* 34 (1999); "Old H-P Unit Adjusts to Life with New Name," *Wall Street Journal,* July 29, 1999.

50. See "One-Stop Shopping Strategy Claims a High-Profile Victim, Leaving Doubts About Its Functionality," *Wall Street Journal,* February 10, 2005, p. A8; "Why Carly's Big Bet Is Failing," *Fortune,* February 7, 2005, pp. 50–64.

Global Strategy: Harnessing New Markets

What you will learn

- *Why companies need to develop strategies to expand across national borders*

- *The key environmental factors that promote the need to expand into overseas markets*

- *The two basic strategies used for expanding overseas: global strategy and multidomestic strategy*

- *Balancing the benefits and costs of overseas expansion*

- *How companies can continue to grow by becoming global players*

Building Global Capabilities at Nokia[1]

One of the world's leading providers of digital wireless phones, Nokia has made great strides toward becoming a household name in the United States and around the world. Based in Helsinki, Finland, Nokia has become extremely adept at designing and manufacturing an ever-expanding variety of mobile phones that have set the standard for performance, design, versatility, and looks in global markets. Considered by many analysts to be the technology leader in developing current and next-generation digital phone and mobile Internet networks, Nokia is gearing itself up to become a potent force in other businesses as well, including software, color display screens, Internet browsers, and much of the hardware needed to deploy "broadband" telecommunications networks. By the end of 2003, Nokia generated over $37 billion in revenues and over $1.7 billion in profits for an industry that is now attracting dozens of rivals from the United States, the Far East, and even from parts of the developing world. Yet, Nokia's stunning growth and performance comes at a time when the market for wireless phones appears to be fast maturing. As Nokia can no longer count on double-digit sales gains from selling wireless phones, the company must now consider new strategies and actions to learn, build, and renew its sources of competitive advantage—particularly in the wake of new competitors from China, South Korea, and elsewhere. Of the company's revenues, 56 percent came from Europe and Africa, 21 percent from North and South America, and 23 percent were from Asia, as of early 2004.

Although Nokia is now investing in new products and technologies to strengthen itself for future competition, the company has been remarkably able to reinvent itself time and again. Started in 1966 as a diversified Finnish conglomerate, Nokia originally managed such diverse businesses as forestry products, paper goods, rubber, and even color television sets. Under CEO Jorma Ollila, who took over the top job in 1992, Nokia made a concerted decision to focus exclusively on wireless phones, which Ollila and his management team believed had a bright future. The company divested itself of all its remaining businesses and proceeded to invest in state-of-the-art manufacturing plants that could churn out brand-new phones twenty-four hours a day, six days a week. Compared to such technology giants as Motorola and Siemens, Nokia believes that it should design and build its own factories to become the lowest-cost producer in the world. By controlling its own production, Nokia can speed up the process in which a newly designed phone can be ready for manufacture. For other companies that choose to outsource most of their phone production, it can take upwards of a month to prepare a production line for a new model. By contrast, at one of Nokia's most advanced factories in Finland, the company only needs four days, not five weeks, to ramp up to full production of a new phone model.

As Nokia begins to manufacture phones in different parts of the world, the company has also taken significant steps to work more closely with its key suppliers. For example, at a new plant under construction in China, Nokia is working with IBM, Philips Electronics, Sanyo, and other companies to build next-generation phones using a just-in-time manufacturing system. Under ideal conditions, Nokia is hoping to build phones for the huge Chinese market with almost no inventory in the production system. As demand for one particular phone model surges, the factory will be able to reconfigure its production line quickly to take advantage of growing sales. When demand slows down, the factory will also be able to retool itself in preparation for another line of phone products under development. By working closely with suppliers, Nokia also wants to ensure that its partners do not get caught with large amounts of inventory that they cannot easily sell. To make this vision a reality, Nokia is relying on its key suppliers for real-time information about the production status and unit cost of the phone's components and parts. Likewise, Nokia will instantaneously inform its suppliers of emerging trends and changes in market demand based on the latest retail sales results. In this way, both Nokia and its suppliers will be less likely to find themselves with large inventories of components or phones that do not sell well.

Nokia's management realizes that as new competitors enter the digital phone market (for example, Sony-Ericsson, Samsung, LG Electronics, Kyocera, China's TCL and Ningbo Bird), it will face growing price pressures that will lower its profit margins. To counter this trend, Nokia is aiming to build its brand image around the world, as well as construct new low-cost factories that can help the company survive potentially severe price wars. To promote the style and quality of Nokia's phones, the company is also promoting its leading-edge digital phone as a new fashion accessory. Senior management hopes that as phones become more popular around the world, new customers will buy Nokia phones to make a fashion statement as much as to place a phone call. In fact, by some accounts, Nokia was sixth in the top ten most valuable brands as surveyed in 2003.

To sustain the high growth of digital phones, Nokia has invested heavily in developing new models using cutting-edge designs and the latest in color screen technologies. In 2004 alone, Nokia is expected to have introduced over forty new models, with an emphasis on those that perform multiple functions. Some of these phones, such as the 6250 and 7200 series, will have a bigger display, built-in video recorder, and even an MP3 music player. Many of today's leading-edge cell phones have vastly increased capability to perform multiple functions, and the trend will likely continue as new features are built into future generations of technology. Almost all of these phones will allow users to access the Internet as well. Yet, as new competitors become more efficient in developing their own lines of advanced wireless phones, Nokia believes that it must create new markets for its innovations. Perhaps the boldest new line of products coming from Nokia in late 2003 was the N-Gage handheld device. Designed to include a full-color screen, FM radio, MP3 player, and a versatile phone, the N-Gage is Nokia's first foray into the world of online video gaming. Users are able to download games into their N-Gage devices through removable memory cards that are sold in stores. Nokia is working with such well-known game publishers as Activision, Eidos, Sega, Taito, and THQ to design games for the N-Gage. In the future, Nokia is expected to design newer generations of N-Gage devices that will allow users to download games over the airwaves as new transmission equipment becomes available to do so. To strengthen its influence in the fast-evolving arena of digital music players, Nokia in February 2005 joined forces with software giant Microsoft to use a version of Windows Media Player in future Nokia phones. By working together around a common digital music player technology, both Nokia and Microsoft hope to develop phones that will share features with the wildly popular and ubiquitous iPod designed by Apple Computer.

Yet, despite the growing ubiquity of Nokia's digital phones around the world, there is another side to the Finnish giant. Nokia's broadest technology-based initiative is its push toward 3G networks. 3G refers to "third generation," which describes the technology that allows phones to carry voice, data, text, video, and other information either in real-time or as stored information. Nokia is also a major player in developing and installing the telecom infrastructure that is the backbone of next-generation wireless voice, video, and Internet transmission. This is the equipment that Internet service providers (ISPs) deploy to enable customers to surf the web and send pictures from their digital phones. The company is creating a comprehensive new set of technical standards that aims to provide wireless Internet and communications access to any user at any time, in any place around the world. These initiatives are also expected to help Nokia sell even more advanced versions of its N-Gage devices that will allow two or more game players to compete against each other anywhere in the world.

To remain on the forefront of new technology, Nokia has also begun investing in new start-up companies to keep abreast of the latest developments. In 1998, the company created a new unit called Nokia Ventures, whose purpose is to identify and incubate new ideas—both within the company and from outside. Since its inception, Nokia Ventures has invested in over twenty-five different companies around the world to learn more about developments in mobile communication technology. Based in Menlo Park, California, Nokia Ventures has recently begun investing in new markets, such as Israel, where there is a considerable talent base and experience in software engineering. The company believes that Nokia Ventures can serve as a "greenhouse" for venturing and learning new ideas. This greenhouse also includes the Nokia Entrepreneurial Web—a new type of network organization designed to promote the exchange of business ideas among scientists and other personnel. Some of the technologies that Nokia Ventures has recently targeted include Internet security systems, new types of color display screens, and mobile alert messaging. Nokia believes that its new venture will help the company not only gain exposure to the new skills it must learn to stay competitive but also create

entirely new markets and industries for the Internet economy. In effect, Nokia recognizes that it must scour the world for the best people and the best ideas, no matter where they originate. Consequently, Nokia's R&D efforts are now located in many parts of the world to take advantage of the specialized talent and deep resources that have emanated from those regions. This reliance on external talent, combined with internal R&D capabilities, will help Nokia sustain its innovative approach to learning and applying new technologies in a variety of arenas.

To ensure that the company's designers, engineers, manufacturing people, and salesforce work together, Nokia uses a novel organizational format that combines people from different functions into flexible product teams. These product teams share knowledge and insights to accelerate time-to-market. Equally important, when designers and engineers are at the early stages of creating a new phone line, people from manufacturing are already at work figuring out how best to manufacture the phone at the lowest possible cost. In addition, manufacturing specialists provide critical data and feedback to the designers and engineers on different ways to improve the phone's design for smoother and easier production.

A core pillar behind Nokia's enormous technological success is the company's long-standing belief in promoting the self-worth of any individual. Even though Finns dominate the company's senior management and engineering staff, Nokia views itself "as a multicultural organization doing business in a multicultural environment." Nokia believes that it must hire people from different parts of the world because people from different regions view and address problems from different perspectives. Putting people together on Nokia's teams enables the company to gain from a wide-ranging set of ideas and viewpoints that would not have been possible if the company confined itself to its Northern European region.

Introduction

This chapter focuses on how firms can develop strategies for global expansion that extend their competitive advantage to worldwide markets. For firms in almost every imaginable industry, the need to think about strategies for global expansion and operations is rising fast. In fact, in some industries (for example, high fashion, pharmaceuticals, cell phones, Hollywood movies, semiconductors, video game consoles, digital music players, and Internet-driven, online businesses) where products are in such high demand, the need to think about global expansion begins on day one. Rapidly changing technologies, the growth of computer networks that make the Internet ever-more pervasive around the world, the rise of new competitors from newly developed markets, the global desire for exciting new products and services, and the availability of new sources of production make global strategy issues a critical consideration for senior managers in all types and sizes of companies. Business leaders from North and South America, the Far East, and Europe all agree that going global is essential to their future business success. Yet, few managers actually agree on which factors are most important in pursuing successful global expansion strategies.[2]

At the same time, however, globalization can introduce its own set of economic and organizational challenges. Competing in many parts of the world often requires the firm to understand the needs of new customers, build facilities, and establish goodwill in new markets—all very time-consuming tasks. Also, managing far-flung operations can tax the best company's organizational efforts, since global strategies place a premium on attaining a balance between meeting customers' needs in different parts of the world with maintaining cost parity with competitors. In other words, the term *globalization* often conjures up different images in the minds of people from different industries. In this book, we define **globalization** as viewing the entire world as a potential market or source of inputs for the firm.

The issue of globalization is a complex one. Firms operating in many national markets face different strategic considerations and issues than do firms operating solely in their home market. Developing effective global expansion strategies requires managers to think beyond their home market and across many markets. When carefully understood and matched to their firm's products and practices, global expansion strategies can dramatically help firms extend their distinctive competence and sources of competitive advantage to new markets.

We begin by examining the environmental changes and factors that accelerate the trend toward globalization in many industries. Second, we focus on the broad types of global expansion strategies that firms can undertake to expand their operations overseas. Third, we look at the benefits and costs that underscore global operations and examine how managers can balance the risks and rewards inherent in each type of global strategy. Finally, we examine some of the ethical issues that surround globalization. As firms move to set up operations abroad, managers begin to realize that other cultures sometimes have their own interpretation of what constitutes sound business practices and ethics.

globalization:
Viewing the world as a single market for the firm; the process by which the firm expands across different regions and national markets. On an industry level, globalization refers to the changes in economic factors, such as economies of scale, experience, and R&D, that make competing on a worldwide basis a necessity.

Environmental Factors That Accelerate Globalization

Over the past two decades, companies in a growing range of industries have looked overseas to expand their operations. Industries ranging from semiconductors to consumer electronics, automobiles, computers, watches, tools, medical equipment, aerospace, and others have also

Exhibit 7-1   **Factors Promoting the Globalization of Industries**

- Narrowing of demand characteristics
- Escalating costs of R&D
- Cost reduction pressures and economies of scale
- Government industrial policies
- Reduction of factor costs (e.g., labor, capital)
- Rise of new distribution channels
- Reduction of transportation, communication, and storage costs
- Internet access
- Reduction of tariffs worldwide

seen global competitors from other nations make serious inroads into the United States. Some of the most important environmental factors that promote globalization within and across industries are the following: (1) narrowing of demand characteristics among countries and regions; (2) escalating costs of R&D; (3) pressures for cost reduction and higher economies of scale; (4) the rise of government "industrial" policies that promote globalization; (5) the reduction of factor/capital and labor/costs in many markets; (6) the availability of new distribution channels; and (7) lower transportation, communication, and storage costs[3] (see Exhibit 7-1).

Narrowing of Demand Characteristics Across Markets

One of the most important factors promoting faster globalization is the rising level of incomes and awareness of new products and services in regions around the world. Since the 1970s, rising prosperity in countries such as Brazil, Chile, China, South Korea, Taiwan, Singapore, South Africa, Saudi Arabia, Greece, and Turkey has vastly increased the amount of disposable income available for purchasing new products. In addition, more mature markets, such as Europe, North America, and Japan, have been experiencing steadily rising incomes as well, albeit at a slower rate. Even though many countries still exhibit varying rates of economic development, the rise of new middle classes in once underdeveloped nations has opened up new markets for products such as Sony Walkmans, Levi's jeans, McDonald's restaurants, Coca-Cola, and even Nokia or Motorola or Samsung digital cell phones. Entirely new markets are being created over the span of a few years.

Products and services that once were confined primarily to wealthier people in the United States and Europe (such as financial services, luxury automobiles, commercial banking, golfing equipment, tennis rackets, cellular phones) are now available to anyone, anywhere in the world, who can afford them. In fact, rising prosperity around the world is opening up huge new markets annually—to firms willing to enter and serve them—populated by millions of wealthier people. In the new millennium, even greater opportunities may abound. The economic stabilization of Latin America, the opening up of Eastern Europe, and the massive growth of new middle classes in Indonesia, India, and Southeast Asia are all contributing to the marked rise of incomes, aspirations, and business opportunities for designing and selling new products.

Consider the case of China alone. In just the past four years, the enormous growth of China has completely reshuffled the supply and demand balance for many industries. For example, the rising level of prosperity in China has created a middle class that is almost a third the size of that of the United States. The country is installing as many new telephone lines each year as there are in the state of California. Put in another way, China is installing the equivalent of Verizon's entire fixed-line telephone operation each year. In 2003 and 2004, China is believed to have consumed up to one-third of the world's cement production and almost a quarter of the world's steel production.[4] Industries as diverse as beer, cell phones, semiconductors, automobiles, chemicals, textiles, apparel, toys, and food processing have only just begun to feel the massive impact of China's bourgeoning demand for these products (and its growing capability to produce them at low cost).

Increasing demand worldwide has direct and more specific effects on the competitive nature of many industries. In some industries, globalization of demand means a leveling of demand patterns, whereby people's desires for products and services are becoming steadily more homogeneous. **Homogeneity of demand** means that regardless of where customers are physically located, buyers are likely to want the same kind of product or service with certain similar features. In other words, customers are becoming increasingly similar in some industries where tastes, preferences, and desires for certain product attributes are converging into one larger, more homogeneous market. Demand characteristics in one region are likely to be nearly, if not altogether identical to those characteristics found in another region. For example, in the wireless phone industry, a number of companies (for example, Motorola of the United States, Siemens of Germany, TCL of China, LG Electronics and Samsung of South Korea) compete with Nokia to design, produce, and distribute millions of cell phones and handheld digital devices to customers worldwide, with few substantive changes in the way the products look or function.

Perhaps the most enduring example of the growing homogeneity of demand in the consumer electronics industry is the Sony Walkman. Consumers in New York, Nanjing, and Nairobi are all likely to be wearing the same style of headset and listening to music from a radio/cassette player that is interchangeable across markets. Today, the Apple iPod is emblematic of such fast global change. However, a product does not necessarily have to be tangible to be wanted by millions of global consumers. For example, blockbuster movies and television shows produced by Hollywood studios are clearly hits wherever they are shown worldwide. See Exhibit 7-2 for examples of products with worldwide markets and increasingly shared tastes and uses.

Homogeneity of demand, however, is perhaps more prevalent in industries that produce and sell products that serve as components to some other product or cannot be truly differentiated in their use. For example, semiconductors, flat-panel displays, telecommunications

homogeneity of demand:
Similarity of demand patterns and wants across customers, regardless of where they are located.

Examples of Growing Homogeneity of Demand	Exhibit 7-2

- Communications equipment
- Cellular phones
- Sony Walkmans
- Apple iPod
- Levi's jeans
- Commercial banking
- Financial services
- Flat-screen technologies
- Semiconductors
- Machine tools
- Computers
- Pharmaceuticals
- Construction equipment
- Commercial aircraft
- Hollywood films
- Television shows
- Data and computer networks

equipment, and other electronic devices are clearly designed to serve the same purpose and function, no matter where the end user is located. Microprocessors run computers, telephones, and even automobile engines, regardless of where the end product is located. Fiber optics transmits telephone calls across regions, countries, and continents, no matter what language is spoken. Commercial aircraft, such as the Boeing 747 and 777, serve the same purpose of carrying passengers and freight, whether they are sold to American Airlines, Air France, or Aerolineas Argentinas. Homogeneity of operating standards, such as software and word-processing systems, also contributes to rising globalization of these industries. Witness the impact of Microsoft's various operating systems (Windows 2000, XP, and NT) in shaping the evolution of future add-on software, video games, and other programs created by software design companies throughout the world. Other industries exhibiting a growing convergence of tastes and demand characteristics include certain types of automobiles (luxury, sport utility, four-wheel drive, and sporty segments), soft drinks (Coke vs. Pepsi), and even high fashion to some degree (the prevalence of Italian-cut suits in Europe, Asia, and the Americas), where a growing common desire for high-quality products transcends languages, ethnic differences, political systems, and religions.

Escalating Costs of Research and Development

The exponentially rising costs of research and development (R&D) in some industries make it absolutely essential for companies in these industries to sell their products globally. The semiconductor, biotechnology, pharmaceutical, and composite materials industries also face a similar economic imperative of rising R&D costs. In 2001, Intel alone spent $7.5 billion for both research and capital equipment, despite the fact that the semiconductor industry went into a downturn for much of the year. Intel realizes that it must not only prepare for next-generation chips regardless of the immediate economic climate but also establish facilities to sell its chips on a global basis. Its next-generation Itanium chip was so complex and expensive that Intel developed it in conjunction with Hewlett-Packard, which committed significant design expertise to the project. In the biotechnology and pharmaceutical industries, designing a new line of anticancer drugs is a costly proposition. The research and development costs of testing, developing, and finally commercializing new medications can easily exceed $800 million, so selling globally as fast as possible is a must. Companies that manufacture "new wave" materials, such as hybrid composites used in tennis rackets (graphite), golf clubs (titanium, tantalums, and carbon fibers), engineering resins and alloys (superstrong composite metals or engineered plastics), and new synthetic fibers (advanced polyester blends) must also amortize their R&D costs over a global volume of business. For example, graphite tennis rackets are expensive to develop and sell, but few people in one market alone are likely to buy enough of them to justify a firm's initial investment in that business. Likewise, carbon fiber developed for the aerospace business needs to be produced on a global basis to justify the massive investment in these complex manufacturing plants. Companies in this and other industries must view the entire world as their market before they can undertake costly product development. Thus, firms in industries that face rising R&D costs accelerate the broader trend toward globalization. See Exhibit 7-3 for examples of global, R&D-intensive industries.

Rising Economies of Scale and Cost Pressures

minimum efficient scale (MES):
Level of production volume that a factory must reach before it achieves full efficiency.

Many industries are currently exhibiting rising levels of economies of scale in production. For example, the steel industry is characterized by a high minimum efficient scale (MES). **Minimum efficient scale** refers to the production volume at which a plant must operate to achieve full efficiency. New integrated steel mills that turn out high-quality, continuously cast

| Examples of R&D-Intensive Industries | Exhibit 7-3 |

- Semiconductors
- Software
- Biotechnology
- Communications systems
- Pharmaceuticals
- Commercial aircraft
- Electronics
- Composite materials
- Advanced imaging systems
- Medical equipment
- Fiber optics

steel face rising levels of MES to the point where a brand-new steel mill must be able to produce a sizable fraction of total world demand before it breaks even. During the early 1990s, South Korea's newest integrated steel mill, owned and operated by the Pohang Iron and Steel Company (POSCO), at one point could produce high-quality steel for export at 75 percent of the cost of comparable U.S. integrated mills. However, POSCO's plant is so huge that it must produce approximately 3 percent of total world demand before it achieves full efficiency. Now, POSCO faces the prospect of inevitable global competition from even larger and newer mills now coming on line in China. Although surging domestic demand continues to exceed China's internal steel production capacity, many analysts feel that China will likely become an important export player in the steel market by the end of the decade. Thus, high economies of scale in production mandate a global view of supply and demand.

Global economies of scale can also promote related experience curve effects in production. Experience curve effects (see Chapter 3) resulting from global volume production are important, because they can help firms reduce costs even further. In technologies where costs decline from both cumulative volume and learning, firms may be more inclined to sell more products across different regions. As costs decline, the company will be better able to price its product to penetrate new markets. In addition, faster learning and experience means that the company will be able to remain at a lower cost position than its rivals for an extended period. This motivation is a big reason why Nokia has chosen to design and manufacture its line of digital phones and N-Gage handsets within its own factories. By capturing all of the scale and experience benefits that accrue from running its own plants, Nokia hopes to be able to remain an even lower-cost producer than its rivals that prefer to outsource production and component design. Economies of scale is clearly an important factor in most information-driven industries, because once the fixed costs are amortized, there is enormous profit in selling to new markets and new customers. Computer hardware and their components exhibit significant economies of scale, especially in storage and memory devices. The economies of scale and cumulative experience effects gained by Japanese automakers, such as Toyota, Honda, and Nissan, have helped these companies penetrate both the U.S. and European markets, while sustaining the momentum of global volume production. See Exhibit 7-4 for examples of products in industries with rising economies of scale.

Role of Government Policy

Government policy can often accelerate the trend toward globalization in one or a group of industries. For example, the rise of Japanese integrated steel producers during the 1960s and

Exhibit 7-4   Examples of Rising Economies of Scale/Cost Pressures

- Steel
- Automobile engines
- Color television tubes
- Semiconductors
- Fiber optics
- Office equipment
- Telecommunications
- Aircraft
- Chemicals

STRATEGIC COMPETENCY *in action*

Creating Distinctive Value: China's TCL[5]

TCL is probably one company that few people outside its home country have ever heard of. Yet, it has become the largest manufacturer of televisions in the world, producing such well-known brands as RCA in the United States, Thomson in France, and Schneider in Germany. The company is expected to produce over 15 million sets annually. This same company now employs more than forty thousand people making everything from televisions to mobile phones, laptop computers, refrigerators, and air conditioners. TCL has ambitions to become a leading Fortune Global 500 company by the end of the decade.

Who is TCL? Founded in 1982 as a state-owned manufacturer of small cassette tape recorders, TCL is a new breed of Chinese enterprise that is aspiring to become a top-tier, branded producer of consumer electronics to serve markets anywhere around the globe. Led by charismatic chairman Li Dongsheng, TCL has aggressively invested in new technologies and manufacturing facilities in China, Europe, the United States, and Southeast Asia to produce low-cost television sets and other electronic products. By 2002, TCL was already making over eleven million televisions a year, with almost four million sold overseas under such brand names as Philips, Thomson, and Panasonic. In April 2004, TCL signed an agreement with Alcatel of France to take over the production of the entire telecommunications firm's line of cellular phones and other handheld devices. Alcatel sold the technology and the factories to TCL because it could not ramp up production to capture global economies of scale. Yet, TCL eagerly bought the business because it now has an important beachhead to sell both Alcatel-branded and eventually its own line of phones in Europe and elsewhere. In November 2003, TCL signed a similar deal with Thomson of France, where the company would assume majority ownership of all of Thomson's worldwide television production. This gives TCL effective control over Thomson's plants in France, Poland, Thailand, and Bloomington, Indiana. These moves demonstrate TCL's fierce determination to carve its own dominant position and name in the global marketplace.

More important, TCL symbolizes the kind of enterprise that many other Chinese manufacturers hope to become—a company that can not only produce state-of-the-art products at low cost, but can also develop a vibrant brand that could possibly rival those of Sony, Sharp, Samsung, and other well-known global companies. TCL is following the same pattern that once unknown companies such as Matsushita, Toshiba, Ricoh, and LG followed before they became powerful brands.

TCL's core strategy is to build up manufacturing capabilities that enable the company to capture huge economies of scale. By constructing and owning a network of large factories, TCL plans to break into Europe and the rest of Asia with big flat-screen televisions, DVD players, and other consumer electronic products. It is the only Chinese television producer that has consistently gained market share and shown a profit over the past five years. The deals with Thomson, Schneider, and Alcatel give TCL direct, immediate penetration into Europe. Already, the combined cell phone output with Alcatel makes TCL the world's seventh largest producer, with over 19 million units a year. Although that is a far cry from such behemoths as Nokia, Motorola, and Samsung, TCL is scaling up even more future production in China to serve its own domestic market's enormous needs. At the same time, TCL is beefing up its R&D capabilities, especially in the technologies vital to building flat-screen televisions. In July 2004, TCL announced a partnership with U.S. semiconductor firm Genesis Microchip. The two companies will codesign and coproduce digital HDTV chips for flat-screen televisions. In November 2004, TCL entered into a broad agreement to develop advanced home appliances and refrigerators with Japan's Toshiba. The two companies will create joint ventures that will share manufacturing and marketing know-how to expand both companies' positions in China and throughout Southeast Asia. Toshiba hopes to rapidly expand in the fast-growing Chinese market and wants to use TCL as a manufacturing base to lower its cost structure.

Chairman Li has been pushing to manage TCL more like a true, unconstrained free-market enterprise firm in a country where the government typically owns big shares of large companies. Li believes that TCL can become a global powerhouse, but only if it is able to compete on its own. Through a series of stock offerings to the public, Li has whittled down the Chinese government's stake to less than 25 percent, with the rest of it distributed among the general public and large foreign partners, including Philips Electronics, Toshiba, and several Hong Kong companies. Li himself owns 6 percent of the company.

Li is a survivor of the Cultural Revolution in China during the 1960s, when the Communist Party sought to eliminate all types of foreign-influenced ideas, knowledge, and practices. Forced to raise crops on an agricultural commune, Li reportedly read books in secret. Ironically, according to *Fortune* magazine, he is now more likely to quote the wisdom of such former executives as General Electric's Jack Welch and IBM's Lou Gertsner than that of Mao or Marx. He is known for his aggressive marketing and relentless searching for new ways to cut costs.

Some of the big challenges still confronting TCL are the company's lack of strong marketing, distribution, and customer service capabilities that will be required in global markets. Li recognizes these weaknesses and hopes to continue acquiring other companies that can help compensate for these shortfalls in their home markets. Yet, TCL faces enormous competition its own domestic Chinese market from other like-minded firms. Several other Chinese firms have recently built their own huge factories to support their global ambitions. Already, Haier Group has successfully penetrated the U.S. and European markets with compact refrigerators and is moving up the value chain by producing wine-cooler cabinets and even flat-screen televisions. Haier hopes to innovate new products faster than all of its competitors, both domestic and foreign based. Haier sells its refrigerators through Wal-Mart and other major appliance chains. Recognizing the importance of marketing to build its brand name, Haier has even begun advertising by placing its name on luggage carts at JFK Airport in New York.

1970s was largely due to the coordination and preferential tax treatment (particularly in depreciation) accorded to steelmakers by the government. Companies such as Nippon Kokan, Nippon Steel, Sumitomo Metal, and others were encouraged by the government to share their technological innovations and to build steel mills that exhibited ever-higher minimum efficient scale (such policies can, of course, have a very mixed blessing when these industries enter a protracted cyclical downturn, as is the case with Japan now). In turn, many of these steel companies started to export to the United States, where older mills owned by a variety of existing and previous firms, such as U.S. Steel, Bethlehem Steel, Jones and Laughlin, and National Steel, could not compete as effectively.

Numerous tools of government policy, such as subsidies, preferential tax treatment, and other support for critical industrial sectors can accelerate the trend toward globalization. "Industrial policies" such as these are fairly common in the Far East and Latin America, where governments often intervene in ways to promote their strategic industries. Until very recently, for example, South Korea's government provided generous subsidies or indirect loans to its electronics and semiconductor companies (for example, Samsung), which in turn are able to invest in newer equipment and larger plants for export. Europe's numerous government-sponsored collaborative projects in semiconductors, aircraft, and other industries (for example, JESSI and Airbus Industries) have spurred the rise of pan-European global competitors that are seeking to challenge U.S. and Japanese strongholds in a number of industries. Even to this day, France and Germany speak openly about the creation of "national champion" firms.[6] These companies are chosen by their respective governments to serve as flagship leaders for that particular industry. The pursuit of this policy enabled France to prevent a takeover of Aventis (a Franco–German leader in pharmaceuticals) by Novartis, a leading Swiss drug firm, in February 2004. Instead, the French government actively encouraged its other large drug firm, Sanofi-Synthelabo, to serve as a "white knight" and rescue Aventis from other interested merger partners. Likewise, in 2003 and 2004, the United States filed a number of complaints with the Chinese government over its domestic tax policies that were designed to favor domestic production of advanced semiconductors at the expense of foreign competitors. Imports of foreign-made chips were

Exhibit 7-5   *Examples of Government Initiatives to Promote Industrial Development*

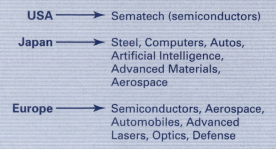

taxed at a higher level than those made in China, thus giving domestic firms a big leg up in a fast-growing market. The dispute was tentatively resolved in July 2004.[7] Thus, government policy can accelerate the rise of new global competitors in industries by removing some of the initial impediments to globalization. Exhibit 7-5 presents some industries in the United States, Japan, and Europe that have been the recent focus of government-backed initiatives or industrial policies.

Conversely, government policy can impede the trend toward globalization in some industries. Subsidies to weak domestic producers, and protectionist measures such as tariffs, quotas, and other import limitations, can actually prolong the decline of certain industries that are ripe for global competition. For example, many governments protect their domestic producers of agriculture, textiles, steel, electronics, and other businesses that in many cases would ordinarily have been subject to global competitive pressures earlier were it not for protective policies. Even government-sponsored "industrial policies" can backfire in unintentional ways. For example, South Korea's generous support of its numerous semiconductor manufacturers caused a massive oversupply of memory chips during the late 1990s that hurt competitors from around the world, including its own. Two of its own domestic producers of memory chips, Lucky-Goldstar (now better known as LG Electronics) and Hyundai Electronics, were unable to remain profitable without domestic subsidies. Hyundai Electronics, now known as Hynix Electronics, has repeatedly turned to its creditors for extensions on loan payments and has even sought debt relief. As recently as 2004, Hynix was able to survive by selling off smaller operations to other companies, but it continues to depend heavily on the largess of many South Korean banks, many of whom are partially owned by the state (and therefore unwilling to see a large domestic producer go out of business). Japan's long-cherished policy of promoting its own industrial growth has resulted in serious economic distortions, especially as many of its export-oriented companies confront currency fluctuations and overcapacity in many industries. In fact, several Japanese companies, such as Hitachi, NEC, Toshiba, Mitsubishi Motors, Nissan, and Fujitsu, during the past several years have been forced to resort to layoffs across their disparate businesses, an amazing turnabout for a country that has long prided itself on preserving a policy of lifetime employment at its largest companies. Even though this restructuring process of Japanese firms appears to be gaining speed, it is likely to be a decade-long event before Japan is able to rid itself of industry overcapacity and large numbers of teetering enterprises. Even to this day, Mitsubishi Motors continues to receive large capital infusions from affiliated Mitsubishi-related companies to keep the automotive concern afloat, even though the company faces enormous debt and a poor reception from customers in its home Japanese market.

Change in Factor Costs Around the World

One of the most important factors that have accelerated the globalization of different industries is the prevalence of low-cost labor and resources in different parts of the world. Low-cost labor attracts companies from other countries to set up operations in the hope of lowering the cost of their end products. During the 1960s and 1970s, many U.S. companies such as General Electric, United Technologies, Westinghouse Electric, Ford, Texas Instruments, and General Motors established factories and other production facilities throughout the Far East and Latin America to take advantage of lower labor costs to manufacture consumer electronics and automotive components. Now many other firms, such as Dell, Hewlett-Packard, Intel, Nortel Networks, and Lucent Technologies, have begun to establish design, assembly, and customer-service operations in many of these same countries and elsewhere in their pursuit of even lower costs. Toy companies, such as Mattel and Hasbro, and garment makers/retailers Liz Claiborne, Evan Picone, and Bloomingdale's have significant production and sourcing operations in the Far East that enable them to offer high-quality goods at lower cost. The presence of these companies has also helped stimulate the development of local economies, which, in turn, have become important customers and competitors in different industries.

In fact, the sustained growth and increased prosperity of the Mexican border areas near California and Texas have resulted from massive investment by both U.S. and Japanese firms to establish assembly plants in the region to take advantage of lower labor costs. These assembly plants, known as *maquiladoras,* play a vital role in bringing new technology and new opportunities for Mexico, which in turn has spawned a whole new set of suppliers and distributors in the region. U.S. investment in Mexico is certainly not confined to the border area alone. For example, General Motors and Ford build some of their most popular-selling vehicles deep inside Mexico, in places such as Ramos Arizpe (GM), Monterrey (GM and Ford), and Hermosillo (Ford and Volkswagen). Japanese automotive firms have established a strong presence in many of the same places to serve both the Mexican and U.S. markets with greater local presence. Yet, as new countries enter the global marketplace, Mexico may be losing some of its traditional sources of comparative advantage. Ironically, in a remarkable twist of fate, many Mexican companies are now complaining about the massive competition they now feel from Chinese exporters, who have actually displaced Mexican producers of tourist items that are sold in places such as Los Cabos and Cancun. Along a similar vein, U.S. manufacturers that invested in Mexico twenty years ago are now considering a shift in their operations to lower-cost China and India, even for such increasingly sophisticated products as automotive parts.[8]

The continued presence and attraction of low-cost, skilled labor in China, India, Indonesia, and other Southeast Asian countries encouraged many Japanese producers to build factories in this region during the 1990s, because labor had become a scarce and high-cost commodity in Japan. In fact, some economic analysts have noted that the Japanese have built as much manufacturing capacity in Southeast Asia as exists in all of France. Many well-known Japanese products, such as Sony's television sets and Matsushita Electric's air conditioners, are made in China, Singapore, Thailand, and elsewhere.

Lower costs of energy and other resources can also accelerate globalization. Metal smelting and fabrication costs for aluminum, copper, iron, and other resources are highly sensitive to processing costs. As a result, Alcoa has invested over $5 billion in new smelting plants around the world, including Brazil, Trinidad, China, and even Iceland! Alcoa's desire to enter newly developing markets has also pushed the company to locate plants near much cheaper sources of electricity as well, since smelting aluminum is a power-intensive business.[9] Not to be outdone by its large American rival, Canadian aluminum firm Alcan has begun buying up equity stakes and other positions in Chinese aluminum producers for many of the same reasons.[10] Dramatically cheaper costs of energy may encourage miners and producers of these metals to shift their value-adding functions to cheaper locations. For example, the mining of bauxite (the ore that becomes aluminum) takes place globally, but its processing into higher, value-added metal parts and components occurs closer to aluminum's end markets, where energy, transport, and distribution costs are lower. Many U.S. firms are locating some of their most sophisticated operations according to where they can find abundant sources of highly skilled, technical personnel. Countries such as Taiwan, India, and Israel are becoming important engineering and development centers for key skills such as software and computer design. For example, Texas Instruments (TI) has long experience managing a state-of-the-art software development site in Bangalore, India, to work with a rich source of exceptionally skilled technical expertise. TI's engineers in India communicate with their U.S. and European counterparts by way of the company's proprietary satellite transmission system that offers real-time communication. In fact, software competency in India has become so sophisticated that almost all U.S. and European computer and telecommunications companies have established operations in both Bangalore and around the country. Because of the nation's rich educational traditions and rigorous educational standards, India has become a world leader in producing some of the highest quality software talent found anywhere. India's combination of deep talent and low wage costs has attracted scores of leading U.S. firms to invest heavily there. Companies such as General Electric, Dell, IBM, Hewlett-Packard, and Citigroup have established major operations in India that range from simple call center operations to entire chip design capabilities. As the Indian economy gains further steam, it will also become an important provider of many services beyond software and other high-tech applications.[11] Even India, though, is not immune to global competition in this extremely advanced industry. Japanese companies such as NEC and Omron Electronics are now starting to tap into China, which over the last decade has begun educating and graduating legions of software engineers. In fact, General Electric has plans to establish over twenty R&D facilities in China alone in the next several years.

The trend of tapping into the world's abundant pools of ever-rising talent will likely accelerate as companies further invest and implement new internal computer networks that use the Internet to link up their disparate subsidiaries into a cohesive, real-time information system. In turn, companies that use the Internet to build strong relationships with local talent can often take advantage of important first-mover advantages, not only in developing new technology, but also in understanding how local market conditions may differ. Motorola, Intel, and other U.S. semiconductor firms have set up R&D facilities in Israel to accelerate new product design and testing activities. Taiwan is fast becoming the center of production and development expertise for a range of important products, including PCs, MP3 players, and flat-screen television sets. Equally important, Taiwan in just the past four years has become the epicenter for much of the world's semiconductor fabrication and testing processes. Companies unheard of as recently as the late 1990s (for example, Semiconductor Manufacturing and United Microelectronics in Taiwan, and Chartered Semiconductor Manufacturing in Singapore) now do much of the production work for such U.S. and European semiconductor firms as Altera, Xilinx, Broadcom, Vitesse Semiconductor, and even Philips Electronics.

Leveraging Technology: Using Advanced Technology to Keep It Made in the U.S.A.

As globalization begins to impact every industry and company, America faces both a crisis and an opportunity. There is a growing consensus among economists that lower-skilled jobs making mass-produced, standardized goods will continue to move abroad where labor is cheaper and more abundant. Dozens of industries will face the prospect of even more intense foreign competition. Yet, a big opportunity exists for many companies who are willing to embrace the latest advances in manufacturing technology to stay competitive. Product and process innovation are key.

In America's best-running factories today, enormous productivity, low cost, world-class quality, and product customization are coming together in one system. State-of-the-art factories use computer-integrated manufacturing (CIM) to harness the power of the Internet to directly tie production with sales forecasts and even specific customized orders for individual customers. The brains and nerve center of the modern factory has moved away from physical hardware to leading-edge software, skills, and Internet-driven technologies to make manufacturing a much more nimble and flexible corporate resource. These assets now give firms an unparalleled flexibility to produce more varieties of products at lesser cost with greater ease—something that factories using large numbers of lesser-skilled workers are unable to do. Firms are just beginning to feel the impact of CIM technology on their productivity strides. Computer-controlled machine tools can work just as well making one hundred units of a single design as one hundred units of different designs. For a growing number of companies, making one unit or making many is now economically the same. These advances have also boosted U.S. manufacturing across many sectors, including machine tools, aerospace, and high-tech components. These concepts have even been used to sequence and understand DNA in the field of biotechnology.[12]

Consider the Ingersoll Milling Machine Company. Ingersoll uses an advanced manufacturing system that links design with manufacturing and process control. Ingersoll's CIM system can machine more than twenty-five thousand different prismatic parts used for specialized machine tools and motor controls. Seventy percent of its production occurs in lot sizes of one. Half of the different parts this machine can make will never be made twice. Unit production cost is approximately the same as for a long run of a single standard part.[13]

The $10 million flexible machining system of Vought Corporation (now part of Lockheed Martin) began operations during the mid-1980s. This advanced technology allows the aerospace maker to produce some six hundred designs of specialized aircraft parts using the same equipment—even one design at a time in random sequence. This CMI is expected to save Vought over $25 million annually in machine costs by performing, in seventy thousand hours, work that would have taken more than two hundred thousand hours by conventional machining methods.[14]

Many other U.S. companies are not only keeping ahead of their foreign rivals, they are also beating them to market with better, newer products. Timken, a leading producer of bearings (parts that make machines work), invested over $150 million in a state-of-the-art North Carolina factory that can manufacture small batches of bearings without a long downtime to refit the tools between orders. Using advanced design and process control software, Timken's skilled factory technicians can modify product designs in under half an hour—a process that used to require more than a half a day in the past. Moreover, the same technology enables Timken to use the data on each individual part to identify new ways of maintaining equipment in the field for Timken's customers.[15]

One key result of CIM is that design and manufacturing will become much more closely linked. New computer-assisted design (CAD) tools will be able to test new product ideas and prototypes immediately. The resulting designs, stored as program files in the CIM computer, allow for immediate ramp-up of production when needed. The trend of compressing design together with manufacturing is making huge strides in boosting the productivity and innovation of U.S. companies embracing the idea. They are also helping to reduce manufacturing job losses in the U.S. However, the nature of these jobs is changing markedly.

To succeed in the new CIM factory, employees will need multiple sets of skills to compete. Factory jobs in the past were specialized and narrowly defined. Workers were often unable to work on other factory jobs that needed different skills. Formal workplace rules and strictly defined tasks limited employees' ability to do other tasks. The rise of CIM means that employees will have to engage in a much greater variety of activities. Fewer workers will be needed, but those retained will have to learn many types of skills. Workers will need a better understanding of computer technology; they must know how to use software and how to adapt the system to changing products that come through the factory. These requirements put a premium on organizing employees into cross-functional teams that include people from design, manufacturing, and marketing who work together on a focused project. The teams need to be small and versatile enough to learn and apply new skills quickly. They must also move from one part of the factory or firm to another as needed. Tomorrow's factory workers will differ substantially from their predecessors. More than likely, they will look more like technicians or knowledge workers. Formal job

(continued)

classifications will matter little. In the most advanced factories, there is no unskilled labor at all.

Hutchinson Technology is a small Minnesota-based company that produces the microscopic suspension assemblies needed to keep computer hard drives running. It supplies more than half of the world's output of this vital component. At Hutchinson's four factories, computer-driven production and inspection lines continuously but gently fabricate ultra-miniaturized parts, requiring only a few workers at each line.

Direct labor now accounts for less than 15 percent of cost of goods sold. A big advantage that Hutchinson enjoys over Asian companies is that it is able to build small volumes to better serve the needs of smaller disk-drive companies that appreciate Hutchinson's operating flexibility. Hutchinson prefers to stay in the United States because it can work more closely with its customers, and because it leads in the kind of advanced engineering and precision manufacturing skills that have kept Asian producers at bay—at least for now.[16]

Rise of New Distribution Channels

The rise of new distribution channels can also accelerate globalization of product trends. For example, the rise of hypermarts—huge supermarkets—in Germany and other parts of Europe has greatly increased the availability of American-made products (for example, Tex-Mex food) that ordinarily would have had a much more limited market presence. New distribution channels that supplement or replace more costly existing channels may indirectly act to stimulate demand for newer products. For example, the rise of the Toys "R" Us chain in Japan not only lowered the cost of Japanese-made toys for the local population, but also brought in competing imports from U.S. and other Far Eastern toy makers. The rise of department store chains (Sears and J. C. Penney in Brazil and Mexico), mammoth retailers (Wal-Mart in Canada and Mexico, France's Carrefour in China), and specialized, low-cost retailers (Toys "R" Us in Japan, The Home Depot in Chile) is hastening the convergence of tastes and the demand for new global products that are made elsewhere. In Mexico, Wal-Mart has become an important domestic competitor for the hard-earned pesos of Mexican consumers who are attracted to the company's wide product offerings and low prices. Operating in conjunction with its Mexican partner Cifra SA, Wal-Mart has even outmuscled other U.S. firms such as Sears and J. C. Penney in setting up similarly large stores throughout Mexico as it did in the United States.

Overall Reduction in Transportation, Communication, and Storage Costs

The expanding availability of lower-cost transportation has helped stimulate the globalization of many industries. For example, few people probably realize that the United States is the largest importer of fresh flowers and tulip bulbs from South America and the Netherlands. Although fresh-cut flowers would seem to represent the one product least subject to global shipment and export (because of perishability), the ability to mass-produce and to ship flowers on airplanes overnight to the United States has instantly transformed the growing of flowers and plants into a new global business. Growing and shipping flowers has become an important industry for many South American countries such as Ecuador and Peru. Custom-made Swiss chocolates and candies are now often shipped directly from Switzerland to the United States to serve niche markets in New York and other cities. The greater availability of low-cost, overnight transportation is not limited to specialty products either. Caterpillar, the leading U.S. manufacturer of construction equipment, routinely promises and delivers replacement parts to its distributors anywhere around the world in less than forty-eight hours. More broadly, the long-run decline in real costs of transportation over the past thirty years has been a fundamental, although subtle, factor that has accelerated globalization across every type of industry.

Communication costs also decline each year. Most recently, the single greatest accelerating factor that promotes globalization and homogeneity of demand is the Internet's presence in every corner of the globe. The massive proliferation of personal computers, state-of-the-art communication networks using fiber optics, and the establishment of huge "server farms" has brought the Internet to some of the most remote villages of the world. New satellites, electronic mail, and broadband-based video communications connect the world more tightly than could have ever been imagined as recently as five years ago. Fiber optics that transmit voice, video, and data over telephone lines, combined with wireless communications over a growing range of the electromagnetic spectrum, have lowered the cost of communications every year. Communications technology has advanced to the point where IBM is now actively designing and installing voice recognition chips able to translate languages over the telephone without the need for a translator. Advances in search engine technologies (for example, Yahoo! and Google) on the Internet enable information access from a variety of different global and domestic sources using multiple languages. During the late 1990s, this technology had already far surpassed conventional mail in terms of commercial application and the amount of communications sent.

Storage costs have also declined along with transportation and communication costs in recent years. Improvements in inventory control, such as just-in-time (JIT) production and scheduling, and innovations in containerization and intermodal shipping have contributed to the decline in storage cost for durable products. Merchant ships now routinely carry boxed "containers" that are then directly hooked on to the back of trucks or loaded onto specialized railway wellcars or flatcars (which in turn lowers transport costs even further). This simplification of transportation and storage of products across vast reaches of ocean and land contributes greatly toward faster globalization. For example, shipping companies such as Maersk of Denmark, NYK and K-Line of Japan, Sea-Land of the United States, and Hapag-Lloyd of Germany work closely with other shippers and railroad companies in each country to ensure that containers are off-loaded from ships and quickly loaded onto trucks or rail cars for fast delivery. Many of these companies have even begun deploying advanced Global Positioning System (GPS) technologies to provide customers with the ability to instantaneously track the location and status of their shipment anywhere around the world. These companies also find that utilizing GPS technologies helps them to use their containers far more productively by reducing the time they sit empty or in port. Exhibit 7-6 summarizes some of the key triggers that have lowered the costs of transportation, communications, and storage over the past decade.

Examples of Declining Transportation, Communication, and Storage Costs   Exhibit 7-6

Transport costs
- Containerization
- Intermodal shipping/rail
- Air freight

Communication costs
- More global long distance carriers
- Massive proliferation of fiber optic cable lines
- Internet access everywhere

Storage costs
- Refrigeration
- Just-in-time inventory
- Reduction of perishability
- Supply chain management
- Virtual production/design

The growth of the Internet can only enhance the prospects for even greater opportunities for firms of all sizes to reach and distribute to customers globally. Already, such existing Internet giants as Amazon.com and eBay have set up virtual retail and transactions-based operations in Europe and China, respectively. Both firms view their U.S.-grown distribution models as ideal for reaching customers in markets that were untouchable as recently as a few years back. However, in many ways, it is the large industrial firms, such as Dow Chemical, DuPont, General Electric, Hewlett-Packard, and IBM, that have made enormous strides in harnessing the power of the Internet to dramatically cut their logistics and documentation costs as they strive to enter new markets around the world. At the same time, they have been able to use their enormous buying power to lower the costs of the components and products they source from local markets.

Strategies for Global Expansion

Firms need to address two basic questions when thinking about developing effective strategies for competing globally: (1) How can we extend our advantage by competing across many markets? and (2) How do we minimize our vulnerabilities and maximize our opportunities when competing globally? The first question focuses on the issue of leveraging a critical resource, distinctive competence, or competitive advantage from one market to another. In the Nokia example, the design, manufacture, and distribution of advanced digital phones and telecommunications networks compels the firm to think globally by virtue of the sheer demand for its products, the widespread proliferation of new customers in emerging markets, and also the growing strength of many domestic competitors that have global aspirations for themselves. Consider the alternatives for Boeing and Coca-Cola also. Even though these firms' products are vastly different, both companies realize that competing globally is an effective and necessary way to extend their sources of competitive advantage and to carry out their visions of their home industries. Thus, the underlying issue behind global expansion is similar to that of expanding across industries in corporate strategies. Global expansion strategies concentrate on matching the firm's distinctive competence and line of products with the markets it will serve.

The second question addresses a different issue. Here, the focus is on building and managing global operations in a way to counter the actions and moves of other global competitors. Since global competition by its very nature involves strategies and actions that cut across multiple markets, the actions of a competitor in one market could very well present both vulnerabilities and opportunities in other markets. Individual global expansion strategies will thus require particular practices and ways of managing operations to deal with competitors' actions.

In other words, the issues surrounding global expansion strategies are similar to corporate strategy issues discussed in the preceding chapter. In corporate strategy, the decision to enter new activities, industries, and businesses should be based on the extent to which enlarging the firm's scope of operations reinforces and extends its distinctive competence. That issue was summarized in the question: Does a firm's presence in one set of activities or businesses benefit from expansion into another set? When examining globalization, a similar question exists: To what degree does expansion into different regional markets help extend and reinforce the firm's distinctive competence?

Global expansion involves creating and running large operations in markets outside the firm's home base. We now focus on two fundamentally different global expansion strategies for competing across multiple markets. One of the most important strategic choices firms must make is deciding whether to compete on a global basis or a multidomestic basis.[17] Firms pursue a **global strategy** when they seek to operate with worldwide consistency and a highly standardized approach across different markets. Firms pursue a **multidomestic strategy** when they adjust their products and operations according to each country or market they serve. Each strategy, to a large extent, is shaped by the economic requirements of the industry and the product.

Global Strategy

Over the past twenty years, many companies have adopted global strategies because their markets have moved toward increasing standardization. Popular images of firms pursuing a global strategy, for example, include huge Japanese firms acting as economic juggernauts seeking to dominate every market in which they compete, or legendary IBM (Big Blue) developing and manufacturing all of the computers used in the world. In reality, a number of specific industry-driven factors have prompted firms from around the world to develop a global strategy. Global strategy can also raise concern that local industries will be decimated due to lower-cost competition. Throughout the United States, the rising economic prowess of China has already begun to make have an impact on a growing range of manufacturing industries, and even some areas of high technology. Chinese exports of new products of increasing quality have forced U.S. manufacturers in many industries to find new ways to become productive or shut down their operations. Yet, regardless of how firms from different nations seek to build their global sources of competitive advantage, there are some important economic factors that shape a firm's global strategy. These factors include growing homogeneity of demand, rising economies of scale, increasing technological intensity of new products, the pressure to amortize high costs of R&D or other proprietary investments, and the need to avoid duplication of critical value-adding activities. These industry drivers oblige the firm to compete along a highly standardized and consistent manner across different markets.

A global strategy emphasizes operating with worldwide consistency and standardization of key processes and product designs at low relative cost. Firms pursuing a global strategy view all of their markets and subsidiaries as being highly interdependent and mutually supporting to achieve a high level of internal cohesion and consistency. Key to pursuing a global strategy is an integrated view of building and extending sources of competitive advantage that link up all of the firm's operations to create a unified value-adding delivery system. Firms undertaking a global strategy view each market in which they compete as a platform to learn new skills and techniques that are then applied in other markets. At the same time, this strategic posture enables the firm to increase its bargaining power over its suppliers, thus enhancing the prospects for even lower costs in key sourced inputs. In other words, when a firm pursues a global strategy, actions or results that occur in one market can often impact the others. This approach enables firms to maximize the benefits of exploiting worldwide economies of scale, rising technology intensity of new products, and growing homogeneity of demand. Moreover, a global strategy helps firms extend their distinctive competences to build leverage across markets. The mutually interdependent, systemwide view of a global strategy is shown in Exhibit 7-7. Firms pursuing global strategies tend to undertake the following actions to build leverage across markets: (1) standardize products as much as possible, (2) build their plants and factories in locations that maximize systemwide global competitive advantage, (3) leverage their technology across many regional markets, (4) coordinate marketing and sales worldwide, and (5) compete against other global competitors through cross-subsidization. (See Exhibit 7-8.)

global strategy:
A strategy that seeks to achieve a high level of consistency and standardization of products, processes, and operations around the world; coordination of the firm's many subsidiaries to achieve high interdependence and mutual support.

multidomestic strategy:
A strategy that seeks to adjust a firm's products, processes, and operations for markets and regions around the world; allows subsidiaries to tailor their products, marketing, and other activities according to the needs of their specific markets.

Exhibit 7-7   *Global Strategy of Expansion*

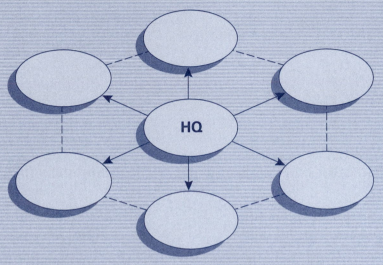

- Systemwide approach to competing worldwide
- Mutually interdependent subsidiaries
- Centralized control and reporting of activities
- Facilitates cross-subsidization policies across markets

Exhibit 7-8   *Key Characteristics of a Global Strategy*

- Standardized products
- Global economies of scale in key components and activities
- Leverage technology across many markets
- Global coordination of marketing and sales systemwide
- Cross-subsidization policies to respond to competitive moves by other global strategy firms

A Strong Tilt Toward Standardization. Global firms seek to standardize their product designs, components, and even their core value-adding processes wherever they can. In a full-blown global strategy, a high level of product design and component standardization is essential to capture low-cost economies of scale in production. In turn, standardized products often convey the image of design excellence, global acceptance, and world-class quality, as demonstrated by such highly regarded products as Sony Trinitron television sets, Minidisc-mans, DVD players, Walkmans, Citizen and Seiko watches, Nokia phones, Hewlett-Packard calculators and laser printers, Toyota and Ford automobiles, and Caterpillar and Komatsu heavy construction equipment. Companies seek a high level of product design standardization (with some minor adaptation or variation according to local power requirements, laws, or sizes) because it enables them to produce global volumes at low cost. Moreover, well-conceived and standardized product designs do much to increase the firm's marketing image. A strong image eases the firm's entry task of producing another line of products to serve the same markets in later periods.

In the case of Nokia, commercializing a new line of phones every few months is made faster when the firm is able to build around a core set of product designs and standardized components. Although Nokia has recently unveiled an entirely new line of N-Gage digital handheld devices that offer multiple functions, the N-Gage shares many of the same components that are used in its Communicator line of digital phones. Components and development costs are shared across the company's entire line of communication products. Although customers in different national markets may have distinct preferences for varying phone styles (for example, candy bar vs. clamshell handsets), Nokia is able to respond to these differing needs by incorporating these design variations in its manufacturing facilities quickly.

Locating Plants to Maximize Systemwide Advantage. Another central facet of a global strategy is to maximize the total systemwide competitive advantage of the firm across multiple regional markets. Global strategy firms must invest in the newest production technologies to reap the benefits of economies of scale from serving all of its markets. Key to doing so is locating plants, factories, laboratories, facilities, and other crucial infrastructure in those worldwide sites that maximize the firm's sources of global leverage and scale economies. In other words, the decision to build plants and factories is based not only on the economics of serving individual local markets but also on maximizing the firm's competitive advantage and economies of scale across all of its subsidiaries and markets. For example, firms may locate some plants in low-cost countries to further reduce labor costs (as is the case with the textile or consumer electronics industries); they may choose to build plants where energy costs are the lowest (for example, aluminum smelting); they may locate their most sophisticated plants closest to their most important markets (digital phones and handheld devices, construction equipment, and automotive industries); or they may build only one or two giant, world-scale plants to serve the entire global market (steel, flat display screens, semiconductor fabrication). Thus, the decision to locate plants, laboratories, and other facilities globally is predicated on a systemic view of extending and leveraging the firm's scale-driven production base across all of its key markets, as opposed to scattering plants across many markets in a host of countries.

Ford Motor Company, for example, centralizes the production of many standardized engines and components in the United States but builds many of its transmissions and drivetrain parts in Brazil and Mexico, where the cost of engineering and building such complex parts is lower. On the other hand, some of Ford's newest multivalve engines come from Ford factories and affiliates in Japan, where a greater abundance of multivalve technology and advanced production techniques is available. Cars that are to be sold in the United States are assembled here, whereas cars destined for Europe are assembled in locations throughout Britain and Germany. Thus, Ford's decisions to build and locate plants and facilities around the world are based on maximizing the firm's overall objective of being competitive and a low-cost producer for each critical component of the car.[18] In recent years, Ford's luxury line of Lincoln LS cars has shared the same chassis and drivetrain platforms with those used for the Jaguar XJS. Even though Ford seeks to maintain the unique identities of its European automotive acquisitions (Jaguar, Aston Martin, Volvo Cars), the company still actively searches for ways to use a common set of suppliers to lower its total procurement costs. Ford will even share components among all lines of vehicles (U.S. and European) to the extent that they do not compromise the unique experience that a customer feels when driving that particular line or type of car.

Not to be outdone, General Motors announced in June 2004 that it would also shift the responsibilities for core product design and engineering for its steering, braking, and other chassis-related parts to its German subsidiary, Open. Many of GM's midsize cars use a basic set of components known within the company as the Epsilon architecture. Likewise, GM also announced that its U.S. operations will take over the engineering responsibilities for full-size trucks and sport utility vehicles (SUVs) for its global operations. Strategically, GM is hoping to capture significant cost savings, greater economies of scale, and increased component standardization by concentrating product development and engineering in those subsidiaries that possess the deepest competences in that field.[19]

IBM also pursues a global strategy in its various computer, networking, consulting, and semiconductor operations. Many of IBM's mainframe computers are designed and built in the United States, but its most advanced laptop, notebook-sized computers are built in IBM facilities located in Japan, where there is an abundance of skills and expertise in manufacturing flat-panel display screens. On the other hand, IBM has completely contracted out the manufacturing of its entire line of personal computer products to Sanmina-SCI and other contract manufacturers. At the same time, IBM supplies key semiconductor manufacturing capabilities to a number of other electronics firms as well, thus helping it gain economies of scale in semiconductors, disk drives, displays, and power systems. These components are actually more profitable for IBM than the PC itself. Over the past few years, IBM has faced the paradoxical situation wherein it is cheaper for the company to supply the parts for PCs rather than to make the entire PC itself. Having lost money in PCs over the past several years, IBM in December 2004 chose to sell its entire PC operation to Lenovo Group, a Chinese firm that has big ambitions to enter different high-technology fields.

In the commercial aircraft industry, the majority of Boeing's aircraft manufacturing and assembly operations takes place in its flagship plant in Everett, Washington, as well as in St. Louis and Long Beach where the company has refurbished some of McDonnell-Douglas' preexisting facilities. In facilities around Seattle, 65 percent of total world demand for commercial aircraft can be assembled in that one region. The size and sophistication of Boeing's recent manufacturing investments exemplify Boeing's commitment to economies of scale in component manufacture and final airframe assembly. Advanced machining and metal-cutting operations needed for aircraft wings are located in nearby supporting plants, whereas centralized development laboratories and facilities provide new composite or resin materials that help further reduce the weight and eventual cost of operating the plane. Also central to Boeing's enormous base of production expertise is the company's commitment to total quality management and continuous improvement. Boeing is constantly searching for new techniques that steadily improve the cost, quality, and durability of its airframes. Novel assembly techniques are continuously explored and tested to see if they can further reduce waste to speed up development time.

Leveraging Technology Across Multiple Markets.   Rising technological intensity of new products makes them correspondingly more expensive to develop and commercialize. High R&D costs that accompany more sophisticated products mean that global production volumes are necessary to recoup the firm's initial outlays. R&D represents a huge fixed cost in which large amounts of money and time are spent to test and finally develop a new product. Only by selling to the entire world can firms recoup their development costs. Thus, firms possessing highly proprietary technologies or distinctive, hard-to-imitate R&D skills and facilities often seek to blitz the world with their products.

For example, Honda Motor Company of Japan retains a distinctive technological capability in small combustion engine design and manufacture. Because of its expertise, Honda has been able to design and market engines for use in outboard motorboats, generators, lawnmowers, motorcycles, snowblowers, and, of course, its best-selling line of cars in the United States and Japan. The existence of a technological competence or skill encourages the firm to develop a full-blown global strategy, in which new applications of the underlying skill help build reputation, market share, and a global presence.

In highly scientific industries, such as pharmaceuticals, biotechnology and specialty plastics or chemicals, firms possessing highly proprietary technologies or patents on their products have also pursued a global strategy. Patents give the firm a temporary monopoly over its product, and thus entering worldwide markets greatly raises the firm's earnings potential. Companies such as Pfizer and Merck have steadily been moving toward incorporating many aspects of a global strategy, and have even become competitive in the fierce Japanese market.[20]

One of the major reasons why Nokia has taken such an active role in promoting next-generation 3G technology in so many national markets is that the firm hopes to lead the wave as consumers begin to use the company's even more advanced digital phones. Nokia envisions that these digital handheld devices will enable consumers to do many things from the ease and convenience of their versatile phone/radio/e-mail device/game player/digital music player. As a result, Nokia has been encouraging other national telecom companies to adopt its technology as the centerpiece of their future wireless phone systems. By pushing an advanced wireless network design across multiple national boundaries, Nokia hopes to leverage the costs of its technology development across many markets that will ultimately look to purchase some of Nokia's transmission equipment as well.

Worldwide Marketing Efforts. Most marketing efforts by their very nature must be carried out within individual local markets. Marketing requires close contact with customers to ensure that the firm meets their needs. Yet, some marketing activities lend themselves well to supporting a global strategy. The most obvious case would be a centralized, global marketing team or salesforce that specializes in selling highly sophisticated, expensive products that are purchased infrequently. In some industries, such as aircraft, power generation equipment, and telecommunications, a common salesforce travels the globe providing customers with specifications, costs, and individual features of the products. For example, in the power generation equipment industries, General Electric, ABB, Siemens, Toshiba, and Mitsubishi use global marketing and sales teams to compete with one another in selling large nuclear plants or intricate turbines that are used in hydroelectric and coal-burning electricity plants. The sales task is often highly complex, in that it involves discussing the specifications of the project with the customer over a lengthy period. Moreover, the number of people who have the detailed, technical knowledge behind such complex products and projects is few. This scarcity compels companies such as General Electric and ABB to rely on the same marketing team to travel the world in search of customers for power generation equipment.

Boeing, Airbus, Embraer, and other commercial aerospace firms have centralized their marketing efforts as well. Whether the customer is in Saudi Arabia, China, Brazil, or Japan, these companies will send the same team that is knowledgeable about their line of aircraft and their specifications to meet with potential customers. In this way, all of these firms hope to spread the fixed costs of a highly sophisticated, technically fluent salesforce over its many markets.

Competing by Cross-Subsidization. Firms pursuing a global strategy often engage in a policy known as cross-subsidization. **Cross-subsidization** refers to using the financial resources and technological skills learned from one market to fight a competitor in another. It is a powerful process that enables firms competing globally to build leverage across markets by transferring funds, skills, low-cost production, or market insights from one market to another. Cross-subsidization, in its most sophisticated form, is the deployment of resources and products across markets to maximize opportunities to build leverage. Companies who practice cross-subsidization often view the entire globe as one large "chess map." Each player seeks to position itself in a position of maximum competitive advantage in order to have the greatest sway over customers and competitors. The presence of several large, global firms competing for the same

cross-subsidization:
Using financial, technological, and marketing resources from one market to fight a competitor in another; involves extensive use of "parry and thrust" tactics to gain new market positions.

market often indicates a strong potential for cross-subsidization. For example, Japanese and South Korean consumer electronics firms practice cross-subsidization in the sale of consumer electronics globally. The earnings they receive from their home market often allow them to fund expensive promotion efforts in the United States and Europe. Also, the earnings from a comparatively mature product (for example, televisions) provide the cash necessary for next-generation technologies (flat-screen displays) that become the basis of future product development. Simultaneously, the marketing skills and techniques they learn from selling in one overseas market help them refine their techniques to enter another. Thus, cross-subsidization, when carried out effectively, enables firms pursuing a global strategy to build on success in one market to penetrate and fight competitors in another. Some authors have termed this type of global cross-subsidization fight as "parry and thrust," which is also the phrase used to describe how fencers maneuver around one another when searching for weakness and advantage.[21] The careful coordination of the actions of its subsidiaries through cross-subsidization allows firms to achieve a systemwide view of competition and market share.

Cross-subsidization is a vital tool that enables firms to deal with the second issue of global expansion: How do we minimize our vulnerabilities and maximize our opportunities against the actions of similarly minded competitors? Cross-subsidization is directly concerned with the actions of competitors across shared markets. The actions and earnings of Sony in the European television market, for example, may have direct effects on the way it will compete in the U.S. market. Sony could use the potentially high profits earned from Europe to develop a new line of less costly televisions to penetrate the U.S. market even further, thus escalating its fight with other firms jockeying for the American market. Or, Sony could use its European profits to pour more money into its advanced DVD business in any of the markets it serves, with the hope of beating out other competitors with similar market ambitions for that product category. Based on Sony's capability to use cross-subsidization in this manner, existing competitors in the U.S. market such as Philips, Toshiba, Sanyo, Sharp, LG, Samsung, and Matsushita Electric have reason to watch and monitor Sony's moves in Europe and all of its other markets. Conversely, Sony needs to keep a watchful eye on Matsushita Electric, which may seek to build share in both the United States and adjacent markets. Matsushita's large domestic market in Japan and growing presence in Latin America will give Matsushita a source of funds that it could use to battle Sony elsewhere, perhaps in Southeast Asia or the Middle East. Sony certainly has to keep watch on Philips, a European firm that has a long tradition of innovating breakthrough products in a number of fields. Thus, the competitive moves of firms that practice cross-subsidization resemble a global game of chess or Go, whereby a move anywhere on the board (world markets) will eventually have ripple effects elsewhere.[22]

Boeing's early 1990s strategy against global competitors Airbus and McDonnell-Douglas shows how cross-subsidization applies even when an industry has only three competitors. Both Boeing and Airbus sought to build market positions around the world, while McDonnell-Douglas was largely concerned with protecting its U.S. market base. Boeing frequently offers superior financing, servicing, and other buying incentives to its vital European customers, such as Lufthansa and Air France. A strengthened position in Europe gives Boeing more room to maneuver against Airbus in its home base. By selling more planes to European customers, Boeing squeezes Airbus' cash position and market share. On the other hand, Airbus is likely to offer its own set of superior and possibly more attractive financing terms to its customers in North America, such as United Airlines and American Airlines. If Airbus is successful (and it has become even more so in recent years), then it gains a valuable beachhead from which to penetrate Boeing's home market with other types of aircraft in the future. Airbus has even secured commitments from FedEx to purchase its A380 aircraft for cargo shipment applications. Thus, Boeing and Airbus are engaged in constant parrying and thrusting into each other's markets.[23]

Note that McDonnell-Douglas, a weak third player in the 1980s and early 1990s, was largely unable to move against Boeing or Airbus successfully, since its excessive reliance on the U.S. commercial market gave it little leverage against either firm elsewhere. Thus, it is no accident that both Airbus and Boeing gained strength at the expense of McDonnell-Douglas, since its lack of a global presence handicapped it against better-armed competitors. Boeing's recent acquisition of McDonnell-Douglas occurred at a time when McDonnell-Douglas could no longer afford to commit vast sums of money into development expenditures for a market base that was increasingly squeezed by two larger competitors practicing cross-subsidization.

Thus, global strategies are designed to link the firm's operations in many markets into a systemwide perspective for building and extending competitive advantage. Global strategy seeks to exploit technologically driven sources of leverage. Leverage results when the firm can extend and transfer its skills and resources across markets that are interdependent and mutually reinforcing. When pursued successfully, global strategy maximizes a firm's opportunities to transfer its products, processes, and competences from one market to another.

Multidomestic Strategy

A multidomestic strategy is often the preferred way to compete when regional markets contrast with one another in terms of consumer tastes and preferences and competitive conditions. The more diverse the regional or national market condition, the greater the appeal of the multidomestic strategy. A multidomestic strategy is really a collection of country or region-based strategies, where each region or country (defined by the firm's economic reach and organizational approach) possesses its own set of value-adding activities or value chains. Popular images of firms pursuing a multidomestic strategy, for example, include various sizes and tastes of Maxwell House coffee or Snapple teas in China, India, and other locales where these offerings are considered new and perhaps exotic products. Nestlé's assortment of chocolate candies that are mixed to suit varying tastes in different countries also represents a multidomestic strategy. A number of economic and industry-driven factors promote the use of multidomestic strategies for a given industry. These industry drivers include heterogeneous demand patterns across markets, few economies of scale in production, high product transportation costs, variations in distribution channels across markets, and the need to source products locally because of perishability, legal requirements, or specific types of ingredients or components.

Firms pursuing a multidomestic strategy adjust and tailor their products and practices to the individual needs of each market. As opposed to a global strategy, a multidomestic strategy treats each market independently and separately. Firms pursuing multidomestic strategies also view competitive challenges in the context of local conditions and therefore do not attempt to form a completely unified, systemwide approach to building and extending competitive advantage. Key to a successful multidomestic strategy is treating each market as a unique arena from which to differentiate the firm's products as much as possible from those of local producers or other multidomestic competitors. Thus, value chains in one market may be significantly different from value chain configurations designed for another market with very different economic or environmental settings. In other words, a firm pursuing a multidomestic strategy must deal with the very real possibility that each market will require its own value chain, with few opportunities to share costs or activities among them. The lack of sufficient economies of scale across multiple markets is a critical industry factor that promotes a multidomestic strategy. The multidomestic strategy's independent and separate treatment of markets and subunits is shown in Exhibit 7-9.

Exhibit 7-9 *Multidomestic Strategy of Expansion*

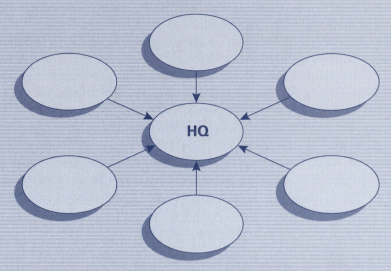

- Competitive advantage built in each separate national or regional market
- Markets and subunits treated independently from one another
- Control of activities are decentralized, reporting back to headquarters

Although firms undertaking a multidomestic strategy can sometimes transfer what they have learned from one market to another, this transfer is difficult to do on a consistent basis because of the numerous value chains dedicated to each market. Because the individual markets are often so unlike one another, the firm must essentially retrace its steps to build competitive advantage in each market, making it difficult to leverage highly tangible skills or resources across markets. Firms pursuing a multidomestic strategy tend to exhibit the following practices to build competitive advantage in each market: (1) adapt and change their products frequently, (2) conduct key value–adding activities and operations in each market locally, (3) coordinate marketing and sales within individual markets, and (4) leverage a brand name or reputation globally to build image. (See Exhibit 7–10.)

Frequent Product Adaptation.   Central to the multidomestic strategy is frequent product adaptation and modification to match the specific tastes and consumer preferences of a firm's individual markets. In stark contrast to a global strategy, in which standardization of product design often conveys the image of quality, frequent product adaptation in a multidomestic

Exhibit 7-10   *Key Characteristics of a Multidomestic Strategy*

- Customization or frequent adaptation of products for each separate market
- Few systemwide opportunities for economies of scale
- Value-adding activities performed and duplicated in each market
- Coordination of marketing and sales within each market
- Quality and image across markets are important sources of competitive advantage

strategy is required because the product or service does truly differ along some critical attribute across markets. Superior quality in such products as food, beverages, banking, clothing, and even some categories of industrial goods and supplies is not based on standardized features, but rather on how closely the products fit the targeted market. Often the nature of product adaptation goes beyond design modification; some products must be entirely redesigned, reformulated, or incorporate entirely different ingredients to successfully appeal to customers in different markets. For example, most competitors in the food processing and consumer nondurable industries, such as Procter & Gamble, H. J. Heinz, General Mills, Kraft Foods, and PepsiCo, all practice some variation of a multidomestic strategy. Tide detergent, Heinz ketchup, processed foods, and Pepsi cola drinks, to note a few examples, are actually quite different, depending on where you purchase the product. Other industries characterized by a high level of multidomestic competition include textiles, brewing, automotive motor oils, local telephone services, and personal banking. In each of these cases, the product or service in question is customized to the individual market segment that is targeted.

In a multidomestic strategy, each firm seeks to identify the most important attributes of a product to a specific market and then to closely tailor its offerings to that market. McDonald's restaurants are found worldwide, but the servings offered in a restaurant in France or Germany, for example, are likely to differ significantly from those in the United States and Japan. McDonald's serves beer and a particular menu of sandwiches in its German restaurants, whereas in Japan it offers a special kind of fish sandwich and beverages that taste unlike those in the United States. In the personal care and cosmetics industry, firms such as Estée Lauder, Procter & Gamble, Revlon, and Lancôme often customize the blends that become ingredients used for eye makeup, face creams, cleansing solutions, and other care products. A cosmetic company must often consider such region-specific factors as the daily amount of sun, water hardness or acidity conditions, skin complexions, and likely personal habits of customers in deciding how to tailor its products to each market.

Product adaptation is sometimes necessary because of local laws and regulations stipulating that certain products use a high percentage of domestic content. For example, certain segments of the machine tool industry are multidomestic in nature because host governments demand that multinational firms produce a given portion of their product using local labor and supplies of materials. This is particularly the case for those industries that a local government considers strategic or vital to its national development. Thus, although machine tools such as lathes and drills would ordinarily exhibit economic characteristics favoring a more global strategy, local restrictions can sometimes make a multidomestic strategy the best alternative for a firm serving local markets.

Coke practices a high degree of product adaptation and modification across every market it serves. Rapid product testing, introduction, and adaptation are the hallmarks of Coke's product strategy worldwide. Product testing and development are performed in each individual market, since market research for one country or region is unlikely to show trends that are identical to another market. In the United States, Coke is best known for its Coca-Cola, Diet Coke, Sprite, Diet Sprite, and Mello Yellow carbonated beverages. Although Coke offers its cola-based drinks in a similar form and taste in Japan and Europe, the sweetness levels are altered from one market to the next. Also, Coke develops and introduces new brands in many of its markets besides the United States. For example in Japan, the company has pioneered and sold large quantities of its beta carotene–based beverages aimed at a specific health-conscious segment. In Australia, flavored carbonated beverages sold under the brand names Skysurfer and Lift are unlike beverages that people are accustomed to in the United States. The sizes of containers that Coke uses for its beverages vary greatly across regions. Even the size of aluminum cans used for convenience packaging of Coke's products is adjusted.

Local Value-Adding Activities. Another key facet of the multidomestic strategy is to perform all critical value-adding functions locally. In effect, a pure multidomestic strategy is an aggregate collection of many separate value chains, each of which is found within the market it serves. Each market has its own R&D, manufacturing, and marketing functions to perform the value-adding activities needed to compete there. Thus, firms in multidomestic industries tend to produce or source their products locally. Several economic factors promote the need to establish separate value-adding activities in each market, including high perishability of product, the lack of economies of scale in production, and high transportation costs resulting from a low value-added/weight ratio.

perishability:
The loss of economic value that occurs when a product or service is not used within a given time period, often used to describe the ease with which a product spoils or decays; a major economic consideration that promotes the use of multidomestic strategies.

High perishability is often a factor promoting multidomestic strategies. **Perishability,** in the broadest sense, occurs when a product or service is not used by a certain time. The most obvious case of high perishability as a significant strategic factor is the food-processing industry, in which eggs, meat, and dairy products spoil rapidly, in days if not hours. The need for extensive refrigeration, warehousing, and careful packaging is best performed in local facilities, since transportation costs associated with moving highly fragile or perishable products are prohibitive. Perishability is the primary reason why milk (which actually exhibits a high degree of consistency worldwide) is not a global industry.

The lack of significant production economies of scale is a major factor in keeping manufacturing activities within each regional market. Many products still do not offer sufficient global economies of scale to warrant central production. For example, leather and tanning products remain largely multidomestic in nature, although some Brazilian and Italian firms are starting to export large quantities of their fine quality shoes to Europe, the United States, and other markets. The building controls industry is another example where the need to adapt and produce parts locally outweighs any large economies of scale in components. Companies such as United Technologies, Honeywell, and General Electric have traditionally managed their building controls businesses in a multidomestic approach, since it is easier to build or source low-voltage transformers and other mature electrical supply products locally. Other products by their very nature must be built locally, such as engineering-intensive projects. Engineering, contracting, and construction companies such as Bechtel, Morrison-Knudsen, and Halliburton's Kellogg Brown and Root subsidiary often establish local offices to manage their projects under contract. The "components" or raw ingredients used for their products and services (reinforced cement and gravel) are products and supplies best provided locally. High cost prohibits their shipment, but more important, local rock and mineral conditions dictate what kinds of materials can be used for a particular project. Even though these firms have world-class engineers (located both locally and around the world) who are highly mobile, the need to deal with the customer on a day-to-day basis for several years after the contract is signed means that the actual building, servicing, and management operations remain local.

Another factor that favors the multidomestic strategy is low value-added/weight ratio. Perhaps the best example of a low value-added/weight ratio product is that of reinforced cement, mentioned in the preceding paragraph. Cement is a highly standardized product with numerous uses. It also faces a market with homogeneous demand. Yet, the costs of shipping reinforced concrete anywhere is prohibitive. That is why even in the United States, local highway projects, shopping centers, office buildings, and subway construction use cement that is actually manufactured or mixed on-site. Its use of ingredients with a low value-added/weight ratio is also why most construction and building industries remain a multidomestic industry throughout the world. On the other hand, architectural and engineering talent is becoming more global in nature, since technical knowledge and experience can easily be leveraged from one project to another. Other products that exhibit a low value-added/weight ratio include unprocessed farm crops (wheat, corn, oats), raw pulp, and other intermediate products that are refined into more valuable products further down the value chain. To the extent a firm can innovate a new way to ship unprocessed grains in a way that dramatically improves shipping and loading time, reduces perishability or spoilage, and/or standardizes a method for transporting them, then the prospects for this industry to become more global are greatly enhanced.

Local Distribution Channels. Firms competing in multidomestic industries must understand and manage a broad range of distribution channels. Each country is likely to have its own distinct way of distributing products throughout its economic system. Even across Europe, stark differences in the distribution and shopping habits can be observed within individual nations. In Germany, a large volume of products is sold through huge hypermarts that are even bigger than the shopping warehouse clubs found in the United States. In Italy, on the other hand, the distribution channels are highly complex and convoluted. Instead of large supermarkets and hypermarts, small retailers (almost overwhelmingly family-owned) tend to dominate distribution, even in large cities such as Milan and Florence. Numerous middlemen and wholesalers make it difficult for firms to sell their products without maintaining substantial operations there. France and Great Britain contrast with Germany and Italy in that distribution channels are even more region specific within the same country.

Multidomestic firms develop their own distinctive strategies for each market's distribution channels and other unique, region-specific features. Procter & Gamble, for example, has its own sophisticated, computer-driven warehousing system that ships vast quantities of Tide detergent and other products to its German wholesalers and retailers quickly. On the other hand, Procter & Gamble relies on an array of middlemen to manage the inventory flow of Tide to reach customers in Italy and France. In recent years, P&G has restructured its European operations in an attempt to centralize more of its product development and distribution activities to cater to a greater, pan-European market. New products are designed to serve a broader market base, although so far the reception has been mixed. Entrenched middlemen, wholesalers, and retailers in a number of countries, plus shifting currency exchange rates, complicate P&G's ability to price its products uniformly across the continent.

Procter & Gamble's largest competitors (such as Colgate-Palmolive, Unilever, Henkel, and Kao of Japan) have confronted similar problems in trying to develop a wider, pan-European strategy. Like Procter & Gamble, Nestlé has attempted to concentrate its efforts on key products that appear to attract large, similar segments from different markets. Its white chocolate candy bars, for example, are a hit in both the United States and Europe. On the other hand, some of Nestlé's other products, such as instant chocolate drinks, confront more traditional multidomestic issues, such as separate distribution systems for highly perishable products. Kmart, the large U.S. discount retailer, commenced operations during 1995 in Prague, Czech Republic, after having bought out an existing retailer a few years back. It is finding that despite the Czech population's zeal for lower-priced goods and imports, managing the distribution system that brings products into its flagship stores is an arduous task, particularly in a nation that was previously more accustomed to state-run distribution systems where pricing flexibility and wide product choice were nonexistent. Kmart must deal with a host of middlemen and other distribution players (often relics of previous state ownership) that eat into its cost advantage.

Leveraging a Global Brand Name. Multidomestic strategies by their very nature require firms to locate their key value-adding activities in each market they serve. Yet, firms pursuing multidomestic strategies can still attempt to build sources of leverage and competitive advantage across markets. The most important source of leverage for each firm comes from cultivating and extending its well-known quality image to new products and markets. Many of the companies that practice multidomestic strategies (Nestlé, H. J. Heinz, Kellogg, Procter & Gamble, Unilever, McDonald's, PepsiCo, and Philip Morris, to name just a few) have tried to develop and foster their own corporate images of quality that help with entry into new markets. On the one hand, the nature of these firms' product offerings—foods, restaurants, laundry detergents, soft drinks and beverages, and personal care products—makes local value-adding activities a necessity. On the other hand, these firms have been careful to build up a strong corporate association with high product quality. Thus, markets around the world can come to expect a certain level of high quality with McDonald's restaurant offerings, with PepsiCo's soft drinks and snack foods, and with P&G's or Henkel's laundry detergents and soaps. Even though each firm's products are multidomestic, these companies can still develop strong global images. In effect, a strong quality reputation provides competitive strength in each local market and helps provide a unifying framework for developing a global brand franchise.

Thus, multidomestic strategies are an aggregate collection of the firm's many distinct and discrete operations in multiple markets. Unlike a global strategy, a multidomestic strategy does not explicitly seek to link up markets and subsidiaries through shared technologies, products, and processes. Even as the Internet begins to connect a firm's local subsidiaries into an integrated information and communication platform, the specific strategies and marketing programs for each subsidiary remain largely autonomous. The need to satisfy local customers often continues to outweigh the gains of centralized coordination of subsidiary actions and local strategies. Instead, firms that compete multidomestically do so on a market-by-market basis. Each subsidiary is free to formulate and execute its own strategies for the market it serves, since pricing, local tastes and customs, regulations, distribution channels, and product differences still represent major strategic considerations. Leverage in a multidomestic firm is not based on shared technologies, products, or production processes, but rather on creating a well-known, high-quality, worldwide image.

Benefits of Global Expansion

Global expansion can help the firm achieve numerous benefits. Whether its strategy is global or multidomestic, global expansion can create numerous sources of value and help the firm reinforce its competitive advantage. Some of the most important value-creating benefits of global expansion include (1) market growth and expansion, (2) the recovery of investment costs, (3) the creation of a strong image, and (4) accelerated learning and transfer of new knowledge and skills (see Exhibit 7-11).

Exhibit 7-11   *Benefits of Global Expansion*

- Market growth and expansion opportunities
- Recovery of R&D and investment costs
- Creation of a distinct image
- Accelerated learning and transfer of new skills

Market Growth and Expansion

Globalization allows firms to overcome the limits of domestic growth. For U.S., European, and Japanese companies in particular, global expansion is a necessity because many domestic markets are maturing and growth rates are slowing down. Numerous sectors of the U.S. economy, including service-oriented businesses, such as fast foods, packaged goods, retail/grocery store chains, beverages, and even telecommunications, are not growing as fast as they used to. On the other hand, the opening of vast new markets in China, Eastern Europe, and Latin America means that U.S. firms such as McDonald's, Colgate-Palmolive, Wal-Mart Stores, and Anheuser-Busch can continue to grow and create new sources of value. Thus, companies can expand globally to achieve benefits similar to diversifying into new industries; they can maintain their growth momentum and extend their competitive advantage in new markets.

Globalization also enables the firm to outperform local domestic competitors in their home markets. When a firm expands globally, it develops new insights and identifies new product opportunities that may not be available to competitors who remain domestic in orientation. Many Japanese firms explicitly viewed their initial forays abroad during the 1970s as the necessary costs to learn how best to design products for the U.S. market. The trials of going abroad helped the firm refine and reinforce its competitive advantage. Lack of global awareness was a big problem with the Big Three automakers during the 1970s and 1980s. Although General Motors and Ford had substantial European operations, senior management in the United States was primarily concerned with "milking" the domestic market. Japanese competitors, such as Toyota, Nissan, and Honda, on the other hand, were looking to expand beyond their small domestic base. They made deep inroads into the U.S. market that not only persist, but also continue to grow even today. In turn, GM has begun to rely more heavily on its numerous equity holdings or national subsidiaries (for example, Fuji Motor, Isuzu, Suzuki, Daewoo, Opel of Germany, Saab of Sweden). Through global expansion, a firm can realize the related benefit of keeping competitors at bay and effectively barring them from cross-subsidizing into the firm's home market. For example, Caterpillar maintains a small presence in Japan to keep tabs on Komatsu, its most important competitor in the construction, earth-moving, and heavy equipment industry. If Caterpillar did not maintain even a small presence in Japan, Komatsu would likely feel less constrained about taking on Caterpillar more aggressively in the United States and other national markets. IBM Japan serves an extremely valuable purpose for all of IBM. Having a major presence in Japan helps IBM learn critical new technologies that can be applied to its entire line of computer and semiconductor products. More important, IBM Japan serves to constrain the actions of such key competitors as Fujitsu, Toshiba, NEC, and Hitachi. Despite fierce competition from these companies, IBM Japan serves as a vital "strategic window" that IBM can use to monitor its competitors. Most recently, IBM Japan in 2001 was actually beginning to gain significant market share from Fujitsu and NEC in mainframe computers. In September 2001, IBM Japan's efforts in rebuffing its competitors were so successful that Fujitsu even announced that it would no longer make IBM-compatible mainframe computers—an effort that Fujitsu once considered to be its core undertaking during the 1970s and 1980s.

In a similar vein, Xerox once owned 50 percent of Fuji-Xerox Corporation. Fuji-Xerox played a major role in helping the U.S. copier giant learn how to compete using such Japanese manufacturing techniques as lean production, total quality management, and just-in-time inventory systems. As Xerox Corporation almost went into financial collapse during the 1980s, many observers believe that Fuji-Xerox's presence in Japan helped Xerox not only to learn how to make better copiers but also to constrain the actions of fierce Japanese competitors such as Canon, Sharp, Minolta, and Ricoh. Even though Xerox recently sold off part of its interest in

Fuji-Xerox to restructure its domestic U.S. operations, the company still retains a 25 percent share of Fuji-Xerox to keep abreast of new technologies and manufacturing techniques.

Recovery of Investment Costs

Globalization is a powerful method to help recover the investment costs required for new products and processes. As noted earlier, selling at global volumes is a requirement for innovation in many industries. The recovery of huge investments for R&D and production facilities is an overwhelming incentive for firms in high-technology industries to expand globally. Semiconductor, pharmaceutical, aircraft, communication and medical equipment, advanced materials, and other industries need global markets to build sufficient economies of scale to recover their sunk costs. Multidomestic firms also can recover investments in brand names by expanding globally. Although multidomestic firms do not share the same economies of scale that global firms do, companies such as Coca-Cola, Nestlé, Colgate-Palmolive, and Unilever have invested heavily into their brand names that are effectively intangible assets that can be applied abroad. **Intangible assets** represent firm-based resources, skills, or other hard-to-imitate assets that are not physical in form. These can include investments in brand equity, human talent, a unique approach to product development, means to foster innovation, and other resources that help make the firm distinctive.

intangible assets: *Resources based on skills or other hard-to-imitate assets that are not physical in form; examples include brand equity, fast product development, management techniques, proprietary means of developing knowledge, innovation, and so forth.*

Creation of a Strong Image

Both multidomestic and global firms enhance their image when they expand globally with quality products. A strong image works as an investment that can ease entry into new markets later, thus extending a competitive advantage over time. In other words, a strong, globally recognized image becomes an intangible but vital building block of competitive advantage that lays the foundation for creating future value. For many firms, their brand names and quality image have become almost synonymous with their distinctive competences, and thus represent durable but intangible assets that serve to implement an "umbrella" strategy.

Consider the wide line of products that Sony uses to enter new markets. Because Sony's television sets and other consumer electronics are so well built and engineered, new Sony products, such as electric shavers, food mixers, and even air conditioners, are likely to receive a warm reception in new markets as well. Sony's distinctive competence in designing and producing high-quality, technically advanced consumer electronics and gadgets (a key aspect of a global strategy) thus "spills over" into emerging high-tech household appliances and new markets. Consequently, Sony's task of entering new markets with new products becomes much easier over time, since Sony's highly burnished image helps extend its competitive advantage in unforeseen ways. Sony's image thus serves as an umbrella that protects its new products from fierce competition and consumer skepticism. For example, Sony's rapid rise to challenge Nintendo in the fiercely competitive video game business stems from many consumers' experience and belief that a Sony-made product will consistently be world-class. As Sony begins to enter other electronic and Internet-driven arenas, the company's strong brand equity allows it to lower the cost of entry and risk in pursuing new ventures. In other words, strong brand equity and images are fixed investments in value-creating assets; reputation and quality give these firms (both global and multidomestic) a decided and enduring competitive advantage, which facilitates new market entry. This same emphasis on building and sustaining a strong brand equity and presence for packaged foods and beverage companies has also enabled many U.S. multinational giants to establish strong market positions overseas.[24]

The American Express Company also realizes the benefits of a well-known and well-defined image that brings forth the idea of quality, security, and safety. One of American Express' strategic missions is to create the "world's most respected brand name." Travelers around the world recognize the reliability and quality that are behind the blue square American Express logo. Although each American Express region pursues its own specific advertising and marketing (multidomestic strategy), all travel offices follow a common set of procedures to help people in need (common practices to reinforce quality and image). Travelers or tourists who encounter trouble can go to an American Express office for emergency replacement of travelers' checks or lost or stolen credit cards. In addition, all American Express offices are equipped to send emergency telegrams and messages to families, consulates, and other contacts of the people in need.

Accelerated Learning

One of the most important benefits of globalization is the ability to learn and transfer new knowledge within the firm. Global and multidomestic firms, through their exposure to numerous environments, products, and markets, are constantly receiving vast amounts of information concerning competitors, customers, and new technologies. Firms with large operations become storehouses of new knowledge and skills, especially if they possess distinctive competences in core R&D, production, or marketing techniques. The need to seek a return on proprietary technologies and brand names encourages expanding firms to design new products and to enter new markets. In turn, by doing so, firms accumulate new insights that can be used to generate products for other markets. Global and multidomestic firms acquire their knowledge and skills from high-intensity competition with other global and domestic firms. Thus, global competition among firms with subsidiaries and technology development efforts located in many key markets has the effect of accelerating the diffusion of new product ideas worldwide.

The effect of global competition on these firms is the building of a substantial value-adding infrastructure that allows for faster transfer of ideas, insights, and skills across their subsidiaries. Such information has helped Nokia to develop a wider range of advanced communication products and technologies that flow through its vast R&D, production, supply, and distribution systems. Moreover, Nokia is an excellent position to learn how changing customer demands for a particular type or style of phone in one market can become a similar trend in another market. By competing in a global posture among many markets, Nokia hopes to be able to respond to these changes faster than other digital phone companies, which may not have the same global breadth and reach as Nokia. Similarly, multidomestic firms such as Coca-Cola, Nestlé, Procter & Gamble, Diageo, Henkel, Electrolux, and PepsiCo can take advantage of the insights and new ideas learned from one market to enter new markets under a well-recognized global umbrella of brands.

Costs of Globalization

Although global expansion strategies can provide firms with huge benefits, managing overseas operations also involves substantial costs. Many of these expansion-related costs are organizational. Coordinating operations across multiple, diverse markets generates significant organizational tensions, pressures, and tradeoffs within a company. For example, companies are exposed to the volatilities and idiosyncrasies of operating in different markets. Although regions in one part of the world may prosper, others may be entering recessions. During the late 1990s, as Southeast Asia entered a difficult period of recession and recovery, many U.S. firms with extensive operations there, such as 3M, Boeing, and IBM, reeled from the effects of lessened demand.[25]

In many ways, global expansion can present a double-edged sword, since such expansion can often expose firms to different types of economic cycles and practices they would not have ordinarily incurred with a more domestic approach.[26] Nonetheless, markets have become more integrated, and technology now links people from around the world through the Internet and other communication modes. The costs of global expansion should still be viewed in the context of building a wide base of firm capabilities that enable firms to plant the seeds for new sources of competitive advantage. These efforts are especially important if market demand becomes more homogeneous, technologically similar, or when emerging markets recover. Thus, even though economic conditions in one part of the world may be less than favorable, they also create opportunities for firms willing to strengthen their positions by buying out their joint venture partners or increasing management control over ventures and activities in that region.

For example, despite the great turmoil and recessionary pressures that confronted firms competing in Southeast Asia in the late 1990s, many Japanese firms continued to invest in local operations in Thailand, Malaysia, Singapore, and other nations because they believe it is an opportunity to further strengthen their investment hold and market position when other foreign rivals are contemplating exit. Management in several Japanese firms believes that Southeast Asia's troubles open up opportunities to solidify their market positions even at a time when they are likely to lose money in the short term. For example, Nissho Iwai Corporation, a leading Japanese trading corporation, increased its ownership of Thai Central Chemical Republic Co., a leading fertilizer firm in the region in 1998. Nissho Iwai increased its ownership stake from 24 percent to 42 percent by purchasing additional shares in Thai Central Chemical at a substantial discount. Moreover, other Nissho Iwai–affiliated companies have also increased their ownership of the same firm to over 11 percent, thus giving Nissho Iwai effective control over its Thai partner's operations. In another case, Honda Motor Company says it will use its Thailand-based operations to increase exports of its Honda Accord models to Australia and New Zealand to take advantage of the region's depreciating currency effects. Honda believes the regional downturn is temporary and is willing to continue investing there, despite short-term profitability pressures. Now, this Honda plant will build Accords for export throughout the region.[27]

A few U.S. firms have begun to view their joint ventures in Asia as opportunities to increase their presence at a time when domestic competitors in Korea, Indonesia, Thailand, and elsewhere are feeling the pressures from recessionary downturns. Great Lakes Chemical, a leading U.S. specialty chemical manufacturer, expanded its equity stake in Miwon Chemical of Korea. The two companies have operated a joint venture in Korea for a number of years, but management at Great Lakes Chemical believes it can further expand its presence throughout Asia by forming additional joint ventures with companies that need a partner for financial and technological assistance. Parker Hannifin, a leading U.S. manufacturer of industrial controls and fluids, viewed the economic difficulties in Asia as a buying opportunity. In March 1998, Parker Hannifin bought out two majority-owned joint venture stakes from its long-standing partner, H S Group of Korea. By selling out, H S Group receives badly needed cash, whereas Parker Hannifin gains control of some key plants that manufacture air-conditioning components.

Other U.S. firms have noted that the Asian economic downturn offers tremendous opportunities to gain access to markets that were previously difficult to penetrate. For example, in January 1999, GE Capital, a unit of General Electric, bought over $6 billion worth of assets from Japan Leasing Corp., a unit of Long-Term Credit Bank of Japan. Likewise, GE Capital also

| Costs Associated with Global Expansion | Exhibit 7-12 |

Costs of strategic leverage
- Sustained investment required
- Preserving and extending image

Costs of flexibility
- High interdependence of subsidiaries (and businesses)
- Change or development affecting all markets

Costs of cooperation
- Compromise
- Accountability

purchased Koei Credit Company and Lake Credit, two Japanese lenders in the subprime market in 1998. GE Capital hopes that its investment in Asian companies will enable it to earn significant returns in the next few years.

In a similar move to bolster its Southeast Asian market presence, U.S. foods company H. J. Heinz bought out its Indonesian joint venture partners in the local food processing industry. Heinz believes that growth in Southeast Asia will continue in the future, but that economic downturns offered significant opportunities to acquire new assets to compete in the future. In fact, Heinz strengthened its position in the Japanese market by forming a tighter alliance with another Japanese food producer, Kagome Company, that has strong distribution advantages in its own home market. Kagome is Japan's largest producer of tomato-processed foods and vegetable juices, which are natural complements to Heinz's enormous strengths and market presence for ketchup, seasonings, and other condiments. Heinz has also solidified its relationship with other Asian companies, such as Universal Food Corp. and Southeast Asia Food, both of the Philippines.[28]

Among the most serious costs often associated with globalization are those arising from (1) strategic leverage, (2) loss of flexibility, and (3) efforts required to coordinate businesses across market lines (see Exhibit 7-12).

Cost of Strategic Leverage

One of the more significant costs imposed on a firm by global expansion is the cost of identifying and leveraging sources of competitive advantage across diverse, multiple markets. Identifying points of leverage requires the firm to focus on critical value-adding activities. These are applied to build and sustain advantage across its markets. Building systemwide leverage applies especially to global strategy firms. In these companies, leverage comes from interdependent and mutually supporting subsidiaries working together. However, the costs of building leverage are also present with multidomestic firms, although in a different way. In these firms, leverage comes primarily from cultivating strong brand images, as opposed to technology-driven investments in global firms. Because the sources of leverage are distinct for global and multidomestic firms, the costs of building leverage will depend upon the specific configuration of the firm's strategy.

Successful global strategies require firms to manage and view their subsidiaries as a single system, not as a loose collection of national markets. Shared production forces managers to allocate resources and investments according to criteria that support the firm's competitive advantage. The biggest cost of leverage in global firms is the sustained, continued investment in a key source of competitive advantage. In other words, resources committed to a particular competence or skill are likely to require sustained investment over time to upgrade that capability. Thus, building leverage in global firms imposes on managers an ongoing need to fund one or more key resources. In the case of Nokia, investment funds are needed to support the company's commitment to leading-edge designs, manufacturing, and new forms of transmission technologies that will be the core of next-generation wireless networks. New software, Internet browsers, instant messaging systems, and color screen developments that are part of every new generation of wireless digital handheld device are critical bastions of knowledge and skills that Nokia must harness to prosper in the wake of intense competition from Siemens, Samsung, LG Electronics, Motorola, and China's TCL.

In multidomestic firms such as Coca-Cola, Nestlé, Procter & Gamble, Hershey Foods, PepsiCo, and McDonald's, leverage comes from global brand recognition based on high-quality products that cater to local market tastes. However, the nature and cost of leverage in multidomestic firms does not come from making expensive technology-driven investments that are shared across subsidiaries. Instead, leverage in multidomestic firms arises from the cumulative market successes of many subsidiaries' efforts over time. The biggest cost of building leverage in multidomestic firms is ongoing investment that preserves and extends the image.

Loss of Flexibility

An important cost associated with globalization is the potential loss of flexibility in managing operations. Across all industries, quick responsiveness to market needs is vital to building new sources of competitive advantage. This need for responsiveness applies in every industry from consumer electronics to advanced composite materials, where new technologies allow scientists to custom design hybrid materials made of both new plastics and metals. Expanding globally raises the risk that the firm will lose its ability to respond to new technological or market trends that could be critical in creating new, valuable products. The potential loss of flexibility could occur in both global and multidomestic firms, although the kind of flexibility lost will depend upon the specific strategy employed.

In firms pursuing global strategies, the loss of flexibility is likely to result from the high level of interdependence and shared investment found between subsidiaries. Because the actions of one subsidiary may affect the behavior of another, the response time to adjust to new market developments slows considerably in global firms. Managers need to communicate and convince their counterparts in other subsidiaries why a particular market development should receive attention. Even though advances in e-mail and the Internet have linked subsidiary operations more closely, these technologies can introduce so much information that they actually overwhelm managers' priorities and cognitive ability to process it. Information pouring in on a daily basis may lose its sense of urgency. What may be vital or urgent to one subsidiary manager may not be to another. Thus, the immediate, day-to-day priorities confronting each subsidiary may cause systemwide inflexibility in response to a potential threat.

Consider IBM's situation in mainframe computers. IBM knew for a long time that personal computers (and now the Internet and client-server architecture) would eventually displace mainframe computers in many applications. Yet, IBM's huge systemwide investment in plants, laboratories, and distribution facilities geared to making and servicing large mainframe computers slowed down its response to this new trend. IBM's loss of flexibility in dealing with new environmental developments that threatened its systemwide investments resulted in the company's slow recognition of the personal computer threat. Even though this inflexibility cost the company valuable lost time and market share, IBM eventually was able to undertake the transition to new technologies and investments that allow it to gain strength against Japanese and European competitors in the industry.

In firms pursuing multidomestic strategies, the loss of flexibility occurs differently. Unlike global firms, multidomestic firms can respond quickly to changing product needs within their own markets. But multidomestic firms are less able to respond to a change that may affect all of its markets simultaneously. Subsidiaries that operate as discrete, stand-alone units, such as those found in Coca-Cola, 3M, Colgate-Palmolive, Henkel, Unilever, PepsiCo, and Procter & Gamble, have sufficient local resources, initiative, and incentive to respond promptly to local market changes. On the other hand, a multidomestic firm faces a potentially serious problem if a new technology renders its existing products obsolete across all of its markets. For example, if Coke were confronted by a new technological development that extended the shelf life of soft drink concentrate, then it would almost certainly need to restructure its numerous multido- mestic distribution arrangements to take advantage of this change. Instead of organizing multidomestically as it does now, Coke would be forced to consider adopting a more global strategy. This move, in turn, would likely undermine goodwill and initiative among Coke's many local distributors and bottlers.

Costs of Cooperation

Global strategies, in particular, require a high level of cooperation and coordination among business units and subsidiaries to achieve systemwide leverage. Cooperation is especially relevant for global firms practicing cross-subsidization policies across numerous markets in ef- forts to dislocate other global competitors. Yet, achieving cooperation can engender significant costs of its own. These include (1) costs of compromise and (2) costs of accountability. To a large extent, multidomestic strategies do not generate high costs of compromise and accountability. Because these firms do not have a systemwide perspective for building competitive advantage, they are not subject to many of the costs associated with high cooperation.

Costs of Compromise. Global firms allocating scarce resources to develop new tech- nologies and investments must often compromise on what goals and products should proceed first and where key operations should be located. A huge semiconductor or automobile engine plant, for example, is likely to engender debate within the company on which markets to target first, how much to produce for each market, how long the product should be produced, and which subsidiaries should bear the costs of the plant. In addition, considerable debate is likely to take place over the plant's location. Some managers might wish their subsidiary to be the one that houses this plant, since it may generate internal prestige among their colleagues and allow it to control a significant portion of components used by other subsidiaries. Yet, these same man- agers are probably unwilling to assume the full costs of the plant, since much of the plant's out- put will be shared among other subsidiaries and markets. The costs of compromise include, for example, long committee meetings, time spent negotiating between subsidiary managers, and deciding how to share critical resources and their internal pricing.

In multidomestic firms, the goals and specific products of each subsidiary are determined according to that subsidiary's market conditions. Subsidiaries are independent from one another and are less likely to engage in debate about shared resources or joint projects across subsidiaries. Still, such debate tends to occur within each subsidiary over issues on how best to serve its local market.

Costs of Accountability. Global firms also face the issue of accountability of their sub- sidiaries. Building competitive advantage systemwide means that some subsidiaries must bear a higher cost of R&D or new product development, for example, than other subsidiaries. Some subsidiaries will also gain less benefit from such efforts than others. These discrepancies mean that using a uniform set of measures to assess the performance of each manager may cause some subsidiaries to appear to be underperforming. In reality, subsidiaries investing heavily in new equipment will appear to be high-cost units, whereas those firms that invest little will have higher profitability and greater cash flow. In particular, shared resources and costs, as well as joint development efforts, will distort the financial performance of each subsidiary. For multidomestic firms, calculating the costs and returns of each subsidiary is an easier task. The independent nature of the subsidiaries within multidomestic firms enables performance evaluations to be specific to each subsidiary. As each subsidiary is responsible for its own market (and thus its own set of value-creating activities), it is easier for senior management to isolate and evaluate each subsidiary's contribution to the firm's overall profitability.

Balancing Global and Multidomestic Approaches

The multiple illustrations of companies pursuing a global vs. multidomestic strategy clearly represent two distinct, almost polar opposite strategies or approaches to expanding globally. Companies such as Caterpillar, Boeing, Intel, and Samsung have implemented full-blown global strategies to compete in their respective industry environments that are driven by homogeneity of demand, huge R&D costs, rising economies of scale, and proprietary manufacturing technologies. Other firms, such as Nestlé, Procter & Gamble, Coca-Cola, Colgate Palmolive, and H. J. Heinz, have successfully built strong market positions by relying on a well-defined multidomestic strategy. Extensive product modification means that these firms tend to rely heavily on local managers, production sites, market research staffs, distributors, and relationships with established wholesalers and retailers in each market. Even though they compete in each market separately, they have cultivated a strong corporate quality image.

In practice, however, most firms attempting to enter and build new market positions discover that they must ultimately combine the benefits of both global and multidomestic strategies when expanding abroad. The latest developments in manufacturing technology, for example, make it possible for companies in an increasing number of industries to be able to produce highly customized products at low unit costs. For example, a wide range of products such as toys, clothing, automotive parts, motor controls, doors, furniture, and even aircraft parts can now be produced in ever-smaller lot quantities without a cost penalty. Moreover, even though middle-class incomes and tastes are reaching vast numbers of people around the world, there appears to be a limit in just how far demand will become even more homogeneous in the future. As tens of millions of people each year approach middle-class incomes, they are discovering not only the power to purchase distinctively branded products from the developed countries, but also the desire to buy an increasing amount of home-grown products as well. Many people with a middle- or upper-level income may well prefer products that demonstrate the highest quality and performance standards, but customized to their specific tastes and needs (for example, cell phones, MP3 players, fashionable clothing, nonperishable foods, software applications). A hybrid or blended strategy that seeks to combine the benefits of both global and multidomestic approaches is growing in a number of companies producing consumer electronics, automobiles, personal care products, and even financial services and high fashion. Let us examine how companies in a few of these industries have attempted to move toward a blended global/multidomestic strategy to secure the benefits of both.

Automobiles: Combining Global Scale with Local Response

Over the past decade, several leading companies in the automobile industry are moving toward a blended global/multidomestic strategy to balance low-cost production with high product customization and fast response to local markets. One of the most important considerations facing the global automotive industry is that it is difficult to build a single model with few variations to serve the entire world. In April 1994, then-CEO Alex Trotman put forth a new organizational architecture for the Ford Motor Company. Known as Ford 2000, the company's reorganization combined its European and North American automotive operations into one unit. The objective of the reorganization was to create a company in which global product teams had the capability to design around a central type of car platform a series of car models that could then be sold around the world with minor modifications. By integrating these once-separate divisions into a single unit, Trotman hoped to transform Ford into a much more nimble company that could compete with fast-moving Japanese and other competitors around the world. This single automotive division was organized around five product vehicle development centers, four in the United States and one in Europe. Each vehicle development center was responsible for a particular type of vehicle platform (for example, small car, midsized car, luxury car, sport utility vehicle, commercial truck) that would then be developed and sold around the world under its authority. The general thrust of the organization was to create a set of vehicle and component designs that would lower the economic and organizational costs of rolling out new models. For example, instead of designing two separate lines of Taurus midsized cars for sale in the United States and Europe, the company sought to create one basic midsized vehicle platform in North America and then modify it for individual markets anywhere around the world. Over time, Ford confronted significant organizational difficulties with this global realignment, because managers were unable to prioritize the tasks needed to accomplish both low-cost production with fast response to local market needs. Now, the company is seeking to introduce even newer Japanese-style manufacturing techniques to rapidly produce new designs to meet fast-changing market needs through its Japanese affiliate, Mazda Motors. Ford is now developing at least ten models of Lincoln and Mercury cars based on variations of the Mazda 6 series sedans. Much of the design work will occur in Japan, but production is envisioned to occur in the United States and elsewhere. In fact, one variation of the Mazda 6 series sedan will be built in Ford's Hermosillo plant in Mexico, where the factory will use flexible manufacturing technology to build eight different models off two basic chassis platforms.[29]

Along with Ford, all the world's major automobile companies followed a similar path to combine the benefits of global scale in manufacturing and procurement without sacrificing the ability to design a car according to each local market's specific conditions and needs. Despite the fact that an increasing number of vehicles share a common platform (for example, unitized body, chassis, drivetrain, braking systems), buyers are increasingly looking for distinctive, if not unique, styling. General Motors, DaimlerChrysler, Toyota, Mazda, Honda, and Hyundai are among a growing number of firms seeking to build critical core components of their cars, such as engines, transmissions, air-conditioning compressors, and fuel-injection systems, in world-scale facilities to lower their unit costs. On the other hand, these same companies are looking to use design talent and assembly sites in local markets to perform much of the automobile design work and car assembly tasks for individual markets. By producing scale-sensitive components in one or two key plants and assembling the final product in local markets, these auto firms are hoping to combine the benefits of global and multidomestic approaches.

Consider the illustration of the Honda Accord, one of the most popular cars in the United States.[30] Honda produces its various lines of engines, transmissions, and other components for the Accord in scale-efficient plants in Japan to reduce costs and to share proprietary manufacturing processes across auto-part families. Advanced automobile engines often require extremely costly development of new materials (aluminum heads and magnesium-alloy engine blocks) that demand global volume to cover R&D costs. On the other hand, all of the Honda Accords sold in the United States are now assembled in plants in Ohio and elsewhere. Engines and transmissions are shipped from Japan and assembled in the United States, often with a high mix of U.S.-made parts, such as glass and rubber, from local manufacturers. Thus, Honda seeks to blend the benefits of a global strategy for its core scale-sensitive and technology-intensive components (to secure low-cost production and shared development of advanced designs) with a multidomestic strategy for assembly and distribution of the finished car (the final product comes together in local markets).

Honda's evolution to combining both aspects of a global and multidomestic production strategy is leading the way in the automotive industry. More recently, Honda originally decided to make all of its highly popular CR-V line of vehicles in Japan. But because of currency fluctuations and the need to better understand U.S. consumers, Honda has decided to make some of its vehicles in the United States. Moreover, because Honda also faces a potential overcapacity problem in Europe, Honda will actually begin to make some CR-Vs in Britain, and then re-export them to the United States. In turn, Honda will start making a hatchback version of its popular Civic in the United States and begin shipping them to Europe. The reason Honda has been so effective in being able to ship to the location of production around the world is because of the company's commitment and investment to building highly flexible factories that are capable of switching from one car model to another without significant retooling or downtime. Both Honda and its archrival Toyota are now capable of putting a new model into production in as little as three months.

DaimlerChrysler is also pushing ahead its own version of a blended global/multidomestic strategy. The company has begun to increasingly rely on its affiliates Mercedes and Mitsubishi Motors to participate in the costs of designing and manufacturing cars that can be sold anywhere around the world. For example, one of the company's newest models, the Crossfire, is a Mercedes in a Chrysler body. Up to 39 percent of the car's core components, including the engine and transmission, are made by Mercedes in Germany. By sharing parts with its far-flung global affiliates, DaimlerChrysler aims to slice the time and cost required to bring a new model on to the market. Other well-known Chrysler models will follow a similar path: The midsize Dodge Stratus and Chrysler Sebring will receive upgraded engineering from Mitsubishi, whereas the Dodge Intrepid and the Chrysler 300M will contain an increasing number of core Mercedes parts. Of course, one of the biggest risks in pursuing such a blended strategy is that the company may lose the distinctive brand-name recognition and quality associated with each of these brands.[31] More recently, however, the scale and size of this enormous coordination, brought about by the original merger of Daimler-Benz with Chrysler in 1998, has created its own set of complex issues. In particular, transferring managers across these two proud organizations has resulted in serious costs of compromise and accountability as DaimlerChrysler endeavors to forge a truly global strategy for this industry. These coordination issues have become particularly exacerbated recently as the automotive industry faces growing overcapacity worldwide and reduced demand.[32]

Perhaps the one company that has made the furthest strives in attaining the finely tuned balance of global vs. multidomestic is Toyota Motor Company of Japan. The company has just begun implementing a fully integrated, global, flexible manufacturing system. In this new configuration, local plants anywhere in the world will be designed to accommodate and customize cars for local markets. At the same time, these same plants can rapidly adjust to surges in demand for a given model in another market by shifting production almost instantaneously. By tapping to a plant's capacity in one country to meet the unexpected demand in another, Toyota believes it can save over $1 billion that is usually required to build an entirely new factory. The company is also in the midst of its own CCC21 plan, abbreviated for Construction of Cost Competitiveness for the 21st century. Toyota is implementing this plan to dramatically slice the costs of its core components, which make up 90 percent of parts expenses. Innovations in the factory also enable superior quality improvements, as well as reduce the number of steps to assemble new vehicles. In the huge U.S. market, Toyota is currently engaging in a plan to "Americanize" its operations. The company views the American market as a natural testing laboratory to design cars with cutting-edge, avant-garde features. It is also seeking to promote more Americans to senior management in a company that has long been regarded as insular. This move is a big change for Toyota, because it has long designed cars in Japan before exporting them to other markets. Perhaps the one car that symbolizes Toyota's push into advanced automotive technologies as well as its leading-edge designs is its rollout of the hybrid Prius line of cars.[33]

Personal Care Products: Matching Local Response to Global Development

A growing number of companies producing personal health care products appear to be moving away from a pure multidomestic strategy to a blended multidomestic/global strategy. Personal care products such as diapers, shampoos, and toothpastes still clearly require a strongly multidomestic focus to tailor activities to local market conditions. Rapid product introduction and product customization still essentially define the basis of competitive success in regional markets. Yet, consumer products firms such as Unilever, Colgate-Palmolive, Procter & Gamble, Henkel, and Kao are developing new R&D facilities that can obtain some of the benefits of shared product development and testing across national markets. The R&D costs of developing new personal health care products that use, for example, new mixtures of chemicals and environment-friendly and less perishable ingredients are rising. This trend means growing opportunities for companies that will consider adopting a more global approach to develop and test future products.

For example, the "tilt" toward incorporating several key aspects of a global strategy has become more evident in the worldwide personal care products industry. Products such as laundry detergent, toothpaste, and even toothbrushes are sharing global brand recognition. Moreover, the costs of R&D have grown significantly in recent years as many of these products incorporate the latest ingredients that are designed to enhance the product's performance and value. In the case of Procter & Gamble, the pursuit of a hybrid or blended strategy has occurred over two decades. Procter & Gamble has several key R&D facilities in Europe, Japan, and the United States to share research, product development, and testing. P&G has long been a major producer of laundry detergent, competing against such well-heeled competitors as Germany's Henkel, the Anglo-Dutch Unilever, and Japan's Kao. However, further refinement of Liquid Tide, which now incorporates advanced surfactant technology to eliminate tough stains, occurs on three different continents. P&G's laboratories in Japan fostered many of the innovations that are vital to improving the cleaning quality of detergents. At the same time, its European labs are busily engaged in finding new ways to make the detergent workable in a variety of water conditions. This will become an important factor in helping P&G produce variations of Liquid Tide for a broader range of markets by using a common set of ingredients that can be produced anywhere around the world. Such a move will help P&G attain significant benefits from greater economies of scale. The company also recently purchased German shampoo company Wella in 2003 to extend its reach into hair-care products, in both Europe and the United States. Likewise, Japanese competitor Kao has staked out R&D facilities in the United States, Europe, and Southeast Asia to avoid duplication of product development efforts. Kao, for example, acquired the Andrew Jergens company in the United States to strengthen its technical and marketing reach. Both firms are using a network of globally situated laboratories to develop high-value products for their global operations.

Consider the illustration of Bausch & Lomb in the contact lens and eye-care industry. Bausch & Lomb is a leading firm in the development and production of contact lens, sunglasses, and associated cleaning solutions for markets worldwide. Bausch & Lomb has conducted its operations on a strictly multidomestic basis because of its goal of developing and cultivating a strong local presence in each market. The company realized that customers had to become more aware of the quality standards and image of Bausch & Lomb's products before people would trust their eyes to them. Working with and supporting local opticians and distributors have been critical to competitive success. Local managers knew best how to understand and penetrate their markets. Moreover, the shape and fit of a pair of glasses actually depends on the contours of a person's nose and cheekbones, characteristics that vary markedly around the world. Thus, Bausch & Lomb has endeavored to produce and market eye-care products in each of its regional markets separately. More recently, Bausch & Lomb has begun to develop new contact lenses based on expensive proprietary technologies developed in key laboratories in South Korea, Japan, and the United States. These advances enable Bausch & Lomb to formulate a more global approach to its strategy.

These examples point to the growing likelihood that firms in a number of industries will move to implement some combination of a blended global/multidomestic strategy to expand their overseas operations. Balancing the dual need for low-cost economies of scale with fast-response product customization will be a significant factor in determining competitive advantage and success. The numerous examples above demonstrate how firms can combine the benefits of pursuing a hybrid, blended strategy. Yet, these same strategies also require the firm to remain agile and responsive enough to respond to important organizational challenges, such as rising costs in communication and coordination among many distant operations.

Strategic Application to Nokia

Let us now summarize by examining how Nokia's strategies fit the underlying patterns of global competition that were described earlier. The massive success that Nokia has enjoyed over the past decade in the wireless phone industry has emanated from the company's many distinctive competences: strong manufacturing capabilities that provide both low-cost operations and flexibility, proprietary technologies that have enabled the company to chart a new direction in telecommunications equipment, and certainly a brand name that has become synonymous with both quality and leading-edge design. All of these attributes enable Nokia to compete effectively in an industry that exhibits very strong global characteristics: homogeneity of demand, increasing sensitivity to economies of scale, escalating R&D costs, and the growth of new ways for people to communicate with one another.

Nokia has sustained its global strategy by building world-class scale plants in key markets around the world. All of these factories utilize the latest manufacturing technologies to produce vast quantities of digital cell phones, N-Gage handsets, and other telecom-related equipment.

The components used within its broad line of cell phones are all standardized to the extent possible, thus providing important savings and greater ease of assembly. Nokia also believes in a high degree of vertical integration by producing many of its core components in-house, thus enabling the firm to lower manufacturing costs even further. Nokia's manufacturing prowess even extends into China, where the company has recently confronted a host of new domestic competitors attempting to grab market share from the Finnish giant. Even in this vast market, Nokia has been able to make steady inroads against such long-entrenched firms as Motorola and Alcatel.

Nokia has long pursued a long-range, global strategy in its pursuit of advanced R&D for next-generation phones and telecommunications equipment. By leading the charge for newer versions of 3G transmission standards, Nokia hopes that the world's cellular phone service providers will buy into the company's proprietary standard. There is a risk, however, that other companies may seek to develop their own version of a transmission standard that may not be fully compatible with that of Nokia's. Thus, in order to ensure that its wireless phones work anywhere around the world, Nokia has built a "dual-mode" capability into the devices that it sells in many countries. "Dual-mode" means that a customer can use the phone in one country (which may operate cell networks on one particular standard), and not lose the ability to use the same phone in another country (which may operate on a different technical standard).

Nokia envisions that software will be the next core technology that the company must develop to stay ahead of its competitors. As phones become more versatile and allow different forms of communication (for example, voice, video, music, online gaming, data, text), Nokia feels that it must become the leader in the key technologies that support each application. The company is also making a push toward becoming a next-generation Internet portal company through its Club Nokia wireless Internet site. Customers subscribe to Club Nokia simply by owning a Nokia phone. Members are then able to surf the web through Nokia's custom-designed Internet site and send e-mail and other messages through Nokia's browser and software. Club Nokia offers members the opportunity to personalize their phones, such as composing their own distinctive rings, creating their own choice of icons on the phone, and even customizing pictures that can be sent to their Nokia Picture Messaging–enabled digital camera phones.

Nokia is also competing in an industry where customers increasingly view their cell phones and digital handheld devices as fashion accessories as well. This means that as these products continue to evolve, there will be an increasing demand for more customized versions of phones that will have to appeal to ever-smaller niches of customers. As a result, Nokia must formulate and implement future hybrid, blended strategies that enable it simultaneously to attain global economies of scale and low unit costs, but become even more responsive to the needs of an extremely diverse set of customers. The company's investments in flexible manufacturing technologies enable Nokia to produce phones in ever-smaller lot sizes to help sustain this strategy. More important, Nokia has been actively hiring technical personnel and managers from around the world to help it better understand the distinctive needs of customers in fast-growing markets. Like Procter & Gamble and other personal care product firms, Nokia has established large R&D facilities in key markets around the world such as China, the United States, and the United Kingdom to promote innovation and to keep abreast of the latest technological developments.

Ethical Dimensions

Globalization presents significant strategic opportunities for firms willing to take the risk of going overseas and committing themselves to serving customers worldwide.[34] Yet, global expansion obliges a firm to deal with a wide range of competitors, customers, and market needs, thereby compelling it to deal with a broad range of ethical beliefs and practices. Many of these beliefs and practices contrast starkly with those found in U.S. firms. The issue of ethics when competing globally has become especially noteworthy over the past ten years, as we witness the assortment of values and different business practices found around the world.

Much of the current interest in ethics that accompanies global expansion can be traced to the numerous scandals in Europe and the Far East that occurred during the 1980s and continued through the 1990s. For example, a major scandal in London's posh Lloyd's of London insurance firm surfaced when numerous investors were defrauded by Lloyd's agents who allegedly expropriated funds for their own use. In 1989 and 1990, several stock market scandals and insider-trading scams took place in France and Germany, while in 1995, several major financial firms were taken to the brink of disaster because of alleged insider training and misuse of funds to engage in global commodities speculation (for example, Sumitomo Metals, Daiwa Securities of Japan). Despite all of the effort the United States has devoted to making insider trading illegal here (for example, the investigation of Michael Milken's bond trading), officials in Europe have a different perspective on what constitutes the ethical boundaries of insider trading.

In 1997 and 1998, Japan faced its own set of political and economic scandals rocking its close-knit financial and industrial establishment. Several politicians were forced to step down from office and face indictments because they allegedly received payoffs from construction interests, the local Yakuza (the Japanese "mob"), and industrial companies seeking preferential treatment in the allocation of government contracts. In fact, several leading Japanese brokerage firms pleaded guilty to having loaned considerable sums of money in secret deals to underworld characters. Yet, despite having committed apparently extremely serious criminal acts, many of the officials investigated and indicted received only minor punishments because Japan has not acted on its recently adopted set of formal regulations, laws, or ethical codes of conduct that prohibit these activities.

More recently, business practices and codes of ethical conduct have become important global competitive issues in Italy, China, and South Korea, as firms in those countries engage in a variety of questionable behaviors. In December 2003, Italian investigators uncovered a series of fraudulent transactions involving the Italian diary giant Paramalat, whose senior management is accused of concocting false revenue numbers and bank deposits that never actually existed. Much of Parmalat's money was spent on other family-oriented interests; a significant portion of it remains unaccounted for. Many senior managers and founding family members remain under investigation in order to uncover transferred assets and hidden income.[35] This investigation has shaken the Italian business establishment to the core, since it reveals the extent to which Italian business and politics have become cozy. Likewise, in 2002, the FBI undertook a sting operation that revealed the extent to which Huawei Technologies, a leading Chinese telecom equipment firm, engaged in industrial espionage against U.S. networking giant Cisco Systems. Engineers at Huawei apparently stole leading-edge router designs from Cisco and incorporated them into their own products, including many of the same errors and software bugs that were found in other Cisco equipment. On a much smaller scale, Citigroup engaged in a series of highly questionable business practices in both Japan and Europe in 2003 and 2004. Citigroup's Japanese subsidiary was forced to apologize to its customers and regulators after its local managers approved the use of questionable marketing approaches to win over Japanese customers in its retailing market. Citigroup was also forced to temporarily suspend some of its retail operations. In Europe, Citigroup faced serious inquiries from several European governments after its bond traders engaged in questionable trading practices that produced quick profits, but at the cost of heightened bond market volatility.

The differences in attitudes and what defines ethical practices across nations is strongly rooted in public expectations and local history. In the United States, ethical behavior transcends what is simply considered legal or even legitimate. Managers, employees, suppliers, and even customers are implicitly expected to follow their own personal codes of conduct that prohibit embezzlement, insider trading, and a host of other practices that most of us take for granted as somehow "crossing the line." In many other nations, however, practices such as preferential treatment to long-standing financial and business partners, gift giving, relaying insider information, and other actions are considered discreet and appropriate ways of smoothing business relations between people who know each other well. Although criminal investigation and prosecution has accelerated in Europe for insider trading and other corporate transgressions, the pace of reform to a large extent is slower in the Far East, where local customs and traditions mandate that close ties require a different set of standards be applied to "insiders" and "outsiders."

Differences in business ethics across the globe are rooted in the way ethics is defined. In the United States, where individualism defines many of our institutions and legal codes, ethics is strongly based on personal behavior and attitudes that condemn actions that clearly do not fit the spirit of what was intended, even if these actions are not overtly illegal. People are expected to decide what is right and wrong largely through their own moral beliefs and conscience. In effect, when a company does something perceived as wrong, employees often feel great discomfort. In many other countries with less strongly rooted individualism, the distinction between company and individual actions may be more vague. In other words, individual managers in Europe and the Far East may perhaps be more likely to conform their own beliefs to that of their companies' needs. The role of the individual is not as well defined or cherished in Europe and elsewhere. Thus, managers may be more inclined to overlook ethical breaches committed for company-related goals as opposed to personal goals, since the company might benefit from these actions in the long term. In the Far East, the distinction between individual employee and company is even more vague. Many workers in Japan, Korea, and elsewhere see themselves as "industrial soldiers," where their primary function is to carry out their companies' strategy, mission, and other objectives to whatever extent they best can. As recipients of generous corporate benefits, these workers will often do whatever they feel is necessary to preserve and to strengthen their company's strategies, including the potential use of industrial espionage. Considerations that Americans value highly, such as the protection of intellectual property and the preservation of open markets, may not carry the same weight in many other countries. As a result, patent theft and violation of intellectual property are taken for granted if it helps local companies become more competitive.

The net effect of these divergent ethical beliefs and practices around the world is that U.S. firms in particular face great dilemmas when dealing in other nations. The business practices of competing firms may even conflict with practices of U.S. firms. Moreover, what constitutes legal or ethical behavior may be specific to different situations. U.S. companies, for example, are prohibited from offering bribes to foreign officials because of the Foreign Corrupt Practices Act passed in the mid-1970s. Unfortunately, many global competitors of these U.S. firms may not face the same restriction when competing for lucrative contracts in third-party countries. These countries often have more liberal definitions of what defines gift giving as opposed to bribes and payoffs. In many cases, U.S. managers will face great moral dilemmas in designing ethical and appropriate strategies to counter such actions. On the one hand, securing a lucrative contract may be imperative to building market share and profitability. Yet, on the other hand, U.S. managers realize they are held to a difficult standard, one that is often more restrictive and that calls upon the individual to make a personal judgment when ethical boundaries are less clear.

The cumulative effect of these contrasting ethical backgrounds and beliefs is the likelihood of more government regulation in the United States and elsewhere. Governments in many cases are being forced to scrutinize the actions of firms and individuals more closely because of growing public outrage at blatantly unethical acts and transgressions. For example, in Japan, the Liberal Democratic Party (LDP) has never really regained its firm control over parliament (the Diet) and the confidence of the Japanese people as a result of its scandal-plagued administrations during the 1990s. We witnessed a similar situation develop in South Korea in 2001 and 2002, as the government investigated allegations that executives from Hyundai secretly made payments to North Korea in order to encourage dictator Kim Jong-Il to engage in peace talks with the South. However, few prime ministers or elected officials have demonstrated much vigorous action to attain these objectives. The ethical transgressions found in both the developed and the developing world will likely result in continued calls for increased government oversight and regulation around the world.

Summary

- Global expansion enables firms to build and extend their sources of competitive advantage to new markets.
- Firms need to consider global expansion because of increasing demand around the world, rising R&D costs to develop new products, growing economies of scale, the change in factor (labor and capital) costs, and greater ease of communications, transportation, and storage.
- Global expansion strategies are of two basic types: global and multidomestic. Industry drivers are important factors that influence the firm's choice of a global or multidomestic strategy.
- Firms pursue a global strategy when they seek to operate with worldwide consistency, standardization of products and practices, and a systemwide perspective to extend competitive advantage.
- Firms pursue a multidomestic strategy when they adjust their products and operations according to the particular markets being served.
- Benefits of global expansion include entering fast-growing markets, recovering investment costs, creating a strong image, and accelerating learning and knowledge transfer.
- The expense of building leverage, potential inflexibility, and the challenges of cooperating across subsidiaries are all costs of global expansion.
- Many companies are currently formulating their own strategies that combine the benefits of both global and multidomestic approaches. The imperative to combine these strategies becomes especially relevant as companies strive to find the right balance between the need to serve different customers with efforts to reduce costs of operations and other activities.

Exercises and Discussion Questions

1. What are some important environmental and economic factors that firms must consider when choosing to compete in global markets? How are these factors significantly different from those facing the firm in its domestic market?
2. The growth of the Internet has been a major factor that has substantially reduced the costs of communications around the world. What are some things that a small firm

can do to use the Internet as a tool to enter global markets? Can a small firm that shrewdly uses the Internet still become an important global player?

3. Most recently, many U.S. firms have sustained losses in profits and market share as the economies of Southeast Asia have entered a recession. If you were a consultant to 3M, for example, what are some steps that you would recommend to senior management to protect your market position and perhaps even use the recession to your advantage? Likewise, in 2004, as European markets face continued sluggish growth, how would you advise a large American company seeking to bolster its market position in the Continent?

4. As new technologies make mass customization strategies more commonplace, which type of overseas expansion strategy is likely to dominate in the future: global or multidomestic? What are some attributes of mass customization strategies that make them particularly powerful weapons in the fight for global market share and position?

Endnotes

1. Data and facts for the Nokia Strategic Snapshot were adapted from the following sources: "Will Rewiring Nokia Spark Growth?" *Business Week*, February 14, 2005, pp. 46-47; "Has Nokia Lost It?" *Fortune*, January 24, 2005, pp. 98–106; "Nokia to Compete in Games Market," *Wall Street Journal,* October 24, 2004, p. B4; "Nokia Bets One Global Message Will Ring True in Many Markets," *Wall Street Journal,* September 27, 2004, p. B6; "Nokia Maintains its Market Share, but at Steep Cost," *Wall Street Journal,* July 13, 2004, p. B5+; "Can Nokia Get the Wow Back?" *Business Week,* May 31, 2004, pp. 48–50; "No-Growth Nokia Sees Rivals Gain," *Wall Street Journal,* April 15, 2004, p. B5; "Nokia to Fall Short of Sales Forecast," *Wall Street Journal*, April 7, 2004, p. B7; "Nokia Clicks with Camera Phones," March 29, 2004, p. B3; "Nokia Profit Sends a Signal," *Wall Street Journal,* January 9, 2004, p. A9; "Guiding Nokia in Technology's Rough Seas," *Wall Street Journal,* November 24, 2003, pp. B1, B2; "Nokia's Big Leap," *Business Week,* October 13, 2003, pp. 50–52; "Nokia Calling," *Barron's Online,* September 29, 2003, pp. 1–6; "Phone Providers Develop Hybrid Handsets," *Wall Street Journal,* September 18, 2003, pp. B9, B10; "China's Makers of Cellphones Thrive at Home," *Wall Street Journal,* August 21, 2003, pp. B1, B4; "Beyond 1.0 Megapixel," *Wall Street Journal,* June 17, 2003, pp. B1, B11; "Nokia to Challenge Game Boy," *Dallas Morning News,* February 13, 2003, p. 4D.

2. An excellent landmark work that first investigated the relationship between headquarters and subsidiaries as the foundation of a global strategy is by J. M. Hulbert and W. K. Brandt, *Managing the Multinational Subsidiary* (New York: Holt Rinehart and Winston, 1980).

Also see P. Almeida and A. Phene, "Subsidiaries and Knowledge Creation: The Influence of the MNC and Host Country on Innovation," *Strategic Management Journal* 25, nos. 8–9 (2004): 847–864; Y. Gong, "Subsidiary Staffing in Multinational Enteprises: Agency, Resources, and Performance," *Academy of Management Journal* 46, no. 6 (2003): 728–739; Y. Gong, "Toward a Dynamic Process Model of Staffing Composition and Subsidiary Outcomes in Multinational Enterprises," *Journal of Management* 29 (2003): 259–280; U. Andersson, M. Forsgren, and U. Holm, "The Strategic Impact of External Networks: Subsidiary Performance and Competence Development in the Multinational Corporation," *Academy of Management Journal* 23, no. 11 (2002): 979–996; A. M. Rugman and A. Verbeke, "Subsidiary-Specific Advantages in Multinational Enterprises," *Academy of Management Journal* 22, no. 3 (2001): 237–250; T. S. Frost, "The Geographic Sources of Foreign Subsidiaries'

Innovations," *Academy of Management Journal* 22, no. 2 (2001): 101–124; S. Watson O'Donnell, "Managing Foreign Subsidiaries: Agents of Headquarters, or an Interdependent Network," *Academy of Management Journal* 21, no. 5 (2000): 525–548; J. M. Birkinshaw and N. Hood, "Multinational Subsidiary Evolution: Capability and Charter Change in Foreign-Owned Subsidiary Companies," *Academy of Management Review* 23, no. 4 (1998): 773–795; J. H. Taggart, "Strategic Shifts in Multinational MNC Subsidiaries," *Academy of Management Journal* 19, no. 7 (1998): 663–681; J. Birkinshaw, N. Hood, and S. Jonsson, "Building Firm-Specific Advantages in Multinational Corporations: The Role of Subsidiary Initiative," *Academy of Management Journal* 19, no. 3 (1998): 221–242; G. S. Yip, *Total Global Strategy: Managing for Worldwide Competitive Advantage* (Englewood Cliffs, NJ: Prentice Hall, 1992); C. A. Bartlett and S. Ghoshal, "What Is a Global Manager?" *Harvard Business Review* (September–October 1992): 124–133; and R. F. Maruca, "The Right Way to Go Global: An Interview with Whirlpool CEO David Whitwam," *Harvard Business Review* (March–April 1994): 150–160; M. Schrage, "A Japanese Giant Rethinks Globalization: An Interview with Yoshihisa Tabuchi," *Harvard Business Review* (July–August 1989): 70–76; G. Hedlund, "The Hypermodern MNC: A Heterarchy?" *Human Resource Management* 25 (1986): 9–36.

3. An enormous amount of literature has developed in the past several years on global strategy. The following seminal pieces have provided much of the groundwork for this chapter. For a study on how firms become more global or multinational over time, two landmark studies are J. M. Stopford and L. T. Wells, Jr., *Managing the Multinational Enterprise* (New York: Basic Books, 1972), and M. Z. Brooke and H. L. Remmers, *The Strategy of Multinational Enterprise: Organization and Finance* (London: Longman, 1970). Within the strategic management literature, for example, see T. Hout, M. E. Porter, and E. Rudden, "How Global Companies Win Out," *Harvard Business Review* (September–October 1982): 98–108. Also see B. Kogut, "Designing Global Strategies: Comparative and Competitive Value-Added Chains," *Sloan Management Review* 26 (1985): 15–28; M. E. Porter, "Changing Patterns of International Competition," *California Management Review* 28 (Winter 1986): 9–40; S. Ghoshal, "Global Strategy: An Organizing Framework," *Academy of Management Journal* 8 (1987): 425–440; S. Ghoshal and C.A. Bartlett, "The Multinational Corporation as an Interorganizational Network," *Academy of Management Review* 15 (October 1990): 603–625. Excellent books that survey the requirements for success in global strategies include C. A. Bartlett and S. Ghoshal, *Managing Across Borders: The Transnational Solution* (Boston: Harvard Business School Press, 1989); M. E. Porter, *The Competitive Advantage of Nations* (New York: Free Press, 1990); C. K. Prahalad and Y. L. Doz, *The Multinational Mission: Balancing Local Demands and Global Vision* (New York: Free Press, 1987); Y. Doz and C. K. Prahalad, "Managing DMNCs: A Search for a New Paradigm," *Academy of Management Journal* 12, Special Issue (1991): 145–164; N. Nohria and C. Garcia-Pont, "Global Strategic Linkages and Industry Structure," *Academy of Management Journal* 12, Special Issue (1991): 105–124; H.V. Perlmutter, "The Tortuous Evolution of the Multinational Corporation," *Columbia Journal of World Business* 4, no. 4 (1969): 9–18; J. Fayerweather, *International Business Strategy and Administration* (Cambridge, MA: Ballinger, 1978); J. H. Dunning, *International Production and the Multinational Enterprise* (London: Allen & Unwin, 1981); P. J. Buckley and M. C. Casson, *The Economic Theory of the Multinational Enterprise* (London: Macmillan, 1985); A. K. Sundaram and J. S. Black, "The Environment and Internal Organization of Multinational Enterprises," *Academy of Management Review* 17 (1992): 729–757; P. M. Rosenweig and J.V. Singh, "Organizational Environments and Multinational Enterprise," *Academy of Management Review* 16 (1991): 340–361. The economics of globalization are shown in C.W.L. Hill and W. C. Kim, "Searching for a Dynamic Theory of the Multinational Enterprise: A Transactions Cost Model," *Academy of Management Journal* 9 (1988): 93–104; B. Mascarenhas, A. Baveja, and

M. Jamil, "Dynamics of Core Competencies in Leading Multinational Companies," *California Management Review* 40, no. 4 (1998): 117–132.

Some critical studies that have examined different modes of global competition, entry strategies, and the relationship with financial performance and firm-based innovation include the following: H. Barkema and F. Vermeulen, "International Expansion Through Start-up or Acquisition: A Learning Perspective," *Academy of Management Journal* 41, no. 1 (1998): 7–26; J. H. Taggart, "Strategy Shifts in MNC Subsidiaries," *Academy of Management Journal* 17, no. 7 (1998): 663–682; M. A. Hitt, R. E. Hoskisson, and H. Kim, "International Diversification: Effects on Innovation and Firm Performance in Product-Diversified Firms," *Academy of Management Journal* 40, no. 4 (1997): 767–798; S. Tallman and J. T. Li, "Effects of International Diversity and Product Diversity on the Performance of Multinational Firms," *Academy of Management Journal* 39, no. 1 (1996): 179–196; J. F. Hennart and Y. R. Park, "Greenfield versus Acquisition: The Strategy of Japanese Investors in the United States," *Management Science* 39 (1993): 1054–1070; K. Roth, "International Configuration and Coordination Archetypes for Medium-Sized Firms in Global Industries," *Journal of International Business Studies* 23 (1992): 533–549; K. Roth, D. Schweiger, and A. Morrison, "Global Strategy Implementation at the Business Unit Level: Operational Capabilities and Administrative Mechanisms," *Journal of International Business Studies* 22 (1991): 361–394.

More recent work includes the following studies examining the impact of globalization: "M. T. Hansen and B. Lovas, "How Do Multinational Companies Leverage Technological Competencies? Moving From Single to Interdependent Explanations," *Academy of Management Journal* 25, nos. 8–9 (2004): 801–822; S. E. Feinberg and A. K. Gupta, "Knowledge Spillovers and the Assignment of R&D Responsibilities to Foreign Subsidiaries," *Academy of Management Journal* 25, nos. 8–9 (2004): 823–846; A. Goerzen and P. W. Beamish, "Geographic Scope and Multinational Enterprise Performance," *Academy of Management Journal* 24, no 13 (2003): 1289–1306; R. Belderbos, "Entry Mode, Organizational Learning, and R&D in Foreign Affiliates: Evidence from Japanese Firms," *Academy of Management Journal* 24, no. 3 (2003): 235–260; L. Tihanyi, R. A. Johnson, R. E. Hoskisson, and M. A. Hitt, "Institutional Ownership Differences and International Diversification: The Effects of Boards of Directors and Technological Opportunity," *Academy of Management Journal* 46, no. 2 (2003): 195–211; X. Martin and R. Salomon, "Tacitness, Learning, and International Expansion: A Study of Foreign Direct Investment in a Knowledge-Intensive Industry," *Organization Science* 14, no. 3 (2003): 297–311; D. Denis and K. Yost, "Global Diversification, Industrial Diversification, and Firm Value," *Journal of Finance* 57 (2002): 1951–1980; J. W. Lu and P. W. Beamish, "The Internationalization and Performance of SMEs," *Academy of Management Journal* 22, Issues 6–7 (2001): 565–586; S. J. Chang and P. M. Rosenzweig, "The Choice of Entry Mode in Sequential Foreign Direct Investment," *Academy of Management Journal* 22, no. 8 (2001): 747–776; D. G. McKendrick, "Global Strategy and Population Level Learning: The Case of Hard Disk Drives," *Academy of Management Journal* 22, no. 4 (2001): 307–334; Y. Luo and S. H. Park, "Strategic Alignment and Performance of Market-Seeking MNCs in China," *Academy of Management Journal* 22, no. 2 (2001): 141–156; A. Rugman and R. Hodgetts, "The End of Global Strategy," *European Management Journal* 19 (2001): 333–343; E. Autio, H. J. Sapienza, and J. G. Alameda, "Effects of Age at Entry, Knowledge Intensity, and Imitability on International Growth," *Academy of Management Journal* 43, no. 5 (2000): 909–924; J. M. Geringer, S. Tallman, and D. M. Olsen, "Product and International Diversification Among Japanese Multinational Firms," *Academy of Management Journal* 21, no. 1 (2000): 51–80; S. Thomsen and T. Pedersen, "Ownership Structure and Economic Performance in the Largest European Companies," *Academy of Management Journal* 21, no. 6 (2000): 689–705; S. A. Zahra, R. D. Ireland, and M. A. Hitt, "International Expansion by New Venture Firms:

International Diversification, Mode of Market Entry, Technological Learning, and Performance," *Academy of Management Journal* 43, no. 5 (2000): 925–950; P. P. McDougall and B. Oviatt, "International Entrepreneurship: The Intersection of Two Research Paths," *Academy of Management Journal* 43, no. 5, pp. 902–908; A. Delios and W. J. Henisz, "Japanese Firms' Investment Strategies in Emerging Economies," *Academy of Management Journal* 43, no. 3 (2000): 302–323; A. Delios and P. W. Beamish, "Geographic Scope, Product Diversification and Corporate Performance of Japanese Firms," *Academy of Management Journal* 20, no. 8 (2000): 711–727; L. G. Thomas III and G. Waring, "Competing Capitalisms: Capital Investment in American, German and Japanese Firms," *Academy of Management Journal* 20, no. 8 (2000): 729–739; Y. Pan and P. S. K. Chi, "Financial Performance and Survival of Multinational Corporations in China," *Academy of Management Journal* 20, no. 4 (1999): 359–374.

4. See, for example, "China's Steel Industry Looks Abroad," *Wall Street Journal,* March 31, 2004, p. A6; "China's Growing Thirst for Oil Remakes the Global Market," *Wall Street Journal,* December 3, 2003, pp. A1, A6; "China Saps Commodity Supplies," *Wall Street Journal,* October 24, 2003, pp. C1, C9.

5. Data and facts for the TCL example were adapted from the following sources: "France's Alcatel Feels Pressure From the East," *Wall Street Journal,* February 10, 2005, pp. B3, B4; "Toshiba, TCL to Set Up Joint Venture in China," *Wall Street Journal,* November 4, 2004; "Global Business Briefs: TCL Corp.," *Wall Street Journal,* July 20, 2004, p. C12; "Alcatel Shifts Production to China, Venture with TCL, Maker of TV Sets, Will Take Over Manufacture of Cellphones," *Wall Street Journal,* April 27, 2004, p. B5; "Riding China's Coattails: An Export-Hungry Mainland Is the Force Behind Japan's Recovery," *BusinessWeek,* March 1, 2004, p. 50; "TV's Mr. Big," *Fortune,* February 9, 2004, pp. 84–88; "After Years Behind the Scenes, Chinese Join the Name Game," *Wall Street Journal,* December 26, 2003, pp, A1, A2; "Bursting Out of China: TCL's Deal with Thomson Puts It in Reach of a Global Electronics Market," *BusinessWeek,* November 17, 2003, p. 20; "Thomson to Create Venture with China's TCL to Make TVs," *Wall Street Journal,* November 3, 2003, p. B4; "Breaking into the Name Game," *BusinessWeek,* April 7, 2003, p. 54; "TCL Mobile Is Leader of a New Breed," *Wall Street Journal,* August 29, 2002, p. B4.

6. See, for example, "Europe's Goal: 'Industrial Champions,'" *Wall Street Journal,* May 14, 2004, pp. A3, A6.

7. See "Pact May Boost Confidence in China Tech Sector," *Wall Street Journal,* July 12, 2004, p. A15; "U.S. Settles China Trade Spat, Tightens Import-Duty Rules," *Wall Street Journal,* July 9, 2004, p. A2.

8. See "U.S. Auto Makers Find Promise—and Peril—in China," *Wall Street Journal,* June 19, 2003, pp. B1, B4.

9. See "The Cosmopolitan Touch," *Forbes,* June 21, 2004, pp. 133–138.

10. See "Alcan Gets Foothold in China," *Wall Street Journal,* October 24, 2003, p. B2.

11. See "India's Elephantine Economy May Be Poised to Run," *Wall Street Journal,* September 25, 2003, p. A17. "In India's Outsourcing Boom, GE Played a Starring Role," *Wall Street Journal,* March 22, 2005, pp. A1, A12.

12. See, for example, "Why U.S. Manufacturing Won't Die," *Wall Street Journal,* July 3, 2003, pp. B1, B2; "Heroes of Manufacturing," *Fortune,* March 17, 2003, pp. 124C–124L; "Brave New Factory: From the Line to the Supply Chain, All Goes on Autopilot," *BusinessWeek,* July 23, 2001; "Heroes of U.S. Manufacturing: America Remains the World's Top Industrial Power with the Help of Innovators Like These," *Fortune,* March 19, 2001; "Cutting Edges: Better Machine Tools Give Manufacturers Newfound Resilience," *Wall Street Journal,* February 15, 2001, pp. A1, A8.

13. D. Lei and J. D. Goldhar, "Multiple Niche Competition: The Strategic Use of CIM Technology," *Manufacturing Review* (September 1990): 195–206.

14. A. T. Talysum, M. Z. Hassan, and J. D. Goldhar, "Uncertainty Reduction Through Flexible Manufacturing," *IEEE Transactions on Engineering Management* EM-34, no. 2 (May 1987): 85–91.

15. See "The Flexible Factory," *BusinessWeek,* May 5, 2003, pp. 90–91 for a discussion of Timken's manufacturing advances.

16. See "Still Made in the U.S.A.," *Wall Street Journal,* July 8, 2004, pp. B1, B4.

17. T. Levitt, "The Globalization of Markets," *Harvard Business Review* (May–June 1983): 92–102. Also see M. E. Porter, ed., *Competition in Global Industries* (Boston: Harvard Business School Press, 1986).

18. S. Wetlaufer, "Driving Change: An Interview with Ford Motor Company's Jacques Nasser," *Harvard Business Review* 77 (March–April 1999): 76–91.

19. "GM to Shift Basics of U.S. Cars to German Unit in Big Overhaul," *Wall Street Journal,* June 21, 2004, p. A6.

20. See "Merck, Pfizer Battle in Japan," *Wall Street Journal,* October 2, 2003, p. B4.

21. See, for example, G. Hamel and C. K. Prahalad, "Do You Really Have a Global Strategy?" *Harvard Business Review* (July–August 1985): 139–148. Also see C. K. Prahalad and Y. L. Doz, *The Multinational Mission: Balancing Local Demands and Global Vision* (New York: Free Press, 1987).

22. Go is an ancient game of strategy that requires players to capture large swathes of territory on a map measuring nineteen squares on each side. Conceived in China over two thousand years ago, it remains an enormously popular game in Japan to this day, where contestants have been known to spend months, if not years, contemplating highly intricate moves on a single game.

23. See "Big Plane May Give Lift to EADS," *Wall Street Journal,* January 10, 2005, pp. C1, C4.

24. See, for example, R. Kerin and R. Sethuraman, "Exploring the Brand Value–Shareholder Value Nexus for Consumer Goods Companies," *Journal of the Academy of Marketing Sciences* 26, no. 4 (1998): 260–273.

25. See, for example, "3M Expects Earnings to Decline Due to Asia's Turmoil," *Wall Street Journal,* June 16, 1998, p. B4.

26. "U.S. Firms' Global Prowess Is Two-Edged," *Wall Street Journal,* August 17, 1998, pp. C1, C2; "To Battle Asian Slump, Multinationals Import Lean-and-Mean Ways," *Wall Street Journal,* August 19, 1998, pp. A1, A6.

27. See "Many Japanese Firms Cling to Troubled Southeast Asia," *Wall Street Journal,* September 18, 1998, p. A8.

28. See "H. J. Heinz, Japan's Kagome Agree to Investments as Part of Alliance," *Wall Street Journal,* July 26, 2001, p. B11; "U.S. Firms Reassess Asian Joint Ventures," *Wall Street Journal,* September 23, 1998, pp. A2, A10; "GE Capital's Tokyo Treasure Hunt," *BusinessWeek,* February 18, 1999, p. 39.

29. See, for example, "Bill's Brand New Ford," *Fortune,* June 28, 2004, pp. 68–76; "Ford to Expand Mexican Plant for Production of New Sedan," *Wall Street Journal,* October 7, 2003, p. D5; "Revived Mazda Serves as School for Parent Ford," *Wall Street Journal,* August 28, 2003, pp. B1, B6; "Ford to Boost Europe Output," *Wall Street Journal,* August 20, 2003, p. B7; "Bill Ford's Next Act," *Forbes,* June 23, 2003, pp. 74–80.

30. See "Fickle Consumers Force Auto Makers to Be More Flexible," *Wall Street Journal,* September 10, 2001, p. B8; "Tailoring World's Cars to U.S. Tastes," *Wall Street Journal,* January 15, 2001, pp. B1, B6; "Honda to Halt Civic, Accord Exports to the U.S.," *Wall Street Journal,* September 20, 1993, p. B5; "Toyota Is Expected to Build New Car at Kentucky Plant," *Wall Street Journal,* October 12, 1993, p. A18; "A New Export Power in the Auto Industry? It's North America," *Wall Street Journal,* October 18, 1993, pp. A1, A5; "Japan's Car Makers Seek Solutions From U.S. Big Three," *Wall Street Journal,* November 15, 1993, p. B4; "Ford Aggressively Increases Its Visibility in Japan as U.S. Brands Make Inroads," *Wall Street Journal,* February 11, 1994, p. A6; "Toyota Studies Fourth North American Plant," *Wall Street Journal,* February 10, 1995, p. A3.

   A recent academic piece that examines the role of global product development is M. Subramaniam and N. Venkatraman, "Determinants of Transnational New Product Development Capability: Testing the Influence of Transferring and

Deploying Tacit Knowledge Overseas," *Academy of Management Journal* 22, no. 4 (2001): 359–378; also see L. Thomas and K. Weigelt, "Product Location Choice and Firm Capabilities: Evidence From the U.S. Automotive Industry," *Academy of Management Journal* 21, no. 9 (2000): 897–910; A. K. Gupta and V. Govindarajan, "Knowledge Flows Within Multinational Corporations," *Academy of Management Journal* 21, no. 4 (2000): 473–496; M. Subramaniam, S. Spear, and H. K. Bowen, "Decoding the DNA of the Toyota Production System," *Harvard Business Review* 77 (September–October 1999): 96–108; S. R. Rosenthal and K. J. Hatten, "Global New Product Development: Preliminary Findings and Research Propositions," *Journal of Management* Studies 35, no. 6 (1998): 773–796; S. Ghoshal, H. Korine, and G. Szulanski, "Interunit Communication in Multinational Corporations," *Management Science* 40, no. 1 (1994): 375–384.

31. See "Just Another Sexy Sports Car? Sure. But It's Also a Whole New Way of Doing Business at Chrysler," *Fortune,* March 17, 2003, pp. 76–80; "Crossbreed: Is It a Chrysler or a Mercedes? Only Your Engineer Knows for Sure," *Fortune,* March 17, 2003, p. 54. "DaimlerChrysler Ponders 'World Engine' in Bid to Transform Scope into Savings," *Wall Street Journal,* January 8, 2002, pp. A3, A4.

32. See "Slide in Mercedes's Performance Dent's Chrysler's Recent Revival," *Wall Street Journal*, February 9, 2005, pp. A1, A6.

33. See "Toyota's Bid to Be Number 1 in Market Share Takes Toll on Earnings and Shareholders," *Wall Street Journal,* March 23, 2005, pp. C1, C3; "Toyota's Group May Not Be Safe From Hot Suitors," *Wall Street Journal,* March 23, 2005, p. C3; "Toshiba to Supply Hybrid Motors to Toyota Affiliate," *Wall Street Journal,* March 20, 2004, p. B5; "The Americanization of Toyota," *Fortune,* December 8, 2003, pp. 165–170; "Can Anything Stop Toyota?" *BusinessWeek,* November 17, 2003, pp. 114–122; "Toyota to Produce Camry in China," *Wall Street Journal,* October 31, 2003.

34. An excellent article that examines the globalization of business ethics is D. Vogel, "The Globalization of Business Ethics: Why America Remains Distinctive," *California Management Review* 35, no. 1 (1992): 30–49.

35. See "How Parmalat Spent and Spent," *Wall Street Journal,* July 21, 2004, p. C2.

Chapter 8

Strategic Alliances: Partnering for Advantage

Chapter Outline

What you will learn

- *The characteristics of a strategic alliance*

- *Why companies around the world are forming strategic alliances*

- *The different broad types of strategic alliances, including licensing, joint ventures, and multipartner consortia*

- *The benefits and costs of entering into strategic alliances*

- *How to balance the need for cooperation with competition*

IBM's Microelectronics Alliance Strategy[1]

Throughout the 1990s, International Business Machines (IBM), the world's largest computer company, entered into a wide array of strategic alliances with numerous partners in the United States, the Far East, and Europe. During the past twenty years, IBM, popularly known as Big Blue, has shifted from relying on mainframe computer products for its huge revenue base ($89.1 billion for 2003). Already, IBM is a leading provider of many leading-edge products and services such as advanced semiconductors, storage devices and servers, mainframe computers, software development tools, Internet e-commerce tools, personal computers, disk drives, telecommunications equipment, and corporate Internet and intranet websites. Many of these technologies require more than one firm to perfect and to rush to market. This development is especially revealing as twenty-first-century technologies become more expensive and risky to develop.

As an entire organization, IBM has established over five hundred different alliances with partners in almost every high-technology sector. However, our focus is much more limited. We look at a very distinct part of IBM—its Microelectronics unit that has provided important leadership for the semiconductor industry along a number of dimensions. IBM Microelectronics has long remained at the cutting-edge of technological research to produce breakthroughs in chip design and chip manufacturing. However, IBM Microelectronics provided important strategic leadership for the entire U.S. semiconductor industry throughout the 1990s as it architected a series of vital strategic alliances that protected and demonstrated the continued prowess of U.S. manufacturing in this critical industry. In recent years, IBM has entered into a broad array of strategic alliances with partners from around the world to exploit its technological leadership in the key chip industry. These strategic alliances involve not only shared marketing and technology development efforts, but also major commitments of investment funds to build ultramodern facilities that are beyond the financial means of any one company. These two themes, providing leadership for industry competitiveness and building new relationships, are the bases for our discussion. Exhibit 8-1 portrays some of the most significant alliance semiconductor-based relationships that IBM has entered as of October 2004.

Alliance Initiatives During the 1990s: Rebuilding Competitiveness

Perkin–Elmer, Silicon Valley Group, and Etec Systems. According to many industry observers, IBM took on a major role to help the United States preserve its high-technology manufacturing base from Japanese assault during the early 1990s. In late 1989, Perkin–Elmer, a leading maker of scientific instruments, put its critical semiconductor manufacturing equipment division on the sale block. Perkin–Elmer represented one of the last viable U.S. manufacturers of chip-making equipment. Its sale or transfer to foreign investors would hasten the erosion of U.S. manufacturing capability in this field.

Key Pillars of IBM Microelectronics' Alliance Strategy — Exhibit 8-1

Rebuilding U.S. Semiconductor Competitiveness (late 1980s–early 1990s)

- Perkin-Elmer (wafer steppers/lithography)
- Etec Systems (electron-beam etching)
- Silicon Valley Group (lithography equipment)
- Motorola (X-ray lithography techniques)
- Apple Computer and Motorola (PowerPC microprocessor architecture)

Building Ever More Sophisticated Chips (early 1990s–present)

- Toshiba and Siemens (256 megabit memory chips)
- Toshiba, Siemens, Motorola (1 gigabit memory chips)
- Novellus Systems (copper interconnect technology)
- Intel and Motorola (deep ultraviolet (DUV) technology)
- Philips Electronics (microcontrollers)
- Sony and Toshiba (advanced microprocessors used in consumer electronics)
- Samsung Electronics (advanced chip designs)
- Seiko-Epson (advanced microcontrollers)

Manufacturing Chips for Other Firms

- Nvidia (advanced graphics chips for Xbox video game consoles)
- Xilinx (contract manufacturing of programmable logic devices)
- Advanced Micro Devices (development of advanced manufacturing techniques)
- Chartered Semiconductor Manufacturing (process technology sharing)
- Nintendo (advanced processor chips for GameCube video systems)

Advanced Semiconductor Applications

- Medtronic (wireless technology for pacemakers)
- Scientific-Atlanta (set-top boxes)

In early 1990, IBM joined forces with DuPont to transfer Perkin-Elmer's photolithography division to the Silicon Valley Group, and the electron beam operation to Etec Systems, two smaller Silicon Valley firms that possessed cutting-edge technology vital to next-generation chip design and production at the time. IBM, DuPont, and three other domestic strategic investors were dominant co-owners of both Silicon Valley Group and Etec Systems during the 1990s. In effect, IBM's oversight of Perkin-Elmer's transfer of key manufacturing assets into the hands of other friendly, strategically aligned investors ensured that the United States retained a strong domestic manufacturing capability for semiconductor capital equipment. In January 2000, Etec Systems merged with Applied Materials, a leader in developing a broad line of semiconductor capital equipment that is used throughout the entire chip-making industry.

In August 2001, ASM Lithography, a Dutch company that has become a leader in photolithography technology, acquired Silicon Valley Group. IBM had already developed strong relationships with both Applied Materials and ASM Lithography over the past few years.

Motorola. During the 1990s, IBM worked with Motorola on a number of key technologies to bolster U.S. competitiveness in chip making. These alliances have been instrumental for both companies to learn and apply new technologies, particularly in the area of semiconductors and new forms of communications equipment. Some of the IBM–Motorola relationships included such technologies as etching and lithography techniques for chip making, mobile data networks, and new generations of microprocessors. Both IBM and Motorola are members of the U.S. semiconductor consortium, Sematech. Starting in 1989, IBM and

Motorola began to share the earliest versions of X-ray lithography technology used in currently produced semiconductors. Motorola was also the third "leg" of IBM's highly touted joint venture with Apple Computer to develop multimedia operating systems and advanced chip technologies.

During the early 1990s, all three firms attempted to develop a new operating system based on Motorola's 88000 series microprocessor. This new microprocessor, known as the PowerPC, was expected to have many of the same capabilities as Intel's Pentium series of chips, but ultimately the three-way venture never experienced the same market penetration as Intel did. Although IBM and Motorola continue to work jointly on cutting-edge semiconductor technology, they have recently begun to take different paths in using the PowerPC architecture for consumer electronics, telecommunications, and other applications. More recently, the two firms joined with Intel to work on even more advanced semiconductor capital equipment to produce chips for the current decade. By working with both Intel and Motorola, IBM hopes to sustain America's lead in developing the equipment and technologies that are needed for tomorrow's semiconductor industry. In late 2004, Motorola's semiconductor unit was spun off into a separate entity known as Freescale, which continues to design leading-edge semiconductors.

Apple Computer. IBM formed a complex series of alliances with Apple Computer during the early 1990s. One venture, named Kaleida, was designed around operating software and emerging multimedia technology and enabled both firms to share information regarding the industry's technical standards. The second venture, Taligent, joined with Motorola to develop a new line of PowerPC microprocessors. These PowerPC chips were originally developed to compete with Intel's Pentium chips and offer customers faster speed at lower cost. These alliances were designed to assist each partner to work to mutual benefit. For example, IBM was to have gained access to Apple's proprietary Macintosh operating system, while Apple received development help and a steady supply of chips for its new computers. Both Kaleida and

Taligent endeavors were highly welcomed at the time, especially when numerous customers were increasingly wary of Microsoft and Intel's growing dominance in Windows-driven software applications. Although the broad framework of cooperation was designed to counter some of Microsoft's dominant market position in PC software, both pillars of the alliance, Kaleida and Taligent, eventually dissolved throughout 1995 and 1996. Neither IBM, Apple, nor to a lesser extent, Motorola were able to resolve some key differences about how best to manage the organization and operations of the alliance.

Toshiba. IBM clearly saw many Japanese companies posing a direct threat to U.S. competitiveness in chip making and computers. Despite that fact, IBM took steps to enlarge the scope of cooperation with some of its Japanese partners. Many of these alliances were designed with two purposes in mind: to learn new technologies from the Japanese partner and, simultaneously, to "contain" the Japanese partner. Over the past decade, Toshiba has become IBM's most important Japanese alliance partner. It has worked with Big Blue in a number of different ventures, ranging from mainframe computers to semiconductors to flat-panel displays. Flat-panel displays represent screens that use liquid crystal display (LCD) and other means to generate digital images. These screens are used in notebook and palm-sized, handheld computers. From September 1989 to May 2002, IBM and Toshiba jointly manufactured active matrix and liquid crystal display technologies in an ultramodern plant and fabrication facility in Japan. The development and manufacture of flat-panel displays are still extremely costly and difficult. Early generations of screen technology used over one million transistors to control the transmission of images back and forth between the screen and the computer. Current flat-screen technology uses several million transistors, and the number will continue to grow.

Siemens. In July 1992, IBM broadened the scope of its alliance with Toshiba to include the semiconductor business of German firm Siemens. (This semiconductor business is now known as Infineon

Technologies when it was spun off from Siemens a few years ago.) This three-way venture continues to work on extremely advanced chip design and manufacturing skills. The $1 to $2 billion cost of designing the first chip is so expensive that no one firm can afford to undertake the project alone. In October 1996, this three-way venture was expanded to include longtime IBM partner Motorola. Now, this complex alliance includes four different partners with complementary skills to forge ahead with extremely costly chip development. Much of this work is concentrated at IBM's East Fishkill, New York facility.

Sony. In another related venture signed in May 2001, IBM and Toshiba agreed to work with Sony to build even faster computer chips. Known as "The Cell," these chips are designed to operate at speeds of current supercomputers, and they will be used for next-generation multimedia and entertainment applications. The first application of "The Cell" will be in Sony's next generation of PlayStation video game consoles that will debut in 2006. IBM continues to work with both Japanese partners at one of its semiconductor laboratories in Austin, Texas.

Philips. In October 1994, IBM formed a joint venture with European consumer electronics giant Philips to codesign and coproduce new forms of microcontroller chips for use in television sets, CD players, stereos, and home appliances. By linking up with one of the world's biggest and most advanced electronics firms, IBM gains access to Philips' expertise in consumer products. The deal helps both companies learn how to develop new products and technological applications that will be important for the emerging multimedia industry. For IBM, this was an important deal since it enabled Big Blue to understand the kinds of chips that were needed for the fast-changing consumer electronics industry.

Current Strategic Alliance Initiatives

Today, IBM's umbrella of chip-driven strategic alliances covers almost every region of the world. In particular, IBM Microelectronics has repositioned itself to become a key chip "foundry" to build chips according to other firm's technical specifications. Chip "foundries" are companies that specialize in the manufacture of chips, while relying on other companies to provide the underlying designs. Chip foundries have especially proliferated in the Far East, with Taiwan Semiconductor Manufacturing and United Microelectronics (both in Taiwan) and Chartered Semiconductor Manufacturing (out of Singapore) the best known. In July 2002, IBM constructed a $3 billion ultramodern manufacturing facility in East Fishkill, New York, to become one of the biggest players in the chip foundry business. Compared to its Far Eastern rivals, IBM Microelectronics has the distinction of being able to design cutting-edge chips and manufacture them at low cost, a rarity in the semiconductor industry. Only Intel matches IBM's skills in chip manufacturing. Some of IBM Microelectronics' biggest partners are the following:

Xilinx. In mid-2002, Xilinx announced a coproduction arrangement with IBM. Xilinx is a small U.S. semiconductor design firm that has developed new types of programmable chips that enable customers in the automotive, industrial, and other sectors to use them according to their own specific needs. Known as system-on-a-chip technology, programmable chips are extremely difficult to manufacture at low cost. Xilinx benefits from gaining access to IBM's state-of-the-art manufacturing; IBM benefits because Xilinx enables the new plant to become much more efficient and experienced at building very complex chips.

Chartered Semiconductor Manufacturing. In December 2002, IBM announced that it would help this Singapore-based company develop its own manufacturing expertise in return for referring customers to IBM. Facing deep financial difficulties, Chartered agreed to send customers who needed the most advanced manufacturing skills to IBM. IBM, however, has agreed to help Chartered participate in jointly developing advanced chip-manufacturing processes that will be used in both East Fishkill (the New York location of IBM's ultramodern semiconductor plant) and Singapore.

Nvidia and Microsoft. These two companies provide important technologies for the Xbox gaming system. Nvidia provides the graphic chips that give the Xbox stunning visual effects; Microsoft has invested billions in its Xbox system to compete against rivals Sony and Nintendo in the video game industry. Both companies have turned to IBM to provide it with the chips needed to power the next-generation Xbox console. Nvidia turned to IBM because it did not want to become excessively reliant on its previous manufacturing partner, Taiwan Semiconductor. Microsoft, in turn, chose IBM Microelectronics in order to reduce its dependence on Intel, which has long worked with Microsoft to provide microprocessors for PCs. Microsoft's newest Xbox consoles will use the PowerPC architecture.

Nintendo. IBM also provides chip-manufacturing expertise for the microprocessors that power Nintendo's GameCube video game consoles.

Alliances in New Smart Technologies. IBM continues to invest in strategic alliances that help the company learn new hardware-based technologies as well. The company is also working with Scientific-Atlanta to design next-generation interactive television set-top boxes designed to provide Internet and other forms of telecommunications access through cable television networks. It has also signed a variety of alliance agreements with LSI Logic and Kymata to develop next-generation communication chips using optics and other technologies. With the Carrier unit of United Technologies, IBM will participate in designing new web-enabled air-conditioning systems. Both IBM and Carrier will develop new technologies that allow customers to control their air-conditioning systems through the Internet—a valuable service for many customers that would like to better manage their electricity costs during the summer. In addition, Carrier's air conditioners would use IBM's "smart technology" that notifies customers when important mechanical components or fluids need service. In more advanced versions of this technology, the air conditioner will send a diagnostic report to a Carrier service center, which in turn will contact the customer to schedule a maintenance checkup and preventive repair.

Health Care. IBM has started to form alliances with companies in the medical device and health care fields as well. In January 2000, IBM signed a deal with Medtronic, Inc. IBM will jointly design the chips and wireless networks that will power Medtronic's future pacemakers and cardiac defibrillators. Medtronic hopes to use IBM's technology to develop pacemakers that would automatically notify a patient's doctor or the nearest hospital in case the patient suffers an early heart attack or other abnormality. By designing ultraresponsive pacemakers, Medtronic hopes to save most patients from suffering a full-blown cardiac event.

Strategic Snapshot

The Global Airline Industry[2]

During the 1990s, many airline companies began to form close strategic alliances with their counterparts from different parts of the world. As the demand for air transportation increases with global business growth, tourism, the rise of discretionary incomes, and the need for airfreight services, many airlines are seeking to extend their reach and revenue streams from domestic markets into new regions of the world. In particular, alliances among different airline partners took on greater impetus during the mid-1990s as many governments (particularly those in Europe) encouraged a wave of consolidation to improve efficiency and to promote competition within the industry. Alliances have begun to pervade the airline industry as they have in the telecommunications, semiconductor, financial services, and pharmaceutical industries. In all of these industries, firms have begun to realize that building a large, critically massed network is key to establishing competitive advantage and market position. As no one airline can afford to reach and serve every market in every region on a cost-competitive basis, alliances among once-fierce rivals have begun to mushroom, especially in the highly lucrative transatlantic market. Some of the most noteworthy globe-spanning, multipartner alliances are presented in Exhibit 8-2.

Although most airlines continue to retain their own corporate identities and marketing programs, the massive growth of strategic alliances in this industry has meant that most airlines have become highly interdependent on their alliance partners in order to reach different markets around the world. Alliances and mergers in the global airline industry are likely to accelerate as all the carriers face renewed cost pressures and difficult market conditions. As a result, each major carrier needs to develop strategies for entering new markets and serving new customers. Thus, individual airline companies are becoming a part of a larger airline alliance network.

From Code Sharing to Combined Operations

Airline alliances once started as simple "code-sharing" arrangements that enabled cooperating partners to sell each other's seats using the same ticket for a passenger. When conceived in the early 1990s, code-sharing arrangements were an extremely important development in the industry, since they allow airlines to rationalize their passenger flights and airline capacity to maximize the number of revenue miles per flight. In effect,

airlines working together in code-sharing arrangements could streamline and improve the profitability of their operations by coordinating different schedules and ticket pricing for various markets. Airlines would link up and share their flight codes through central computer reservation systems in such a way that the passenger's ticket reflected a single itinerary that might include a flight that is on an airplane owned by an alliance partner. The effect of code-sharing is to help participating carriers better coordinate their schedules and operational planning in key markets where governments allow the practice. However, beyond that of selling seating capacity, code-sharing alliances are relatively simple mechanisms, since most code-sharing arrangements precluded the airline partners from more closely coordinating their schedules or pricing structures.

In the mid-1990s, however, airline alliances evolved from simpler code-sharing arrangements toward much closer, more intricate joint alliance planning between partners. In 1992, the U.S. Department of Transportation in a landmark decision granted antitrust immunity to Northwest Airlines and KLM Royal Dutch Airlines that enabled the two companies to coordinate their transatlantic flights as if they were one single entity. This move helped both carriers reduce their costs significantly. This decision set the pattern for more sophisticated alliances that allowed partners to unite their entire fare structures, flight schedules, marketing initiatives, frequent-flier programs, baggage handling facilities, and time and gate slots at different airports. These partnerships have worked to create significantly easier international connections for passengers traveling from one region to another, and it brought nonstop service to new, interior markets that were previously required to fly passengers to another "departing hub" or "gateway" location before they could actually catch their international flight. In recent years, governments have steadily approved of such expanded partnership arrangements because there are more choices of international routings served through multiple hubs, thus preserving competition among competing airline alliances. The

Exhibit 8-2   Global Strategic Alliances in the Airline Industry

TRANSATLANTIC LINKAGES/RELATIONSHIPS

Airlines	Type of Alliance
• United Airlines • Lufthansa	Full partnership (antitrust immunity) part of Star Alliance
• Delta Air Lines • Swissair • Sabena • Austrian Airlines	Full partnership (antitrust immunity) Relationship unwound in 1998/1999
• Continental Airlines • Alitalia	Code sharing, joint marketing (antitrust issues pending)
• American Airlines • British Airways	Code sharing, joint marketing (antitrust request withdrawn in 2002)
• Delta Airlines • Air France/KLM • CSA Czech Airlines • Alitalia • Aero Mexico • Continental Airlines • Northwest Airlines	Sky Team alliance

GLOBE-SPANNING LINKAGES/RELATIONSHIPS

Airlines	Type of Alliance
• United Airlines • Lufthansa • Scandinavian Airline System (SAS) • Thai International • Varig Brazilian Airlines	Star Alliance: Code sharing, joint marketing; includes up to 15 partners in 2004
• American Airlines • British Airways • Cathay Pacific • Qantas Airways • Aer Lingus • Lan Chile • Finn Air • Iberia	Code sharing, joint marketing, arrangement for global flights. New alliance now known as **one**world.
• Northwest Airlines • Continental Airlines • Japan Air System	Code sharing for transpacific flights

net effect of these alliance-driven, combined operations is to give partners an ability to leapfrog into new markets that they previously could not have served because of government regulations, pricing difficulties, overwhelming market dominance by a local carrier, or the high cost of establishing infrastructure at a newly served airport. These alliances provide the basis for a global network without the associated costs of high capital investment. Alliances receiving antitrust immunity are the only way that airlines can become even more global in their reach, particularly when there are still numerous government restrictions imposed by many nations.

Network versus Network

Airlines were forming alliances and combining their operations at a dizzying pace in the late 1990s and continuing in this decade as well. Northwest Airlines and KLM have extended their core Detroit–Amsterdam passenger routes to extend farther into continental Europe and the United States. These have included such other gateways as Minneapolis, New York, and Seattle-Tacoma. At one point, Delta Air Lines worked very closely with partners Swissair, Sabena, and Austrian Airlines to provide frequent nonstop service from New York, Atlanta, Cincinnati, and Salt Lake City to several European locations. However, this series of relationships eventually dissolved, and Delta began working with Air France to form a new transatlantic network relationship, which won antitrust immunity in 2001. Delta's former alliance partners could not provide the kind of high-frequency flight schedules that were needed to battle those of American Airlines and United Airlines. Now, United Airlines closely coordinates its flight schedules and pricing closely with Lufthansa to gain access to Northern Europe and the rest of the continent.

In May 1996, American Airlines sought governmental permission to enter into a broad-ranging alliance with British Airways to create a new global airline network. Far more vast than the Northwest–KLM or the previous Delta–Swissair–Sabena–Austrian Airlines alliances, the original two-way American–British alliance began to rapidly overshadow the existing transatlantic division of labor among competing alliances in terms of sheer size of the parent companies, projected number of passengers carried, and the stranglehold that both American and British Airways would control at London's key Heathrow Airport. In linking up with British Airways, American gained the ability to ticket its customers for travel beyond Heathrow and into the continent. American is currently second to United in serving the trans-atlantic market and could not extend its reach to such cities as Rome, Budapest, Vienna, Athens, or any other points beyond without a partner. British Airways, on the other hand, sought American as a partner because it offered a strong passenger network into much of the United States and Latin America, where American has steadily gained strength against many of the nationally based local airlines. The vast scale of the proposed American–British Airways alliance prompted numerous protests from other competing airline partners, such as United Airlines and Lufthansa, which demand greater access to Heathrow and other European hubs before they will approve of the deal. In January 2002, the two carriers decided not to petition their respective governments for antitrust immunity. Even nine years after the original petition was filed with the U.S. and British governments, neither British Airways nor American Airlines has received full antitrust immunity for their coordinated transatlantic schedules.

The proliferation of alliances in the profitable transatlantic market is giving way to more complex multipartner operations that are now linking up partners from different parts of the world into a series of interwoven code-sharing and joint marketing arrangements. These broader multiairline alliances have not yet received antitrust immunity for other markets (for example, transpacific), so their scope of coordination is somewhat more limited than that found in the core transatlantic market. However, the transatlantic alliance experiences for United Airlines, Delta Air Lines, and American Airlines have provided these carriers important experience and learning opportunities to broaden their relationships to other parts of the world where they have not intensively served before. From a competitive standpoint, these globe-spanning alliances will now pit entire global networks of airline alliances against other rival alliances to capture customers, lucrative airport hubs, and market shares. Thus, the industry is moving to a new form of jointly managed cooperation and competition between entire collections of firms.

For example, the Star Alliance (formed in May 1997) enlarged a preexisting United Airlines–Lufthansa alliance to include a code-sharing arrangement with Thai International, SAS, and Varig Brazilian Airlines, which represented the five founding partners. By June 2002, the original five-member Star Alliance grew to include seventeen members, including ANA of Japan, British Midland, Air Canada, and a number of different carriers serving the Pacific. Star Alliance strengthened the reach of Lufthansa and United, the biggest carriers, to gain better access to Southeast Asia, Scandinavia, Latin America, and now the Pacific. By significantly broadening what is already a powerful alliance, Lufthansa in particular gains a much larger share of the profitable long-haul traffic from Europe to the Far East, especially from business travelers who contribute a disproportionate amount of airline profits. Even now, Star Alliance is currently negotiating to expand its alliance membership to other carriers throughout the world. Meanwhile, American Airlines has been forming relationships with a number of important carriers to both Asia and Latin America throughout the past few years. Not to be outdone, American and British Airways formed a global partnership spanning Europe, North America, the Far East, and Australia by forming a series of alliances with Cathay Pacific of Hong Kong and Qantas Airways of Australia. Cathay Pacific and American Airlines both need each other in particular because neither has the critical mass to serve North America or the Pacific, respectively. In particular, Cathay Pacific has come under severe margin pressures recently with the economic recession now plaguing Southeast Asia. American, however, needs Cathay Pacific as a key partner to circumvent the need to fly to Tokyo before reaching other Asian destinations. In March 1999, American Airlines, British Airways, Canadian Airlines, Cathay Pacific, and Qantas Airways formally unveiled their globe-spanning **one**world alliance. **One**world is designed to help all five carriers (and future participants) reach parts of the world they were unable to access before. Newer partners also include Iberia (routes in Spain and Portugal), Finn Air (routes in Scandinavia), and Aer Lingus (Ireland). Some analysts believe that because American and British Airways did not receive antitrust immunity, the relationship between the two megacarriers may weaken in future years as both companies look for more suitable partners. For now, they remain committed to the **one**world alliance. American Airlines has also formed separate code-sharing alliances with a host of smaller regional airlines, including TAM of Brazil and Turkish Airlines, to further its reach beyond that of **one**world alliance cities.

Perhaps the most important developments in the evolution of global airline alliances are the rapid inclusion and consolidation of several key players that form the third competing alliance, SkyTeam. Delta's core relationship with Air France paved the way for the massive expansion of the SkyTeam alliance, which was designed to counter rival transatlantic alliances. By working with Korean Air, Delta gains access to the Pacific and Far Eastern markets. On the other hand, Delta has made some major inroads into the Latin American market by working more closely to integrate its flight schedules with long-standing partner Aero-Mexico, which has also become part of SkyTeam. New partners in the alliance include Alitalia and CSA Czech Airlines as part of SkyTeam. Within the United States, Delta has more closely coordinated its frequent-flier program with Continental Airlines and Northwest Airlines, both of which became partners in SkyTeam in March 2003. In October 2003, Air France and KLM merged to create a mega-European airline in a bid to gain further economies of scale and better coordination of transatlantic and cross-European flight schedules. The current SkyTeam alliance, which consists of nine partners, now flies to over six hundred different destinations, and has become an extremely formidable competing alliance network to both Star Alliance and **one**world.

Introduction

This chapter shows how companies can use strategic alliances to learn and build new sources of competitive advantage. The role of strategic alliances in shaping corporate and business strategy has grown significantly over the past decade. In almost every industry, alliances are becoming more common as companies realize that they can no longer afford the costs of developing new products or entering new markets on their own. Alliances are especially prevalent in industries or technologies that change rapidly, such as semiconductors, airlines, automobiles, fuel cells, flat-screen televisions, pharmaceuticals, telecommunications, consumer electronics, and financial services.[3] What is also interesting about strategic alliances is that we are beginning to see intensely competitive rivals now working together, often in ways unimaginable even a few years back. For example, we are seeing collections of competitors working together to architect new types of digital home entertainment technologies, including such firms as Hewlett-Packard, Microsoft, Samsung, Sony, and Cisco Systems, to devise new types of personal computers that can control all aspects of a "digital living room." On a broader global level, many U.S. and Japanese firms in the automobile and electronics industries have teamed up to develop new technologies, especially in the areas of advanced batteries and fuel cells that use alternative sources of energy. And yet, in both the digital entertainment and automotive industries, *firms will partner with one another while simultaneously competing to sell products and enter each other's markets.*

Strategic alliances are linkages between companies designed to achieve an objective faster or more efficiently than if either firm attempted to do so on its own. The role of strategic alliances in shaping the future course of both industries and individual firms is likely to become even more profound in the next century. For organizations of all sizes and types, teaming and allying with other companies are becoming powerful vehicles for entering new markets, learning new technologies, and developing new products. Yet, strategic alliances are not without risks. Coordinating the efforts of another partner (or set of partners) requires management to carefully balance cooperation and competition. Alliance relationships can prove extremely turbulent and can result in the unforeseen creation of a direct competitor if they are poorly managed. Many companies have discovered that the costs of undertaking internal development programs, especially for new drugs or high-technology products, are extremely high and risky. Other companies want to grow and expand, but they realize that mergers and acquisitions can present significant difficulties related to integrating newly acquired companies or businesses. On the other hand, strategic alliances serve a vital role in extending and renewing a firm's sources of competitive advantage because they allow companies to limit certain kinds of risk when entering new terrain.

We begin by examining some of the key objectives that firms seek to accomplish by forming strategic alliances. Second, we examine the different types of strategic alliances. We examine both single-partner relationships, as well as more complex, multipartner arrangements. Third, we analyze the costs and risks of cooperation that underscore all strategic alliances. Finally, we focus on alliance-based implementation issues, examining how companies can balance cooperation and competition to maximize the benefits and minimize the costs of alliance-based activities.

strategic alliances:
Linkages between companies designed to achieve an economic objective faster or more efficiently than either company could do so alone.

Key Strategic Alliance Objectives

Alliances work to extend a firm's competitive advantage in several important ways. In many situations, firms enter into strategic alliances because an alliance can potentially provide *benefits that are not possible through either internal development or external acquisition.* Thus, companies form alliances to acquire some of diversification's benefits without assuming the full costs of going it alone. Alliances represent a potent alternative to internally formulated diversification strategies to enter new industries that companies pursue on their own. Unlike do-it-yourself internal development, a firm must work with a partner to develop new technologies and/or products. Also, unlike full-scale acquisitions, an alliance does not give a firm total control over its partner; the firm does not completely merge with its partner. In this sense, alliances serve as an intermediate or transitional step to enter new industries and markets. Alliances can assist the firm's learning and diversification into new areas of activity. Consequently, alliances provide the partner with a strategic option on future growth opportunities. However, they generate a very different series of organizational issues that management must consider, since a firm cannot fully "control" or rule over its partner(s).

Strategic alliances can help firms extend and renew their sources of competitive advantage when expanding globally. The successful pursuit of global or multidomestic strategies often requires firms to establish operations in distant markets. Yet, these commitments in many cases are high risk, especially when companies are not familiar with the local environment. Alliances thus act as *potential risk reduction vehicles for firms seeking to enter new markets that they do not know well.* As such, firms may find that alliances provide useful platforms to test their products in new markets before they commit themselves to establishing their own self-contained units and subsidiaries in global markets. By teaming up with a partner that has more experience and knowledge about a particular market's conditions, a firm can better understand how to compete in a new region at lower cost and risk. Even companies that have already established their own operating subsidiaries in distant markets can benefit from strategic alliances. Working with a partner can help overcome or sidetrack other economic obstacles to further expansion.

Firms engage in strategic alliances for a number of reasons, but they all involve some form of *risk reduction*. Strategic alliances can help firms accomplish one or more of the following key economic objectives: (1) new market entry, (2) vertical integration, (3) shaping of industry evolution, (4) learning and applying new technologies, and (5) rounding out a product line. These categories are not mutually exclusive. In practice, many firms will employ strategic alliances in order to manage and deal with several overlapping types of risks.

New Market Entry

Companies have formed strategic alliances to speed market entry. In the global pharmaceutical industry, for example, Merck, Fujisawa, and Bayer aggressively cross-license their newest drugs to one another. These arrangements help all three firms reduce the high fixed costs of R&D and global distribution. Fujisawa distributes Merck's and Bayer's drugs in Japan, while Bayer does so for Merck and Fujisawa in Europe. In this way, all three firms avoid duplicating the high fixed costs of development, distribution, and marketing worldwide. Pharmaceutical firms will often work with one another to promote the fast distribution and acceptance of a new drug. For example, GlaxoSmithKline recently entered a wide-ranging strategic alliance with Schering-Plough to further strengthen its U.S. market position across a broad range of drugs.

In the beverage industry, Nestlé works with Coca-Cola to gain access to the other's distribution channels. This is a long-standing relationship that combines both companies' marketing and distribution clout in ways that enhance each firm's competitive position in businesses that are more central to them. Coca-Cola distributes Nestlé's line of fruit juices and coffees, while Nestlé works with Coke on other soft drink products distribution worldwide. Without teaming up, both companies would have to spend more time and resources on their own "reinventing the wheel" to enter certain market segments.

The rise of numerous alliances in the airline industry is directly related to partners seeking access to serve new markets they previously could not enter. In particular, U.S. and European airlines have been rapidly teaming up with one another to serve the profitable transatlantic market in such a way that they can reach into the European continent and the U.S. interior, respectively. Transatlantic airline alliances enable partners to extend their reach without incurring a disproportionate high cost of capital investment. Likewise, many of the same U.S. carriers are beginning to formulate a broad range of alliances to help them enter promising transpacific markets, especially Japan, China, and Southeast Asia, which U.S. airlines have typically had difficulty reaching (largely because of government regulations and agreements needed between nations to allocate flights).

Vertical Integration

Trying to attain the benefits of vertical integration (without the costs of doing it alone) is a critical reason why many firms enter strategic alliances. Vertical integration is designed to help firms enlarge the scope of their operations within a single industry. Yet, for many firms, expanding their set of activities within the value chain can be an expensive and time-consuming proposition. Engaging in full vertical integration is especially risky for companies that compete in fast-changing industries. Alliances can help firms retain some degree of control over crucial supplies at a time when investment funds are scarce and cannot be allocated to backward integration. Also, alliances can assist firms to achieve the benefits of vertical integration without saddling them with higher fixed costs and risks. This benefit is especially appealing when the core technology used in the industry is changing quickly.

In the semiconductor industry, the rapid rise of highly innovative, small firms has reshaped the economics of developing leading-edge technologies. In particular, small semiconductor companies such as Nvidia, PMC-Sierra, Altera, Xilinx, and Broadcom are hotbeds of design innovation. They specialize in pioneering and using cutting-edge technologies to design new types of chips to power the Internet. However, these firms typically do not have the funds, size, capital investment, or technical competence to engage in large-scale manufacturing on their own. Many have outsourced their manufacturing to larger, dedicated chip foundry firms that possess distinctive competences in skills such as cost control, process and yield improvement, and manufacturing scale economies. These small, leading-edge firms have instead concentrated their scarce capital and resources to focus on what they do best: innovative designs, creativity, and pushing the limit of technology. In Silicon Valley, they are known as "fabulous fab-less" companies because of their lack of manufacturing operations. More often than not, these companies have established a strong production, division-of-labor relationship with semiconductor foundries, such as Taiwan Semiconductor Manufacturing Company (TSMC) and United Microelectronics Company (UMC), both of which are Taiwan-based firms that provide contract manufacturing services.[4] Thus, partnering enables the smaller firms to capture the benefits of vertical integration without incurring the high fixed costs of in-house investments.

In the highly capital-intensive chemical and petroleum industries, alliances are becoming more common as firms seek to divvy up the high fixed costs required for managing ever more scale-intensive production processes. In both industries, production is highly dedicated and continuous in nature, meaning that it is difficult for firms on their own to build sufficient scale and profitability in products that often face highly volatile pricing and deep cyclical downturns when markets collapse. For example, Royal Dutch/Shell Group and Texaco have worked closely to coordinate their production and marketing activities in the United States to rationalize their production capacity and thus lower costs.

In the airline industry, firms receiving antitrust immunity to coordinate their pricing, marketing, and scheduling operations in the transatlantic market are effectively seeking the benefits of vertical integration without its commensurately high costs. By coordinating flight schedules and other key activities (for example, baggage handling, landing slots in airports, vendor relations, crew facilities, ticket gates, and maintenance), partnering airlines can avoid duplicating some of the costly infrastructures that are needed each time they serve a new airport. Whether a plane is full or empty, the airline still incurs the costs of maintenance, crew handling, scheduling, and slot fees imposed by each airport. With an alliance, however, many of these fixed costs are shared, and capital investment for each partner is kept to a minimum.

Shaping Industry Evolution

Strategic alliances can help shape what an industry may look like in the future. In the semiconductor and biotechnology industries, many firms have formed alliances to define emerging standards or new products (see Exhibit 8-3). For example, Texas Instruments began working with European partner STMicroelectronics to develop key software tools and instructions that will enhance the capabilities of new generations of digital signal processing (DSP) chips. These DSP chips power next-generation cellular phones, digital cameras, printers, and other consumer electronics. By working together, both Texas Instruments and STMicroelectronics hope to participate in a fast-evolving segment of the semiconductor industry where demand is expected to grow more quickly than the rest of the industry. The semiconductor industry has been replete with alliances that enable smaller firms to pool resources and to share the risks of developing in cutting-edge technology.[5]

Qualcomm has used strategic alliances to establish a near 90 percent dominance of chips in cell phones that use a technology known as CDMA.[6] CDMA technology is a digital standard used to handle cell phone calls. Some market researchers believe that CDMA-enabled phone devices could become dominant in many parts of the world over the next decade. Qualcomm has worked extensively with Nokia and Samsung to provide the CDMA chips needed to power their phones. Qualcomm's near-monopoly position has enabled the firm to define many of the technical standards for how video, voice, and data are transmitted over the airwaves. To stay ahead of its competitors, Qualcomm is investing in newer types of CDMA chips that allow cell phone users to "roam" anywhere around the world, a task that is currently difficult because of conflicting transmission standards. Qualcomm's latest chips will enable users to watch full-motion, streaming video on their cell phones and laptop computers in the next few years. In turn, cell phone manufacturers look to Qualcomm for the latest technical advances to boost sales of newer models.[7]

More and more frequently, teams of companies possessing different technologies or skills will compete against other teams to see which group will ultimately produce a dominant industry-wide standard. For example, Toshiba, Matsushita, and Time Warner cooperated extensively during the mid-1990s to design highly versatile, digital video discs (DVDs) for the consumer electronics industry. Sony and Philips Electronics had their own alliance to codesign and produce their respective version of DVD technology that used a different set of design tools and layers to record and store video and other forms of data. These DVDs have already replaced VCRs as the primary consumer electronics device to complement the television set in many homes. Both the Sony–Philips alliance and the Toshiba–Matsushita–Time Warner alliance produced numerous variations of DVD prototypes and software platforms before the two sides were able to come to a mutual understanding and agree on a common set of technical standards in early 1996. Both alliance teams realized that if they failed to come to an agreement early in the product development stage, then it was highly unlikely that consumers would buy either

| Representative Alliances in the Semiconductor Industry | Exhibit 8-3 |

Partners	Technology
IBM Motorola Toshiba Siemens	256-megabit memory chips Advanced flash memories
Advanced Micro Devices Fujitsu	Advanced flash memories
Intel AT&T	Wireless communication chips
Texas Instruments Qualcomm	Technology cross-licensing pact
Advanced Micro Devices Motorola	Copper deposition technology in chip circuitry
Intel Hewlett-Packard	64-bit Itanium microprocessor (earlier known as Merced Project)
Lucent Technologies NEC Mitsubishi Electric	Custom-designed chips for communications equipment
Toshiba Samsung	Advanced memory chips
Philips Electronics STMicroelectronics Taiwan Semiconductor	90-nanometer chip technology
IBM Xilinx	System-on-a-chip technology using Power PC architecture
Toshiba Infineon Technologies	Advanced DRAM chips
Intel Analog Devices	Advanced DSP chips

competing DVD standard, since movies made on one version of DVD were not compatible with the other.[8]

The current nature of DVD technology is likely to change again with a new level of competition taking shape in 2005. A new DVD technology, known as "Blu-Ray," is based on an advanced laser that enables a recordable DVD to pack thirteen times more data onto a single disc than a traditional DVD. Developed by Sony and supported by its partners (for example, Matsushita Electric, Hewlett-Packard, Dell Computer), Blu-Ray faces another competing technology known as HD-DVD, which was developed by Toshiba and NEC. Both the Blu-Ray and HD-DVD alliances are vying with one another to seek the support of Hollywood film studios. Because film studios control the films that will be available on these high-definition discs, they are vital players in determining which industry standard wins. This confrontation between competing alliances over technical standards will certainly shape what future generations of consumer electronics products will look like by the end of 2005.[9]

More recently, telecommunications equipment companies have begun working closely among themselves to design an industry standard for new types of wireless communications. Here, the alliance efforts have been significantly more fragmented. During the late 1990s, Ericsson, Motorola, and Nokia joined forces to promote a new wireless standard known as Wireless Application Protocol (WAP). This standard was designed to enhance the creation of new technologies and applications for wireless Internet usage. Other companies, however, formed their own relationships to promote their vision of what wireless technologies should be able to do. Some of these technologies use different software algorithms to transmit digital information (for example, TDMA vs. CDMA vs. GSM standards). For example, Qualcomm (U.S. based), Nokia (Finland based), Symbian (U.K. based), and even Microsoft worked with a broad array of their own partners to create the technology platform for what is known as 2.5G and 3G technologies (G stands for generation). These are technologies that allow video streaming, wireless Internet transmission, and even the use of digital cameras on next-generation cellular phones. In addition, these phones will be designed to work together with future personal digital assistants (PDAs), such as Palm's Palm Pilot line of products and Handspring's future Visor offerings.

Learning and Applying New Technologies

Companies form alliances to learn or to gain access to new technologies. In the telecommunications industry, for example, a broad array of alliances has arisen over the past few years as existing telephone networks quickly converge with new Internet-driven communications and computer technologies. For example, a number of new upstart firms that promise to offer faster, clearer, and multipurpose communications services (voice, video, data) along broadband networks have found important strategic partners with the capital and technology to invest in them. Until it became a publicly traded company in June 1999, Juniper Networks worked closely with IBM and other companies to develop an ultrafast, terabit capability (transmission speeds of one trillion bits per second) router that will transform much of current Internet and voice traffic. At that time, Juniper was an upstart in a field dominated by the likes of Cisco Systems, Lucent Technologies, Nortel Networks, and other networking companies that were seeking to enter the telecom and broadband networking equipment area. Now, Juniper Networks has begun challenging market leader Cisco Systems to develop even faster routers that will power next-generation telecommunications and optical networks. More important, Juniper has even begun to develop its own technology that many telecommunications firms are currently reviewing for their own use. Nortel Networks even entered into a joint marketing alliance with Juniper in summer 2000 to sell its ultrafast routers to other telecommunications firms. Nortel will provide much of the marketing and distribution clout that Juniper currently lacks.[10]

This same rationale to learn new technologies and to tap into new sources of talent drives many pharmaceutical firms to establish close alliance relationships with young biotechnology firms. Exhibit 8-4 shows just a few of the hundreds of relationships that have taken root over the past several years. For example, Bayer AG of Germany entered into an alliance with Millennium Pharmaceuticals to develop cancer-fighting drugs based on recent discoveries of a new gene that causes tumors to form. Both Bayer and Millennium will work over a six-year period to use computers and other advanced techniques to speed up the discovery of new genetic-based treatments for everything from cancer to osteoporosis. In a related manner, AstraZeneca formed an alliance with Orchid BioSciences, a leading biotechnology firm that specializes in discovering the specific genetic proteins that may be important triggers for disease formation. Orchid's technology is designed to foster the creation of drugs that are unique to each individual human being, using genetic materials to deliver very specific treatments that limit side effects and other downside risks.

Representative Alliances in the Biotechnology Industry — Exhibit 8-4

Partners	Technology/Product
Biogen GlaxoSmithKline	Tissue regeneration
Amgen Kirin Brewery	Blood platelet growth factor
Onyx Pharmaceuticals Bayer AG	"Arrow" drug delivery technology
Chiron Novartis	Genetic mapping technology
Genentech Hoffman-LaRoche	Tissue plasminogen activator
Neurocrine Biosciences Eli Lilly	Corticotropin releasing factor (CRF) hormones
Agouron Pharmaceuticals Roche Holding, Ltd.	Anticancer drugs
Human Genome Sciences GlaxoSmithKline	Genetic mapping technology
Millennium Pharmaceuticals American Home Products	Genetic mapping technology
Creative BioMolecules Biogen	Kidney treatments
Incyte Pharmaceuticals Monsanto	Genetic engineering software
Pioneer Hi-Bred DuPont	Genetically engineered seeds for agriculture
Bayer AG Millennium Pharmaceuticals	Genetically engineered cancer-fighting compounds
Merck Sunesis Pharmaceuticals	Alzheimer's drugs
AstraZeneca PLC Orchid Biosciences	Advanced single nucleotide polymorphisms (SNPs)

In these alliances, pharmaceutical firms have the resources, marketing, distribution, regulatory knowledge, and R&D facilities that almost all the small biotechnology firms lack. On the other hand, biotechnology firms, often founded by recently trained microbiologists, possess cutting-edge techniques that are of great interest to more mature drug companies. These techniques include the use of computer-generated software algorithms to map out the human genetic sequence (genomic technologies), protein synthesis (using amino acid technologies), and the design of new genetic engineering techniques that specifically isolate different sources of hard-to-treat diseases. Often, younger biotechnology firms will develop and use techniques that are so new that they are hard to replicate within the established procedures and development patterns found in many incumbent pharmaceutical firms. Thus, large drug companies will often enter into mutually benefiting alliances with biotechnology companies to jointly learn and develop exotic new drug and drug delivery technologies.[11]

Sony's desire to upgrade its skills to produce the newest generations of flat-screen televisions motivated the Japanese giant to team up with its once-rival Samsung Electronics of South Korea. For more than thirty years, Sony has led the world in designing and producing the most desirable televisions, stereo systems, portable music players, and other sleek appliances. However, Sony fell behind in the race to develop flat-screen televisions as senior management misjudged how quickly consumers would readily purchase these expensive sets. Samsung, on the other hand, invested heavily into new flat-screen technologies based on liquid crystal displays (LCDs) and soon became the world's largest producer in 2003. Samsung's growing technological and manufacturing prowess enabled it to steadily improve its quality and its global brand recognition as well. Realizing that it could not afford the $2 billion to build a factory on its own, Sony teamed up with Samsung in October 2003 to build a leading-edge LCD screen plant where both partners would share the cost equally.[12]

In another technology-driven industry, Mitsubishi, Fuji Heavy Industries, and Kawasaki Heavy Industries have long worked closely with Boeing to learn new assembly techniques used in the aerospace industry. These three Japanese companies serve as chief subcontractors to Boeing for key parts of commercial aircraft, such as the fuselage and tail sections. For example, Mitsubishi Heavy Industries assembles about 60 percent of the fuselage used in many Boeing aircraft. In addition, Boeing's relationship to all three companies has grown closer as they cooperate on studying new fuselage designs that use composite materials. All three Japanese firms have long-term ambitions to enter the commercial aviation industry. Realizing that these three firms could pose a potential long-term threat, Boeing carefully manages the degree of technological sharing it conducts with its Japanese partners. On the other hand, Boeing finds its Japanese partners to be useful teachers of lower-cost Japanese assembly and fabrication techniques that Boeing can then incorporate in its operations in the United States, especially as Boeing learns to adopt new streamlined manufacturing techniques that call for closer supplier relationships and the use of computer networks to design leading-edge airframes.[13]

IBM has teamed up with Motorola and Toshiba to further improve its semiconductor-manufacturing prowess in making superdense chips. IBM gains access to Toshiba's manufacturing and miniaturization skills and its expertise across a whole range of technologies, including flat-panel display screens and specialized skills used for making chips in consumer electronics. With Motorola, IBM learns how to design new products for emerging wireless technologies. Both IBM and Motorola work together to develop new X-ray photolithography techniques that neither company can afford on its own. This technology is an integral part of designing and producing new types of microprocessors and memory chips. By working with two partners simultaneously, IBM hopes to learn the best techniques and designs from both.

Rounding Out the Product Line

Some companies use strategic alliances to round out or fill their product line. See Exhibit 8-5 for an overview of alliances that shape much of the global automotive industry. In the U.S. market, the typical pattern during the 1980s and 1990s involved a U.S. firm working closely with a Japanese firm that possesses valuable experience in building compact and more fuel-efficient cars. In return, the Japanese partner gains access to the U.S. firm's distribution facilities and market. U.S. automakers are often strapped for resources to invest in leading-edge technologies that are vital for smaller cars, and more recently, for cars that use hybrid engines and fuel cells. For example, General Motors uses joint ventures with Suzuki, Isuzu, and Toyota to

Creating Distinctive Value: GE Honda Aero Engines[14]

STRATEGIC
COMPETENCY *in action*

In October 2004, General Electric and Honda Motor Company of Japan formed a 50/50 joint venture known as GE Honda Aero Engines. The formation of this alliance represents a major culminating point in Honda's evolution to become an important player in the aerospace and jet engine business. For Honda, the deal signifies the long-term effort and investment that Honda has made to develop new types of engine-based competencies that enable it to enter new markets. For GE, the relationship is an opportunity to work with Honda to create an entirely new family of smaller jet engines designed for regional jets.

The joint venture will work to further develop and manufacture the HF118, a small jet engine that Honda has devoted over twenty years to perfect. The HF118 offers lower emissions and noise than other comparable engines. It also delivers 10 to 30 percent greater fuel efficiency. More important, Honda views all forms of engine expertise as the source of its distinctive competence. By investing together with GE, Honda will also expand its range of engine technologies, including automotive, generator, marine, motorcycle, lawn and garden equipment, and other uses. Honda's superb automotive engines have enabled the Japanese firm to become a very powerful competitor in building highly desirable cars, light trucks, and motorcycles around the world. Honda now views its investment in aerospace engines as another step toward building airframes and even complete aircraft systems in the next decade. Honda CEO Takeo Fukui views the joint venture as helping the company build the "Honda Civic of the Air." Honda has already experimented with building a small, four-to-five passenger jet that will have more cargo and passenger space than existing models.

For GE, the new relationship with Honda opens up the opportunity to learn new ways to design smaller, more fuel-efficient engines. GE Transportation Systems, which will over-see the new venture, is already the world's largest producer of jet engines, and competes against Pratt & Whitney (a unit of United Technologies) and Rolls-Royce (of the United Kingdom). General Electric will contribute advanced materials and its own engine design technology to the venture. For several years, GE has been working to create its own line of smaller engines for regional jets.

The market for the GE–Honda joint venture appears very promising as large airline companies invest in much more efficient jets that fly short distances between cities. In addition, a host of upstart companies are looking to enter the "air taxi" market, in which a regional jet flies a small number of people between small airports not serviced by major air carriers. "Air taxis" may become even important if some of the weaker big carriers eliminate service to less frequently traveled destinations to cut costs. Former CEO Robert Crandall of AMR's American Airlines and People Express founder Donald Burr have plans to start their own air taxi service named Pogo. Named after a stick that bounces, Pogo will begin service in 2005 with a new class of six-seat mini-jets that will fly the East Coast from North Carolina to Maine, once it passes FAA certification. Pogo will also fly a new line of jets made of reinforced carbon fiber and built by Adam Aircraft Industries of Englewood, Colorado. Honda and GE see a market for over two hundred air taxis a year, and they are aiming to sell the HF118 to just this type of company.

Both GE and Honda are negotiating with several aircraft manufacturers to use the HF118 to power their jets. One potential customer is Brazil's Embraer, which has already captured larger orders from U.S. carriers for regional jets. Within the venture, GE and Honda will share key leadership positions, and each company will appoint a president that will serve rotating three-year terms.

Sample Alliances in the Global Auto Industry   Exhibit 8-5

U.S. Unit/Product	Partner	Location of Manufacture
DaimlerChrysler	General Motors	Transmissions and fuel cells in United States
DaimlerChrysler	BMW	Joint investment in Latin America
United Technologies	Nissan	Automotive components
DaimlerChrysler	Mitsubishi	Advanced modular engines
	Hyundai	
Caterpillar	DaimlerChrysler	Medium-duty engines
General Motors	Toyota	Fuel cells and hybrid engine technology
General Motors	Isuzu	40% equity stake
General Motors	Fuji Motor	20% equity stake
Ford	Toyota and Toshiba	Hybrid motors

coproduce many of its compact cars. Now, Ford is beginning to work with Toyota's suppliers to develop hybrid engines for its cars and SUVs. DaimlerChrysler's U.S. unit relied on Mitsubishi Motors to produce a broad line of Chrysler, Plymouth, and Dodge cars in the subcompact and sports lines. In all of these cases, the U.S. firm needs the competence and skills that the Japanese partner brings to manufacture quality compact cars that help provide a full lineup of cars.

In the financial services industry, both Fidelity Investments and Charles Schwab & Co., two leading discount brokerage houses, have offered other mutual fund companies' offerings through their own fund distribution systems. Both firms believe that cooperating with other fund companies works to mutual advantage because it enables Fidelity and Schwab to participate directly in timing the new funds' rollout, setting minimum balance requirements, and other marketing considerations. Fidelity and Schwab directly benefit from cooperating with other companies because not only do they receive a fee for helping with the funds' launch, but they also provide a wide variety of product and fund offerings to fill in the "shelf space" of these discount brokerages' vast distribution system.[15]

In Japan, Mitsubishi and Hitachi resell mainframe and notebook computers built by IBM to complement their existing products. These alliances are especially important for Hitachi, which recently announced that it would no longer produce its own line of IBM-compatible mainframe computers. IBM achieved low-cost volume production of mainframe computers in Japan to accomplish its goals of breaking into the Japanese market, and Hitachi needed IBM's PowerPC semiconductor line to fulfill its own line of consumer electronics and computers. Over time, as the two companies diversified their operations into other lines of business, both Mitsubishi and Hitachi needed to fill out their mainframe product lines but did not have the manufacturing capacity or advanced semiconductor technology to do it on their own. Mitsubishi's ties with IBM have also grown recently as the two companies begin to cooperate on designing the chips needed for new types of handheld computers. Hitachi has also recently committed itself to using more IBM-manufactured PowerPC microprocessors in its line of personal computers and other electronic equipment. IBM, in turn, sold its disk-drive operations to Hitachi in 2002 to sharpen its focus on its core software and services businesses. Hitachi will now manufacture IBM-designed disk drives that will store data across a broad range of computers.

Star Alliance, which encompasses United Airlines, Lufthansa, Thai International, SAS, Varig Brazilian Airlines, Air Canada, and a dozen other carriers, allows each partner to offer a truly global range of cities and service. The alliance helps each airline partner serve many parts of the world that it previously could not access without significant cost or lengthy government petitions and regulatory processes. Star Alliance enables each of its partners to develop and coordinate a unified marketing theme (worldwide travel to anywhere) that ideally is designed to transport passengers from any region of the world to another using an alliance member's aircraft. In this way, each member of the alliance benefits from providing services that capture the full stream of revenues from each paying passenger. This global network allows the participants of Star to better compete against the likes of similarly emerging alliance networks around the world.

Types and Benefits of Strategic Alliances

Firms can enter into a number of different types of strategic alliances. These could include comparatively simple, more "distant" arrangements in which firms work with one another on a short-term or "arms-length" basis. In these alliances, the two parties effectively do not combine their managers, value chains, core technologies, or other skill sets. Firms working in arms-length relationships do not blend or integrate any of their activities. On the other hand, companies may seek to increase the level of coordination in their cooperative ventures. Such alliances combine managers, technologies, products, processes, and other value-adding assets in varying degrees and ways to bring the companies more closely together. Thus, firms may work together to design new products, share the risks of new technology development, or even coproduce a limited range of products using the same factories. Finally, partners can choose to tightly integrate many more aspects of their operations. For example, they could combine their value chains, core technologies, management systems, and skills outright. These tightly coordinated relationships may even approximate the organizational and strategic characteristics of a full-blown merger or acquisition.

A firm can design its alliance strategy to involve only one partner, or a host of multiple partners. Also, a firm can choose how closely it works with its partners: (1) simple, arms-length relationships, (2) highly coordinated alliances, or (3) tightly integrated alliances. Exhibit 8-6 presents an overview of the broad types of strategic alliance relationships that a firm can choose.

We will examine several different types of strategic alliance vehicles that are positioned in Exhibit 8-6. Each broad type of cooperative relationship can, in turn, result in specific types of strategic alliances, such as licensing, coproduction arrangements, joint ventures, knowledge webs, and so on. These arrangements can help a firm accomplish several different objectives simultaneously.

In practice, a firm will likely work with its partners using a variety of different alliance vehicles to achieve different objectives. For example, an automotive firm may work only with one key supplier to develop a core electronics-based technology, but work with several companies to share the risks in designing next-generation fuel cells. From the perspective of the automotive firm, it is working in a single-partner relationship with the electronics firm. However, the same automotive firm is working with multiple companies to develop fuel cells. Thus, firms can rely on simple or highly complex webs of relationships depending on the economic objectives confronting them.

Alliance Configurations | Exhibit 8-6

	Arms-Length Relationships	Highly Coordinated Relationships	Tight Integration
Single Partner	• Licensing • Comarketing	• Outsourcing • Coproduction • Knowledge sharing	• Joint ventures • Equity stakes
Multipartner	• Industry-wide licensing • Industry standards committees	• Industry consortia • Knowledge webs • Cross-holdings • Equity stakes	• Multipartner joint ventures

Simple, Arms-Length Relationships

Examples of simpler, arms-length alliance relationships between two or more companies include licensing agreements and comarketing agreements.

Licensing. In most manufacturing industries, licensing represents a sale of technology- or product-based knowledge in exchange for market entry. In service-based firms, licensing is the right to enter a market in exchange for a fee or royalty. Licensing arrangements have become more prominent across both categories. In many ways they represent the least sophisticated and simplest-to-manage form of strategic alliance. Licensing arrangements are simple alliances because they allow the participants greater access to either a technology or market in exchange for royalties or future technology sharing than either partner could do on its own.

In the software industry, for example, Microsoft has used licensing very effectively to promote its Windows-based operating systems for use in personal computers, servers, and large commercial networks. Microsoft gets a small royalty in exchange for allowing another firm to incorporate its software offering into a hardware-based product.

Companies enter into licensing agreements for several reasons. The primary reasons are (1) a need for help in commercializing a new technology and (2) global expansion of a brand franchise or marketing image.

Technology Development. In many cases, firms will freely license their newest technologies to other firm in order to define industry standards that shape the industry's evolution. Because few firms can establish a commanding position in a new industry on their own, licensing becomes vital to building industry support. Firms want as many prospective users as possible to generate future sales and product applications. During the 1980s, Matsushita Electric of Japan licensed its VHS technology to anyone interested in building VCRs, including its rivals. Matsushita's liberal licensing policies allowed it to fill the distribution pipeline rapidly with the now famous VHS standard, eventually displacing Sony's Betamax system in the marketplace. During the 1990s, we witnessed much the same replay of licensing arrangements between the two different camps of firms that wanted to create and disseminate their own DVD technical standards and architectures for the post-VCR world of entertainment and consumer electronics. In a desire to avoid a replay of the Betamax–VHS wars of the 1980s, Matsushita, Toshiba, and Time Warner eventually cross-licensed their designs and specifications with those of Sony and Philips to prevent the emerging DVD market from cannibalizing itself as a result of product and technical incompatibilities in future products. Without a single DVD standard, consumers would be much more reluctant to buy DVD players that could not reliably play movies that were made by different companies.

Licenses are designed to keep the industry dynamic and to reduce the high fixed cost of duplication. For example, competitors in both the pharmaceutical and chemical industries freely exchange ideas and license their newest products to one another, since everyone has an interest in spreading out R&D and distribution expenses. On the one hand, all key industry players compete with one another; yet, they exchange information to maintain industry discipline and to further enhance their R&D competences.

Global Expansion. Many firms use licensing to gain fast market entry for existing products. For example, McDonald's, Anheuser-Busch, Frito-Lay International, Nestlé, KFC, and Coca-Cola view licensing as a valuable market entry tool. Licensing generates royalties and builds market share. It can also build a firm's standardized global image with comparatively little cost. At KFC, its licensing strategy provided fast entry into Japan's economy at reasonable cost. Without this licensing arrangement, KFC could not establish itself in Japan because of government regulations that prohibit foreign firms from entering Japan's restaurant businesses without a domestic partner. Coca-Cola works with a number of licensed franchisees to enter newly opened markets. The firm believes that franchising is an effective way to build market presence quickly, plus it provides access to local managers who are knowledgeable about market and competitive conditions.

Cross-Marketing Agreements. Cross-marketing agreements are very similar to licensing deals. Companies will often work together to promote each other's products in the hope of boosting sales for both. For example, McDonald's has worked with the Walt Disney Company to promote Disney's children-oriented films by giving away toys with its Happy Meals. Cell phone companies will often cross-promote their offerings with retailers, as Sprint-Nextel does with Radio Shack to broaden its customer reach.

In the airline industry, code-sharing arrangements represent a form of cross-marketing. Code-sharing helps airline partners gain indirect access to new parts of the world and helps them rationalize and streamline capacity. They also work to increase an airline's revenue and increase brand awareness through alliance arrangements. Thus, code sharing is equivalent to cross-marketing arrangements found in many service industries (for example, retail gasoline operations), whereby partners cooperate to promote, distribute, and divide the royalties and revenues by selling each other's products or offerings. By coordinating reservations and ticket codes, airline partners are able to sell seats on each other's planes and thus potentially capture more passengers who prefer an integrated travel itinerary rather than a series of tickets that must be exchanged with each airline separately.

Highly Coordinated Alliances

When partners work together to design products, share the cost of manufacturing, or rely upon each other for a key value-adding activity, there is much more coordination involved than that found in simpler licensing and cross-marketing arrangements. Highly coordinated alliances introduce greater levels of *dependency* among partners. The actions of one partner have a direct effect on the other partner's capabilities. Moreover, these relationships often require partners to share knowledge and skills in ways that they cannot fully control. Examples of alliance relationships that require coordination include outsourcing arrangements, coproduction deals, knowledge-sharing relationships, and industry-wide consortia. Also, when a firm owns a partial equity stake in another firm, it may also involve coordination of some operational activities as well.

Outsourcing. Outsourcing relationships occur when a firm becomes dependent on a key supplier to provide inputs or activities that were once conducted in-house. Outsourcing has become especially prevalent in many high-technology industries, where high capital costs and rapid product change make it difficult to sustain in-house manufacturing. For example, smaller semiconductor firms increasingly rely on dedicated chip foundries that perform much of the fabrication and testing needed to bring new chips to market. In fact, the long-term trend toward greater outsourcing of manufacturing activities has given rise to an entire new industry: contract electronics manufacturers (CEMs). These firms purchase or build large factories solely to provide low-cost manufacturing to other firms who once built their own products. CEMs include companies such as Flextronics, Solectron, Sanmina-SCI, and Celestica. Flextronics, for example, builds the Xbox gaming system for Microsoft, which has no desire to invest billions in factories to manufacture these devices. At the same time, Flextronics also works with Nortel Networks to build advanced telecom switches and other high-tech equipment. In 2004, Flextronics concluded a deal where it will purchase all of Nortel Networks's manufacturing facilities in North America. In another example, Sanmina-SCI is IBM's exclusive supply partner to build PCs. Because IBM is a high-cost producer, it decided to completely outsource all PC manufacturing to Sanmina-SCI to focus on other more productive activities.

Many U.S. and European firms are outsourcing their back-office operations to lower-cost providers around the world, particularly in China and India. For example, call centers, billing operations, and routine accounting operations are increasingly performed by external suppliers who can perform these activities at significantly lower cost. In fact, the outsourcing of service and back-office operations has stimulated the growth of an entire industry in India. Companies such as Infosys Technologies, Wipro Limited, and Satyan Computers are taking advantage of their superior labor cost position to perform many back-office and service activities for U.S. firms. As these companies strengthen their capabilities and business acumen, they will likely become important competitors to such established firms as IBM, EDS, and Accenture in the United States.

Coproduction. When companies share the cost of building key factories and facilities together, they are coproducing a product. IBM has long relied on coproduction agreements with key partners Motorola, Toshiba, and Infineon Technologies to jointly develop and produce leading-edge memory chips. IBM views coproduction as an effective vehicle to share the costs and risks of developing next-generation technology, but without completely ceding a core skill and technology to its partners. Coproduction arrangements are especially prevalent in aerospace and defense industries, where partners work together to develop key components or to assemble the final airframe.[16] For example, the latest generation of European fighter aircraft involves extensive coproduction of key parts in Britain, Germany, Spain, and Italy. Likewise, in the United States, coproduction is common for many defense-related technologies and components because the government prefers to have a "secondary source" in case of national emergency.

Industry Consortia. In many high-tech industries, competing firms will actively cooperate to share the costs and risks of developing cutting-edge technology that represents important breakthroughs. In the United States, Sematech represents the best example of a multipartner, technology-based consortia.[17] Based in Austin, Texas, Sematech involves more than fifteen U.S. firms interested in sharing ideas to promote new ways to manufacture semiconductors and chip-making equipment. Sematech aims to link up all participating U.S. semiconductor manufacturers to improve domestic design and manufacturing skills. Funded in part by the U.S. Defense Department, this multipartner arrangement was originally defined by the underlying need to upgrade the U.S. chip industry and protect it from Japanese competition. Members include smaller firms, such as Micron Technology, along with such giants as IBM, Lucent Technologies, Intel, Texas Instruments, and Motorola. Over the past decade, Sematech has been instrumental in helping U.S. firms learn and share new technologies and manufacturing skills that are vital to making even more dense memory chips and microprocessors. Sematech promotes specialization of chip-making skills among its member companies by encouraging interfirm sharing of new developments in advanced materials and new manufacturing techniques. This cooperative effort helped its member companies become less dependent on Japanese chip-making equipment during the mid-1990s. In 1992, Sematech was also instrumental in helping several U.S. member companies secure domestic production facilities for flat-panel display screens used in laptop computers and flat-screen television sets.

In a separate industry-wide effort, major U.S. semiconductor firms are now pushing for the creation of a national institute to examine new technologies and approaches to design ever-smaller chips as current technology approaches the limit of its usefulness. In 2004, the Semiconductor Industry Association pushed for the creation of a Nanoelectronics Research Institute that will direct and coordinate a massive research effort to assure U.S. leadership in future semiconductor manufacturing. The proposed institute would represent a shared effort that brings together government, academia, and semiconductor companies.[18]

In Europe, several consortia have formed to protect and reinforce such industries as semiconductors, video display technologies, and aircraft. JESSI (Joint European Submicron Silicon Initiative) was organized in the 1990s to help European semiconductor manufacturers attain the manufacturing and design capabilities of U.S. and Japanese firms. It is Europe's equivalent to Sematech in the United States. JESSI includes such well-known European electronics firms as Siemens, Philips, and STMicroelectronics. Each member company contributes its expertise on some critical aspect of designing and manufacturing next-generation semiconductors. Another European consortium initiative, ESPRIT, is designed to advance the learning and application of new defense technologies among member companies.

Industry Spanning Alliance Networks. Competition and value creation in many industries now involve product and technology development that spans multiple firms. In particular, breakthrough developments in high-technology industries and pharmaceuticals are often beyond the means and capability of an individual firm. As a result, firms in these and other industries are beginning to work more closely with one another than ever before. Oftentimes, a firm will work with a number of different partners to share knowledge, costs, and risks, rather than just a single one. As a result, firms are finding themselves in a more complex alliance environment, where companies are forming a larger industry-wide network. More important, the growth of such alliance networks within and across industries means that each firm is now contributing its own distinctive competence in a way that requires it to work interdependently with other partnering companies, each of which will likely specialize in some value-creating activity.[19]

In what is perhaps the most complicated form of alliance evolution that has yet transpired, companies in many industries are now becoming members of what might be termed a larger knowledge-creating web. **Knowledge webs** are groups of companies that work together to shape the overall evolution of an industry. For example, in the wireless telecommunications industry, a wide range of companies, including Nokia, Motorola, Ericsson, Qualcomm, Symbian, Vodafone, Deutsche Telecom, Japan's NTT DoCoMo unit, and even Microsoft, are working to shape what could be the industry's next generation of wireless telephone and data communication systems. For example, NTT DoCoMo was the first company in the late 1990s to develop and commercialize very user-friendly, next-generation wireless cell phones that can access the Internet, store MP3 music files, and even host a digital camera in which the user can then send images through wireless e-mail. NTT's "I-mode" technology was seen as a model for some of the newer 3G networks that are now in development.

In industries that are characterized by fast change, high levels of uncertainty, and extremely high fixed costs, industry-spanning alliance networks are now becoming important forces that shape how the marketplace will evolve. These alliances are in some cases becoming so important that the development activities of the entire network are becoming more important than the actions taken by an individual firm working alone. Although becoming more common in such industries as multimedia, entertainment, software, personal computers and servers, telecommunications, consumer electronics, Internet access and health care, industry-spanning alliance networks also occur in other mature industries as well, such as those found in

knowledge web:
A collection or group of companies that work in tandem to shape the evolution of an industry.

airlines and transportation companies. For example, individual railroad companies in the United States (such as CSX, Burlington Northern Santa Fe, Union Pacific) are now jointly working with container shipping companies (such as Denmark's Maersk, Japan's NYK and K-Line, and Taiwan's Evergreen) to coordinate low-cost, global transportation of containers to anywhere in the United States and even around the world. Within the United States, the major railroad companies are now tying their schedules closely to automotive manufacturers who are now implementing just-in-time inventory systems (to reduce inventory). In addition, Burlington Northern Santa Fe is now closely coordinating its rail schedules to work in conjunction with the warehousing and shipping operations of United Parcel Service (UPS) to lower each firm's costs and improve delivery times. In general, U.S. railroad companies are now repositioning themselves to act as full-service providers of documentation, shipping, customs clearance, and container tracking services that are tightly integrated with those of other firms around the world, including shipping, trucking, barge traffic, and even delivery.[20]

In the global airline industry, the number of industry-spanning networks has risen significantly in the past few years. Airline companies realize that they must form broader networks in order to capture the benefits of serving new markets without assuming even more fixed costs. For example, the relationship among American Airlines' **one**world alliance partners is growing closer whereby partners are now actively dividing the world among member airline carriers to maintain capacity and to stabilize costs. Also, the competing United- and Lufthansa-organized Star Alliance incorporates seventeen (and growing) members who work closely together to reach different parts of the world through active code-sharing activities that help lower costs. Gaining access to new markets and reducing costs simultaneously motivated the rapid expansion of Delta-led SkyTeam over the past few years. Although the vast majority of global airline alliances has not yet received the kind of broad antitrust immunity that allows for tight coordination as a single entity (as is the case with several transatlantic arrangements), it is likely that more network alliance configurations will evolve over the next few years as carriers seek to establish a strong, integrated network in each regional market. On the other hand, even though there is a high level of interdependence among partners, alliance networks are not permanent relationships. For example, Delta Air Lines was not able to continue working with its original transatlantic partners Sabena, Swissair, and Austrian Airlines for more than a few years. Although the three European firms served as a valuable linchpin in Delta's transatlantic strategy, they were also smaller carriers that could not provide the same degree of shared scale and access that American Airlines found in British Airways or what United Airlines obtained with Lufthansa. Some observers have also noted that American Airlines worked behind the scenes to provide incentives to Swissair and Sabena to switch their allegiance away from Delta and more toward American. Eventually, Delta began working with Air France, a large carrier that also needed a big transatlantic partner.

Knowledge webs, on the other hand, are a highly complex variation of industry-spanning alliance networks because the primary contribution of each firm participating in the network tends to be innovation-driven or related to knowledge creation of some type. In the telecommunications industry, for example, firms contribute their distinctive skills along such dimensions as software, algorithms, semiconductors, Internet browsers, voice recognition systems, video streaming, and even the actual "content" that could flow along future airwaves. Knowledge webs also characterize the nature of the entertainment industry, where broadcast networks interact heavily with film studios, production houses, Hollywood agencies, special effects firms, syndication firms, cable television systems, and even publishing firms.

By carefully working with other partners in the knowledge web, a firm attempts to position itself to determine or influence future industry standards. For example, Microsoft has been extremely successful in making its DOS and Windows operating systems the de facto software standard of the personal computer industry. It is now seeking to dominate the market for corporate networks in the same way. Microsoft also hopes to become a bigger player in the evolving knowledge web for digital music players that are converging with cell phones and handheld gaming devices. As such, it cooperates but also vies for influence with Nokia. Likewise, Intel hopes to parlay its success in microprocessors for personal computers into communication chips that dominate the Internet. Nokia hopes to do the same for next-generation 3G wireless networks by innovating a new wireless phone that contains its own Internet browser and video-streaming technology. Texas Instruments in the semiconductor industry is attempting to establish its dominance over DSPs, which will be the silicon brains of many future electronic and Internet products. All of these companies also work closely with other firms in order to better position themselves within their respective industries. Industry-spanning alliances help each of these firms to shape the evolution of their respective industries and technologies.

Cross-Holding Consortia. Cross-holding consortia are alliances in which companies hold equity-stakes in one another to achieve a high degree of coordination among members. Some of the more complex cross-holding alliance relationships are found in the Far East. Examples of cross-holding consortia include the large Japanese keiretsus and Korean chaebols. These collections of companies involve extensive equity cross-holdings among all of the member companies. Examples of Japanese keiretsus include Sumitomo, Mitsubishi, and Mitsui.[21] Korean chaebols include Daewoo Group, LG Group, Hyundai, and Samsung.

Two defining features of cross-holding consortia are building long-term focus and gaining technological critical mass among affiliated member companies. First, strong supplier–buyer relationships among keiretsu or chaebol members work to stabilize production volume and promote long-term focus. For example, producers of television sets or DVDs in this consortia arrangement could access the components needed for their products from other members in the consortia. This vertically integrated arrangement makes investment planning for high, fixed-costs investments easier and more predictable for the member firms. Because considerable sharing takes place among different member companies for key technologies, firms are able to cooperate in making huge, fixed costs investments; the consortia provide at least some degree of a "guaranteed" internal market for components or products to be used or sold by member companies.

Second, these consortia arrangements can provide member companies with the technological critical mass needed for investing in world-scale efficient plants. Take the case of semiconductors, for example. Because these devices are becoming the "brains" of many products ranging from television sets to cars and telephones, member companies that produce these products benefit from sharing the costs for a semiconductor plant that can serve all their needs. Instead of having each company build its own chip plant (with individually high fixed costs for each firm and lower economies of scale), the member companies contribute funds to build a more optimally sized plant that serves their collective needs, with correspondingly greater economies of scale and thus lower unit costs. Consequently, consortia arrangements allow firms to share the costs and develop the critical mass needed for building and running world-scale plants. The main drawback to these arrangements is that valuable capital is often tied up in investments that may be less productive or lacking the same depth of core competences as compared with a much more focused competitor. In addition, these cross-holdings may slow down a member firm's ability to react quickly to new developments.

In the last few years, the continued slowdown of the Japanese and South Korean economies has caused some of the major companies to rethink the way they manage this cross-holding arrangement. In particular, companies such as Toshiba, Mitsubishi, NEC, Hitachi, and

Fujitsu have begun to sell some of their holdings in other companies, largely because they need the funds to invest in more central operations. Likewise, the South Korean government has issued a series of directives that companies such as Samsung, LG Group (formerly Lucky-Goldstar), Daewoo, and Hyundai spin off their noncore businesses in order to free up capital from unproductive uses. Both Japanese and South Korean cross-holding relationships represent large portions of each company's manufacturing base, and if their assets are not used productively, these alliances can actually hold back an entire nation's capacity to restructure and to grow. Because capital is tied up in relationships that are more tradition-bound, productivity of asset use has sagged in recent years. Another major factor that has accelerated the unwinding of some of these complex cross-holdings is the greater clamor that investors have been voicing for more "transparent" financial reporting of profitability and losses. Japanese and South Korean companies in the past have been able to occlude or evade some of their financial reporting through alliance arrangements by transferring losses from one affiliate member's accounting books to another.

Tightly Integrated Alliances

Some alliances can involve even more extensive blending and sharing of value-adding activities among the partners. In some instances, alliances among partners may result in the creation of a completely new entity with its own management system and set of operational activities. This new entity may even grow to become a vibrant, competitive enterprise in its own right. Tightly integrated alliances introduce many issues akin to those found in companies that merge and acquire other firms.[22]

Joint ventures are substantially much more complex than other alliance arrangements. Joint ventures involve the partners' creation of a third entity representing the interests and capital of the two or more partners. Partners contribute their own proportional amounts of capital, distinctive skills, managers, reporting systems, and technologies to the venture. Joint ventures often entail complex coordination between partners in carrying out value chain activities. Some joint ventures may focus on a division of labor among partners (for example, one partner manufactures, another partner distributes and markets the product) to promote a high degree of specialization within each firm. Other joint ventures may combine all of the partners' operational activities (such as R&D, manufacturing, marketing) to achieve greater economies of scale, critical mass, or improvements in efficiency.

Joint ventures are prevalent in the global automotive industry. In the automotive industry, firms will often outsource production of key components to their partners in order to lower costs and reduce in-house investment in fixed assets. Many firms (for example, GM, Ford, DaimlerChrysler, and Toyota) have formed joint ventures to share the costs and risks of developing hybrid engines and advanced fuel cells in next-generation cars. Other joint ventures in the automotive industry have involved two or more partners building larger-sized plants with improved scale economies to manufacture cars for the U.S. and other markets. During the 1980s and 1990s, U.S. firms formed many ventures with Japanese firms to learn new manufacturing techniques to boost the quality of American-built cars. These ventures have helped both partners streamline their capacity requirements as global demand slows down. For example, General Motors uses joint ventures with Suzuki, Isuzu, and Toyota to produce many of its compact cars, including the Chevrolet Cavalier. DaimlerChrysler's U.S. unit relies on Mitsubishi Motors to produce a broad line of Chrysler, Plymouth, and Dodge cars in the subcompact and sports lines. In both cases, the U.S. firm has sought out a Japanese ally. The Japanese firm often commands superior manufacturing skills, quality processes, and fast changeover capability. In turn, Toyota, Isuzu, and Suzuki further reduce their own manufacturing fixed costs by producing for a U.S. company.

In other cases, global automotive manufacturers may create a joint venture to pool all of their value-adding activities together to gain critical mass in a key market. For example, the legendary joint venture between General Motors and Toyota to form New United Motor Manufacturing Incorporated (NUMMI) combined both companies' manufacturing, distribution, and marketing operations. Located in Fremont, California, the plant produces cars for both GM and Toyota for sale throughout the United States. Likewise, U.S., German, and Japanese car makers have accelerated the formation of joint ventures with Chinese car makers to sell in this promising and huge market. Shanghai Volkswagen, for example, is a decade-long venture that combines the R&D, manufacturing, and distribution capabilities of Germany's Volkswagen with a partner selected by the Chinese government. General Motors, Ford, Honda, and Toyota are all currently forming their joint ventures that seek to produce an entire line of vehicles in the Chinese market with a local partner. Shanghai GM is a 50/50 joint venture that makes Buicks and Cadillacs for the Chinese market and is becoming a major player in the Chinese market. General Motors also owns a 50 percent stake in Jinbei GM Automotive Company to produce pickup trucks and SUVs in China and continues to own substantial equity stakes in Isuzu, Suzuki, Fuji Heavy Industries (maker of Subaru), and even a Russian automaker (AvtoVAZ).[23]

Joint Ventures and Learning. Firms often enter into joint ventures to learn another firm's distinctive skills or capabilities in some key value-creating activity. In many high-technology industries, many years of development are required before a company possesses the proprietary technologies and specialized processes needed to compete effectively on its own. These skills may already be available in a potential partner. A joint venture can help firms learn these new skills without retracing the steps of innovation at great cost. For example, Texas Instruments worked closely with Japanese partner Hitachi during the 1990s in designing and producing 16- and 64-megabit chips necessary for today's newest computers. By working with Hitachi, Texas Instruments hoped to learn the new types of etching and other fine manufacturing processes required for high-quality production of even denser chips. Although these earlier generations of memory chips seem like ancient history now, these relationships have helped TI become much more efficient in its semiconductor production expertise. In particular, these relationships were also useful in helping both companies transfer new sources of knowledge between each other when it came to testing and developing new types of chip-manufacturing processes. Although the TI–Hitachi joint venture has recently ended, TI learned key manufacturing skills from its Japanese partner. The venture ended because of financial constraints and TI's decision to exit the memory chip business. TI now focuses its efforts on DSP chips that are the future for numerous applications in telecommunications, consumer electronics, and other applications.

ChevronTexaco formed a 50/50 joint venture with Energy Conversion Devices (ECD) to develop new alternative energy technologies in 2000. This venture, known as Cobasys, is working to develop advanced batteries and fuel cells using nickel-metal hydrides that are the key to today's hybrid vehicles. Cobasys recently completed a massive, automated battery plant in Troy, Michigan, that will make over a million battery modules a year. Management believes the technology will have great applicability to customers in the telecommunications and computer industries as well. In a separate relationship, ECD licensed its nickel-metal hydride battery technology to Sanyo Electric of Japan, which produces batteries that now power Ford's Escape SUV.[24]

Multipartner Joint Venture Arrangements. Firms can cooperate in a multipartner joint venture to develop and commercialize new technologies that may significantly influence an industry's future direction. For example, during the 1990s, AT&T (and later Lucent Technologies) worked closely with Zenith Electronics to design and produce the next generation of digital-based high-definition television (HDTV) technology. Together, they joined General Instrument, RCA, Philips, and NBC to commercialize and standardize today's emerging HDTV standards already found in different broadcasting markets. Thus, companies can ally with others in competing joint ventures in a race to develop the newest breakthrough technology or next-generation industry standard. Without using joint ventures, none of these companies would have been able to design and produce a vital HDTV standard in a timely manner. All of the companies involved in various aspects of HDTV development—AT&T, Zenith, General Instrument, RCA, Philips, and NBC—combined their various competing technologies into one Grand Alliance. The goal of this Grand Alliance, as it was formally known, was to gain agreement among all U.S. participants on a common digital standard that now shapes today's HDTV broadcasts.

Corning Incorporated has formed a network of joint ventures with more than twenty individual firms throughout the world. These joint ventures help Corning shape the evolving glass and advanced materials industry. Corning works with Samsung, Iwaki Glass, and Asahi Glass to design and produce advanced quality television tubes. In turn, each partner learns how to improve its own glass fabrication techniques. With Siemens of Germany, Corning has become one of the world's largest suppliers of fiber optics used in telecommunications. Most recently, it has investigated purchasing the optical-fiber unit of competitor Lucent Technologies, which has struggled to realign its operations in the wake of declining demand in the telecommunications industry. Corning also has a separate joint venture with NGK of Japan. NGK is one of the world's largest auto parts makers (spark plugs) and has invested significant resources in commercializing advanced ceramics. In the future, some analysts believe that automotive engines may actually be made of ceramics rather than steel or aluminum. In each of Corning's joint ventures, a partner contributes a skill or market position that Corning does not have or could not develop quickly on its own.

The need to maintain industry dynamism and momentum in research is a motivating force that drives drug companies to engage in joint ventures, even when they compete in existing product lines. For example, the task of finding a drug that can kill the AIDS virus is so complex and daunting that many U.S. firms are seriously considering joint research ventures to pool their efforts. Competing chemical firms often team up in formal joint ventures to commercialize costly development processes. For example, U.S. chemical giant DuPont teamed up with Japanese firm Toray to accelerate the learning and transfer of new product applications for carbon fibers. Toray is the world's leader in producing carbon fiber and has used DuPont's original technology to build a strong market position in this critical field. Although originally pioneered for aerospace and defense applications, carbon fiber has begun to play an important role in many other industries. Today, many state-of-the-art golf clubs, other sporting equipment, and automotive parts are built from carbon fiber composite materials.

Perhaps the most prominent example of a multipartner European-based joint venture/consortia to date is Airbus Industries. Conceived originally as a loosely organized, coproduction-sharing consortium, Airbus has more tightly integrated the alliance substantially in recent years. The Airbus consortium, once involving a cumbersome organizational arrangement among companies from four European companies, has now become a much more centralized company that reports along the lines of a single, integrated firm (a parent company now known as EADS). Throughout its long history, Airbus brought together four European aerospace firms from Britain, France, Germany, and Spain. Each firm committed its entire aerospace business to a formal joint venture/consortium arrangement. The goal of Airbus Industries has been to dethrone Boeing from its dominant position in the global commercial aircraft market.[25] By pooling their member firms' resources, Airbus Industries has become a major competitor for the U.S. giant. Without such pan-European cooperation, it is unlikely that any of the individual firms would have been able to challenge Boeing on a low-cost basis.

Risks and Costs of Strategic Alliances

Through alliances, firms can acquire new products, skills, and knowledge that are otherwise not available to them. Regardless of how the alliance is arranged (for example, licensing, joint venture, equity stake, knowledge web), the firm faces a set of important potential trade-offs. Working with an alliance partner to learn and build new sources of competitive advantage, however, is not a cost-free proposition. Without clearly understanding the risks and costs inherent in alliances, cooperation may unintentionally damage a firm. In the worst case, loss of a firm's proprietary know-how or skills to a partner could create a new competitor.[26] Four general types of risks and costs are associated with alliances: (1) rising incompatibility between partners, (2) risk of knowledge or skill leakage, (3) risk of dependence, and (4) strategic control costs associated with day-to-day operational issues.

Rising Incompatibility of Partners

Even the best-conceived alliances face the potential danger that partners may become incompatible over time. For example, firms that once needed each other to design a new product or enter a new market may feel that their strategic interests no longer match as the market or industry evolves. When partners find that their long-term strategies have changed, they must then redefine the basis of the alliance. In many situations, firms that once enjoyed a harmonious, close working relationship discover that changes in their strategies or industry conditions often result in growing incompatibility between their goals. In some cases, rising incompatibility may transform a once-close partner into a direct competitor.

Consider the evolution of Independence Air, a new low-cost regional carrier that flies in the Northeastern United States. Independence Air is the newly created subsidiary of Atlantic Coast Airlines, which provided regional jet service for its long-term partners United Airlines and Delta. In June 2004, Atlantic Coast decided to compete directly with its former partners because it felt that it could become more profitable, especially as United Airlines attempted to restructure itself in bankruptcy court. Management at Atlantic Coast believed that as long as its fate was tied so closely to that of United Airlines, it would encounter many of the same economic difficulties facing its larger partner. By forming Independence Air, the company hopes to be able to compete directly with United Air and other major carriers through its own more efficient cost structure. As a result, United Airlines must cut its air ticket prices even further to blunt the growth ambitions of its former partner.[27]

When Dell Computer announced in July 2002 that it would begin to enter the printer business on its own, Hewlett-Packard immediately ended its eight-year agreement that allowed Dell to sell HP-branded printers. Hewlett-Packard did not want to provide Dell with the printers that Dell needed to compete against it. Instead, Dell chose Lexmark International to make printers so that Dell could sell them under its own brand name. Hewlett-Packard envisioned Dell as another distribution channel partner that could expand the reach of HP's well-recognized brand name; however, Dell looked at Hewlett-Packard as simply a supplier of printers. Dell had further ambitions to build upon its own brand and chose another partner who would manufacture printers according to Dell's specifications. Now, Dell is competing with HP across a broad line of printers and even seeks to enter the replacement printer cartridge business, which is a big source of profits to HP.[28]

Rising incompatibility between the Walt Disney Company and Pixar Animated Studios resulted in the dissolution of a twelve-year alliance between these two firms in February 2004. Using leading-edge, computer-driven animation technologies, the companies had worked together to produce such blockbuster films as *Toy Story, A Bug's Life, Finding Nemo,* and *Monsters, Inc.* Since 1999, Pixar has become an even more important partner for Disney, contributing over 35 percent of Disney's studio profits. As animation moves away from hand-drawn pictures to computer-generated 3-D modeling with heavy use of virtual reality, Disney has lagged behind the rest of the industry in its ability to produce what viewers want to see. The two companies have clashed over the number of movies that Pixar agreed to coproduce with Disney through the year 2006. For example, Pixar believes that a sequel to an original movie (for example, Toy Story 2) counts against the original number of films that it agreed to coproduce with Disney. Disney, for its part, claims that because a movie is a sequel, it does not represent a new product. Pixar will be free to coproduce films with other movie studios once the agreement with Disney is completed sometime by 2006.[29]

In the restaurant industry, a two-year joint venture between Arby's, a leading fast-food chain specializing in roast beef sandwiches, and ZuZu, an upstart Mexican restaurant chain, went sour in 1997 after the two companies could not agree on how best to coordinate their various menu items in different cities. Designed originally as a joint venture to bring together two companies that were struggling to define themselves in a saturated industry, the alliance intended to help both partners combine their talents and offerings for two distinctive market segments into one restaurant platform. Arby's originally needed ZuZu because its sales of roast beef sandwiches had plateaued, although it had plenty of seating capacity in many of its urban markets. ZuZu, on the other hand, found Arby's retailing and distribution system a real plus because it lacked the critical mass to "roll out" its offerings by itself. However, the venture collapsed for both operational and marketing reasons. From an operations perspective, Arby's restaurant crews were more used to processing, cooking, and serving food quickly—skills critical to serving customers in the fast-food segment. They were not able to cope with the more complicated and time-intensive ingredients required for ZuZu's nouveau Mexican cuisine. Also, Arby's food tends to be served in paper wrappers, whereas ZuZu's items typically came with metal utensils on a crockery plate designed to keep the food warm and fresh from the oven. Over time, managers in the venture realized that both Arby's and ZuZu were incompatible in terms of how they viewed their customers, food selection, and operational methods of preparation.[30]

Risk of Knowledge/Skill Drain

Many forms of cooperation require partners to share their knowledge and skills to develop a new technology or product. The central problem of sharing knowledge is the impossibility of strictly limiting how partners will use knowledge gained from cooperation. This problem is especially critical for firms that face industry convergence. For example, the computer, communications, and consumer electronics industries are growing more similar, which means that an alliance based on designing new types of computers will have an impact on communications devices as well. Consider the situation of Apple Computer during the early 1990s. Apple's experimental product developed in the early 1990s combined a Macintosh computer, CD-ROM, and a screen that also receives television signals. This new Apple product merges technologies and skills required for competing in both the computer and consumer electronics businesses. However, Sony built many of Apple's laptop computers in a long-standing alliance. Sony has benefited substantially through its long-term relationship with Apple as it learned how to use Apple's distinctive consumer electronics skills and capabilities. This knowledge helped Sony enter the personal computer industry in the late 1990s. These skills are also instrumental to Sony's development of its PlayStation line of video games. Sony thus acquired a superb position to learn and to see how Apple's products are likely to perform.

When IBM works together with Toshiba in designing flat-panel display screens used for laptop computers, IBM is limited in its ability to control how Toshiba uses the shared technology for other applications outside the venture. This joint venture, known as Display Technologies, Inc., is based in Japan, where Toshiba has a home-field advantage in learning new technologies from IBM. Until its dissolution in late 2001, Display Technologies was the world's epicenter for developing flat-screen technologies for many years. Other applications in which Toshiba could apply IBM's technology include potential products such as flat-screen color television sets. Likewise, Toshiba cannot unconditionally limit IBM's use of what Big Blue learns from Toshiba in terms of new manufacturing technology and process improvement skills. IBM, in turn, could apply the new manufacturing skills that it learns from the joint venture to improve its cost position in developing new forms of handheld computers that are not covered within the scope of the current alliance. By allying on a critical core technology of the future, neither IBM nor Toshiba can actually control the other firm's pace in using the technology to develop future commercial products. Recently, the two companies have differed in their strategic vision for that venture. Toshiba wants to use the displays for cellular phones and personal digital assistant products that are close to Toshiba's core strengths in consumer electronics and telecommunications. IBM, on the other hand, wants to use the venture's manufacturing capacity to produce displays for scientific instruments, laptop computers, and desktop computers—areas that are considered more crucial to IBM's core businesses. Because the two companies diverge in how best to utilize their jointly owned plant's manufacturing operations, both partners agreed to dissolve the Display Technologies venture, even though IBM and Toshiba continue to cooperate across a wide range of high-technology arenas.[31]

Matsushita Electric of Japan has taken important steps to protect its core technology when investing in joint ventures with Chinese partners. Although Matsushita wants to greatly expand its sales of advanced consumer electronics products in China, it also faces tough, low-cost partners that could ultimately become competitors to Matsushita. To prevent key technology from leaking to competitors, Matsushita separates its core and noncore technologies. It leaves basic research and advanced production technology in Japan. Where possible, it delegates noncore technology to China-based plants for further engineering work that is performed locally. Matsushita has also devised new ways to package and protect its technology so that products cannot be easily disassembled and reverse engineered by competitors.[32]

Firms taking part in a strategic alliance must therefore carefully identify and isolate what types of knowledge can be safely shared with a partner. They need to recognize that technologies previously developed for one set of products may later be applicable to other products as well. This likelihood is particularly strong in industries that are converging, or where future products increasingly use similar components or manufacturing skills. *A firm always runs the risk of giving the partner more insight into its knowledge base than intended.*

Risk of Dependence

Alliances can often make a firm too dependent on its partner.[33] This dependence can occur without the firm's awareness of the process. For example, many U.S. automakers believe that their joint ventures with Japanese and other firms have saved them time and money in their production of small cars. These alliances free up capital for other uses. Over time, however, firms can become overreliant on their partners to build new lines of cars for them. As a result, the firm's skills—especially those in manufacturing—can deteriorate, while those of the partner improve. In other words, a company that serves as a critical supplier of an underlying technology or production process to another firm will be able to exercise a high degree of control over its partner's activities. Thus, firms can find that alliances will "hollow out" their skills. This process is shown in Exhibit 8-7. Both General Motors and Chrysler experienced this problem in their automobile ventures with Japanese suppliers in the early 1990s. Chrysler, in particular, became highly dependent on Mitsubishi Motors for a steady supply of high-performance engines, transmissions, and other key components required for its subcompact and sports car lines, including the former Dodge Daytona, Dodge Stealth, Chrysler Laser, and Eagle Talon. In the recent past, General Motors' former Geo line of cars was manufactured by three different Japanese firms: Isuzu, Suzuki, and Toyota. Consequently, neither GM nor Chrysler was in a position to compete in this segment on its own for a long time because they lacked the critical manufacturing skills during the early 1990s.

The United States does not produce any of its own VCR- or DVD-related technologies because U.S. consumer electronics firms have eagerly outsourced their manufacturing operations to Far Eastern companies. For example, all DVD players bearing U.S. labels such as RCA, General Electric, and Zenith come from major Japanese, Korean, and even Chinese manufacturers who compete fiercely for market share with both quality products and highly efficient manufacturing operations. In turn, these same U.S. firms remain largely unable to compete in other consumer electronics, because the manufacturing skills required for ever-more versatile DVD and MP3 players are directly applicable to other uses. Once U.S. firms "surrendered" their VCR, DVD, and other consumer electronics skills to their alliance partners, they faced an uphill battle to recapture control over critical value chain activities. As new Internet-based electronic appliances become more popular, U.S. firms will have difficulty serving this market without further relying on their manufacturing partners in the Far East and elsewhere. This means that U.S. firms will continue to be forced to share their profits in ways they may not have intended. Japanese, Taiwanese, Korean, and Chinese companies appear likely to dominate Internet-based electronic appliances as they continue to invest in upgrading their manufacturing skills.

In the semiconductor industry, similar attempts by some U.S. firms to avoid building state-of-the-art chip fabrication facilities have made many companies dependent on Japanese

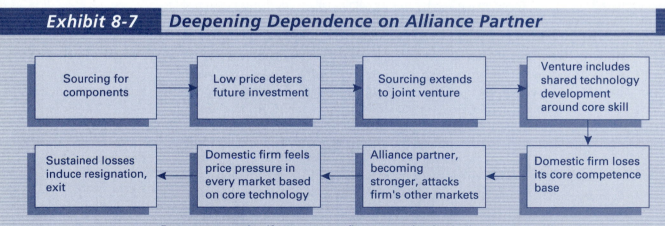

Exhibit 8-7   Deepening Dependence on Alliance Partner

Sourcing for components → Low price deters future investment → Sourcing extends to joint venture → Venture includes shared technology development around core skill → Domestic firm loses its core competence base → Alliance partner, becoming stronger, attacks firm's other markets → Domestic firm feels price pressure in every market based on core technology → Sustained losses induce resignation, exit

Process repeats itself across every firm competing in similar industry or line of business. Eventually, U.S. industry loses ground in cumulative effect.

and especially Taiwanese suppliers for chips. This pattern now appears to be repeating itself as Motorola and Texas Instruments are now turning to Taiwan Semiconductor Manufacturing Company (TSMC) and United Microelectronics Company (UMC) to share in the costs of manufacturing leading-edge semiconductors. As the fixed costs of building new fabrication facilities continue to rise, outsourcing and alliances appear much more attractive to companies. Smaller U.S. firms, such as Altera, Broadcom, Nvidia, and Xilinx, use Taiwanese chip foundries as an explicit part of their strategy, since they are too small to invest in their own manufacturing facilities. However, continued and growing reliance on Taiwanese manufacturers by larger manufacturers such as Motorola and Texas Instruments may damage their internal capability to master newer manufacturing processes that are required to enter new markets on their own.[34] On the other hand, both IBM and Intel are hoping to avoid such an outcome. These two giants continue to invest substantial sums in ultramodern manufacturing facilities. Intel alone spent $7.5 billion in 2001 on capital expenditures to build state-of-the-art facilities for its Pentium 4 chips, and it continues to pour money into cutting-edge fabrication technology each year. These investments enable Intel to make newer classes of Pentium 4, Itanium, and other chips more efficiently—a critical factor in Intel's ability to remain competitive and even dominant in microprocessors.

Merck, a leading U.S. pharmaceutical firm, appears to be increasingly dependent on external sources of new drug development technology as its own internal R&D efforts face growing difficulties. Known for its fiercely independent R&D approach, Merck is now relying on an expanding array of licensing deals to help spur new drug products. Merck is now working aggressively with smaller biotechnology and early-stage drug development companies to learn new genetic engineering techniques. As Merck works more closely with its new partners, it will likely become increasingly dependent on them for new ways to think about new compounds, molecules, and drug delivery systems.[35]

Costs of Alliance Control and Operations

In day-to-day alliance operations, managers face three types of costs: (1) costs of coordination, (2) costs of learning, and (3) costs of inflexibility.

Costs of Coordination. Benefits of alliances can result only when the two partners work closely. Yet, working with an alliance partner can be a challenging and frustrating series of events, especially if the partner's values, organization, or operating methods are different from one's own. This may represent a significant latent challenge for airlines now engaged in multi-partner alliances with firms from different parts of the world. Organizational cultures and styles are likely to clash as managers from separate regions come together. Likewise, companies may differ in their interpretation of what each partner should contribute, how much, and for how long. When parties are unable to agree upon the definition and terms used in the original contract, the relationship is likely to become rocky, as both Pixar and Disney discovered in 2003. Strategies, budgets, plans, and product layouts must be carefully worked out and managed, as managers at Arby's and ZuZu came to realize belatedly. Managers must also hammer out such key issues as accounting formats and human resource practices within the alliance, including such questions as whether a manager works for one partner or the other and whether an assignment is temporary or permanent.[36] Such difficulties became apparent when managers from IBM, Toshiba, and Siemens got together to design and build 256-megabit chips. IBM managers felt that their colleagues from Toshiba were excessively group oriented and wanted consensus on every step of the design and experimental process. Also, IBM managers felt that the German managers from Siemens were overly concerned with the costs and details of technical planning.

Conversely, Japanese and German managers became frustrated with the apparent American penchant for taking on high-risk, uncertain experimental design approaches without getting approval from higher-up managers. Cooperation was also complicated by subtle differences in languages and in translation.

Cooperation is further inhibited by the natural reluctance of partners to divulge proprietary technology, knowledge, or skills to their partners. Such skills or technologies could later be used against the partner even as the alliance continues. For example, when General Motors teamed up with Japanese robot maker Fanuc, GM benefited in the short term from a low-cost supply of reliable robots and numerical control (NC) tools from its Japanese partner. Fanuc, on the other hand, learned from GM the core technologies to make its robots more advanced and "smarter" by assimilating GM's skills in sensor and vision systems, advanced software, machine language, computer systems integration, and other machine design concepts. Ultimately, Fanuc ended up competing against General Motors in selling industrial robots to other U.S. manufacturers, such as makers of construction equipment, farm equipment, and major home appliances. Fanuc was able to learn and apply skills from General Motors to make its own robots better than those of GM. Fanuc could then compete against other robotics companies with the technologies it acquired from GM. Now, Fanuc is believed to have as much as 75 percent of the world's market share for numerical control tools and other critical factory automation equipment.

Thus, the costs of coordinating and managing an alliance extend far beyond the simple management structure of the alliance. Coordination costs extend to the day-to-day management styles and issues surrounding the partnership. The struggles in getting partners to agree on management issues are often unforeseen. In addition, coordination involves deciding the degree of knowledge sharing as well. This is particularly true for firms that face the delicate situation of competing and cooperating with the same partner when developing products in high-tech industries. In many cases, two or more partners may work together on an underlying core technology, but compete with one another to develop new products to sell to new markets.

Likewise, firms that participate in industry-spanning alliance networks or knowledge webs are particularly susceptible to difficulties in coordinating activities with other member firms. The real balance of power between partners is found in the knowledge flows between partners. Too much of a one-way knowledge flow to its partner could put a firm in a dangerously dependent position.

Costs of Learning. Firms must also concentrate on learning from their partners. This requires assuming the role of student rather than teacher. Firms cannot learn if they are smug or overconfident about what they can learn from their alliance partner. Korean firm Daewoo formed a joint venture with Caterpillar to learn how to make forklift trucks and other related construction equipment and machinery. Once Daewoo was able to master the design and production skills needed to make the equipment on its own, it bought out Caterpillar's interest in the venture and began competing against it in global markets. Samsung followed a similar series of events with U.S. forklift maker Clark Equipment. Apparently, neither Daewoo nor Samsung had expectations of working with their American partners over an extended period. Once they had learned what they needed, they bought out their partners. Both examples show that managers must take the initiative to learn new management techniques and skills from their partner quickly, while protecting their own core technology from excessive encroachment from an aggressive partner.

Learning means improving not only current products but also core skills, processes, and technologies that underpin the firm's competitiveness. This effort generates additional costs, since skill-based learning requires extra effort and attention to identify emerging or useful technologies and to bring them home effectively. To learn effectively, partners must be careful not to be overconfident when working with another firm. For example, in the 1970s, U.S. VCR manufacturer Ampex believed that it could "teach" Toshiba of Japan how to make better VCRs, since it possessed a proprietary magnetic head technology at the time. Ampex found over time that Toshiba not only learned how to make better VCRs but also improved on Ampex's video head design to improve the quality of Toshiba's own line of VCRs.

Learning is also much more difficult when managers are kept on alliance assignments for only a short time period. Those managers do not have the time to establish informal contacts or to tap into the "grapevine" to learn new sources of information. When managers are rotated through the alliance too quickly, they lose the incentive to assimilate the necessary skills and technologies that will be useful to the parent firm when they return. Short-term assignments compromise managers' ability to learn new insights and skills from their partners. Much of this learning occurs informally as managers communicate with one another on a daily basis.

Costs of Inflexibility. Alliances paradoxically can constrain a firm's future strategy, despite offering immediate benefits of risk and cost reduction. Even the best-negotiated contracts and arrangements cannot prespecify the future events that may disturb or change the conditions of the alliance. Thus, managers need to be flexible in dealing with various situations that are likely to arise when working with a partner. Long-standing alliances should be evolving relationships that reflect a close understanding of the partner's intentions and what the firm intends to gain from the alliance. Otherwise, alliances can actually limit the firm's ability to perform new sets of activities. In some instances, for example, alliances can limit the firm's ability to enter new markets where a partner is already situated. Consider the case of General Electric. GE cannot further enter and serve the medical equipment business in Japan without the help of its partner, Yokogawa Electric. The venture between GE and Yokogawa, known as GE Yokogawa, produces X-ray and CT (computer tomography) scanners for both the Japanese and other major markets around the world. However, Yokogawa acts as a "brake" on General Electric's speed and ability to maneuver, particularly if GE wants to use its Japanese manufacturing base to supply new markets. In a separate venture, GE works with Japanese giant Toshiba in several different ventures, including power generation equipment, power transmission equipment, and major home appliances. Toshiba has become an important partner for GE to sell major home appliances in the Japanese market. Yet, GE's alliance with Toshiba specifies what appliance distribution channels and what regional Japanese markets GE may enter. GE is limited in how far it can sell its major appliances to Japanese customers.

Other day-to-day issues can collectively result in alliance inflexibility. Cash flow earned from a venture must be shared with a partner, such as between Fuji and Xerox. Jointly conducted research may lead to patents that require both partners to tell the other what their new products will be, as is the case in certain pharmaceutical and biotechnology alliances. Thus, alliances can lead the firm into a series of unanticipated obstacles. For example, the Kaleida and Taligent alliances between Apple and IBM to develop new operating systems and multimedia technologies for personal computers ran into a series of problems. Both IBM and Apple realized that they needed to cooperate closely to design a user-friendly operating system that could compete effectively against Microsoft's Windows and other new offerings. However, neither firm realized the degree of day-to-day negotiation that was required to reach consensus on key details of developing new types of software and multimedia computer formats. Long negotiations were needed to ensure that future products would be compatible with each firm's existing array of products. The time required for both firms to learn how to work with each other comfortably came at a high price, since the software industry is fast moving and product delays often mean potentially big losses of market share. Moreover, both IBM and Apple suffered from additional operating delays that resulted from the feeling that neither firm was willing to truly "commit" to the joint venture's final products.[37]

Balancing Cooperation and Competition

Alliances involve both benefits and risks. As such, all alliances involve careful assessment of unavoidable trade-offs. Many of the risks associated with alliances—knowledge/skill leakage, deepening dependence, and coordination costs—result when managers rush into alliances. The heaviest costs and highest risks of alliances manifest themselves when managers view alliances as a complete substitute for their own firm's internal development or global expansion strategy efforts. All too often, senior managers will regard alliances as a long-term "crutch" that enables them to avoid real commitments to developing the basics of a business. However, when managers use alliances as a substitute for internal development or market expansion efforts, they often feel they have surrendered control over their businesses. In fact, surrender more often than not results from business neglect and from misreading partners' strategic goals. Overreliance on alliances to learn, to build, and to extend new sources of competitive advantage can be a serious mistake. On the other hand, carefully designed and implemented alliance strategies can help firms attain many important benefits while limiting knowledge-sharing and competitive risks.

Western firms, with few exceptions, have been unable to use alliances as effectively as Japanese partners to learn new skills. They often become excessively dependent on their partners for key skills and products. Western managers fail to realize that cooperation and competition need to be balanced in a relationship. On the other hand, Japanese managers often run their alliances "in parallel" with internal development. For example, Toshiba works closely with IBM in developing newer models of flat-panel display screens for use in notebook computers. Yet, Toshiba ensures that it simultaneously has its own self-contained factory to apply the lessons from working with IBM to its own products. Alliances work best when they are implemented in conjunction with the firm's own internal development and market expansion efforts. A few basic guidelines managers can use to design effective alliances that protect and extend their firm's distinctive competence are described in the following sections.

One key characteristic of all alliances is that *a participating company will actually cooperate and compete simultaneously with all of the partners.* Some researchers have also described this phenomenon as co-opetition.[38] **Co-opetition** refers to the strategic paradox in which a firm cooperates and competes with another firm at the same time. For example, in the fast-moving corporate server and data storage market, Sun Microsystems and EMC are both involved in a state of co-opetition. Sun Microsystems needs EMC's advanced data storage solutions in order to sell a full range of products to its corporate customers. EMC considers Sun Microsystems a critical partner that helps it sell more storage products. At the same time, however, Sun Microsystems competes with EMC to develop even newer forms of storage technology in order to achieve a breakthrough on some critical dimension that relates to the product's performance. Thus, both firms find themselves in a strategic paradox in which they actually need one another, but are taking steps to learn from each other in order to supplement their own internal development efforts to create the next breakthrough technology. Likewise, Intel and Microsoft are engaged in their own sort of co-opetition in the personal computer industry, in which both giants simultaneously work together to develop new PC offerings but also compete to see who can develop an innovation first (and therefore claim more profits from each personal computer that is sold).

co-opetition:
The strategic situation whereby a firm cooperates and competes with another firm(s) at the same time. Firms in co-opetitive relationships often race with one another to learn each other's skills and to develop new sources of knowledge or value-creating activities.

In all types of alliances, firms will race one another to contribute a new source of knowledge, capability, or skill in order to capture a disproportionately high level of profitability of the alliance network's products or services that are sold to customers. This type of knowledge-based competition is especially prevalent in industry-spanning, knowledge-driven webs and networks. Companies that can innovate faster than others will be in a better position to set the tone for the future path of product development within that industry. For example, a firm hopes to develop an underlying architecture, technology, production process, or product platform that becomes the basis for the industry's future standard. By setting a key standard, the innovating company can exert a disproportionate influence on the shape of future products that the industry will develop in ensuing years.

Understand the Firm's Knowledge and Skill Base

The single most important step to prepare for an alliance is to understand how the firm's skills and knowledge contribute to competitive advantage. By knowing what skills are essential to the firm's future, managers can define the scope, goals, and limits of cooperation with a partner. First and foremost, companies must understand how their distinctive competence contributes to building competitive advantage. A firm's distinctive competence lays the foundation for learning and applying new technologies and core skills that are translated into new products. However, working with an alliance partner certainly exposes the firm's core skills and distinctive competence to some degree. All too many firms, such as General Electric, General Motors, and Chrysler, have failed to recognize how quickly critical skills and knowledge can leak to an alliance partner if management is not careful. This unintended transfer happens frequently when both senior management and the alliance manager do not protect the firm's distinctive competence. Despite its desire to work with more partners to reach new customers and markets, IBM has been extremely careful and deliberate in managing its growing array of alliances. IBM has long understood how mismanaged alliances can rapidly expose the firm's core skills and technologies to its partners. For example, IBM's joint venture with Toshiba in flat-panel screens has been conducted in a separate, jointly owned plant away from other IBM operations in Japan. This isolation limits how far Toshiba is able to "snoop" around or access other core IBM product development or technology areas and proprietary manufacturing processes. It also helps keep IBM attuned to its partner's interests and requests for technology. IBM is fully aware that as it reconfigures its relationship with Toshiba, the Japanese firm remains a potent, current competitor in other markets and products.

IBM's Microelectronics unit has generally preferred to work with domestic U.S. partners, such as Motorola, Novellus Systems, and Applied Materials, on critically sensitive technologies, such as photolithography and etching techniques used in making advanced semiconductors. Novellus Systems helped IBM become the first semiconductor manufacturer to substitute copper for aluminum in building the complex circuitry within microchips. IBM is a leading supporter of Sematech's efforts to deepen U.S. manufacturing skill in advanced chips. Working with domestic partners eases some of the costs of coordination. In recent years, IBM has also entered into a broad array of coproduction arrangements with a number of firms such as Advanced Micro Devices (AMD), National Semiconductor, Transmeta, Cirrus Logic, Xilinx, and other smaller firms to help these companies gain access to vital manufacturing capabilities they do not have. It also enables IBM to compete indirectly with Intel by introducing new competitors' offerings of microprocessors into the PC industry where Intel has an overwhelming market position. At the same time, IBM has also begun working closely with Intel and Motorola to accelerate the development of newer X-ray and deep ultraviolet (DUV) lithography tools needed to push chip circuitry even further. This is another example where IBM, Intel, and Motorola are working together in a co-opetitive relationship. Yet, neither firm wants to be overly dependent on Japanese and other suppliers of critical semiconductor capital equipment.[39]

In the past few years, IBM Microelectronics has expanded the reach of its alliances. In particular, IBM is using its technology-based strengths to enter a series of co-opetitive relationships with Japanese firms, once considered the primary threat to IBM's dominance in a broad array of businesses. These relationships are co-opetitive in nature because IBM realizes that even though it will share the costs in developing new chips with its Japanese partners, Big Blue cannot fully control how they will use their newly acquired skills to develop future products— some of which may compete with IBM's offerings in ways that no one could have predicted. In 1999, IBM became the primary manufacturing source to provide microprocessors for Nintendo's newest video game systems. In April 2001, IBM announced plans to work with Sony and Toshiba to build a new "supercomputer on a chip" for introduction in the latter part of this decade, now known by its industry name as "The Cell." By locating this venture in Austin, Texas, IBM is in a superior position to control the extent to which its partners can learn from IBM's core skills. Although Sony clearly wants to use this chip to further its own strategy for the multimedia and entertainment industries, IBM remains wary of Sony's renowned skills in manufacturing and thus wants to make sure that the consumer electronics giant does not get the upper hand in future semiconductor development. At the same time, IBM's relationship with Toshiba remains close, even though one of their oldest ventures that produced flat-panel displays dissolved a few years ago. Still, IBM has more strongly asserted its presence in the Japanese market, working with new firms across a broad array of products and services. IBM's newest semiconductor alliance—with Seiko-Epson of Japan—is designed to help both companies develop newer chips for Japan and other Asian markets.

IBM Microelectronics is also looking to serve as a chip foundry for other emerging semiconductor firms that do not have the capital or skills to engage in self-manufacture. IBM hopes to gain significant market recognition for its semiconductor prowess. In its most recent marketing campaign, IBM is now promoting its "Built with IBM Technology" logo in a move that imitates the Intel Inside campaign used in personal computers.

Choose Complementary Partners

Alliances are less likely to result in crippling dependence if firms are careful in selecting their partners. Alliances are apt to be smoother and less dangerous if two firms cooperate on a project that is not central to their interests or if they collaborate in a marketplace where their interests are not likely to collide. Partners with similar skills, technologies, and products/services designed for the same market or region often find themselves competing against each other relatively quickly. This development is most likely to occur when firms realize that their long-term goals may actually converge in the future, especially if the sharp distinction between industries or technologies begins to blur. Similarly, firms competing in the same marketplace or region will often find their partners becoming unintended competitors simply because their individual ambitions may override an earlier desire to cooperate. Consequently, co-opetition can ultimately become full-blown, direct competition. Thus, firms with complementary technological skills or firms that have complementary market strengths in different regions may make better partners because of the reduced potential for direct competition in end products and markets. The Nestlé and Coca-Cola alliance is an example of a complementary partnership that has worked well over the past few years. Nestlé has little interest in penetrating the soft drink market. Coca-Cola has few interests in the flavored drink and coffee segments. Yet, both firms have benefited from using each other's distribution channels and marketing programs. Both partners also strengthen themselves against other competitors in their respective markets.

The airline industry demonstrates the clear necessity of choosing partners that have complementary interests. Star Alliance, which encompasses United Airlines, Lufthansa, Scandinavian Airline System (SAS), Thai International, Air Canada, and Varig Brazilian Airlines, involves partners from different parts of the world that are seeking cooperation to enter each other's markets carefully. Each partner directly complements the others in terms of knowledge of local markets, best ways to deal with host governments in regulatory matters, and in providing key infrastructure (for example, maintenance, aircraft service, crew handling facilities) at hub airports. Moreover, each airline is strong in one part of the world, but comparatively weak or nonexistent in the other parts. This makes the choice of complementary partners not only a necessity, but also a basis for longer-term, sustainable cooperation. Although airline alliances involving complementary partners can sometimes unwind (for example, Delta Air Lines and Singapore Airlines), close coordination among partners to form transatlantic, transpacific, and even fully global networks helps each alliance member better serve its customers in those parts of the world where it has little previous experience. Still, alliance members will have to devote considerable effort to mesh and harmonize their disparate organizational cultures, styles, and decision-making processes.

Keep Alliance Personnel Long Term

Learning and applying new skills and technologies require patience and time. Thus, it is imperative that corporate managers keep their alliance personnel long term. This step ensures that a sufficient "gestation" period occurs for effective learning and insight. Unfortunately, U.S. managers often perceive that alliance assignments are less valuable or "fast-track" than working in headquarters. Often, the alliance site is far from headquarters. Alliance assignments lack visibility to aspiring managers and offer little opportunity to network with other managers and superiors. These factors often bias U.S. companies toward short-term alliance assignments, which are viewed as tangential to the company's key activities. On the contrary, Japanese companies often commit their managerial and technical personnel to the life of the venture. This strategy ensures a vastly more receptive and fertile ground to learn their partner's skills. The managers' personal success now depends almost exclusively on what they can learn and bring back to the parent firm.

Planning and Administration: Fuji Xerox[40]

Perhaps one of the most enduring alliances ever constructed is Fuji Xerox, a joint venture that has spanned over four decades. Formed in 1962, Fuji Xerox is "considered the most successful joint venture between an American and a Japanese company."[41] By 2004, Fuji Xerox had endured many changes and challenges within the relationship, but it continues to thrive as a vibrant powerhouse in the fields of digital imaging, copiers, fax machines, and printers. Founded originally as a 50/50 partnership, Fuji Xerox is owned by Fuji Photo Film and Xerox Corporation. Led by distinguished CEO Yotaro Kobayshi, Fuji Xerox has become the technological epicenter for Xerox's worldwide operations and is now a key vehicle for helping Xerox to become an important player in the emerging Chinese market for office automation equipment.

Fuji Xerox's role within the larger Xerox Corporation underwent a series of important changes since the alliance's inception. During the 1960s and 1970s, Fuji Xerox served as a distant marketing operation that helped Xerox sell copiers in the fast-growing Japanese market. Xerox transferred a number of core technologies to Fuji Xerox, which in turn refined them to better suit the needs of Japanese customers. For example, most of Xerox's U.S.-designed copying machines were extremely large and complex. However, because of the small size of Japanese offices, Fuji Xerox effectively redesigned Xerox's machines to become much smaller and more energy efficient. In the process, Fuji Xerox developed its own set of core miniaturization skills that would prove useful in making high-performance, highly compact copying machines. At one point during the 1970s, a Fuji Xerox machine cost half as much to make as a comparable Xerox-designed machine.

As a result of its own indigenous R&D skills, Fuji Xerox gradually set its own strategy to compete against larger Japanese
(continued)

STRATEGIC COMPETENCY *in action*

competitors such as Canon, Ricoh, and Minolta. It became increasingly difficult for parent Xerox to manage joint venture operations from such a distance. In the early 1970s, Fuji Xerox instituted a company-wide commitment to total quality control. Fuji Xerox sought to eliminate waste in every part of its operations and to accelerate its product development efforts. By 1980, Fuji Xerox earned the highly coveted W. E. Deming award, an annual prize given to the Japanese firm that made the greatest stride in developing products of the highest quality. Ironically, Deming was an American statistics expert who jump-started the quality movement in Japan at a time when U.S. firms turned a deaf ear to his advice. Fuji Xerox also committed itself to learning and applying the latest technological developments in fine optics that laid the foundation for advanced lens and better copy resolution. By 1980, a growing portion of Fuji Xerox's business was sales of small and medium-sized copiers to U.S. parent Xerox. Around this time, Xerox's senior management decided to give Fuji Xerox even greater latitude to develop its own technologies and products, and even started to help pay for part of Fuji Xerox's development costs.

During the 1980s, Fuji Xerox played a decisive role in helping Xerox transform its operations. Xerox lost its core patents on the copying process (reprographics), and such competitors as Canon and Ricoh captured significant U.S. and global market share. Canon's machines used advanced technology to sell through a nationwide dealer network. More important, Canon's machines demonstrated exceptional reliability, whereas Xerox's copiers suffered frequent breakdowns and quality issues. Yet, Xerox took too long to recognize the impact of this new competition; instead of being satisfied with selling smaller, less expensive machines, Japanese firms started aiming for Xerox's leadership at the top end, which was the source of most of its profits. Fuji Xerox's core skills in miniaturization, optics, and quality control became the basis for Xerox's U.S. turnaround. Xerox sent dozens of its managers to visit and learn from Fuji Xerox's total quality control program. Yet, Fuji Xerox's vast influence extended to all parts of Xerox's organization; Xerox sought to embrace and teach quality principles in every part of its operations. By 1989, Xerox's product quality had improved by such a quantum leap that the company earned the distinguished Malcolm Baldrige National Quality Award, an annual U.S.-based competition that seeks to emulate the Deming Prize in Japan.

During the 1990s, Fuji Xerox's role evolved to the point where the joint venture took on an even greater role in pioneering and commercializing new optics-based technologies. Fuji Xerox became the manufacturing center for most of Xerox's smaller and medium-sized copiers and printers. Equally important, Fuji Xerox began investing in newer technology fields, such as lasers, digital document storage systems, and advanced software that enables employees to work in an "open office environment." Fuji Xerox envisions an "open office" to become a borderless workplace where people can perform their tasks anywhere, including outside of the office itself. Fuji Xerox began providing consulting services to customers throughout the Far East and Pacific regions.

In this decade, Fuji Xerox has evolved into a self-contained, fully autonomous company with its own strategy. Facing renewed financial difficulties, Xerox reduced its long-time 50/50 stake in Fuji Xerox by selling another 25 percent to Fuji Photo Film, with Xerox owning a minority equity stake. Although this move represents a substantial retreat for parent Xerox, Fuji Xerox still provides significant technology for all of Xerox's imaging and printer products. Fuji Xerox is now investing in new production and distribution centers along the Chinese coast to take advantage of business growth. In addition, Fuji Xerox is now in the midst of creating its own set of strategic alliances to further enhance its technological leadership. It jointly developed a new type of microcontroller with Motorola that integrates printing and scanning functions on one chip. This new chip can control all of the key functions of low- and medium-speed copiers, and it will help Fuji Xerox slice manufacturing costs by as much as half. Moreover, the new integrated chip will help accelerate Fuji Xerox's product development time, requiring only six months as opposed to three years to develop a new copier. Fuji Xerox is also working with Samsung of Korea to build multifunctional copiers and scanners in one device. In January 2004, both Xerox and Fuji Xerox entered into a supply agreement with Dell, who will start sourcing key products from both companies in the future.

Ethical Dimension

The rise of strategic alliances should encourage managers to think about the ethical problems likely to emerge when undertaking such arrangements. Two dominant ethical issues surrounding strategic alliances are (1) balancing collaboration and competition within the alliance and (2) the issue of loyalty among personnel assigned to an alliance.

Cooperation and Competition in Alliances

The formation of strategic alliances often raises a critical ethical question concerning the boundaries of cooperation and competition with partnering firms. On the one hand, strategic alliances are designed to give firms an opportunity to apply their distinctive skills and capabilities jointly to accomplish some objective (the collaboration side of alliances). On the other hand, alliances are also designed to help the firm learn from its partner new skills or technologies that it currently does not have (the competitive side of alliances). Although alliances involve cooperation, a firm must set definite limits on how far it will go to cooperate with other partners. Knowing how far to go and when to exit are key to successful alliance planning and negotiation. Firms need to protect their interests in an alliance by ensuring they do not "give away the store" in terms of losing control over their core technologies and proprietary knowledge. In other words, alliances involve a certain duality wherein partners work together (cooperate) on a certain objective but also attempt to learn new skills (compete). Thus, managing this tightrope balance with a partner involves a high degree of relationship building, while at the same time, communicating that certain areas are off limits for discussion.

Their day-to-day operations allow alliance partners to become more familiar with the habits and practices of their partners. This familiarity, in turn, enables them to build a stable relationship based on mutual respect and mutual benefit (cooperation). However, the workings of any alliance still depend upon a certain give-and-take quality, whereby partners trade information or technology in exchange for something of value from the partner (competition). Thus, every alliance in some sense has "two faces" to it. Genuine cooperation requires trust and stability to accomplish some jointly desired objective; learning from a partner requires negotiation or give-and-take that represents competition within the alliance. The ethical balance in alliances comes from a certain level of trust that partners build to ensure that they treat each other openly, while simultaneously not attempting to gain the upper hand on each other by demanding or covertly stealing technology that is clearly beyond the scope of the agreement.

Regardless of the alliance vehicle (licensing, joint ventures, networks, knowledge webs, consortia), firms always face the potential problem of partners attempting to take advantage of their relationship to learn or "steal" technology that was not part of the original arrangement. This ethical issue becomes paramount when firms are collaborating on large-scale projects that involve highly proprietary or emerging technologies representing many years of investment and effort. Unscrupulous partners can sometimes use alliances as a method to learn new technologies and processes from their partners "cheaply," thereby avoiding their own R&D to advance their efforts. This problem is likely to become more salient and problematic as firms become increasingly interwoven in alliances that bring in partners from other cultures and nations, where the ethical distinction between cooperation and competition may be much more blurred.

Alliance Personnel Issues

Another pertinent ethical issue is the staffing of alliances. Oftentimes, managers and technical personnel assigned to an alliance will experience a certain degree of confusion about where to place their loyalties. This problem will also affect their feelings toward their parent company and the alliance they are assigned to, particularly if they are to work with the alliance partner over a long time. Namely, are alliance personnel supposed to be loyal to their parent firm that assigned them there, or are they supposed to be loyal to the alliance as a new entity? Employees who think their primary loyalty should be with their parent firms may feel more prone to view the alliance as a "dispensable" vehicle, in which their only goal within the alliance is to learn as much as they can from the partner and then return to headquarters. On the other hand, employees who believe they must work more intimately with their partner's managers and employees may face the danger of "going native." In other words, people assigned to an alliance may begin to start thinking like their partners and to assimilate their partner's values and culture over time, particularly if they feel they have been neglected or forgotten by their parent firms. Employees may sometimes develop a new loyalty toward the alliance as an entity in its own right. Thus, senior managers must carefully evaluate these issues before assigning key personnel to an alliance. Staffing the alliance with too many people who are simply out to "get" the partner's technology or skills will destroy the fabric of trust within an alliance. However, sending out people to staff an alliance without giving them opportunities to return home will raise the potential of their "going native."

Summary

- Alliances represent a useful intermediate step for firms seeking to gain the benefits of diversifying into new areas of activity.
- Alliances can serve as a lower-risk vehicle for firms seeking to enter new markets as part of a measured strategy of global expansion.
- The need for some form of risk reduction promotes alliance formation. These risks include new market entry, industry evolution, learning and applying new technologies, and filling out a product line.
- Allying with other firms enables the company to secure added benefits, especially benefits from the opportunity to develop new products and technologies that are too costly for the firm to undertake by itself.
- Alliances come in three broad categories: licensing arrangements, joint ventures, and consortia distant arms-length arrangements, highly coordinated arrangements, and tightly integrated arrangements.
- Industry-spanning alliance networks are now taking on a greater importance in shaping the evolution of many new products and services, especially in entertainment, high-technology arenas, and health care.
- Firms that participate in industry-spanning alliance networks may find themselves members of a larger knowledge web. In this context, firms attempt to outrace one another to innovate new forms of technologies and knowledge to dominate the evolution of an industry. Frequently, firms will find themselves cooperating and competing with their partners at the same time.
- Managers must understand how their firm's distinctive competence benefits from working with a partner. Managers must also take steps to protect their firm's distinctive competence from excessive exposure to the firm's partners.
- All alliance configurations or forms impose risks. These risks are rising incompatibility of partners, knowledge/skill leakage to the partner, deepening dependence, and strategic control costs of coordination, learning, and inflexibility.
- Allying will be fruitful only to the extent that the benefits outweigh the costs.
- Understanding how the firm's skills and technologies relate to building competitive advantage is a vital step in defining the limits and scope of cooperation.
- Firms with complementary skills tend to make better alliance partners because they offer less potential for direct competition in end products or markets.
- Keeping alliance personnel long term is critical to effective learning.
- All alliances involve a simultaneous degree of collaboration and competition when working with a partner. Cooperating effectively to accomplish some desired objective requires relationship building and trust; however, learning new skills and technologies from a partner involves day-to-day negotiations and give-and-take that are more competitive in nature.

Exercises and Discussion Questions

1. Over the past year, the telecommunications industry has seen a large number of alliances form between local telephone companies and other firms. Using the Internet, look up the website for Verizon Communications, a major local telephone company in many parts of the nation. What type of companies is Verizon allying with? What appears to be the rationale for Verizon's multiple array of alliances? Which ones appear to be complementary partners? Which ones appear to be technology development relationships?

2. Why is it important to understand the strategic motivations of a potential alliance partner? What are some things to consider when assessing the relative compatibility of a future partner?

3. Assume you are the CEO of a leading technology company. You are currently manufacturing state-of-the-art notebook computers and have a wildly successful brand name to your credit. A Japanese firm wishes to form an alliance with you. The proposed partnership would involve manufacturing a large portion of your notebook computers in Japan using the partner's factories and employees. The partner insists on using his or her factories in Japan because they have a reputation for quality products. What are some of the benefits and risks that you face in the relationship? How would you manage this relationship over the long term? Does manufacturing in Japan make a difference to your long-term competitive advantage? What are some key issues you need to think about when entering the alliance?

Endnotes

1. Facts and data used for the IBM case are adapted from the following sources: "IBM Discovers the Power of One," *BusinessWeek*, February 14, 2005, pp. 80-81; "Sony, IBM, Toshiba To Offer First Peek of 'Cell' Chip Design," *Wall Street Journal*, February 7, 2005, pp. B1, B2; "IBM to Unveil a Powerful Chip for Home Entertainment Market," *Wall Street Journal,* November 29, 2004, p. A3; "Big Blue Plant Is Stuck in Red," *Wall Street Journal,* June 23, 2004, p. B10; "Toshiba Outlines $9.4 Billion Focus on Screens, Chips," *Wall Street Journal,* April 12, 2004, p. B6; "Soaring Costs Forcing Chipmakers to Team Up," *Investor's Business Daily,* March 25, 2004, p. A4; "Taiwan's VIA Selects IBM as Foundry for Tiny Chips," *Wall Street Journal,* January 5, 2004; "Microsoft's Xbox to Use IBM Chips," *Wall Street Journal,* November 4, 2003; "IBM Alters Silicon to Increase Speed of Computer Chips," *Wall Street Journal,* September 8, 2003, p. A6; "IBM Unit Hatches Heart Monitor," *Wall Street Journal,* August 5, 2003; "IBM Grabs Business From Asian Foundries," *Wall Street Journal,* May 8, 2003; "IBM, Xilinx Pass a Milestone in Race to Shrink Circuitry," *Wall Street Journal,* December 16, 2002; "IBM Bets Big on Chips as Industry Slumps," *Wall Street Journal,* July 31, 2002, p. B4; "IBM Cites Circuit Breakthrough," *Wall Street Journal,* March 18, 2004, p. B4; "IBM, Seiko Epson Negotiate to Form Asian Chip Venture," *Wall Street Journal,* May 24, 2001; "IBM, Toshiba Launch Talks to End Venture That Produces LCDs," *Wall Street Journal,* May 17, 2001; "IBM, Carrier to Unveil Joint Internet Venture in Air Conditioning," *Wall Street Journal,* April 9, 2001; "Joint Project to Develop Supercomputer on a Chip," *Semiconductor International,* April 1, 2001; "IBM Receives Sony Contract for New Chips," *Wall Street Journal,* March 12, 2001; "IBM, Cisco Extend Mobile Networking Alliance," *Fiber Optic News,* March 5, 2001.

2. Facts and data for the airline industry were adapted from the following: "Alitalia Can't Stanch Red Ink," *Wall Street Journal,* April 21, 2004, p. A16; "Air France, KLM

Forge New Order," *Wall Street Journal,* October 1, 2003, p. D7; "Air France Votes to Merge with KLM," *Wall Street Journal,* September 30, 2003, pp. A2, A6; "Global Partners May Get Roiled by Turbulence," *Wall Street Journal,* December 6, 2002, pp. B1, B5; "United to Boost Revenue Via Lufthansa Link," *Wall Street Journal,* November 15, 2002, p. B6; "Airlines Scurry to Make Connections," *Dallas Morning News,* August 24, 2002, pp. 1F, 2F; "American Air, British Air Drop Plans for Venture," *Wall Street Journal,* January 28, 2002, pp. A3, A16; "Delta and Air France Set Initial Agreement under 'Open Skies' Deal," *Wall Street Journal,* October 22, 2001, p. B7; "Delta Air to Request Antitrust Immunity for Foreign Alliance," *Wall Street Journal,* August 15, 2001; "Alitalia Board Approves Bid to Forge Air Alliances," *Wall Street Journal,* July 10, 2001, p. A15; "AMR, British Air Renew Push for Alliance," *Wall Street Journal,* August 6, 2001; "More Airlines Will Crash If Mergers Are Blocked," *Wall Street Journal,* July 3, 2001; "Air New Zealand Spurns Qantas, Woos Singapore Airlines," *Wall Street Journal,* June 20, 2001; "American and British Air's Alliance Bids Again for Antitrust Immunity," *Wall Street Journal,* June 12, 2001; "Delta Instigates Broad Talks with 2 Airlines," *Wall Street Journal,* January 31, 2001; "American Air Says Huge Deal Helps Consumers," *Wall Street Journal,* January 11, 2001, pp. B3, B10; "Cathay Pacific May Join Alliance with British Air," *Wall Street Journal,* September 21, 1998, p. A22; "In Asia's Stormy Weather, Airlines Find Strength in Alliances," *Wall Street Journal,* August 19, 1998, p. A15; "United, Delta Air Unveil Big Alliance, Close Scrutiny by Regulators Expected," *Wall Street Journal,* May 1, 1998, p. A6; "American Airlines, US Airways Plan Marketing Accord to Vie with Rivals," *Wall Street Journal,* April 24, 1998, p. A4.

3. A growing literature on strategic alliances has developed over the past ten years. Some of the representative research pieces include the following: J. E. Oxley and R. C. Sampson, "The Scope and Governance of International R&D Alliances," *Strategic Management Journal* 25, nos. 8–9 (2004): 723–750; A. C. Inkpen and S. C. Currall, "The Coevolution of Trust, Control, and Learning in Joint Ventures," *Organization Science* 15, no. 5 (2004): 586–599; D. Gerwin and J. S. Ferris, "Organizing New Product Development Projects in Strategic Alliances," *Organization Science* 15, no. 1 (2004): 22–37; D. Gerwin, "Coordinating New Product Development in Strategic Alliances," *Academy of Management Review* 29, no. 2 (2004): 241–257; M. G. Colombo, "Alliance Form: A Test of the Contractual and Competence Perspectives," *Strategic Management Journal* 24, no. 12 (2003): 1209–1229; M. Kotabe, X. Martin, and H. Domoto, "Gaining From Vertical Partnerships: Knowledge Transfer, Relationship Duration and Supplier Performance Improvement in the U.S. and Japanese Automotive Industries," *Strategic Management Journal* 24, no. 4 (2003): 293–316; P. Kale, J. Dyer, and H. Singh, "Alliance Capability, Stock Market Response, and Long-Term Alliance Success: The Role of the Alliance Function," *Strategic Management Journal* 23, no. 8 (2002): 747–768; Y. Luo, "Contract, Cooperation and Performance in International Joint Ventures," *Strategic Management Journal* 23, no. 10 (2002): 903–920; M. Zollo, J. Reuer, and H. Singh, "Interorganizational Routines and Performance in Strategic Alliances," *Organization Science* 13, no. 6 (2002): 701–713; B. R. Koka and J. E. Prescott, "Strategic Alliances as Social Capital: A Multidimensional View," *Strategic Management Journal* 23, no. 9 (2002): 795–816; E. W. K. Tsang, "Acquiring Knowledge by Foreign Partners in International Joint Ventures in a Transition Economy: Learning-by-Doing and Learning Myopia," *Strategic Management Journal* 23, no. 9 (2002): 835–854; A. Takeishi, "Bridging Inter- and Intra-Firm Boundaries: Management of Supplier Involvement in Automobile Product Development," *Strategic Management Journal* 22, no. 5 (2001): 403–434; J. E. Salk and O Shenkar, "Social Identities in an International Joint Venture: An Exploratory Case Study," *Organization Science* 12, no. 2 (2001): 161–178; R. C. Schrader, "Collaboration and Performance in Foreign Markets: The Case of Young High-Technology Manufacturing Firms," *Academy of Management Journal* 44, no. 1

(2001): 45–60; T. E. Stuart, "Interorganizational Alliances and the Performance of Firms: A Study of Growth and Innovation Rates in a High-Technology Industry," *Strategic Management Journal* 21, no. 8 (2000): 791–812; H. Merchant and D. Schendel, "How Do International Joint Ventures Create Shareholder Value?" *Strategic Management Journal* 21, no. 7 (2000): 723–738; A. C. Inkpen, "A Note on the Dynamics of Learning Alliances: Competition, Cooperation, and Relative Scope," *Strategic Management Journal* 21, no. 7 (2000): 775–780; A. Kaufman, C. H. Wood, and G. Theyel, "Collaboration and Technology Linkages: A Strategic Supplier Typology," *Strategic Management Journal* 21, no. 6 (2000): 649–664; T. Chi, "Option to Acquire or Divest a Joint Venture," *Strategic Management Journal* 21, no. 6 (2000): 665–688; P. Dussauge, B. Garrette, and W. Mitchell, "Learning From Competing Partners: Outcomes and Durations of Scale and Link Alliances in Europe, North America and Asia," *Strategic Management Journal* 21, no. 2 (2000): 99–126; T. K. Das and B. S. Teng, "Instabilities of Strategic Alliances: An Internal Tensions Perspective," *Organization Science* 11 (2000): 77–101; M. Koza and A.Y. Lewin, "The Co-evolution of Strategic Alliances," *Organization Science* 9, no. 3 (1998): 255–264; T. Khanna, "The Scope of Alliances," *Organization Science* 9, no. 3 (1998): 340–356; T. Khanna, R. Gulati, and N. Nohria, "The Dynamics of Learning Alliances: Competition, Cooperation and Relative Scope," *Strategic Management Journal* 19, no. 3 (1998): 193–210; A. C. Inkpen and A. Dinur, "Knowledge Management Processes and International Joint Ventures," *Organization Science* 9, no. 4 (1998): 454–468; S. Kumar and A. Seth, "The Design and Coordination and Control Mechanisms for Managing Joint Venture-Parent Relationships," *Strategic Management Journal* 19, no. 6 (1998): 579–600; R. Kumar and K. O. Nti, "Differential Learning and Interaction in Alliance Dynamics: A Process and Outcome Discrepancy Model," *Organization Science* 9, no. 3 (1998): 356–367; P. J. Lane and M. Lubatkin, "Relative Absorptive Capacity and Interorganizational Learning," *Strategic Management Journal* 19 (1998): 461–478; J. F. Hennart, D. J. Kim, and M. Zeng, "The Impact of Joint Venture Status on the Longevity of Japanese Stakes in U.S. Manufacturing Affiliates," *Organization Science* 9, no. 3 (1998): 382–395; R. N. Osborn and J. Hagedoorn, "The Institutionalization and Evolutionary Dynamics of Interorganizational Alliances and Networks," *Academy of Management Journal* 40, no. 2 (1997): 261–278; P. Dickson and K. M. Weaver, "Environmental Determinants and Individual-Level Moderators of Alliance Use," *Academy of Management Journal* 40, no. 2 (1997): 404–425; A. C. Inkpen and P. W. Beamish, "Knowledge, Bargaining Power, and the Instability of International Joint Ventures," *Academy of Management Review* 22 (1997): 177–202; P. F. Swan and J. E. Ettlie, "U.S.-Japanese Manufacturing Equity Relationships," *Academy of Management Journal* 40, no. 2 (1997): 463–479; J. F. Hennart and S. Reddy, "The Choice between Mergers/Acquisitions and Joint Ventures: The Case of Japanese Investors in the United States," *Strategic Management Journal* 18 (1997): 1–12; T. K. Das and B. S. Teng, "Between Trust and Control: Developing Confidence in Partner Cooperation in Alliances," *Academy of Management Review* 23, no. 3 (1998): 491–512; Y. L. Doz, "The Evolution of Cooperation in Strategic Alliances: Initial Conditions or Learning Processes?" *Strategic Management Journal* 17, Summer Special Issue (1996): 55–83; M. A. Lyles and J. E. Salk, "Knowledge Acquisition From Foreign Parents in International Joint Ventures: An Empirical Examination in the Hungarian Context," *Journal of International Business Studies* 27 (1996): 877–904; R. Gulati, "Does Familiarity Breed Trust? The Implications of Repeated Ties for Contractual Choice in Alliances," *Academy of Management Journal* 38, no. 1 (1995): 85–112; B. Gomes-Casseres, "Group versus Group: How Alliance Networks Compete," *Harvard Business Review* (July–August 1994): 5–10; R. M. Kanter, "Collaborative Advantage: The Art of Alliances," *Harvard Business Review* (July–August 1994) 96–108; N. Nohria and R. G. Eccles, eds., *Networks and Organizations: Structure Form and Action* (Boston: Harvard Business Press, 1993); D. Mowery, ed., *International Collaborative Ventures in U.S.*

Manufacturing (Cambridge, MA: Ballinger, 1988); J. Hagedoorn and J. Schakenraad, "The Effect of Strategic Technology Alliances on Company Performance," *Strategic Management Journal* 14, no. 4 (1994): 291–309; J. Bleeke and D. Ernst, *Collaborating to Compete* (New York: Wiley, 1993); A. Parkhe, "Messy Research, Methodological Predispositions, and Theory Development in International Joint Ventures," *Academy of Management Review* 18, no. 2 (1993): 227–268; L. L. Blodgett, "Factors in the Instability of International Joint Ventures: An Event History Analysis," *Strategic Management Journal* 13 (1992): 475–481; D. Lei and J. W. Slocum, Jr., "Global Strategy, Competence-Building and Strategic Alliances," *California Management Review* (Fall 1992): 81–97; P. S. Ring and A. H. Van de Ven, "Structuring Cooperative Relationships Between Organizations," *Strategic Management Journal* 13 (1992): 483–498; J. L. Badaracco, *The Knowledge Link: How Firms Compete through Strategic Alliances* (Boston: Harvard University Press, 1991); J. M. Geringer, "Strategic Determinants of Partner Selection Criteria in International Joint Ventures," *Journal of International Business Studies* 22 (1991): 41–62; G. Hamel, "Competition for Competence and Interpartner Learning Within International Strategic Alliances," *Strategic Management Journal* 12 (1991): 83–103; D. Lei and J. W. Slocum, Jr., "Global Strategic Alliances: Payoffs and Pitfalls," *Organizational Dynamics* 1 (1991): 44–62; R. N. Osborn and C. C. Baughn, "Forms for Organizational Governance for Multinational Alliances," *Academy of Management Journal* 33 (1990): 503–519; B. Borys and D. Jemison, "Hybrid Arrangements as Strategic Alliances: Theoretical Issues in Organizational Combinations," *Academy of Management Review* 14 (1989): 234–249; G. Hamel, Y. Doz, and C. K. Prahalad, "Collaborate with Your Competitors and Win," *Harvard Business Review* (January–February 1989): 133–139; K. R. Harrigan, "Joint Ventures and Competitive Strategy," *Strategic Management Journal* 9 (1988): 141–158; B. Kogut, "Joint Ventures: Theoretical and Empirical Perspectives," *Strategic Management Journal* 9 (1988): 319–332; H. Thorelli, "Networks: Between Markets and Hierarchies," *Strategic Management Journal* 7 (1986): 37–51; K. Ohmae, *Triad Power: The Coming Shape of Global Competition* (New York: Free Press, 1985).

4. See, for example, "Toshiba in Pact to Produce Chips for Xilinx of the U.S.," *Wall Street Journal,* October 14, 2004; "Shift in Making Chips Bears Fruit," *Wall Street Journal,* February 5, 2004, p. B5.

5. An empirical piece that examines the formation of alliances in the semiconductor industry, especially among smaller firms is: S. H. Park, R. Chen, and S. Gallagher, "Firm Resources as Moderators Between Market Growth and Strategic Alliances in Semiconductor Start-Ups," *Academy of Management Journal* 45 (2002): 527–545. Also see W. Vanhaverbeke, G. Duysters, and N. Noorderhaven, "External Technology Sourcing Through Alliances or Acquisitions: An Analysis of the Application-Specific Integrated Circuits Industry," *Organization Science* 13, no. 6 (2002): 714–733.

6. CDMA stands for code-division multiplexing access. CDMA technology is a digital phone standard that has been rapidly gaining in popularity in many parts of the world, especially China and India. CDMA differs from other cell phone technologies, including GSM, GPRS, and EDGE—all of which transmit cell phone signals using a different series of underlying algorithms.

7. See "Chipping Away at Qualcomm's Chips," *BusinessWeek,* June 16, 2003, pp. 66–68; "Heads We Win, Tails We Win," *Fortune,* March 3, 2003, pp. 142–150.

8. "Sony, Partners Plan Own Format on Rewritable Compact Disks," *Dallas Morning News,* August 14, 1997, p. 2D.

9. See "Blu-Ray Group Plans Smaller DVD Format for Camcorder Use," *Wall Street Journal,* October 7, 2004; "News Corp. Unit in Blu-Ray Race," *Wall Street Journal,* October 5, 2004.

10. See, for example, "Juniper Posts a $29.7 Million Net Loss, but Stock Nevertheless Jumps on Results," *Wall Street Journal,* October 12, 2001, p. B3; "Juniper, Sonus Share Converged Vision," *Fiber Optic News,* May 14, 2001.

11. Literally hundreds of biotechnology alliances have been formed over the past several years. See, for example, "Bayer, Millennium Say Genomic Drug That They Developed Fights Tumors," *Wall Street Journal,* January 11, 2001, p. B4; "AstraZeneca Forms Alliance with Orchid," *Wall Street Journal,* February 13, 2001, p. B6.

    A recent empirical piece that examines the role of alliances to explore new technologies using the biotechnology industry setting is R. S. Vassolo, J. Anand, and T. B. Folta, "Non-Additivity in Portfolios of Exploration Activities: A Real Options-Based Analysis of Equity Alliances in Biotechnology," *Strategic Management Journal* 25, no. 11 (2004): 1045–1062. Also see F. Rothaermel and D. L. Deeds, "Exploration and Exploitation Alliances in Biotechnology: A System of New Product Development," *Strategic Management Journal* 25, no. 3 (2004): 210–222; L. G. Zucker, M. Darby, and J. S. Armstrong, "Commercializing Knowledge: University Science, Knowledge Capture, and Firm Performance in Biotechnology," *Management Science* 48 (2002): 138–153; J. Baum, T. Calabrese, and B. Silverman, "Don't Go It Alone: Alliance Network Composition and Startups' Performance in Canadian Biotechnology," *Strategic Management Journal* 21, no. 3 (2000): 267–294.

12. See "Rivals Samsung, Sony Unit in Flat-Screen TV Venture," *Wall Street Journal,* July 15, 2004, p. B1.

13. "Boeing Is Negotiating Wing-Parts Pacts with Japanese Firms for New Large Jet," *Wall Street Journal,* September 5, 1996, p. A4.

14. Data and facts were adapted from the following sources: "Honda Takes to the Skies," *Forbes,* November 15, 2004, pp. 184–185; "Honda Teams with GE with Dreams of 'Honda Civic of the Air,'" *FinancialWire,* October 13, 2004; "Honda Venture in Talks to Supply Jet Engines to Aircraft Makers," *Wall Street Journal,* October 12, 2004, p. B5; "General Electric Co. and Honda Motor Co. Establish Joint Company," *Market News Publishing,* October 12, 2004; "GE, Honda Form Joint Venture to Market Honda's Jet Engines," October 12, 2004; "Sky Kings," *Forbes,* August 16, 2004, pp. 76–80.

15. "Schwab Expands Role in Launching Other Firms' Funds," *Wall Street Journal,* July 21, 1998, pp. C1, C25.

16. See "Defense Industry Sees More Deals on the Horizon," *Wall Street Journal,* September 25, 2002, pp. C1, C3.

17. See, for example, L. D. Browning, J. M. Beyer, and J. C. Shetler, "Building Cooperation in a Competitive Industry: SEMATECH and the Semiconductor Industry," *Academy of Management Journal* 38, no. 1 (1995): 113–151. Also see W. J. Spencer and P. Grindley, "SEMATECH after Five Years: High Tech Consortia and U.S. Competitiveness," *California Management Review* 35 (Fall 1993): 9–32; C. H. Ferguson and C. R. Morris, *Computer Wars: How the West Can Win in a Post-IBM World* (New York: Times Books/Random House, 1993).

18. See "Chip Firms Seek a National Institute," *Wall Street Journal,* June 10, 2004, p. B6.

19. The concept of applying network-based theories from other disciplines can help contribute to our understanding of the dynamics of strategic alliances, particularly those involving multiple firms. An outstanding research piece that highlights some of these issues from a competitive perspective is D. R. Gnywali and R. Madhavan, "Cooperative Networks and Competitive Dynamics: A Structural Embeddedness Perspective," *Academy of Management Review* 26, no. 3 (2001): 431–445. Recent pieces that examine the relationship between knowledge-sharing and competitive advantage are J. W. Spencer, "Firms' Knowledge-Sharing Strategies in the Global Innovation System: Empirical Evidence From the Flat Panel Display Industry," *Strategic Management Journal* 24 (2003): 217–234; and M. Sakakibara, "Formation of R&D Consortia: Industry and Company Effects," *Strategic Management Journal* 23, no. 11 (2002): 1033–1050. Also see R. Gulati, N. Nohria, and A. Zaheer, "Strategic Networks," *Strategic Management Journal* 21 (2000): 203–215; T. E. Stuart, "Inter-organizational Alliances and the Performance of Firms: A Study of Growth and

Innovation Rates in a High-Technology Industry," *Strategic Management Journal* 21, no. 8 (2000): 791–811; R. Gulati, "Network Location and Learning: The Influence of Network Resources and Firm Capabilities on Alliance Formation," *Strategic Management Journal* 20 (1999): 397–420; T. Stuart, "Network Positions and Propensities to Collaborate: An Investigation of Strategic Alliance Formation in a High-Technology Industry," *Administrative Science Quarterly* 43 (1998): 668–698; B. Uzzi, "Social Structure and Competition in Interfirm Networks: The Paradox of Embeddedness," *Administrative Science Quarterly* 42 (1997): 35–67; J. Gimeno and C. Woo, "Economic Multiplexity: The Structural Embeddedness of Cooperation in Multiple Relations of Interdependence," *Advances in Strategic Management* 13 (1996): 323–361; W. W. Powell, K. W. Koput, and L. Smith-Doerr, "Interorganizational Collaboration and the Locus of Innovation: Networks of Learning in Biotechnology," *Administrative Science Quarterly* 29 (1996): 329–346.

20. See, for example, "Union Pacific Seeks to Boost Revenues in Unlikely Places," *Wall Street Journal,* October 16, 2001, p. B4.

21. An excellent discussion of Japanese keiretsu may be found in C. H. Ferguson, "Computers and the Coming of the U.S. Keiretsu," *Harvard Business Review* (July–August 1990): 55–70. See also F. Kodama, *Emerging Patterns of Innovation* (Boston: Harvard Business School Press, 1995).

22. See, for example, "Y. L. Doz, P. M. Olk, and P. S. Ring, "Formation Processes of R&D Consortia: Which Path to Take? Where Does It Lead?" *Strategic Management Journal* 21 (2000): 239–266.

23. See "Global Motors," *Forbes,* January 12, 2004, pp. 62–68.

24. See "New Hybrid Cars Drive a Company, and Its Stock," *Wall Street Journal,* October 13, 2004, p. C1.

25. See, for example, "Airbus Goes into Overdrive," *Wall Street Journal,* January 14, 2003, p. B4.

26. Issues and costs surrounding strategic alliances are further discussed in the following works: S. H. Park and G. R. Ungson, "Interfirm Rivalry and Managerial Complexity: A Conceptual Framework of Alliance Failure," *Organization Science* 12, no. 1 (2001): 37–53; J. J. Reuer and M. J. Leiblein, "Downside Risk Implications of Multinationality and International Joint Ventures," *Academy of Management Journal* 43, no. 2 (2000): 203–214; C. Saunders, M. Gebelt, and Q. Hu, "Achieving Success in Information Systems Outsourcing," *California Management Review* 39, no. 2 (1997): 63–79; P. C. Grindley and D. J. Teece, "Managing Intellectual Capital: Licensing and Cross-Licensing in Semiconductors and Electronics," *California Management Review* 39, no. 2 (1997): 8–41; S. H. Park and M. Russo, "When Competition Eclipses Cooperation: An Event History Analysis of Alliance Failure," *Management Science* 42 (1996): 875–890; B. Kogut and N. Kulatilaka, "Operating Flexibility, Global Manufacturing, and the Option Value of a Multinational Network," *Management Science* 40 (1994): 123–139; R. A. Bettis, S. P. Bradley, and G. Hamel, "Outsourcing and Industrial Decline," *Academy of Management Executive* (February 1992): 7–22; C. C. Snow, R. E. Miles, and J. E. Coleman, "Managing 21st Century Network Organizations," *Organizational Dynamics* (Winter 1992): 5–20; D. Lei and J. W. Slocum, Jr., "Global Strategy, Competence-Building and Strategic Alliances," *California Management Review* (Fall 1992): 81–97; J. Bleeke and D. Ernst, "The Way to Win in Cross-Border Alliances," *Harvard Business Review* (November–December 1991): 127–135; D. Lei and J. W. Slocum, Jr., "Global Strategic Alliances: Payoffs and Pitfalls," *Organizational Dynamics* 1 (1991): 44–62; G. Hamel, Y. Doz, and C. K. Prahalad, "Collaborate With Your Competitors and Win," *Harvard Business Review* (January–February 1989): 133–139.

27. See "Regional Carrier Sheds Its Partners to Fly Solo," *New York Times,* June 16, 2004.

28. See "As Alliances Fade, Computer Firms Toss Out Playbook," *Wall Street Journal,* October 15, 2002, pp. A1, A8; "Lexmark Will Make Cartridges and Printers Under Dell Brand," *Wall Street Journal,* September 25, 2002, p. B4.

29. See "The Man Who Built Pixar's Incredible Innovation Machine," *Fortune,* November 15, 2004, pp. 207–212; "Disney to Raise Its Gaming Profile," *Wall Street Journal,* November 8, 2004, p. B4; "Freeze Frame: Pixar Still Lacks a Partner for Post-Disney Era," *Wall Street Journal,* October 25, 2004, pp. B1, B4; "Can Disney Still Rule Animation After Pixar?" *Wall Street Journal,* February 2, 2004, pp. B1, B4; "Disney Decides It Must Draw Artists into Computer Age," *Wall Street Journal,* October 23, 2003, pp. A1, A15; "Is Steve About to Move His Cheese?" *BusinessWeek,* February 10, 2003, p. 72.

30. "Mexican-Food Joint Venture Gives Arby's Indigestion," *Wall Street Journal,* August 12, 1997, pp. B1, B2.

31. See "IBM, Toshiba Launch Talks to End Venture That Produces LCDs," *Wall Street Journal,* May 15, 2001.

32. See "A Tricky Transition in China," *Wall Street Journal,* November 23, 2004, p. A17.

33. See, for example, R. B. Reich and E. D. Mankin, "Joint Ventures with Japan Give Away Our Future," *Harvard Business Review* (March–April 1986): 78–86.

34. See "Taiwan Semi to Spend Billions on Chip Plants," *Wall Street Journal,* October 26, 2001, p. A13; "Focus on Taiwan: UMC on the Move," *Semiconductor International,* September 1, 2001; "Taiwan's Manufacturers Climb the 'Food Chain,'" *Wall Street Journal,* December 13, 2000, p. B10.

35. See "Merck Licenses Insomnia Drug From Lundbeck," *Wall Street Journal,* February 11, 2004, p. B2; "Merck Looks Outside for Help," *Wall Street Journal,* October 16, 2003, p. B2.

36. See R. N. Osborn and C. C. Baughn, "Forms of Interorganizational Governance for Multinational Alliances," *Academy of Management Journal* 33 (1990): 503–519. Also, A. Parkhe, "Strategic Alliance Structuring: A Game Theoretic and Transaction Cost Examination of Interfirm Cooperation," *Academy of Management Journal* 36 (1993): 794–829.

37. See, for example, "Apple-IBM Goal of Universal Computer Faces Hurdles," *Wall Street Journal,* November 9, 1994, p. B4.

38. See, for example, A. M. Brandenburger and B. Nalebuff, *Co-opetition: A Revolutionary Mindset That Combines Competition and Cooperation* (New York: Doubleday, 1996).

39. See "Group of Tech Companies, 3 Labs to Unveil Chip-Making Machine," *Wall Street Journal,* April 11, 2001, p. B6.

40. Data and facts were adapted from the following sources: "Fuji Xerox to Offer Business Document Digitization Service," *Nikkei Report,* September 18, 2004; "Fuji Xerox Wants to Be a Pioneer in Open Office Frontier Concept," *Business Times,* August 24, 2004, p. 6; "Fuji Xerox to Open Design Offices in Major Asian Cities," *Asia In Focus,* August 11, 2004; "Fuji Xerox Launches Enhanced Laser Printers," *New Strait Times,* March 15, 2004, p. 6; "Motorola, Fuji Xerox Develop System Chip for Digital Copiers," *Nikkei Report,* January 19, 2004; "Xerox International Partners and Fuji Xerox Align with Dell to Expand Imaging and Printing Marketplace," *Pressi.com,* January 9, 2004; "Fuji Xerox to Provide ASICs to Xerox," *Nikkei Report,* January 8, 2004; see "Seeking a Big Lift, Xerox to Launch Big Color Printer," *Wall Street Journal,* August 28, 2001, B1, B6; "Canon on the Loose," *Forbes,* July 23, 2001, pp. 68–69; "Xerox, Beset by Problems, Lost Ground to Rival Canon in 2000, Study Finds," *Wall Street Journal,* March 9, 2001, p. B6; "Xerox Nears Sale of Half Its Stake in Fuji Venture," *Wall Street Journal,* March 2, 2001, p. B6.

41. An excellent formal case that examines Fuji Xerox's growth and role within Xerox Corporation is Harvard Business School case "Xerox and Fuji Xerox," Number 9-391-156.

Organizing for Sustainable Advantage

Designing Organizations for Advantage

What you will learn

- *How strategy implementation contributes to a firm's competitive advantage*

- *Why organizational issues are a significant part of strategy implementation*

- *How organizational structure lays the foundation for strategy implementation*

- *The broad types of organizational structures that companies are likely to use*

- *The concept of loose coupling and the network organization*

- *The evolution and ingredients of the virtual organization*

- *Why no single type of organizational structure is likely to fit all companies*

Cisco Systems[1]

Cisco Systems is one of the world's leading technology companies. The company is a leader in developing computer routers, switches, networking gear, and leading-edge telecommunications equipment that are at the heart of the Internet. When the company first went public in early 1990, few people had ever heard of the company, and even fewer knew about the products that Cisco designed and sold. Now, Cisco is synonymous with a number of different things: the Internet, a vibrant high-technology flagship company, even as a bellwether for the Nasdaq stock market on which it is a leading company. In fact, most people hardly ever see an actual product developed by Cisco Systems, since routers and switches are usually found in computer and telecommunication servers and networks that serve to direct the flow of data to desktop computers in businesses and other organizations. Yet, without networking products made by companies such as Cisco Systems, the Internet would not be nearly as advanced, fast, and versatile as it is today.

By the late 1990s, many people had come to view Cisco Systems as synonymous with the Internet. By July 2004, Cisco had become a $22 billion company, and many of its competitors envied and imitated its organizational model. In fact, until the recent downturn that afflicted the economy in 2000–2001, Cisco Systems had continuously grown at rates exceeding 20 and even 30 percent each year. Its computer networking gear is considered some of the most advanced products available, and Cisco has become an important rival to many high-technology companies, including Alcatel, Juniper Networks, Lucent Technologies, Nortel Networks, and Ciena Corporation in selling cutting-edge technologies to telecommunications firms that are upgrading their own transmission infrastructure. At the peak of its growth rate in 1999, Cisco developed and sold over 80 percent of the networking gear used to transmit and direct Internet traffic. At one point in March 2000, the firm had become the most valuable company in the world with a market capitalization close to $550 billion. By July 2004, Cisco still had over $19 billion in cash, no long-term debt, and significantly increased its profitability by earning $4.4 billion for that fiscal year. Even with the economic downturn, the company still has an overwhelming market share for all key networking gear products that are needed to power the Internet. As the economic recovery gained steam in late 2003 and early 2004, Cisco even appeared to be taking market share away from some of its competitors. More important, Cisco has expanded its growth to include several key new product categories, including intelligent networks, Internet security, Voice over Internet Protocol (VoIP) phones, and wireless technologies. Its latest technology initiative is the Cisco CRS-1 Carrier Routing System, which can handle 92 terabits of data per second. According to the company, that is the equivalent of transferring the entire collection of the U.S. Library of Congress in five seconds. Cisco sees itself as the provider of technologies that will allow people to communicate with each other in any medium—voice, video, data—over a single secure network that possesses its own intelligence and capability to change whenever needed.

Cisco's meteoric rise to technological preeminence over the past decade is due in part to the company's leading-edge technologies and its ability to innovate rapidly. Equally important, Cisco Systems from its earliest days relied on a different organizational model that allowed it to become a highly agile yet focused competitor. Cisco became extremely profitable because it did not have the same degree of fixed costs in manufacturing plants that saddled many of its more established competitors, including Alcatel, Lucent Technologies, and Nortel Networks. Cisco believes that it needs to be able to respond quickly to its customers' changing needs, especially in the telecommunications industry where technology moves fast. To compete on the basis of speed and leading-edge technology, Cisco Systems during the 1990s grew its revenue astronomically by acquiring dozens of companies each year to fill out its product line. Under its longtime CEO John Chambers, Cisco has prided itself on acquiring young, innovative companies that developed promising technologies. CEO Chambers designed Cisco's organization so that it its newly acquired companies could find the breathing room, capital, and access to customers to further grow their ideas. Unlike other companies where many preexisting employees left after their companies were acquired, Cisco cultivated and retained many such employees to power its growth. Chambers believed that keeping business units small and giving them plenty of autonomy was key to innovation. Newly acquired companies were organized as small businesses to "incubate" their best ideas. In turn, Cisco benefited enormously from the collective and massive effort put forth by thousands of newly acquired engineers and managers. Until recently, Cisco did comparatively little internal R&D on its own. Thus, retaining these brilliant people became the basis for Cisco's rocketlike growth and ability to create cutting-edge technology products.

Since the economic downturn of 2000–2001, Cisco has deemphasized its strategy of acquiring dozens of companies each year to grow. Instead, the company has begun to spend more money ($3 billion in fiscal 2004) to develop more products through its own R&D. Cisco is now gaining market share, and 14 percent of its revenues now come from new products. These products include wireless gear, as well as faster routers and switches that power the Internet. With a greater focus on internal growth rather than external acquisition, Chambers has realigned Cisco's organization to achieve greater coordination of key value-adding activities. Although Cisco is now a huge company, it has pushed ahead with many important organizational innovations so that it can continue to respond quickly to its customers' needs. Some of the most defining characteristics of Cisco's approach to organizing its people and activities are described in the following sections.

Near Total Reliance on Suppliers and Manufacturing Partners

One of the most important hallmarks of Cisco's organizational model is its almost total reliance on its suppliers and manufacturing partners to build, assemble, test, and even deliver Cisco's entire line of products. In fact, most of the high-tech components and chips that go into Cisco's products are manufactured by third-party companies that specialize in a particular network component or assembly of the final product. These chips and components are then assembled into Cisco's final end products. Over the past decade, Cisco has established strong working relationships with these contract manufacturers that have become an integral part of Cisco's web of suppliers. These suppliers include such companies as Solectron, Flextronics, Celestica, and Sanmina-SCI, which are able to produce vast quantities of key components for Cisco's networking gear at low cost. Cisco relies so heavily on its manufacturing partners that it even teaches them how to perform quality control according to Cisco's high standards. Cisco also delegates to its manufacturing partners highly intricate, customized product designs that fit each customer's unique specifications. As Cisco's manufacturing partners become more sophisticated in their capabilities, they are also better able to help Cisco become more flexible and agile in responding to fast-changing technologies. By 2000, these manufacturers had become so important to Cisco that they built more than 60 percent of Cisco's products and would even ship them directly to customers' locations. To cut costs even further, Cisco cut the number of suppliers from 1,300 to around 400. Now, Cisco relies on its key suppliers for over 90 percent of its production. These relationships have helped Cisco become one of the most efficient companies in managing its inventory and in reducing the amount of fixed costs required to produce more complex products. Equally important, Cisco has been able to shrink delivery times to customers from ten weeks to three weeks in most cases.

Fast Product Design Capability

Another important facet of Cisco's organizational model is the company's renowned capability to design new generations of networking equipment faster than its rivals can. To make sure that Cisco can build the right products for its customers, the company actively encourages its key enterprise and telecommunications customers to work directly with Cisco's designers and engineers to test new product designs. Although Cisco has a wealth of talent that it acquired through scores of acquisitions, the company believes that product development and innovation should focus on a customer's specific technology needs. Cisco actively woos its customers for ideas, suggestions, criticisms, and other input to sharpen its product development skills. CEO Chambers is well known throughout business circles for visiting customers and treating them as long-standing partners. In fact, Cisco fervently believes that much of the company's product development activity should be performed in conjunction with its customers, since they can provide unique yet realistic insights into how products should perform. Cisco asks its customers what kinds of products and technologies they feel they will need in future years. More important, Cisco wants to use customers' input as the basis for exceeding their expectations with next-generation products that are specifically made for each customer's needs. Customers can work in person with Cisco's engineers or directly with the company through the Internet. Cisco even allows its customers to design and order products through its website, where customers can check on the status of their orders through a real-time, continuously updated database that is tied in with Cisco's manufacturing partners. By encouraging customers to use the Internet, Cisco also listens directly to their complaints and suggestions on how best it can improve future networking gear to make it easier to use and less costly to install. In effect, under CEO Chambers, Cisco has made its growing customer base a key source of its R&D ideas for future innovations.

Retention of People From Acquisitions

Chambers has long believed that for Cisco to remain on the cutting edge of technology, the company should seek new ideas and technologies from wherever they may be developed. During the 1990s, this belief led Cisco on a massive buying spree of many leading-edge companies that possess brilliant design and engineering talent. Cisco won over many skeptical soon-to-be-acquired employees and managers by showing how their efforts and knowledge will make Cisco a leader in that technology field. Cisco has grown so successfully through its acquisitions that comparatively few of its products are "homegrown." In fact, CEO Chambers felt that acquisitions, if done correctly, would help Cisco fill gaps in its product line much more quickly than if everything were done internally alone. Many corporate executives and analysts believe that Cisco Systems is one of the few companies that have been successful in retaining the people that it acquired through buyouts of companies. Cisco makes sure that when it buys companies, they share some important characteristics: (1) ambitious and talented engineers, (2) products or technologies that complement Cisco's own offerings, and (3) management who tend to stay and become important team leaders within Cisco after the buyout is completed.

Cisco has been especially successful in retaining people after making an acquisition because it not only offers generous compensation but also encourages newly acquired talent to become project leaders within Cisco. Senior managers that accompany the acquisition are asked to stay as well; in fact, CEO Chambers set up a direct reporting relationship where newly acquired managers are able to oversee many of the same talented people they worked with before the acquisition. Now, even though Cisco is placing greater emphasis on internal R&D over acquisitions, Chambers wants to encourage the same exciting level of innovation and energy that the company enjoyed before the economic downturn. Chambers has encouraged Cisco's managers to look at new ways to improve the company's productivity and to do things better. Cisco also created a series of committees to make sure that all parts of the company are better able to work together. The company is hoping that these moves will enhance its ability to capture new and larger corporate customers.

The Key Role of Strategic Implementation

So far, we have focused on ways a firm can build and extend its sources of competitive advantage. We have analyzed how companies from various industries formulate specific strategies to create new sources of value from their activities. However, strategy formulation is only part of the equation in developing competitive advantage. Once a particular strategy has been chosen, the firm must then devote considerable effort to ensure that managers and employees are united in their efforts to execute the strategy.

This chapter will focus exclusively on the "architecture" of designing an organization. Managers must see that individual activities within an organization work together to build and sustain competitive advantage. In its simplest definition, **strategy implementation** refers to converting strategies into desired actions and results. In a broader sense, strategy implementation is concerned with efforts to build a more effective organization to continuously execute desired results.[2] Successful strategy implementation depends on both a well-managed organization and a solid base of committed, competent personnel to execute plans and objectives. Execution delivers results. Management can formulate any number of strategies to build competitive advantage, but the success of any given strategy is only as good as the organization and the people behind it. Execution ultimately determines the success or failure of any given strategy.[3]

We begin by providing some reasons why strategy implementation is an imperative issue. In the second section, we focus exclusively on the topic of organizational structure. We look at how a firm may select a particular organizational structure to support its strategy. In the third section, we examine how firms organize themselves to balance the dual needs of stability and fast responsiveness. Finally, we revisit Cisco Systems to see how it has used specific organizational structures to support its strategies.

strategy implementation:
The process by which strategies are converted into desired actions.

A Framework for Designing Organizational Structure

The basis for successful strategy implementation rests on designing an effective organization. People working within an organization must be able to understand how their actions interrelate with the actions of others to support and execute the firm's strategy. Yet, in many instances, talented people in even the best-managed firms are sometimes left groping to understand their own roles in supporting the firm's strategy. Organizational structure is vital in clarifying the roles of managers and employees that hold the company together.

structure:
The formal definition of working relationships between people in an organization.

Structure refers to the underlying design or configuration of authority, responsibilities, and relationships within an organization. Organizational structure serves a twofold purpose. First, structure distinguishes and separates the specific tasks that make up the firm's activities: what people should do. On the other hand, structure provides the basis to integrate these tasks into a coherent whole: how people should work together. Structure defines the working relationships within an organization.[4]

A company's strategy will require a particular form of organizational structure to implement it. The strategy a firm selects will determine the general guidelines for grouping activities and tasks, the choice of practices and procedures to attain consistency of performance, and the delegation of authority within the firm.

Basic Ingredients of Organizational Structure

Three important ingredients, or dimensions, compose organizational structure: (1) specialization, (2) standardization, and (3) centralization. Each of these ingredients of organizational structure influences how managers and employees interact (see Exhibit 9-1).

Specialization

specialization:
The assignment of particular tasks and activities to those people who are best able to perform them.

Specialization refers to identifying and assigning particular activities or tasks to the appropriate individuals, teams, or units capable of performing them. When used effectively, specialization enables an organization to divide many activities and tasks and allocate them to those people best equipped to handle them. The dimension of specialization can be found at all levels within an organization.

Every company uses the concept of specialization in some way. For example, within an automotive factory, welders perform only those tasks that relate to welding; assemblers do their jobs by putting the parts of the car together; painters work the specialized machinery that paints

Exhibit 9-1	*Key Dimensions of Organizational Structure*

Specialization
- Matching activities with people who are best able to perform them
- Found at all levels within an organization

Standardization
- Practices, procedures, and guidelines that provide the basis for consistent performance
- Focused on achieving internal order within a given structure

Centralization
- Delegation of authority throughout the organization's ranks

each car to a glowing finish. The skills of painters are different (specialized) from those of assemblers. In a fashion salon, customers can also find specialization at work. For example, some stylists are particularly skilled at cutting and shaping hair to current styles or perms, other stylists are better trained at choosing the right mix of dyes to modify hair color according to a customer's skin complexion or tone, while other stylists specialize in care for the hands and feet as manicurists and pedicurists. People conduct particular activities according to their skills and capabilities.

Specialization is also found when we examine larger units of a firm. For example, an automotive manufacturer may decide to group all of its assembly activities in one part of the factory, while placing the specialized paint machinery in another. On an even larger scale, the same automotive company can group all of its assembly operations in one unit that reports to senior management, while placing all of its engine-manufacturing operations in another specialized unit dedicated to producing engines. In the hair salon example, a company such as Supercuts could group all of its U.S. salons and shops in one unit, while placing all of its Latin American salons in another unit. Supercuts may choose to do this because the fashion and hair-styling requirements of U.S. customers (time spent on makeup, time spent on perms, type of shampoos used, type of advertising) may vary from those of Latin American customers. Thus, for Supercuts as a company, dividing up its markets may help management better understand specific market conditions. Specialization is vital to any organization, because it matches activities with people and units best able to perform them.

Standardization

Standardization is the process of defining the organization's work, procedures, and practices in such a way that people do their jobs in a consistent manner. Standardization is concerned with achieving internal order and performance within a given structure. The concept of standardization focuses on ensuring that people, teams, and larger units perform "up to a given standard." It is found in many forms and at all levels, even within a single company. For example, standards for quality and ethical behavior exist at the personal level, whereas financial performance standards are used for larger units in a company. Regardless of level, the purpose behind standardization is to attain and to measure consistency of performance.

Standardization can take the form of rules, practices, procedures, and the criteria by which people are evaluated and measured on their performance. For example, the quality of welding and assembly in the automobile factory will be evaluated according to exacting, precisely defined measures of the car's fit, whereas the quality of a paint job will be assessed according to the luster and consistency of the car's appearance. In the fashion salon example, hair stylists are evaluated according to a quite challenging set of standards—those of the customer. Customers can tell whether their hair "looks and feels right" when they look in the mirror. Yet, in both the car factory and fashion salon examples, a defined set of practices, procedures, and criteria is used to measure and ensure consistent performance.

The concept of standardization also applies to larger units within a company. Here, the focus of standardization tends to be on attaining consistency of financial or operating performance. For example, a division in an automobile company producing luxury cars is likely to have a different standard for profitability as compared to a division producing subcompact, economy cars for young people in their first jobs. For example, at Ford, senior managers will probably hold the division producing luxury cars to a higher standard of profitability than the division producing economy cars for a less wealthy group of customers. Thus, standardization is concerned with organizational practices, procedures, and criteria that provide the basis for consistent performance.

standardization:
The process of defining the organization's work practices and procedures so that people can repeatedly perform them at a given level or measure of performance.

Centralization

centralization:
The degree to which senior managers have the authority to make decisions for the entire organization.

Centralization refers to the degree to which senior managers have the authority to make decisions for the entire organization. Delegating authority to lower-level personnel is an important aspect of organizational structure because it involves choosing which people have the right to decide and act. In a highly centralized organization, senior management retains most of the authority to decide how subunits will act. Senior managers in a centralized company decide strategy and objectives, even for smaller subunits within the firm. In contrast, a highly decentralized organization places wide discretion with lower-level managers and employees. Senior management plays a lesser role in setting goals and objectives for the company's subunits. By delegating authority to lower-level managers and personnel, decentralization allows senior management to harness the decision-making capabilities of many people throughout the company.

Companies differ widely in the amount of authority they delegate to lower-level subunits. For example, in chemical and pharmaceutical companies such as Dow, DuPont, Monsanto, Merck, Schering-Plough, and Pfizer, top managers make many key decisions and communicate them to lower-level managers and employees. On the other hand, many high-tech and software firms such as Microsoft, Adobe Systems, Electronic Arts, Apple Computer, and Hewlett-Packard prefer a high degree of decentralization that encourages their lower-level managers to make decisions on their own. Centralization is concerned with the degree of delegation of authority throughout the organization's ranks.

STRATEGIC COMPETENCY *in action*

Planning and Administration: The Home Depot[5]

Founded by Bernie Marcus and Arthur Blank after they were fired from a hardware store in 1979, The Home Depot has mushroomed to over 1,700 stores throughout the United States from a single store in Atlanta, Georgia. For many customers, Home Depot has become synonymous with tools, gardening and electrical supplies, lawnmowers, lumber, cabinetry, and everything else that is needed for the home. By January 2004, Home Depot had earned $4.30 billion on net sales of $64.8 billion and was the nation's second largest retailer after Wal-Mart. Despite its tremendous growth, Home Depot for its first twenty years encouraged its store managers to operate with a high degree of autonomy to ensure that they could best serve their customers. Believing that paperwork from headquarters interfered with individual decision making and initiative, Bernie Marcus once communicated a simple message to all store managers: "It's your store; do what's best."

This emphasis on running each store as its own business injected a strong entrepreneurial spirit throughout the company. Passionate store managers took great personal interest in running their operations, and they gained a deep knowledge about what their customers wanted for home improvement projects. Many employees at Home Depot had worked in the electrical, plumbing, and carpentry trades before, and they provided extremely knowledgeable and helpful service that kept customers coming back. Each store typically ordered merchandise best suited for its individual market; for example, stores located in the suburbs kept their shelves well stocked with topsoil, gardening tools, light fixtures, lawnmowers, and other items that families would use to maintain their homes. Stores located in the more rural "exurbs" ordered more lumber and building supplies that contractors would need to complete home building projects in growing neighborhoods. Individual stores would also promote and advertise those products best suited for their local markets, and merchandise was arranged within each store according to customer preferences. As Home Depot grew nationally, the company created nine regional buying offices that would source merchandise for a group of stores in a given market. Each of these buying centers also enjoyed considerable autonomy in selecting suppliers and products.

During the late 1990s, Home Depot experienced much slower growth as markets saturated. In particular, the company faced intensified competition from Lowe's Companies, a rival that began competing in much the same way. Although Lowe's was an older outfit (founded in 1921), it traditionally built smaller stores with a more of a "hardware-store" atmosphere (about one-fifth the size of a Home Depot store). By the late 1980s, Lowe's offered a similar line of home improvement and building supply products, and it started to build much larger stores in fast-growing suburbs, especially in the eastern United States. As Home Depot's growth slowed down, Lowe's planned a massive expansion.

In 2000, Bernie Marcus left the CEO post and the company hired Robert Nardelli from General Electric to succeed him. Nardelli was a newcomer to retailing, after having served a long career in the lighting and power equipment businesses at General Electric under CEO Jack Welch. Nardelli was an expert in manufacturing, and he was extremely steeped in the General Electric approach to management: a focus on measuring and boosting productivity, an emphasis on understanding your financial numbers, and strategic thinking. When Welch retired in 2000, Nardelli was one of the front-runners to succeed him. Nardelli became CEO of Home Depot when another GE successor was chosen (Jeffrey Immelt from GE Medical Systems, now GE Healthcare).

Realizing that Home Depot faced real constraints on future growth, CEO Nardelli undertook an ambitious plan to completely reshape the way that Home Depot organized and ran its operations. Nardelli believed that Home Depot could become a $100 billion company, but its existing management practices limited its full potential to grow. Visiting stores himself, Nardelli believed Home Depot could substantially boost productivity and operational efficiency in both individual stores and systemwide. Believing that his previous manufacturing expertise could readily apply to retailing operations, Nardelli was stunned to realize that he could not send a company-wide e-mail that reached all store managers from Atlanta headquarters. The first objective Nardelli set out was to modernize the company's entire "infrastructure." Computers were installed in each store to facilitate communication and to pursue a unified direction from headquarters. Computers also help headquarters track the individual sales and performance results of each store. Nardelli's second major objective was to redesign the way that Home Depot sourced and purchased merchandise from its suppliers. Instead of relying on the nine preexisting regional buying centers, Nardelli centralized all purchasing decisions in Atlanta. He believed that with Home Depot's enormous purchasing clout, it could demand and receive much bigger discounts from vendors for everything from tools to gardening supplies. By centralizing purchasing, Nardelli took away each store's ability to order what it wanted for its particular market. Third, Nardelli wanted to develop store managers into leaders. Using a leadership development model he learned at GE, Nardelli wanted store managers to become more comfortable with using hard numbers to measure and improve their performance. Previously, store managers ran their operations in the way they best saw fit, and they paid scant attention to headquarters' directives. To boost store efficiency levels, Nardelli insisted that store managers drive results and think strategically.

Nardelli's imprint on Home Depot aroused enormous controversy and outright criticism from many long-term managers and employees. Many managers at all levels within the company quit because Nardelli took away the high degree of freedom they previously enjoyed. Even former CEO Marcus was alarmed at the direction Nardelli took the company. The emphasis on centralizing purchasing and building a systemwide, computer-linked supply chain threw store managers into fits. Store managers who previously were accustomed to ordering their own products regionally now felt compelled to take what Atlanta ordered for them. Headquarters went even so far as to demand that each Home Depot store arrange the merchandise and shelves along a standardized format that would fit a nationwide model. Many store managers grew frustrated with the need for continuous reporting of financial numbers. They thought this activity took away from their ability to work with customers more closely. Even long-term store employees who worked in trades previously grew tired of dealing with more centralized procedures that dictated how they were supposed to do their jobs. Some employees were even clamoring for Mr. Marcus to come back to lead the company.

Nardelli's efforts to centralize Home Depot's operations, although resented by some, have begun to produce important results. Centralized purchasing has boosted Home Depot's gross margins, and many stores have installed computerized self-checkout counters to speed up the lines. Nardelli is also changing the way that Home Depot develops its store managers. Instead of relying on plumbing and electrical experts, Nardelli has pushed Home Depot to begin recruiting a new breed of managers—many of whom have military backgrounds and are accustomed to reporting to managers in a well-defined hierarchy. Nardelli believes that ex-military officers, who are smart, intense, and hardworking, can become leaders that further transform the way that Home Depot does business in the future.

Broad Forms of Organizational Structure

The interaction of these three dimensions—specialization, standardization, and centralization—will vary according to each firm's strategy. Managers need to find the right combination of specialization, standardization, and centralization to implement their firm's strategy most effectively.

Four common combinations of these elements are (1) functional, (2) product, (3) geographic, and (4) matrix structures. Each of these broad structures involves different choices with respect to specialization, standardization, and centralization to implement a given strategy.[6]

Functional Structures

functional structure:
An organizational structure that groups managers and employees according to their areas of expertise and skills to perform their tasks.

In a functional structure, each subunit is assigned responsibility for firmwide activities related to a particular function. Functions are the broad tasks that every organization performs to create value: production, marketing, engineering, finance, human resources. **Functional structures** group managers and employees according to their areas of expertise and the resources they use to perform their jobs. For example, in a functional structure, all company manufacturing activities are assigned to the same subunit regardless of where they are conducted or to what products they apply; all company marketing activities are grouped under another subunit that deals solely with marketing issues; all company development and engineering activities are grouped in a common subunit, and so on (see Exhibit 9-2).

A functional structure permits the firm to *achieve a high degree of specialization in key value-adding activities*. Functional structures are usually found in firms engaged in high-volume production of a single or narrow range of products or services. Thus, functional structures are particularly useful in supporting low-cost leadership strategies. Technical competence and specialization of skills in value-adding activities are concentrated in each of the functions. Grouping activities by way of a functional structure is efficient and cost-effective when technical, marketing, or product development expertise is scarce. Functional structures exhibit a high degree of standardization of procedures. Tight cost control, frequent detailed reports on operating efficiency, and well-defined assignment of responsibilities are the hallmarks of a functional structure in firms seeking to lower their costs. Operating practices, such as quality improvement and efficient flow of work, tend to follow strict procedures within each function. In addition, functional structures in low-cost leadership firms tend to be highly centralized. Top management monitors, oversees, and makes decisions concerning all of the functional activities occurring within the firm.

The functional structure can also be used to support differentiation strategies, but its application in such a setting is unlike its use in firms practicing low-cost leadership strategies. Recall that differentiation strategies place a high premium on quality, strong marketing skills, creative flair, innovative technologies, and often a distinctive company reputation. Firms practicing differentiation can therefore use a functional structure to develop especially distinctive or

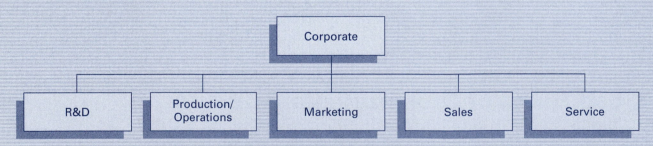

Exhibit 9-2   **Diagram of a Typical Functional Structure**

- Each function is responsible for its own set of tasks and activities.
- Each function has its own set of goals and objectives that require coordination with other functions.

specialized marketing or R&D skills. Production efficiency, although important to firms that practice differentiation, is less likely to be as critical as other issues such as product design, marketing capabilities, and innovative technologies. Instead, these latter areas of activity are likely to receive continuous attention from top management.

Functional structures are particularly common in the petroleum, mining, and other resource-extractive industries. These firms organize their value-adding activities according to the specific stages of exploration, production, refining, distribution, and marketing. ExxonMobil, ChevronTexaco, ConocoPhillips, and other large oil companies use a functional structure to organize their petroleum-based activities. Functional structures are also common in other firms that have high levels of vertical integration. Steel, glass, aggregates (for example, gravel, rock), and rubber companies have traditionally relied on functional structures to manage the stages of production, refining, and fabrication of their products. Companies in the telecommunications industry also frequently use a functional structure, because it allows them to achieve low-cost, efficient management of their transmission operations. All of the local "Baby Bell" (or Regional Bell Operating Companies) firms, such as SBC Communications, Bell South, and Verizon, typically employ a functional structure to manage their telephone operations. A functional structure is a very efficient vehicle to coordinate activities, such as repair, installation, and switching for homes and businesses.

Functional structures are particularly suitable for firms that are small. They are equally suitable for firms that do not diversify into new businesses or areas of activity. In other words, functional structures support the needs of a single-business firm quite well. A functional structure consumes little overhead because it has only one general manager and one set of functional managers that oversee activities for the entire firm (high centralization). When businesses are very small or confine their activities to a narrow range of products/markets, functional structures work well to concentrate expertise (high specialization and standardization). For example, small food-processing firms, such as bakeries and canneries, often organize functionally for these reasons.

Advantages of Functional Structures. Functional structures provide economies of scale for management and administration of each function; therefore, they are excellent in reducing overhead costs for a firm. Functional structures hold down administrative costs because everyone in a department shares the training, experience, and resources devoted to a particular function. In addition, senior management can easily identify and promote those people who have the necessary technical expertise to manage their particular function. A key advantage of the functional structure is the high degree of centralized decision making it allows within each functional area. Functional structures are simple structures and are highly suitable for small firms, less diversified firms (big and small), and growing start-up firms. For large companies, such as those in the petroleum and telecommunications industries, functional structures are excellent in supporting high-volume, low-cost, dedicated production or operations. Functional structures support large economies of scale for each functional activity, and encourage the preservation of key skills and knowledge that drive that subunit's activity.

Disadvantages of Functional Structures. The Achilles' heel of a functional structure is the difficulty it poses for coordination, especially if the firm expands into a broad range of products. When a functional structure is used, individuals within functional units will tend to develop loyalty to their specialties, which frequently makes them unwilling to accommodate the needs of other functional units. Consider, for example, a proposal by marketing personnel to expand a company's product line. Such a change will complicate the tasks of manufacturing

Exhibit 9-3   Key Characteristics of a Functional Structure

Advantages	Disadvantages
• Economies of scale in administrative costs/activities	• Coordination difficulties arise when firm diversifies
• Good for small-sized firms	• Difficult for each function to accommodate needs of other functions
• Easy to identify talent	
• Fosters high centralization of decision making	• Divergent goals and objectives based on each function
• Promotes high task and activity specialization	• Inflexible with broad-based global or multidomestic strategies
• Supports a low-cost leadership strategy	• Needs extensive modification to support differentiation strategies
• Supports vertical integration in a business	• Poor fit for highly diversified firms
• Best for undiversified firms	

personnel by increasing the number of designs, components, equipment variations, and production setups they must handle. Manufacturing personnel are therefore likely to object to such a change. Thus, a big disadvantage of the functional structure is that each function is likely to have its own set of values, priorities, goals, and even time perspectives on what constitutes an urgent versus routine matter. This narrowness often limits functional managers' perspective concerning the entire firm's operations. Functional managers may generally place their priorities above that of others for additional resources—sometimes to the detriment of the entire firm. (See Exhibit 9-3 for a summary of advantages and disadvantages of a functional structure.)

In some ways, management control that spans functional activities may be difficult to achieve, because no common performance criteria are available by which to measure, for example, marketing effectiveness and manufacturing efficiency. Measuring performance involves comparing apples and oranges in the sense that each function is unlike the other. Although performance standards are easy to set and measure within a function, they do not mix well when comparing across functions.

Product Divisions

As a firm expands into new products, businesses, or areas of unrelated activity, the functional structure often loses many of its advantages. High product diversity often leads to serving many types of customers and involves the firm in multiple technologies. In response to these developments, senior management will often utilize a **product divisional** structure. Product divisions are structures that divide the organization into self-contained units responsible for developing, producing, distributing, and selling their own products and services for their own markets (see Exhibit 9-4).

product divisions:
The most basic form of product structure, in which each division houses all of the functions necessary for it to carry out its own strategy and mission.

A product division structure establishes a separate organizational unit (and management team) for each product (or group of related products) in the firm. Product divisions are the most commonly used organizational structures in large U.S. corporations. Most companies in the Fortune 500 have expanded into new businesses at some point and exhibit some degree of related or unrelated diversification. Product division structures tend to fit companies exhibiting wide diversification because each individual business unit is likely to face a different set of product, technology, market, and customer requirements.[7]

Product divisions in effect *represent small, self-contained businesses within a company.* Although a large company can have many product divisions, these divisions tend to remain fairly autonomous. Thus, managers and individuals assigned to a particular product division often

Diagram of a Typical Product Division Structure — Exhibit 9-4

- Each division is self-contained and responsible for its own products and markets it serves.
- Each division contains its own set of functions.

become expert about that division's products and markets. Still, each division reports to senior management. Each product division also contains its own functional specialists and resources that are usually organized into departments. These functional departments are designed to support the needs of various products within the division. Most product divisions are evaluated on the basis of their own financial performance and the competitive success of their products. Consequently, each product division has the opportunity to develop its own distinctive competence or sources of competitive advantage for its own products.[8]

Product divisions display a high level of specialization based on the products the firm develops and produces. Unlike functional structures, in which specialization is based on operational activities and tasks, product divisions are organized in such a way that managers and employees become specialists and experts about the products they develop, produce, and sell. A product structure, therefore, encourages modifying and directing functional activities to support particular products.

Product divisions also differ from functional structures in terms of how performance is measured. Product divisions are evaluated on the basis of their profit contributions to the entire corporation. Since each division represents a product or group of similar products, senior management can easily isolate the financial performance of each division according to some benchmark or performance standard (usually a rate of return on investment or assets). Thus, individual divisions may be evaluated along different performance criteria, even within the same company. Consequently, senior management has great leeway in applying performance standards across divisions. For example, at General Electric, the standard for profitability may be quite high for mature businesses, such as light bulbs. Because GE light bulbs are well established in the marketplace, senior management may place a high priority on the lightbulb division to earn a big return on investment. On the other hand, GE's senior management may consider using another performance standard for a fast-growing business, such as medical equipment or plastics. In these businesses, GE must continue to invest large sums of money building new factories and laboratories. Consequently, these divisions may be evaluated along other performance criteria, such as growth in market share or number of customers added.

Some firms using product divisions display a high degree of centralization, with senior management closely monitoring and even participating in the shaping of a business unit or product strategy. For example, in the automotive industry, senior managers may work closely with managers to plan production schedules for new product rollouts. Other firms using product divisions may be much more decentralized. For example, in diversified food companies, management typically makes few decisions about product offerings, timing of rollout, discounts, promotions, and other details specific to the division. Thus, the use of product division structures by themselves does not reveal much about the degree of centralization.

Advantages of Product Divisions. Product divisions offer enormous advantages in allocating, assigning, and defining the responsibilities required for each product or group of products. It allows managers to concentrate their expertise on their assigned products lines or markets. In addition, each product division has its own self-contained functional departments designed to support the needs for individual products. Thus, product divisions allow for considerable specialization that enables firms to develop a base of managerial and technical expertise for each product. A big advantage of the product division is that it enables senior management to locate and identify the costs, profits, and potential problems accurately within each line of business.

Product divisions also tend to help managers develop a cross-functional perspective that is important to achieving fast response. Since each product division has a self-contained set of functional departments, managers tend to learn fast and know what it takes to coordinate these functional departments effectively to build competitive advantage.

Product division structures are also excellent mechanisms by which to train and develop future senior and general managers, since this type of structure holds each division manager accountable for results of an entire business. Thus, opportunity for advancement presents considerable incentive for division managers to learn how to manage their businesses effectively.

Product divisions also work very well to promote a high degree of competition within the company, which stimulates innovation. Many high-technology companies deliberately keep their product divisions small to encourage a free flow of ideas within each division. At the same time, all divisions compete with one another to accelerate the time-to-market for new products.

Organizing along a product division format gives senior management considerable flexibility in rearranging the shape of the company's portfolio of businesses. Management can decide to sell different pieces of the company that are underperforming or do not have attractive prospects for the future. Since product divisions are self-contained units that house their own functions and centers of expertise, senior management can more readily put divisions on the block for sale if they no longer fit the company's long-range strategy.

Disadvantages of Product Divisions. Several important disadvantages are associated with product divisions. First is the potential for inefficient use of functional resources. Remember that each product division has its own self-contained set of functional departments. If a firm's products are actually quite similar in terms of development, production, or marketing, multiple functional departments duplicate time and effort across divisions that may be striving to accomplish the same objective.

Second, a product division structure duplicates administrative, management, and staff activities. Since each product division by design is highly autonomous, high overhead costs are associated with this structure. Each division is likely to possess its own administrative setup, including accounting and other staff functions.

Third, firms using product divisions tend to measure individual divisional performance by way of quantitative financial measures. This emphasis could induce a significant bias toward

Key Characteristics of Product Division Structures	**Exhibit 9-5**

Advantages

- High autonomy of divisions for each product/business
- Allows for specialization based on products/markets
- Enhances and supports needed change in products
- Allows for easy measurement of financial performance
- Standardizes performance measurement
- Cross-functional perspective
- Supports highly diversified strategies (related and unrelated)

Disadvantages

- Duplicates functions within each product division
- Duplicates administrative and staff functions
- Leads to short-term thinking if not careful
- Promotes high internal competition between divisional managers
- May underinvest in firm's core competence and skills; discourages company-wide "mega" projects

short-term thinking. Since division managers must meet a certain level of financial return (return on investment, assets, or sales), they may be inclined to run the business "according to the numbers." This may cause them to delay important investment in new process technologies, R&D, or other future sources of competitive advantages because of the daily short-term pressures to produce. Divisional managers may reinterpret "competitive advantage" as current return on investment, as opposed to building and applying new skills or capabilities that may not come to full fruition until much later. Thus, product division structures may instill a short-term orientation in divisional managers that, if uncontrolled, could lead to steady deterioration of overall corporate competitive advantage and distinctive competence.

When taken to an extreme, product division structures may go overboard in encouraging excessive internal competition among divisional managers. Since product divisions within the same company are often highly autonomous, their financial performance is easily compared, one against the other, by senior management. Divisional managers may attempt to outdo each other in trying to beat some performance target or goal, particularly when the potential for bonuses and future promotions is based on current divisional performance. This possibility is especially pronounced when division managers know that senior management may sell off divisions of the company that appear to be underperforming. Internal competition may also strongly discourage managers from working together on joint investment activities or "megaprojects" that could help all divisions involved.[9] (See Exhibit 9-5 for a summary of advantages and disadvantages of a product division structure.)

Variants of the Product Division Structure. Many U.S. companies have attempted to modify their product division structures in response to some of the disadvantages noted earlier. Three important modifications involve the use of strategic business units, groups or sectors, and the conglomerate or holding company structure. Related diversification firms tend to use the strategic business unit and group/sector modifications, whereas companies pursuing unrelated diversification tend to rely on the conglomerate, holding company structure.

Strategic business units, or SBUs, represent a collection of individual product divisions that produce related or similar products (see Exhibit 9-6). SBUs are used by related diversified companies such as General Electric, American Express, Citigroup, Motorola, Texas Instruments, DuPont, IBM, Procter & Gamble, and Honeywell International to manage the great expanse of

strategic business unit:
Form of organization that often represents larger product divisions or collections of smaller product divisions under one reporting relationship.

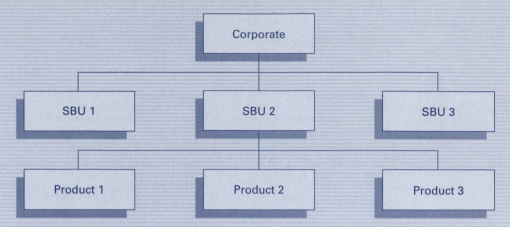

Exhibit 9-6　*Diagram of a Strategic Business Unit Structure*

- The SBU structure is a collection of product divisions that produce related or similar products.
- Supports related diversification because similar products that are grouped together share a common underlying technology, market, skill, or resource.

products and businesses under their umbrella. If these companies were to use a pure product division structure for each type of product they produce, they would have literally hundreds of product divisions that would report to senior management at corporate headquarters. This vast number would make it extremely cumbersome for senior management to understand and monitor what is going on in each business. The SBU concept, on the other hand, attempts to identify and group together similar product divisions that share an underlying common characteristic, such as technology used, customer served, and so on. By shrinking a hundred different product divisions into ten SBUs, for example, senior management can monitor and oversee operations more easily and effectively.

In theory, SBUs attempt to group several product divisions to achieve important operational synergies. First, SBUs can enhance the prospects for sharing and transferring activities between businesses in related diversified firms. Second, by putting together divisions that share similar technological or market characteristics, the SBU form may reduce the potential for excessive internal competition. In turn, skillful use of the SBU concept may encourage divisional managers to undertake joint investment projects that help each division accomplish some objective that it could not accomplish alone.

In practice, though, the SBU concept in many companies has not overcome an important deficiency of the product division structure—that of short-term orientation by managers. Both divisional and SBU managers still face the same intense pressures to perform, as the product and SBU structures make it easy for senior management to isolate and pinpoint financial performance. Even worse, in some cases, the SBU concept may aggravate the tendency toward short-term thinking, since it enables senior management to allocate cash and other resources more easily by dealing with groups or clusters of divisions, instead of many separate divisions working by themselves. Even though the SBU concept was originally designed to help senior managers build closely related clusters of divisions, in practice SBUs suffer from the same potential for short-term thinking that occurs with conventional product divisions.[10]

Groups or sectors occur when companies go beyond the SBU concept to form large collections of SBUs. Sectors are simply groups of SBUs (composed of product divisions) lumped together in a grander unit. Groups and sectors add another layer of management between senior managers and SBU general managers. In effect, they add a third layer of management between the product division and senior management (with SBU and group/sector layers in the middle). They are extremely costly to operate. In the late 1990s, many companies, such as General Electric and Honeywell International, moved away from using groups and sectors for this reason. GE found that this additional layer of management generated enormous administrative, staffing, and overhead costs. Instead, GE relies primarily on the simpler SBU concept to organize its many lines of businesses.[11]

Conglomerate structures represent the last important modification of the pure product division structure. In contrast to the SBU and group or sector organization, the conglomerate structure emphasizes an *extremely lean administrative staff* at corporate headquarters.[12] Companies such as Textron and Tyco International that pursue unrelated diversification strategies use the holding company structure to keep overhead costs low. Conglomerates are often called holding companies in the sense that the lines of business currently under the corporate umbrella can be readily sold to a willing buyer (an advantage for organizing businesses by way of product divisions). Conglomerate firms "hold" these assets until they are ready to sell them. Product division managers within the conglomerate holding company structure are given high autonomy (very decentralized) to run their businesses in ways they see fit. In turn, however, divisional managers are under extreme pressure to perform, especially to provide high cash flow and fast return on investment.[13]

Geographic Division Structures

Some firms operate in a number of geographic regions. For example, many fast-food chains fall in this category, as they must prepare food, serve it, maintain facilities, run local promotions, and perform other activities in many different restaurant market locations. Such firms often find the functional structure and the product division structure cumbersome because they provide for no direct way to coordinate activities within geographic regions. Functional and product structures also do not lend themselves well to developing expertise about what it takes to compete in a specific geographic region. A **geographic division** structure helps firms organize activities operated in many locations. Also known as place or area structures, geographic division structures allow firms to develop competitive advantage in particular regions according to that area's customers, competitors, and other factors. Many organizations use a geographic structure, such as the federal government, UPS, FedEx, and other delivery services. Restaurant chains, grocery stores, department stores, airlines, and other similar businesses also tend to employ geographic structures to organize activities (see Exhibit 9-7).

A geographic structure sets up a separate organizational subunit and management team for each region served by the firm. Geographic structures display a high level of specialization based on the markets the firm serves. If each unit is in close contact with its market, it can adapt readily to changing environmental demands. As is the case with product divisions, geographic divisions also contain all of the necessary functional activities (again, organized in departments) to achieve the company's objectives for that region. Geographic structures encourage rapid change in functional activities to adapt products and services to local markets. Thus, each region possesses its own administrative, marketing, financial, manufacturing, R&D, and other value-adding activities necessary to support a given regional strategy.[14]

Geographic division structures, like product division structures, are extremely versatile. Thus, the practices, procedures, and performance criteria used can vary according to regional

group or sector:
A larger version of the SBU structure that often houses many different SBUs under one reporting relationship.

conglomerate:
Firm that practices unrelated diversification.

geographic division:
An organizational form that divides and organizes the firm's activities according to where operations and people are located.

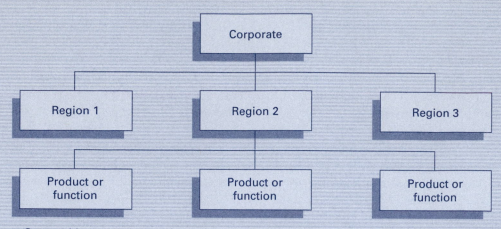

Exhibit 9-7   Diagram of a Typical Geographic Structure

- Geographic structures are excellent in responding to the needs of local, regional markets.
- Geographic structures have their own self-contained product and/or functional structures to meet the operation and marketing needs of that region's customers.
- These structures promote a high level of decentralization.

competitive conditions, as well as the order of priorities senior management attaches to each region. Managers in geographic division structures are evaluated according to the financial targets and desired performance levels for their particular region or market. Consequently, senior management can vary the choice of standards used to assess divisional performance according to market conditions.

One of the most important reasons why firms organize geographically is to get closer to their customers. In turn, this closeness often encourages a high degree of decentralization, with regional and subregional managers enjoying considerable authority and leeway to run their operations. Although senior management may require each region to perform up to some level, it often leaves the details of managing day-to-day operations with regional division heads.

In practice, organizing geographically gives senior management enormous discretion to divide up or to consolidate the various subunits of a geographical structure. Regions may be defined as small subunits, such as the individual counties and states within the United States, or quite large subunits covering entire countries and even continents. Firms can even organize geographically based on similar market characteristics that span regions and continents. For example, a firm could divide up the world according to similarities in tastes, incomes, buying habits, or any combination of demand factors. Consequently, many multinational firms often turn to geographic structures to coordinate their global expansion and operations. For example, until recently, Procter & Gamble organized its operations around the world under a modified form of a geographic/regional structure for similar reasons. Detergents (for example, Liquid Tide) and shampoos often need specific blends and mixtures to accommodate local conditions, such as water hardness and purity, advertising campaigns, pricing flexibility, and distribution channels. Customers in different regions often demand variations in product design (as they do in Ford's automobile business). This feature is especially important when we examine the impact of the various organizational structures on global operations in a later part of this chapter.

Advantages of Geographic Structures. Firms use geographic structures to develop functional capabilities within each region. A geographic structure facilitates timely adaptation of a firm's activities to local conditions without requiring managers to go beyond that region for resources. Organizing geographically can be a major source of strength when firms want to stay closely attuned to customers' needs. A key advantage of the geographic structure is that it puts the firm's operations close to its customers or suppliers. For manufacturing activities, it means that the firm may be able to source lower-cost labor and other supplies to achieve competitive advantage; locating near suppliers has been particularly beneficial for textile and garment manufacturers that have built sourcing operations in the Far East and Latin America. In other cases, locating near the customer means better response and service. Both FedEx and UPS have organized their operations geographically to improve customer service and competitive advantage.

Another advantage of organizing geographically is that it develops extremely seasoned managers who are aware of what it takes to compete in a given region. Geographic structures promote excellent specialization and knowledge about particular markets. Managers of geographic subunits generally reside in the regions they oversee, so they become familiar with local labor practices, governmental requirements, and cultural norms. Such individuals are ideally suited to supervise local operations. Subunit managers in functional and product structures, by contrast, generally reside at company headquarters. They are often less able to provide effective supervision of distant operations.

A final advantage of the geographic structure is its flexibility. Senior management can easily consolidate smaller regions to become bigger ones. Conversely, it is easy to divide up a large region into a series of smaller ones as market conditions change or fragment.

Disadvantages of Geographic Structures. A major disadvantage of the geographic structure is that it duplicates in each geographical region all of the functional activities needed to serve a particular region. Organizing geographically fragments functional activities by allocating a portion of each to a different geographic region. Such fragmentation reduces a firm's ability to achieve economies of scale.

One drawback of organizing geographically is that managers operating in a geographic structure often feel little need to coordinate their actions with managers in other regions. This drawback can be serious if companies need to protect a quality image across regions (as do fast-food chains, rental car firms, haircut and beauty salon chains, and travel agencies). This separation can result in disagreement over objectives between regions and corporate headquarters.

Finally, geographic structures may suffer an important disadvantage when it comes to setting standards for quality and image across markets or regions. For example, McDonald's, Wendy's, Burger King, and 7-Eleven prefer to organize their operations geographically so as to best serve their customers. On the other hand, they also insist that all regional managers and operators produce and serve their products at a quality standard that is uniform across regions. Managers in geographically organized firms may have to develop extensive rules and regulations to ensure quality across regions. For example, Domino's Pizza has numerous rules and procedures to ensure pizza quality, pizza temperature, and driver safety in all regions of the United States. (See Exhibit 9-8 for a summary of advantages and disadvantages of geographic structures.)

Matrix Structures

In a rare number of firms, however, senior management has chosen a matrix structure. **Matrix structures** organize activities along multiple (two) lines of authority. Instead of organizing solely along a functional or product structure, a firm using a matrix structure *requires lower-level managers to report to two bosses.* Matrix structures are designed to help coordinate functional,

matrix structure:
An organizational form that divides and organizes activities along two or more lines of authority and reporting relationships.

Exhibit 9-8   *Key Characteristics of Geographic Structures*

Advantages

- High specialization according to market needs
- High autonomy from other geographic units
- Promotes a high degree of decentralization
- Fast response to market needs
- Highly flexible structure; easy to create smaller geographic units
- Allows for full use and development of local talent/managers
- Excellent support for multidomestic strategies

Disadvantages

- Duplicates functions within each region
- Places coordination demands on senior management
- Needs other support measures to ensure high quality and uniform image
- May not work well in fast-changing, technologically intensive businesses or industries

product, and regional activities across divisions or other subunits. Most U.S. firms using a matrix structure have combined a basic product division structure with that of a functional structure. Thus, two lines of authority and reporting relationships exist: one based on product and the other based on function[15] (see Exhibit 9-9).

Matrix structures became popular during the 1960s and 1970s as aerospace firms found that building new types of technologically advanced aircraft required extensive coordination between functions (engineering, production, fabrication, advanced materials, testing, assembly, distribution) and the product divisions that eventually sold the final aircraft product to specific markets (small aircraft, small corporate jets, large jetliners, specialized military aircraft). Aerospace companies such as Boeing, Lockheed–Martin, and Northrop Grumman have used some variation of a matrix structure to handle the high-tech development activities common with new types of aircraft at some point in time.

Matrix structures work to combine two lines of authority into one system. Thus, all matrix structures require lower-level managers to report to two immediate superiors representing different product, regional, or functional orientations. The term *matrix* came about from the crisscrossing of reporting relationships, as shown in Exhibit 9-9. Matrix structures may overlay a product division with a geographic division, or they may blend a product division with a functional structure.

In most U.S. firms using them, matrix structures attempt to capture the benefits of both the product division structure and the functional structure, while minimizing the disadvantages that are found in each. Matrix structures in their ideal form enable the firm to benefit from specialization of both function and product. The key benefit of using matrix structures is that information flows both vertically (within a given function from employee to manager to senior manager) and horizontally (across managers with comparable rank, authority, and responsibility) between divisions. Matrix structures thus try to remove some of the organizational barriers that impede fast information flow and transfer of knowledge or technical skills between product groups that use a common underlying technology. The ideal matrix organization is one where information flows smoothly and unimpeded between divisions (horizontally) and within divisions (vertically).

Advantages of Matrix Structures. Matrix structures work best when firms confront an environment in which product and technological change occurs rapidly. In addition to the

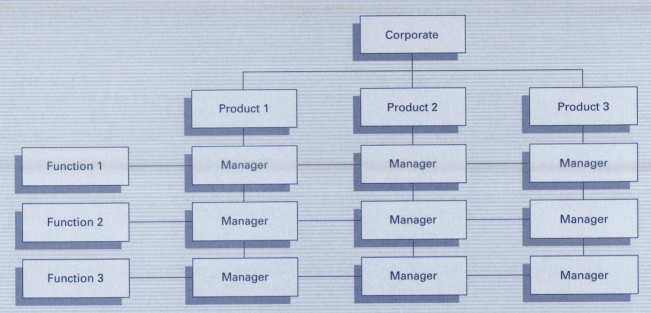

Diagram of a Typical Matrix Structure **Exhibit 9-9**

- Each lower-level manager reports to two bosses—one product division superior and one functional superior.
- Although they promote technology sharing, matrix structures are extremely costly and difficult to manage.
- Matrix structures lost favor over the 1980s; most companies that adopted them ultimately switched to another structure.

aerospace industry, many other industries face such high change, including advanced composite materials, electronics, and communications equipment. Matrix structures also work best when functional resources and technical expertise are scarce but must be spread across product divisions that share a common core technology or distinctive competence.

Matrix structures in their smoothest implementation allow for considerable flexibility of operations, movement of people between formal divisions, and fast flow of technologies from the lab to the final product. Matrix structures tend to work best when they are focused on a particular project that has a time deadline. Senior managers can freely move highly skilled people from function to division and vice versa according to the timetables of specific product development needs. In addition, matrix structures also provide a strong basis for interdepartmental and interdivisional cooperation.

Disadvantages of Matrix Structures. The single biggest disadvantage of matrix structures is that they are extremely cumbersome and costly to manage. If managers do not know how to manage and run a matrix structure, the firm is saddled with the disadvantages of both the product division and the functional structure. From a financial standpoint, a matrix structure imposes high administrative costs because two lines of authority, accounting systems, reporting systems, and other support staff must be duplicated. In other words, a matrix organization would have to support two parallel sets of administrative staffs.

Equally important, matrix structures in practice can actually inhibit fast response and quick adaptability if managers are unable to work in such a structure. Imagine the following dysfunctional matrix structure used in a large electronics firm. The product divisions (or SBUs) operate independently of one another with an excessively short-term financial orientation, while managers in the functional structures jealously hide and restrict their technical expertise from each other and from other divisions. Functional managers will not work with product division managers and vice versa. Information and technical expertise does not flow from one division or structure to another; instead, managers impede information flows to protect themselves. Thus, in the worst case, matrix structures can induce organizational paralysis as managers from individual divisions and functions fail to cooperate. In effect, a matrix structure that is poorly implemented will achieve none of the special benefits for which it was designed, but leave the organization saddled with huge costs and slow responsiveness.

By their very nature, matrix structures are designed to encourage dual loyalties and responsibilities. Matrix structures impose a high human cost on the managers who must report to two bosses. Most lower-level managers who report to one boss or superior generally will have developed the interpersonal skills and ability to work with that person in planning subunit strategy or in resolving conflict and other issues. When the same lower-level manager must report to a second superior (from either functional or geographic structures), then that manager must now deal with two people who have their own personalities, styles, and agendas. Moreover, lower-level managers must balance priorities and assess which of the two superiors is really more powerful than the other. In practice, however, few managers can really handle the day-to-day "balancing act" of working easily across divisional lines.

The disadvantages and high personal stress found in matrix structures often outweigh the advantages. During the 1980s, many U.S. firms outside the aerospace and high-tech industries experimented with using a matrix structure to improve coordination of activities across functions and divisions. Companies such as Dow Chemical, Digital Equipment, Citigroup, and IBM all attempted to adopt some type of matrix structure. Most, however, retreated from it because of the difficulties noted earlier. (See Exhibit 9-10 for a summary of advantages and disadvantages of a matrix structure.)

Special Organizational Structures for Global Operations

Firms using a functional structure group activities by function. Product division structures group activities by product. Geographic division structures organize by region or market. Matrix structures combine two of the other structures (usually product and function) in attempting to gain the benefits of both. All these structures have been used in some form by U.S. firms as they seek to build and sustain competitive advantage. However, when firms seek to expand operations globally, these structures are often modified in varying degrees because of the

Exhibit 9-10	**Key Characteristics of Matrix Structures**

Advantages	Disadvantages
• Promotes sharing of key resources and skills • Enhances fast change and flexibility • Helps when resources are scarce • Allows for transfer and movement of people • High specialization along key activities and products	• Very high cost structure • Slows down decision making in practice • Lower-level managers often unable to feel comfortable in this structure • High tension and stress • Could generate conflict between superiors who are the "arms" of the matrix

market-specific economic, technological, and competitive factors that accompany global operations. Problems of distance and distribution channels, competing in new markets, and different types of competitors arise.

Firms expanding globally often use some variation of a basic organizational structure discussed earlier. They include (1) international division structure, (2) worldwide product division structure, (3) worldwide geographic structure, (4) worldwide functional structure, or (5) worldwide matrix structure.[16] Let us briefly highlight the basic features of each structure and examine how well it supports the implementation strategies of international expansion.

International Division Structures. The international division structure represents one of the easiest ways to organize for global operations. As the name suggests, all of the firm's non-domestic operations simply report to an international division. Domestic operations and sales are separated from foreign operations (see Exhibit 9-11).

Those that use the international division structure most extensively first begin to invest and to conduct operations outside their home country. More often than not, firms using the international division structure have a relatively low percentage of sales from abroad. The international division enables senior management to house all of its internationally seasoned and knowledgeable managers in one unit. This attractive feature of an international division helps the firm achieve a critical mass of knowledge about competing abroad that otherwise might be diffused throughout the rest of the company. Almost every firm in the Fortune 500 at one point or another has used the international division structure when it first ventured abroad.[17]

The most important disadvantage facing the international division is its general unsuitability for managing large global operations. In other words, when a firm's global expansion is successful and becomes a significant portion of total revenues, the international division often cannot handle the huge volume of information and resources needed to conduct and coordinate global operations. Once the firm shifts away from the international division, it usually adopts either a worldwide product division structure or a worldwide geographic structure.

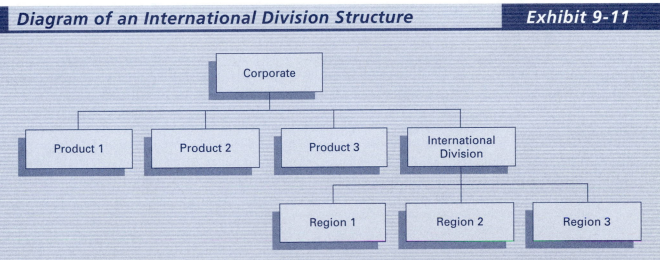

Diagram of an International Division Structure — Exhibit 9-11

- International division structures are excellent to support a firm's early global expansion efforts.
- These structures promote a high level of specialization for overseas knowledge and activities.

Worldwide Product Divisions. Worldwide product divisions are extremely common for firms that have a large portion of their revenues and operations occurring outside their home country. Many U.S. firms use a worldwide product or SBU structure to organize their global operations once they have disbanded their international division structure. The key distinction between a domestic product division and a worldwide product division is that the manager of the latter has global responsibility for all of the division's or SBU's products. This type of structure is especially well suited to the firm that is highly diversified with products that require little modification for the local market. Worldwide product or SBU structures work best in high-tech or scale-intensive industries. Products there often face homogeneous demand characteristics and require little or only moderate customization in local markets, but they also demand state-of-the-art manufacturing facilities and use proprietary technologies or design skills based on expensive R&D costs. The worldwide product or SBU structure assigns key functional activities to products. As a consequence, the worldwide product or SBU structure is best suited for those firms pursuing a global strategy. Examples of companies that have given worldwide authority to their product division or SBU managers include General Electric, United Technologies, and Texas Instruments. Both Caterpillar and Komatsu—two leading firms that produce construction and earth-moving equipment—use a worldwide product structure to centralize pricing to avoid market distortions caused by foreign exchange fluctuations.

For example, Philips Electronics of the Netherlands has steadily adopted a worldwide SBU structure to implement full-blown global strategies in its array of diversified businesses. This structure enables Philips to build critical mass and economies of scale in such related businesses as semiconductors, computers, lighting, compact discs, consumer electronics, and medical equipment. By relying on SBUs with global capabilities and responsibilities, Philips is better positioned to build scale-intensive plants that enable the company to compete with large Japanese firms (Sony, Hitachi, Toshiba, Matsushita) in high-tech products, such as high-definition televisions, semiconductors, office equipment, and home appliances. Over the past ten years, Philips closed down an additional 100+ plants around the world in order to gain even greater economies of scale to compete in newer high-tech markets.[18]

Worldwide Geographic Division Structures. Some firms expanding abroad may opt for the worldwide geographic structure when their overseas operations become a substantial portion of their total sales. Oftentimes, U.S. firms will move from an international division structure to a worldwide geographic structure as a matter of course; senior management breaks up a big, cumbersome international division into a series of smaller regional divisions.

Worldwide geographic structures, in principle, are quite similar to the geographic structures discussed earlier. The primary difference is that distinct parts of the world represent lines of authority, rather than parts of an individual country or region. As may be expected, managers in a worldwide geographic structure have authority for all markets that compose their individual region. The worldwide geographic structure is especially well suited to firms with products that require extensive modification or local production to serve local markets. Thus, worldwide geographic structures are excellent in supporting those firms that pursue multidomestic strategies. For example, Nestlé of Switzerland uses a regional structure to encourage managers to adapt its food, candy, and other nutrition products to local regulations, preferences, and distribution channels found in their operating areas. The high perishability of food requires Nestlé to build production and distribution facilities for its various food businesses in the regions in which they sell these products.

Worldwide Functional Structures. In some companies, global expansion requires few modifications to their existing organizational structure. For example, firms in the petroleum and other resource-extractive industries continue to undertake their same extractive, refining, production, fabrication, and distribution activities, whether mines and refining facilities are located in the United States or elsewhere. Thus, some firms that expand globally will organize their global operations under a worldwide functional structure. ExxonMobil, ChevronTexaco, Royal Dutch Shell, and other petroleum firms use a worldwide functional structure to organize their global operations. The functional structure suits these firms extremely well, since the high level of vertical integration means that senior management must be able to closely monitor and understand all of the activities that contribute to refining and distributing the end product. This structure varies little from the basic functional structure outlined earlier in the chapter.

Worldwide Matrix Structures. In the past, a small number of firms from the United States, Europe, and the Far East utilized a worldwide matrix structure, which blended a worldwide product division structure with a worldwide geographic structure. Firms that used such a structure hoped to achieve low-cost economies of scale with rapid adaptation to local markets. As mentioned previously, the matrix structure is complicated, and it takes talented managers— at all levels—to understand and implement it smoothly.[19] Firms that used worldwide matrix structures attempted to achieve the benefits of global and multidomestic strategies while avoiding some of their disadvantages. The high cost of these structures makes their current use comparatively rare.

Building Global Businesses: Organizational Realignment at Procter & Gamble[20]

STRATEGIC **C**OMPETENCY *in action*

For the past few years, Procter & Gamble (P&G) has realigned its organizational structure to build and sustain new sources of competitive advantage. As a world leader in consumer packaged goods and personal care products, P&G is well known for such products as Tide detergent, Pantene shampoo, Pampers diapers, Crest toothpaste, Oil of Olay facial products, Charmin hygiene products, and Iams pet foods. As a $51 billion company, P&G derives half of its revenues from outside North America. Thus, P&G serves a globally diverse set of customers in many regions, each of which has its own unique competitive and customer needs.

In the 1930s, P&G in the United States created a new type of organization based on brand management. To spur internal innovation, P&G organized marketing teams around each brand and encouraged them to compete against each other. This approach compelled brand managers to think strategically and to learn general management skills. Some well-known alumni of P&G's brand management system include Jeffrey Immelt (CEO of General Electric), Steve Case (America Online), Meg Whitman (CEO of eBay), and Steve Ballmer (president of Microsoft). The brand management structure also facilitated P&G's rapid growth through acquisition during the 1980s and 1990s, because managers can oversee each product line separately from others. During this same period, P&G stepped up its expansion into overseas markets. As sales growth in the United States started to plateau, rising incomes abroad generated steady demand for P&G products.

Managing expansive, global operations became a highly complex task at P&G. To simplify operations, P&G traditionally relied on a regional organizational structure that measured country-based sales and profitability. This structure worked especially well in helping P&G to better learn and serve its customers' needs. For example, Tide detergent is formulated differently in each part of the world according to local water chemistry and other factors. Distribution channels and marketing requirements also vary significantly across regions. However, as the number of P&G products grew, so did the responsibilities of regional managers. By the 1990s, the sheer number of P&G products in any given region or country meant that managers could not really devote sufficient time and resources to managing all of them effectively. There was growing organizational tension in trying to balance regional needs with overall corporate growth objectives.

After a long study of its competitive position, P&G restructured its organization on very different lines in 1999. P&G's reorganization came at a time when the company started facing a smaller number of global competitors. Under an initiative known as Organization 2005, P&G realigned all of its products into global business units. These include global beauty care; global household care; and global health, baby,

(*continued*)

and family care products. Each global business unit (GBU) oversees several product categories that share a common denominator, such as an underlying product development or marketing, or common customer need. The purpose of each GBU is to achieve significant economies of scale and cost efficiencies by ensuring that core innovations are spread rapidly around the world. Previously, under the country-based regional structure, a technical innovation or product concept developed for one region may not spread to another region for many years. With the GBU structure, an innovation will cut across regional lines much faster. With each GBU, P&G has created a market development organization (MDO) that focuses on developing key region-specific skills. People working within a MDO cultivate a deep understanding of specific customer needs, unique distribution requirements, nurturing relationships with local retailers, and working with local communities.

P&G's creation of GBUs and MDOs are designed to achieve a balance between global scale and local responsiveness. Some of P&G's newest products require an increasing amount of advanced science and technology to commercialize. For example, new facial treatments require expensive innovations in surface chemistry, blending technologies, and proteins. Once a key innovation is harnessed into a new product, P&G seeks to launch the product on a global basis to recoup its investment costs. The GBU is organized so that technical innovations and new products are shared across all regions. The GBU is also responsible for decisions regarding product manufacturing and sourcing. Each GBU seeks to develop and produce P&G products in ways that leverage maximum global efficiencies. However, selling a new product requires a sensitive understanding of how customers use the product and purchase it. This means that P&G must rely on local managers and talent to manage distribution channels and to work with retailers to promote the product. The MDO is organized so that P&G's employees are better synchronized with each market's specific requirements. The MDO manages a broad portfolio of P&G brands to meet a wider range of needs for local customers.

It is likely that P&G's newest organizational format will face a significant test as it completes its January 2005 acquisition of Gillette, a leading maker of razors and batteries. Gillette also has far-flung global operations, and it prides itself on its ability use technology to innovate mundane products (for example, razors and blades) into highly profitable, sought-after items. Under P&G's Organization 2005 initiative, both companies hope to combine their renowned fast innovation skills with a powerful worldwide presence that captures more customers in new markets.

Balancing Flexibility and Stability: Moving to a Networked Organization

Rapid technological change, the emergence of new products and markets, globalization, and the need for greater productivity are among the many tensions forcing senior management to make their organizations more flexible. Percy Barnevik, former CEO of Asea-Brown-Boveri (ABB), stated the crux of the problem: "We want to be global and local, big and small, radically decentralized with centralized reporting and control. If we resolve those contradictions, we create real organizational advantage."[21] In both new and existing companies, management is experimenting with a wide array of new organizational formats and management practices. These practices are designed to make firms more responsive and flexible in every aspect of their operations and activities, regardless of function, product, or region. The resulting trend is toward an agile organization that combines the benefits of existing structures while reducing some disadvantages of rigidity and slow responsiveness.[22]

Efforts to achieve both flexibility and fast response, on one hand, and efficiency and stability, on the other, have led many firms to experiment with new organizational concepts. Firms can modify their existing organizational structures to become more responsive and agile at any level or size. In fact, organizations are attempting to become more "loosely coupled" to manage operations. **Loosely coupled** means a deemphasis on relying on in-house activities (vertical integration) to perform every aspect of producing a good or service. In effect, a firm practices loose coupling when it seeks to break down some of the longstanding organizational

loose coupling:
An organization design and structure that fosters a balance between the need to centralize and decentralize activities.

Different Configurations of Broad Organization Designs — Exhibit 9-12

- Traditional Organizations
- Network Organizations
- Virtual Organizations

Emphasis on vertical integration in product, area, functional structures; fosters high stability

Emphasis on high responsiveness and partnering; balances stability with flexibility

Emphasis on extreme specialization; tight focus on one or two key activities

boundaries that separate it from its suppliers, customers, and other partners. Loose coupling is designed to give all parts of the firm more "breathing room" and latitude to work with external entities.

A key facet of loose coupling is that firms are moving away from relying on traditional organizational structures to manage their activities.[23] Instead, firms are relying far more heavily on working with customers, suppliers, and alliance partners to perform many value-creating activities that they once performed in-house. Thus, firms moving toward a loosely coupled organizational format are attempting to achieve a broad division of labor with other firms. This means that firms are becoming increasingly more specialized in those activities they choose to perform. At the same time, they must communicate more frequently with customers, suppliers, and alliance partners in order to synchronize their activities and to share information.

Exhibit 9-12 portrays the extent to which firms can choose to become more or less loosely coupled. On the left side of Exhibit 9-12, firms can choose to perform most, if not all, of their value-creating activities in-house. This heavy emphasis on internal vertical integration means that the firm must coordinate all of its value-creating activities among many subunits. The traditional organizational structures described from the previous chapter provide the basic framework for strategy implementation and reporting relationships among the firm's people. As a firm chooses to become loosely coupled, it can move toward becoming a networked organization, or even a virtual organization that is portrayed on the far right side of Exhibit 9-12. In the virtual organization, the firm is seeking to become extremely specialized in what it does. Often, the firm will perform only one or two tasks and outsource all of its remaining activities in order to keep vertical integration to a minimum. Let us now examine some of the key characteristics of both the networked and virtual organizational forms.

All companies seek to combine the stability and efficiency of their existing structures with a capability for fast response and flexibility. However, relying on traditional organizational structures to attain such a balance is a very difficult, if not impossible, task. Broadly speaking, an increasing number of companies are trying to become "networked" organizations. **Network organizations** are firms that attempt to balance their reliance on performing value-creating activities in-house with an emphasis on becoming more responsive and open to the environment.[24]

Although network organizations still rely on conventional structures to provide the basic architecture of the firm, they differ from traditional firms in several important ways. The three primary characteristics of a networked organization are (1) semipermeable boundaries, (2) reliance on external alliances, and (3) an organizational focus on core processes and technologies. These characteristics are outlined in Exhibit 9-13.

network organization: *Organizational format in which firms try to balance their reliance on performing internal value-creating activities with the need to stay responsive and open to the environment.*

Exhibit 9-13 | *Characteristics of the Network Organization*

Semipermeable Boundaries
- Looser organizational "walls"
- Faster information flow among subunits

Alliances and Partnering
- Divide up the industry value chain
- Specialize among partners

Focus on Core Processes/Technologies
- Specialization along a core activity
- Redefining ways to create value in core activity

Semipermeable Boundaries

Conventionally organized firms employ a strict division of tasks and activities along well-defined functional, product, or geographic lines. Although conventional structures may facilitate senior management's task of monitoring and measuring subunit performance, they tend to isolate individual subunits from each other. Thus, conventional structures create "walls" or boundaries among subunits that slow down information flow and impede the firm's responsiveness to environmental change. Network organizations differ from traditional firms in that their structures have semipermeable boundaries. **Semipermeable boundaries** are designed to open up organizational boundaries to speed up the flow of communication, knowledge, information, and even people throughout the firm. The assignment of tasks, activities, and responsibilities is less strict along functional, divisional, or geographic lines within the organization. Network firms use semipermeable boundaries to keep the subunits of conventional structures more flexible. Functions and divisions are not eliminated; only the walls or boundaries that separate subunits from one another are opened up to encourage faster information flow, thus enhancing the firm's responsiveness to environmental changes and new customer needs.

In the 1990s, Corning Incorporated redesigned its organizational structure to make its divisions more flexible. One of the most important steps in this direction was Corning's move to relax some of the formal boundaries that prevented the domestic product divisions from working closely with geographic divisions operating outside the United States. With its domestic product divisions working independently and separately from geographic divisions, Corning was previously unable to take quick advantage of newly emerging market opportunities for many of its products. In many of Corning's technologically advanced businesses (for example, fiber optics, advanced fuel cells, drug development technology, and LCD glass), fast response to the needs of global customers and low-cost production are necessary to sustain competitive advantage. During the 1990s, Corning's CEO James Houghton spent considerable time and effort convincing product division and regional managers of the need to communicate and cooperate more extensively with each other. Since much of Corning's growth now occurs outside the United States, regional managers located abroad increasingly need the product and technological expertise housed in Corning's domestic product divisions. Corning's senior management has exerted great effort to make its organizational boundaries more semipermeable, thereby significantly boosting the firm's competitiveness in commercializing new products faster for customers around the world.

semipermeable boundaries:
Flexible separations between organizational subunits across which communication, knowledge, and information flow more readily.

Other firms in the United States are attempting similar organizational changes to make their structures more semipermeable. For example, industrial giants Honeywell International and United Technologies have restructured their operations several times throughout the past decade in order to become more responsive to their customers' needs. Both Honeywell International and United Technologies compete with each other (as well as with General Electric) to meet the demanding needs of key customers in the aerospace, automotive, building controls, and industrial equipment businesses. As their customers become more technologically savvy, Honeywell and United Technologies need to be able to "turn on a dime" to meet their ever more specific and exacting requirements. Both companies have "delayered" their organizations by removing the sector and group reporting levels between key SBUs and senior management. Now, more SBU managers report directly to senior management. At the same time, Honeywell and United Technologies are attempting to reduce the functional boundaries that separate R&D from manufacturing and marketing within each SBU to cut down on the amount of time needed for product development.

Reliance on External Alliances

Network organizations also differ from conventional firms by relying more extensively on strategic alliances to become more responsive to external change. Compared with traditional firms, network organizations do not seek to maintain full control over all assets and value-adding activities required to produce a product or service. Thus, network firms do not seek complete control over the entire value chain. They place less emphasis on attaining full vertical integration. Strategic alliances represent a key external dimension of a network organization. These benefits include reduced risks in entering new markets, participating in new industries, learning and applying new technologies, and achieving faster product development. Firms often form networks of alliances to access the distinctive competences and skills of alliance partners. Firms that cooperate closely can divide up value chain activities according to their own distinctive competences and ability to contribute. In many cases, network organizations use strategic alliances as more formal extensions of long-standing supplier–customer relationships. By closely integrating the activities of both suppliers and customers, firms using network organizations have broken down the once-distant (and impenetrable) walls that traditionally kept them separated from their key partners and customers.

Organizational Focus on Core Processes and Technologies

The third key dimension of a network organization is its emphasis on organizing around core processes and technologies. **Core processes and technologies** are the key levers that form the underlying basis of the firm's distinctive competence and critical value-adding activities. The network firm attempts to combine the low-cost efficiency of the functional structure with the high degree of autonomy found in product divisions and the responsiveness of geographic structures.

Core processes are key activities and technological drivers that cut across all divisions, whether based on product or geography. *Core processes are not the same as functions such as engineering, manufacturing, and marketing; instead, they represent a common skill or technology that all of the firm's subunits use in varying degrees to develop systemwide competitive advantage.* Core processes and technologies are cross-functional in nature; that is, they overlay across product development, engineering, manufacturing, marketing, and distribution activities. They become the basis for specializing, prioritizing, and delegating activities within the network firm.

core processes and technologies:
The key levers or drivers that form the basis of a firm's distinctive competence and critical value-adding activities.

Core processes and technologies could include, for example, the cross-docking distribution system that Wal-Mart Stores uses so effectively to compete against other retailers and department stores, the miniaturization and microelectronics skills that Sony uses to produce new generations of consumer electronics and PlayStation video game consoles quickly, or even the satellite and Internet-based transmission networks that FedEx and UPS use to coordinate overnight delivery operations.

Walt Disney Company uses the concept of core processes to organize its Magic Kingdom and other amusement park operations. A core process for Disney is close and friendly customer contact. Disney personnel are taught to consider and treat all customers as guests. All activities within Disney's amusement parks are organized and positioned in such a way that guests are treated exceptionally well. Almost every possible guest need or request has been anticipated in advance: park rides and events are organized around considerations of human comfort and convenience; so are information booths; kiosks that sell ice cream, camera film, and souvenirs; and first aid kits that are located throughout the parks. Disney is customer service at its ultimate. Although every Disney amusement park contains vital functions (engineering, operations, maintenance and repair, sales), Disney's approach to customer service blends all functions into a defining core process. The overriding priority placed on fast and friendly customer service transcends the parochial interests of each of the individual functions. In fact, a growing number of firms from other service industries are studying the Disney approach to organizing its core activities around the customer. By making friendly customer service its core process, Disney lays the foundation for its distinctive competence—providing memorable emotional experiences, or the special "Disney Magic."

The concept of core processes and technologies is not limited to for-profit organizations in industry. Hospitals, for example, are becoming networked organizations as well. Core processes and technologies for large hospitals include intensive care, emergency trauma, burn units, oncology, and specialized treatment centers. The growing use of digital patient records will go a long way in helping hospitals better monitor and track their patients' needs. Information will flow from treating physician to pharmacy to guest services and to billing without the loss of critical data along the way. Digital patient records also will enable subsequent physicians to understand each patient's individual needs without taking a long and detailed patient history with each visit. On the other hand, hospitals are beginning to view certain medical procedures as increasingly noncore, such as routine examinations, day surgery, testing, diagnostics, and even advanced imaging (MRI and CAT scans) techniques that can be performed more cheaply in specialized, nonhospital facilities on an outpatient basis. The massive growth of medical and professional offices in plazas surrounding hospitals reveals the extent to which hospitals have begun relying on physicians and key service providers whose practices and offices are becoming more loosely coupled with those of hospitals' core activities.

Moving to a Virtual Organization

The need for fast response has not been limited to companies that compete in the fast-moving high-tech and health care industries. In fact, many companies in a broad array of industries are finding that they must become even more specialized and focused in their strategies and activities in order to respond quickly and effectively to their customers' needs. Although network organizations can help many firms become more responsive and open to the environment, some firms are choosing to become even more agile in their operations. In the most extreme form of loose coupling, these firms are becoming virtual organizations. In the broadest sense, a **virtual organization** seeks to coordinate and link up people and activities from many different locations to communicate and act together, often on a real-time basis. In many instances, a virtual organization encompasses not only the firm's own people but also those of suppliers, customers, and even alliance partners to create value together. Often, people in virtual organizations will work so closely with suppliers and customers that the firm will have effectively transformed itself into a complex network or web of value-creating activities.

In many high-tech industries, virtual organizations rely heavily on internal computer networks, or even the Internet, to provide instantaneous communications and access to people who may be in many different locations, perhaps even around the world. However, firms do not have to be exclusively in high-tech industries to capture some of the benefits of the virtual organization format. Organizations in other industries or professional fields can still apply the underlying virtual organization concept in order to achieve speed, agility, and fast response. Although firms in many industries will claim "to be going virtual," the precise shape and look of the virtual organization will depend on how it is used in a specific industry. The virtual organization format will evolve to accommodate the particular types of products, services, technologies, and processes that are at the basis for defining what people will do and how their work is coordinated.[25]

The production of movies in the entertainment industry, for example, has long displayed many characteristics of a virtual organization. Filmmakers, directors, producers, actors, agents, makeup artists, costume specialists, special-effects artists, technicians, and lawyers come together from many different companies and agencies to produce a film. Although they are all independent economic entities, they closely coordinate and communicate among one another to produce a film according to very exacting specifications. After film production is complete, these contributors disband and then regroup, often with different people, to produce another film with a different set of actors, producers, directors, technical specialists, and so forth. Thus, the entertainment industry is actually composed of many different specialist firms, each of which is highly dependent on the people, knowledge, skills, and inputs of other firms to create a product that is often beyond the scope and capability of any given firm alone. Working together with people from different mind-sets, backgrounds, expertise, and age groups has become a vital core competence for entertainment-based firms that must undertake such a complex coordination task. At the same time, these firms must stay especially receptive to new ideas, technologies, creative techniques, and market trends that might become the basis for future films.

Thus, the concept of coordinating the actions of people with highly specialized capabilities from many locations to focus on a core task captures the essence of a virtual organization. Such coordination is a complex, ongoing task that places enormous emphasis on effective and open communication. Yet, the concept of a virtual organization is still evolving. Although research on virtual organizations is a relatively recent academic endeavor, the virtual organization does appear to share the following three characteristics: (1) high specialization of knowledge, (2) rapid assembly/disassembly of project-based teams, and (3) ability to interconnect quickly with other firms. These characteristics are outlined in Exhibit 9-14.

High Specialization of Knowledge

One of the hallmarks of the virtual organization is that the firm will focus on one or two core value-creating activities to drive its strategy and organization. In some instances, a firm may choose to become extremely specialized in an even narrower range of activities. Typically, it will concentrate its resources to dominate a central knowledge-driven activity or capability that is a key focal point within an industry. For high-tech firms, activities that are key focal points

virtual organization:
An organizational format that coordinates and links up people and activities from different locations to communicate and act together, often on a real-time basis.

Exhibit 9-14 | Key Characteristics of Virtual Organizations

- High specialization of knowledge
- Rapid assembly/disassembly of project teams
- Ability to interconnect quickly with other firms

include unique software, a distinctive approach to product design, highly refined manufacturing skills, or specialized marketing or distribution skills. In many professional-service industries, firms that utilize a virtual organization format will also become highly specialized, such as the "boutiques" found in advertising and financial services industries, "specialty practices" in different fields of medicine (such as radiology, oncology, plastic surgery), and even narrow specialty fields in law (such as patents, corporate litigation, bankruptcy, estate planning). Thus, building up a distinctive competence in a central knowledge-based activity or focal point endows the virtual firm with strong influence. It can become an important player to influence or directly provide a given product or service to customers in the industry, especially in the earliest stages of the product's or service's life cycle.

Consequently, firms that adopt the virtual organization format must ensure that they continue to invest in upgrading and refining their knowledge base and human capital. Organizing virtually allows firms to compete on agility by learning and applying knowledge rapidly to create valuable products and services. This means that virtual organizations will likely do best in more formative industries experiencing high growth rates and rapid product change. Although specialization and distinctive knowledge gives the firm considerable negotiating power with its suppliers, customers, and other partners, its core competence faces the ongoing risk of becoming obsolete if there are new entrants or competitors that can match the firm's resources and skill level. Moreover, since firms using the virtual organization format will outsource all of their noncore activities, they typically will not have the same size or degree of staying power as compared with larger, more vertically integrated firms if they must conduct a prolonged price war in the industry. For example, the very distinctive offerings of boutique firms in advertising and financial services, as well as the unique skills of physicians who practice in specialized fields of medicine, face potential imitation and even low-cost competition by other providers when their skills and knowledge become much more commonplace within their respective professions. Thus, as an industry or field of practice begins to enter maturity, the virtual organization will face growing dangers of being "outmuscled" by larger firms that will likely compete on the basis of economies of scale as products and services become more standardized. As a result, virtual organizations must ensure they cultivate the kinds of human resource practices that promote innovation, experimentation, and a willingness to take on risky projects. Since the firm's knowledge base almost entirely resides in its people's minds, the virtual organization is only as competitive as the quality and resourcefulness of the people that work in it.

Rapid Assembly/Disassembly of Project Teams

Another important facet of the virtual organization is the ability to assemble people with different insights into project-based teams that work exclusively on a given product, service, or technology. When a given project is completed (for example, developing a new product or process), these teams will just as quickly disassemble. People are then assigned to another project, where they may likely work with another group of people who bring a different set of skills according to what the new project needs. Therefore, virtual organizations depend heavily on facilitating and managing lateral relations among people who bring a different perspective to a project. **Lateral relations** means coordinating work and communication among people who are at the same reporting level within the organization.[26] For example, lateral relations in project-based teams might require people from engineering, manufacturing, marketing, sales, and finance to work together to share information and to communicate freely in order to develop a product or service. Project-based teams in virtual organizations place a high premium on fostering open communications among people from wherever they may be located. However, it is important that the people who work on these project-based teams possess strong interpersonal and relationship skills so that work proceeds smoothly. People with different insights and backgrounds need to be able to work smoothly together and to communicate their views effectively in order to respond quickly to customer demands or fast-changing technologies. This is especially important as project-based teams in a number of industries begin to expand membership *to include personnel from the firm's suppliers and customers as well.* When project-based teams combine individuals from suppliers and customers, they can promote even faster product and technology development and new insights. The interest and use of project-based teams will grow as more firms harness Internet-driven technologies to link up with their suppliers and customers. With the advent of the Internet in particular, project-based teams can very well include people who are geographically distant from one another.

Certainly, the Internet plays a major role in enhancing lateral relations and spawning project-based teams. In fact, a growing number of industries use project teams that actually involve coordinating the work of people who are located around the world. In the software industry, for example, project-based teams will frequently bring together designers and engineers from the United States, India, Israel, and even Russia to share insights in how best to create a new software program. AT&T, Sun Microsystems, Intel, Hewlett-Packard, Texas Instruments, and Microsoft are just a few companies that have organized software development project teams on a virtual basis. Project members work together by sharing their designs and knowledge through the Internet and through videoconferencing that let people communicate openly. Japanese companies such as Hitachi, NEC, and Matsushita Electric are beginning to implement their own versions of project teams that include software engineers from China to accelerate their own product development for telecommunications and semiconductors. In some industries, firms have already become so intricately interwoven with their suppliers that it is hard to separate each party's specific contribution to the design or fulfillment of a total product or service.

Yet, virtual project teams are rising in importance in almost every technical and professional endeavor. Managers, copy editors, and designers in the advertising industry are now relying on highly flexible project teams that are dedicated to serving the needs of a given client. People interact not only within the firm but also with the client through the Internet and videoconferencing to determine which advertising message and copy is best suited for the client. In the aerospace industry, engineers are sharing their designs with key suppliers to assess which types of engines, airframe designs, and metallurgical alloys are needed for next-generation aircraft. Even in the field of medicine, specialty physicians and surgeons are now able to consult and work with one another through the Internet on how best to treat an individual patient's specific condition. The Internet even allows for real-time, video-conferencing of many doctors that can provide their unique insights on one patient's case. Increasingly, patients will be able to request multiple "second opinions" from medical specialists from anywhere around the world. This rising phenomenon is expected to bring a broad array of medical talent and insights ultimately to serve the patient through virtual means as well, and it is becoming an integral part of telemedicine.

lateral relations:
Coordinating work and communications among people who are at the same reporting level within the organization.

Ability to Interconnect Quickly with Other Firms

Finally, firms adopting the virtual organization format need to work and coordinate activities with a wide variety of different suppliers, customers, and partners. Equally important, these firms have to be able to connect and link up with other firms quickly, as well as to adjust easily to different product development time schedules, product development practices, design formats, communication patterns, customer order fulfillment systems, and process technologies. In other words, virtual organization firms must work "seamlessly" with other companies and adjust quickly to their methods, practices, and processes. Using a metaphor from the personal computer and electronics industries, we might even go as far to say that companies using a virtual organization format need to make themselves "plug-compatible" with other firms. Just as a personal computer can accommodate such add-on products as scanners, digital cameras, printers, MP3 players, CD burners, and joysticks to play video games with little difficulty, firms competing with a virtual organization format need to be able to rapidly adjust and connect their skills, knowledge base, and activities with those of their suppliers, customers, and other partners. Virtual firms therefore need to make themselves flexible and compatible with the operational approaches, knowledge bases, and communication patterns of other firms. Thus, virtual organizations are designed to promote faster coordination and communications not only within the firm but also among firms.

Across many industries, we are seeing how companies are using the virtual organization format to become more actively involved with their suppliers, customers, and partners. In the semiconductor industry, many so-called "fabulous fab-less" companies have achieved significant competitive advantages by cultivating their specialized design expertise. Companies such as Altera, Broadcom, Xilinx, and others are leaders in designing next-generation communications chips, but they outsource all of their manufacturing to such Taiwanese chip foundries as Taiwan Semiconductor Manufacturing and United Microelectronics, which in turn do comparatively little product design work. Even pharmaceutical companies such as Pfizer and GlaxoSmithKline are using some aspects of the virtual organization format. Drug companies are phasing out their own internal production of basic chemical compounds that are used in their pharmaceuticals, relying on such companies as DSM Catalytica to produce them. In addition, many drug companies are also starting to work closely with specialized research firms to test and market new drugs. Companies such as Quintiles Transnational and Covance are two specialists that do little else than manage the clinical trials of pharmaceutical companies' drugs in the development pipeline. Even the large automotive companies are beginning to rely on their key suppliers to design and even manufacture major portions of each car or truck's interior. In fact, General Motors has shifted some one thousand of its own engineers to work at the firm's major suppliers. These auto suppliers will in turn begin training GM's engineers and workers to make components that will eventually be assembled in GM's products.

Consider the fast evolution of strategy and organization at Amazon.com. In many ways, Amazon.com has built important sources of virtual advantage (for example, speed, fast response) by way of its modified virtual organization format. Amazon.com owns its own warehouses to stock inventory but prefers to rely on its suppliers and logistics/delivery firms to provide fast replenishment of books, CDs, and videos to fill its customers' orders. Amazon specializes in gathering information from its customers so that it can provide personalized recommendations and solutions to people who visit its website. Yet Amazon does not perform every aspect of its retailing and distribution activities. People at Amazon.com are as likely to work together with the company's suppliers and partners as they do among themselves. Amazon seeks to build close and lasting relationships with a vast number of different publishers, distributors, manufacturers, "brick-and-mortar" retailers, and logistics/delivery firms to ensure fast delivery to customers using its cybermall website. To strengthen its market reach, Amazon fostered the ability to interconnect quickly with other companies who want to become part of Amazon's Internet-based system. One of the major reasons why Amazon.com is becoming synonymous with on-line retailing is because of its expanding capability to serve as the "hub" that links up a growing number of retailers (such as Circuit City, Target, Toys "R" Us, sporting goods firms, clothing and apparel companies) with logistics firms (such as UPS) to ensure speedy fulfillment of customers' orders. Thus, Amazon is able to build significant competitive advantage by way of its central position in a larger web of interconnected firms.

Strategic Application to Cisco Systems

As a giant in the computer networking and telecom equipment industries, Cisco is considered a flagship organization that many other firms seek to emulate. Even those firms in other industries regard Cisco Systems as a bellwether company that is able to respond quickly, and yet grow exponentially.

The evolution of Cisco Systems' strategy and organization is based on its decade-long commitment to applying the latest technologies to enter new communications-based markets. As such, the company has grown very fast by acquiring small, innovative companies that possess promising ideas and enthusiastic people. Cisco's organizational structure during the 1990s emphasized buying small companies and keeping them as "incubators" of new technologies so that newly acquired personnel would have great autonomy to follow through on their product ideas. During its peak period of acquisition activity during the late 1990s, Cisco acquired over twenty companies a year in such disparate fields as optical networking, advanced routers and switches, wireless technologies, and security software. Thus, Cisco emphasized external acquisition over internal R&D to seek growth.

After the telecom implosion of 2000–2001, CEO John Chambers overhauled Cisco's strategy and organization to make the company even stronger. Instead of relying on dozens of annual acquisitions to grow, Cisco started emphasizing internal R&D to create new technologies for new markets. In fiscal 2004, Cisco spent over $3 billion on R&D and maintained over one thousand labs with twelve thousand engineers worldwide. Cisco's organizational structure reflected this change in strategy. In 2001, Cisco began to centralize engineering decisions and activities to better coordinate product development and resource allocation across products. Cisco has also sliced the number of products in its inventory by over 25 percent, thus emphasizing more controlled growth. As a result, Cisco consolidated its organizational structure around larger business units that report directly to the CEO. Chambers now oversees thirteen top executives directly, thus avoiding the need for costly group and sector-based structures. These top executives are also expected to coordinate business planning across business units. This reorganization is especially important, since Cisco now wants to sell to large telephone companies that seek to purchase all of their products and service solutions from one company. Coordinating the activities of many business units is essential to satisfying the needs of such large corporate customers. Individual Cisco managers also began assuming more responsibility to avoid more adding more layers to the organization. Yet, the recent shift towards internal R&D over external acquisitions, combined with larger business units, means that each senior manager must now oversee a much broader range of products.

Even with the economic downturn of the past few years, Cisco tries to stay true to original entrepreneurial roots. Despite its earlier emphasis on acquiring companies for promising ideas, Cisco believes in staying agile. This is why Cisco focuses only on product development and customer relationships as its two core activities. Cisco wants to make sure it stays on the cutting edge of new product design and development activities by cultivating new talent wherever it comes from. Yet, Cisco listens closely and works intimately with its customers to ensure that they receive the best possible technology the fastest possible way. Cisco even regards its best customers as a key part of its knowledge base. Cisco's networking gear and levels of customer service have often set the standard for other competitors to imitate. To preserve its competitive edge, Cisco is building up its own internal R&D capabilities in priority businesses. Yet, Cisco delegates almost all of its manufacturing operations to its partners who are better able to manage this function.

Developing and retaining people drives Cisco's efforts to learn and apply new sources of highly specialized knowledge. This is a key factor behind Cisco's competitive success in growing so fast. Cisco takes careful steps to ensure that it is able to retain the engineers and senior managers when it acquires small companies with promising technologies. CEO John Chambers has always realized that if Cisco is not able to hold onto these key people, then the company's long-term competitive posture suffers. Even with Chambers's fervent belief in Cisco's people, the company was unable to avoid layoffs when revenues declined over 18 percent in 2001. To ease the painful situation, Chambers insisted on rich severance packages for those affected.

Cisco's product development activities focus on using project teams that are able to share and bring together different insights and technologies to create new product concepts faster. Many of Cisco's project teams also include key personnel from its customers, who provide the needed "reality check" to make sure that products are not designed overly complex. This emphasis on working with customers has helped Cisco to grow faster than its competitors. Moreover, Cisco has begun using the Internet as a means to create virtual product teams whereby project engineers from different locations can use the company's internal network to share knowledge and data in order to work on a new router or switch together.

Cisco Systems has purposely designed its organization to be flexible to work together with an ever-expanding array of suppliers and customers. Cisco practices loose coupling by relying heavily on alliances and partnerships to manufacture products and service large customers. Cisco's product design data and ordering systems are closely meshed with those of key manufacturers, such as Flextronics and Solectron. When a customer orders a specific network router or switch, the information is fed directly into Cisco's order fulfillment system through the Internet. In turn, Cisco transmits this information to its manufacturing partners, who respond by informing Cisco when the order is likely to be ready for delivery. In most cases, the manufacturing partner will actually ship the finished product directly to the customer's location, where Cisco personnel will work with the customer to provide installation and support. Cisco believes that its ability to quickly connect with any given supplier of high-tech components is a big advantage that allows it to respond quickly to changing customer needs. In turn, Cisco has begun to work more closely with Ericsson, IBM, and Hewlett-Packard to serve large corporate customers. Alliances help Cisco fill gaps in technology and give Cisco exposure to customers who have worked with IBM for a long time.

No Single Structure Is Perfect

As each organization formulates its own unique strategy, it must select the organizational structure that best fits its implementation needs. However, no single structure is appropriate for all strategies. Even two very similar firms, competing in the same industry with a similar set of products, technologies, and markets, may find that a structure that works for one firm may need some modification in another.

Choosing the right structure is critical because switching from one structure to another is a laborious and costly process. Oftentimes, a structure chosen to support one strategy will become less useful as the organization is forced to deal with new developments, such as changing markets, technologies, and cost structures. For example, in 1999 and 2000, Exide Corporation, a leading U.S. manufacturer of industrial and automotive batteries, faced many of the same organizational dilemmas. Under then–CEO Robert Lutz, Exide moved away from a country-centered organization (geographic divisions) to one that emphasized reporting along different lines of battery products (product divisions). However, this realignment caused numerous problems for Exide. Managers clashed over who would report to whom. More important, managers were confused about how best to meet and satisfy customers' needs. European managers, in particular, had developed close relationships with key automotive customers that spanned many decades and personal friendships. On the other hand, the new battery-centered organization required German and other European marketing managers to transfer their accounts to a new set of managers who reported directly to a superior who oversaw a specific battery line. This caused numerous problems and confusion for customers, who did not know how best to receive help with their accounts. Regional managers lost direct contact with the customers and suppliers with whom they had worked for a long time. On the other hand, product managers now faced the difficulty of attempting to modify battery sizes and power requirements for uses in different regions of the world. Product managers did not have the knowledge that resides in regional managers' minds; regional managers in turn were unwilling to help product managers gain access to their customer relationships. Turf battles roiled Exide over the past few years, and more than half of Exide's Europe-based managers resigned. Finally, the company settled on a mixed geographic/product division structure that attempts to capture the benefits of both organizational formats.[27]

Other companies facing similar challenges in redesigning their organizations include General Motors, which recently realigned its massive organizational structure. For many decades, GM has grown to become a huge global company that develops, produces, and sells cars in every corner of the world. GM's organization reflected this global expansion by allowing regions to enjoy considerable autonomy to design new car models for each market. In many parts of the world, GM's executives coordinated very little of their activities with any other GM affiliate. Even in the United States, GM's Cadillac, Chevrolet, Buick, and Pontiac divisions all acted and performed as separate business units with their own R&D, manufacturing centers, distribution facilities, and marketing plans. Now, GM is seeking to achieve global coordination and centralization of key value-adding activities to lower its cost structure in order to better compete against Toyota, Honda, Renault-Nissan, Hyundai, and other automotive giants. GM is now realigning the entire company by organizing along large, worldwide product divisions that can better share common parts and work together. GM hopes to slice the number of different parts and components that are used across its massive car lineup. For example, engineers in India, China, and South Korea will work with engineers in the United States and Europe to design common parts for the internal subassemblies of future vehicles. By harnessing the Internet, GM hopes to closely coordinate engineers' idea-sharing to build vehicles faster and at lower cost. Just a few years ago, these GM engineers would work only on local projects with little consideration of sharing costs and ideas with their counterparts elsewhere in the company. Now, GM is hoping to build future SUVs using a common platform that will allow the final vehicle to be sold anywhere around the world with simple modifications. In Europe, traditionally autonomous GM subsidiaries, such as Opel of Germany, Saab of Sweden, and Vauxhall of Britain, will now work together with U.S. engineers to construct common engine components that will allow small and medium-sized cars to be built in any GM factory around the world.[28]

GM's search for the right balance of local autonomy and global coordination is something that every large company with worldwide operations has faced. GM's rival Ford Motor Company also underwent a series of major changes in its organizational structure to find the right balance as well. Other companies, such as IBM, Hewlett-Packard, Unilever (Anglo-Dutch), Henkel (Germany), and Sony (Japan), have encountered such issues as well. Throughout the 1990s, all of these firms realigned their product division structures, alternating between an emphasis on achieving stability (greater product standardization, more central control of operations) with faster responsiveness to local customers (less product standardization, greater decentralization of operations). In January 2005, Unilever sought to improve its cost structure by reorganizing and centralizing to promote greater resource sharing among its many business units in Europe and the United States.

Yet, choosing the right structure is a necessary but not sufficient condition to implement strategy. Selecting an organizational structure is much like deciding on the best "architecture" for a building. Architecture can provide the basic design, outline, and shape of the final building, but it requires careful application of mortar to keep the bricks solid and tightly held together. Organizational structure may be thought of as the framework on which bricks are laid into place. In addition, firms continue to experiment with different types of organizational structures to find the right balance between stability and responsiveness. The move to virtual organizational models that implement loose coupling, specialization, and alliance-based partnerships prompts firms of all sizes to focus on what they do best—their distinctive competences and core processes. Yet, changing the organizational chart alone will not result in superior strategy execution. Managers must consider other key aspects of the organization, such as rewarding and evaluating people for their performance, developing a supportive corporate culture, dealing with resistance to change, and instilling new ways for the organization to learn. These are topics that will be examined in greater detail in Chapter 10.

An Overview of Organizational Structure

Obviously, choosing the right organizational structure to support strategy implementation is a complex task. Understanding the differences between various types of structure is essential because each offers certain strengths and weaknesses in supporting strategy implementation. No single organizational structure is suitable for all strategies. Any given strategy requires a particular kind of structure to achieve high performance. Finding the right match of strategy with organizational structure is a key task facing senior management. Securing the right match creates a strong foundation upon which senior managers, lower-level managers, and employees can work together to implement the firm's strategy.

Firms that are small or exhibit little diversification often find the functional structure the best match for their strategies. Functional structures allow for the development of specialized knowledge, technologies, and skills required to support the end product or service. Functional structures also allow senior management to centralize key decisions and to closely monitor the firm's activities. Functional structures also fit the needs of vertically integrated companies, since the stages or activities that make up the final product can be divided and specialized into functional units.

Diversified firms often find the product division structure (or modifications of it) best matched to their corporate strategies. Product divisions offer firms considerable flexibility and specialization concerning products or groups of products. These divisions encourage divisional managers to become experts concerning their products and the technologies behind those products. Product divisions also allow senior managers to isolate and identify key strengths, weaknesses, and the financial performance of each division.

Related diversified firms, or those that attempt to build synergies among their products and businesses, often use a modification of the product division, such as strategic business units (SBUs) or groups and sectors. Unrelated diversifiers are more likely to use a modification of the product division known as the conglomerate or holding company structure. All product division structures (including these modifications) suffer from the disadvantage of encouraging a short-term financial orientation in their managers, which can lead to deterioration of the firm's competitive advantage if senior management is not careful.

Some firms organize their operations geographically because of the need to get closer to their customers. Geographic structures encourage fast response to changes in local markets and tend to be highly decentralized. Companies with large international operations often use a geographic structure.

Matrix structures combine two of the structures already mentioned. Although matrix structures may enhance internal communication and flexibility, in practice they are difficult to apply and costly to operate.

Firms expanding globally use some variation of organizational structure to manage the special conditions of going abroad. Firms in the early stage of global expansion tend to use international division structures. Firms with multidomestic strategies prefer geographic structures to organize their overseas operations, whereas firms with global strategies are more likely to use a worldwide product division structure to support implementation.

Summary

- Strategy implementation is a vital issue because any strategy is only as good as the effort behind it to move it forward.
- Strategy implementation is intimately concerned with building the right kind of organization that can support a chosen strategy.
- One of the most important organizational building blocks that is needed to implement strategy is organizational structure.
- Organizational structure has three dimensions: specialization, standardization, and centralization. The four broad types of organizational structure that companies can use to support their strategies include functional structures, product division structures, geographic division structures, and matrix structures.
- A functional structure promotes company-wide scale in carrying out each functional activity; a product structure facilitates scale in performing activities associated with each product; and a geographic structure promotes responsiveness in operating activities in each geographic region. A matrix structure is a combination of two of the three structures already mentioned.
- These three basic structures—functional, product, and geographic—also promote the firm's distinctive competences in other areas. Thus, a functional structure conserves scarce general management talent; a product structure fosters ability to adapt a company's activities to the needs of specific products; a geographic structure promotes both the adaptability of a firm's activities to needs of geographic regions and the effective supervision of local activities.
- Strategies to expand the firm's operations globally also depend on the appropriate organizational structure. Global organizational structures include international

division; worldwide product, geographic, or functional structures; or worldwide matrix structures.

- Worldwide product structures best support global strategies; worldwide geographic structures best support multidomestic strategies.
- Network organizations seek to achieve balance between relying on in-house activities with an emphasis on become more open and responsive to the environment.
- The three characteristics of the network organization include (1) semipermeable boundaries, (2) reliance on external alliances, and (3) a focus on core processes and technologies.
- Virtual organizations seek to coordinate and link up the actions of people from independent firms to communicate and work together, often on a real-time basis.
- Key characteristics of a virtual organization include (1) high specialization of knowledge, (2) rapid creation/disassembly of project-based teams, and (3) the ability to interconnect quickly with other firms.
- No single organizational structure is perfect for all strategies.

Exercises and Discussion Questions

1. Many companies in the United States have undergone significant restructuring and reengineering initiatives to improve their organizational capabilities. What are some of the drawbacks of traditional, functional structures that have previously been in place in many of these companies, especially those with a growing line of products and services? How well does a functional structure support a company that seeks to diversify into new industries and lines of business?

2. The Internet, e-mail, and other computer-driven technologies have become a powerful set of internal communications tools for many companies. How do you see the Internet's role in helping compensate for some of the trade-offs of conventional organizational structures? How can companies use the Internet to improve the quality and speed of information flow in their companies?

3. Many companies are now seeking to expand their operations globally. Which organizational structures best support different types of global expansion strategies? What are some economic factors and considerations that should influence the choice of organizational structure?

Endnotes

1. Data for the Cisco Systems Strategic Snapshot were adapted from the following sources: "Can Cisco Settle for Less Than Sizzling?" *BusinessWeek,* February 21, 2005, pp. 62-65; "Will Cisco Rewire Asia?" *BusinessWeek,* February 7, 2005, pp. 50-51; "Cisco Gets Internet-Phone Pact From Bank of America for U.S.," *Wall Street Journal,* September 28, 2004, p. A2; "What Makes Cisco Run," *Forbes,* July 26, 2004, pp. 66–74; "The Cisco Kid Rides Again," *Fortune,* July 26, 2004, pp. 132–140; "Cisco's Comeback," *BusinessWeek,* November 24, 2003, pp. 116–124; "Why Cisco's Comeback Plan Is a Long Shot," *BusinessWeek,* May 21, 2001, p. 42; "Cisco Fractures Its Own Fairy Tale," *Fortune,* May 14, 2001, pp. 105–112; "Behind Cisco's Woes Are Some Wounds of Its Own Making," *Wall Street Journal,* April 18, 2001, pp. A1–A8; "How Cisco Makes Takeovers Work with Rules, Focus on Client Needs," *Investor's Business Daily,* November 20, 2000, p. A1; "Cisco Not the Top Choice of Every

Network Builder," *Investor's Business Daily,* November 13, 2000, p. A6; "Cisco Keeps Growing, but Exactly How Fast Is Becoming an Issue," *Wall Street Journal,* November 3, 2000, pp. A1, A12; "Juniper Taking a Fast Route in Its Battles with Cisco," *Investor's Business Daily,* October 16, 2000, p. A6.

2. A recent research study that examined the relationship between different organizational processes with strategies is S. W. Floyd and P. J. Lane, "Strategizing Throughout the Organization: Managing Role Conflict in Strategic Renewal," *Academy of Management Review* 25, no. 1 (2000): 154–177. See also L. J. Bourgeois and D. Brodwin, "Strategic Implementation: Five Approaches to an Elusive Phenomenon," *Strategic Management Journal* 5 (1984): 241–264; J. Galbraith and R. Kanzanjian, *Strategy Implementation: The Role of Structure and Process* (St. Paul, MN: West, 1985); J. Frederickson, "The Strategic Decision Process and Organizational Structure," *Academy of Management Review* 11 (1986): 280–297; D. Nadler and M. Tushman, *Strategic Organization Design* (Boston: Scott, Foresman, 1987); D. C. Hambrick and A. A. Cannella, Jr., "Strategy Implementation as Substance and Selling," *Academy of Management Executive* 3 (November 1989): 278–285. Also see J. R. Galbraith and D. A. Nathanson, *Strategy Implementation: The Role of Structure and Process* (St. Paul, MN: West, 1978), for a discussion of the key issues behind implementation.

Works examining the concept of organizational structure include some of the following: L. W. Fry and J. W. Slocum, Jr., "Technology, Structure and Workgroup Effectiveness: A Test of a Contingency Model," *Academy of Management Journal* 17 (1984): 221–246; C. C. Miller, W. H. Glick, Y. D. Wang, and G. P. Huber, "Understanding Technology-Structure Relationships: Theory Development and Meta-Analytic Theory Testing," *Academy of Management Journal* 34 (1991): 370–399; J. M. Pennings and F. Harianto, "Technological Networking and Innovation Implementation," *Organization Science* 3 (1992): 356–382; D. Miller, "The Architecture of Simplicity," *Academy of Management Review* 18 (1993): 116–138; C. Gresov, H. A. Haveman, and T. A. Oliva, "Organization Design, Inertia and the Dynamics of Competitive Response," *Organization Science* 4 (1993): 181–208; H. L. Boschken, "Strategy and Structure: Reconceiving the Relationship," *Journal of Management* 16 (1990): 135–150. See also M. A. Hitt, R. E. Hoskisson, and H. Kim, "International Diversification: Effects of Innovation and Firm Performance in Product-Diversified Firms," *Academy of Management Journal* 40, no. 4 (1997): 767–798, for an excellent discussion and overview of the impact of different kinds of structural modifications used to implement diversified and global strategies. Also see S. E. Human and K. G. Provan, "An Emergent Theory of Structure and Outcomes in Small-Firm Strategic Networks," *Academy of Management Journal* 40, no. 2 (1997): 368–403.

Also see N. S. Argyres and B. Silverman, "R&D, Organization Structure, and the Development of Corporate Technological Knowledge," *Strategic Management Journal* 25, nos. 8–9 (2004): 929–957; X. Lin and R. Germain, "Organizational Structure, Context, Customer Orientation, and Performance: Lessons from Chinese State-Owned Enterprises," *Strategic Management Journal* 24, no. 11 (2003): 1131–1152; R. Sabherwal, R. Hirschheim, and T. Goles, "The Dynamics of Alignment: Insights From a Punctuated Equilibrium Model," *Organization Science* 12, no. 2 (2001): 179–197; R. T. Keller, "Cross-Functional Project Groups in Research and New Product Development: Diversity, Communications, Job Stress, and Outcomes," *Academy of Management Journal* 44, no. 3 (2001): 547–556; H. K. Steensma and K. G. Corley, "Organizational Context as a Moderator of Theories on Firm Boundaries for Technology Sourcing," *Academy of Management Journal* 44, no. 2 (2001): 271–291; R. G. McGrath, "Exploratory Learning, Innovative Capacity, and Managerial Oversight," *Academy of Management Journal* 44, no. 1 (2001): 118–133; J. Sandberg, "Understanding Human Competence at Work: An Interpretive Approach," *Academy of Management Journal* 43, no. 1 (2000): 9–25; G. Lorenzoni and A. Lipparini, "The Leveraging of Interfirm Relationships as a Distinctive Organizational Capability: A Longitudinal Study," *Strategic Management Journal* 20, no. 4 (1999): 317–338; M. S. Kraatz, "Learning by Association? Interorganizational Networks and Adaptation to Environmental Change," *Academy of Management Journal* 41, no. 6 (1998): 621–643.

3. See, for example, Q. N. Huy, "In Praise of Middle Managers," *Harvard Business Review* 79, no. 8 (September 2001): 72–81. Also see J. H. Davis, F. D. Schoorman, R. C. Mayer, and H. H. Tan, "The Trusted General Manager and Business Unit Performance: Empirical Evidence of a Competitive Advantage," *Strategic Management Journal* 21, no. 5 (2000): 563–576; J. E. Dutton, S. J. Ashford, R. O'Neill, E. Hayes, and E. Wierba, "Reading the Wind: How Middle Managers Assess the Context for Selling Issues to Top Managers," *Strategic Management Journal* 18 (1997): 407–425; C. G. Smith and R. P. Vecchio, "Organizational Culture and Strategic Management: Issues in the Management of Strategic Change," *Journal of Managerial Issues* 5 (1993): 53–70; B. Wooldridge and S. Floyd, "The Strategy Process, Middle Management Involvement and Organizational Performance," *Strategic Management Journal* 11 (1990): 231–241; W. Guth and I. MacMillan, "Strategy Implementation versus Middle Management Self-Interest," *Strategic Management Journal* 7 (1986): 313–327.

4. Numerous classic works examine the concept of structure. Some of them include the following: P. Lawrence and J. Lorsch, *Organizations and Environment* (Homewood, IL: Irwin, 1967); J. D. Thompson, *Organizations in Action* (New York: McGraw-Hill, 1967); D. S. Pugh, D. J. Hickson, C. R. Hinings, and C. Turner, "The Context of Organization Structure," *Administrative Science Quarterly* 13 (1968): 65–105; M. Aiken and J. Hage, "The Organic Organization and Innovation," *Sociology* 5 (1971): 63–82; L. B. Mohr, "Organizational Technology and Organizational Structure," *Administrative Science Quarterly* 16 (1971): 444–459; J. Child, "Predicting and Understanding Organizational Structure," *Administrative Science Quarterly* 18 (1973): 168–185; A. H. Van de Ven and A. Delbecq, "A Task Contingent Model of Work Unit Structure," *Administrative Science Quarterly* 19 (1974): 183–197; H. K. Downey, D. Hellriegel, and J. W. Slocum, Jr., "Environmental Uncertainty: The Construct and Its Application," *Administrative Science Quarterly* 20 (1975): 313–327; J. D. Ford and J. W. Slocum, Jr., "Size, Technology, Environment and the Structure of Organizations," *Academy of Management Review* 2 (1977): 561–575; H. Mintzberg, *The Structuring of Organizations* (Englewood Cliffs, NJ: Prentice Hall, 1979); J. L. Pierce and A. L. Delbecq, "Organizational Structure, Individual Attitudes and Innovation," *Academy of Management Review* 2 (1977): 26–37; J. Hage, *Theories of Organization* (New York: Wiley, 1980).

5. Data and facts were adapted from the following sources: "Thinking Outside the Big Box," *BusinessWeek*, October 25, 2004, pp. 70–72; "It's His Home Depot Now," *Fortune,* September 20, 2004, pp. 115–119; "House Call," *Forbes,* September 6, 2004, p. 93+; "Home Depot's Hardware Warriors," *Fast Company,* September 1, 2004, p. 37; "Home Depot's CEO Led a Revolution, but Left Some Behind," *Wall Street Journal,* March 16, 2004, p. B1, B4; "Great Expectations: General Electric Alumni Find It Harder to Shine," *Wall Street Journal,* May 13, 2003, p. A1+; "Can Home Depot Get Its Groove Back?" *Fortune,* February 3, 2003, p. 110+; "What Worked at GE Isn't Working at Home Depot," *BusinessWeek,* January 27, 2003, p. 40; "Under Revolution: A Hardware Chain Struggles to Adapt to a New Blueprint," *Wall Street Journal,* January 17, 2003, p. A1+.

6. See, for example, A. D. Chandler, *Scale and Scope* (Boston: Harvard University Press, 1990). Also see J. D. Ford and J. W. Slocum, Jr., "Size, Technology, Environment and the Structure of Organizations," *Academy of Management Review* 2 (1977): 561–575, for a discussion of how specialization, centralization, and standardization can differ among basic organizational structures. For a recent examination on the implications of choosing different organizational structures, see the following representative

research piece: K. Atuahene-Gima and A. Ko, "An Empirical Investigation of the Effect of Market Orientation and Entrepreneurship Orientation Alignment on Product Innovation," *Organization Science* 12, no. 1 (2001): 54–74.

7. A landmark work that examines the product division structure is J. Lorsch and S. Allen, *Managing Diversity and Interdependence* (Boston: Division of Research, Harvard Business School, 1973). Also see R. Rumelt, *Strategy, Structure and Economic Performance* (Boston: Harvard Business School Press, 1974).

8. R. E. Hoskisson, "Multidivisional Structure and Performance: The Contingency of Diversification," *Academy of Management Journal* 30 (1987): 625–644.

9. See, for example, M. A. Hitt, R. E. Hoskisson, and R. D. Ireland, "A Mid-Range Theory of the Interactive Effects of International and Product Diversification on Innovation and Performance," *Journal of Management* 20 (1994): 297–326; R. E. Hoskisson, R. A. Johnson, and D. D. Moesel, "Corporate Divestiture Intensity in Restructuring Firms: Effects of Governance, Strategy, and Performance," *Academy of Management Journal* 37 (1994): 1207–1251; R. E. Hoskisson, M. A. Hitt, and C. W. L. Hill, "Managerial Incentives and Investment in R&D in Large Multiproduct Firms," *Organization Science* 4 (1993): 325–341; R. E. Hoskisson, M. A. Hitt, and C. W. L. Hill, "Managerial Risk Taking in Diversified Firms: An Evolutionary Perspective," *Organization Science* 2 (1991): 296–314; M. A. Hitt, R. E. Hoskisson, and R. D. Ireland, "Acquisitive Growth and Commitment to Innovation in M-Form Firms," *Strategic Management Journal* 11 (1990): 29–47.

10. An excellent discussion of the shortfalls of using SBUs to organize global-scale businesses is G. Hamel and C. K. Prahalad, "Strategic Intent," *Harvard Business Review* (May–June 1989): 63–76.

11. "Allied-Signal's Chairman Outlines Strategy for Growth," *Wall Street Journal,* August 17, 1993, p. B4; "Allied-Signal Streamlines into a Startling Turnaround," *Wall Street Journal,* May 20, 1992, p. B4.

12. R. A. Pitts, "Strategies and Structures for Diversification," *Academy of Management Journal* 20 (1977): 197–208; N. A. Berg, "What's Different About Conglomerate Management?" *Harvard Business Review* 47 (1969): 112–120.

13. For example, see "ITT to Spin Off Rayonier Paper Unit, Concentrate on Its Higher Return Lines," *Wall Street Journal,* December 9, 1993, p. A4; "Allied-Signal Agrees to Buy Textron Unit," *Wall Street Journal,* May 13, 1994, p. A6. Also see "A New Mix: Conglomerates Make a Surprising Comeback—With a '90s Twist," *Wall Street Journal,* March 1, 1994, pp. A1, A6.

14. J. D. Daniels, R. A. Pitts, and M. J. Tretter, "Organizing for Dual Strategies of Product Diversity and International Expansion," *Strategic Management Journal* 6 (1985): 223–237. Also see M. A. Hitt, R. E. Hoskisson, and H. Kim, "International Diversification: Effects on Innovation and Firm Performance in Product-Diversified Firms," *Academy of Management Journal* 40, no. 4 (1997): 768–798; S. Tallman and J. T. Li, "Effects of International Diversity and Product Diversity on the Performance of Multinational Firms," *Academy of Management Journal* 39, no. 1 (1996): 179–196.

15. W. F. Joyce, "Matrix Organization: A Social Experiment," *Academy of Management Journal* 29 (1986): 536–561. Also see E. Larson and D. Gobeli, "Matrix Management: Contradictions and Insight," *California Management Review* 29 (Summer 1987): 126–138. An excellent book that discusses how the matrix organization works is S. Davis, *Matrix* (Reading, MA: Addison-Wesley, 1977).

16. C. A. Bartlett and S. Ghoshal, *Managing Across Borders: The Transnational Solution* (Boston: Harvard Business School Press, 1989). Also see J. D. Daniels, R. A. Pitts, and M. J. Tretter, "Organizing for Dual Strategies of Product Diversity and International Expansion," *Strategic Management Journal* 6 (1985): 223–237.

17. W. G. Egelhoff, "Strategy and Structure in the Multinational Corporations: A Revision of the Stopford and Wells Model," *Strategic Management Journal* 9 (1988):

1–14. Also see C. A. Bartlett, "MNCs: Get Off the Organizational Merry-Go-Round," *Harvard Business Review* (March–April 1983): 138–146.

18. See, for example, "Philips Plans to Unveil Digital Videodisc Machine," *Wall Street Journal,* August 24, 2001, p. B7.

19. For a discussion of the use of matrix arrangements in multinational enterprises, see S. M. Davis and P. R. Lawrence, *Matrix* (Reading, MA: Addison-Wesley, 1977); R. Pitts and J. Daniels, "Aftermath of the Matrix Mania," *Columbia Journal of World Business* 19, no. 2 (1984): 48–54. Also see Bartlett and Ghoshal, *Managing Across Borders;* L. R. Burns and D. R. Wholey, "Adoption and Abandonment of Matrix Management Programs: Effects of Organizational Characteristics and Interorganizational Networks," *Academy of Management Journal* 36 (1993): 106–138; L. R. Burns, "Matrix Management in Hospitals: Testing Theories of Matrix Structure and Development," *Administrative Science Quarterly* 34 (1989): 349–368; C. Bartlett and S. Ghoshal, "Matrix Management: Not a Structure, a Frame of Mind," *Harvard Business Review* (July–August 1990):138–147.

20. Data and facts were adapted from the following sources: "It Was a No-Brainer," *Fortune,* February 21, 2005, pp. 98–102; "P&G to Buy Gillette for $54 Billion," *Wall Street Journal,* January 28, 2005, p. A1, A5; "P&G Has Rivals in a Wringer," *Business Week,* October 4, 2004, p. 74; "P&G: Teaching an Old Dog New Tricks," *Fortune,* May 31, 2004, pp. 167–180; "Aisle 9 to Saks: P&G Brings Its $130 Skin Treatment to U.S.," *Wall Street Journal,* March 12, 2004, pp. B1, B3; "Kid Nabbing," *Forbes,* February 4, 2004, pp. 84–87; "P&G: New and Improved," *Business Week,* July 7, 2003, pp. 52–63; "The Un-CEO," *Fortune,* September 16, 2002, pp. 88–96; "Why P&G's Smile Is So Bright," *Business Week,* August 12, 2002, pp. 58–60. Also see Procter & Gamble Annual Reports, 2004, 2003, and 2002.

21. See W. Taylor, "The Logic of Global Business: An Interview with ABB's Percy Barnevik," *Harvard Business Review* (March–April 1991): 90–105.

22. See, for example, "As Orders Slump, ABB Speeds Plan to Cut Jobs, Debt," *Wall Street Journal,* October 25, 2001, p. A16; "New ABB Chairman Unveils Overhaul, Reacting to Rival GE," *Wall Street Journal,* January 12, 2001, p. A16.

23. An excellent research piece that discusses the notion of loose coupling is K. E. Weick, *The Social Psychology of Organizing* (Reading, MA: Addison-Wesley, 1979). Also see an earlier landmark organizational theory piece by M. S. Granovetter, "The Strength of Weak Ties," *American Journal of Sociology* 78 (1973): 136–138.

24. The research literature on network organizations has grown considerably in recent years. Listed here are some representative works that have identified and developed taxonomies or other measures for understanding network-based forms across a variety of settings: M. Zeng and X. P. Chen, "Achieving Cooperation in Multiparty Alliances: A Social Dilemma Approach to Partnership Management," *Academy of Management Review* 28, no. 4 (2003): 587–606; P. Kenis and D. Knoke, "How Organizational Field Networks Shape Interorganizational Tie-Formation Rates," *Academy of Management Review* 27, no. 2 (2002): 275–293; D. R. Gnyawali and R. Madhavan, "Cooperative Networks and Competitive Dynamics: A Structural Embeddedness Approach," *Academy of Management Review* 26, no. 3 (2001): 431–445; R. T. Sparrowe, R. C. Liden, S. J. Wayne, and M. L. Kraimer, "Social Networks and the Performance of Individuals and Groups," *Academy of Management Journal* 44, no. 2 (2001): 316–325; A. Madhok and S. Tallman, "Resources, Transactions and Rents: Managing Value Through Interfirm Collaborative Relationships," *Organization Science* 9, no. 3 (1998): 326–339; J. Sydow and A. Windeler, "Organizing and Evaluating Interfirm Networks: A Structurationist Perspective on Network Processes and Effectiveness," *Organization Science* 9, no. 3 (1998): 265–284; R. N. Osborn and J. Hagedoorn, "The Institutionalization and Evolutionary Dynamics of Interorganizational Alliances and Networks," *Academy of Management Journal* 40, no. 2 (1997): 261–278; K. Smith, S. Carroll, and S. Ashford, "Intra- and Interorganizational

Cooperation: Toward a Research Agenda," *Academy of Management Journal* 38 (1995): 7–23; J. M. Pickering and J. L. King, "Constructing the Networked Organization: Content and Context in the Development of Electronic Communications, *Organization Science* 6, no. 4 (1995): 475–500; K. Provan, "Embeddedness, Interdependence, and Opportunism in Organizational Supplier-Buyer Networks," *Journal of Management* 19 (1993): 841–856; A. Larson, "Network Dyads in Entrepreneurial Settings: A Study of the Governance of Exchange Processes," *Administrative Science Quarterly* 37 (1992): 76–104; C. C. Snow, R. E. Miles, and H. J. Coleman, Jr., "Managing 21st Century Network Organizations," *Organizational Dynamics* (Winter 1992): 5–20; R. E. Miles and C. C. Snow, "Causes of Failure in Network Organizations," *California Management Review* (Summer 1992): 53–73; H. Bahrami, "The Emerging Flexible Organization: Perspectives from Silicon Valley," *California Management Review* (Summer 1992): 33–52; J. C. Jarillo, "Comments on Transaction Costs and Strategic Networks," *Strategic Management Journal* 11 (1990): 497–499; J. C. Jarillo, "On Strategic Networks," *Strategic Management Journal* 9 (1988): 31–41; R. E. Miles and C. C. Snow, "Network Organizations: New Concepts for New Forms," *California Management Review* (Spring 1986); B. Kogut, W. Shan, and G. Walker, "Competitive Cooperation in Biotechnology: Learning Through Networks?" in *Networks and Organizations: Structure, Form and Action,* eds. N. Nohria and R. Eccles (Boston: Harvard Business School Press, 1993), 348–365; A. Larson, "Network Dyads in Entrepreneurial Settings: A Study of the Governance of Exchange Relationships," *Administrative Science Quarterly* 37 (1992): 76–104; W. E. Baker, "Market Networks and Corporate Behavior," *American Journal of Sociology* 96 (1990): 589–625; G. Walker, "Network Position and Cognition in a Computer Software Firm," *Administrative Science Quarterly* 30 (1985): 103–130; R. G. Eccles and D. B. Crane, "Managing Through Networks in Investment Banking," *California Management Review* 30, no. 1 (1987): 176–195.

25. A growing amount of research interest is beginning to flourish on virtual organizations. Some of the more representative research pieces include the following: M. L. Maznevski and K. M. Chudoba, "Bridging Space over Time: Global Virtual Team Dynamics and Effectiveness," *Organization Science* 11, no. 5 (2000): 473–492; G. DeSanctis and P. Monge, "Communication Processes for Virtual Organizations," *Organization Science* 10, no. 6 (1999): 693–704; M. K. Ahuja and K. M. Carley, "Network Structure in Virtual Organizations," *Organization Science* 10, no. 6 (1999): 741–757; R. Kraut, C. Steinfield, A. P. Chan, B. Butler, and A. Hoag, "Coordination and Virtualization: The Role of Electronic Networks and Personal Relationships," *Organization Science* 10, no. 6 (1999): 722–740; H. W. Volberda, "Toward the Flexible Form: How to Remain Vital in Hypercompetitive Environments," *Organization Science* 7 (1996): 359–374; R. Benjamin and R. Wigand, "Electronic Markets and Virtual Value Chains on the Information Superhighway," *Sloan Management Review* 35 (1995): 62–72; H. C. Lucas and J. Barudi, "The Role of Information Technology in Organizational Design," *Journal of Management Information Systems* 10 (1994): 9–23.

    A book that examines the competitive dimension of virtual organizations is S. Goldman, R. Nagel, and K. Preiss, *Agile Competitors and Virtual Organizations: Strategies for Enriching the Customer* (New York: Van Nostrand Reinhold, 1995).

26. See, for example, R. T. Keller, "Cross-Functional Project Groups in Research and New Product Development: Diversity, Communications, Job Stress and Outcomes," *Academy of Management Journal* 44, no. 3 (2001): 547–556; K. Lovelace, D. L. Shapiro, and L. R. Weingart, "Maximizing Cross-Functional New Product Teams' Innovativeness and Constraint Adherence: A Conflict Communications Perspective," *Academy of Management Journal* 44, no. 4 (2001): 779–793; R. Reagans and E. W. Zuckerman, "Networks, Diversity and Productivity: The Social Capital of Corporate R&D Teams," *Organization Science* 12, no. 4 (2001): 502–517; I. Bouty, "Interpersonal and Interaction Influences on Informal Resource Exchanges Between R&D

Researchers Across Organizational Boundaries," *Academy of Management Journal* 43, no. 1 (2000): 50–65; K. Kusunoki, I. Nonaka, and A. Nagata, "Organizational Capabilities in Product Development of Japanese Firms: A Conceptual Framework and Empirical Findings," *Organization Science* 9, no. 6 (1998): 699–718. Also see J. Lipnack and J. Stamps, *Virtual Teams: Researching Across Space, Time and Organizations with Technology* (New York: Wiley, 1997); D. Denison, S. L. Hart, and J. Kahn, "From Chimneys to Cross-Functional Teams: Developing and Validating a Diagnostic Model," *Academy of Management Journal* 39, no. 5 (1996): 1005–1023; M. D. Aldridge and P. M. Swamidass, *Cross-Functional Management of Technology* (Chicago: Irwin, 1996).

27. See "Place vs. Product: It's Tough to Choose a Management Model," *Wall Street Journal,* June 27, 2001, pp. A1, A4.

28. See "Reversing 80 Years of History, GM Is Reining in Global Fiefs," *Wall Street Journal,* October 6, 2004, p. A1.

Chapter 10

Organizing and Learning to Sustain Advantage

Chapter Outline

What you will learn

- *The concept of organization design practices*

- *The broad types of reward systems used by many companies*

- *How corporate culture can contribute to competitive advantage*

- *The dangers of relying too long on established organizational practices and corporate cultures*

- *The concept of a learning organization*

- *The key practices found in learning organizations*

- *Why static organizations have difficulty in responding to change*

- *The steps senior managers use in dealing with resistance to change*

Strategic Snapshot

The Transformation of General Electric[1]

As America's largest company, General Electric has always been considered a bellwether of the entire U.S. economy. If there has been one company over the past two decades that has instilled the idea of making perpetual change an integral part of its corporate culture, it is General Electric—especially under the leadership period of CEO John "Jack" Welch (1981–2001). As of January 2005, General Electric is America's most valuable company, as defined by its market capitalization exceeding $370 billion. Investors have long viewed GE very positively as CEO Welch implemented aggressive actions to ensure that GE remains agile, lean, and noncomplacent about its competition. Yet, the transformation of GE took well over twenty years and is continuing today.

Early Years

boundaryless organization:
An organization design in which people can easily share information, resources, and skills across departments and divisions.

Before Jack Welch took over as CEO in 1981, GE was profitable and grew slowly each year. Its home appliances, aircraft engines, lighting, plastics, consumer electronics, and motors businesses, for example, were largely mature, profitable, and ripe for global competition. Each business unit was finely attuned to competing in its own environment, with competition and technology fairly predictable and stable. General Electric was regarded as a venerable leader of U.S. industry, although each of its businesses faced rising undercurrents of major change. In consumer electronics, new rivals from Japan meant fierce, price-based competition for GE's televisions. The home appliances and lighting businesses generated significant cash, but growth opportunities in the United States remained few. GE's factories were underproductive and management layers were thick. This meant that there was very little incentive for people to change.

Jack Welch was a rising star that came from one of GE's newer businesses—plastics. Unlike other CEOs who traditionally came from the power generation or other traditional business lines, Welch was also younger than most CEOs. He ascended to the CEO position at age forty-two. More important, he brought an intensely competitive personal spirit to the job. During his tenure, Welch would fundamentally rewrite the way that GE would compete and grow. Exhibit 10-1 shows the implementation of numerous changes that have pushed GE more toward a learning organization.

Becoming Boundaryless

One of Welch's first steps was to make GE a "boundaryless" organization. A **boundaryless organization** means that people in one department or division talk with people in other departments/divisions to share ideas, resources, and insights. In its most ideal form, a boundaryless organization encourages people to learn from one another, no matter where they may be located within or outside the organization. Welch fervently believed that people should be free to learn and adapt the best ideas to improve their businesses. These ideas can come from people from other levels or places within the organization (internally), or from customers, suppliers, and even competitors (externally). A boundaryless organization means that people should be willing to listen and implement new ways of doing things, no matter where they originated.

Corporate Transformations in the 1990s: Making General Electric Boundaryless

Exhibit 10-1

1980	1986	1988–1992	1994 →
• GE vulnerable to change	• Reduce number of peripheral businesses	• Form strategic alliances	• Reduce SBU walls even more
• Slow growth	• Sell nonperforming assets	• "Work Out"	• Invest in Asia/Europe
• Average earnings	• Break down strong SBU lines	• Team with suppliers/ customers	• Foster continual training and development
• Big bureaucracy	• Acquire strong performers elsewhere	• Share knowledge and skills across GE's SBUs	• Encourage best practices and benchmarking
• High divisional walls	• Delayer management hierarchies	• Promote those who take risks	• Productivity focus
• Lots of protected turf	• Adopt new reward systems	• Invest in streamlined product development time	• Promote common vision
• Resistance to change			• Emphasize service businesses
			• Hire people with entrepreneurial tendencies
			• Healthcare push
			• "Six Sigma"
			• Streamline reporting structures

Removing or reducing formal department-divisional boundaries is an important first step in becoming a learning organization. Welch believed that making GE boundaryless would pave the way to building an organization that could change faster and begin to learn new skills. Welch needed to uproot and replace deeply ingrained practices and habits that inhibited change. To accomplish his goal, Welch dissolved many layers of management that separated employees from managers and each other. Some of the directives that Welch and his team took during the early 1980s resulted in large layoffs; the business press started calling the CEO "Neutron Jack" for his massive firings that left GE significantly depopulated in many business units.

Number One or Number Two

Welch demanded high performance from every GE business. Despite heavy criticism, Welch moved to make each GE business unit much leaner and more agile over time. Each GE business was expected to become either "number one or number two" in its respective industry. Those businesses that could not make the cut were sold. Even such well-known businesses as consumer electronics, small appliances, industrial controls, and broadcasting equipment were eventually divested. During his first four years as CEO, Welch sold off over a hundred different GE businesses—all of them slow growers or unprofitable. By selling some of the businesses that served as icons of the old GE, Welch sent a very clear message that no business is sacred or immune from the need to change.

At the same time, GE acquired numerous other companies that helped each surviving GE business attain a number one or two position in its industry. For example, in 1986 GE completed the acquisition of RCA, a leading industrial and broadcasting company that also owns the NBC network. Since Welch took over, GE has made hundreds of acquisitions, usually of smaller companies, to bolster GE's growth rate and market share. Despite frequent communications to managers and employees that GE needed to change, Welch faced a difficult road. His efforts initially encountered significant resistance from lower-level managers who feared that change would erode their power bases. Many veteran GE managers left; others were asked to join management development programs designed to convince them of the need to change.

Training New Leaders

Welch later instituted other practices designed to enhance the firm's capacity for change. These include extensive managerial rotation and training programs to promote openness and idea exchange at all levels of the company. The company maintains an executive and employee development facility in Crotonville, New York. Every day, GE managers and employees enter courses and other training programs designed to keep them aware of environmental developments and the need to change. In the late 1980s, General Electric instituted a company-wide program known as "Work Out." Everyone is encouraged to participate in an ongoing internal overhaul of the company to locate and remove hidden inefficiencies and wasteful practices. People with the best and most workable suggestions are given authority to implement their recommendations.

To this day, General Electric is still working to make continuous learning and improvement a key part of its organizational practices. Since 1995, GE has greatly expanded the Work Out concept to further empower and encourage all of its employees and managers to identify and isolate what they believe to be inefficient or wasteful practices that detract from the company's profitability. With even newer quality management techniques available, GE is now in the midst of a massive quality improvement program known as "Six Sigma." Using a program that is similar to Motorola's own quality initiative, GE is attempting to revamp all of its operations and core processes to promote those practices that best support and improve quality. The objective of Six Sigma is to identify and eliminate all sources of waste, thus unleashing even greater improvements in quality and productivity. Every GE employee is expected to undergo a series of classes regarding Six Sigma, until he or she graduates with a "black belt" in process improvement. By training and allocating resources to its Six Sigma program throughout the company, GE has been able to locate and remove "hidden factory" after "hidden factory" that represented underused equipment or inefficient procedures that detracted from full-capacity utilization. According to the company, each hidden factory thus represented a source of capital or asset base that was not previously used to its fullest extent. In effect, GE's reengineering and Six Sigma program enabled the company to save capital expenditures and to squeeze much more productivity out of its existing assets. Six Sigma has attained an almost religion-like status throughout GE.

Going Abroad and Focusing on Services

During the late 1990s, Welch pushed GE to become much more aggressive in its efforts to expand into new markets around the world, as well as into new service-based businesses. Since 1998, GE has placed a high priority on investing in Asia, with the explicit goal of making Asian consumers aware of GE's wide range of quality products and services, especially in Japan. GE Capital has purchased important financial assets in Japan. GE also purchased its joint venture partner Tungsram of Hungary to solidify its lighting business in Eastern Europe. GE initiated many strategic alliances with European and Far Eastern firms to enter new markets across all of GE's businesses. At the same time, GE is moving to expand its service-based businesses to bolster the profitability of its traditional business lines. GE wants to further differentiate itself from competitors by using new technology to offer exceptional value and skills to its customers. Such GE businesses as aircraft engines, medical systems, power systems, lighting, plastics, and transportation systems are moving to become even closer to their customers by setting up service operations directly on their customers' sites. GE believes it can earn customers' loyalty and future business by offering in-depth, fast, ongoing services that complement its traditional manufacturing expertise. In GE Healthcare for example, the business unit invested heavily in new computer and database systems that make storing and retrieving digital patient records much easier for hospitals and other care providers. GE's Healthcare unit continues to develop hospital-wide information systems that help them to reduce their own costs and improve their patient responsiveness and productivity. GE hopes to use new technology to improve the productivity of its customers and therefore capture more of their business. In another example of this service focus, GE Transportation Systems is now beginning to work closely with the largest railroad companies in the United States (for example, Union Pacific, Burlington Northern Santa Fe, CSX, Norfolk Southern) to provide immediate and on-site maintenance and repair work for their locomotives.

The Post-Welch Era: GE Under Jeffrey Immelt

In September 2001, Jack Welch retired from his CEO position at General Electric after twenty years of service. His replacement, forty-five-year-old Jeffrey R. Immelt from GE Healthcare, faced an even more challenging task. Under Welch's stewardship, GE grew its earnings from $1.5 billion

in 1980 to $12.7 billion in 2000. Revenues since 1981 also quintupled to $130 billion. When Welch took over in 1981, GE's market capitalization was $13 billion (the nation's seventh most valuable company at the time). By early 2002, GE was worth over $400 billion. An economic recession took root in the United States at the same time that Immelt became CEO. Numerous questions surrounded Immelt as to what he would do to sustain Welch's legendary performance. Before assuming the CEO's job, Immelt had already shown that he could lead change at GE Healthcare (formerly known as GE Medical Systems). Under his leadership, the business unit made dozens of acquisitions and introduced many new products. Immelt was also well known for being a "high contact person" with customers and employees.

Now, CEO Immelt wants to continue transforming GE's businesses with an even greater focus on technology and services. In 2002, he consolidated the lighting and appliances businesses into one unit. A newly formed GE Transportation unit now holds both locomotives and aircraft engines. Welch's former GE Plastics unit now oversees advanced materials (such as high-energy ceramics, silicon, diamonds). Immelt considers it his primary task at GE to promote the development of new ideas. Perhaps most important, Immelt realizes that GE now lives in a world with much more volatility and higher risks. Consequently, Immelt has now greatly expanded GE's R&D efforts, both in the United States and around the world. New GE laboratories are now found in India, China, and Germany that will work on hydrogen fuel cells and even advanced medical treatments. Under Welch's reign, R&D focused on small projects that offered a quick return. Under Immelt, R&D will undertake bigger, bolder projects that offer much greater payoffs over the long term. Even though Immelt is undoing some of Welch's earlier emphasis on faster return projects, Welch himself has even acknowledged that GE needs to invest more in its future in order to grow.

Immelt has already begun to make an imprint on GE. While continuing his predecessor's zealous use of Six Sigma to improve quality and productivity, Immelt is also trying to reach out further to GE's customers. Under a company-named program known as "At the Customer, For the Customer," GE will develop best practices to improve its operations and share them directly with its customers. Immelt believes that the more successful GE's customers are, the more successful GE will be. In addition, Immelt has pushed to make everyone answer exactly what he or she has done to serve customers lately. He often gets deeply involved with his customers through personal visits. Immelt believes in personally updating employees each week about GE's latest developments—new products developed, missed opportunities, nuggets for new ideas—through the company's internal e-mail system. E-mail is sent in five languages, sometimes even a dozen, to ensure that it reaches everybody around the world in GE's vast empire.

In April 2004, Immelt led the effort to acquire U.K.-based Amersham PLC, a global leader in the field of medical diagnostics and protein separation systems for $10.3 billion. Amersham is best known for "contrast agents," which are injected into the body to enhance the image of organs during medical scans. Amersham's expertise complements GE Healthcare's leading market position in medical equipment such as PET, MRI, and CT scanners. The acquisition of Amersham sent an important message throughout GE on another front. To signify the company's deep commitment to promoting globalization, innovation, and technological leadership, CEO Immelt made the head of Amersham, Sir William Castell, a vice-chairman of GE. Castell will now share that title with Robert Wright and Dennis Dannerman, who are considered the "wise men" of GE and served the longest time with Jack Welch.

Alumni of GE

An enduring legacy of Jack Welch is the growing number of former GE managers who now preach and practice many of these same ideas at other companies. For example, in 1991 Lawrence Bossidy, a former GE vice-chairman, took over the reigns at Allied-Signal, an industrial conglomerate that eventually purchased Honeywell in 1999. Under his leadership through 2002, Bossidy became the CEO of both companies under the Honeywell International name and insisted that each Honeywell manager train a group of leaders for that business. Executive search firms actively seek to hire away dozens of top GE managers each year for companies in every industry that seek to reinvent themselves in the way that GE did. These ex-GE managers are now transforming other companies. The choice of Jeffrey Immelt as new CEO of General Electric led to an exodus of many leading GE managers who competed for the top job. In turn, however, these ex-GE alumni are now beginning to transform the companies that hired them in mid-2001. For example, firms such as Albertsons, The Home Depot, 3M, and Conseco now have their own CEOs who once worked closely with Welch to transform GE for much of the 1990s. All of these managers are now committed to making their companies leaders in their respective industries by instilling many of the same practices they pushed forth at GE.

Organization Design Practices

organization design practices:
Support mechanisms that facilitate the implementation of a strategy within the framework of a given structure.

Organizational structure provides the "architecture" for executing a firm's strategy. However, "architecture" alone is insufficient. Effective strategy execution also depends on ensuring that the right kind of mortar holds the bricks together. The nature of this "mortar" is known as organizational design practices. **Organization design practices** are the means by which a firm implements strategy within the framework of its structure. A growing number of companies are making important modifications to their organization design practices to respond more effectively to changes in their competitive environments. Organization design practices will be found in any firm—no matter if it relies on a traditional organizational structure, a networked

| *Some Key Organization Design Practices* | *Exhibit 10-2* |

Reward and Performance Evaluation Systems
- Hierarchy-based systems
- Performance-based systems
- Impact on corporate performance

Shared Values and Corporate Culture

organization form, or a virtual organization form. Although every structure gives rise to its own set of tradeoffs, organization design practices possess the ability to work around some of their disadvantages. In well-managed companies, senior management can use effective design practices to enhance decision making, information flow, and smoother strategy implementation.

Many kinds of design practices are used to supplement organizational structure. Some of the most important design practices include reward and performance evaluation systems, and shared values and corporate culture (see Exhibit 10-2). In the next sections, we explore these key organization design practices. Collectively, they represent the mortar that seals together the organization so that it can fully implement its strategy.

Reward and Performance Measurement Systems

A firm's reward system represents a powerful means of implementing strategy. The reward system defines the relationship between the firm and its employees by specifying the values and behaviors it desires from them. Reward systems in many cases are even more effective design tools than organizational structures to enhance desired performance. A company's reward system addresses the following two questions: What behaviors, practices, and outcomes should be rewarded? What should be the type and amount of our rewards? Strategy and reward systems should be designed to work in tandem to produce high performance. The firm benefits from the collective efforts of its people when each individual knows what to do and how he or she will be rewarded. The two major kinds of reward systems are *hierarchy based* and *performance based*.[2]

Hierarchy-Based Systems

The hierarchy-based system puts a premium on the supervisor's subjective evaluation of the subordinate's performance. Numerous qualitative factors, such as team performance, cooperation with other people or units, long-term relationships with suppliers and customers, joint efforts and projects among people and divisions, and personal management styles and abilities, are often just as important as quantitative measures of performance, such as return on investment (ROI), production volume, or market share (see Exhibit 10-3).

Close Superior–Subordinate Relationship. The most important characteristic defining the hierarchy-based reward system is the relationship between superior and subordinate. The hierarchy-based system measures individual performance at a specified time interval, usually every year. These measures of performance contain both quantitative aspects and subjective, qualitative judgments made by superiors. Employees are informed of their performance,

Exhibit 10-3	Reward Systems: Key Characteristics of a Hierarchy-Based System

- Close superior-subordinate relationships
- Extensive use of subjective and objective criteria to measure performance
- Superiors will guide the career and actions of subordinates
- Emphasis on group and team efforts and results
- Emphasis on long-term thinking and actions that help the organization
- Supports differentiation strategies at the business unit level
- Supports related diversification and global strategies at corporate and business levels

socialization:
The process by which shared values and ways of behaving are instilled in new managers and employees.

usually in the form of both formal feedback from the superior, as well as informal comments throughout the given time period. Often, superiors will take on the role of a mentor. Superiors will guide the career paths and steps of their subordinates to ensure that all employees know how best to implement the firm's strategy. Managers using hierarchy-based reward systems will often take advantage of their continuing contact with subordinates to transmit and teach the firm's key values and ideals. In this sense, hierarchy-based reward systems, by fostering close superior–subordinate contact, are excellent vehicles to transmit core organizational values and ideals to all employees. **Socialization,** or the process of instilling core values and beliefs in people, is a natural outcome of the hierarchy-based reward system. People in hierarchy-based reward systems often strongly identify with the organization. They feel that their efforts to work across formal organizational boundaries are recognized and rewarded.

Emphasis on Group or Team Efforts. Hierarchy-based reward systems place a great premium on group efforts and results, as opposed to individual results, in assigning bonuses and promotions. Often, corporate- or systemwide performance measures are given considerable weight in devising the formula for allocating individual bonuses. The hierarchy-based system considers team-based efforts and team output as primary benchmarks in assigning rewards and emphasizes the crucial nature of a long-term perspective, systemwide thinking, and coopera-tion. Hierarchy-based systems, because of their reliance on close superior–subordinate relation-ships and preference for team-based performance measures, tend to promote managers from within the firm.

For many years, IBM has relied on hierarchy-based reward systems and socialization to help managers and employees improve their ability to work across formal divisional lines. IBM has en-couraged its sales personnel to understand the role of how different IBM products work together to produce a "solution" for a given corporate customer. This broader view of understanding the customer requires the cooperation of many divisional and product managers to coordinate their efforts closely. Thus, IBM has traditionally placed a great premium on rewarding team-based efforts that promote close working relationships among people from different divisions.

Link with Strategies. Within a business unit or single-business firm, hierarchy-based sys-tems tend to work best in firms practicing differentiation. Differentiation strategies that put a strong premium on high quality, solid marketing skills, creative flair, and highly innovative en-gineering require people who can work together. At companies such as Black & Decker, Cross Pens, or Citizen Watch, joint projects often cut across functions. Technological or quality-based leadership demands people who can perform under a variety of conditions and can cooperate closely with suppliers and customers. The subjective evaluation criteria of hierarchy-based reward systems encourage these attributes. Quality, engineering, and other marketing tasks often do not lend themselves well to strict, concrete measures of output. Moreover, quality-based strategies take time to develop and implement. Differentiation strategies need a longer-term outlook than do low-cost strategies, which tend to emphasize strict cost controls and a rigidly standardized approach to managing operations.

Hierarchy-based reward systems are also helpful for firms implementing related diversification and global strategies. Related diversifiers, such as 3M, Nokia, and many other electronics firms, need to ensure that their different subunits (divisions or SBUs) organize their activities around a crucial distinctive competence or central technology. To nurture the success of related diversification, senior management often uses a hierarchy-based reward system to ensure that managers and employees are rewarded for efforts that span across divisions or SBUs. In other words, related diversifiers need to make sure their managers and employees have sufficient incentive to think and act in ways that promote systemwide competitive advantage. Hierarchy-based reward systems are designed to promote cooperation across business units. These systems have worked well for such successful related diversifiers as DuPont, Dow Chemical, H. J. Heinz, IBM, and Motorola.

Firms that implement global strategies also tend to use a hierarchy-based reward system. Recall that global strategies require firms to coordinate subsidiaries and subunits tightly, no matter where they are located. The hallmarks of a global strategy, such as product standardization, economies of scale, and cross-subsidization, all require a reward system that promotes systemwide, global thinking. Companies using a hierarchy-based system to support their global strategies include Boeing, Pfizer, Novartis, Merck, Toyota, Matsushita Electric, Whirlpool, and Sony. Many European industrial and financial giants have long used a hierarchy-based system to promote people from within and to transfer them across subsidiaries across different parts of the world. Such companies include Allianz, Deutsche Bank, Nestlé, Philips Electronics, and Unilever. The strong emphasis on teamwork, joint tasks and efforts across subunits, and close superior–subordinate relationships in hierarchy-based systems support the global strategy well.

Performance-Based Systems

The alternative to a hierarchy-based reward system is a performance-based system. As the name suggests, the performance-based reward system puts a great premium on quantitative measures of performance, such as ROI and market share. In contrast to the hierarchy-based reward system, the performance-based system assigns overwhelming priority to tangible measures of output and results (see Exhibit 10-4).

Reward Systems: Key Characteristics of a Performance-Based System

Exhibit 10-4

- Superior-subordinate relationships not typically close
- Emphasis on tangible, concrete measures of output or performance
- Focus on individual, not group, measures of performance
- Bonuses are a big portion of total compensation
- Enhances individual initiative, entrepreneurial thinking, and personal efforts to excel
- Supports low-cost leadership strategies at the business unit level
- Supports unrelated diversification and multidomestic strategies at the corporate and business levels

Concrete Measures of Performance.

In the performance-based system, promotion and bonuses are based exclusively on the degree to which subordinates meet well-defined output and performance standards. Performance evaluation occurs frequently and formally in this system. Unlike the hierarchy-based system, qualitative and informal measures are not considered important to the process. The hallmark of the performance-based reward system is its emphasis on a distant, almost "market-based" approach between superior and subordinate. A market-based approach means that superiors measure their subordinates as if they were external contractors or agents. In other words, a subordinate's loyalty and affiliation with the firm contribute little to the manager's assessment of employee performance; both older and younger subordinates are expected to meet the same concrete, direct measures of performance. Consequently, little of the close personal interaction or relationship between superior and subordinate found in hierarchy-based systems is fostered in performance-based systems. The superior's personal care and mentoring that determine the subordinate's career path in the hierarchy-based system are replaced with the performance-based, "numbers-only" approach to rewards.

Emphasis on Individual Performance.

Rewards in a performance-based system are strictly allocated according to individual results; team and cross-unit or corporate performance results are deemphasized. A concern for the development of the individual and that person's career path falls by the wayside, overshadowed by individual results. Performance-based systems often have an "up-or-out" nature to them—people are expected to perform at a high level; those who cannot do so are asked to leave the organization. On the other hand, the performance-based system does tend to reward generously; individual bonuses, which represent the essence of the system, can often amount to the equivalent of a year's salary. From an organization-wide perspective, performance-based systems reinforce a different set of values, such as individual initiative, entrepreneurial thinking, and personal effort. Performance-based systems do not attempt to socialize managers and employees. Consistent with this lack of socialization are the lack of managerial prerequisites and other "symbols" of group identity or affiliation. In performance-based systems, promotion from within the ranks is not considered a priority. Every person's individual potential for promotion is assessed solely according to well-defined measures of output.

Link with Strategies.

Within a business unit or a single-business firm, performance-based reward systems work well to support low-cost leadership strategies. Low-cost leadership strategies emphasize intense supervision of people, task specialization, process engineering skills, and products designed for easy manufacture and distribution. As compared with differentiation strategies, low-cost strategies place comparatively less emphasis on creative flair, strong marketing skills, and innovative product designs. The need for subjective measurement of each individual's performance is therefore reduced. Rather, low-cost leadership strategies require tight cost controls, frequent reports on output and production rates, and well-defined responsibilities that tend not to span functions. Large, integrated steel and aluminum companies such as U.S. Steel and Alcoa tend to use performance-based reward systems when evaluating functional or other subunit managers. Likewise, major airline carriers in the United States such as American Airlines, United Airlines, and Continental Airlines typically use rigid performance-based reward systems to evaluate people. CEOs of these airline companies know that they are competing in a nasty, often brutal business where cost containment is an absolute necessity for competitiveness. The high cost of acquiring and maintaining large aircraft fleets, as well as centralized hub-and-spoke airline hub systems, demand an unflinching eye to manage the bottom line. All of these steel and airline firms face very high fixed costs and operate in industries with little opportunity to practice differentiation. Their senior managers feel little need to cultivate a close relationship between superiors and subordinates. Performance-based systems, with their emphasis on tangible measures of performance, thus fit the needs of low-cost strategies quite well.

Performance-based reward systems are also suitable for firms practicing unrelated diversification and multidomestic strategies. Recall that conglomerate-based firms actively acquire and sell unrelated businesses across industries. When measuring performance, they place a high premium on financial measures of individual division or SBU performance. Unlike related diversifiers, unrelated firms such as Textron and Tyco International are made up of businesses that share no distinctive competence. Senior managers can therefore evaluate performance solely according to financial criteria. Businesses (and their managers/employees) that make the grade are kept within the corporate portfolio; those that fail to do so are sold. Tyco International, in particular, is well known for laying off thousands of employees after making an acquisition to ensure that businesses perform up to their targeted numbers. This kind of "market-based" approach is practiced in rewarding the firm's people as well; managers at Tyco can make several times their base salary if they exceed the performance standards given to them.

Firms that pursue multidomestic strategies of global expansion also tend to use some variant of the performance-based reward system. Unlike their global strategy counterparts, firms that practice multidomestic strategies tend to view the world as separate, discrete markets. Because their operations are not based on a common underlying technology and are separated from one another by distance and distinct local conditions, their individual performance is easy to gauge and measure. Subsidiaries and product brands are typically evaluated according to local profitability and market share measures. Companies using some format of a performance-based system to support their multidomestic strategies include PepsiCo, Citigroup, and Altria (formerly known as Philip-Morris). Yet, firms pursuing multidomestic strategies are flexible in their use of the performance-based reward system. Thus, even though senior managers will assess the performance of their subunits through largely quantitative means, they must balance such measures with informed subjective judgment as well. Also, management must be careful not to alienate critical people in local markets. Senior managers therefore still need to encourage some degree of close superior–subordinate relationships.[3]

Performance Measurement at the Corporate Level

Denominator Management. Most corporate managers use financial measures such as ROI to some extent when assessing divisional performance. Corporate managers need to realize that divisional managers can often manipulate the numbers that determine such measures. Such subterfuge is more popularly known as "denominator management." Remember that all financial return measures are calculated by dividing profitability by assets or investments to come up with a final figure (for example, ROI = return/investment). Denominator management occurs when managers try to understate the value of the assets or investment contained within their division. By shrinking the denominator, managers try to appear to be performing better than they really are. In the worst situation, divisional managers, if left unmonitored, may actually choose not to invest in their business over time. By not investing, the denominator will never grow. Yet, the business presents the illusion of competitiveness and high profitability. The end result is that a division or business unit may look financially attractive on paper but conceal deep problems that may fester for a long time. Ultimately, these problems can grow so severe as to pose a danger to the entire company.

Consider Westinghouse Electric's series of disasters that the company faced when it did not have an adequate appreciation of how managers could use financial ratios to "manage performance" of their respective units. Westinghouse took big hits in its financial services unit in the early 1990s and in its robotics unit in the 1980s. The lack of sufficient effort by senior management to evaluate each SBU's performance in a balanced way resulted in severe problems for Westinghouse. Westinghouse's management relied on quantitative data submitted by divisional managers as the sole barometer of unit performance. Emphasis was placed on using performance-based reward systems, which fit Westinghouse's almost conglomerate-like corporate strategy. However, the crucial flaw in Westinghouse's performance-based system was that senior management paid little attention to how managers were actually determining the numbers for each division. Over time, denominator management became the basis for implementing divisional strategies. Senior management paid little attention to how the numbers were devised. The result was that individual managers within each of Westinghouse's divisions did anything they could to generate "the right numbers." The problems that festered in the financial services subsidiary during the 1990s acted like a ticking time bomb. In the end, senior management's inattention cost the firm well over $3 billion in write-offs.

Westinghouse's checkered history of facing numerous difficulties in its multiple lines of business eventually resulted in an erosion of the firm's long-term competitiveness. Facing much tougher competition from the likes of General Electric, Siemens, Toshiba, ABB, and other similar firms, Westinghouse continued to diversify into numerous industries to avoid some of these competitive pressures. Ultimately, the firm lost all sense of corporate coherence, and the company was sold in pieces to different buyers. Ironically, many of Westinghouse's previous business units are now thriving. These include Knoll Group, a leading designer of office furniture, as well as the avionics and defense electronics businesses, which are now part of Northrop Grumman. Westinghouse Plasma is now a leading innovator in the use of high-temperature techniques to incinerate dangerous materials and garbage to avoid the need for landfills. Westinghouse's electrical distribution and controls business is a strong contributor to Eaton Corporation, a diversified firm with many industrial lines of business. The core Westinghouse nuclear power unit is now owned by a British firm with strong ties to the UK government.[4]

Early detection of potentially dangerous actions and denominator management of the sort engaged by Westinghouse's SBUs is necessary, especially in firms that practice conglomerate or unrelated diversification strategies. Corporate managers must delve deeply into the operations of each business to understand how the numbers are derived. They must assess various factors affecting each business, such as the risk associated with divisional decisions and the degree of internal investment. Such assessments naturally entail a high level of informed judgment. Still, they are necessary to limit some of the toxic side effects of relying on numbers alone.[5]

Shared Values and Corporate Culture

shared values:
The basic norms and ideals that guide people's behaviors in the firm and form the underpinning of a firm's corporate culture.

corporate culture:
The system of unwritten rules that guide how people perform and interrelate with one another.

Yet another means of supporting effective strategy implementation is to instill a well-defined set of shared values and corporate culture within the firm. Deeply held shared values can strongly influence implementation of strategy. Shared values and corporate cultures help implement strategy by shaping the behavior of managers and employees.[6]

Shared values lay the foundation for the norms and ideals that guide behavior. Related to the concept of shared values is the concept of corporate culture. **Corporate culture** is the embodiment of shared values. It is the system of norms and unwritten rules that guide people in how they should act and interrelate with one another. Corporate culture is the company's "personality" or "psychology." Culture represents the way of thinking and doing things within the company. In this sense, corporate culture causes employees to "internalize" the firm's values. Both shared values and their embodiment in corporate culture work to influence behavior on a day-to-day basis. Shared values and corporate cultures in organizations represent a big part of the mortar that binds together the bricks of a firm. They hold people together and give them a sense of belonging and purpose. All these intangibles provide vital support to strategy implementation efforts throughout the organization.[7] Once shared values become part of the rubric of the corporate culture, they serve as psychological rudders, guiding employees to behave in ways that are congruent with the company's interests. Corporate culture thus provides a common, but distinctive, way of seeing, processing, interpreting, and acting on information.

Balancing Stakeholders: Cultural Change at Southwest Airlines[8]

The airline industry is perhaps one of the least attractive industries in which to compete. Fixed and operating costs for labor and fuel are very high, and buyer loyalty remains fairly low. Yet, Southwest Airlines has long distinguished itself from its rivals by making $448 million when the rest of the entire U.S. airline industry lost nearly $5.8 billion in 2003. Southwest also enjoys a market valuation of $11.7 billion, which is larger than all of its competitors put together. It has become the nation's fourth-biggest airline in terms of domestic service. What has been the secret of Southwest Airlines' success? In short, low-cost operations and a strong, people-oriented culture. Yet, as Southwest expands, its distinctive culture is now feeling the pressure of nationwide growth, rising costs, and a changing labor force.

For most of its thirty-plus year history, Southwest has pursued a successful low-cost/focused strategy by serving short-haul routes, rather than fighting major airlines for a losing share of long-distance, transnational flights. To this day, Southwest Airlines practices low-cost policies in almost every value-adding activity. Its planes are frugal, its offices are spartan, and it does not serve fancy meals on its planes. Employees recycle everything and reuse paper clips to keep costs down. Moreover, its procurement policies are also frugal; it buys only one type of plane (Boeing 737s) to keep maintenance costs low and to use common spare parts. Fast turnaround of aircraft is one key to Southwest's success in sustaining its low costs. Yet, to promote a high degree of customer service, Southwest carefully recruits the people that it believes have the best attitude that reflects the company's fun and efficient way of doing business. Colleen Barrett, Southwest Airlines' president, feels that it is Southwest's way of selecting and managing its people that gives the firm a uniquely low-cost structure, despite the comparatively high pay that it offered. The major airlines are wary of Southwest, since Southwest offers the lowest fare on any route that it chooses to serve and can destroy route profitability for other higher-cost airlines. In effect, traditional competitors such as American Airlines, Continental Airlines, US Airways, and United Airlines are forced to lower their fares in response to Southwest's initiative. US Airways, in particular,

has felt the real brunt of Southwest's low-cost strategy. When Southwest entered the short-haul California market in the 1980s (for example, San Francisco–Los Angeles), US Airways enjoyed over 50 percent market share. By the mid-1990s, Southwest forced US Airways to completely exit the market. A similar pattern repeated itself as Southwest became the biggest player in Baltimore and drove out US Airways from its long-standing hub.

For much of Southwest Airlines' history, former legendary CEO Herb Kelleher (who retired in June 2001) made it a personal point to directly work with flight attendants and ticket agents to create a memorable experience and personal touch with customers. One day a week, Kelleher dressed in a sport shirt and shorts (just like the rest of Southwest's flight attendants) and went down the aisle telling jokes as he handed out drinks and snacks. Sometimes, Kelleher would wear outrageous clothes to create a stir within the plane. By doing so, Kelleher exemplified Southwest Airlines' core values of warmth, friendly service, and fun. Kelleher believes that only through friendly customer service can Southwest Airlines keep its customers on its short-haul routes. Through his actions, Kelleher conveyed to employees his belief that customers on Southwest should have fun as they receive great value. Other Southwest Airlines senior managers are still required to practice these same customer service values by serving customers in airplanes as well.

Together with President Colleen Barrett, Kelleher helped instill a unique culture throughout Southwest. Many employees regarded Kelleher more as a father figure rather than a boss. One of Kelleher's most important innovations was the creation of a stock-ownership plan for employees. As Southwest prospered, so did flight attendants and mechanics, many of whom became millionaires over the years. (The stock has risen over a thousand times since 1972). Flight attendants developed an intense loyalty to both Kelleher and the company and pitched in numerous ways to keep costs down. For example, they would work together to clean planes and get them back in the air within twenty-five minutes—a real key to Southwest's exceptionally low operating costs. Pilots have been known to work with ramp agents to get bags unloaded. Even

(continued)

though everyone works extremely hard, they feel encouraged to find new ways to cut costs and improve operations. These collective efforts generated huge long-term results. For example, in 2003, Southwest's unit labor costs were 22 percent below that of Continental Airlines, even though the two companies' average salaries remained comparable at $60,000.

Although Kelleher retired from Southwest in early 2001, his senior management team (Colleen Barrett remains president; Gary Kelly became CEO in July 2004 after Jim Parker, Kelleher's immediate successor, resigned) continues to emphasize Southwest's fun-loving and customer-caring culture. Yet, the reality of the September 11 attacks, rising fuel costs, and difficulties in attaining further cost reduction are starting to change Southwest's unique culture. Southwest's stock price has stagnated as the entire airline industry remains mired in a tough operating environment. Keeping costs controlled and its culture vibrant are now Southwest's biggest challenges. One major threat that Southwest may likely face is the risk that its fun-loving, treat-workers-as-family culture will begin to fray at the edges as the company grows and expands operations throughout the United States. As Southwest starts serving more cities nationwide, it risks becoming more like its major airline rivals. The number of planes will expand and the complexity of operations will grow. Already, many flight attendants and mechanics have begun to grow weary over the long hours they put into the company. As the company's stock price continues to stagnate, a growing number of employees have complained about the extra productivity they have contributed without commensurate pay increases. Growth has also made middle and upper management seem somewhat distant to employees. New hires, in particular, may have a different set of expectations from Southwest, as compared with long-standing employees, who represent Southwest's special culture. In an unprecedented move, flight attendants staged a light-hearted picket at home base Dallas Love Field on February 14, 2003 (Valentine's Day), to demonstrate their dissatisfaction with protracted wage negotiations. Mechanics have also become more strident in their demands and have begun to reject initial offers from management, something that is also unprecedented. In July 2004, Southwest's flight attendants were awarded a new contract that boosts pay over 31 percent over a six-year period. Combined with other labor contracts, Southwest's costs are rising and it appears that it is no longer the lowest-cost carrier (a title now held by new rival Jet Blue). Although Southwest remains profitable (an amazing feat), its cost advantage over major rivals has been narrowing as well. Over time, if Southwest Airlines eventually becomes more of a "professionally managed" company, then we can expect that its ability to sustain its unique culture will become even more difficult.

Characteristics of Shared Values That Define Culture

To develop a distinctive corporate culture, the values that define a firm's culture should be (1) simple and clear, (2) crystallized at the top, and (3) consistent over time. All of these characteristics represent important ingredients of the mortar that holds the organization together (see Exhibit 10-5).

Exhibit 10-5	**Ideal Key Characteristics of Shared Values**

- Simple to understand

- Crystallized at the top

- Consistent over time

- Examples

McDonald's ⟶ QSCV
Southwest Airlines ⟶ Fun, warm, friendly
Wal-Mart ⟶ Efficient service and low prices
Motorola ⟶ Quality is key
Intel ⟶ Execution is key
Johnson & Johnson ⟶ Do the right thing

Simple and Clear Values. Values must be simple and clear so they can be understood and practiced by everyone. If values are to convey the same meaning, ideas, and sense of purpose to all employees within the firm, they must be identifiable to individuals from various backgrounds. The values must reflect some general belief about the company's commitment to a particular ideal or how the company's existence creates a unique identity that makes it distinctive from other competitors. Values that are explicit and give a sense of belonging, purpose, or self-confidence provide an esprit de corps, and assist managers in better understanding, cooperating, and relating to one another.

At McDonald's Corporation, the firm follows what it calls "QSCV" as the basis for defining its value system. Quality, service, cleanliness, and value are the four elements of QSCV that define the practices of every McDonald's restaurant, no matter where it is located worldwide. The best-quality ingredients in the food that McDonald's serves, the fastest possible service to its customers, the highest standards of cleanliness for its restaurants, and good value for the price together define McDonald's key values. The essence of QSCV is that everyone in the company, from cook to manager, understands each element. QSCV requires no explanations and no complex interpretations. QSCV serves as the internal guidepost that channels the activities of employees in every McDonald's restaurant. It is the foundation for McDonald's relationships with its suppliers as well and has long been the basis for its corporate mission.

Crystallized at the Top. The most enduring values are those found and practiced at the top of the organization. Senior managers must believe, uphold, and practice the same values they expect their subordinates to follow. When people throughout the company can see their senior managers personally embody and practice the company's values, they will know what behaviors and actions will be consistently rewarded over time.

For example, several companies that continue to cultivate a strong sense of employee loyalty and dedication are the same firms led by CEOs who practice honesty and close interaction with employees. At J. M. Smucker, this family-led company practices very simple values: listen, look for the good in others, and have a sense of humor. Co-CEOs Tim and Richard Smucker encourage high performance by offering employees special rewards for jobs well done. The company has enjoyed very little employee turnover (3 percent), and became number one on *Fortune* magazine's list of the 100 Best Companies to Work For in 2004.[9] CEOs can also personify the values they want imbued in their companies. At fast-growing Whole Foods Market, unconventional CEO John Mackey leads the company with his shared beliefs in libertarianism and social consciousness. Mackey does not act like most CEOs, and he seeks to infuse values of "truth, love, and beauty" into his nationwide chain of conventional and natural food stores.[10]

Consistent over Time. Values must be consistent and stable over time to preserve their integrity and to be effective in implementing strategy. Consistency is essential to making sure that the values are well cherished, unspoiled, and almost "pristine." Values that are constantly redefined, reinterpreted, and changed lose their meaning.[11] When values have little current relationship to a firm's strategy and no real roots in the organization, their importance will diminish in the eyes of managers and employees. Values that are timely must also be timeless. Many highly successful firms practice a consistent set of values over an extended period. McDonald's QSCV works anywhere, anytime. In fact, for McDonald's, its enduring QSCV values have reinforced its competitive advantage and reputation in the face of ongoing wars with Burger King and other fast-food outlets. Customers of Burger King, which had a much looser set of values and organizational practices, often experience less consistency. In many instances, the lack of a well-defined, consistent set of shared values at Burger King has resulted in high personnel turnover, even at senior management levels. As a business, Burger King has had numerous corporate owners over the past two decades, and its problems have frustrated every attempt by a new senior management team to turn its operations around.

At companies such as 3M, Nokia, Agilent Technologies, and Intel, innovation is a timeless value that is constantly reinforced in these firms' day-to-day practices. Managers encourage their technical personnel to experiment and to develop new technologies or novel products using whatever conventional or unorthodox techniques may work. In fact, 3M actively cultivates "legends" about renegade engineers who managed to invent hugely successful products in the face of difficult bureaucratic constraints.

STRATEGIC COMPETENCY *in action*

Creating a Unifying Corporate Vision: Johnson & Johnson[12]

Johnson & Johnson (J&J) is a leading health care company that generated $41.8 billion in revenues for 2003 (net income of $7.2 billion). Led by CEO William Weldon, J&J is aggressively pursuing new growth opportunities through internal innovation and external acquisitions. The 118-year-old company operates more than two hundred different business units that cover pharmaceuticals, advanced medical devices, and new diagnostic techniques. While many of its competitors (such as Merck, Pfizer, GlaxoSmithKline) are facing increasingly difficult competitive pressures, J&J has thrived on creating and acquiring new businesses that have consistently boosted the company's earnings over the past decade.

To manage such a large number of business units, J&J practices extreme decentralization. Each business formulates its own strategy and possesses its own functional units. Even the businesses that J&J acquired are given total autonomy to run their own show. The role of headquarters is to negotiate financial targets with each business, but allow them to determine how best to achieve them. Although this organizational structure results in duplication of activities and occasional friction, the company believes that encouraging entrepreneurship is well worth the higher overhead costs. This decentralization policy has kept J&J intensely competitive and allows each business unit to innovate new products in the way that it best sees fit. Despite this managing vast assortment of businesses, J&J also practices a long tradition of doing the best things for its customers, employees, and investors. The company regularly makes the ranks of *Fortune* magazine's Most Admired Companies and Best Companies to Work For.

One of J&J's most important assets is its corporate credo that articulates the deeply held values and standards that the company must live by. J&J's credo spells out the company's core responsibilities to its customers, employees, communities, and investors. (See www.jnj.com to read the credo.) Crystallized in a one-page document in 1943, J&J's credo outlines what current

and future management should do to make it an ingrained part of business practices and philosophy. Although the credo does not specifically state how employees should behave in specific situations, it communicates the very core principles that should guide their behavior. J&J's employees willingly embrace the company's credo because they accept its standards. Employees are given periodic surveys to evaluate just how well the company performs and lives by its credo responsibilities. The principles behind the credo have become a constant throughout the company. Former CEO Ralph Larsen stressed the essential importance of J&J's credo, claiming, "The Credo shouldn't be viewed as some kind of social welfare program. It's just plain good business."

Guided by its credo, ethical behavior remains a cornerstone of J&J's strategy. From 1982–1985, when saboteurs contaminated the company's flagship Tylenol product with cyanide, J&J initiated a nationwide recall that took every Tylenol package off the shelves to ensure public safety. Although the company took a major earnings hit, J&J management acted swiftly to introduce new tamper-proof packaging and to offer new bottles of Tylenol at such deep discounts that they were almost free. The credo served as the conscience and ethical guide for managers' actions during this tremendous crisis. Establishing trust and doing the right thing with its customers has always driven J&J's corporate values throughout its long history.

An important part of J&J's credo is the company's commitment to its Contributions Program, which is a worldwide social responsibility effort, as well as its Signature Program that is designed to help local communities. For example, in March 2004, J&J announced that it would give away a promising AIDS drug to a nonprofit organization in order to accelerate the development and use of experimental medicines in developing countries. J&J believes that it can work together with AIDS activists to find new ways to commercialize expensive drugs for widespread use in poorer nations.

Ways to Transmit Shared Values	*Exhibit 10-6*

Myths and Legends
- Develop internal folklore
- Heighten awareness of key cherished values

Socialization
- Learning "proper" behaviors and ways of doing things
- Extensive mentoring and coaching

Methods of Transmitting Shared Values

Shared values can be transmitted and learned in a number of ways (see Exhibit 10-6). Two of the most important mechanisms are myths and legends and socialization processes.

Myths and Legends. A common method of transmitting values is recounting stories involving individuals who have accomplished great feats on behalf of an enterprise. Over time, such accounts often develop a life of their own, embellishing the exploits of protagonists in much the same way that myths and legends exaggerate the feats of ancient heroes. Despite—or perhaps because of—this exaggeration, such stories can have a powerful effect in securing employee commitment to shared values. Legends are often passed on through storytellers who help maintain cohesion and unity of effort. Sometimes these myths and legends are used to convey an important message about what it takes to succeed within the company.

Consider the case of 3M, for example. It has achieved a stunning record of successful new product introductions, many pioneered by low-level "champions" deep within its organization. To encourage the perseverance needed to realize such achievement, stories about successful past champions have become an integral part of 3M's folklore. These legends have become so enduring that people use them as guides to their own efforts. One story that has taken on mythical proportions describes an engineer who, many years ago, became so interested in a project that he often worked on it rather than on assigned tasks. When his supervisor objected, he persisted whenever he could steal a moment and began coming in on Saturdays to work on his project. His supervisor soon objected to these weekend activities on the grounds that they consumed raw materials and tied up test equipment. But the engineer persevered, even secretly obtaining a lab key when his own was taken away. The engineer was eventually caught and fired, but he was so convinced of the project's worth that he kept working on it in his own garage.

This myth, as with many used by companies to communicate key values, has a positive ending. Months later, having perfected and market tested his invention, the engineer was able to interest one of 3M's top executives in his idea. Soon thereafter, the product was introduced to the market and in time it became one of the company's most successful (though no one ever knew exactly which product it was). This achievement led to the engineer's ultimate reemployment at a substantial increase in compensation. This legendary success story has been so widely cherished, repeated, and practiced at 3M that people now believe the story can apply to any of 3M's leading-edge, innovative products.

Socialization. Another vehicle that transmits shared values is socialization, which can serve to influence the way employees behave. In most companies, socialization occurs through extensive training and development programs. Learning the proper behaviors, routines, and the path to success in an organization helps socialize people. Companies with shared values develop their own ways to socialize their people. Usually, socialization takes place through extensive training, mentoring, coaching, involvement in company-wide activities, and pointing out past successful role models from the company's history.

Socialization processes are especially prevalent in large professional-service firms. Accounting, advertising, law, and management consulting firms often possess their own set of special values and professional cultures. Newly hired professionals are often extensively trained and mentored by senior managers to ensure that they have "learned the ropes" of how to perform and behave. Instead of relying on formal training programs, professional-service firms practice intensive mentoring of newly hired trainees. Mentoring, coaching, and advising help transmit core values, operating practices, and the right behaviors to people over time. In many ways, young employees act as "apprentices" with older mentors who spearhead the socialization process.[13]

Japanese firms explicitly use the socialization process as a key vehicle to develop and foster corporate loyalty. Companies such as Sony, Toshiba, Mitsubishi, Hitachi, and Matsushita Electric take newly hired college graduates and train them in all aspects of proper corporate behavior and values. Managers show these graduates all the details of how to perform, how to make budgetary requests, and even what phrases to use to address a superior or a customer. Also, newly hired personnel are given tours of the company's key plants and an overview of the firm's corporate strategy. In this way, people become thoroughly familiar with the company's mission and shared values. Over time, a "company" man or woman is created. Even though the concept of lifetime employment is fading in Japanese corporations, socialization remains important in guiding the actions of younger employees as they enter their careers.

Unilever uses an elaborate socialization process to create its own distinctive global culture that spans six continents. A European-based company that sells soap, foods, shampoos, and other packaged goods in numerous markets, Unilever employs extensive training and development to instill the company's operating practices and a corporate culture based on flexibility, cooperation, and consensus. Every new management trainee is assigned to a group of twenty-five to thirty people recruited for similar-level management positions. By focusing its efforts on training groups and teams of managers at the same stage of career development, Unilever infuses in them a feeling of shared experience and camaraderie. This exchange is especially important in a company that hires from so many cultures. The role of training to socialize managers is so important at Unilever that insiders have joked that the company is really a management-training center financed by soap and margarine. Extensive training, managerial rotation across assignments, frequent committee meetings, and executive retreats all work to bond Unilever's managers.[14]

Corporate Culture and Strategy Implementation

Each company is likely to have its own set of shared values and corporate culture; but whatever the shared values and corporate culture may be, they influence strategy implementation in two general, yet crucial ways:

- They provide the invisible mental and behavioral framework that guides the actions of managers and employees.
- They enable people to better relate to one another, while making the company distinctive from its competitors.

Well-defined and widely understood values lay the foundation for smoother strategy implementation, because people are likely to have a common set of operating assumptions and responses when dealing with environmental changes. Shared values put strategy implementation on an elevated plane, driven by the degree of common ground that transcends organizational structure and formal procedures.

Corporate Culture as Competitive Advantage. In many successful companies, a distinctive corporate culture has become a a vital source of competitive advantage in itself. Corporate cultures based on timeless and widely shared values often provide an important mental basis for fast response, flexibility, and risk taking that spans organizational and geographic boundaries and "walls." A distinctive corporate culture acts as an "invisible structure" and "glue" that represents a powerful competitive advantage.[15] A corporate culture shapes the norms, behaviors, and unwritten rules that employees follow. Culture that influences behavior, in turn, influences performance. A strategy is more likely to succeed if it is promoted throughout the firm in ways that are consistent with the corporate culture. Corporate culture is an invisible asset that helps unify the firm and keeps managers and employees from straying too far. It is an intangible, but powerful, resource that provides an underlying focus, mindset, and common problem-solving approach for the firm's people.[16]

Distinctive corporate cultures are especially important to companies with extensive global operations. For example, Coca-Cola gives its managers and subsidiaries a high degree of leeway to formulate and implement marketing strategies for their particular regions. Moreover, the numerous affiliated companies—distributors, wholesalers, and bottlers—that supply and distribute Coke's products come from every part of the world. Keeping this giant, diverse group of people together and unified in purpose is no easy task. Organizational structures and reward systems help but cannot substitute for Coke's core values and a global image that span many cultures and beliefs. Quality, fun, joy, and refreshment represent core values that define the way Coke views itself. These values form the invisible bond that ties together Coke's numerous subsidiaries and relationships around the world. Not surprisingly, they are also the basis for Coke's distinctive global image.

Double-Edged Sword. A set of shared values and corporate culture may also inhibit fast response to a changing environment. Over time, a longstanding way of doing something, such as developing products, improving process technologies, or selling to customers can "imprint" itself into the company's culture. Oftentimes, the particular way a company does things becomes the underlying dominant reference point and mental benchmark for undertaking future projects. Moreover, this dominant reference point or way of thinking makes itself felt in the corporate culture. Insights into new product ideas or technologies are viewed from a "strategic lens" that is colored with this perspective. A dominant design or approach leads to a dominant mind-set. This often results in strong corporate cultures that support an existing competitive advantage but also lead to difficulties in learning and building a new competitive advantage when the environment demands it. Even when the company is able to ultimately learn and incorporate a new technology or product design, it often encounters real difficulties in exploiting it.

For example, Procter & Gamble, a leading firm in the personal-care products industry, is trying to reinvent its culture to encourage a high level of diversity, experimentation, and willingness to engage in higher-risk projects. Throughout most of its history, Procter & Gamble has prided itself on developing and refining a culture that subtly encouraged a high degree of conformity and set of behaviors and norms that molded each manager and employee's viewpoints. As P&G's operations become more global and faster product innovation becomes more important to building competitive advantage, the corporate culture that supported P&G for so long has become a gradual hindrance to bolder experimentation and risk taking. According to senior management, although P&G actively recruits job candidates from a variety of economic and ethnic backgrounds, over time all of these people begin to sound alike, think alike, and even look alike. Within the company, people are known as "Proctoids." To ensure that the firm stays innovative, senior management is hoping to transform P&G's culture into one that encourages both consistency of behaviors and a willingness to think in new, innovative ways.[17]

The transformation of IBM into a high-tech developer of new Internet-based electronic-commerce tools, advanced semiconductors, web-driven software, and other computer peripherals required Big Blue to change its internally focused culture gradually to one that was more customer responsive over an extended period. Consider the numerous difficulties IBM has encountered in its mainframe computer business. The explosive growth of IBM's mainframe computer business during the 1960s through the late 1980s helped infuse a highly elaborate "mainframe" culture throughout the company. This culture embodied values and practices such as exclusive relationships with customers, technological leadership based on proprietary machines and software, and close cooperation among IBM business units. Within IBM, mainframe computers were known as "Big Iron," signaling that powerful computers process and transmit information in much the same way that railroads transported goods in the nineteenth century. This culture helped IBM totally dominate U.S. and global markets for mainframe computers.

Over time, this culture began to overshadow other IBM businesses, such as personal computers, semiconductors, advanced network systems, and software development. Because of this mainframe culture, problems and issues in other businesses were approached from the mainframe point of view. In fact, senior management took drastic steps to protect the flagship mainframe business and culture—even going so far as to delay commercialization of competing technologies, such as RISC. However, competitive success in rapidly evolving personal computers, Internet-driven solutions, electronic-commerce technologies, and software requires fast market response, aggressive risk taking, and constant new product development as opposed to proprietary machines, technology, and software. Technological leadership and customer service as applied to mainframe computers—bigger proprietary machines, extended leasing and service agreements, and exclusive relationships with customers—did not apply to these new areas. Competitive success in personal computers, electronic commerce, Internet-driven solutions, and other fast-moving businesses required a culture radically different from IBM's mainframe-driven culture. Thus, the corporate culture and behaviors that emanated from IBM's mainframe business may have greatly impeded IBM's ability to detect and to respond to the fast growth in the personal computer industry. As a result, IBM in some ways is still trying to stay as competitive with its more agile competitors such as Apple Computer, BEA Systems, Dell Computer, EMC, Hewlett-Packard, and Sun Microsystems.[18]

The transformation of IBM into a more nimble, agile competitor remains an ongoing process. IBM has become much more aggressive in developing new technologies to help companies establish viable competitive market space positions using the Internet. IBM is a key player in working with a host of firms in the airline, financial services, health care, and retailing industries to manage their computer, web-hosting, and even inventory management systems. Under its "on-demand" computing and business strategy, IBM is helping companies that want to integrate their businesses processes and technical capabilities across divisions and subunits. "On-demand" symbolizes IBM's goal of making computing capabilities more like a "utility," in which its customers will view Big Blue as a provider of web-based business services. IBM itself has been actively acquiring innovative software developers such as Lotus Development, Tivoli, and

Rational Software—companies that are vital in helping IBM establish a stronger position in the relational database market. It has also formed scores of alliance relationships with Ariba, I2 Technologies, Commerce One, Oracle, PeopleSoft, and other firms that develop business-to-business software and Internet platforms.

These initiatives reveal some of the growing dilemmas that will continue to haunt IBM. On the one hand, mainframe computers exert a disproportionate influence on IBM in terms of revenues, profits, and corporate culture influence. Yet, on the other hand, components, e-commerce, "on-demand" computing, and software represent the current vision for IBM's future. How well IBM is able to manage and navigate the ongoing tension between these two broad initiatives will largely shape the company's ability to compete in the early part of the next decade.

Thus, shared values and corporate cultures can prove to be a double-edged sword. On the one hand, they provide the invisible bond and implicit guidance of behavior that make strategy implementation easier. On the other hand, they can impede a firm's ability to detect and respond to new developments in the environment. Managers will often "see" things through the lenses of an established culture.[19] They will then "interpret" new developments in terms of the existing culture, frequently viewing them as threats to the culture. This rigid view can work to slow down the company's recognition of a growing threat and the creation of new skills to compete for the future.

Keeping the Organization Vital. Firms with distinctive corporate cultures that match their strategies possess a huge advantage over competitors that do not enjoy such a match. Yet, distinctive corporate cultures can in some instances impede a firm's ability to respond to new developments and changes. Companies, as with people, often need a shake-up to keep themselves from becoming too complacent over time.

Hiroyuki Itami, a leading Japanese management scholar, notes that firms must sometimes take steps to prevent themselves from becoming too insular or protected by their cultures. Itami suggests that firms undertake a process of "creative tension," in which senior management deliberately chooses a small-scale new strategy that stretches the boundaries of organizational consensus and current behaviors.[20] **Creative tension** seeks to introduce new activities, ideas, and ways of thinking to the company's people. Careful use of creative tension can help managers think beyond the confines of their existing operating procedures, learned behaviors, and existing culture. For example, a new product strategy that uses an untried or novel technology or entry into a new market whose characteristics are unfamiliar to the firm can help stimulate creative tension. On the one hand, the chosen strategy should not be too radically different from the firm's traditional strategy; otherwise, managers and employees are likely to reject the idea outright. On the other hand, the chosen strategy should not be so familiar that it fails to create a reasonable level of creative tension. Too easy a consensus means that the strategy is not sufficiently novel. In its ideal form, a "creatively tense" strategy should pit old and new ways of thinking against each other to generate sparks. The new strategy should not initially involve the entire organization, but rather a portion of its operations with the expectation that its effects will later spread systemwide.

For example, Microsoft's currently limited efforts to enter the emerging interactive cable television and entertainment fields to further deploy new forms of Internet-driven technology demonstrate a good example of creative tension. As a software company, Microsoft's culture puts a premium on individual creativity, flexibility, confrontation, and aggressive risk taking. These values have helped Microsoft's people excel in designing and quickly producing successive

creative tension:
A process in which senior management systematically attempts to encourage people to think about new strategies and directions, which prevents the firm from becoming complacent.

waves of new software that are the foundation for numerous applications. Yet, the evolving multimedia, Internet-related technology and distribution arenas may require new types of skills, outlooks, and business practices than those traditionally fostered at Microsoft. Microsoft senses that multimedia and new entertainment applications are bound to grow and impact the company at some point in the future. To learn more about potential Internet software and technology-based applications, Microsoft has entered a series of small-scale joint projects with Intel, Nokia, Hewlett-Packard, RealNetworks, Comcast, Time Warner, General Electric's NBC unit, and Samsung to see how multimedia and interactive television are likely to evolve, especially to create a "digital living room" in the home. These projects are sufficiently different from Microsoft's core PC-based software business to promote creative tension within Microsoft. Yet, these small-scale projects are not so unrelated as to distract Microsoft from its core business. By participating directly in these emerging technologies, Microsoft has taken steps to prevent itself from being shut out of what appears to be a promising new industry that has exploded with high-speed Internet access.[21]

Building the Learning Organization

Most industries and their competitive environments are rapidly changing. With change comes the necessity of learning new skills and developing new sources of competitive advantage. Thus, all types of firms (large and small, established and new entrant, diversified and single-business) cannot rely on their existing sources of competitive advantage for long-term survival; they must be able to learn and create new ones as their environments change. Building and sustaining competitive advantage in the midst of rapid change requires the organization to learn new technologies, new markets, and new ways of managing. In the future, the only truly sustainable source of competitive advantage will be the organization's ability to change and learn new skills.[22]

Successful learning of new skills demands management's focused effort. Often, learning new skills and technologies can be a traumatic experience. The large-scale, ongoing restructurings of firms such as IBM, Sears, Fidelity Investments, J. C. Penney, United Technologies, and Eastman Kodak are just a few examples in which one can see the dramatic effects of rapid environmental change. However, bringing about organizational change that facilitates learning is not an easy task. Managers and employees at all levels frequently resist the process of change, since it may alter their existing practices and web of relationships. Senior managers who seek to induce organizational changes that promote the learning of new skills and distinctive competences must therefore be sensitive to potential resistance. Their challenge is to take steps that encourage lower-level managers and employees to join and facilitate needed changes.[23]

learning organizations:
Firms that view change as a positive opportunity to learn and create new sources of competitive advantage.

Learning organizations are firms that view change as a positive opportunity to learn and create new sources of competitive advantage. We focus on various organizational practices that promote this kind of proactive, change-oriented learning. Although instilling new forms of learning can be a difficult task, companies that are successful in doing so can better adjust and thrive in a rapidly changing environment.

Some firms possess characteristics that greatly enhance their capabilities to adapt to rapid change. Exhibit 10-7 highlights key organizational practices that contribute to a firm's potential for learning: (1) frequent rotation of managers, (2) continual training of personnel, (3) decentralization of decision making, (4) encouragement of multiple experiments, (5) high tolerance for failure, and (6) openness and diversity of many viewpoints. These practices encourage managers to be truly open to ideas that identify trends and generate choices. Under these conditions, adapting to the environment becomes easier and more likely to succeed.

Management Practices of Learning Organizations   **Exhibit 10-7**

Frequent Rotation of Managers

Managers new to their positions are less likely to be wedded to a particular set of values or way of operating than individuals who have held the same position for many years. Long-standing managers of a department are likely to be proponents of their department's current strategy and, therefore, emotionally tied to its success. Over time, these individuals have a tendency to become less accepting of new strategies, approaches, and ways of doing things. For example, at companies such as Eastman Kodak, Polaroid, Timex Watch Company, and Merrill Lynch, managers who stayed with their respective lines of business were often unable to under-stand the nature of the changes facing their products and technologies; change became more difficult when managers were locked into a particular "lens" and functional perspective through which they defined and solved problems.

One organizational practice that enhances a firm's ability to change is periodic rotation of managers throughout the firm. Rotating managers across business lines exposes them to experiences, perspectives, functional skills, and competences that were developed elsewhere. Managerial rotation also promotes the building of interrelationships and synergies that span departmental and divisional lines. At Sony, for example, managerial rotation infuses managers with new insights and ideas and gives them greater awareness of a wide range of technologies and products that consumers may want. Managers are thus able to see how employees from other departments work together smoothly to get new products to market fast. In turn, they become more aware of their own competitive environment. Frequent managerial rotation greatly enhances Sony's ability to adapt to environmental change.

General Motors' Saturn operation practices managerial rotation to encourage its people to visit other parts of the factory. Rotating both managers and employees throughout Saturn's many work areas helps convince people of the need to do their best in producing quality prod-ucts. This system enables Saturn employees to see how their efforts and work contribute to the entire car's production and assembly. Managers and employees also learn multiple sets of skills that are used in auto manufacturing and assembly. In turn, the quality of the car improves, and people learn and share manufacturing insights and skills throughout the factory.[24]

Continual Training of Personnel

An insidious source of resistance to change is fear that change will render obsolete many managers' and employees' current skills, promotion opportunities, and career paths. Regular training and development through which managers and employees learn new skills lessen such fears and thus reduce resistance to change. Many researchers and analysts have noted that continuous training is one key pillar of Japanese firms' success in learning new technologies to develop fresh products quickly.[25]

Sony maintains an internal training program designed to impress young Japanese employees with the firm's newest technologies. It also instills the company's management procedures, corporate values, and operating practices. Additionally, Sony trains its managers extensively to prepare them for overseas assignments. Overseas customs and practices are taught regularly. In particular, by sending highly talented, young managers to places such as the United States, Latin America, and Europe, Sony is able to see firsthand the emerging lifestyle and technology-driven trends that may first start in other markets. In turn, by actively researching and listening to what future consumers want from their products, Sony's managers can then develop those products that it thinks will capture people's desires. This type of training helps Sony's managers spot new trends and potential opportunities in consumer electronics markets and understand what each market wants in Sony's products.

Decentralization of Decision Making

Lower-level managers, sales representatives, and front-line employees are much closer to the action than most senior managers. They are therefore often the first to become aware of potential new developments and changes. A firm can improve its responsiveness by pushing decision-making responsibility down to these individuals; therefore, a firm should practice some degree of decentralization wherever possible. Careful decentralization facilitates organizational change and learning because it encourages managers and employees to participate in making decisions that directly affect them. It also gives them room to experiment with new methods they feel are appropriate. Yet, decentralization should not go so far that it results in excessive and extreme duplication of activities across businesses, the dilution of a well-defined corporate mission and culture, or other inefficiencies. When carefully implemented, decentralization increases the number of employees who can deal with change, and mobilizes the energies of many people. Making the right level of decentralization work requires trust among managers and employees throughout the company. If managers cannot trust their employees or vice versa, then unfettered decentralization can cause numerous problems for the firm.

Well-thought-out decentralization works to promote change and learning because the flow of information is less likely to be distorted.[26] People on the front line (especially marketing, sales, customer service) are constantly exposed to numerous sources of timely information vital to detecting potential developments or opportunities. On the other hand, thick layers of management (particularly in companies organized along strictly functional lines for long periods) often distort or delay information flows. Managers tend to "reinterpret" information from their employees and pass it on in a distorted form to their superiors.

Of course, decentralization must be balanced with a strong sense of shared values to promote change and learning. Decentralization frees up the creative energies of managers and employees but can result in chaos if people do not share some common goals and values.

Johnson & Johnson is another example of how effective decentralization can foster the creation of new sources of competitive advantage. J&J's senior management has divided the company into more than fifty operating divisions (or "companies") that produce everything from surgical sutures to Tylenol, anesthesia, advanced surgical implements, medical instruments, diagnostic equipment, toothbrushes, baby oils, shampoos, and blood monitors. J&J's senior management believes in giving each division the power to do whatever is needed to succeed in its market. This high degree of decentralization has enabled J&J business units to become some of the most successful innovators and marketers in the United States. The CEO of Johnson & Johnson compares his role to that of an orchestra conductor: he gives his players inspiration and direction, but his subordinates get complete freedom to execute the desired objective.[27]

Encouragement of Multiple Experiments

Developing new products and technological processes are often complicated tasks. Sometimes several initiatives need to be tried simultaneously to determine which is better. Running multiple projects reduces the likelihood that a superior approach will be overlooked. As separate groups or teams work on a solution to the same problem, people develop skills and insights that can prove useful in thinking about future products. In other words, companies need to "parallel-process" their efforts to learn new technologies and develop new products. Parallel processing enables a firm to see which technologies, product standards, marketing approaches, and management methods work best. This approach harnesses a healthy degree of internal competition with a dual focus on continuous improvement and search for best designs and best value. In turn, people are exposed to different ways of thinking about and doing things.

Multiple experiments are one key to Honda's enormous success in developing a broad range of engine technologies for automobiles, motorcycles, lawn mowers, power boats, and power generators. Honda keeps an "idea file" that includes numerous prototypes and designs for models previously developed but never produced. Many of these ideas have later become the basis for motorcycles, automobiles, and lawn mowers when opportunities opened up.[28] Oftentimes, ideas developed in one business unit to serve a particular customer have had considerable future, unanticipated value serving Honda's customers in another market.

Timex's early unwillingness to experiment with new technologies that redefined the inner workings of the watch ultimately shut the company out from new generations of products. The company's cadre of mechanical engineers was unable to assimilate electronic displays and other new technologies in watch designs, because they saw mechanical springs and gears as superior to emerging electronic technologies being developed by other companies. For example, competing manufacturers such as Citizen Watch, Seiko, Casio, and Texas Instruments were already producing watches made with electronic components, which were often derived from other product applications, such as calculators and measuring instruments.

High Tolerance for Failure

If people are punished for working on projects that eventually are not selected, then few will be willing to take on risky projects in the future. Firms must be careful not to discourage people associated with projects that do not work out if they want to sustain high creativity. Instead, senior managers should continue to reward them if their efforts are meaningful and reasonable. This approach ensures that employees receive the encouragement they need to "venture off the beaten path" when exploring new solutions.

Many innovative companies, including Sony and 3M, have experienced failures, some of them rather large. For example, during the 1980s, Sony pioneered a new digital camera called the Mavica. The company believed the public was ready for a new filmless camera that could take clearer pictures faster. Yet, the Mavica was ahead of its time and few consumers were interested, so Sony withdrew the product. Not until the mid-1990s did Sony reintroduce the Mavica and the even more improved Cybershot line of digital cameras. This product is now a real winner in the marketplace. Even with this early failure, Sony gained many insights into digital technology that led to new generations of compact disk players, Minidiscs, advanced integrated circuits, and DVD technology. Sony did not penalize its managers or employees for this product's failure. Instead, it gave these individuals important positions in which they could borrow upon their newly acquired experiences and skills. They were encouraged to apply their expertise to designing new products and technologies. Ultimately, Sony is now well positioned to compete across a whole spectrum of digital imaging technologies for use in advanced consumer electronics applications.

3M is another company that seeks to utilize failures as a way to create new technologies and market opportunities. The company has long believed that it is far better to encourage people to make mistakes and stumble, rather than to wait too long before other competitors pounce on new market ideas. 3M's senior management has long believed that scientists need to keep their fertile minds active, and explicitly allow them to work on projects that may have no immediate payoff. During the 1990s, 3M instituted programs to provide internal grants of as much as $50,000 for scientists to work on individual special projects. Product and technology failures are legendary at 3M for creating new applications elsewhere. For example, one 3M division developed an easy-to-apply sticky coating for the aerospace industry. Unfortunately, the coating did not meet the aerospace customer's exacting needs. However, with a slight modification of the coating's chemical properties, another 3M division was able to pioneer today's wildly popular Post-It Notes. In fact, many of 3M's products resulted when scientists either failed in an initial experiment or accidentally "stumbled" onto something that turned out to be a future winner.

At Sony and 3M, managers are encouraged to learn from their experiences instead of being fired for their decisions. Failures are defined as part of the learning process and personal growth. The knowledge gained by personnel associated with failures became instrumental in developing new products that helped the company enter other markets. In other companies, the very prospect of failure causes organizational paralysis rather than growth.

Openness and Diversity of Viewpoints

True openness by managers to new ideas, suggestions, and criticisms is rare in most firms. Openness means not only a *willingness to listen to new ideas and face reality but also encouragement of a diversity of viewpoints and perspectives throughout the firm*. Openness demands that managers suspend their need for control. The need for constant and direct control often limits the potential for effective learning, since it suppresses people from bringing up contrary viewpoints, "bad news," or alternative problem solutions that may cause internal political problems. Excessive control sharply narrows the manager's attention to short-term objectives. For example, if managerial attention is riveted solely to quantitative performance measures such as return on investment (ROI), managers will be less attuned and sensitive to environmental developments with potential long-term impact. During the 1980s and 1990s, managers at Westinghouse Electric were so obsessed with "making their numbers" that they even went so far as to undertake actions that ultimately resulted in the financial collapse of several Westinghouse business units. Moreover, managers fixated on control are often unable to draw useful suggestions and ideas from their employees, many of whom may be afraid of their superiors. Control usually focuses managers' attention on specific details of high-urgency projects; this reduces the amount of time and effort that managers need to discover and understand important long-term trends.

Another essential ingredient to openness is the ability to understand diverse perspectives and viewpoints. Managers must be able to appreciate other people's values, backgrounds, and experiences as being no less important than their own. In other words, true openness means a willingness to accept and listen to other people's ideas and perspectives. The hidden belief that one's own background or experience is superior to another's seriously hinders learning. This phenomenon is especially dangerous for firms whose top management is overly represented by a particular function. For example, engineering-dominated firms, such as Raytheon, Rockwell International, and Texas Instruments, have experienced difficulty in entering the consumer market for such products as calculators, digital watches, and personal computers. During the 1980's, TI's inability to view marketing as a function equal in importance to engineering and production is partly to blame. Consequently, TI developed consumer products (calculators, personal computers) in the same way it developed products for the government and other large companies. The result was a series of consumer products that were overpriced and lacking many user-friendly features. Resources that TI allocated to the consumer market were not as great as those dedicated to industrial markets that were more familiar to its senior managers. As a result, TI's managers were unable to get a feel for the consumer market.

Implementing Change in Static Organizations

A handful of firms have fully incorporated the practices described in the preceding sections into their management systems. Because of their ability to create new sources of competitive advantage rapidly, these learning organizations can adapt quickly to environmental change. On the other hand, many companies perceive change as a threat to their existing sources of competitive advantage and established procedures. In these firms, managers often resist efforts to change. Exhibit 10-8 presents a spectrum of how firms differ in their adaptability and responsiveness to change.

Learning organizations are found on the far right side of Exhibit 10-8. In learning organizations, managers view change as an opportunity for improvement and renewal of competitive advantage. At the far left are firms that have not adopted the organizational practices that promote learning and change but instead focus on doing better what they are already doing. Such firms we call "dinosaur" or static organizations.[29] **Static organizations** are akin to dinosaurs in that they have adapted themselves well to current environmental conditions but have little ability to change. They have a management system well attuned to a particular environment. These firms are often wedded to a particular technology, distribution channel, or other way of doing things that makes them vulnerable to new products or new competitors. Such

static organizations: *Firms that have adapted extremely well to a particular environment but lack the ability to respond quickly to change.*

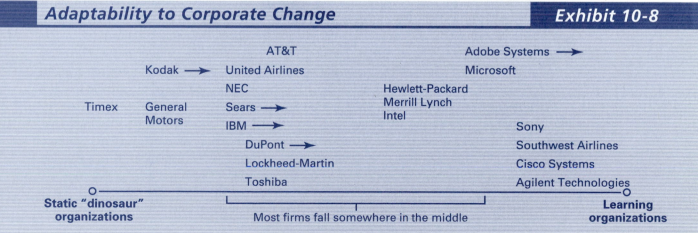

Adaptability to Corporate Change   **Exhibit 10-8**

firms often perform well for a considerable period but tend to become insular and averse to change. Senior management loses the ability to see the ripples of change occurring in both the immediate competitive environment and the larger general environment. Managers at all levels within the firm become more inwardly focused rather than understanding what customers, competitors, and new entrants may be doing in the marketplace. In effect, their existing sources of competitive advantage have become extremely brittle and inflexible and thus especially vulnerable to new entrants, new products developed by competitors, or new technologies developed elsewhere in the industry (or beyond). As a result, when their competitive environments eventually change, they lack the ability to readily adapt.

For example, companies such as American Express, General Motors, J. C. Penney, and Sears during the late 1980s displayed many characteristics of a static, dinosaur-like organization. Each company was superbly adapted to its own previous low-change environment. In the automotive and retailing industries, GM, J. C. Penney, and Sears considered themselves as "definers" and incumbent leaders of industries they thought would not change very quickly. Yet, these companies came close to extinction because of rapidly changing environments brought about by new entrants, new technologies, and shifting customer needs. General Motors steadily lost market share to both Japanese imports and domestic competitors for over twenty years, dropping from 50 percent of the U.S. market to a low of somewhere around 27 percent. The company initially attempted to reverse its slide by investing in advanced manufacturing technologies, robotics, software, acquisitions of Electronic Data Systems (EDS) and Hughes Aircraft, accelerated product development, quality improvement programs, and new car designs. Yet, despite all of these massively expensive undertakings, thick layers of bureaucratic management impeded fast information flow and made GM unresponsive to its customers' needs. To this day, although it made tremendous advances in quality improvement and factory productivity, some doubt persists as to whether General Motors can truly match or exceed the best Japanese competitors in developing new car models as quickly. Nevertheless, it has shortened the time of new car model development by including suppliers, customers, and people from every function on its product development teams. GM also started practicing continuous improvement by asking its suppliers for ways to improve its manufacturing operations and reduce its inventory costs. Yet, even today, GM continues to struggle with declining market share and is looking for further wage and benefit concessions from its managers and rank-and-file workers.[30]

Sears continues to face the same kind of problem in the retailing industry. Confronted with new "boutique" retailers and "category killers" such as Benetton, Abercrombie & Fitch, The Limited, and The Gap and new broad-line competitors such as Wal-Mart Stores, Sears was unable to provide the wide variety of products demanded by younger generations of consumers. Boutique retailers and category killers focus their efforts on specific niches. Their dedicated focus enabled them to command much higher customer loyalty and superior margins. Sears even lost ground to other mainline department stores and larger, megaretailers such as Federated Department Stores and Wal-Mart Stores, respectively. These retailers were better able to provide brand-name merchandise at lower prices. In 2002, Sears acquired Lands' End, a specialty retailer that offers a distinctive fashion style, to broaden its customer reach in both stores and on the Internet. In late 2004, Sears announced that it would merge with Kmart Holdings to form a new mega-retailer that is better able to compete with the likes of Wal-Mart and Target. However, even this merger of two second-tier retailers will likely present major organizational challenges that need to be fixed before the combined entity can truly become competitive in the fast-changing retailing industry.

The majority of companies are located somewhere in the middle of the spectrum shown in Exhibit 10-8. Change can and does occur in these firms but not without varying degrees of resistance and difficulty. However, most companies need to change or adapt within a very short time period. Rapid environmental change, particularly when unanticipated, can seriously erode the value of a firm's distinctive competence and other sources of competitive advantage.

Consequently, a static or slowly changing organization faces a significant challenge. Caught between the proverbial rock and a hard place, a static organization must often adapt quickly to an environmental development or be left behind in the wake of more nimble competitors. Yet, it may lack many of the organizational practices that enhance its ability to learn. Furthermore, the learning practices described previously often require considerable time to take effect. For example, several years may be required to generate value from a program of management rotation.

All too often, a static organization remains behind the curve when adapting to a new competitive environment. It is easy to imagine how change can be so fast in some industries (for example, software, semiconductors, consumer electronics, financial services, and entertainment) that a change program initiated in one time period may already be obsolete before it is fully embraced by the organization. To bring about change in a static organization, senior managers must take a much more active role in the change process. The following section identifies some of the obstacles senior management experience in trying to carry out this role. We first discuss the resistance that senior managers of a static organization often encounter when attempting to bring about change. Then we describe a series of steps managers can take to overcome such resistance.

Resistance to Change in Static Organizations

Senior managers interested in promoting change in static organizations often possess insufficient knowledge to determine precisely how a firm should respond. They therefore need help designing and implementing a change program from managers and employees who have more specialized knowledge in specific areas. The need for such assistance is particularly great if a senior manager has been brought in from outside the company and possesses little industry experience. A senior manager interested in bringing about change in a static organization faces another kind of obstacle. Such an individual must also rely on managers and employees to implement the new response once it has been developed. Consequently, senior management needs the support of managers and employees in designing a change initiative and in implementing it. Unfortunately, managers and employees in static organizations often withhold such support. Among the most common reasons for withholding support are (1) lack of awareness of the need to change, (2) lack of interest in the opportunity that environmental change presents, and concern about (3) incompatibility, (4) cannibalization, and (5) personal loss (see Exhibit 10-9).

Common Reasons for Organizational Resistance to Change

Exhibit 10-9

- Lack of awareness of need to change
- Lack of interest in opportunity for change
- Incompatibility of change with existing values or interests
- Fear of cannibalization
- Fear of personal loss

Lack of Awareness

An appreciation of the need to change often requires a broad view of both the competitive and general environments. Managers and employees, especially functional managers and technicians preoccupied with their daily operating tasks, are often too focused on current activities to develop this kind of perspective. Therefore, people become overly short-sighted and too narrowly focused to be aware of potential changes over the horizon. As a result, they often fail to appreciate the need for change, especially if change means learning new methods, processes, or techniques that are significantly different from what they currently practice. The recent challenges facing companies as wide ranging as Eastman Kodak, Timex, Sears, Merrill Lynch, and companies in the music industry showed how people can become riveted to an earlier product, technology, way of serving a customer, or problem-solving approach.

Lack of Interest

Even when managers and employees recognize the need for change, they often perceive it as having only marginal impact on them. This kind of reaction is common even with new developments that could have severe consequences for the firm. It often occurs when a firm's own business is growing rapidly. People's energies remain fully engaged with current activities. People also tend to ignore developments that represent transient or relatively small opportunities for expansion. Too often, an unproven or unorthodox approach is dismissed because of people's inability to understand the nature of the change.

Unfortunately, arrogance becomes a significant barrier to understanding the implications of new developments. For example, many former U.S. companies in the consumer electronics industry, such as RCA, Philco, Motorola, General Electric, and Zenith, did not perceive the Japanese quality and low-cost advantage in making color televisions until it was too late. U.S. firms did not believe that Japanese manufacturing skills would help Japanese products penetrate the U.S. market, where domestic firms had long commanded a strong market position. Ultimately, all of these companies exited the consumer electronics business or were acquired by larger, more efficient foreign competitors. Japanese success in this activity underscores the vital roles of openness and experimentation to promote learning and competitive advantage.

Incompatibility with Cherished Values

Firms frequently develop their own sense of shared values and corporate culture that define the company's outlook and future strategies over time. In many cases, strongly held values or corporate culture can become significant obstacles to change. Managers and employees oppose new strategies, products, or approaches that appear to conflict with established practices. Strong corporate culture can often have the unintended effect of filtering out and neutralizing badly needed information and trends from the environment, since people are not used to thinking about their company's strategy and operations from a totally different perspective.

Consider the former experience of Japanese computer and consumer electronics giant Nippon Electric Corporation (NEC) in the early 1990s. NEC invested heavily in its own proprietary personal computer (PC) software language. The company assigned great value to internal development of all key parts of its computers, including the software. Using an IBM-, Apple-, or Microsoft-based software operating system would violate NEC's cherished value of independence and self-directed innovation. As U.S. companies steadily penetrated the Japanese market, NEC lost market share to Compaq Computer, Dell Computer, Apple, and even IBM itself, in its own home market. NEC ultimately abandoned its internal project and was even forced to retreat from many computer-related businesses as it sought to restructure itself.[31] Even now, the company is still struggling with how best to grow, and it has recently decided to exit some of its core high-technology businesses to refocus its efforts.

Fear of Cannibalization

Cannibalization is one of the greatest fears that prevent companies from investing in new technologies or products before competitors compel them to do so. Developing new products that are distinct from those of the firm's current lineup means admitting the possibility that alternative or substitute products do indeed exist. Facing the threat of substitute products or radically new product concepts is hard for any company to do. On the one hand, it means recognizing that the firm's strategic approach, assumptions, distinctive competences, and investments up to this point could quickly become obsolete. On the other hand, it may also require that the firms' people learn an entirely new set of skills and technologies to compete effectively in the new environment.

For example, by developing the personal computer and newer computer networking technology, IBM was forced to acknowledge that its core mainframe business would eventually face significant decline. Within IBM, people vigorously resisted this move, from fear that growing sales of emerging technologies would cannibalize sales of the firm's traditional products. The dominant approach that IBM used to develop, manufacture, sell, and service mainframe computers became part of the dominant mind-set of the entire firm. Anything that threatened IBM's dominance in the business was either dismissed (because IBM was too big), or ignored (because of a lack of understanding or urgency). Ironically, IBM during the early 1970s was the inventor of the RISC microprocessor used in smaller computers, but failed to commercialize it because of its likely impact on mainframe sales. Instead, for most of the 1990s, sales gains by Hewlett-Packard, Sun Microsystems, and even Intel have grabbed big portions of the specialized RISC-based computer and workstation market.

In addition, industry leaders and other established firms generally enjoy higher profit margins in their traditional businesses than in newly emerging markets that they begin to explore (or prospect). This financial reality adds to the fear of cannibalization. For example, the Big Three U.S. automakers failed to innovate fast enough in smaller subcompact cars during the 1970s. Their hesitation to invest in worker training and to learn new assembly techniques accelerated Japanese import penetration into the United States. One can only hope that the Big Three will avoid these same steps when it comes to adopting new types of automotive technologies such as advanced fuel cells, batteries, and advanced materials and electronics. Fear of cannibalizing film sales was a major factor that held Kodak back from fully committing to learning new digital technologies for many years. This hesitation enabled new competitors, such as Hewlett-Packard, Canon, and Sony to grab significant market share and technological leadership during the 1990s. However, Kodak must now fight an uphill battle to reclaim its previous leadership role.[32]

Fear of Personal Loss

Fear of personal loss is perhaps the most significant obstacle that prevents firms from becoming successful learners. The fear of restructurings that would eliminate entire divisions and businesses, along with all of the people involved, makes corporate change painful. Strategic change greatly impacts the personal well-being of employees in many ways. It alters how they interact with others and affects their bases of power. Also, change may render obsolete their skills, reduce their career opportunities, and even cost them their jobs. In recent years, dozens of firms have been forced to lay off hundreds of thousands of employees. Concern about layoffs often leads people to resist strategic change vigorously. For example, the United Auto Workers union has consistently fought General Motors' efforts to reclassify jobs to streamline the number of workers needed to produce cars and engaged in a costly strike against GM in 1998. This strike revolved around what GM could and could not do to outsource production to other nonunion U.S. plants or even foreign subsidiaries. Now, union members across many industries are fighting to retain their jobs and benefits as U.S. companies face even greater pressures to control their costs. In the airline industry, pilots, mechanics, and flight attendants have been forced to accept massive cuts in pay and benefits (sometimes twice in two years) to keep the major airlines out of bankruptcy, often to no avail. Japanese and Korean firms are not immune from the need to change either. They now face continued sluggish domestic demand and the rise of more efficient Chinese exporters. Many Japanese (such as Hitachi, Toshiba, NEC, Mitsubishi, and Nissan) and Korean (such as Samsung, Hyundai, and Daewoo) have been forced to engage in painful restructurings that led to layoffs and plant closures. These moves are especially painful in Japan, where lifetime employment remains a corporate ideal.[33]

Change Steps

Senior managers implementing new initiatives in static organizations must deal with the issues of resistance brought about by the factors described in the preceding paragraphs. Some sources of resistance, such as fear of personal loss, remain extremely difficult, if not impossible, to resolve. However, these factors can also serve as important markers of where the firm needs to focus its change efforts. Also, the need for restructuring and decisive action opens up opportunities to make change and learning an integral part of the firm. To implement change effectively in static organizations, senior managers need to build commitment for some kind of change program or initiative.[34] Key steps in the process of building such commitment include (1) sensing the need for strategic change, (2) building organizational awareness of this need, (3) stimulating debate about alternative solutions, (4) strengthening consensus for a preferred approach, (5) assigning responsibility for implementation, and (6) allocating resources to sustain the effort (see Exhibit 10-10). These steps are especially valuable for firms that have just begun to recognize environmental developments that are starting to erode their existing sources of competitive advantage.

Exhibit 10-10   *Key Steps to Implement Strategic Change*

Sense need

↓

Build awareness

↓

Foster debate

↓

Create consensus

↓

Assign responsibility

↓

Allocate resources

↓

Act quickly

Sense the Need for Strategic Change

To fulfill their roles as change agents, members of senior management must develop an early awareness of the need for change. Information leading to such awareness can come from a variety of sources. Functional managers (vice presidents of manufacturing, marketing, and other departments) are one common source. A senior manager is likely to have frequent contact with such people during the course of everyday activities. During these interactions, valuable information about potential changes will sometimes come up. However, information supplied by these individuals will rarely be complete. For example, functional managers typically see only a portion of the firm's overall environment. They often suffer from specialty biases, especially in firms that do not have a well-developed system of managerial rotation and development. Thus, senior management should not rely exclusively on subordinates for information about environmental developments.

Another potential source of information about environmental developments is a firm's strategic planning process. Formal planning processes, however, can be real mixed blessings. On the one hand, they help managers identify near-term changes and the rise of potential competitors or new markets. On the other hand, planning processes can sometimes instill a rote method of analysis that can dangerously blind the firm to radical types of change. This danger results from reliance on the previous period's results as the basis for future assumptions within the planning process. Planning also tends to be dominated by managers in charge of major functions. As a consequence, planning reviews often become little more than a projection of historic trends and a rededication to past practices. Thus, a company's planning process can oftentimes be unreliable as a source of information about new developments, and certainly not a stimulant for creative thinking.

To secure reliable information about developments, senior managers generally need to spend time talking to people outside their own firms. A wide variety of external sources can be useful. Customers can provide especially valuable information about emerging product and service needs. For example, Canon successfully entered the U.S. copier and office equipment markets by asking secretaries what attributes they prefer in photocopiers. By building a reliable machine that did not require expensive maintenance, Canon was able to displace Xerox as market leader in the smaller and medium-sized copier categories. Information about new technologies and production techniques can often be acquired from suppliers. Suppliers are often more aware of shifts in the cost and availability of raw materials and of components that are likely to be introduced in new products. Companies can engage in benchmarking to measure their progress vis-à-vis their rivals along such key metrics as unit cost, quality, and efficiency. **Benchmarking** provides an important source of ongoing information about the firm's practices and competitiveness vis-à-vis its competitors. Another source of information is scientific and professional associations, which may know more about developments in product and manufacturing technologies. Lobbyists who are typically aware of pending governmental regulations may also be a useful source of information. Examining the actions of competitors in closely related fields gives managers an additional lens through which to monitor the environment. These are just a few of the external sources of information available to top management. Outsiders still have their own biases but can provide fresh perspectives not available from within the firm.

benchmarking:
A firm's process of searching for, identifying, and using ideas, techniques, and improvements of other companies in its own activities.

Build Awareness of Need to Change and Learn

Once top managers have gained a general idea of the kind of change required, they must begin to build awareness of this need among employees in the firm, particularly among subordinates who possess expertise needed to shape a proper response, since such individuals have the power either to promote or to derail it. Senior management's objective at this point must be to target such individuals and encourage them to think about and evaluate important environmental developments and their significance for the firm.

Senior managers can take specific, direct steps to build awareness for the need for change. An immediate step is to share their concerns verbally with lower-level managers and employees during routine contacts with them. These conversations will stimulate people's thoughts about possible change without raising anxieties too quickly. This step also reinforces the vital role of trust in airing problems and working through them. As they listen to people throughout the ranks, senior managers can surmise who is likely to support and oppose needed changes. Sharing information and establishing trust are critical in helping senior management build support for change.

A useful next action is to establish a task force to study the possible need for change more systematically. The group's composition must be carefully determined so that enough supporters are included to ensure that an initiative moves forward. A few opponents should also be included, however, in the hope that their interaction with supporters will convert them. Also, opponents often present arguments that have considerable merit. Failure to consider the value of these arguments only solidifies the opponents' resistance and raises the fear level among employees. This failure damages much of the firm's effort to instill new practices that promote learning. Opponents with special expertise may be able to contribute a unique perspective that turns out to be instrumental in solving problems.

Foster Debate

Stimulating debate about alternative solutions is essential, and a diversity of perspectives is vital to prevent the debate from being a one-sided exercise. Debate encourages new thinking that may produce insights not forthcoming from previous meetings. These debates also contribute to building a commitment to new goals. A task force can be useful in fostering healthy debate as well. By including proponents of several approaches, top management can ensure that the task force examines various solutions. Sometimes more than one task force can be formed to explore potential solutions. The results can then be compared at a later date to determine which approach is superior.[35]

Multiple teams are especially useful when new technology is involved. Diversity of ideas raises the chance that both the best and worst aspects of each alternative are brought to light. Bringing customers into the discussion is worthwhile, since they are the best judges of whether a new or modified product idea will work. Highly innovative companies such as Procter & Gamble and Cisco Systems mandate customer participation when developing new products or service offerings. Customers test and comment on new product prototypes. For example, McDonald's numerous successes with different types of hamburgers and breakfast offerings were tested with customers in trial runs. Customers are encouraged to give their candid feedback about new products.

Create Consensus

As results from debates come in, evidence will accumulate in favor of a particular approach. This evidence will itself help create consensus about the direction change should take. It will rarely persuade all parties, however, and some skeptics are likely to remain. Since resistance from such people can undermine further progress, a firm's management must strive to convert or at least neutralize these remaining "foes." Steps to do so can be extremely precarious, however, especially when the firm wants to become more open. Retaining entrenched opponents to a change initiative can result in further trouble. On the other hand, removing them too quickly without debate and consideration can seriously demoralize people, raising fears instead. Personal judgment, ethics, and leadership become vital guideposts at this stage.

Fortunately, opponents to a new initiative can often be converted by milder measures. Time alone can do much to transform opponents into allies. By giving an organization plenty of time to prepare for the new approach, management can provide opportunities for troubled or fearful personnel to work through resentment and frustration. At this stage, continuous training and management development can reap big dividends in implementing change. By teaching new skills to people threatened by a new approach, management can eliminate fear—one of the major sources of resistance to transformation. The reduction of fear can make employees valuable contributors to the change process. Companies can also take other steps to signal the positive effects of change. A change in the location of company headquarters or in a company's name can help signify the higher aspirations and positive benefits of change.

For example, the strategic integration and redirection of Textron's Avco subsidiary after its takeover by Associates First Capital in 1997 relied on many of these steps. Associates First Capital (now part of Citigroup) solicited Avco managers' and employees' ideas and feelings concerning what the company should do to compete in its many commercial and credit card businesses. By directly helping people recognize the certainty of change and finding a new role for them, management was able to reduce skepticism among Avco employees. Associates First Capital also hosted discussion groups in locations distant from the workplace as yet another vehicle for overcoming resistance to proposed change. Most likely, the enthusiasm of employees in favor of change worked to convert less enthusiastic members within focus and discussion groups.

Assign Responsibility

Once the appropriate response to an environmental change has been determined, responsibility for carrying it out must be assigned. Two basic approaches are available. First, a new effort toward change can be placed within an existing department. Second, it can be set up as a newly autonomous unit. The first approach will generally be less costly in the short run, since it enables a new activity to draw on resources and expertise of an existing unit. However, the new effort may lose urgency when the existing unit has priorities that lie elsewhere. To ensure that an initiative receives proper attention, it may need to be established as a separate unit headed by someone who has only its welfare in mind.

Who should be selected to administer such a unit? Candidates who have championed a new initiative in the past should be candidates for this position. Their past advocacy is testimony to their belief in the effort's worth, and it raises the likelihood that the initiative will receive the attention it needs to prosper. Also, longtime champions often possess skills needed to make the effort succeed. Motorola has used this approach successfully in implementing new manufacturing technologies to make quantum leaps in quality improvement during the 1990s. Previous process champions have been asked to participate and to initiate the changes required to make new factories work.

Allocate Resources

A variety of resources may be needed to carry out a new initiative. For example, cash may be needed to develop a new technology, construct a prototype product, or conduct market research. Technical personnel and legal assistance may also be required. Management must ensure that sufficient resources are available for the initiative. Otherwise, the initiative will atrophy for lack of sustenance. Allocating these resources is the final step of the change process.

Embracing Change as a Way of Life

Perhaps the most important legacy that former General Electric CEO Jack Welch has left for both his company and for management in general is the need for constant change.[36] Welch understood that for companies to learn and build new sources of competitive advantage, a business within an industry must change and reinvent itself faster than the rate at which the industry is changing. In other words, *competitive advantage at the business unit level stems from the actions of each individual business to embrace and utilize change to create new opportunities at a rate faster than that at which competitors, customers, and suppliers are changing.* At the corporate level, competitive advantage comes when *the entire organization is able to leverage new ideas, skills, technologies, and insights in ways that other competitors cannot.* By doing those things that competitors cannot imitate, the company becomes increasingly distinctive. Distinctiveness, in turn, leads to stronger sources of competitive advantage—which ultimately translates into higher sustained profitability.

Undoubtedly, the issue of learning and change is highly complex. Yet, even such relatively new and innovative companies as Cisco Systems and Microsoft are making change part of their culture. More than ever, Microsoft has become much more of a mature company, even in the eyes of its employees. Microsoft realizes that it must rapidly adjust its business model and software development methods, especially as new threats from open-source Linux and other technologies take root. Many smaller companies and even foreign governments have been shifting to a Linux-based software platform because of its very low cost and the perception that Microsoft remains an arrogant competitor. Even within the company, the culture has changed markedly over the past five years. Before the economic downturn of 2000–2001, Microsoft employees would willingly spend long hours working together to develop newer and better software. The prospect of fast riches and working in a winning company proved to be a very powerful combination during the 1990s. Now, Microsoft's employees are seeking a better balance between their professional and personal lives. As the prospect for immediate riches fades with slowing demand for technology products, Microsoft employees want to spend more time with their families. The company is also changing significantly in the wake of invigorated competition. Microsoft continues its ongoing diversification into video games (Xbox system), communications (equity stakes in cable companies), and new technologies for the digital living room.[37]

Cisco Systems realizes that it, too, must devise new strategies to change its operations and new product development approaches as the telecommunications and computer networking industries' growth rates slow down. Throughout the 1990s, Cisco consistently grew its revenues and earnings over 25 percent per year. Yet, facing the same downturn as Microsoft did, Cisco was forced to scale back operations significantly in the past few years. Demand for advanced routers and switches plummeted, and Cisco was even forced to lay off several thousand employees, some of them after just a month on the job. Yet, Cisco used the downturn to upgrade its R&D capabilities and to reorganize itself to streamline costs. Under CEO John Chambers, Cisco realizes that it must continue to learn new skills and ideas to compete effectively. Even Chambers has admitted that as companies become larger, the more difficult it is to innovate.[38]

Promoting the need for learning and embracing change within a company is a tough sell, even for the best leaders. Its treatment in this chapter is at best rudimentary, since so many human relationship issues are involved. Many of the measures discussed in this chapter represent only the first steps of learning and change. Yet, they are applicable to all firms that find change at their doorstep. The rise of new technologies, markets, and competitors will surely accelerate the tempo of change in all industries.

Summary

- Reward systems are the set of incentives used to attain high performance and strategy implementation.
- Hierarchy-based reward systems encourage close superior–subordinate interaction, place a premium on team and group results over individual results, and use a high degree of informed subjective judgment to assess performance.
- Performance-based systems focus on tangible, concrete measures of output and results. They generally do not encourage close interactions between superiors and subordinates. Individual effort and results are the primary means to evaluate people.
- Shared values define the norms and ideals of the firm. Corporate culture is the embodiment of the firm's shared values.
- Distinctive corporate cultures can provide an important source of organizational competitive advantage. As a double-edged sword, they can also impede the firm's ability to detect and respond to new environmental developments.
- Building a learning organization helps firms create new sources of competitive advantage. As environments change more quickly, organizations must be able to reconfigure their products and technologies faster.
- Management practices that promote learning include (1) frequent rotation of managers, (2) continual training of personnel, (3) decentralization of decision making, (4) encouragement of multiple experiments, (5) high tolerance for failure, and (6) openness to diverse perspectives.
- Dinosaur organizations are extremely well tuned and adapted to a no-change or even low-change environment. These firms are wedded to a particular technology, product design, or distribution channel. They are most vulnerable to new competitors or other environmental developments.
- Managers and employees often resist initiatives designed to enhance the organization's ability to adapt to change. Managers and employees resist change for many reasons; they (1) lack awareness of the need to change, (2) lack interest in the opportunity that change presents, (3) feel that an initiative is incompatible with cherished values, (4) fear cannibalization, and (5) worry about personal loss. The last factor is often the most troublesome.
- Senior managers interested in implementing a change initiative must undertake steps to overcome resistance. Often, opponents to change can become persuaded over time to see the necessity and merits for change if there is sufficient openness in the organization.
- Senior managers are responsible for creating a setting conducive to expressing various perspectives and arguments for and against change. Key steps in this process are (1) sensing the need for change, (2) building organizational awareness of this need, (3) stimulating debate about alternative solutions, (4) strengthening consensus for a preferred approach, (5) assigning responsibility for implementation, and (6) allocating resources to sustain the effort.
- Even today's most innovative organizations will ultimately confront the need for change.

Exercises and Discussion Questions

1. Is the concept of corporate culture applicable only to businesses or can it be used in other organizational settings? What are some ways that teams in professional sports can use aspects of corporate culture to develop stronger, better performing teams?

How would you classify the culture that defines a hospital, for example, or even that in a university?

 2. Using the Internet, look up the website for Korn/Ferry International, the world's largest executive search firm. How has Korn/Ferry used the Internet to develop new types of products and services to help companies meet their staffing needs? Do you see the Internet helping you attain some of your immediate job or career objectives?

3. Many companies over the past few years find themselves struggling in the wake of faster environmental change and the advent of new competitors. Within the restaurant industry, who are some established companies now feeling the pressure of new entrants? What about the music industry, especially the market for digital music players?

4. If you were the CEO of a large industrial company, what are some change steps that you would implement immediately to help prepare yourself for the arrival of lower-cost, foreign competition? Which steps would be supported within your company? Which change steps would be opposed?

Endnotes

1. For an excellent discussion of GE's transformation and the leadership of GE's CEO Jack Welch, see N. M. Tichy and S. Sherman, *Control Your Destiny or Someone Else Will* (New York: Doubleday, 1993); R. N. Ashkenas and T. Jick, "From Dialogue to Action in GE Work-Out," in *Research in Organizational Change and Development,* Vol. 6, eds. W. A. Pasmore and R. W. Woodman (Greenwich, CT: JAI, 1992), 267–287; L. Hirschhorn and T. Gilmore, "New Boundaries of the Boundaryless Company," *Harvard Business Review* (May–June 1992); "GE: Keep Those Ideas Coming," *Fortune,* August 12, 1991, pp. 41–49; N. M. Tichy, "GE's Crotonville: A Staging Ground for a Corporate Revolution," *Academy of Management Executive* 3, no. 2 (1989): 99–106. An excellent discussion of the change process at both GE and other large U.S. firms can be found in F. J. Aguilar, *General Managers in Action* (New York: Oxford University Press, 1994).

See "Managing the GE Way: Reaping the Wind," *BusinessWeek,* October 11, 2004, pp. 201–202; "GE Breaks the Mold to Spur Innovation," *BusinessWeek,* April 26, 2004, pp. 88–89; "With New Chief, GE Healthcare Breaks Tradition," *Wall Street Journal,* April 8, 2004, pp. B1, B10; "GE, Amid Slow Growth, Streamlines," *Wall Street Journal,* December 5, 2003, p. A6; "Will Jeff Immelt's New Push Pay Off for GE?" *BusinessWeek,* October 13, 2003, pp. 94–98; "GE Makes Overture to Buy Amersham," *Wall Street Journal,* October 9, 2003, pp. A3, A14; "GE Discusses 'Clean Coal' Plants in Bid to Market New Technology," *Wall Street Journal,* October 4, 2003, p. A3; "GE Chief Is Charting His Own Strategy, Focusing on Technology," *Wall Street Journal,* September 23, 2003, p. B1; "GE's Immelt Starts Renovations on the House That Jack Built," *Wall Street Journal,* February 6, 2003, pp. A1, A6; "What's So Great about GE?" *Fortune,* March 4, 2002, pp. 65–67; "At GE, New Pride in the Peacock," *BusinessWeek,* November 19, 2001, pp. 79–81; "Welcome to the Frying Pan, Jeff," *BusinessWeek,* October 8, 2001, pp. 82–84; "GE Foresees Growth Despite Big Hit From Terrorist Attack," *Wall Street Journal,* September 24, 2001, p. B4; "It's All Yours, Jeff. Now What?" *Fortune,* September 17, 2001, pp. 64–68; "GE's Immelt Frets over Economy, Not Icons," *Wall Street Journal,* September 5, 2001, pp. B1, B11; "The Immelt Revolution," *BusinessWeek,* March 28, 2005, pp. 64–73; "GE's Jeffrey R. Immelt," *Investor's Business Daily,* November 28, 2000, p. A4.

See "Why Jack Welch's Brand of Leadership Matters," *Wall Street Journal,* September 5, 2001, pp. B1, B10 for a discussion of Welch's view on perpetual change.

2. See, for example, J. Kerr and J. W. Slocum, Jr., "Managing Corporate Culture Through Reward Systems," *Academy of Management Executive* 1, no. 1 (1987): 99–110. This is an excellent article that portrays the key differences between hierarchy-based and performance-based reward systems. Recent work examining the nature of different reward systems on strategy implementation includes the following select works: H. G. Barkema and L. R. Gomez-Mejia, "Managerial Compensation and Firm Performance: A General Research Framework," *Academy of Management Journal* 41, no. 2 (1998): 135–145; T. M. Welbourne, D. E. Johnson, and A. Erez, "The Role-Based Performance Scale: Validity Analysis of a Theory-Based Measure," *Academy of Management Journal* 41, no. 5 (1998): 540–555; H. Tosi, J. P. Katz, and L. R. Gomez-Mejia, "Disaggregating the Agency Contract: The Effects of Monitoring, Incentive Alignment, and Term in Office on Agent Decision Making," *Academy of Management Journal* 40 (1997): 584–602; R. D. Naker, S. Y. Lee, G. Potter, and D. Srinivasan, "Contextual Analysis of Performance Impacts of Outcome-Based Incentive Compensation," *Academy of Management Journal* 39, no. 4 (1996): 920–948; J. M. Pennings, "Executive Reward Systems: A Cross-National Comparison," *Journal of Management Studies* 30 (1993): 261–281; L. R. Gomez-Mejia, J. Tosi, and T. Hinkin, "Managerial Control, Performance and Executive Compensation," *Academy of Management Journal* 30 (1987): 51–70; R. S. Schuler and S. A. Jackson, "Linking Competitive Strategies with Human Resource Management Practices," *Academy of Management Executive* 1, no. 3 (1987): 207–219.

Also see D. Lei, J. W. Slocum, Jr., and R. W. Slater, "Global Strategy and Reward Systems: The Key Roles of Management Development and Corporate Culture," *Organizational Dynamics* (Winter 1990): 27–41. This article focuses on the interrelationships among various global strategies with reward systems to implement them. A full-blown study that examines the relationship between diversification strategy and reward systems is J. L. Kerr, "Diversification Strategies and Managerial Rewards: An Empirical Study," *Academy of Management Journal* 28 (1985): 155–179. Another study is that by D. Norburn and P. Miller, "Strategy and Executive Reward: The Mis-Match in the Strategy Process," *Journal of General Management* 6 (Summer 1981): 17–27.

3. Reward systems also exert a strong influence on the firm's culture and even its "organizational climate." See, for example, J. W. Slocum, Jr., and E. Jackofsky, "A Longitudinal Study of Organizational Climates," *Journal of Organizational Behavior* 9 (1988): 319–334, for a thorough coverage of what constitutes "organizational climate." Also see J. W. Slocum and W. Joyce, "Strategic Context and Organizational Climate," in *Organizational Climate and Culture,* ed. B. Schneider (San Francisco: Jossey-Bass, 1990), 130–150.

4. See, for example, "Whatever Happened to the Old Westinghouse?" *Wall Street Journal,* October 30, 1998, p. B1; "Westinghouse Power Unit Is Purchased From CBS," *Wall Street Journal,* August 21, 1998, p. C14; "CBS to Sell Nonmedia Lines to Consortium," *Wall Street Journal,* June 29, 1998, p. A4; "How Westinghouse's Famous Name Simply Faded Away," *Wall Street Journal,* November 20, 1997, p. B6.

5. The eventual difficulties that result from "managing by the numbers," or denominator management, are elaborated in C. K. Prahalad and G. Hamel, *Competing for the Future* (Boston: Harvard Business School Press, 1994).

6. The research literature examining organizational culture issues is vast. See, for example, M. J. Hatch, "The Dynamics of Organizational Culture," *Academy of Management Review* 18 (1993): 657–693; J. E. Sheridan, "Organizational Culture and Employee Retention," *Academy of Management Journal* 35 (1992): 1036–1056; J. Martin, *Cultures in Organizations: Three Perspectives* (New York: Oxford University Press, 1992); W. F. Joyce and J. W. Slocum, Jr., "Strategic Context and Organizational Climate," in *Organizational Climate and Culture,* ed. Schneider, 130–150; G. S. Saffold, "Culture Traits, Strength and Organizational Performance: Moving Beyond 'Strong'

Culture," *Academy of Management Review* 13 (1988): 546–588; W. G. Ouchi, "Markets, Bureaucracies and Clans," *Administrative Science Quarterly* 25 (1980): 129–141; A. Pettigrew, "On Studying Organizational Cultures," *Administrative Science Quarterly* 24 (1979): 570–581; E. Abrahamson and C. J. Fombrun, "Macrocultures: Determinants and Consequences," *Academy of Management Review* 19 (1994): 728–755; C. R. O'Reilly, "Corporations, Culture and Commitment: Motivation and Social Control in Organizations," *California Management Review* 32 (1989): 9–25; R. H. Kilmann, M. I. Saxton, and R. Serpa, eds., *Gaining Control of the Corporate Culture* (San Francisco: Jossey-Bass, 1990); S. Cartwright and C. L. Cooper, "The Role of Culture Capability in Successful Organizational Marriage," *Academy of Management Executive* 7 (1993): 57–70; J. P. Kotter and J. L. Heskett, *Corporate Culture and Performance* (New York: Free Press, 1992); J. R. Harrison and G. R. Carroll, "Keeping the Faith: A Model of Cultural Transmission in a Formal Organization," *Administrative Science Quarterly* 36 (1991): 552–582; S. A. Sackmann, "Culture and Subcultures: An Analysis of Organizational Knowledge," *Administrative Science Quarterly* 37 (1992): 140–161; N. Nohria and S. Ghoshal, "Differentiated Fit and Shared Values: Alternatives for Managing Headquarters–Subsidiary Relations," *Strategic Management Journal* 15, no. 6 (1994): 491–502.

A recent piece that examines the applicability of American culture to other settings is C. F. Fey and D. R. Denison, "Organizational Culture and Effectiveness: Can American Theory Be Applied to Russia?" *Organization Science* 14, no. 6 (2003): 686–706.

7. For excellent discussion of this subject, see T. Peters and R. Waterman, *In Search of Excellence* (New York: Harper & Row, 1982). Chapter 9 of this work, entitled "Hands-On, Value-Driven," is particularly useful.

8. Data and facts for Southwest Airlines were adapted from the following sources: "Dressed to Kill...Competitors," *Business Week,* February 21, 2005, pp. 60–61; "At Southwest, New CEO Sits in a Hot Seat," *Wall Street Journal,* July 19, 2004, pp. B1, B3; "Southwest Air's Flight Attendants Get Tentative Deal," *Wall Street Journal,* July 2, 2004, p. B2; "Southwest Airlines: The Hottest Thing in the Sky," *Fortune,* March 8, 2004, pp. 86–103; "Inside Southwest Airlines, Storied Culture Feels Strains," *Wall Street Journal,* July 11, 2003, pp. A1, A6; "Southwest's Handle on the Future," *Dallas Morning News,* June 19, 2003, pp. 1D, 13D; "Is Lovin' Feeling Gone?" *Dallas Morning News,* February 14, 2003, pp. 1D, 11D; "Holding Steady," *Business Week,* February 3, 2003, pp. 66–68; "The Chairman of the Board Looks Back," *Fortune,* May 28, 2001, pp. 62–79.

9. See "Keeping Out of a Jam," *Business Week,* October 4, 2004, pp. 104–106; "J.M. Smucker in The 100 Best Companies to Work For," *Fortune,* January 12, 2004, pp. 58–78.

10. See "No Preservatives, No Unions, Lots of Dough," *Fortune,* September 15, 2003, pp. 127–130.

11. See, for example, J. J. Jermier, J. W. Slocum, Jr., L. W. Fry, and J. Gaines, "Organizational Subcultures in a Soft Bureaucracy: Resistance Behind the Myth and Facade of an Official Culture," *Organization Science* 2 (1991): 170–194.

12. Data and facts were adapted from the following sources: "J&J to Give Away New AIDS Drug," *Wall Street Journal,* March 29, 2004, p. B6; "J&J: Toughing Out the Drought," *Business Week,* January 26, 2004, pp. 84–85; "Staying on Top," *Business Week,* May 5, 2003, pp. 60–68; "Johnson & Johnson: A Shopping Spree Waiting to Happen," *Business Week,* June 17, 2002, pp. 58–60; "Can J&J Keep the Magic Going?" *Fortune,* May 27, 2002, pp. 117–122; "J&J Stops Babying Itself," *Business Week,* September 13, 1999, pp. 95–98; "Leaders of the Most Admired," *Fortune,* January 29, 1990, p. 50.

13. See, for example, B. E. Ashforth and A. M. Saks, "Socialization Tactics: Longitudinal Effects on Newcomer Adjustment," *Academy of Management Journal* 39, no. 1 (1996):

149–178; J. A. Chatman, "Matching People and Organizations: Selection and Socialization in Public Accounting Firms," *Administrative Science Quarterly* 36 (1991): 459–484; G. R. Jones, "Socialization Tactics, Self-Efficacy, and Newcomers' Adjustments to Organizations," *Academy of Management Journal* 29 (1987): 262–279.

14. See, for example, F. A. Maljers, "Inside Unilever: The Evolving Transnational Company," *Harvard Business Review* (September–October 1992): 46–52.

15. See H. Itami, *Mobilizing Invisible Assets* (Cambridge, MA: Harvard University Press, 1987), for an excellent discussion of how corporate cultures are invisible assets.

16. See J. Barney, "Organizational Culture: Can It Be a Source of Sustained Competitive Advantage?" *Academy of Management Review* 11, no. 3 (1986): 480–481.

17. See "New CEO Preaches Rebellion for P&G's 'Cult,'" *Wall Street Journal,* December 11, 1998, pp. B1, B4.

18. "Is Gerstner Too Cautious to Save IBM?" *Fortune,* October 3, 1994, pp. 78–90.

19. See, for example, M. A. Hitt and B. Tyler, "Strategic Decision Models: Integrating Different Perspectives," *Strategic Management Journal* 12 (1991): 327–351.

20. H. Itami, *Mobilizing Invisible Assets* (Cambridge, MA: Harvard University Press, 1987), 153–155.

21. See "Microsoft May Be A TV Star Yet," *BusinessWeek,* February 7, 2005, pp. 78–80; "Media Moguls," *BusinessWeek,* November 8, 2004, pp. 124–126.

22. A growing research literature on organizational learning examines the relationship of organizational practices and the organization's ability to change. Suggested references for further reading include the following: C. Argyris and K. A. Schon, *Organizational Learning: A Theory of Action Perspective* (Reading, MA: Addison-Wesley, 1978); C. M. Fiol and M. A. Lyles, "Organizational Learning," *Academy of Management Review* 10 (1985): 803–813; G. Huber, "Organizational Learning: The Contributing Processes and the Literatures," *Organization Science* 2, no. 1 (1991): 1–18; J. S. Brown and P. Duguid, "Organizational Learning and Communities of Practice: Toward a Unified View of Working, Learning, and Innovation," *Organization Science* 2 (1991): 40–57; and A. Van de Van and D. Polley, "Learning While Innovating," *Organization Science* 3 (1992): 92–116. Readers may also want to consider P. M. Senge, *The Fifth Discipline* (New York: Doubleday, 1990), and B. Levitt and J. G. March, "A Model of Adaptive Organizational Search," *Journal of Economic Behavior and Organization* 2 (1988): 307–333. An evolving typology of the different forms of organizational learning can be found in D. Miller, "A Preliminary Typology of Organizational Learning: Synthesizing the Literature," *Journal of Management* 22 (1996): 485–505.

A recent review of the key issues surrounding organizational change can be found in H. Tsoukas and R. Chia, "On Organizational Becoming: Rethinking Organizational Change," *Organization Science* 13, no. 5 (2002): 567–582; A. Pettigrew, R. W. Woodman and K. S. Cameron, "Studying Organizational Change and Development: Challenges for Future Research," *Academy of Management Journal* 44, no. 4 (2001): 697–714; L. Heracleous and M. Barrett, "Organizational Change as Discourse: Communicative Actions and Deep Structures in the Context of Information Technology Implementation," *Academy of Management Journal* 44, no. 4 (2001): 755–778; B. L. Kirkman and D. L. Shapiro, "The Impact of Cultural Values on Job Satisfaction and Organizational Commitment in Self-Managing Work Teams: The Mediating Role of Employee Resistance," *Academy of Management Journal* 44, no. 3 (2001): 570–579.

Some important streams of theoretical and empirical research studying organizational learning and its antecedents have emerged in the past few years. A sample of representative works includes the following: D. Vera and M. Crossan, "Strategic Leadership and Organizational Learning," *Academy of Management Review* 29, no. 2 (2004): 222–240; N. W. Hatch and J. H. Dyer, "Human Capital and Learning as a Source of Sustainable Competitive Advantage," *Strategic Management Journal* 25, no. 12, (2004): 1155–1178; M. Crossan and I. Berdrow, "Organizational Learning and

Strategic Renewal," *Strategic Management Journal* 24, no. 11 (2003): 1087–1106; J. B. Thomas, S. Watts Sussman, and J. C. Henderson, "Understanding 'Strategic Learning': Linking Organizational Learning, Knowledge Management and Sensemaking," *Organization Science* 12, no. 3 (2001): 331–345; F. Vermeulen and H. Barkema, "Learning Through Acquisitions," *Academy of Management Journal* 44, no. 3 (2001): 457–476; R. G. McGrath, "Exploratory Learning, Innovative Capacity, and Managerial Oversight," *Academy of Management Journal* 44, no. 1 (2001): 112–133; D. Z. Levin, "Organizational Learning and the Transfer of Knowledge: An Investigation of Quality Improvement," *Organization Science* 11, no. 6 (2000): 630–647; H. W. Volberda, "Toward the Flexible Form: How to Remain Vital in Hypercompetitive Environments," *Organization Science* 7, no. 4 (1996): 359–374; B. L. Simonin, "The Importance of Collaborative Know-How: An Empirical Test of the Learning Organization," *Academy of Management Journal* 40, no. 5 (1997): 1150–1174; W. W. Powell, K. W. Koput, and L. Smith-Doerr, "Interorganizational Collaboration and the Locus of Innovation: Networks of Learning in Biotechnology," *Administrative Science Quarterly* 41 (1996): 116–145; R. M. Grant, "Prospering in Dynamically Competitive Environments: Organizational Capability as Knowledge Integration," *Organization Science* 7, no. 4 (1996): 375–387; E. Bruderer and J. V. Singh, "Organizational Evolution, Learning, and Selection: A Genetic-Algorithm-Based Model," *Academy of Management Journal* 39, no. 5 (1996): 1322–1349; J. M. Pennings, H. Barkema, and S. Douma, "Organizational Learning and Diversification," *Academy of Management Journal* 37 (1994): 608–640; H. Barkema, O. Shenkar, and J. M. Pennings, "Foreign Entry, Cultural Barriers, and Learning," *Strategic Management Journal* 17 (1996): 151–166; A. Parkhe, "Interfirm Diversity, Organizational Learning, and Longevity in Global Strategic Alliances," *Journal of International Business Studies* 22 (1991): 579–601.

23. This section is adapted from M. McGill, J. W. Slocum, Jr., and D. Lei, "Management Practices in Learning Organizations," *Organizational Dynamics* (Summer 1992): 5–17; D. A. Garvin, "Building a Learning Organization," *Harvard Business Review* (July–August 1993): 78–91; K. Jones and T. Ohbora, "Managing the Heretical Company," *McKinsey Quarterly* 3 (1990): 20–45; C. Argyris, "Education for Leading-Learning," *Organizational Dynamics* 22, no. 2 (1993): 5–17; M. E. McGill and J. W. Slocum, Jr., *The Smarter Organization* (New York: Wiley, 1994); D. Miller, *The Icarus Paradox: How Exceptional Companies Bring About Their Own Downfall* (New York: Harper Business, 1990); J. W. Slocum, Jr., M. E. McGill, and D. Lei, "The New Learning Strategy: Anytime, Anything, Anywhere," *Organizational Dynamics* 23, no. 2 (1994): 33–48; C. Argyris, "The Executive Mind and Double-Loop Learning," *Organizational Dynamics* 11, no. 1 (1982): 5–22.

   Also see M. Marquardt and A. Reynolds, *The Global Learning Organization* (New York: Irwin, 1994); E. C. Nevis, A. C. DiBella, and J. M. Gould, "Understanding Organizations and Learning Systems," *Sloan Management Review* 36, no. 2 (1995): 73–85; I. Nonaka, "A Dynamic Theory of Organizational Knowledge Creation," *Organization Science* 5 (1994): 14–37; D. Levinthal and J. G. March, "The Myopia of Learning," *Strategic Management Journal* 14 (1993): 95–112; B. Kogut and U. Zander, "Knowledge of the Firm, Combinative Capabilities and the Replication of Technology," *Organization Science* 3 (1992): 383–397; A. Van de Van and D. Polley, "Learning While Innovating," *Organization Science* 3, no. 1 (1992): 92–116. R. Stata, "Organizational Learning—The Key to Management Innovation," *Sloan Management Review* 30, no. 3 (1989): 63–74.

24. See "Can Caddy's Driver Make GM Cool?" *BusinessWeek,* September 20, 2004, pp. 105–106; "Detroit Tries It the Japanese Way," *BusinessWeek,* January 26, 2004, pp. 76–77; "Rick Wagoner's Game Plan," *BusinessWeek,* February 10, 2003, pp. 50–60.

25. See, for example, H. Itami, *Mobilizing Invisible Assets* (Cambridge, MA: Harvard University Press, 1987), and W. Ouchi, *Theory Z: How American Business Can Meet the*

Japanese Challenge (Reading, MA: Addison-Wesley, 1981), for an early overview and discussion of the high-premium Japanese firms place on continuous training.

26. See, for example, T. Peters, "Rethinking Scale," *California Management Review* 35, no. 1 (1992): 7–29.

27. See "Johnson & Johnson Is on a Roll," *Fortune,* December 26, 1994, pp. 178–195.

28. See T. Hout, M. E. Porter, and E. Rudden, "How Global Companies Win Out," *Harvard Business Review* (September–October 1982): 98–106; C. K. Prahalad and Y. Doz, *The Multinational Mission* (New York: Free Press, 1987); and "A U.S.-Style Shakeup at Honda," *Fortune,* December 31, 1991, pp. 115–122.

29. See, for example, D. Dougherty and C. Hardy, "Sustained Product Innovation in Large, Mature Organizations: Overcoming Innovation-to-Organization Problems," *Academy of Management Journal* 39, no. 5 (1996): 1120–1153; E. E. Lawler III and J. R. Galbraith, "Avoiding the Corporate Dinosaur Syndrome," *Organizational Dynamics* 23, no. 2 (1994): 5–17; W. Weitzel and E. Johnson, "Reversing the Downward Spiral: Lessons from W. T. Grant and Sears Roebuck," *Academy of Management Executive* 5, no. 3 (1991): 7–22; E. C. Shapiro, *How Competitive Truths Become Competitive Traps* (New York: Wiley, 1991); "History Is Full of Giants That Failed to Adapt," *Forbes,* February 28, 1994, pp. 73–78.

30. See, for example, "GM Hits the Skids," *Fortune,* April 4, 2005, pp. 71–74; "Wide Gap Exists Between GM, Rivals in Labor Productivity, Report Says," *Wall Street Journal,* July 16, 1998, p. A4.

31. See "Japan's PC Market Bows to U.S. Makers as NEC Stronghold Continues to Loosen," *Wall Street Journal,* February 14, 1995, p. B4.

32. See "Kodak to Reorganize Its Business Again," *Wall Street Journal,* November 15, 2001, p. B12.

33. See "Japan Chip Makers Suffer From 'Structure,'" *Wall Street Journal,* November 13, 2001, p. A18.

34. The discussion in this section draws heavily on James Brian Quinn's excellent treatment of this subject in *Strategies for Change: Logical Incrementalism* (Homewood, IL: Irwin, 1980). These ideas, although frequently drawn from firms competing in low-change environments, are also applicable as initial steps to firms considering change in fast-changing environments. An enhanced and more elaborate discussion of these ideas can be found in M. Goold and J. B. Quinn, "The Paradox of Strategic Controls," *Strategic Management Journal* 11 (1990): 43–57.

35. James Brian Quinn refers to such comparisons as "shoot-outs" (p. 126) in *Strategies for Change: Logical Incrementalism* (Homewood, IL: Irwin, 1980).

36. See "The Welch Legacy: Creative Destruction," *Wall Street Journal,* September 10, 2001, p. A18.

37. See "This Is War," *Forbes,* August 16, 2004, pp. 65–68; "Cultural Evolution," *Wall Street Journal,* July 11, 2003, pp. B1, B6.

38. See "The Cisco Kid Rides Again," *Fortune,* July 26, 2004, pp. 132–140; "A Do-It-Yourself Plan at Cisco," *BusinessWeek,* September 10, 2001, p. 52.

Part Four

Corporate Governance

Chapter **11**   *Corporate Governance: Instilling Long-Term Value*

Corporate Governance: Instilling Long-Term Value

Chapter Outline

Morrison Knudsen[1]

On August 6, 1996 Judge Peter Walsh of the U.S. Bankruptcy Court, District of Delaware, approved Morrison Knudsen's plan of reorganization. It called for merger of Morrison Knudsen (MK)—a major engineering firm that built dams, bridges, electrical generating plants, and other large facilities—into Washington Construction Group (WCG). Holders of MK's $360 million secured debt would receive 45 percent of the common shares of the merged company; the remaining 55 percent would go to WCG shareholders. MK shareholders would receive only warrants entitling them to buy 5 percent of the merged company's common stock at a fixed price for six years. One knowledgeable observer valued these warrants at just $.08 per MK share. This outcome represented a devastating loss of market value for MK's shareholders, since MK's shares had sold for as much as $30 just eighteen months earlier.

According to observers, a major contributor to MK's difficulties was the company's CEO William Agee. Following his appointment as CEO in 1989, Agee steered the company toward larger, riskier projects—including a particle accelerator in Texas and a rapid transit system in Honolulu. Many of these projects turned out to be money losers. He instituted a policy of retaining an operating interest in more of the projects built by the company. A contract to build an 8.4-mile toll bridge from New Brunswick to Prince Edward Island and another to build a toll road to the new Denver airport, for example, were negotiated on this basis. Most of these arrangements failed to pan out. He spearheaded a disastrous diversification into railroad car assembly, a business the company

knew very little about. By 1995, this effort was producing large losses.

Having lost confidence in his ability to deal with the company's problems, MK's board finally forced Agee to resign. However, by the time this decision was reached in mid-1995, the company's strategic and financial positions and its stock market value had deteriorated very significantly. Had MK's board stepped in sooner, it might have been able to rescue the company before such damage had been inflicted. Why didn't the board act sooner? Several factors appear to have contributed to the board's inaction.

During his six and a half years as CEO, Agee systematically removed inside directors (that is, senior MK managers) from MK's board and replaced them with outside directors (individuals who were not employed by the company). As a result of this process, by 1995 Agee was the only inside director on MK's twelve-person board. Without any other inside director included in its membership, the board was deprived of a vital source of information about the true state of the company's welfare, which might have been useful to directors in evaluating Agee's overoptimistic assertions about the company. The problem was aggravated by Agee's habit of holding board meetings at sites far from Boise, Idaho, where the company was headquartered. This practice further reduced the ability of board members to query MK managers about the true state of the company's affairs. One director noted, "By doing that, you limit the board's access to knowledge and information."

Some of Agee's choices for board positions were well-known public figures: Peter Lynch, the fabled mutual fund manager from Fidelity; Peter Ueberroth, former baseball commissioner and organizer of the Los Angeles Olympic Games; and Zbigniew Brzezinski, former national security adviser. Several were very rich: Christopher Hemmeter, owner of gambling casinos and of the Hyatt Regency Waikoloa Resort in Hawaii; and John Arrillaga, a Silicon Valley real estate tycoon. Others were quite obscure: John Rogers, head of a small Chicago-based money management firm; and Irene Peden, an engineering professor in Seattle. MK's directors all shared two traits, however. None had any direct experience in MK's major industrial area of project construction and management; and none had ever been CEO of a large company. As a consequence, there was no one on MK's board during the period of Agee's mismanagement with sufficient background to challenge Agee on major issues.

This problem was exacerbated by personal considerations. Several directors (for example, Lynch, Ueberroth) were close personal friends of Agee. Several others had a common interest in a charity, founded by Agee's wife, which offered assistance to pregnant women as an alternative to abortion. At one point, half the members of MK's board had wives on the charity's board. This overlap was so extensive that the boards of the two organizations often met at the same time in the same city, with husbands and wives traveling together on MK's corporate jet. Agee and his wife worked hard to make such get-togethers festive affairs. According to one director who was present on a number of such occasions, "Agee was spectacular with the board. He kept the fun up. He knew when to bring the wives. He made directors look forward to meetings." Directors were, perhaps understandably, reluctant to criticize such a gracious host.

However, as the company's problems increased, criticism mounted from other sources. During fall 1994, a group of concerned top executives, shareholders, and company retirees sent a lengthy letter to the board "documenting the deteriorating financial performance" of the company.

The letter cited Agee's inept management, his "aggressive if not illusory balance sheet accounting," the high turnover of his management staff, his high pay, his long absences from the company's Boise headquarters following the move of his residence to Pebble Beach, California, and his use of company funds to acquire art objects for himself and his wife. Although most directors ignored the letter, William Clark, a former California Supreme Court justice who was the newest member of MK's board, was sufficiently concerned to begin an investigation. During subsequent weeks, he interviewed dozens of MK executives, retirees, bankers, and customers, and in due course reported his highly critical findings to other members of the board. According to one director, "What Clark told us was extremely damaging. Management had lost confidence in Bill [Agee]. Clark said management, in its dealing with the board, was told only to put the most optimistic stuff up on the projector."

As evidence of Agee's deviousness and ineptitude mounted, directors reluctantly reached the conclusion that he must go. At the February 9, 1995, board meeting held in San Francisco, Agee was asked to wait outside while the rest of the board debated his fate. After three and a half hours, Lynch and others finally emerged to inform Agee that he was fired. Shortly thereafter, the company announced that it would write off an additional $135 million not previously reported, bringing 1994 losses to $310 million. With cash draining away during ensuing months and bankers unwilling to provide additional financing, the board sought protection under Chapter 11 of the Bankruptcy Code. The bankruptcy court's solution for MK's difficulties was to merge the company with Washington Construction Croup, a successful competitor. As described earlier, MK's shareholders came away with very little in the transaction. The market value of their MK holdings declined from more than a half billion in 1989, the year Agee was appointed chairman, to a mere fraction of that following the 1996 announcement of MK's merger with WCG.

Introduction

When left to their own devices, CEOs sometimes pursue initiatives that are at variance with shareholder interests. Some CEOs may do so because they lack the wisdom to make decisions that truly foster shareholder interests. For example, Agee's decision to enter the railcar assembly business may represent a failure of this sort. He may not have envisioned how difficult a business this would be for the company. CEOs may also pursue initiatives that are contrary to shareholder interests for reasons of pride, ego, or greed. They may raise their personal interests over those of shareholders. CEO pay in some companies is closely tied to firm size. Agee may have moved MK into the railcar business not with any idea that it would increase shareholder welfare, but as a means to boost his own compensation. Agee's decision to move his home from Boise to Pebble Beach, California, appears to have been motivated primarily by personal considerations. He and his wife most likely preferred the excitement and elegance of California to the more austere conditions of southern Idaho. He probably also wanted to distance himself from critics in Boise who were becoming increasingly outspoken about his mismanagement of the company. As a result, Agee became increasingly isolated from overseeing important corporate operations.

corporate governance:
The set of policies designed to ensure the creation of long-term sustainable value for the firm's shareholders.

This chapter focuses on the broad issue of corporate governance. **Corporate governance** is the set of policies designed to ensure the creation of long-term sustainable value for the firm. Over the past five years, numerous corporate scandals have prompted a renewed interest in corporate governance, especially as the U.S. government instituted new laws and regulations that mandate increased oversight and auditing of business operations and financial reporting. Issues related to corporate governance are particularly relevant for large corporations, since ownership is widely diffused among shareholders. However, CEOs and senior managers oversee strategy formulation and implementation, as well as day-to-day operations. In most cases, they do not own a significant portion of the company. Thus, corporate governance focuses on how best to align the actions of management with the desires of shareholders.[2]

CEOs and managers are actually employees of the owners (shareholders). However, since CEOs and managers actually run the firm, there is little that shareholders can do to determine if managers' actions are in their best interests. Thus, there is always the potential risk that managers may not always act to preserve shareholders' interests; in fact, managers may seek to protect and enlarge their own interests at the expense of shareholders. This phenomenon is broadly known as the agency problem. An **agency problem** occurs when there is a conflict between the interests of managers and shareholders.[3]

agency problem:
When managers seek to protect and enlarge their own interests at the expense of shareholders. A conflict between the interests of managers and shareholders.

Our purpose in this chapter is to highlight some of the key issues related to the broad topic of corporate governance. Dealing with the agency problem requires a strong Board of Directors and other organizational mechanisms that limit the ability of managers to engage in self-serving actions. In addition, internal auditing systems are needed to oversee managerial behavior and to ensure accurate financial reporting. Over the past few years, the U.S. government has implemented a number of laws and regulations that are designed to eliminate corporate malfeasance and enhance the accuracy of financial reporting.

In this chapter, we will examine how a company's Board of Directors plays a pivotal role in corporate governance. We will consider some important factors that historically have led boards to neglect their obligations to shareholders. We will also describe recent developments that have caused boards to take their responsibilities to shareholders more seriously. Renewed board diligence has also brought about important changes in board operation. In particular, the Sarbanes-Oxley Act of 2002 has compelled large U.S. companies to dramatically strengthen the power, independence, and liability of boards to oversee senior management. In addition, we will review additional changes currently being debated to make boards even more responsive to shareholder needs. We will also examine trends in corporate governance that are occurring outside the United States as well.

The Board of Directors

The primary legal mechanism that is designed to align CEO actions with shareholder interests is a company's Board of Directors (BOD). Elected annually by a firm's shareholders, directors are responsible for ensuring that the CEO behaves in ways that promote shareholder interests. In the mid-1990s, the "typical" board of a public U.S. company consists of about thirteen members called directors.[4] Approximately one-quarter of this number are "insiders" (members of the enterprise's management), while the remaining three-quarters are "outsiders" (individuals who are not employees of the company). Most of the latter are full-time senior executives at other companies, many themselves holding the position of president or CEO.

Directors are elected annually at the company's annual meeting. Almost always, a single slate of nominees for each annual election is developed by the current board and presented to shareholders for their approval. Shareholders vote on this slate either by personally attending the firm's annual meeting or, more typically, by sending in a mail proxy before the date of the annual meeting. Once elected, directors attend on average about seven directors' meetings a year, each session lasting somewhat less than a day in length. Most outside directors also serve on one or more board committees, the most common of which are nomination (to recommend nominees for election to the board), compensation (to determine CEO compensation), audit (to gather information needed to evaluate CEO performance), finance (to evaluate investments proposed by management), and executive (to communicate with the CEO on critical issues in between board meetings). The total amount of time the typical director spends attending full board meetings and working on board committees is about a hundred hours per year. For this service, he or she receives an average annual compensation of about $40,000.

Directors have at their disposal powerful tools to motivate the CEO to act in the interests of shareholders. For example, they have final say in determining who will be the firm's CEO. They also determine how much the CEO will be paid. They can, if they choose, veto measures proposed by the CEO. Finally, they can discharge a CEO who fails to meet their expectations to enhance the company's long-term value to shareholders.

Why Directors Often Neglect Shareholder Interests

Over the past decade, however, directors, have often failed to carry out this mandate. Indeed, boards of altogether too many firms have allowed the CEO to pursue with relative impunity initiatives that have harmed shareholder interests—some actions leading to outright bankruptcy. In more notorious cases (for example, Enron, WorldCom), there has been evidence of potentially significant breaches of criminal law. In the case of Morrison Knudsen, the board remained passive for years while Agee pursued policies seriously detrimental to the company's shareholders. Only after MK suffered heavy losses and experienced a severe loss of competitive position did the board finally act. By that time, it was too late to save much of value for the shareholders.

With powers such as these at their command, why have boards so frequently failed to stand up to CEOs who neglect shareholder interests? Among the most important reasons for this failure are (1) time constraints that board members face, (2) the inordinate power exerted by most CEOs, (3) CEO-related factors, including the placement of inside managers on the board and outside directors' personal considerations, and (4) the inherent difficulties shareholders face when trying to oust directors who fail to carry out their duties.

Time Constraints

As noted earlier, about three-quarters of directors on the typical board are outsiders holding demanding executive positions at other firms. Such individuals understandably have limited time to devote to board oversight duties. This problem is compounded by the fact that many outside directors serve on several boards. For example, approximately 65 percent of all outside directors serve on at least two boards, and 20 percent serve on as many as four.[5] Directors with such heavy responsibilities often do not have sufficient time to develop a deep understanding of each company on whose board they sit. Yet, such understanding is necessary to make sound evaluative judgments of CEO performance. Two knowledgeable experts of board activities comment on this problem:

> Based on our experience, the most widely shared problem directors have is lack of time to carry out their duties. The typical board meets less than eight times annually. Even with committee meetings and informal gatherings before or after the formal board meeting, directors rarely spend as much as a working day together in and around each meeting. Further, in many boardrooms, too much of this limited time is occupied with reports from management and various formalities. In essence, the limited time outside directors have together is not used in a meaningful exchange of ideas among themselves or with management/inside directors.[6]

CEO Factors

The CEO is a member of the board of virtually every public U.S. company. A CEO's presence on the board makes honest evaluation more difficult. The CEO is then present at all formal deliberations of the board, so any criticism of the CEO must be directed face-to-face. Some directors are naturally reluctant to confront the CEO in this way. And the CEO is unlikely to direct criticism to his or her self. Harold Geneen, former CEO of ITT Corporation, commented on the latter problem:

> If the Board of Directors is really there to represent the interests of stockholders, what is the chief executive doing on the board? Doesn't he have a conflict of interest? He's the professional manager. He cannot represent the shareholders and impartially sit in judgment on himself.[7]

CEO/Chairperson combination. The problem is aggravated when the CEO also holds the position of board chairperson. Since a chairperson plays a pivotal role in setting the agenda for board meetings and in leading board deliberations, he or she can steer deliberations away from areas that might invite CEO criticism. Combining the positions of CEO and chairperson thus increases the risk that directors will avoid their oversight duties. Despite the obvious problems created by combining these positions, about three-quarters of all U.S. public companies do so.

Loyalty to CEO. Inside directors are immediate subordinates of the firm's CEO. They are dependent on the CEO for career advancement and compensation increases. As a result, they are generally loyal supporters, reluctant to forcefully criticize the CEO on key issue.

Outside directors often feel such reluctance for different reasons. In many cases, they may have been initially invited or selected for a board position by the CEO. Therefore, they largely owe their position on the board to the CEO. An outside director who criticizes a CEO too harshly risks being excluded from the nominee list for the subsequent year's board election. Loss of a director's seat involves loss of the many perquisites (perqs) that typically accompany board membership. These include elevated status in the business community, large fees for just a few days of work each year, and perqs such as use of the company's private jet aircraft, lavish accommodations during board meetings, generous provision for retirement, lucrative stock grants, and even sizeable consulting contracts. As an example of the latter, RJR Nabisco once granted a $250,000 two-year consulting contract to one of its outside directors, and an $180,000 six-year contract to another.[8] Henry Kissinger earned as much as $500,000 in some years from American Express in consulting fees while serving as a director of the company.[9] Since consulting assignments are at the discretion of management, directors who desire them are understandably reluctant to criticize the CEO too harshly.

Weak Shareholder Power

Ordinarily, one would expect that shareholders of poor-performing companies would quickly expel directors and replace them with individuals more diligent in pursuing shareholder interests. Until recently, however, shareholders have rarely taken such initiative. Morrison Knudsen's shareholders are typical in this respect. During the extended period of MK's declining performance, they made no concerted effort to replace the board. Such apparent passiveness results in part from the difficulty shareholders face removing ineffective directors. In each annual election, shareholders are typically offered a single slate of candidates proposed by the incumbent board. An election of directors is therefore more a ratification of candidates proposed by the incumbent board than an election in any real sense of the term. One observer claims, with some reason, that the process is "procedurally much more akin to the elections held by the Communist party of North Korea than those held in Western democracies."[10] A group of dissident shareholders may, of course, nominate a competing slate of candidates. However, to succeed in getting its slate elected, the group must communicate its nominees to shareholders and persuade a majority to vote favorably. Large corporations often have several hundred thousand shareholders, so building support for an alternate slate of directors can be time-consuming and very expensive. Furthermore, such effort even when attempted is rarely successful, in part because most shareholders have little basis on which to evaluate the merits of a competing slate of directors, so they generally simply go along with the one recommended by the incumbent board. Because of these difficulties, shareholders have, until quite recently, rarely attempted to oust incumbent boards.

Early Forces of Change

Over the past twenty years, a number of developments have caused boards to become more diligent in supervising CEOs in recent years. These include (1) rising public criticism, (2) rising director liability, (3) increased institutional ownership of stock, and (4) prospect for corporate takeovers.

In particular, since 2002, demands for greater director accountability and improved corporate governance have spurred many companies to reform how the board interacts with senior management. Perhaps the single greatest factor that catalyzed the reform of board operations was the numerous corporate scandals and failures that traumatized so many people in 2001 and 2002.

Public Criticism

Knowledgeable observers have long criticized boards for their laxness in supervising CEOs. For example, Myles Mace of the Harvard Business School, writing as early as 1971, argued that directors of most firms are little more than "ornaments on a corporate Christmas tree."[11] A decade later, management scholar Peter Drucker sounded an even more scathing criticism, concluding that "Whenever an institution malfunctions as consistently as boards of directors have in nearly every major fiasco of the last 40 or 50 years, it is futile to blame men. It is the institution that malfunctions."[12] Criticism of board dysfunction continued during the 1980s and 1990s, because many companies began engaging in financial machinations to beat Wall Street's expectations for generating positive earnings reports.

Rising Director Liability

Several spectacular business failures during the 1970s and early 1980s dramatized the incompetence of corporate boards. Included in the list of casualties or near casualties were such revered names as Penn Central Railroad, Rolls-Royce, International Harvester, and Chrysler. These failures led members of the press and other interested parties to ask why the boards of failed companies had not stepped in sooner to correct obvious difficulties. An SEC report on Penn Central, for example, noted that "throughout the entire Penn Central debacle, including the loss of many hundreds of millions of dollars by shareholders, the board had done nothing."[13]

This surge in corporate failures sparked a flurry of lawsuits against directors for neglecting their duty. In 1985, for example, the Delaware Supreme Court found directors of Trans Union Corporation guilty for failing to properly evaluate the value of an outside offer to purchase the company. The court found directors not just negligent, but "grossly" negligent, making them personally liable for damages suffered by shareholders. Many large corporations were terrified by this and similar rulings.[14] These adverse rulings caused insurance companies to reduce liability coverage for directors,[15] and to increase the price of the reduced coverage they did offer. Neglect of shareholder interests thus became significantly more costly to directors.

Increased Institutional Ownership

A significant shift has occurred during the past several decades in the way shares of public firms are held. Ever since the 1970s, large financial institutions have become the dominant holders of shares in public corporations, rather than individuals. As a result of this vast growth, financial institutions now control upwards of 50 percent of the shares of public companies.

Regulations prohibit financial institutions from owning large blocks of shares in any single company.[16] Consequently, institutional owners, like individual investors, rarely control more than a small percentage of the outstanding shares of any company. Nevertheless, institutional owners are in a much better position than individual shareholders to pressure boards to improve company performance. Portfolio managers who oversee the holdings of financial institutions have the expertise needed to correctly evaluate company performance; they have the time required to communicate their wishes to corporate boards; and they have the resources needed to finance proxy battles to force recalcitrant boards to implement desired changes.

Until quite recently, however, financial institutions have been reluctant to vigorously use their formidable powers, preferring instead to simply sell shares of portfolio companies with which they have become dissatisfied. This attitude derives in part from restraints imposed by governmental bodies. Federal regulations, for example, prohibit mutual funds from trading shares of companies in whose affairs they become active.[17] Active involvement in corporate governance can thus limit a mutual fund's ability to trade its holdings.

Pension funds have historically avoided involvement in corporate governance for different reasons.[18] Most pension funds are established by business enterprises to provide retirement benefits for their employees. The monies collected are then turned over to a financial institution such as an insurance company, bank, or investment management firm, which then invests the monies on behalf of pension beneficiaries. To secure pension fund business, financial institutions must be very careful not to alienate top managers of corporations whose pension assets they manage, or wish to manage. One sure way to alienate corporate clients is to become overactive in governance of portfolio firms. Corporate clients generally do not like such involvement because they do not want institutional owners interfering in governance of their own companies. Well aware of how sensitive this issue is for their corporate clients, pension fund managers have historically shied away from active involvement in governance of companies in their portfolios.

The one exception to this generalization is public pension funds—pension funds created by governmental bodies such as states and municipalities to provide retirement benefits for public employees. Since governmental bodies have no shareholders, their top executives do not have the same dread of shareholder activism as their private-sector counterparts. It is not surprising, therefore, that public pension funds have taken the lead in shareholder activism. Particularly prominent in this effort has been the California Public Employees Retirement System (CalPERS), the nation's largest pension fund. Its outspoken former CEO once claimed that "We are no longer into CEO bashing. We are now into director-bashing."[19] CalPERS has submitted numerous resolutions for shareholder vote at annual meetings of companies in which CalPERS owns shares. Other public pension funds are beginning to follow its lead.[20] Although few shareholder resolutions submitted by CalPERS or others ever receive support of a majority of a firm's shareholders, many have been endorsed by a *sufficient* minority to cause boards to change their position on important issues. Such resolutions have also led boards to enter negotiation with sponsors, and in a number of cases, a satisfactory compromise has been worked out without having to put resolutions to full shareholder vote. Public pension funds have thus helped to push corporate boards toward more vigorous oversight of corporate managers.

Prospect for Corporate Takeover

Perhaps the most powerful single force causing directors to pay closer attention to shareholder interests has been the steep rise in corporate takeovers during the 1980s and 1990s. A corporate takeover occurs when an individual or a corporation purchases all outstanding shares of a company. The 1980s witnessed an unprecedented number of such transactions. Many were "hostile" in nature. A hostile takeover occurs when the board of a target company resists efforts by the buying party, commonly referred to as a "raider," to gain control. Typically, a raider trying to gain control of a target company does so by going directly to the company's shareholders with an offer to buy their shares. Companies with a low share price are particularly vulnerable to this tactic since the price a raider has to pay to gain control is then reduced. For example, during the steep recession of the early 1980s, stock market declines drove down the share prices of even well-performing companies, and reduced share prices of poor-performing companies to truly bargain-basement prices. This development made many firms highly vulnerable to corporate raiding. Raiders often financed their takeovers by issuing "junk bonds," a form of financing that became increasingly available as the 1980s progressed. By issuing huge amounts of junk bonds, corporate raiders could often gain control of even quite large companies without having to put up much cash of their own. Famous raiders include T. Boone Pickens and Carl Icahn, both of whom shook up board and senior management practices at a number of companies.

The takeover binge of the 1980s alerted directors to their vulnerability, making them realize that failure to discharge their responsibility to shareholders might lead to their own ousting by a corporate raider. As more and more companies were taken over and their boards replaced, directors increasingly feared that the same thing might happen to them. This growing threat caused directors at many companies to take their oversight duties more seriously.

Fear of corporate raiders led boards at some firms to erect antitakeover devices, the most common of which is the "poison pill." One typical form of poison pill entitles shareholders to purchase additional shares of a company at a steep discount (typically 50 percent) whenever an outside party is close to gaining control of the company against the board's will. The outside party attempting a takeover is of course excluded from this offer. This device helps protect a company from takeover by making it prohibitively expensive for a raider to gain control against the board's will. Shareholders have not been happy with antitakeover devices, since they make it difficult to oust management of poor-performing firms. Shareholders (particularly institutional shareholders) have therefore exerted strong effort to have such devices removed. Two knowledgeable observers described this effort:

> By the end of the 1980's, most large companies bristled with a host of "anti-takeover devices." . . . These protective devices were one of the main reasons for the emergence of shareholder activism, and the dismantling of such devices was one of their main early aims.[21]

Efforts by shareholders to remove antitakeover devices have been largely successful. Firms today that consistently disappoint shareholder expectations are therefore highly vulnerable to corporate takeover.

Catastrophic Corporate Failures

During the past few years, a seemingly unending array of companies were caught engaging in corporate malfeasance, accounting irregularities, or outright theft by members of corporate management. Scandals plagued such companies as Adelphia Communications (family misuse of corporate funds), Enron (off-balance sheet activities and the use of fictitious corporate entities), HealthSouth (CEO greed and falsified accounting), Tyco International (alleged CEO expropriation of corporate loans and cash for personal use), Martha Stewart Living Omnimedia (CEO indicted for lying to federal investigators regarding personal stock sales), WorldCom (biggest bankruptcy in U.S. corporate history and falsified accounting records), ImClone Systems (CEO Sam Waksal's blatant insider trading of company stock), and Qwest Communications (improper accounting and revenue recognition), to name just a few. This cataclysmic explosion of alleged corporate wrongdoing wreaked havoc with the American public's faith in large corporations and business in general. In many cases, employees of these firms lost their jobs as management was forced to retrench and clean up their act. Shareholders of all types (for example, individual and institutional) lost untold billions of equity as the market melted down in 2002. Let us briefly examine the developments behind two of the more notorious examples: WorldCom and Tyco International.

The implosion of WorldCom in July 2002 as the biggest bankruptcy in U.S. corporate history stemmed from the rampant fraudulent accounting that corporate management perpetrated. The accounting fraud at WorldCom will likely total close to $11 billion once everything is tallied. Under CEO Bernie Ebbers, WorldCom is accused of falsifiying as much as $9 billion in earnings going back to 1999. Much of the fraud centered on WorldCom's deliberate mischaracterization of key telecom costs as capital expenditures rather than operating expenses. In addition, when WorldCom's revenues were starting to slow down, management relied on finding and using one-time revenue items to boost its top line. This deceptive combination had the effect of artificially boosting net income. WorldCom's fraud represents a massive breakdown in corporate governance as its management deceived its external auditor by feeding it falsified documents. WorldCom prevented its auditor from gaining access to the company's most important databases where core financial information was kept. Despite this, the auditor (Arthur Andersen) continued to sign off on WorldCom's numbers and did not press its information request before the firm's audit committee. CEO Ebbers also personified greed and extreme ambition at the highest levels of management. Blinded by his own belief that WorldCom could continue growing even when the telecom market became saturated, Ebbers convinced the board to extend him a personal loan of $400 million to cover his losing stock position. Ebbers used the value of his massive WorldCom stock holdings to purchase timberland and other assets. In March 2005, Ebbers was found guilty of a variety of charges related to the WorldCom fraud.[22]

In perhaps one of the most publicized cases of personal greed, the CEO of Tyco International, Dennis Kozlowski, lived a life of extreme luxury in large part using corporate funds. Kozlowski grew Tyco's revenues over tenfold from 1992 to 2001, and he expanded the company through conglomerate-like acquisitions of hundreds of different businesses. By the time Kozlowski's excesses were discovered, Tyco had become a major player in such disparate areas as health care, security systems, electronics, plastics, and engineered products. Although Kozlowski generally acquired solid businesses, Tyco fell under a huge debt load, and rumors about impending bankruptcy became widespread in late 2002. Although new CEO Ed Breen has stabilized Tyco's shaky earnings, Kozlowski himself was indicted and tried for conspiracy and grand larceny charges. The case resulted in a mistrial in April 2004 because of a lone juror's holdout position. Kozlowski will likely face a retrial on these charges, and he faces separate charges for evading New York state sales taxes on the purchase of expensive art. During the trial, the jury and the public learned of Kozlowski's extreme lifestyle that he allegedly supported through company funds totaling near $600 million. For example, he purchased such wildly extravagant items as a $6,000 shower curtain, a $15,000 dog umbrella stand, and threw his wife a $2.1 million birthday bash.[23]

Ironically, Tyco International under CEO Breen has become a model of corporate governance. The first thing that Breen did as CEO was to replace the entire Board of Directors. Breen believed he needed to establish credibility with the financial community that Tyco's former practices would be eliminated. He also established an internal audit staff that reports directly to the board's audit committee. In addition, Breen fired 290 of the 300 top managers at Tyco to purge an older corporate culture that promoted deal making and aggressive acquisitions.[24]

The Sarbanes-Oxley Act of 2002

The collapse of Enron and WorldCom, combined with the apparently rising number of scandals and accounting irregularities at numerous companies, generated enormous public outrage. Managers and employees began wondering if they were working in a company that could become another Enron. Fear and distrust of managers became widespread. Accounting firms came under intense scrutiny after Arthur Andersen's role in destroying documents during the Enron scandal was publicized. In July 2002, Congress passed the Sarbanes-Oxley Act. This landmark piece of legislation dramatically increased the range of criminal and civil penalties that the government could impose on large corporations and accounting firms for violating a strict new set of regulations designed to improve corporate governance. Although the Sarbanes-Oxley Act is extremely complicated, some of the most important provisions related to corporate governance include the following:[25]

- Accounting firms must cooperate with a Public Company Accounting Board to create high ethical standards for auditing companies. Accounting firms must also follow the standards set by the Board to ensure independence and accurate reporting. The largest accounting firms are subject to annual quality reviews, and all others are reviewed every three years.
- The Securities and Exchange Commission (SEC) retains oversight and enforcement authority over the Public Company Accounting Board.
- Accounting firms that audit companies cannot provide consulting or other advisory services to the same company.
- The CEO must certify the accuracy of a company's quarterly and annual financial statements.
- The CEO and other signing officers are responsible for establishing and maintaining internal financial controls.
- The CEO and other signing officers must disclose to the auditor any fraud that might impact the company's internal controls.
- The Act also makes it illegal for any corporate officer or director to mislead, coerce, manipulate, or fraudulently influence auditors during the auditing process.
- If a restatement of financial statements is required because of material non-compliance with financial reporting requirements, the CEO and CFO must return any bonus or incentive-based compensation received during the past twelve months. This also includes any profit on stock or security sales during the same period.
- The SEC can prevent any person who violates the Act from acting as a corporate officer or director of the company.
- The Act also prohibits corporate officers and directors from engaging in stock trades during blackout periods.
- Financial disclosures are significantly strengthened: Every financial report must be filed in accordance with Generally Accepted Accounting Principles (GAAP). Equally important, all material off-balance sheet transactions and other relationships with unconsolidated entities (for example, some types of strategic alliances, leasing arrangements, long-term leases) must be disclosed.
- The Act also prohibits the issuance of personal loans to senior managers, and requires the disclosure of transactions involving corporate officers, directors, and shareholders owning more than 10 percent of the company (by the second day following the transaction).
- Each company's annual report must provide an internal control report that contains an assessment of the effectiveness of the company's reporting system (and attested to by the auditor).
- Senior management must also state if the company has adopted a code of ethics for senior financial officers to promote honest and ethical conduct.
- Wall Street research analysts covering the stock of a company must disclose potential conflicts of interest when they recommend equities in research reports.
- The Act also makes it a criminal offense to knowingly destroy documents or create documents that impede, obstruct, or influence any existing or contemplated federal investigation.

- The Act also imposes white-collar criminal penalties for tampering with records or impeding an official proceeding. The penalties for wire and mail fraud were extended from five to ten years.

There are numerous other complex provisions of the Sarbanes-Oxley Act that are far beyond the scope of this book. Companies have reacted to this Act with some apprehension, since there are questions about the scope and intent of some specific provisions of the law. The fact that CEOs must now attest to the accuracy of their financial reporting has triggered a huge wave of new types of internal controls being instituted within most large corporations. Many CEOs have now compelled their divisional managers to attest to the accuracy of their line of business results as well. The greater degree of regulation by the SEC and accounting boards also means that CEOs will spend more time ensuring the firms' numbers are accurate, possibly resulting in his or her spending less time with operational issues and interacting with customers. Costs of complying with the Act are likely to skyrocket, particularly with respect to new software systems that can better monitor financial performance and reporting.[26] Some analysts and commentators believe that the new law could redefine the very nature of what the Board of Directors does, especially the audit committee. Some fear that in reaction to the law, the board may end up "micromanaging" how a company is run. In addition, the law requires more independent audit committees to ensure a proper distance from corporate management.[27]

In conjunction with the Sarbanes-Oxley Act, the New York Stock Exchange (NYSE) and the Nasdaq stock market have issued a number of proposals that are also designed to improve corporate governance. One NYSE-based proposal includes the expensing of stock options, and ensuring that the board will have a majority of independent directors. Other proposals also include requiring boards to meet without the presence of management to preserve the integrity of their assessment of corporate performance. The issue of expensing stock options is a complex one, but it focuses on the broader issue of compensation. Many growing companies, especially those in high-technology fields, use options as a means to attract and retain talented employees. **Options** represent the right but not the obligation to purchase (or sell) a company's stock at a preset price at some predetermined time in the future. Options are highly sought after, since a company's stock performance directly translates into personal wealth for employees. However, the value of the option can change dramatically, even within a short time period. Companies have issued and given options to employees because they want them to feel that they can strike it rich if they stay with the company and put in their utmost personal efforts to deliver high performance. CEOs and senior managers received the largest proportion and number of options. Many, in turn, engaged in a sort of "gamesmanship" on Wall Street to beat earnings expectations so as to keep their company's stock price high (and thus their options valuable). Yet, the granting of options to managers and employees is controversial because it does represent a form of compensation; however, the actual value of what the manager or employee receives can change substantially. In many cases, if the company's stock price plummets, the employee may be holding options that are financially worthless. During the go-go days of the late 1990s when high-technology companies enjoyed soaring stock prices, these options easily made thousands of employees instant millionaires. However, the cost of these options was not treated as a normal operating expense on the companies' financial statements. Option pricing is highly complex, and developing an appropriate accounting-based formula to value options has aroused considerable debate in the financial and regulatory communities. Starting in late 2002, many large U.S. companies began treating options as an expense, including Coca-Cola and General Electric. However, some of the biggest high-technology companies, including Intel and Oracle, have resisted these efforts.[28]

Options:
The right but not the obligation to purchase or sell a company's stock at a pre-set price within a pre-defined time period.

Leveraging Technology: Complying with Sarbanes-Oxley[29]

As the Sarbanes-Oxley Act of 2002 begins to compel companies to fulfill important federally mandated requirements in 2004 and 2005, many firms are beginning to discover how burdensome the new regulations are. One of the most important aspects of Sarbanes-Oxley is the requirement that senior management testify to the accuracy of their financial reporting and report their findings to investors in a short time period. Moreover, Sarbanes-Oxley will increase the amount of effort and time needed to audit and maintain internal accounting controls to improve financial transparency and to discover potential corporate fraud or misuse of funds in the earliest stages. Companies are now required to establish tighter controls over all sorts of financial reports, ranging from reimbursement of employee expenses to tracking inventory, and to maintaining the integrity of the financial data in their computer systems.

At the time of this writing, it is becoming clear that establishing and maintaining internal controls are growing financial and organizational burdens to companies of all sizes. According to one report, General Electric spent close to $30 million making its systems compliant with the law, whereas giant insurer AIG may have spent close to $300 million. Also, RHR International and Directorship released a survey of corporate boards that indicates annual compliance with Sarbanes-Oxley averages $16 million per company. Although the full cost of complying with Sarbanes-Oxley will likely escalate, it is expected that many firms will begin to invest in new forms of accounting and auditing software systems to authenticate and automate many internal controls once performed manually and stored in paper archives. For example, newly developed security-based software will enable companies to monitor and control every financial record and transaction within the firm. Companies will be able to use this software to track how much was spent, who the recipient was, who approved the expenditure, and whether it was within the budgeted allotment.

Much of the software used for Sarbanes-Oxley compliance is similar to that developed by banks to identify suspicious transactions that may signify money-laundering activities or other illegal transfer of funds. Banks routinely invest in technology upgrades that allow them to track their customers'

balances and to note if they deposited or withdrew very large sums in a short period. In particular, the Patriot Act (passed in response to the September 11, 2001, terrorist act) dramatically tightened the regulations for screening customer transactions and for checking on customer identities to avoid fraud and support of potential terrorist-related funding activities.

Sarbanes-Oxley will likely result in the closer integration of key finance and information technology functions within the firm. Financial officers will have to work much more closely with technology officers and personnel to design financial monitoring systems that track the flow of funds within and outside the company. In turn, accounting firms performing these corporate audits will have to become extremely well versed in all aspects of current and future compliance-based software and technology. The role of the auditor will also reflect these changes as he or she must evaluate and assess the integrity of a company's internal controls, in addition to ensuring the accuracy of the financial reports themselves. Because CEOs and CFOs are now required to personally sign off on their company's financial statements, it is very likely that senior management will now require divisional and middle managers to do the same as part of their jobs. Thus, internal compliance at every level in the organization will mean that each manager with any kind of financial oversight or spending authority will be forced to undertake his or her own intricate audits to better understand and track how funds are used. This growing use of technology-based tools to further strengthen internal controls is part of a larger and longer-term trend whereby companies of all sizes will steadily automate all parts of their business systems.

Yet, Sarbanes-Oxley's biggest challenges will be organizational. New technologies can provide the platform for standardized and smoother corporate financial reporting, but the need for accuracy will likely mean that managers will have to become more accustomed to understanding how "the numbers" are generated in his or her business. Sarbanes-Oxley will likely result in many managers' becoming more risk-averse for fear that they cannot explain how their businesses perform over the short-term, where managers feel they have the most control.

Recent Trends in Board Operation

Even though the last couple of years have witnessed what appear to be monumental steps in reforming corporate governance, board activism has actually increased steadily over the past two decades. During the early 1990s, for example, boards took more aggressive steps to dismiss

CEOs that delivered poor corporate performance. In fact, during an eighteen-month period from 1992 to 1993, more than a dozen CEOs were shown the door. Included on this list were heads of such well-known firms as Compaq Computer, Tenneco, Digital Equipment, GM, IBM, Westinghouse Electric, American Express, and Kodak. Even back then,

> These oustings represented nothing less than a sea-change in American governance. Boards of directors were finally holding managements accountable for poor performance. The "Pharonic CEO had given way to the fired CEO."[30]

The Sarbanes-Oxley Act, combined with widespread public outrage and shareholder-initiated legal action, has only accelerated this trend. There are now many fundamental changes in the way that boards operate. Some of the most important trends that have accelerated since the 1990s include the following:

Smaller Board Size

For the past decade, boards have been shrinking in size. For example, one earlier investigation found that average board size declined from fifteen in 1988 to thirteen in 1993.[31] With fewer directors on the typical board, it is now easier for a group of dissident directors to gather together enough colleagues to confront the CEO on controversial issues.

The more directors on a board, the greater is the opportunity for variety in terms of director background, contacts, and expertise. A large board also provides ample manpower to staff increasingly important board committees. A large board, however, makes it more difficult for a dissident director to muster support for a minority position, because a dissident shareholder must then win over more individuals to gain support for a controversial proposal. Given these trade-offs, what is the proper size for corporate boards? Results of a recent survey indicate that in the eyes of directors, boards of U.S. firms are currently at about the optimal size. The directors surveyed indicated that the ideal size for a corporate board is about twelve—a figure very close to the thirteen directors currently on the typical U.S. board.[32]

Greater Board Independence with Outside Directors

The proportion of outside, relative to inside, directors on corporate boards has been increasing. Thus, while in 1960 fewer than half of all directors were outsiders,[33] this proportion had increased to 75 percent by the early 1990s.[34] Although empirical evidence concerning the impact of outsider directors on corporate performance from earlier studies is mixed, recent legislative and regulatory changes are likely to increase the proportion of outside directors on the board.[35]

Outsiders are less dependent than insiders on the goodwill of the CEO for important things like career advancement and salary increase, so they are often more willing to challenge the CEO on substantive issues. Increased use of outsiders has helped boards be more assertive in promoting shareholder interests.

Inside directors are generally thought to be more dependent on the CEO than outside directors, and therefore are less effective in advocating shareholder positions that might conflict with CEO priorities. According to one authority, inside directors "no doubt owe their seat on the board to the Chair/CEO and are the last directors to pipe up with anything the CEO prefers left unsaid."[36] Insiders, nevertheless, serve a useful board role. Because they are generally more knowledgeable about the company and its industry, they can provide valuable input to board deliberations. The value of such input is well illustrated by the Morrison Knudsen case at the beginning of the chapter. The absence of any inside directors apart from CEO Agee on MK's board deprived directors of vital information about the company needed to properly evaluate

Agee's performance. To ensure that such information is available during board deliberations, a few inside directors should be included on most boards. How many? Directors surveyed about the matter indicated a preference of about one insider for every three outsiders[37]—a ratio that is fairly close to that which currently pertains for boards of most U.S. firms.

In this decade, the search for outside board members who can think and act independently may become more complicated with the passing of Sarbanes-Oxley. Ironically, the need for greater board independence means that there is a greater demand for seasoned people who can actually monitor corporate management. In particular, the amount of time that board members must devote to their much more complicated tasks means that such work in itself has become a full-time job. Vital committees, particularly those regarding audit and compensation, have an especially high demand for independent board members with financial training and experience. The definition of independence in the United States is also strict. Directors receiving more than $100,000 per year in direct compensation cannot be considered independent until three years after such compensation has ended.[38]

The nature of board membership is changing quickly. According to Mercer Delta Consulting, a unit of Marsh & McClennan, a survey of two hundred of the largest one thousand companies in the United States showed that 48 percent of directors have an independent director who provides board leadership. Of those surveyed, 59 percent also said that independent directors will likely have the biggest impact on board effectiveness.[39]

The move to spur greater board independence has not been limited to large public companies. Scandals have also tainted several large mutual fund companies that engaged in illegal forms of trading that ultimately hurt shareholder returns. As a core investment vehicle for many Americans, mutual funds depend on their integrity to earn the public trust to manage their money. In June 2004, the SEC adopted a series of important mutual fund governance requirements that increase the number of independent directors from 40 percent to 75 percent of the board. The chairperson must also be independent, and there are required separate meetings of independent directors at least once a quarter to assess performance.[40] Scandal never touched the two biggest mutual fund companies—Fidelity Investments and Vanguard Group. Both companies' leaders have been calling for even more aggressive governance measures to rebuild investor trust.

Greater Education and Involvement of Board Members

The accounting scandals and other financial irregularities have also highlighted just how much financial expertise is needed for board effectiveness. Paradoxically, many board members serving on companies have comparatively little financial and accounting acumen to evaluate large companies with multiple lines of business and complex operations. Over the past few years, an increasing number of companies are compelling their board members to improve their financial literacy so that they can better ask the kinds of questions that are needed for improved corporate governance. This means that board members need to ask some very fundamental questions about the company they oversee. Awareness of changes in accounting regulations and methods is essential, especially concerning liabilities and off-balance sheet items, such as stock options, pension obligations, synthetic leases, and complex derivatives. Board members need to ask tough questions regarding how a company will go about paying for an expensive acquisition of another company. In the past, many firms have used their elevated stock price as a "currency" to engage in noncash-based acquisitions. Recent changes in accounting regulations regarding the valuation of "goodwill" and other intangible assets have made such practices more difficult, if not prohibited. Thus, board members need to pay special attention to matters of corporate growth and expansion to determine if such moves truly build on a firm's distinctive competence.[41]

At Sempra Energy, the company holds periodic workshops for its board members to provide them with the insight and tools needed for financial literacy. Sempra board members are given intensive courses in accounting and finance to increase their financial oversight effectiveness. With greater awareness of these issues, Sempra hopes that its board members can understand the nature of its business, as well as the financial risks that energy production and trading can entail. In turn, board members will feel more empowered to ask the needed tough questions so that Sempra's senior management do not steer the company in a direction that is far beyond its operational and financial capabilities.[42]

At The Home Depot, board members are required to visit at least twelve Home Depot stores and other operations every year. The purpose of these visits is to keep board members informed about Home Depot's operations at the most basic level—the actual occurrences in the store. Home Depot has implemented this policy for over two decades to ensure that board members are more effective and can understand the nuts-and-bolts of the business. Board members review each store's appearance and provide recommendations on how better to improve customer service. Robert Nardelli, CEO of Home Depot, commented that company-wide changes have benefited significantly from the input provided by mandated board member visits to stores.[43]

Strategic Vision: Board Reform at General Electric[44]

As one of the largest companies in the United States, actions and reforms undertaken by General Electric often become the harbinger of a trend for other companies to follow. In November 2002, CEO Jeffrey Immelt announced a series of landmark changes in corporate governance at GE that will strengthen the board's power to further its involvement in overseeing GE's businesses without the presence of management. According to the *Wall Street Journal*, one of the most important changes will be the complete absence of inside directors on GE's audit, compensation, and governance committees to ensure independent thought and action. In addition, GE will increase the number of outside directors to two-thirds of its total board membership (GE's board has seventeen members), and it will apply a very strict definition of independence. GE will consider a director independent if he or she represents a company that engages in commercial transactions with GE that amount to less than 1 percent of its revenues. GE will also ask its board members to limit the total number of directorships on which they can serve. For CEOs on GE's board, they can serve no more than two other board positions. For non-CEOs, these directors can hold no more than four other board positions. All board members will be expected to visit a minimum of two GE businesses a year to evaluate the quality of operations on their own.

On a broader front, according to *Fortune* magazine, CEO Immelt is hoping to imprint GE with a big commitment to promoting good company values worldwide. Immelt's board reforms are part of a larger picture in which GE seeks to burnish its reputation in everything that it does. According to the CEO, GE needs to remain especially conscious of itself in this post-Enron era where all large companies are considered suspect. As part of its governance reforms, GE has begun to expense stock options to improve financial transparency. Immelt also sees GE making major strides in helping improve the environment through new investments in wind power and water purification technologies. Of course, GE has had long experience in these businesses, and they represent a solid growth opportunity in their own right. However, GE's newfound approach to promoting good values is somewhat complicated by its mixed performance and behavior in some earlier controversies. It has been slow to clean up decades-old industrial pollution in the Hudson River. Some of GE's foreign subsidiaries are known to deal with outcast countries such as Iran, which has nuclear ambitions and a foreign policy hostile to U.S. interests. Despite these lingering issues, GE has actively pursued discussions with environmental and social activist groups to see what it can do to become a better global corporate citizen. It is certainly difficult for any large company to earn the trust of an increasingly skeptical public. Yet, CEO Immelt clearly acknowledges that in the future, GE's values-driven efforts and actions are designed with a key purpose in mind—good values will translate into good business for GE.

STRATEGIC COMPETENCY *in action*

Greater Diversity Among Directors

More minorities are now included on corporate boards. One of the earliest African Americans to join a major corporate board was the Reverend Leon Sullivan, a civil rights leader who joined General Motors' board in 1971. While serving as a GM director, Sullivan drafted a code of behavior for dealing with South Africa. These "Sullivan Principles" were adopted not only by GM, but by several other major corporations as well.

The number of females on corporate boards has also increased. Minorities and women arrived on corporate boards with backgrounds and viewpoints quite different from those of traditional white male directors. Their inclusion in increasing numbers has added voices of dissent previously absent from board deliberations. The importance of this development must not be exaggerated, however. The overwhelming majority of corporate directors are still white males.

Emerging empirical results suggest that board diversity has a positive relationship with shareholder value. One would expect that board diversity will increase in U.S. corporations simply because the marketplace is becoming more diverse. Board diversity can help corporate management broaden their perspectives, which might become overly narrow with a homogeneous board. Moreover, people with different backgrounds, genders, or ethnicity might be inclined to ask questions that would not come from directors with more traditional backgrounds. A diverse board may strengthen the ability of the entire board to act more independently, since board members with nontraditional backgrounds or characteristics might be considered the ultimate outsider.[45]

Agenda for the Future

Major reforms of board activities are clearly underway. Although these modifications have significantly strengthened the power of directors in dealing with the CEO, additional reforms and recommendations to improve board activities are still being considered in numerous quarters. Other important questions regarding board operation include the following:

Multiple Board Responsibilities

Companies looking to fill outside director positions generally seek senior executives of other firms. Especially attractive are executives with high status, wide experience, extensive contacts, and now, financial and accounting acumen.

The impact of Sarbanes-Oxley and other regulatory changes will dramatically increase the effort and time that board members must spend on overseeing corporate management of their companies. Since qualified individuals (particularly presidents and CEOs) are in short supply, they are often inundated with offers to join corporate boards. Some companies are thinking about hiring recently retired CEOs to serve on boards as well. Some board members accept an excessive number of positions, with the result that they are so overextended that they are unable to serve with full effectiveness in any of their assignments. Although this pattern may be fast changing, it was not uncommon in the recent past for executives to serve on as many as a half dozen boards, in addition to holding down full-time senior positions at their own companies.

One solution to this problem is to avoid nominating as director any individual who already sits on more than a specified, small number of boards. Directors queried about the proper limit for this maximum indicated that three board assignments were about the most a full-time executive could handle and still be effective.[46]

An alternate solution to this problem would be to appoint only "professional" directors—individuals who do not hold executive positions, but who instead make a career entirely of serving as outside directors on corporate boards. Because such individuals do not hold full-time managerial positions, they presumably have more time to devote to board duties than do outside directors holding full-time executive positions at other firms. Although this solution has been advocated over the years,[47] it has not yet been adopted by many firms. Even if it were, there would need to be some limit to the number of boards on which professional directors serve. Two prominent advocates of this approach agree a maximum of about six board assignments for professional directors would be appropriate.[48]

Interlocking Relationships

A potential conflict of interest exists when executives of two different companies sit on each other's board. Each executive may then avoid criticizing the other in order to avoid criticism in return. Especially questionable are situations where chief executives from different companies sit on each other's compensation committees. One early study found five pairs of companies where this occurred.[49] An executive in this situation may be tempted to approve an increase in the compensation of his or her counterpart in the hope that the latter will return the favor when determining his or her own salary. Virtually all knowledgeable observers agree that this kind of interlocking board relationship should be avoided.

CEO Presence on the Board

Including a company's CEO on the board can mean that the CEO is put in the position of evaluating his or her own performance. Although including the CEO on the board can thus create a problem, it brings advantages as well. Because of the CEO's unique position to craft strategy for the entire enterprise, he or she understands the company with a depth and perspective equaled by no other individual. When the CEO is a member of the board, other directors have easy access to this valuable information resource. Including the CEO on the board also provides him or her with easy access to the expertise and counsel of outside directors who, as we have seen, are typically seasoned executives in their own right. A CEO who is not a member of the board is cut off from this vital resource.

What is the proper trade-off here? So far, the verdict of practitioners is unambiguous—virtually every public company includes the CEO as a member of its board. In the eyes of practitioners, the benefits of including the CEO on the board appear to outweigh the disadvantages of doing so.

CEO/Chairperson Combination

Because a board's evaluative function is somewhat compromised when the CEO is also given the position of chairperson, some authorities have urged that these two positions be separated. Former SEC Chairman Harold Williams advocated this view as far back as the mid-1970s.[50] A number of shareholder groups have also advocated separating these two positions.

Why do so many U.S. public companies choose to combine these two positions? One possibility is that they do so to enhance accountability. If different individuals were to hold these two positions, directors might have difficulty determining who is really in charge. Another argument advanced for combining the two positions is the inherent weakness of a chairperson who does not also hold the position of CEO. If such an individual is an outsider, as critics generally advocate, he or she will almost certainly have less knowledge of company operations than the CEO, and will enjoy less personal support from managers and employees of the enterprise.

As Ralph Ward has noted, these handicaps can strip a chairperson of the power needed to carry out his or her duties, rendering the individual functionally ineffective.

> The independent outside board chair, who has no other connection to the company, simply would not have enough muscle yet to make a difference. Despite the new powers and self-confidence the boards of major corporations have gained, they still lack the day-to-day strength to counterweigh management. . . . The CEO is a daily presence in the corporation and controls the conduits of information, and every employee works for him or her. The chair, on the other hand, has [only] the board's legal authority and the occasional support of shareholders. Which army would you rather lead? The effectiveness of the chair as a distinct office cannot be separated from the effectiveness of the board. Too often today, the board still lacks this muscle.[51]

There is thus a trade-off here as well. Assigning the positions of CEO and board chairperson to the same individual increases the likelihood that a board may neglect its oversight duties; however, assigning the two positions to different individuals raises problems of accountability. The fact that the two positions are combined in so many U.S. companies suggests that in the eyes of most practitioners the need for accountability takes precedence in this instance.

What steps can a board take to overcome the danger of lax oversight created by combining these two positions? One remedy advocated by some is to designate an outside director to serve as a "lead director."[52] This individual is given distinct administrative duties such as chairing board meetings when a CEO's performance is being evaluated, chairing meetings of outside directors, and consulting with the CEO/chair in shaping board agendas. Conferring such powers on an outside director establishes a counterweight to the CEO/chairperson; thereby reducing the latter's ability to divert the board from forceful evaluation of the CEO.

Director Share Holdings

Directors typically hold only a minimal amount of stock in the companies they serve. As a consequence, their pecuniary interests are not closely tied to those of shareholders. One way to make directors more mindful of shareholder interests is to select as directors only individuals holding a significant amount of shares of the companies they serve. The benefits of such a policy are illustrated by the following remark made by a director of a company whose outside directors each held an average investment of nearly $1 million in the company's shares: "Believe me, that is a board that pays attention . . . I've never seen the pocket calculators come out so quickly in my life."[53] Some advocate increasing director shareholding by having companies make outright gifts of shares to directors, while restricting directors' rights to sell such shares for a certain period.[54] Others prefer substituting shares for cash when compensating directors for their work on corporate boards.[55] Whatever method is used, there is fairly broad consensus that increasing director shareholding would improve the performance of most boards.

Corporate Governance Issues in Other Nations

While much of our previous discussion has focused primarily on corporate governance reform in the United States, many other nations are rethinking and introducing laws to improve board operations and financial integrity as well. Corporate scandals have also surfaced in a few notable cases, such as those involving Royal Ahold (Dutch grocer with extensive U.S.

operations), Parmalat (Italian dairy concern), and Hollinger International (newspaper firm controlled by a British Lord).

Corporate governance regulations in countries such as Japan, Germany, South Korea, and Italy vary significantly from those in the United States.[56] This patchwork of very different, and in some cases, conflicting regulations and legal traditions makes a uniform approach to reforming corporate governance worldwide impossible. In many instances, governance is somewhat weaker because of the stronger presence of founding families on the board. Shareholder activism in many countries is nowhere near as pronounced as that in the United States. However, shareholder activism does appear to be taking firmer root in several countries to exert pressure on global companies.[57] In some countries, governments have actually encouraged practices (such as interlocking relationships and boards) that would be controversial or even illegal in the United States. As far back as 1989, Texas oilman and raider T. Boone Pickens gained enormous notoriety for uncovering Japan's extensive pattern of cross-holdings among companies. This gave the impression that the Japanese stock market in some cases was actually "rigged."[58] In practice, the Japanese government has long encouraged companies to engage in extensive cross-holdings of other affiliated companies to keep foreigners out. Now, many Japanese firms are reversing their traditional pattern of relying on cross-holdings to protect their interests from outsiders. Although cross-holdings effectively keep foreigners from acquiring Japanese firms, they also breed inefficient use of capital. As growing numbers of Japanese firms shed unrelated activities and equity stakes to focus on their core businesses, this nationwide pattern or corporate restructuring is likely to accelerate in the near future.

In a very different legal environment, the German board structure differs radically from its U.S. counterpart. A two-tier, dual board system is required by law. One board is a management board and the other is a supervisory board. The supervisory board is made of up nonexecutive directors, and a significant percentage must be employee representatives.[59] The supervisory board even appoints the management board and approves the company's strategy. By definition, employee representatives are not independent in the U.S. legal sense of the word, and therefore, German companies are incapable of complying with a key provision of the Sarbanes-Oxley Act. In turn, many German firms cannot apply to list their stock on the New York Stock Exchange. Siemens, for example, has taken great steps to comply with U.S. regulations, whereas Porsche AG, the famous automotive firm, has decided to delay its application to list its shares on the NYSE.[60]

Corporate governance reform, nevertheless, is proceeding at its own pace in a number of countries. South Korea, for instance, appears to be making big strides in reforming corporate governance practices. In a country best known for family dynasties controlling the board, many South Korean companies have long engaged in cross-holdings that make it difficult to evaluate true corporate performance. These Korean companies, known as chaebol, have grown enormously through conglomerate-like diversification strategies. It is not unusual, for example, for giant companies such as Samsung Group, LG Group, and Daewoo to own equity stakes in dozens of smaller firms that control each other through cross-holdings. Demand for reform in South Korea initially came from foreign investors, who demanded more transparent accounting. Domestic pressure to reform the chaebols also grew, especially with a new administration that sought to break up the chaebols' overwhelming grip over the Korean economy. In 1999, the government even took the unprecedented step of declaring Daewoo insolvent, a key step to show that no chaebol is too large to fail. Foreigners now own more than a third of the shares of the companies listed on the Seoul stock exchange, and Samsung Electronics (a part of the larger Samsung Group) has even taken steps to fill half its fourteen board seats with outside directors—three of which are foreign investors.[61]

Summary

- Corporate governance deals with the set of policies that are designed to enhance long-term shareholder value of the firm.
- An agency problem occurs when managers put their personal interests before those of the owners of the firm, namely the shareholders.
- Much of the responsibility for ensuring proper corporate governance falls on the company's Board of Directors.
- The Board of Directors is responsible for overseeing the needs of shareholders. All too often, however, boards in many companies have lapsed in this vital duty. Some of the reasons include time constraints, CEO factors, and weak shareholder power.
- A number of factors have pushed boards to become more diligent in protecting shareholder interests. These include public criticism, increased director liability, rising institutional ownership of stock, and the prospect for corporate takeover.
- Corporate governance reforms have made enormous strides in the past few years as a result of catastrophic corporate failures and malfeasance at a number of well-known U.S. companies. Recent U.S. government legislation that has dramatically changed the governance landscape includes the Sarbanes-Oxley Act of 2002, which changes the role of external auditors, and certain key board functions and committees.
- Some key trends that will continue to reshape boards in the future include a move to smaller boards, greater independence of board with more outside directors, greater education and involvement of board members in their companies, and greater diversity of board members.
- Key questions still confronting effective board operation include the following: multiple board responsibilities, the presence of interlocking relationships, the CEO's presence on the board, the CEO/chairperson combination, and director share holdings.
- Corporate governance in each country follows each nation's laws and business practices; efforts to standardize corporate governance worldwide will likely be difficult because of different needs and traditions. However, corporate reform is also taking root in different parts of the world in varying degrees.

Endnotes

1. Data for this case were adapted from the following sources: "Morrison Merging with Washington Construction," *New York Times,* August 27, 1996, p. D4; "MK-Washington Construction Merger Approved," *PR Newswire,* August 26, 1996; "Lemons," *Forbes,* June 17, 1996, p. 228; "Dithering," *Forbes,* May 22, 1995, p. 45; "A Tycoon in the Old Mold," *Forbes,* May 20, 1996, p. 45; "Knudsen Sets Merger with Washington," *New York Times,* May 17, 1996, p. D6; "The King is Dead," *Forbes,* February 27, 1995, p. 16; "Agee's Mess," *Forbes,* February 12, 1996, p. 173; "Agee in Exile," *Fortune,* May 29, 1995, p. 50; "The Imperial Agees," *Forbes,* June 8, 1992, p. 88; "Bill Agee Gets a Second Chance," *Fortune,* March 27, 1989, p. 94.

2. An excellent academic article that provides a concise examination of key issues related to corporate governance is C. Daily, D. Dalton, and A. A. Cannella, Jr., "Corporate Governance: Decades of Dialogue and Data," *Academy of Management Review* 28, no. 3 (2003): 371–382.

3. See A. J. Hillman and T. Dalziel, "Boards of Directors and Firm Performance: Integrating Agency and Resource Dependence Perspectives, *Academy of Management Review* 28, no. 3 (2003): 383–396.

4. Much of the detail in this section is supplied by Robert Monks and Nell Minow, *Watching the Watchers: Corporate Governance for the 21st Century* (Blackwell Publishers, 1996), pp. 169–171.

5. Ibid., p. 188.

6. Martin Lipton and Jay Lorsch, "A Modest Proposal for Improved Corporate Governance," *The Business Lawyer,* 48, no. 1 (Nov. 1992), p. 64.

7. Egon Zehnder International, Corporate Issues Monitor, USA, IV, 1 (1989).

8. Ralph D. Ward, *21st Century Corporate Board* (New York, Wiley, 1997), p. 77.

9. Ibid., p. 76–77.

10. Edward J. Epstein, *"Who Owns the Corporation?" A Twentieth Century Fund Paper* (New York, Priority Press, 1986), p. 13.

11. Quoted in Monks and Minow, *Watching the Watchers,* p. 195.

12. Peter Drucker, "The Bored Board," in *Toward the Next Economics and Other Essays* (New York, Harper & Row, 1981), p. 110.

13. Robert Sobel, *The Fallen Colossus* (New York, Weybright & Taley, 1977), p. 313.

14. Abbass F. Alkhafaji, *Restructuring American Corporations* (Westport, Connecticut, Quorum, 1990), p. 91.

15. Corbette S. Doyle, "Bargaining on D&O Coverage: Corporate Board Special Report on Directors' Liability," July/August 1991, p. 16.

16. See Mark J. Roe, *Strong Managers Weak Owners* (Princeton, New Jersey, Princeton University Press, 1994) for excellent treatment of this subject.

17. Ibid., Chapter 8.

18. Ibid., Chapter 9.

19. Monks and Minow, *Watching the Watchers,* p. 142.

20. Monks and Minow, *Watching the Watchers,* p. 139.

21. Monks and Minow, *Watching the Watchers,* p. 204.

22. See "WorldCom Fraud Was Widespread," *Wall Street Journal,* June 10, 2003, p. A3+; "WorldCom: Hold the Heavyweight Requiem," *Wall Street Journal,* April 15, 2003, p. C1+; "WorldCom Audit Fraud May Rise to $11 Billion," *Wall Street Journal,* April 1, 2003, p. B11; "WorldCom's Latest Headache," *Fortune,* November 25, 2002, p. 34; "Bernie Ebbers' Foolish Faith," *Fortune,* November 25, 2002, p. 52.

23. See "The Big Koslowski," *Fortune,* November 18, 2002, p. 122+.

24. See "Mr. Cleanup," *Fortune,* November 15, 2004, pp. 151–163.

25. The authors would like to extend a special thanks to Professor Wayne Shaw at the Cox School of Business, Helmut Sohmen Distinguished Professor of Corporate Governance, Southern Methodist University, for his help and materials used for this section.

26. See "Call It Sarbanes-Oxley Burnout: Finance Chief Turnover Is Rising." *Wall Street Journal,* April 5, 2005, p. B4; "Companies Complain About Cost of Corporate-Governance Rules," *Wall Street Journal,* February 10, 2004, p. A1+.

27. See, for example, "In Boardrooms, 'Independent' Is Debatable," *Wall Street Journal,* March 3, 2005, pp. C1, C4; "How Real Are the Reforms?" *Wall Street Journal,* July 29, 2002, p. B1.

28. See "In Corporate America, It's Cleanup Time," *Fortune,* September 16, 2002, p. 62+.

29. Data and facts were adapted from the following sources: "Sarbanes-Oxley Compliance Costs Average $16 Million Per Company," *Business Wire,* November 15, 2004, 10:19 a.m., "Companies Rush to Meet Requirement of Sarbanes-Oxley," *Wall Street Journal,* November 15, 2004; "Firms Spend to Boost Accounting in Sarbanes-Oxley Era," *Investor's Business Daily,* November 15, 2004, p. A6.

30. See Monks and Minow, *Watching the Watchers,* p. 142.

31. Monks and Minow, *Watching the Watchers,* p. 170.

32. Korn/Ferry International Board of Directors Survey, 1995, p. 30.

33. Stanley C. Vance, *Boards of Directors* (University of Oregon Press, 1964), p. 19.

34. Monks and Minow, *Watching the Watchers*, p. 170.

35. S. Bhagat and B. Black, "The Uncertain Relationship Between Board Composition and Firm Value," *Business Lawyer,* 54 (1999): 921–963; S. W. Barnhart and S. Rosentein, "Board Composition, Managerial Ownership, and Firm Performance: An Empirical Analysis," *Financial Review,* 33 (1998): 1–16; B. E. Hermalin and M. S. Weisbach,

"The Effects of Board Composition and Direct Incentives on Firm Value," *Financial Management,* 20, (1991): 101–112.

36. Ward, *21st Century Corporate Board,* p. 156.

37. Korn/Ferry International Board of Directors Survey, 1995.

38. See SpencerStuart, "Point of View: Perspectives on Leadership," *Corporate Governance* Special Issue – 2004.

39. See "Corporate Governance (A Special Report): Managers, Keep Out," *Wall Street Journal,* June 21, 2004, p. R4+.

40. See SpencerStuart, "Point of View: Perspectives on Leadership," *Corporate Governance* Special Issue – 2004.

41. See "Ten Questions Every Board Member Should Ask," *Fortune,* November 10, 2003, p. 181+.

42. See "Corporate Governance (A Special Report): Back to School," *Wall Street Journal,* June 21, 2004, p. R3+.

43. See "Corporate Governance (A Special Report): Up Close and Personal," *Wall Street Journal,* June 21, 2004, p. R4+.

44. Data and facts were adapted from the following sources: "Money and Morals at GE," *Fortune,* November 15, 2004, pp. 176–182; "GE Makes Changes in Board Policy," *Wall Street Journal,* November 8, 2002, p. A5; "GE to Announce Set of New Policies to Shore Up Board," *Wall Street Journal,* November 6, 2002, p. A2.

45. M. A. Fields and P. Y. Keys, "The Emergence of Corporate Governance From Wall Street to Main Street: Outside Directors, Board Diversity, Earnings Management, and Managerial Incentives to Bear Risks," *Financial Review,* 38 (2003): 1–33; D. A. Carter, B. J. Simkins, and W. G. Simpson, "Corporate Governance, Board Diversity, and Firm Value," *Financial Review,* 38 (2003): 33+.

46. This, for example, is the maximum suggested by both Martin Lipton, a leading takeover lawyer (see Monks and Minow, *Watching the Watchers,* p. 212), and SpencerStuart, a search firm active in recruiting directors (see Ward, *21st Century Corporate Board,* p. 168).

47. This solution was proposed as far back as 1940 by William O. Douglas, who was then serving as chairman of the SEC (see Ward, *21st Century Corporate Board,* p. 175).

48. Ronald J. Gilson and Reinier Kraakman, "Reinventing the Outside Director," *Stanford Law Review* (April 1991), p. 884.

49. Alison Leigh Cowan, "Board Room Back Scratching?" *New York Times,* June 2, 1993, p. D1.

50. Ward, *21st Century Corporate Board,* p. 244.

51. Ward, *21st Century Corporate Board,* p. 250.

52. Jay Lorsch, for example, author of *Pawns or Potentates,* is a strong advocate of this approach.

53. Lawrence Tucker, *Investor's Business Daily,* July 7, 1993, p. 4.

54. See Marcia Lewis, "Give Directors Restricted Stock," *Directors and Boards,* 16, no. 4 (Summer 1992).

55. Monks and Minow, *Watching the Watchers,* p. 209.

56. See R. V. Aguilera and G. Jackson, "The Cross-National Diversity of Corporate Governance: Dimensions and Determinants," *Academy of Management Review* 28, no. 3 (2003): 447–465.

57. See "Global Companies Face New Pressures From Activist Investors," *Conference Board,* 21 (2000).

58. See "So 'Takeover' Does Translate; Foreigners Are After Japanese Companies," *BusinessWeek,* February 9, 2004, p. 51.

59. See SpencerStuart, "Point of View: Perspectives on Leadership," *Corporate Governance* Special Issue–2004.

60. See "Will Overseas Boards Play By American Rules?" *BusinessWeek,* December 16, 2002, p. 36.

61. See "Crackdown on Korea Inc.," *BusinessWeek,* May 19, 2003, p. 44+.

Glossary

A

Activity Ratios measures used to assess the efficiency of a firm's use of assets (for example, sales divided by assets).

Agency Problem when managers seek to protect and enlarge their own interests at the expense of shareholders. A conflict between the interests of managers and shareholders.

Area Structures an organizational form that divides and organizes the firm's activities according to where operations and people are located (also known as place structures, geographic divisions).

B

Backbone a high-speed transmission line (often of fiber-optic cable) that forms a critical pathway in a telecommunications network. Backbones represent the most important building blocks of modern telephone and Internet-based networks.

Backward Integration a strategy that moves the firm upstream into an activity currently conducted by a supplier (see vertical integration; forward integration).

Bandwidth the defined range of frequencies used by a transmission signal to carry voice, video, data, or other information. The need for greater bandwidth is a fundamental constraint that limits the speed with which all types of information (voice, video, data) is transmitted across the Internet and other networks.

Barriers to Entry economic forces that slow down or prevent entry into an industry.

Benchmarking a firm's process of searching, identifying, and using ideas, techniques, and improvements of other companies in its own activities.

Boundaryless Organization an organization design in which people can easily share information, resources, and skills across departments and divisions.

Bureaucratization the gradual process by which information flow becomes steadily slower within the firm.

Business Managers people in charge of managing and operating a single line of business.

Business Strategy plans and actions that firms devise to compete in a given product/market scope or setting; addresses the question "How do we compete within an industry?"

Business System the subset of value chain activities that a firm actually performs.

C

CAD/CAM Network the linking up of multiple design and manufacturing activities (both within and across) firms through the use of complex networks of computers. CAD stands for computer-assisted design; CAM stands for computer-assisted manufacturing.

Capability Drivers the basic economic and strategic means by which a firm builds an underlying source of competitive advantage in its market or industry. Examples of basic capability drivers include first-mover advantages, economies of scale, experience effects, and interrelationships among business units.

Centralization the degree to which senior managers have the authority to make decisions for the entire organization.

Chaebol a complex arrangement in which Korean firms (often family-owned) assume equity stakes and other ownership positions to maintain a web of companies.

Collaboration cooperation between partners that is often short-term or limited in scope. Collaboration is actually another form of competition between partners seeking to learn and absorb skills from one another.

Comparative Financial Analysis the evaluation of a firm's financial condition across multiple time periods.

Competence-Changing Technology a technology that markedly changes or redefines the structure of an industry; often new processes or innovations that disrupt and erode the market for existing products.

Competing on Time speeding up the time needed to innovate new products and get them to market faster than competitors.

Competitive Advantage allows a firm to gain an edge over rivals when competing. Competitive advantage comes from a firm's ability to perform activities more distinctively or more effectively than rivals.

Competitive Environment the immediate economic factors—customers, competitors, suppliers, buyers, and potential substitutes—of direct relevance to a firm in a given industry (also known as industry environment).

Competitor Intelligence Gathering scanning specifically targeted or directed toward a firm's rivals; often focuses on a competitor's products, technologies, and other important information.

Composite Material a new material made from a distinct combination of metal, polymers, or ceramics that offers great strength and endurance; examples include carbon fibers and graphite used in tennis rackets and golf clubs.

Computer-Integrated Manufacturing (CIM) the use of modern computer and information technologies that closely link up design and marketing activities with those of manufacturing.

Conglomerate Discount an empirical finding of what a conglomerate firm's stock is worth because the market believes management is destroying the value of its individual businesses.

Conglomerates firms that practice unrelated diversification (see unrelated diversification; holding company structure).

Continuous Quality Improvement the deliberate and methodical search for better ways of improving products and processes.

Convergence the blurring of industry boundaries in such a way that the economic and competitive factors shaping one industry begin to influence the evolution of another. Convergence tends to occur most often when the characteristics of a product or service begin to substitute or complement those of an existing offering (for example, Internet and the personal computer, Internet and financial services).

Co-Opetition the strategic situation whereby a firm cooperates and competes with another firm(s) at the same time. Firms in co-opetitive relationships often race with one another to learn each other's skills and to develop new sources of knowledge or value-creating activities.

Core Processes and Technologies the key levers or drivers that form the basis of a firm's distinctive competence and critical value-adding activities.

Corporate Culture the system of unwritten rules that guide how people perform and interrelate with one another.

Corporate Governance the set of policies designed to ensure the long-term creation of sustainable value for the firm's shareholders.

Corporate Managers people responsible for overseeing and managing a portfolio of businesses within the firm.

Corporate Restructurings steps designed to change the corporate portfolio of businesses to achieve greater focus and efficiency among businesses; often involve selling off businesses that do not fit a core technology or are a drag on earnings.

Corporate Strategy plans and actions that firms need to formulate and implement when managing a portfolio of businesses; an especially critical issue when firms seek to diversify from their initial activities or operations into new areas. Corporate strategy issues are key to extending the firm's competitive advantage from one business to another.

Cost Driver a technological or economic factor that determines the cost of performing some activity.

Creative Tension a process in which senior management systematically attempts to encourage people to think about new strategies and directions, which prevents the firm from becoming complacent.

Cross-Functional Teams small units that work across a wide range of functions, technologies, products, and services based in different parts of the firm.

Cross-Subsidization using financial, technological, and marketing resources from one market to fight a competitor in another; involves extensive use of "parry and thrust" tactics to gain new market positions.

Cumulative Volume the quantity that a firm has produced since the beginning of that activity, up to this point in time.

Current Ratio a measure used to assess a firm's ability to make payments to its short-term creditors; current assets divided by current liabilities.

Customer Intimacy a deep knowledge of what motivates a customer to buy; often used in the context of fostering a high degree of communication with the customer to earn his or her loyalty.

Customer-Defined Quality the best value a firm can put into its products and services for the market segments it serves. Customer-defined quality is more important to competitive strategy than what the firm thinks its quality should be.

D

Debt Ratio a measure of a firm's leverage; the amount of debt it possesses divided by stockholder equity.

Defending an activity designed to help the firm shield or insulate itself from environmental change (see prospecting).

De-Integration the process by which a firm becomes less vertically integrated, often by selling off those activities that it once performed in-house.

Delayering the removal of excess levels of management that impede fast information flow within the firm.

Development Policies the training and skill improvement guidelines or practices used by a firm to cultivate its people.

Differentiation competitive strategy based on providing buyers with something special or unique that makes the firm's product or service distinctive.

Digital a method used to capture or represent information by discrete or individually unique signals (usually bits of binary data).

Digitization the conversion of information into binary form (0s and 1s). Digitization is a key reason why information-based industries are rapidly moving to the Internet.

Disintermediation the bypassing of middlemen and other economic entities that once separated firms from their customers.

Distinctive Competence the special skills, capabilities, or resources that enable a firm to stand out from its competitors; what a firm can do especially well to compete or serve its customers.

Diversification a strategy that takes the firm into new industries and markets (see related diversification; unrelated diversification).

Diversified Firm a firm that operates more than one line of business. Diversified firms often operate across several industries or markets, each with a separate set of customers and competitive requirements (also known as a multibusiness firm). Firms can differ in the degree or extent of their diversification.

Downscoping the reduction of a firm's wide-spanning corporate diversification by shrinking the scope of activities it performs.

Downstream Activities economic activities that occur close to the customer but far away from the firm's suppliers. Examples include outbound logistics, distribution, marketing, sales, and service (see also upstream activities).

E

e-Business the use of Internet-based technologies to transform how a business interacts with its customers and suppliers.

Economies of Experience cost reductions that occur from continuous repetition of activities that allow for improvement with each successive act (also known as experience curve effects or learning curve effects).

Economies of Scale the declines in per-unit cost of production or any activity as volume grows.

Economies of Scope an economic characteristic that results when production of two or more goods can be done more efficiently with one set of assets than from separate assets dedicated to each product.

Empowerment delegation of decision-making authority and responsibility to those people most directly involved with a given project or task.

Environment all external forces, factors, or conditions that exert some degree of impact on the strategies, decisions, and actions taken by the firm.

Environmental Scanning the gathering of information about external conditions for use in formulating strategies.

Ethical Dilemmas difficult choices involving moral, legal, or other highly delicate issues that managers must weigh and balance when considering the needs of various stakeholders. Ethical dilemmas work to shape and sometimes constrain a firm's ability to take certain actions.

Exit Barriers economic forces that slow down or prevent exit from an industry.

Experience Curve Effects cost reductions that occur from continuous repetition of activities that allow for improvement with each successive act (also known as economies of experience or learning curve effects).

External Partnering the process of including suppliers and customers in the firm's set of value-adding activities, often through virtual organizational formats.

F

Fiduciary Responsibility the primary responsibility facing top management—to make sure the firm delivers value to its shareholders, the owners of the firm.

First-Mover Advantages the benefits that firms enjoy from being the first or earliest to compete in an industry.

Flexible Factories production facilities capable of producing a variety of products, often by using state-of-the-art computer technologies to promote fast changeover of designs and tools (see flexible manufacturing).

Flexible Manufacturing the ability of equipment in factories to change easily from the production of one good to another (see flexible factories).

Focus Strategies competitive strategies based on targeting a specific niche within an industry. Focus strategies can occur in two forms: cost-based focus and differentiation-based focus.

Forward Integration a strategy that moves the firm downstream into an activity currently performed by a buyer (see vertical integration; backward integration).

Full Integration vertical integration that seeks to control every activity in the value chain. In full integration, firms bring all activities required to design, develop, produce, and market a product in-house (see partial integration).

Functional Structure an organizational structure that groups managers and employees according to their areas of expertise and skills to perform their tasks.

G

General Environment the broad collection of forces or conditions that affect every firm or organization in every industry (also known as macroenvironment).

Generic Strategies the broad types of competitive strategies—low-cost leadership, differentiation, and focus—that firms use to build competitive advantage (see low-cost leadership, differentiation, focus strategies).

Geographic Division an organizational form that divides and organizes the firm's activities according to where operations and people are located.

Global Strategy a strategy that seeks to achieve a high level of consistency and standardization of products, processes, and operations around the world; coordination of the firm's many subsidiaries to achieve high interdependence and mutual support.

Globalization viewing the world as a single market for the firm; the process by which the firm expands across different regions and national markets. On an industry level, globalization refers to the changes in economic factors, such as economies of scale, experience, and R&D, that make competing on a worldwide basis a necessity.

Goals the specific results to be achieved within a given time period (also known as objectives).

Group or Sector a larger version of the SBU structure that often houses many different SBUs under one reporting relationship.

H

Harvesting the systematic removal of cash and other assets from a slow-growth or declining business; may be thought of as "milking" a business before it loses all its value.

Hierarchy-Based Reward System a type of compensation structure that encourages close superior–subordinate relationships, an emphasis on group achievement, use of both qualitative and quantitative measures of performance, and promotion from within (see performance-based reward system).

Holding Company Structure a lean form of a product division structure used by conglomerates in unrelated diversification (see conglomerates; product division; product structure; unrelated diversification).

Hollow Out the process by which a firm becomes steadily less competitive as a result of delegating its core value-adding activities to other firms.

Homogeneity of Demand similarity of demand patterns and wants across customers, regardless of where they are located.

Horizontal Organization an organization design in which teams and small units replace the strict separation of functional activities such as design, manufacturing, marketing, finance, distribution, sales, and service.

Hybrid (or Mixed) Structures combining different basic organizational structures to attain the benefits of more than one.

Hybrid Products products that result from combining or fusing together different sources of technologies (see technology fusion).

I

Industrial Espionage systematic and deliberate attempts to learn about a competitor's technologies or new products through secretive, and often illegal, ways.

Industry Attractiveness the potential for profitability when competing in a given industry. An attractive industry has high profit potential; an unattractive industry has low profit potential.

Industry Environment the immediate economic factors—customers, competitors, suppliers, buyers, and potential substitutes—of direct relevance to a firm in a given industry (also known as competitive environment).

Industry Initiative the ability of a firm to shape, influence, or introduce new product ideas, standards, or technologies within an industry.

Industry Structure the interrelationship among the factors in a firm's competitive or industry environment; configuration of economic forces and factors that interrelate to affect the behavior of firms competing in that industry.

Inertia the difficulty that established firms face when trying to adjust to change; inhibits fast response to new developments in the environment.

Informal Integrators people who act as internal "referees" to resolve disputes and conflicts between divisional managers.

Intangible Assets resources based on skills or other hard-to-imitate assets that are not physical in form; examples include brand equity, fast product development, management techniques, proprietary means of developing knowledge, innovation, and so forth.

Internal Task Forces groups that serve as bridges that forge stronger interrelationships among divisions in an organization.

International Division a structure by which all of the firm's managers and employees in nondomestic activities report to a single senior manager who is separate from other domestic divisional managers; a structure traditionally used by firms that are starting to increase their overseas operations.

Internet the enormous collection of interconnected networks that share the similar use of transmission and delivery protocols (TCP/IP). The Internet evolved from early government-related programs to construct a huge network of research centers, universities, and government installations that would link up computer systems together.

Interrelationships the sharing of activities, technologies, skills, and resources among a firm's subunits, particularly divisions or strategic business units (SBUs).

Invisible Assets intangible sources of competitive advantage such as brands, images, corporate cultures, knowledge, and organizational practices that are hard for competitors to imitate and duplicate.

J

Joint Ventures a form of strategic alliance in which partners work closely—usually through a third company that is set up by both partners—to pursue a mutually shared interest.

Just-in-Time sophisticated approach to inventory management in which firms receive material from their suppliers when it is needed.

K

Keiretsu a complex arrangement in which firms take equity stakes in one another as a long-standing strategic alliance; used in Japan to link up many different companies.

Knowledge-Based Assets intangible assets such as reputation, brand names, scientific skills, or quality techniques that are hard-to-imitate and critical to making a firm's distinctive competence valuable.

Knowledge-Based Competition economic competition and competitive advantage derived from the creation and use of new forms of knowledge, skills, and technologies.

Knowledge Web a collection or group of companies that work in tandem to shape the evolution of an industry.

L

Lateral Relations coordinating work and communications among people who are the same reporting level within the organization.

Learning Curve Effects cost reductions that occur from continuous repetition of activities that allow for improvement with each successive act (also known as economies of experience or experience curve effects).

Learning Organizations firms that view change as a positive opportunity to learn and create new sources of competitive advantage.

Liquid Crystal Displays (LCDs) a display technology that consists of three parts: two glass substrates, a liquid crystal (made from a chemical compound) in the middle, and an electronic device that changes or "stimulates" crystals to produce different colors. LCD technology allows visual display of numbers, images, or other data through the use of crystal, as opposed to conventional tube technology.

Liquidity the ability of a firm or business to pay or meet its obligations (for example, debt payments, accounts payable) as they come due. The more liquid the firm, the easier its ability to meet these obligations.

Location of Activities the physical place where an economic, value-adding activity occurs. Location can be an important source of competitive advantage for some types of firms.

Loose Coupling an organization design and structure that fosters a balance between the need to centralize and decentralize activities.

Low-Cost Leadership a competitive strategy based on the firm's ability to provide products or services at lower cost than its rivals.

M

Macroenvironment the broad collection of forces or conditions that affect every firm or organization in every industry (also known as general environment).

Mass Customization the capability to produce a growing variety or range of products at reduced unit costs. Mass customization is a strategic competitive weapon that helps firms to expand the range of their product offerings and modifications without incurring the high costs of variety.

Matrix Structure an organizational form that divides and organizes activities along two or more lines of authority and reporting relationships.

Mechatronics refers to the fusion of precision, mechanical engineering skills with microelectronics.

Microchip a flat semiconductor device in which tiny (often microscopic) amounts of chemical elements are deposited, etched, and sealed to create integrated circuits. Microchips lay the foundation for the semiconductor industry.

Microprocessor a microchip that performs arithmetic, control, and logic-based operations; used as the central processing unit of personal computers and workstations.

Minimum Efficient Scale (MES) level of production volume that a factory must reach before it achieves full efficiency.

Mission describes the firm or organization in terms of its business. Mission statements answer the questions "What business are we in?" and "What do we intend to do to succeed?" Mission statements are somewhat more concrete than vision statements but still do not specify the goals and objectives necessary to translate the mission into reality (see vision; goals; objectives).

Mixed Structures combining different basic organizational structures to attain the benefits of more than one (also known as hybrid structures).

Modularity an element of product design that allows for the mixing and matching of different components and parts that all share the same interface or means of connecting with one another. A product exhibits modularity if its constituent parts can be rearranged among themselves or with additional parts that share the same pattern of linkage.

Multibusiness Firm a firm that operates more than one line of business. Multibusiness firms often operate across several industries or markets, each with a separate set of customers and competitive requirements (also known as a diversified firm). Firms can possess many business units in their corporate portfolio.

Multidomestic Strategy a strategy that seeks to adjust a firm's products, processes, and operations for markets and regions around the world; allows subsidiaries to tailor their products, marketing, and other activities according to the needs of their specific markets.

Multipoint Competition a form of economic competition in which a firm commits its entire product line against a similarly endowed competitor's array of products.

N

Nanotechnology science and technology based on combining different types of amino acids or molecules to create new types of enzymatic-based circuits and other miniaturized products.

Network Effects an economic condition in which the value of a product or service rises as more people utilize it.

Network Organization organizational format in which firms try to balance their reliance on performing internal value-creating activities with the need to stay responsive and open to the environment.

O

Objectives the specific results to be achieved within a given time period (also known as goals). Objectives guide the firm or organization in achieving its mission (see vision; mission).

Off-Line Coordinators individuals and groups, often experienced managers and staff personnel, outside the formal hierarchy who coordinate activities among subunits.

Option the right but not the obligation to purchase or sell a company's stock at a pre-set price within a pre-defined time period.

Organization Design Practices support mechanisms that facilitate the implementation of a strategy within the framework of a given structure.

Outsource the use of other firms to perform value-adding activities once conducted in-house.

P

Partial Integration vertical integration that is selective about which areas of activity the firm will choose to undertake. In partial integration, firms do not control every activity required to design, develop, produce, and market a product (see full integration).

Performance-Based Reward System a type of compensation structure that puts a premium on a high level of individual performance, a strong reliance on bonuses as part of total compensation, and a relative de-emphasis on close superior-subordinate relationships (see hierarchy-based reward system).

Peripheral Businesses business units or divisions that are not central to the firm's core set of activities, skills, or technologies.

Perishability the loss of economic value that occurs when a product or service is not used within a given time period, often used to describe the ease with which a product spoils or decays; a major economic consideration that promotes the use of multidomestic strategies.

Personalization the creation of a unique mix or set of products and services catered to a specific individual's needs.

Pirating hiring individuals from a competitor specifically to gain their knowledge (also known as raiding).

Place Structure an organizational form that divides and organizes the firm's activities according to where operations and people are located (also known as area structures, geographic structures).

Primary Activities economic activities that relate directly to the actual creation, manufacture, distribution, and sale of a product or service to the firm's customer (see support activities).

Process Development the design and use of new procedures, technologies, techniques, and other steps to improve value-adding activities.

Product Development the conception, design, and commercialization of new products.

Product Differentiation the physical or perceptual differences that make a product special or unique in the eyes of the customer.

Product Divisions the most basic form of product structure, in which each division houses all of the functions necessary for it to carry out its own strategy and mission.

Product Realization the product development process, beginning with product idea and concept and ending with production and distribution.

Product Structure an organizational structure that divides the firm into self-contained units able to perform all of their own activities independently; examples include product divisions, strategic business units (SBUs), sectors or groups, and conglomerate/holding company formats.

Productivity Paradox the economic trade-off that managers must make when using traditional manufacturing technology to achieve low-cost production; flexibility and variety of production are sacrificed.

Prospecting an activity designed to help the firm search, understand, and accommodate environmental change; a proactive attempt by a firm to make an environmental change favorable to itself (see defending).

R

Raiding hiring individuals from a competitor specifically to gain their knowledge (also known as pirating).

Rapid Prototyping a design technology that accelerates the testing of new product concepts, ideas, and designs, often through the use of computer modeling techniques.

Ratio Analysis the use of a proportion of two figures or numbers that allow for consistent comparison of performance with other firms.

Reengineering the complete rethinking, reinventing, and redesign of how a business or set of activities operates.

Related Diversification a strategy that expands the firm's operations into similar industries and markets; extends the firm's distinctive competence to other lines of business that are similar to the firm's initial base (see related industry; unrelated diversification).

Related Industry an industry that shares many of the same economic, technological, or market-based drivers or characteristics as another.

Resource-Based View of the Firm an evolving set of strategic management ideas that place considerable emphasis on the firm's ability to distinguish itself from its rivals by means of investing in hard-to-imitate and specific resources (for example, technologies, skills, capabilities, assets, management approaches).

Resource Sharing the transfer of skills, technologies, or knowledge from one business to another; vital to building synergy in related diversification.

Return on Assets net income divided by total assets.

Return on Capital net income divided by total capital.

Return on Equity net income divided by stockholder equity.

Return on Investment net income divided by total investment.

Revitalization the process of renewing a company's sources of distinctive competence and competitive advantage.

Rightsizing shrinking of the firm's workforce and resource commitment to the firm's businesses.

S

Sarbanes-Oxley Act of 2002 sweeping U.S. legislation designed to change key aspects of corporate governance on a wide scale.

Scope of Operations the extent of a firm's involvement in different activities, products, and markets.

Sector a larger version of the strategic business unit (SBU) that often houses many SBUs under one reporting relationship; sometimes called a group (see group; strategic business unit (SBU); product division; product structure).

Semiconductor electronic device containing many transistors that serve different switching functions on a small chip, usually made of silicon, germanium, or gallium arsenide. Each transistor, in itself, can serve as a switch, amplifier, or oscillator. Semiconductors are vital to the function of many consumer and industrial products. (The term semiconductor actually refers to a type of material or substrate that is part insulator and part conductor.)

Semipermeable Boundaries flexible separations between organizational subunits across which communication, knowledge, and information flow more readily.

Shared Values the basic norms and ideals that guide people's behaviors in the firm and form the underpinning of a firm's corporate culture.

Single-Business Firm a firm that operates only one business in one industry or market (also known as an undiversified firm).

Socialization the process by which shared values and ways of behaving are instilled in new managers and employees.

Specialization the assignment of particular tasks and activities to those people who are best able to perform them.

Spin-Off a form of corporate restructuring that sells businesses or parts of a company that no longer contribute to the firm's earnings or distinctive competence.

Standardization the process of defining the organization's work practices and procedures so that people can repeatedly perform them at a given level or measure of performance.

Static Organizations firms that have adapted extremely well to a particular environment but lack the ability to respond quickly to change.

Statistical Process Controls the use of statistics to measure and control a production process, often with the desired intent of achieving high product conformity.

Strategic Alliances linkages between companies designed to achieve an economic objective faster or more efficiently than either company could do alone; take the basic forms of licensing arrangements, joint ventures, or multipartner consortia.

Strategic Business Unit form of organization that often represents larger product divisions or collections of smaller product divisions under one reporting relationship.

Strategic Groups the distribution or grouping of firms that pursue similar strategies in response to environmental forces within an industry. Firms within the same strategic group will tend to compete more vigorously with one another than with firms from other strategic groups.

Strategic Management Process the steps by which management converts a firm's values, mission, and goals/objectives into a workable strategy; consists of four stages: analysis, formulation, implementation, and adjustment/evaluation.

Strategy refers to the ideas, plans, and support that firms employ to compete successfully against their rivals. Strategy is designed to help firms achieve competitive advantage.

Strategy Implementation the process by which strategies are converted into desired actions.

Structure the formal definition of working relationships between people in an organization.

Support Activities economic activities that assist the firm's primary activities (see primary activities).

Switching Costs costs that occur when buyers or suppliers move from one competitor's products or services to another's.

SWOT Analysis shorthand for strengths, weaknesses, opportunities, and threats; a fundamental step in assessing the firm's external environment; required as a first step of strategy formulation and typically carried out at the business level of the firm.

Synergy an economic effect in which the different parts of the company contribute a unique source of heightened value to the firm when managed as a single, unified entity.

Systemwide Advantage the building and sustaining of competitive advantage across multiple business units to achieve corporatewide strengths.

T

Technological Convergence growing technological similarity of products and businesses, such as components, designs, and production processes among once-distinct industries.

Technology Fusion the blending, or fusing together, of many sources of technology to create new, higher-order products.

Terrain the environment (or industry) in which competition occurs. In a military sense, terrain is the type of environment or ground on which a battle takes place. From a business sense, terrain refers to markets, segments, and products used to win over customers.

Total Quality Management the cultivation and practice of quality in every person's tasks and activities throughout the organization.

Transaction Costs economic costs of finding, negotiating, selling, buying, and resolving disputes with other firms (for example, suppliers and customers) in the open market.

Turnover Ratios measures that assess the speed with which various assets (inventory, receivables) are converted into cash.

U

Undiversified Firm a firm that operates only one business in one industry or market (also known as a single-business firm).

Unrelated Diversification a strategy that expands the firm's operations into industries and markets that are not similar or related to the firm's initial base; does not involve sharing the firm's distinctive competence across different lines of business (see related diversification; related industry).

Upstream Activities economic activities that occur close to the firm's suppliers but far away from the consumer. Examples include inbound logistics, procurement, manufacturing, and operations (see also downstream activities).

V

Value-Added/Weight Ratio a key economic factor that influences the globalization of industries; high value-added/weight promotes global strategies; low value-added/weight ratios promote multidomestic strategies.

Value Chain an analytical tool that describes all activities that make up the economic performance and capabilities of the firm; used to analyze and examine activities that create value for a given firm.

Value Engineering process by which each step in engineering and product development activities directly contribute to the value of the final product.

Value Proposition the products and services that meet customer needs at a price that generates a positive economic return.

Vertical Integration the expansion of the firm's value chain to include activities performed by suppliers and buyers; the degree of control that a firm exerts over the supply of its inputs and the purchase of its outputs. Vertical integration strategies and decisions enlarge the scope of the firm's activities in one industry.

Virtual Advantage a type of competitive advantage based on speed, fast turnaround, and deep knowledge of customers' needs to create value faster than competitors can do, often by focusing on a few core value-adding activities.

Virtual Organization an organizational format that coordinates and links up people and activities from different locations to communicate and act together, often on a real-time basis.

Vision the highest aspirations and ideals of a person or organization; what a firm wants to be. Vision statements often describe the firm or organization in lofty, even romantic or mystical tones (see mission; goals; objectives).

Name Index

Company and Product Index

Note: Page numbers followed by "e" indicate exhibits; "n" indicate notes.

Subject Index

Note: Page numbers followed by "e" indicate exhibits; "n" indicate notes.